KU-601-158

MCAD/MCSD

Self-Paced Training Kit

DEVELOPING

XML WEB SERVICES AND SERVER COMPONENTS

WITH MICROSOFT

VISUAL BASIC® .NET

AND MICROSOFT

VISUAL C#® .NET

Exams
70-310 and 70-320

Microsoft®
.net

PUBLISHED BY
Microsoft Press
A Division of Microsoft Corporation
One Microsoft Way
Redmond, Washington 98052-6399

Copyright © 2003 by Microsoft Corporation

All rights reserved. No part of the contents of this book may be reproduced or transmitted in any form or by any means without the written permission of the publisher.

Library of Congress Cataloging-in-Publication Data
MCAD/MCSD Self-Paced Training Kit: Developing XML Web Services and Server
Components with Microsoft Visual Basic .NET and Microsoft Visual C# .NET / Microsoft Corporation.
      p. cm.
   Includes index.
   ISBN 0-7356-1586-1
   ISBN 0-7356-1925-5 (MCAD Core Requirements)
   1. Electronic data processing personnel--Certification. 2. Microsoft
software--Examinations--Study guides. 3. Microsoft .NET Framework. 4. XML
(Document markup language) 5. Microsoft Windows (Computer file) I. Title:
Developing XML Web services and server components with Microsoft Visual
Basic .NET and Microsoft C# .NET. II. Microsoft Corporation

  QA76.3 .M325565   2002
  005.2'768--dc21   2002033714

Printed and bound in the United States of America.

2 3 4 5 6 7 8 9   QWT   8 7 6 5 4 3

Distributed in Canada by H.B. Fenn and Company Ltd.

A CIP catalogue record for this book is available from the British Library.

Microsoft Press books are available through booksellers and distributors worldwide. For further information about international editions, contact your local Microsoft Corporation office or contact Microsoft Press International directly at fax (425) 936-7329. Visit our Web site at www.microsoft.com/mspress. Send comments to *tkinput@microsoft.com*.

Active Directory, ActiveX, Authenticode, BackOffice, IntelliSense, JScript, Microsoft, Microsoft Press, MSDN, Visual Basic, Visual C++, Visual C#, Visual J++, Visual J#, Visual Studio, Win32, Windows, and Windows NT are either registered trademarks or trademarks of Microsoft Corporation in the United States and/or other countries. Other product and company names mentioned herein may be the trademarks of their respective owners.

The example companies, organizations, products, domain names, e-mail addresses, logos, people, places, and events depicted herein are fictitious. No association with any real company, organization, product, domain name, e-mail address, logo, person, place, or event is intended or should be inferred.

Acquisitions Editor: Kathy Harding
Project Editor: Jean Trenary
Technical Editor: Bob Willer

SubAssy Part No. X09-46565
Body Part No. X08-85375

Contents

About This Book

Welcome to *MCAD/MCSD Training Kit—Developing XML Web Services and Server Components with Microsoft Visual Basic .NET and Microsoft Visual C# .NET*. .NET is a new Microsoft technology that offers new application frameworks such as Web services, ASP.NET, WinForms, and ADO.NET. This revolutionary component technology simplifies development and deployment of components. By completing the lessons and exercises in this book, you will be able to build XML Web services and server components.

This book also addresses the objectives of the Microsoft Certified Professional Exam 70-310 and Exam 70-320.

Note For more information about becoming a Microsoft Certified Application Developer (MCAD) or a Microsoft Certified Solution Developer (MCSD), see "The Microsoft Certified Professional Program" section later in this introduction.

The "Getting Started" section of this introduction provides important setup instructions that describe the hardware and software requirements to complete the procedures in this course. It also provides information about installing or accessing the material provided on the Supplemental Course Materials CD-ROM. Read through this section thoroughly before you start the lessons.

Intended Audience

This book was created for software developers who need to design, plan, implement, and support XML Web services and server components or who plan to take the following related Microsoft Certified Professional exams.

- *Developing XML Web Services and Server Components with Microsoft Visual Basic .NET and the Microsoft .NET Framework* (MCP Exam 70-310)
- *Developing XML Web Services and Server Components with Microsoft Visual C# .NET and the Microsoft .NET Framework* (MCP Exam 70-320)

Prerequisites

This course requires that students meet the prerequisites that follow.

- Be able to create Windows applications using Microsoft Visual Studio .NET in either the Visual Basic .NET or Visual C# .NET programming language.
- Have a basic understanding of the object-oriented programming concepts including classes, properties, methods, and events.

- Be familiar with Windows-based, Web-based, and console-based application development and deployment.
- Have a basic knowledge of COM programming.
- Understand how Web content is stored and accessed over the Internet. This includes being able to explain the roles of Web servers, Internet protocols, and Web clients (such as browsers).
- Be familiar with XML and related technologies such as XPath and XSD.

Reference Materials

You might find the following reference materials useful.

- The Visual Studio .NET online Help
- The Microsoft Developer Network (*http://msdn.microsoft.com*)
- W3C Recommendations for XML and Web Services (*http://www.w3c.org*)
- The XML Web Services Developer Center (*http://msdn.microsoft.com/webservices*)

About the CD-ROM

The Supplemental Course Materials CD-ROM contains a variety of informational aids that can be used throughout this book.

- **eBook.**   A complete electronic version of this training kit.
- **Completed labs.**   Each chapter in this book concludes with a lab containing a series of exercises that reinforce the skills you learned. Completed versions of these applications are included so that you can compare your results. You can also use the completed applications as a reference if you need help while completing an exercise.
- **Sample exam questions.**   To practice taking a certification exam, you can use the sample exam questions provided on the CD-ROM. The sample questions help you assess your understanding of the concepts presented in this book.

About the DVD

The DVD contains a 60-day evaluation edition of Microsoft Visual Studio .NET Professional Edition.

Important   The 60-day evaluation edition provided with this training kit is not the full retail product and is provided only for the purposes of training and evaluation. Microsoft Technical Support does not support this evaluation edition.

For additional support information regarding this book and the CD-ROM and DVD (including answers to commonly asked questions about installation and use), visit the Microsoft Press Technical Support Web site at *http://www.microsoft.com/ mspress/support*. You can also e-mail tkinput@microsoft.com or send a letter to Microsoft Press, Attn: Microsoft Press Technical Support, One Microsoft Way, Redmond, WA 98052-6399.

Features of This Book

Each chapter contains sections that are designed to help you get the most educational value from the chapter.

- Each chapter opens with a "Before You Begin" section, which prepares you for completing the chapter.
- The chapters are then divided into lessons. Each lesson contains the reference and procedural information used for a specific skill or skills.
- The "Summary" section identifies the key concepts from the lesson.
- The "Lab" section provides hands-on exercises that reinforce the skills taught in each of the chapter lessons. The exercises offer step-by-step procedures that give you an opportunity to use the skills being presented or explore the part of the application being described.

Appendix A, "Questions and Answers," contains all of the questions asked in each chapter review and the corresponding answers.

Notes

Several types of notes appear throughout the lessons.

- Notes marked **Tip** contain explanations of possible results or alternative methods for performing tasks.
- Notes marked **Important** contain information that is essential to completing a task.
- Notes marked **Note** contain supplemental information.
- Notes marked **Caution** contain warnings about possible loss of data.

Notational Conventions

The following notational conventions are used throughout this book.

- Characters or commands that you type appear in **bold** type.
- *Italic* in syntax statements indicates placeholders for variable information. *Italic* is also used for book titles and to indicate newly introduced terms.

- Names of files and folders appear in initial capital letters except when you are to type them directly. Unless otherwise indicated, you can use lowercase letters when you type a file name in a dialog box or at a command prompt.

- File name extensions, when they appear without a file name, are in lowercase letters.

- Acronyms appear in all uppercase letters.

- Monospace type represents code samples.

- Square brackets [ ] are used in syntax statements to enclose optional items. For example, [*filename*] in command syntax indicates that you can choose to type a file name with the command. Type only the information within the brackets, not the brackets themselves.

- Braces { } are used in syntax statements to enclose required items. Type only the information within the braces, not the braces themselves.

- Icons represent specific sections in the book as follows:

Icon	Represents
	Supplemental course materials. You will find these materials on the Supplemental Course Materials CD-ROM.
	A hands-on practice. You should perform the practice to give yourself an opportunity to use the skills being presented in the lesson.
	Chapter review questions. These questions at the end of each chapter allow you to test what you have learned in the lessons. You will find the answers to the review questions in Appendix A, "Questions and Answers," at the end of the book.

Chapter and Appendix Overview

This self-paced training kit combines notes, hands-on procedures, and review questions to teach you how to develop XML Web services and server components with Visual Studio .NET. It is designed to be worked through from beginning to end, but you can choose a customized track and complete only the sections that interest you. (See the next section, "Finding the Best Starting Point for You," for more information.) If you choose the customized track option, see the "Before You Begin" section in each chapter. Any hands-on procedures that require preliminary work from preceding chapters refer to the appropriate chapters.

The book is divided into the following sections and chapters.

- This "About This Book" section contains a self-paced training overview and introduces the components of this training kit. Read this section thoroughly to get the greatest educational value from this self-paced training and to plan which lessons you will complete.

- Chapter 1, "Understanding the .NET Framework," introduces the fundamentals of the Microsoft .NET Framework, which is the infrastructure for developing highly distributed applications for the Internet. The chapter discusses the role of the common language runtime in the .NET Framework, the difference between managed and unmanaged program execution, and the use of assemblies in application deployment and configuration. In addition, the chapter describes how to use the tools that the .NET Framework provides for creating, deploying, and managing applications.

- Chapter 2, "Creating and Managing Windows Services," explains the Windows service programming model and includes sections on the creation of Windows services in Microsoft Visual Studio .NET and the mechanisms used to control the behavior of Windows services. You learn to make entries in default event logs, create custom event logs, and record information in custom event logs. You also learn to configure a service dynamically and manage a service manually and programmatically.

- Chapter 3, "Creating and Consuming Serviced Components," describes the serviced components that enable access to COM+ services, such as automatic transaction management, object pooling, and just-in-time (JIT) activation. You learn about the basics of the COM+ programming model, create and register serviced components, utilize COM+ services, and manage serviced components using the Component Services tool.

- Chapter 4, "Creating and Consuming .NET Remoting Objects," demonstrates the use of the .NET Framework to establish communication between objects without having to know about the protocols or the encoding and decoding mechanisms involved in the development of a distributed application. You learn to create, configure, and secure .NET Remoting objects using the classes provided by the .NET Framework.

- Chapter 5, "Database Programming Using ADO.NET," shows you how to use ActiveX Data Objects (ADO) for the .NET Framework. In this chapter, you learn to use the .NET data providers, and create and use ADO.NET DataSets. In addition, you learn to manage and control data using DataReader and Data-Adapter objects.

- Chapter 6, "Accessing and Manipulating XML Data," explains the importance of XML as the core to data exchange between applications in the .NET Framework. This chapter discusses the XML Document Object Model (DOM) and shows how to access XML data in applications. You learn how to read and write data from XML documents, perform queries on XML documents, and validate XML documents with the XML Schema. In addition, you learn to populate a DataSet with data from an XML file and write data from a DataSet into an XML file.

- Chapter 7, "Creating and Consuming XML Web Services," shows you how to build scalable, loosely-coupled, platform-independent applications. XML Web services enable disparate applications to exchange messages using standard protocols such as HTTP, XML, XSD, SOAP, and Web Services Description Language (WSDL).

- Chapter 8, "Advanced XML Web Services Programming," explains how to control characteristics of Web methods using attributes. In addition, you learn to create and use SOAP extensions and create asynchronous Web methods.

- Chapter 9, "Testing and Debugging XML Web Services," shows how to debug XML Web services and serviced components. You also learn how to use tracing and perform code instrumentation.

- Chapter 10, "Deploying XML Web Services and Windows Services," explains the deployment options that the .NET Framework provides. You learn to create setup programs that allow you to install your .NET applications. In addition, you learn to implement versioning and side-by-side deployment.

- Appendix A, "Questions and Answers," lists all of the review questions from the book, showing the page number for each question and the suggested answer.

- Appendix B, "COM Interoperability," provides additional information about how to call unmanaged COM objects from within your managed applications. You learn to export COM types and create interop assemblies from your COM type libraries.

- The Glossary provides definitions for many of the terms and concepts presented in this training kit.

Finding the Best Starting Point for You

Because this book is self-paced, you can skip some lessons and revisit them later. Use the following table to find the best starting point for you.

If you	Follow this learning path
Are preparing to take the Microsoft Certified Professional Exam 70-310 or 70-320	Read the "Getting Started" section. Then work through the remaining chapters in any order.
Want to review information about specific topics from the exam	Use the "Where to Find Specific Skills in This Book" section that follows this table.

Where to Find Specific Skills in This Book

The following tables provide a list of the skills measured on certification Exam 70-310, *Developing XML Web Services and Server Components with Microsoft Visual Basic .NET and the Microsoft .NET Framework*, or Exam 70-320, *Developing XML Web Services and Server Components with Microsoft Visual C# .NET and the Microsoft .NET Framework*. The tables that follow indicate skills and where in this book you will find the lesson or lessons relating to those skills.

Note   Exam skills are subject to change without prior notice at the sole discretion of Microsoft.

Table A.1   Creating and Managing Microsoft Windows Services, Serviced Components, .NET Remoting Objects, and XML Web Services

Skill being measured	Location in book
Create and manipulate a Windows service:	Chapter 2, Lessons 2, 3, 4, 5, and 6
■ Write code that is executed when a Windows service is started or stopped.	Chapter 2, Lessons 2, 3, and 4
Create and consume a serviced component:	Chapter 3, Lessons 2 and 3
■ Implement a serviced component.	Chapter 3, Lesson 2
■ Create interfaces that are visible to COM.	Chapter 10, Lesson 3
■ Create a strongly named assembly.	Chapter 1, Lesson 4
■ Register the component in the global assembly cache.	Chapter 1, Lesson 4
■ Manage the component using the Component Services tool.	Chapter 3, Lesson 4
Create and consume a .NET Remoting object:	Chapter 4, Lessons 1, 2, and 3
■ Implement server-activated components.	Chapter 4, Lesson 2
■ Implement client-activated components.	Chapter 4, Lesson 2
■ Select a channel protocol and a formatter. Channel protocols include TCP and HTTP. Formatters include SOAP and binary.	Chapter 4, Lesson 3
■ Create client configuration files and server configuration files.	Chapter 4, Lesson 6
■ Implement an asynchronous method.	Chapter 4, Lesson 5
■ Create the listener service.	Chapter 4, Lesson 4
■ Instantiate and invoke a .NET Remoting object.	Chapter 4, Lesson 2

(continued)

Table A.1   Creating and Managing Microsoft Windows Services, Serviced Components, .NET Remoting Objects, and XML Web Services *(continued)*

Skill being measured	Location in book
Create and consume an XML Web service:	Chapter 7, Lessons 2 and 4
■ Control characteristics of Web methods using attributes.	Chapter 8, Lesson 1
■ Create and use SOAP extensions.	Chapter 8, Lesson 3
■ Create asynchronous Web methods.	Chapter 8, Lesson 2
■ Control the XML wire format for an XML Web service.	Chapter 8, Lesson 3
■ Instantiate and invoke an XML Web service.	Chapter 7, Lesson 4
Implement security for a Windows service, a serviced component, a .NET Remoting object, and an XML Web service.	Chapter 2, Lessons 4 and 6; Chapter 3, Lesson 5; Chapter 4, Lesson 6; and Chapter 8, Lesson 4
Access unmanaged code from a Windows service, a serviced component, a .NET Remoting object, and an XML Web service.	Appendix B

Table A.2   Consuming and Manipulating Data

Skill being measured	Location in book
Access and manipulate data from a Microsoft SQL Server database by creating and using ad hoc queries and stored procedures.	Chapter 5, Lessons 1, 2, and 3
Create and manipulate DataSets.	Chapter 5, Lesson 3
■ Manipulate a DataSet schema.	Chapter 5, Lesson 3 and Chapter 6, Lesson 6
■ Manipulate DataSet relationships.	Chapter 5, Lesson 3
■ Create a strongly typed DataSet.	Chapter 5, Lesson 3 and Chapter 6, Lesson 6
Access and manipulate XML data.	Chapter 6, Lessons 1, 2, 3, 4, 5, and 6
■ Access an XML file using the Document Object Model (DOM) and an XmlReader.	Chapter 6, Lessons 1 and 2
■ Transform DataSet data into XML data.	Chapter 6, Lesson 6
■ Use XPath to query XML data.	Chapter 6, Lesson 3
■ Generate and use an XSD schema.	Chapter 6, Lesson 4
■ Write a SQL statement that retrieves XML data from a SQL Server database.	Chapter 5, Lessons 2 and 3; and Chapter 6, Lesson 6
■ Update a SQL Server database using XML.	Chapter 5, Lessons 2 and 3; and Chapter 6, Lesson 6
■ Validate an XML document.	Chapter 6, Lesson 5

Table A.3   Testing and Debugging

Skill being measured	Location in book
Create a unit test plan.	Chapter 9, Lesson 1
Implement tracing.	Chapter 9, Lesson 3
■ Configure and use trace listeners and trace switches.	
■ Display trace output.	
Instrument and debug a Windows service, a serviced component, a .NET Remoting object, and an XML Web service.	Chapter 9, Lessons 2, 3, and 4
■ Configure the debugging environment.	Chapter 9, Lesson 2
■ Create and apply debugging code to components and applications.	Chapter 9, Lesson 3
■ Provide multicultural test data to components and applications.	Chapter 9, Lesson 4
■ Execute tests.	Chapter 9, Lesson 1
Use interactive debugging.	Chapter 9, Lesson 2
Log test results.	Chapter 9, Lesson 1 and Chapter 2, Lesson 3
■ Resolve errors and rework code.	Chapter 9, Lessons 1 and 2
■ Control debugging in the Web.config file.	Chapter 9, Lesson 2
■ Use SOAP extensions for debugging.	Chapter 8, Lesson 3

Table A.4   Deploying Windows Services, Serviced Components, .NET Remoting Objects, and XML Web Services

Skill being measured	Location in book
Plan the deployment of and deploy a Windows service, a serviced component, a .NET Remoting object, and an XML Web service.	Chapter 10, Lesson 1
Create a setup program that installs a Windows service, a serviced component, a .NET Remoting object, and an XML Web service.	Chapter 10, Lesson 2
■ Register components and assemblies.	Chapter 10, Lesson 3
Publish an XML Web service.	Chapter 7, Lessons 1, 3, and 4
■ Enable static discovery.	
■ Publish XML Web service definitions in the UDDI.	

(continued)

Table A.4   Deploying Windows Services, Serviced Components, .NET Remoting Objects, and XML Web Services *(continued)*

Skill being measured	Location in book
Configure client computers and servers to use a Windows service, a serviced component, a .NET Remoting object, and an XML Web service.	Chapter 1, Lesson 5
Implement versioning.	Chapter 10, Lesson 4
Plan, configure, and deploy side-by-side deployments and applications.	Chapter 10, Lesson 4
Configure security for a Windows service, a serviced component, a .NET Remoting object, and an XML Web service.	Chapter 2, Lessons 4 and 6; Chapter 3, Lesson 5; Chapter 4, Lesson 6; and Chapter 8, Lesson 4

- Configure authentication type. Authentication types include Windows authentication, Microsoft .NET Passport, custom authentication, and none.

- Configure and control authorization. Authorization methods include file-based authorization and URL-based authorization.

- Configure and implement identity management.

Getting Started

This self-paced training kit contains hands-on procedures to help you learn about developing XML Web services and server components.

Caution   Several exercises might require you to make changes to your servers. This might cause undesirable results if you are connected to a large network. Check with your network administrator before attempting these exercises.

Hardware Requirements

Each computer must have the following minimum configuration. All hardware should be on the Microsoft Windows XP or Microsoft Windows 2000 Hardware Compatibility List.

- Pentium II class processor, 450 MHz
- 160 MB physical memory, 256 MB recommended
- CD-ROM or DVD drive, 12x or faster recommended

Note   A DVD drive is required to install the Visual Studio .NET Professional Evaluation Edition software.

- 3.5 GB on installation drive, which includes 500 MB on system drive
- Super VGA (800 × 600) or higher resolution monitor with 256 colors
- Microsoft Mouse or compatible pointing device

Software Requirements

The following software is required to complete the procedures in this course.

- Microsoft Windows 2000 or Microsoft Windows XP Professional Edition

> **Note** If IIS is not installed on your computer, you can install it by opening Add Or Remove Programs in Control Panel, and selecting Add/Remove Windows Components. Select Internet Information Services (IIS) from the Components list and then follow the onscreen instructions to complete the installation.

- Microsoft Visual Studio .NET Professional Edition or Visual Studio .NET Enterprise Developer Edition. The Professional Edition is recommended, and the Enterprise Developer Edition is ideal.
- Microsoft SQL Server 2000. A free evaluation version of SQL Server 2000 is available for download at *http://microsoft.com/sql/default.asp.*

Setup Instructions

Set up your computer according to the manufacturer's instructions.

The Exercise Files

The Supplemental Course Materials CD-ROM contains a set of solution files to the lab exercises at the end of each chapter.

▶ **To access the solution files**

1. Insert the Supplemental Course Materials CD-ROM into your CD-ROM drive.

> **Note** If Autorun is disabled on your machine, run StartCD.exe in the root folder of the CD-ROM or refer to the Readme.txt file.

2. Click the book's short title on the starting menu and browse the Solution Documents folder. You can then select the chapter number you want to view.

The eBook

The Supplemental Course Materials CD-ROM also includes a fully searchable electronic version of the book. To view the eBook you must have Microsoft Internet Explorer 5.01 or later and the proper HTML components on your system. If your system does not meet these requirements, you can install Internet Explorer 6 SP1 from the CD-ROM prior to installing the eBook.

Note   You must have the Supplemental Course Materials CD-ROM inserted in your CD-ROM drive to run the eBook.

The Exam Questions

The CD-ROM also includes an assessment tool that generates a 50-question practice exam with automated scoring and answer feedback.

▶ **To install the sample exam questions on your hard disk drive**

1. Insert the Supplemental Course Materials CD-ROM into your CD-ROM drive.

   Note   If Autorun is disabled on your machine, run StartCD.exe in the root directory of the CD-ROM or refer to the Readme.txt file.

2. Click Sample Exam Questions on the user interface menu and follow the prompts.

The Microsoft Certified Professional Program

The Microsoft Certified Professional (MCP) program provides the best method to prove your command of current Microsoft products and technologies. Microsoft, an industry leader in certification, is on the forefront of testing methodology. Our exams and corresponding certifications are developed to validate your mastery of critical competencies as you design and develop, or implement and support, solutions with Microsoft products and technologies. Computer professionals who become Microsoft certified are recognized as experts and are sought after industry-wide.

The Microsoft Certified Professional program offers multiple certifications based on specific areas of technical expertise including:

- **Microsoft Certified Application Developer (MCAD) for Microsoft .NET.** Qualified to develop and maintain department-level applications, components, Web or desktop clients, or back-end data services.
- **Microsoft Certified Solution Developer (MCSD).**   Qualified to design and develop custom business solutions with Microsoft development tools, technologies, and platforms and Microsoft Windows architecture.

- **Microsoft Certified Professional (MCP).** Demonstrated in-depth knowledge of at least one Microsoft Windows operating system or architecturally significant platform. An MCP is qualified to implement a Microsoft product or technology as part of a business solution for an organization.

- **Microsoft Certified Systems Engineer (MCSE) on Windows 2000.** Qualified to effectively analyze the business requirements and design and implement the infrastructure for business solutions based on the Microsoft Windows 2000 platform and Microsoft .NET 2003 Enterprise Servers.

- **Microsoft Certified Systems Administrator (MCSA) on Microsoft Windows 2000.** Qualified to implement, manage, and troubleshoot existing network and system environments based on the Microsoft Windows 2000 and Windows .NET Server 2003 operating systems.

- **Microsoft Certified Database Administrator (MCDBA) on Microsoft SQL Server 2000.** Qualified to derive physical database designs, develop logical data models, create physical databases, create data services using Transact-SQL, manage and maintain databases, configure and manage security, monitor and optimize databases, and install and configure Microsoft SQL Server.

- **Microsoft Certified Trainer (MCT).** Instructionally and technically qualified to deliver Microsoft Official Curriculum through a Microsoft Certified Technical Education Center (CTEC).

Microsoft Certification Benefits

Microsoft certification, one of the most comprehensive certification programs available for assessing and maintaining software-related skills, is a valuable measure of an individual's knowledge and expertise. Microsoft certification is awarded to individuals who have successfully demonstrated their ability to perform specific tasks and implement solutions with Microsoft products. Not only does this certification provide an objective measure for employers to consider, but it also provides guidance for what an individual should know to be proficient. As with any skills-assessment and benchmarking measure, certification brings a variety of benefits to the individual, and to employers and organizations.

Microsoft Certification Benefits for Individuals

As a Microsoft Certified Professional, you receive many benefits including:

- Industry recognition of your knowledge and proficiency with Microsoft products and technologies.

- A Microsoft Developer Network subscription. MCPs receive rebates or discounts on a one-year subscription to the Microsoft Developer Network (*msdn.microsoft.com/subscriptions*) during the first year of certification. (Fulfillment details will vary, depending on your location. Please see your Welcome Kit.)

- Access to technical and product information direct from Microsoft through a secured area of the MCP Web site (go to *http://www.microsoft.com/traincert/mcp/mcpsecure.asp*).

- Access to exclusive discounts on products and services from selected companies. Individuals who are currently certified can learn more about exclusive discounts by visiting the MCP secured Web site (go to *http://www.microsoft.com/traincert/mcp/mcpsecure.asp* and click the "Other Benefits" link).

- An MCP logo, certificate, transcript, wallet card, and lapel pin to identify you as an MCP to colleagues and clients. Electronic files of logos and transcripts can be downloaded from the MCP secured Web site (go to *http://www.microsoft.com/traincert/mcp/mcpsecure.asp*) upon certification.

- Invitations to Microsoft conferences, technical training sessions, and special events.

- Free access to *Microsoft Certified Professional Magazine Online*, a career and professional development magazine. Secured content on the *Microsoft Certified Professional Magazine Online* Web site includes the current issue (available only to MCPs), additional online-only content and columns, an MCP-only database, and regular chats with Microsoft and other technical experts.

- A discount on a membership to PASS (for MCPs only), the Professional Association for SQL Server. In addition to playing a key role in the only worldwide, user-run SQL Server user group endorsed by Microsoft, members enjoy unique access to a world of educational opportunities (go to *http://www.microsoft.com/traincert/mcp/mcpsecure.asp*).

An additional benefit is received by Microsoft Certified System Engineers (MCSEs):

- A 50-percent rebate or discount off the estimated retail price of a one-year subscription to *TechNet* or *TechNet Plus* during the first year of certification. (Fulfillment details will vary, depending on your location. Please see your Welcome Kit.) In addition, about 95 percent of the CD-ROM content is available free at the *TechNet* Web site (*http://www.microsoft.com/technet*).

Additional benefits are received by Microsoft Certified System Database Administrators (MCDBAs):

- A 50-percent rebate or discount off the estimated retail price of a one-year subscription to *TechNet* or *TechNet Plus* during the first year of certification. (Fulfillment details will vary, depending on your location. Please see your Welcome Kit.) In addition, about 95 percent of the CD-ROM content is available free at the *TechNet* Web site (*http://www.microsoft.com/technet*).

- A one-year subscription to *SQL Server Magazine*. Written by industry experts, the magazine contains technical and how-to tips and advice—a must for anyone working with SQL Server.

A list of benefits for Microsoft Certified Trainers (MCTs) can be found at *http:// www.microsoft.com/traincert/mcp/mct/benefits.asp*.

Microsoft Certification Benefits for Employers and Organizations

Through certification, computer professionals can maximize the return on investment in Microsoft technology. Research shows that Microsoft certification provides organizations with:

- Excellent return on training and certification investments by providing a standard method of determining training needs and measuring results.
- Increased customer satisfaction and decreased support costs through improved service, increased productivity, and greater technical self-sufficiency.
- Reliable benchmarks for hiring, promoting, and career planning.
- Recognition and rewards for productive employees by validating their expertise.
- Retraining options for existing employees so they can work effectively with new technologies.
- Assurance of quality when outsourcing computer services.

Requirements for Becoming a Microsoft Certified Professional

Certification requirements differ for each certification and are specific to the products and job functions addressed by the certification.

To become a Microsoft Certified Professional, you must pass rigorous certification exams that provide a valid and reliable measure of technical proficiency and expertise. These exams are designed to test your expertise and ability to perform a role or task with a product, and are developed with the input of professionals in the industry. Questions in the exams reflect how Microsoft products are used in actual organizations, giving them "real-world" relevance.

- Microsoft Certified Professional candidates are required to pass one operating system exam. Candidates can also pass additional Microsoft certification exams to further qualify their skills with other Microsoft products, development tools, or desktop applications.
- Microsoft Certified Systems Engineers are required to pass five core exams and two elective exams.
- Microsoft Certified Systems Administrators are required to pass three core exams and one elective exam that provide a valid and reliable measure of technical proficiency and expertise.
- Microsoft Certified Database Administrators are required to pass three core exams and one elective exam that measure technical proficiency and expertise.

- Microsoft Certified Solution Developers are required to pass three core Microsoft Windows operating system technology exams and one BackOffice technology elective exam.

- Microsoft Certified Trainers are required to meet instructional and technical requirements specific to each Microsoft Official Curriculum course they are certified to deliver. The MCT program requires ongoing training to meet the requirements for the annual renewal of certification. For more information about becoming a Microsoft Certified Trainer, visit *http://www.microsoft.com/traincert/mcp/mct* or contact a regional service center near you.

Technical Training for Computer Professionals

Technical training is available in a variety of ways: instructor-led classes, online instruction, or self-paced training available at thousands of locations worldwide.

Self-Paced Training

For motivated learners who are ready for the challenge, self-paced instruction is the most flexible, cost-effective way to increase your knowledge and skills.

A full line of self-paced print and computer-based training materials is available direct from the source—Microsoft Press. Microsoft Official Curriculum courseware kits from Microsoft Press are designed for advanced computer system professionals and are available from Microsoft Press and the Microsoft Developer Division. Self-paced training kits from Microsoft Press feature print-based instructional materials, along with CD-ROM–based product software, multimedia presentations, lab exercises, and practice files. The Mastering Series provides in-depth, interactive training on CD-ROMs for experienced developers. They're both great ways to prepare for the Microsoft Certified Professional (MCP) exams.

Online Training

For a more flexible alternative to instructor-led classes, turn to online instruction. It's as near as the Internet, and it's ready whenever you are. Learn at your own pace and on your own schedule in a virtual classroom, often with easy access to an online instructor. Without ever leaving your desk, you can gain the expertise you need. Online instruction covers a variety of Microsoft products and technologies. It includes options ranging from Microsoft Official Curriculum to choices available nowhere else. It's training on demand, with access to learning resources 24 hours a day. Online training is available through Microsoft Certified Technical Education Centers (CTECs).

Microsoft Certified Technical Education Centers

Microsoft Certified Technical Education Centers are the best source for instructor-led training that can help you prepare to become a Microsoft Certified Professional.

The Microsoft CTEC program is a worldwide network of qualified technical training organizations that provide authorized delivery of Microsoft Official Curriculum courses by Microsoft Certified Trainers to computer professionals.

For a listing of CTEC locations in the United States and Canada, visit the Web site at *http://www.microsoft.com/traincert/ctec*.

Technical Support

Every effort has been made to ensure the accuracy of this book and the contents of the companion disc. If you have comments, questions, or ideas regarding this book or the companion disc, please send them to Microsoft Press using either of the following methods:

E-mail: TKINPUT@MICROSOFT.COM

Postal Mail: Microsoft Press
Attn: *MCAD/MCSD Training Kit: Developing XML Web Services and Server Components with Microsoft Visual Basic .NET and Microsoft Visual C# .NET* Editor
One Microsoft Way
Redmond, WA 98052-6399

The Microsoft Press Web site (*http://www.microsoft.com/mspress/support*) provides corrections for books. Please note that product support is not offered through this Web site. For further information regarding Microsoft software support options, please connect to *http://www.microsoft.com/support*.

For information about ordering the full version of any Microsoft software, please connect to *http://www.microsoft.com*.

C H A P T E R   1

Understanding the .NET Framework

About This Chapter

In this chapter, you will learn the fundamentals of the Microsoft .NET Framework, which is the infrastructure for developing highly distributed applications for the Internet. In addition, you will look at the role of the common language runtime in the .NET Framework, differentiate between managed and unmanaged program execution, and use assemblies in application deployment and configuration. You will also learn how the .NET Framework provides a highly secure and fault-tolerant execution environment. Finally, you will learn to use the tools that the .NET Framework provides for creating, deploying, and managing applications.

Before You Begin

To complete the lessons in this chapter, you

- Must have Microsoft Visual Studio .NET installed on your computer
- Must be familiar with development and deployment of Windows-based, Web-based, and Console-based applications
- Must be able to create, compile, and execute Microsoft Visual Basic .NET and Microsoft Visual C# applications

Each chapter in this book concludes with a lab containing a series of exercises that reinforce the concepts and skills presented in the lessons. Completed versions of these applications are included on the Supplemental Course Materials CD-ROM so that you can compare your results. You can also use the completed applications as a reference if you get stuck while completing an exercise. The \Solution folder on the CD-ROM contains the code required to complete each lab so that you won't need to enter the code manually.

Lesson 1: Overview of the .NET Framework

Microsoft .NET is software that enables you to develop applications for different environments and devices. For example, you can build eXtensible Markup Language (XML) Web services and Web applications for a highly distributed environment such as the Internet. You can also create traditional Windows-based applications, server components, and applications that can run on any device, such as a PC or a mobile device. In addition, .NET enables seamless data exchange between various applications and devices. The .NET Framework is the infrastructure that provides the execution engine and run-time services to applications created using .NET.

After this lesson, you will be able to

- Describe .NET
- Describe the .NET Framework and its role in .NET
- Describe the .NET Framework architecture

Estimated lesson time: 25 minutes

Understanding .NET

.NET provides development tools, run-time environments, server infrastructure, and intelligent software, which enable you to build applications for various platforms and devices. In addition, .NET integrates various applications and devices by using standards such as Hypertext Transfer Protocol (HTTP), XML, and Simple Object Access Protocol (SOAP). .NET overcomes one of the biggest challenges of the software industry: to exchange data between applications written in different languages and for different environments. .NET enables various applications to exchange data by using XML Web services. In addition, .NET provides remoting infrastructure that allows applications running in different processes, on the same or different computers, to exchange data using binary or HTTP protocols.

The tools and operational systems that .NET provides include

- **Smart Client software.**   This software allows a client, a PC, or a mobile device to access data from any location or device by using XML Web services.
- **.NET Server infrastructure.**   This provides a highly secure and scalable platform for deploying .NET applications. The .NET Server infrastructure includes Windows 2000 Servers, Windows .NET Servers, and .NET Enterprise Servers.
- **XML Web services.**   These are core to application integration in the .NET environment. They allow Internet as well as intranet applications, written in different languages and hosted on different platforms, to exchange data using standard protocols such as HTTP, XML, and SOAP. (XML Web services are described in detail in Chapters 7 and 8.)

- **Microsoft Visual Studio .NET and the .NET Framework.**   Visual Studio .NET and the .NET Framework provide a complete solution for building, hosting, and consuming XML Web services. Visual Studio .NET supports a variety of programming environments and languages and provides a single-point access to all the tools that you might need, making it one of the most productive tools available.

Figure 1.1 displays components of .NET.

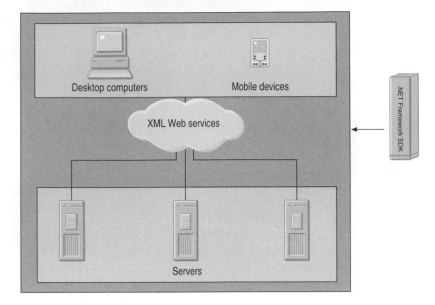

Figure 1.1   Components of .NET

As shown in Figure 1.1, XML Web services comprise the core components that enable a client application to exchange data with another client or server application. Using XML Web services, server applications can also exchange data with each another. In addition, applications running on any device can exchange data with the applications running on any other device.

Understanding the .NET Framework and Its Role in .NET

The .NET Framework is the infrastructure for building applications using .NET. The .NET Framework provides a consistent object-oriented programming model that you can use to build all types of applications. The approach for creating various applications such as Windows-based applications and XML Web services is the same. To create a .NET application, you create a class and define the functionality of the application in terms of properties, events, and methods of the class. Even for Web applications, the code that controls the behavior of the Web page is encapsulated within a class. In addition, classes support object-oriented features such as inheritance, encapsulation, and polymorphism. Therefore, classes are fundamental to programming in the .NET environment. You can create classes in any language supported by the .NET Framework. A class written in one language is reusable by classes written in other languages. You can also inherit classes across language boundaries because the .NET Framework allows language interoperability and supports cross-language inheritance.

The European Computer Manufacturers Association (ECMA) standard defines the Common Language Specification (CLS), which contains the rules for language interoperability. The code written in a CLS-compliant language is interoperable with the code written in another CLS-compliant language because the code written in a CLS-compliant language is compiled into an intermediate language (IL) code. The run-time engine executes the IL code. This ensures interoperability between CLS-compliant languages.

The .NET Framework provides four CLS-compliant languages: Microsoft Visual Basic .NET, Microsoft Visual C#, Microsoft Visual C++ .NET, and Microsoft Visual J# .NET. Visual C# was ratified by ECMA as an international standard on December 13, 2001. The compilers of these languages generate an intermediate code, called Microsoft Intermediate Language (MSIL), which makes programs written in the .NET languages interoperable. Therefore, in the .NET Framework, you can use any language to create applications, and these applications can interoperate with the applications written by others in different languages.

The ECMA standard, Common Language Infrastructure (CLI), defines the specifications for the infrastructure that the IL code needs for execution. The CLI provides a common type system (CTS) and services such as type safety and managed code execution. The .NET Framework provides the infrastructure and services per the CLI specifications. These include

- **Common language runtime.**   This includes the CLI and provides the execution environment to .NET applications. All the .NET language compilers compile the source code into MSIL code, which the common language runtime loads and executes when you run an application.

- **Common type system.**   This provides the necessary data types, value and object types, which you need to develop applications in different languages. All the .NET languages share a CTS. This implies that a String in Visual Basic .NET is the same as a String in Visual C# or in Visual C++ .NET. All the .NET languages have access to the same class libraries. In addition, all languages are equally powerful. There is no superior language in .NET; Visual Basic .NET is as powerful as Visual C# or Visual C++ .NET.

- **Type safety.**   The .NET Framework ensures that operations to be performed on one value or object are performed on that value or object only. To do this, the .NET Framework requires that each value or object has a type and that each reference to a value or an object also has a type.

- **Managed code execution.**   The .NET Framework loads and executes the .NET applications, and manages the state of objects during program execution.

In addition, the .NET Framework automatically allocates memory and provides an automatic garbage collection mechanism, which claims the memory from objects when the objects are no longer required.

- **Side-by-side execution.**   The .NET Framework allows you to deploy multiple versions of an application on a system by using assemblies. *Assemblies* are the deployment units in the .NET Framework. An assembly contains the IL code and metadata. The metadata contains information such as the version of the assembly and the name and version of the other assemblies on which the assembly depends. The common language runtime uses the version information in the metadata to determine application dependencies and enables you to execute multiple versions of an application side-by-side.

Understanding the .NET Framework Architecture

The .NET Framework consists of two main components: the .NET Framework class library and the common language runtime. The .NET Framework class library provides the types that are common to all .NET languages. Programmers can use these types to develop different kinds of applications, such as console applications, Windows and Web Forms, and XML Web services.

The common language runtime consists of components that load the IL code of a program into the runtime, compile the IL code into native code, execute and manage the code, enforce security and type safety, and provide thread support and other useful services.

Figure 1.2 shows the components of the .NET Framework.

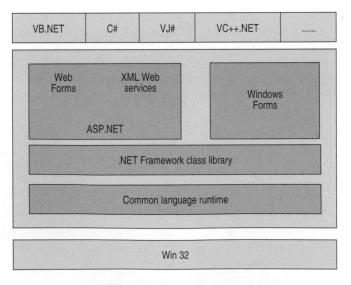

Figure 1.2   .NET Framework components

The code that runs within the common language runtime is called managed code, whereas the code that runs outside the common language runtime is called unmanaged code. The common language runtime provides an interoperability layer, which allows both the managed code and the unmanaged code to interoperate with each other.

Various components within the common language runtime work together to provide the infrastructure and the run-time services. The common language runtime and its components are described in Lesson 2.

Lesson 2: Understanding the Common Language Runtime

As described in the previous lesson, the common language runtime is one of the main components of the .NET Framework. It provides the run-time environment and various run-time services to applications. Various components of the common language runtime work together to provide the run-time infrastructure to the applications that run on the .NET Framework. By learning the common language runtime architecture, the various components of the common language runtime, and the functions of each common language runtime component, you will be able to describe how the common language runtime functions within the .NET Framework

After this lesson, you will be able to

- Describe the architecture of the common language runtime
- Describe how different components of the common language runtime work together to provide the run-time environment and services

Estimated lesson time: 20 minutes

Common Language Runtime Architecture

The common language runtime consists of various components that provide the run-time environment and run-time services for your applications. These components load the IL code of an application into the runtime, compile the IL code into native code, execute the code, and enforce security. In addition, these components implement type safety and provide automatic memory management and thread support. The components of the common language runtime also provide an exception manager, a common debugger, and other system services, such as base class library support and interoperability.

Figure 1.3 shows the various components that constitute the common language runtime.

These components include

- Class loader, which loads classes into the runtime.
- MSIL to native code compiler, which converts MSIL code into native code.
- Code manager, which manages the code during execution.
- Garbage collector, which performs automatic memory management.
- Security engine, which enforces security restrictions.

- Type checker, which enforces strict type checking.
- Thread support, which provides multithreading support to applications.
- Exception manager, which provides a mechanism to handle the run-time exceptions.
- Debug engine, which allows you to debug different types of applications.
- COM marshaler, which allows .NET applications to exchange data with COM applications.
- Base class library support, which provides the types that the applications need at run time.

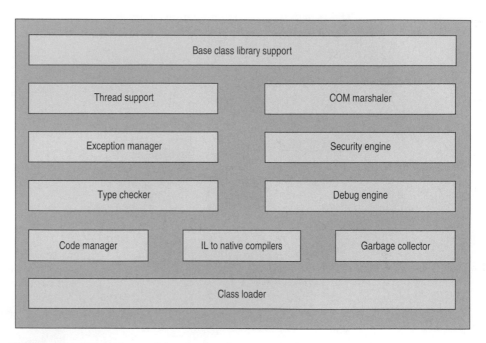

Figure 1.3   Components of the common language runtime

Common Language Runtime Components

For a program to run within the common language runtime and benefit from the managed execution environment, you need to write the source code of the program in a CLS-compliant language. The compilers of CLS-compliant languages compile the source code and generate an intermediate code, called MSIL code, and metadata. The MSIL code contains a CPU-independent set of instructions, which describes how to load, store, initialize, and call methods on objects. MSIL code also contains instructions that enable you to perform arithmetic and logical operations, access memory directly, control the flow of execution, handle exceptions, and perform other operations. Before you execute the MSIL code, you need to compile it into CPU-specific instructions. To execute the code, the runtime requires information about the code that is in the metadata. The metadata describes the code and defines the types that the code contains as well as references to other types that the code uses at run time. The MSIL code and the metadata are located in a portable executable file.

When you execute a portable executable file, the class loader loads the MSIL code and the metadata from the portable executable file into the run-time memory. Before the code is executed, it is passed to the native code compiler for compilation. The IL to native code compiler contains just-in-time (JIT) compilers for different CPU architectures and compiles the IL code into a native instruction set. The IL to native code compilation occurs when a method is called for the first time. For subsequent calls to the method, the existing JIT-compiled code is executed. Figure 1.4 shows the JIT compilation process.

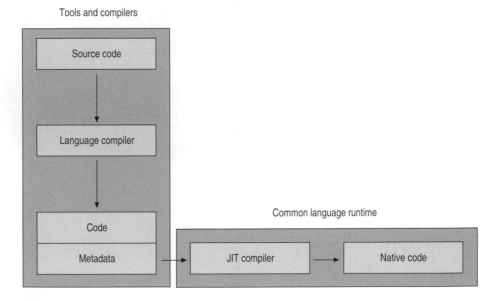

Figure 1.4   Just-in-time compilation

After the MSIL code and the metadata are loaded into memory, the code manager calls the entry-point method, which is the Main, WinMain, or DllMain method. An *entry-point* method is the first method to be executed when you run an application. The IL to native code JIT compiler compiles the entry-point method before it is executed. During the execution of the entry-point method, the code manager places the objects in memory and controls the execution of the program. The garbage collector performs periodic checks on the managed heap to identify the objects that are no longer required by the program and removes them from memory.

During program execution, the type checker ensures that all objects and values, and the references to those objects and values, have a valid type. The type checker also ensures that only valid operations are performed on the objects or values. For example, the type checker ensures that only an integer value is assigned to a variable of integer type. The type checker raises an error if a string value is assigned to an integer variable. In addition, the type checker also ensures that only valid operations such as addition, subtraction, division, and multiplication are performed on an integer value.

The common language runtime controls the code at run time. The security engine of the common language runtime enforces restrictions on the code and controls the access to system resources such as the hard disk, network connections, and other system resources.

The applications running within the common language runtime can utilize the managed multithreading support. The .NET Framework allows a single process to be divided into one or more subprocesses called application domains. Each application domain can contain one or more threads. The runtime monitors all the threads that have executed code within its process.

The common language runtime also allows managed code to interoperate with unmanaged code. One of the components of the common language runtime is the *COM marshaler*, which performs marshaling of data when data passes between managed and unmanaged execution environments. *Marshaling* manages the different representations of data across different execution environments. It performs the necessary conversions in data formats between managed and unmanaged code. In addition, the runtime provides a structured *exception handling* mechanism, which handles exceptions that arise from managed and unmanaged method calls.

During the execution process, a program depends upon the functionality provided by the .NET Framework class library. The common language runtime provides the base class library support to the programs that are running within the managed execution environment.

The common language runtime also provides a common debug engine, which enables you to debug an application written in any language supported by the .NET Framework. The common debug engine supports debugging applications running on local and remote machines.

The process by which different components of the common language runtime provide the infrastructure and run-time services to managed code is called the managed execution process. During managed execution, managed code utilizes the automatic memory management provided by the garbage collector. The next lesson discusses the managed execution process.

Lesson 3: Understanding the Managed Execution Process

The .NET Framework uses the managed execution process to run applications. One of the advantages of the managed execution process is automatic memory management. In this lesson, you will learn how the managed execution process provides automatic memory management.

After this lesson, you will be able to

- Describe the managed execution process
- Describe how the .NET Framework performs automatic memory management

Estimated lesson time: 25 minutes

Defining the Managed Execution Process

Managed execution is the process in which the runtime loads, executes, and provides automatic memory management. Managed execution also performs other useful services, such as performing JIT compilations, ensuring type safety, enforcing security, and handling exceptions.

The managed execution process involves managed code and managed data. Managed code is self-describing code that provides information to the common language runtime for providing various run-time services. In the .NET Framework, this information is stored with the MSIL code in the form of *metadata* inside the portable executable files. Metadata is the information that describes the code and the types that the code contains. Managed data is allocated and released from memory automatically by a process known as garbage collection. You can only access managed data from managed code. However, managed code can access both managed and unmanaged data.

Automatic Memory Management

The .NET Framework uses the garbage collector to perform automatic memory management. Therefore, you do not need to write code to allocate memory when objects are created or to release memory when objects are not required by an application. Automatic memory management overcomes common problems associated with memory management, such as not releasing memory that is no longer required or trying to access released memory. The automatic memory management feature allows you to focus on the solution to the real problem. The process of automatic memory management involves the following tasks:

- Allocating memory
- Releasing memory
- Implementing finalizers

Allocating Memory

Automatic memory management works in the following way. When a process is initialized, the runtime reserves a contiguous address space without allocating any storage space for it. This reserved address space is called a *managed heap*. The managed heap keeps a pointer at the location where the next object will be located. Assume the pointer is called ObjPtr. Initially, ObjPtr points to the base address of the managed heap. When an application uses the *new* operator to create an object, the *new* operator checks whether the memory required by the object is available on the heap. If the memory is available, it is allocated to the object, and the object is created on the heap at the location pointed to by ObjPtr. After the object is created, ObjPtr moves in front of the object. When the next object is created, the garbage collector allocates memory to the object on the managed heap, which is just in front of the first object, and moves ObjPtr in front of the new object. Figure 1.5 shows the object allocation on the managed heap. Note how ObjPtr moves to a new location after the object is created on the managed heap.

Allocating memory to the objects in a managed heap takes less time than allocating unmanaged memory. In unmanaged memory, the pointers to memory are maintained in linked-list data structures. Therefore, allocating memory requires navigating through the linked list, finding a large memory block to accommodate the

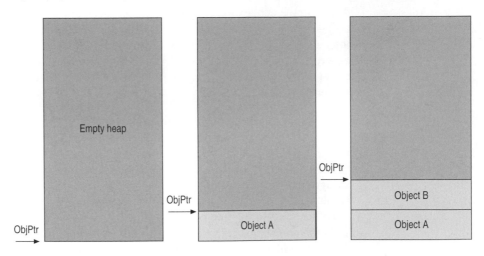

Figure 1.5   Object creation on the managed heap

object, splitting it, and finally, updating the pointers in the linked list. However, in managed memory allocation, the objects are allocated memory at the location to which ObjPtr currently points, and ObjPtr is incremented after the object is created.

You can access objects in managed memory faster than objects in unmanaged memory because in managed memory allocation, objects are created contiguously in the managed address space.

Releasing Memory

When you create an object, enough memory might not be available to be allocated for it. In such cases, the *new* operator, which creates objects, throws the OutOf-Memory exception. However, the garbage collector periodically releases memory from the objects that are no longer required by the application. The process of releasing unused memory is discussed here.

Every application has a set of roots. Roots point to the storage location on the managed heap. Each root either refers to an object on the managed heap or is set to null. An application's roots consist of global and static object pointers, local variables, and reference object parameters on a thread stack. The JIT compiler and the runtime maintain the list of the application roots. The garbage collector uses this list to create a graph of objects on the managed heap that are reachable from the root list. When the garbage collector starts running, it considers all the objects on the managed heap as garbage. As the garbage collector navigates through the application root list, it identifies the objects that have corresponding references in the application root list and marks them as reachable. An object might not be directly reachable from the application roots, but another reachable object might store a reference to that object. The garbage collector also considers such objects as reachable objects. Figure 1.6 shows objects A, D, and F, which are directly reachable from the application root list. Although object B is not directly reachable from the application root list, it is also included in the list of reachable objects because object D references object B.

The garbage collector considers all unreachable objects on the managed heap as garbage. The garbage collector performs a collection process to free the memory occupied by the garbage objects. After the garbage collector performs a round of garbage collection, the layout of the objects in the managed heap no longer remains contiguous. The garbage collector performs the memory copy function to compress the objects in the managed heap. After the objects are moved to the new locations in the heap, the root list becomes invalid. The garbage collector updates the pointers in the application root list so that the application roots correctly point to the objects to which they were pointing earlier. Figure 1.7 shows the managed heap after the collection process.

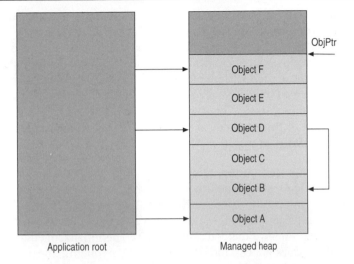

Figure 1.6   Managed heap with allocated objects

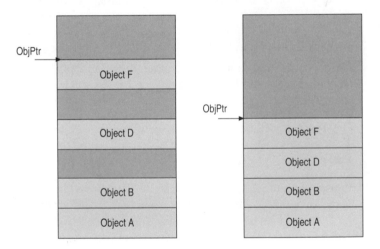

Figure 1.7   Managed heap after collection and compression

The garbage collector uses a highly optimized mechanism to perform garbage collection. It divides the objects on the managed heap into three generations: 0, 1, and 2. Generation 0 contains recently created objects. The garbage collector first collects the unreachable objects in generation 0. Next, the garbage collector compacts memory and promotes the reachable objects to generation 1. The objects that survive the collection process are promoted to higher generations. The garbage collector searches for unreachable objects in generations 1 and 2 only when the memory released by the collection process of generation 0 objects is insufficient to create the new object.

The garbage collector manages memory for all managed objects created by the application. However, the garbage collector cannot clean the system resources used by managed objects. For example, managed objects might use a handle to a file resource or a network connection. In such cases, when the garbage collector releases these objects from memory, the garbage collector does not clean the memory consumed by the system resources. Therefore, you need to explicitly release these system resources by providing the cleanup code in the Dispose method of the object. In addition, you need to explicitly call the Dispose method after you finish working with the object.

The garbage collection mechanism provides another way of cleaning unmanaged objects: finalization. The finalization process allows an object to perform cleanup tasks automatically before garbage collection starts. You need to write the cleanup code to release system resources, such as file handles and network connections, within the Finalize method of the object. The Finalize method ensures that even if the client does not call the Dispose method explicitly, the resources used by the object are released from memory when the object is garbage collected. Once the garbage collector identifies the object as garbage during garbage collection, it calls the Finalize method on the object before releasing memory.

Implementing Finalizers

Finalizers are the methods that contain the cleanup code that is executed before the object is garbage collected. The process of executing cleanup code is called *finalization*. The Dispose and Finalize methods are called *finalizers*.

The Dispose method of an object should release all its resources in addition to the resources owned by its parent object by calling the Dispose method of the parent object.

You can execute the Dispose method in two ways. The user of the class can call the Dispose method on the object that is being disposed, or the Finalize method can call the Dispose method during the finalization process. When a user calls the Dispose method, it can clean managed as well as unmanaged resources. However, when the Finalize method calls the Dispose method, the Dispose method can only clean unmanaged resources because during finalization, the garbage collector might have already removed an object for which Dispose is called. When the Dispose method tries to clean a managed object that is already finalized, the finalization fails.

The Dispose method should call the GC.SuppressFinalize method. This prevents the Finalize method from being called and prevents the cleanup tasks performed by the Dispose method from being repeated.

The following code shows how to implement the Dispose and Finalize methods for parent and child classes.

Note   The Parent class in the following code implements the IDisposable interface. An interface defines the methods that the class implementing the interface must implement. For example, in the following code the IDisposable interface defines the Dispose method that the Parent class implements.

Visual Basic .NET

```
' Implementing IDisposable implies that the
' instances of this class will use unmanaged resources
Public Class Parent
    Implements IDisposable
    ' An unmanaged resource
    Private ptr As IntPtr
    ' A Managed resource
    Private timer As Timers.Timer
    ' Variable to track call to Dispose method
    Private disposed As Boolean = False

    Public Sub New()
        ' Implement constructor
    End Sub

    Public Overloads Sub Dispose() Implements IDisposable.Dispose
        ' Call the overloaded Dispose method
        ' with true as argument, indicating that
        ' Dispose is called by the user of the object
        Dispose(True)
        ' Suppress theFinalizemethod
        ' so that it does not call Dispose again
        GC.SuppressFinalize(Me)

    End Sub

    Protected Overloads Overridable Sub Dispose(ByVal _
        called_by_user As Boolean)
        If Not (Me.disposed) Then
            ' if the user of the object called the Dispose method
            ' Clean managed as well as unmanaged data
            ' Otherwise clean only unmanaged data
            If called_by_user Then
                ' Clean managed data
                timer.Dispose()
            End If
            ptr = IntPtr.Zero
        End If
    disposed = True
    End Sub
```

(continued)

```
            Protected Overrides Sub Finalize()
                Dispose(False)
            End Sub
        End Class

        Public Class Child
            Inherits Parent

                .

                .

                .


        Protected Overloads Overridable Sub Dispose(ByVal _
            called_by_user As Boolean)
            ' Cleanup code for the child object
                .

                .

                .


            ' Call Dispose method of the Parent class
            MyBase.Dispose(called_by_user)
            End Sub
        End Class
```

Visual C#

```
// Implementing IDisposable implies that the
// instances of this class will use unmanaged resources

    public class Parent:IDisposable
    {
        // An unmanaged resource
        private IntPtr ptr;

        // A Managed resource
        private System.Timers.Timer  timer;

        // Variable to track call to Dispose method
        private bool disposed;

        public Parent()
        {
            // Implement constructor

        }

        public void Dispose()
        {
            // Call the overloaded Dispose method
            // with true as argument, indicating that
            // Dispose is called by the user of the object
```

```csharp
            Dispose(true);
            // Suppress the Finalize method
            // so that it does not call Dispose again
            GC.SuppressFinalize(this);
        }

        protected virtual void Dispose(bool called_by_user )
        {
            if  (!this.disposed)
            {
                // if the user of the object called the Dispose method
                // Clean managed as well as unmanaged data
                // Otherwise clean only unmanaged data
                if (called_by_user)
                {
                    // Clean managed data
                    timer.Dispose();
                }
                ptr = IntPtr.Zero;
                disposed = true;
            }
        }
        // C# destructor which is used to execute the finalization code
        ~Parent()
        {
            Dispose(false);
        }

    }

public class Child:Parent
    {.
     .
     .

        protected override void Dispose(bool called_by_user )
        {
            // Cleanup code for the child object
            .
            .
            .

            // Call Dispose method of the Parent class
            base.Dispose(called_by_user);

        }

    }
```

As discussed in the previous lessons, the managed execution process requires the MSIL code and the type metadata, which are both in the portable executable files. The runtime uses the type metadata, which is in assemblies, to provide the run-time services to the managed code.

A portable executable file cannot be executed if it does not contain an assembly manifest. An *assembly manifest* contains information about the assembly and the resources that it depends on. The runtime uses the information in the assembly manifest to load the assemblies into the runtime.

The next lesson discusses assemblies in detail.

Lesson 4: Understanding Assemblies and the Global Assembly Cache

Assemblies are the fundamental units for application development and deployment in the .NET Framework. An *assembly* contains the types and resources that an application requires. In addition, multiple applications can use the types that an assembly contains. An assembly that is shared by multiple applications is called a *global assembly* and is installed in the global assembly cache (GAC). The *global assembly cache* is a machine-wide cache that contains the assemblies that are shared by multiple applications. You use assemblies to perform version control and configure security for your applications. In this lesson, you will learn about assemblies and the role that assemblies play in application development in the .NET Framework.

After this lesson, you will be able to

- Describe assemblies and the role that they play in the .NET Framework
- Describe the types of assemblies
- Create single-file and multiple-file assemblies
- Describe the global assembly cache

Estimated lesson time: 25 minutes

Overview of Assemblies

Assemblies are building blocks of programming in the .NET Framework. An assembly contains the MSIL code, which the common language runtime executes, and the type metadata. The common language runtime uses the type metadata, which is inside the assembly, to provide run-time services to the code. An assembly also contains an assembly manifest that contains the assembly metadata. This metadata contains information about the assembly version, its security identity, the resources required by the assembly, and the scope of the assembly. The common language runtime cannot load and execute the MSIL code that is contained within the portable executable files if the assembly does not contain the assembly manifest.

The assembly manifest contains the version information. An assembly is the smallest unit that you use to define the version of an application. The version of an assembly determines the version of the types and the other resources that it contains. The .NET Framework allows the execution of multiple versions of the same assembly on the same machine. The side-by-side execution of assemblies overcomes the problem known as "DLL hell," which is one of the major problems associated with COM applications.

Assemblies are the smallest units to which the .NET Framework grants permissions. They provide security boundaries within the .NET Framework. You specify the permission required by your application while building assemblies. When the assembly is loaded into the runtime, the assembly sends a request to the runtime to grant the permission. The security engine of the runtime uses certain security policy files to check whether it can grant the permissions requested by the assembly. These security policy files are located on the system in which the application runs. The administrator of the system configures these files by using the security configuration tools provided by the .NET Framework. These tools are described in detail in Lesson 7.

Assemblies provide type boundaries. The type name and the assembly in which it resides determine the identity of the type. Therefore, two types that have the same name but are loaded within the scope of two different assemblies are different from each other. However, an assembly can contain two types with the same name if they are in different namespaces.

Understanding Namespaces

The .NET Framework class library consists of reusable classes, which are organized in hierarchical namespaces. A *namespace* contains logically- and functionally-related classes and divides an assembly into a logical grouping of types. For example, the System.Data namespace contains all the classes that you require to build database applications, and the System.IO namespace contains the classes that you require to perform input and output (I/O) operations within a program. Multiple assemblies can use the same namespace.

Types of Assemblies

Assemblies can be static or dynamic depending upon how they are created and stored. A static assembly is created when you compile the program using any of the .NET language compilers. A *static assembly* contains the types, interfaces, and various resources required by the assembly. A static assembly is stored on the hard disk in the form of a portable executable (.exe or .dll) file. The Visual Studio .NET tool and the language compilers that ship with the .NET Framework enable you to create these portable executable files.

However, dynamic assemblies are not created and stored on the hard disk by default. *Dynamic assemblies* are created at run time when an application requires the types within these assemblies. The .NET Framework provides reflection APIs in the System.Reflection.Emit namespace. *Reflection* APIs allow you to find type information and create objects dynamically at run time. The reflection APIs allow a tool or a compiler to emit metadata and MSIL code and optionally save them as portable executable files on the disk.

An assembly can also be single-file or multiple-file. A single-file assembly contains the assembly manifest, the type metadata, the MSIL code, and the resources. Figure 1.8 shows a single-file assembly and its contents.

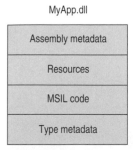

MyApp.dll

| Assembly metadata |
| Resources |
| MSIL code |
| Type metadata |

Figure 1.8   A single-file assembly

You can place the contents of an assembly in multiple files when different modules of the application are written in different languages. In addition, multiple-file assemblies make the downloading process more efficient. They enable you to store the seldom used types in separate modules and download them only when needed. The multiple-file assembly, shown in Figure 1.9, consists of three files. The MyApp.dll file contains the assembly manifest for the multiple-file assembly. The MyLib.netmodule file contains the type metadata and the MSIL code but not the assembly manifest. The Employee.gif is the resource file for this multiple-file assembly. The .NET Framework provides the Assembly Linker (AL) tool, Al.exe, which enables you to create a single manifest file by combining one or more modules and resource files. The AL tool is described in detail in Lesson 7.

Figure 1.9   A multiple-file assembly

Assemblies can also be private or shared. A *private assembly* is installed in the installation directory of an application and is accessible to that application only. On the other hand, a *shared assembly* is shared by multiple applications. A shared assembly has a strong name and is installed in the GAC. A *strong name* consists of an assembly name, version, culture information, digital signature, and public key information. Shared assemblies and the GAC are explained later in this lesson.

Each assembly has an identity, which makes it unique and distinct from other assemblies.

Assembly Identity

The name, version, culture, and strong-name information of an assembly determine its identity. The assembly manifest contains information about the identity of an assembly along with some additional information. Table 1.1 describes the information that is stored in the assembly manifest.

Table 1.1   Contents of the Assembly Manifest

Information	Description
Assembly name	A string value representing the name of the assembly.
Version number	A value in the *x.x.x.x* format. The first two numbers specify the major and minor version numbers. The last two numbers specify the revision and build numbers. The common language runtime uses these numbers to implement the version policy.
Culture	Contains information about the culture and language supported by the assembly.
Strong name	Information about the public key if the assembly has a strong name. The .NET Framework requires an assembly to have a strong name to make it accessible globally. Only strong-named assemblies can be placed inside the GAC.
List of all files in the assembly	The file names and the hash code of each file in the assembly. All files that constitute an assembly need to be in the same directory as the file containing the manifest.
Type reference information	The runtime uses this information to identify the file that contains a particular type declaration and implementation.
Information on referenced assemblies	Information about the assemblies statically referenced by the assembly. The information includes the dependent assembly name, the assembly metadata, and the public key if the assembly is strong-named.

You can define the identity of an assembly by applying certain attributes at the assembly level. Attributes allow you to add information about an assembly or the types contained within the assembly to the assembly manifest. The following code shows how to apply attributes at the assembly level.

Visual Basic .NET

```
Imports System.Reflection
<Assembly: AssemblyVersion("1.1.*")>
```

Visual C#

```
using System.Reflection;
[assembly: AssemblyVersion("1.1.*")]
```

Assembly Deployment

The .NET Framework provides the Xcopy mechanism to deploy assemblies. Using the Xcopy mechanism, you simply Xcopy the files to the installation directory. You need to ensure that all the files that constitute the assembly are installed in the same application directory. The .NET Framework searches for the referenced type declaration and implementation in the files of the application folder. The assemblies deployed in one application directory are not accessible by applications installed in another directory. Such assemblies are called *private assemblies*.

The .NET Framework allows sharing of assemblies between multiple applications. Such assemblies are called *shared assemblies*. The .NET Framework maintains a machine-wide code cache, the GAC, which enables you to store the code shared by multiple applications. You need to assign a strong name to an assembly to place it in the GAC and make it globally accessible. A strong name consists of the assembly identity, a public key, and a digital signature. The .NET Framework provides a tool called the Strong Name Tool (Sn.exe), which allows verification and key pair and signature generation.

Note   The syntax for creating a key pair using the Strong Name Tool is
   sn –k <*filename*>,
where *filename* is the file that contains the new key pair. For example,
   sn –k MyKey.dat
creates a key pair and writes it to the MyKey.dat file.

You specify the name of the file containing the key pair in the AssemblyKeyFile attribute of the assembly to assign it a strong name. The following code shows how to assign a strong name to an assembly.

Visual Basic .NET

```
Imports System.Reflection
<Assembly: AssemblyKeyFile("MyKey.dat")>
```

Visual C#

```
using System.Reflection;
[assembly: AssemblyKeyFile ("MyKey.dat")]
```

After assigning a strong name to the assembly, you can install it in the GAC by using the GAC tool, Gacutil.exe. The GAC tool also enables you to uninstall an assembly from the GAC.

Note   The syntax for installing a strong-named assembly in the GAC using the Gacutil.exe tool is

gacutil /i *<assembly>*

The syntax for uninstalling an assembly from the GAC using Gacutil.exe is

gacutil /u *<assembly>*

You can view the assemblies installed in the GAC from Windows Explorer by opening the %WINDIR%\Assembly folder. The GAC is shown in Figure 1.10.

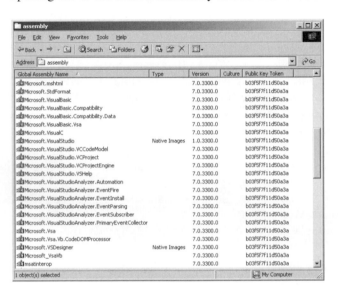

Figure 1.10   The global assembly cache

As mentioned earlier in this lesson, assemblies provide the smallest units for version control and security configuration. The next lesson explains how applications can be configured and secured by modifying the various configuration files.

Lesson 5: Understanding Configuration and Security

The .NET Framework uses various configuration and security policy files to control the behavior of applications at run time. You can manage the settings in these files by using the tools provided by the .NET Framework. In this lesson, you will learn about the configuration files used by the .NET Framework to control the behavior of applications and also learn about the tools that you can use to modify the settings in various configuration files.

After this lesson, you will be able to

- Describe the configuration files used by the .NET Framework
- Use tools to modify configuration files

Estimated lesson time: 25 minutes

Application Configuration

The .NET Framework controls the execution of code. The .NET Framework allows you to control the resources that a program can access, depending upon the origin of the code and the user who is running the code. To control the execution, you configure one or more configuration files. A *configuration file* is an XML document that contains predefined elements. An *element* is a logical structure. It sets the configuration information and is represented by using start and end tags. For example, configuration files contain a <runtime> element that contains another element, <codeBase>. The <codeBase> element determines the location of the assembly. The following sample code shows a small segment of a configuration file.

XML

```xml
<configuration>
   <runtime>
      <codeBase version="1.1.3.0"
          href="http://www.myserver.com/myAssembly.dll"/>

   </runtime>
</configuration>
```

Note The syntax for writing the configuration file is case-sensitive.

The .NET Framework provides different types of configuration files, which include

- **Machine configuration, Machine.config file.** This file is located in the %runtime installation path%\Config directory and contains settings that affect all the applications that run on the machine. This file contains an element called <appSettings>. This element contains application-specific settings, which you can modify to define the settings required by your application. When you run an application, the runtime checks for any additions made to the system configuration file and then checks the settings in the application configuration file.

- **Application configuration file.** This file contains the settings required to configure an individual application. The following code shows how application configuration files are configured.

XML
```xml
<?xml version="1.0" encoding="Windows-1252"?>
<configuration>
  <appSettings>
    <!--   User application and configured property settings go here.-->
    <!--   Example: <add key="settingName" value="settingValue"/> -->
    <add key="ServerButton.Text" value="SQLServer1" />
  </appSettings>
</configuration>
```

Consider an application that needs to connect to a database server to perform transactions. The administrator periodically takes the server offline for routine maintenance work and replaces it with a different database server. The application should be able to connect to the new database server without requiring recompilation. Application configuration files provide a solution for such problems. The application can use the preceding application configuration file and read the value of the ServerButton.Text key. Depending upon the key value, the application can dynamically connect to the database server.

The application configuration files are located in different locations for different run-time hosts. For the executable-hosted applications, Visual Studio .NET creates the <appname>.exe.config file in the same directory as the executable. For ASP.NET-hosted applications, the configuration file is named Web.config and is located in the Web application folder. For example, given the URL *www.microsoft.com/app1/app2*, the configuration file for the Web application app1 is located at *www.microsoft.com/app1*, and the configuration file for the Web application app2 is located at *www.microsoft.com/app1/app2*. The app2 application will be affected by the settings defined in the Web.config files for both applications.

The <link> tag specifies the location of the application configuration file for the applications hosted by Microsoft Internet Explorer. The syntax for the <link> tag is

    <link rel="*ConfigurationFileName*" href="*location*">

where *location* is the URL for the configuration file. This sets the application base. The configuration file needs to be located on the same Web site as the application.

■ **Security configuration files.**   The security configuration files contain security permissions for a hierarchy of code groups. *Code groups* are logical groups of code that are related to each other through common characteristics such as application directory, strong name, URL, site, and zone. You can organize code groups in a hierarchy consisting of the enterprise, machine, and user levels. You grant permissions to code groups based on their characteristics and their positions in the hierarchy. The permissions granted to the code groups at the enterprise level affect the code running on every computer within the enterprise network. The computer-level policy affects the code groups only on a particular computer. The permissions defined at the user level affect the code groups when a particular user executes an application.

When you execute an application, the runtime only grants the intersection of permissions granted to the code group at the enterprise, computer, and user levels.

Table 1.2 provides the locations of various security policy files.

Table 1.2   Locations of Security Policy Files

Configuration file	Location
Enterprise policy	
Windows 2000	%runtime install path%\Config\Enterprisesec.config
Windows NT	%runtime install path%\Config\Enterprisesec.config
Windows 98 and Windows Millennium Edition (Windows Me)	%runtime install path%\Config\Enterprisesec.config
Machine policy	
Windows 2000	%runtime install path%\Config\Security.config
Windows NT	%runtime install path%\Config\Security.config
Windows 98 and Windows Me	%runtime install path%\Config\Security.config
User policy	
Windows 2000	%USERPROFILE%\Application Data\Microsoft\CLR Security Config\Vxx.xx\Security.config
Windows NT	%USERPROFILE%\Application Data\Microsoft\CLR Security Config\Vxx.xx\Security.config
Windows 98 and Windows Me	%WINDIR%*username*\CLR Security Config\Vxx.xx\ Security.config

The .NET Framework provides tools to configure these security policy files. You can use either the .NET Framework Configuration tool (Mscorcfg.msc) or the

Code Access Security Policy tool (Caspol.exe). You should avoid editing the policy files directly because the performance of your application might be affected.

Note A detailed discussion of Mscorcfg.msc and Caspol.exe is provided in Lesson 7.

As mentioned earlier in this lesson, various configuration files allow you to configure and secure your applications. The .NET Framework also provides a fault-tolerant mechanism to execute the applications within the runtime. The next lesson explains application domains and run-time hosts and their roles in providing isolated and secure execution environments.

Lesson 6: Understanding Application Domains and Run-Time Hosts

The .NET Framework provides a secure run-time environment, which ensures that the failure of one application does not affect another application that is running within the runtime. In this lesson, you will learn about application domains and their role in providing a secure, isolated, and fault-tolerant execution environment.

After this lesson, you will be able to

- Describe processes and application domains
- Describe how application domains provide a secure run-time environment

Estimated lesson time: 25 minutes

Understanding Processes and Application Domains

A *process* is the execution boundary within which an application runs. All run-time environments assign an address space to a process when the process starts. The memory addresses within a process are relative to the process, which makes the addresses useless for applications running inside different processes. As a result, applications that are running in different processes cannot access the data of another application directly. This application isolation provided by processes ensures that if the application in one process fails, the applications in other processes remain unaffected.

Before executing an application, the .NET Framework ensures that the references within the application code point to the objects to which they have access. In addition, the .NET Framework ensures that only valid operations are performed on objects. The .NET Framework also ensures that the references never access objects beyond the boundaries of an application. This verification occurs during JIT compilation. The code that passes the verification process is called *type-safe* code. After the code is verified to be type-safe, the .NET Framework loads the code into an application domain.

An *application domain* is the boundary within which an application runs. A process can contain multiple application domains. An application domain provides application isolation that is similar to the isolation provided by processes. An application running inside one application domain cannot directly access the code running inside another application domain. To access the code running in another application domain, an application needs to use a proxy. A *proxy* is an object that enables interprocess communication. This isolation of the application domains ensures that the failure of one application in one application domain does not affect the execution of applications in other application domains. In addition, this low-level isolation enables you to start and stop an application without affecting other applications within the same process.

An application that is running within the common language runtime usually requires functionality from more than one assembly. For example, an application named MyApp.exe might need functionality from a custom class library named MyUtil.dll. The common language runtime needs to load both assemblies into the application domain before executing the application. Applications that run within different application domains might also need functionality from a shared assembly. A shared assembly allows multiple applications to share code between them. However, the applications do not share the data of the shared assembly. The assemblies that are shared between multiple application domains are called domain-neutral assemblies. When an application is loaded into the runtime, the run-time host decides whether to load assemblies as domain-neutral assemblies.

Although the domain-neutral assemblies utilize memory efficiently, these assemblies can adversely affect the performance of applications if the applications frequently access the static data and static methods of assemblies. You can control whether an assembly is loaded as domain-neutral. When you run an application, the run-time host loads the runtime into a process before executing the application. At this point, you can specify whether to load assemblies as domain-neutral. However, the run-time hosts always load assemblies, such as mscorlib, as domain-neutral.

Understanding Run-Time Hosts

When you invoke an application, the runtime is not running in a process. A host needs to load the runtime into a process before the runtime can execute an application. The .NET Framework provides different run-time hosts for different run-time environments. These include the run-time hosts for ASP.NET applications, shell executables, and downloadable components that run within Internet Explorer. These run-time hosts run in an unmanaged environment. The .NET Framework provides interfaces that the run-time hosts use to load and initialize the runtime. The run-time host calls the CorBindToRuntimeEx method that is located in the Mscoree.h API to load and initialize the runtime. While calling the CorBindToRuntimeEx method, the run-time host sets the Loader Optimization value, which determines whether the runtime will host domain-neutral assemblies.

In the previous lessons, you learned that the .NET Framework enables you to develop, configure, and deploy your applications. It provides a fault-tolerant execution environment. In addition, the .NET Framework provides certain tools that make application development, configuration, and deployment simple. The next lesson provides an overview of some of the commonly used tools.

Lesson 7: Introducing the .NET Framework Tools

The .NET Framework Software Development Kit (SDK) provides various tools that enable you to debug, configure, and deploy .NET applications easily. In addition, the .NET Framework SDK provides tools to implement security features in applications and components. In this lesson, you will learn to use some of the tools that the .NET Framework SDK provides.

After this lesson, you will be able to describe and use

- Assembly Linker
- IL Assembler
- IL Disassembler
- Code Access Security Policy Tool
- .NET Framework Configuration Tool

Estimated lesson time: 30 minutes

Assembly Linker

Usually, all Visual Studio .NET compilers generate assemblies. However, if you have modules, you can use the AL tool, Al.exe, to create an assembly with the manifest in a separate file. The AL tool generates a file with an assembly manifest from modules or resource files. You run Al.exe from the command prompt. The syntax for using Al.exe is

    al [*sources*] [*options*]

Tables 1.3 and 1.4 describe the various sources and options that you can use with Al.exe.

Table 1.3   Sources Used with Al.exe

Source	Description
module[,*target*]	Copies the contents of a module to the file name specified as *target*. After copying the contents, Al.exe compiles *target* into an assembly.
/embed[resource]: *file*[,*name*[, private]]	Embeds the resource specified in the image that contains the assembly manifest. Al.exe copies the contents of *file* into the portable executable image. You can specify an internal identifier for the resource by using the *name* parameter.
	You can hide the resource from other assemblies by specifying it as private.
/link[resource]: *file*[,*name*[,*target* [,private]]]	Links a resource file to an assembly.
	You use the *name* parameter to specify an internal identifier for the resource. You use the *target* parameter to specify a path and file to which Al.exe copies the file.
	You can hide the resource from other assemblies by specifying it as private.

Table 1.4   Options Used with Al.exe

Option	Description
/base:*address*	Allows you to specify the address where a DLL loads on a computer at run time.
/bugreport:*filename*	Allows you to specify a file that contains the bugs reported when Al.exe runs.
/fileversion:*version*	Allows you to specify the version of the assembly. This parameter takes a string as a parameter.
/main:*method*	Allows you to specify the fully qualified method name, which is the entry point at which you convert a module into an executable file.
/out:*filename*	Allows you to specify the name of the output file. This is a mandatory option.

This tool allows you to create a multi-file assembly outside Visual Studio .NET. A multi-file assembly is useful to combine modules written in different languages into a single application. The following command creates an assembly, MyApp.exe, by combining the MyModule.netmodule and MyUtil.dll files.

```
al /t:exe /out:MyApp.exe /main:MyClass.Main MyModule.netmodule MyUtil.dll
```

Using the Ilasm.exe Tool

When you compile managed code, the compiler converts the source code to MSIL code. MSIL is a CPU-independent language and its code can be converted to native code. You can use the Ilasm tool, Ilasm.exe, to generate a portable executable file from the MSIL code. You can then run the resulting executable file to determine the performance of your application. This enables you to generate the MSIL code and the metadata without emitting MSIL in the portable executable file format. In addition, Ilasm.exe does not create intermediate object files. It also does not have a linking stage to generate a portable executable file.

You run the Ilasm.exe file at the command prompt. The syntax to run Ilasm.exe is

ilasm [*options*] *filename* [[*options*]*filename...*]

The *filename* used with Ilasm.exe is the name of the .il source file, which contains the metadata declaration directives and symbolic MSIL instructions. You can specify multiple source files to produce a single portable executable file using Ilasm.exe. Table 1.5 describes the options and parameters that you use with Ilasm.exe.

Table 1.5   Options Used with Ilasm.exe

Option	Description
/debug	Allows you to include debug information such as local variable and argument names.
/dll	Generates a .dll file as output.
/exe	Generates an executable file as output.
/key:*keyFile*	Compiles the source .il file with a strong signature using the private key contained in *keyFile*.
/quiet	Allows you to suppress messages that report assembly progress.
/resource:*file.res*	Includes the specified resource file in *.res format in the resulting .exe or .dll file. Only one .res file can be specified with the /resource option.

Using the Ildasm.exe Tool

The MSIL disassembler tool, Ildasm.exe, takes a portable executable file that contains MSIL code as a parameter and creates a text file that contains managed code. You can specify .exe, .dll, .obj, and .lib files as parameters for the Ildasm.exe file. Table 1.6 describes the options and parameters used with the Ildasm tool.

Table 1.6   Options Used with Ildasm.exe

Option	Description
/output:*filename*	Creates an output file with the specified file name rather than displaying the results in a dialog box.
/text	Displays the results to the console window rather than in a dialog box or as an output file.

You can also use the MSIL disassembler tool to view the metadata and disassembled code of a portable executable file, which the GUI of the MSIL disassembler displays in a hierarchical tree structure. To use this GUI, type **ildasm** at the Visual Studio .NET command prompt. To open the Visual Studio .NET Command

Prompt from the Start menu, point to Programs, Microsoft Visual Studio .NET, Visual Studio .NET Tools, and then click Visual Studio .NET Command Prompt. From the File menu of IL DASM, you can navigate to the portable executable file that you want to load into Ildasm.exe, as shown in Figure 1.11. To save the metadata and disassembled code displayed for the selected portable executable, choose Dump from the File menu.

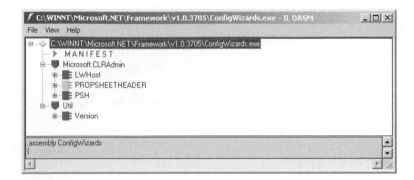

Figure 1.11   The IL disassembler

Using the Caspol.exe Tool

The Code Access Security Policy tool, Caspol.exe, allows you to grant and modify permissions granted to code groups at the user-policy, machine-policy, and enterprise-policy levels.

You run the Caspol.exe file at the command prompt. The syntax to run Caspol.exe is

    caspol [*options*]

Table 1.7 describes various options that you can use with the Caspol.exe tool.

Table 1.7   Options Used with Caspol.exe

Option	Description
-addfulltrust *assembly_file* or -af *assembly_file*	Adds an assembly to the full trust assembly list at a specified level. The *assembly_file* argument specifies which assembly to add. This file needs to be signed with a strong name.
-addgroup {*parent_label* | *parent_name*} *mship pset_name* [*flags*] or -ag {*parent_label* | *parent_name*} *mship pset_name* [*flags*]	Adds a new code group to the existing code group hierarchy. The *parent_label* is the label of the parent code group of the code group that is being added. The *parent_name* is the name of the parent code group of the code group that is being added.

Table 1.7   Options Used with Caspol.exe *(continued)*

Option	Description
-addpset {*znamed_psfile* | *psfile pset_name*} or -ap {*named_psfile* | *psfile pset_name*}	Adds a new named permission set to the policy. The *named_psfile* variable is the permission file written in XML that contains the name of the permissions set. *Psfile* is the file that does not contain the name of the permission set, and *pset_name* is the name of the permission.
-a[ll]	Specifies that the following options apply to the machine, user, and enterprise policies. It always refers to the policy of the currently logged on user.
-e[xecution] {on | off}	Turns the mechanism that checks the code permissions on or off before an application starts.
-h[elp]	Displays all options.
-l[ist]	Lists the code group hierarchy and the permission sets for the specified computer, user, enterprise, or all policy levels.
-reset or -rs	Returns the policy to the default state.
-remgroup {*label* | *name*} or -rg {*label* | *name*}	Removes the code group specified by *label* or *name*.
-s[ecurity] {on | off}	Turns code-access security on or off.

The following command adds the MyApp.exe assembly to the full trust list for the computer policy.

    caspol -machine -addfulltrust MyApp.exe

The following command adds the MyPermset permission set to the user policy.

    caspol -user -addpset MyPermset.xml MyPermissions

The following command removes the code group labeled 1.2. If this code group has any child code groups, those groups are also deleted.

    caspol -remgroup 1.2

Mscorcfg.msc

The .NET Framework Configuration tool, Mscorcfg.msc, is a Microsoft Management Console (MMC) snap-in that enables you to manage and configure assemblies located in the GAC. In addition, it also allows you to manage code access security and remoting services. Open this tool from the Start menu by pointing to Programs, Administrative Tools, and clicking Microsoft .NET Framework Configuration. Figure 1.12 shows the .NET Framework Configuration tool.

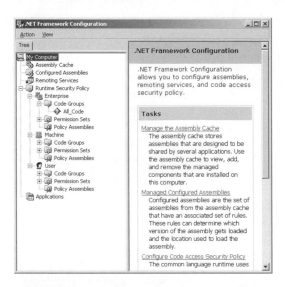

Figure 1.12   The .NET Framework Configuration tool

You use the .NET Framework Configuration tool to create custom code groups at the user-policy, machine-policy, and enterprise-policy levels and to grant them permissions.

Summary

- The .NET Framework is the infrastructure for building applications using .NET. The .NET Framework provides a new programming model that allows applications written in different languages running on different devices to exchange data using standard protocols such as HTTP, XML, and SOAP.

- The .NET Framework consists of the common language runtime and the .NET Framework class library. The common language runtime provides the run-time infrastructure and services, such as type safety, security, and automatic memory management, to .NET applications. The .NET Framework class library provides the common type system for building applications using .NET.

- Assemblies are the fundamental units of application development and deployment. They are the smallest unit for versioning and configuring security. They contain the type metadata, MSIL code, and the assembly manifest.

- The .NET Framework provides a highly secure and fault-tolerant execution environment. It provides application domains, which enable multiple applications to execute in a single process.

- The .NET Framework provides various tools that enable you to develop, deploy, configure, and secure your applications.

Lab: Creating Assemblies and Examining MSIL

In this lab, you will create single-file and multiple-file assemblies. You will examine the MSIL code that the language compilers generate. The solutions to the exercises in this lab can be found in the \Solution folder on the Supplemental Course Materials CD-ROM.

Estimated lab time: 60 minutes

Exercise 1: Creating a Single-File Assembly

In this exercise, you will create a simple console application that displays the sum of two numbers. You will compile the code using the language compilers that ship with the .NET Framework.

1. Open Notepad and type the following code:

Visual Basic .NET

```
<Assembly: System.Reflection.AssemblyVersion("1.1.1.*")>
Module MyModule

    Sub Main()
        Dim n1, n2 As Integer
        n1 = 10
        n2 = 20
        Dim message As String = " The sum of 10 and 20 is " _
            + add(n1, n2).ToString
        System.Console.Write(message)
    End Sub

    Private Function add(ByVal n1 As Integer, ByVal n2 As Integer) _
        As Integer
        add = n1 + n2
    End Function


End Module
```

Visual C#

```
using System;
[assembly: System.Reflection.AssemblyVersion("1.1.1.*")]
namespace MyConsoleAppCS
```

```
{
    class MyClass
    {

        [STAThread]
        static void Main(string[] args)
        {
            int n1,n2;
            n1=10;
            n2=20;
            string message="The sum of 10 and 20 is " +
                add(n1,n2).ToString();

            System.Console.Write(message);
        }

        private static int add(int n1,int n2)
        {
            return n1+n2;
        }
    }
}
```

2. Save the file as MyConsoleApp.vb or MyConsoleApp.cs.

3. Open the Visual Studio .NET Command Prompt from the Start menu by point-ing to Programs, Microsoft Visual Studio .NET, Visual Studio .NET Tools, and clicking Visual Studio .NET Command Prompt.

4. Compile your code using the Visual Basic .NET compiler (Vbc.exe) or C# compiler (Csc.exe). At the Visual Studio .NET Command Prompt, type the fol-lowing command:

   vbc MyConsoleApp.vb
   or
   csc MyConsoleApp.cs

   The compiler creates a single-file assembly called MyConsoleApp.exe.

5. Run the application by typing **MyConsoleApp** at the Visual Studio .NET com-mand prompt.

Exercise 2: Using Ildasm to Examine the MSIL Code

In this exercise, you will use the Ildasm tool to examine the MSIL code and the assembly manifest contained in the assembly that you created in the previous exercise.

1. To open the Ildasm tool, type **ildasm** at the Visual Studio .NET Command Prompt.

2. From the File menu, open the MyConsoleApp.exe assembly. This tool is shown in the following graphic.

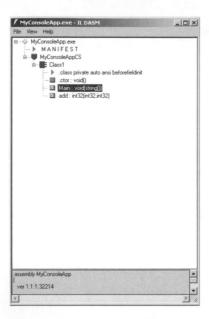

3. Double-click MANIFEST under MyConsoleApp.exe to view the assembly manifest. The assembly manifest for the application created in Visual Basic .NET is shown in the following graphic.

```
/ MANIFEST                                                _|□|x|
.assembly extern mscorlib
{
  .publickeytoken = (B7 7A 5C 56 19 34 E0 89 )
  .ver 1:0:3300:0
}
.assembly extern Microsoft.VisualBasic
{
  .publickeytoken = (B0 3F 5F 7F 11 D5 0A 3A )
  .ver 7:0:3300:0
}
.assembly MyConsoleApp
{
  .hash algorithm 0x00008004
  .ver 1:1:1:33394
}
.module MyConsoleApp.exe
// MVID: {1757E216-194B-427B-A18F-830D426E160E}
.imagebase 0x00400000
.subsystem 0x00000003
.file alignment 512
.corflags 0x00000001
// Image base: 0x03090000
```

What does the assembly manifest contain?

The following graphic shows the assembly manifest for the file created in C#.

```
MANIFEST                                                                    _□×
.assembly extern mscorlib
{
  .publickeytoken = (B7 7A 5C 56 19 34 E0 89 )                    // .z\U.4..
  .ver 1:0:3300:0
}
.assembly MyConsoleApp
{
  // --- The following custom attribute is added automatically, do not uncomment -
  //   .custom instance void [mscorlib]System.Diagnostics.DebuggableAttribute::.cto
  //
  .hash algorithm 0x00008004
  .ver 1:1:1:33468
}
.module MyConsoleApp.exe
// MVID: {DD1F0B9F-2133-4490-B89D-70E0A7D9A08A}
.imagebase 0x00400000
.subsystem 0x00000003
.file alignment 512
.corflags 0x00000001
// Image base: 0x03090000
```

What are the similarities and the differences between the assembly manifests contained within the two assemblies?

4. Double-click the Main method in the MSIL window to view the MSIL code. Is it marked as the entry point for the assembly?

Exercise 3: Creating a Multiple-File Assembly

In this exercise, you will create multiple modules in Visual Basic .NET, Visual C#, and JScript, and combine them into a single assembly. You will examine the contents of the assembly manifest.

1. Open Notepad and type the following Visual Basic .NET code:

Visual Basic .NET

```
namespace Util
    public class HelloUtil
        public shared sub Hello()
        System.Console.writeline("Hello, how are you doing!")
        end sub
    end class
end namespace
```

2. Save the file as HelloUtil.vb.

3. Create and compile the module by typing the following command at the Visual Studio .NET command prompt:

vbc /t:module HelloUtil.vb

The compiler creates the HelloUtil.netmodule file. Open the file within Ildasm to see if it contains an assembly manifest.

4. Close the HelloUtil.vb file.

5. Type the following JScript code in Notepad and save it as GoodByeUtil.js.

JScript
```jscript
import System;
package Util
{
    public class GoodByeUtil
    {
    public static function GoodBye()
        {
                System.Console.WriteLine("Goodbye, see you next time!");
        }
    }
}
```

6. Create a library by typing the following command at the Visual Studio .NET command prompt:

jsc /t:library GoodByeUtil.js

The compiler creates the GoodByeUtil.dll file.

Note   The target for JScript code can be an exe, winexe, or library. You can not compile JScript code into a module.

---

7. Close the GoodByeUtil.js file.

8. Type the following Visual C# code and save it as Main.cs.

Visual C#
```csharp
using System;
using Util;

class MyClass
    {

        [STAThread]
        public static void Main(string[] args)
        {
            System.Console.WriteLine("Hello from Main");
            HelloUtil.Hello();
            GoodByeUtil.GoodBye();
        }

    }
```

9. Create a module by typing the following command at the Visual Studio .NET command prompt:

csc /addmodule:HelloUtil.netmodule
/r:GoodByeUtil.dll,Microsoft.JScript.dll /target:module Main.cs

The compiler creates the Main.netmodule file.

10. Combine the three files into a single assembly using AL by typing the following command at the Visual Studio .NET command prompt:

al /t:exe /out:MyApp.exe /main:MyClass.Main HelloUtil.netmodule
GoodByeUtil.dll Main.netmodule

Note   Ignore the warning: *ALINK: warning AL1020: Ignoring included assembly*. You get this warning because the multi-file assembly is created from the files that include GoodByeUtil.dll, which itself is an assembly. The assembly linker ignores the GoodByeUtil.dll assembly while creating the new assembly MyApp.exe.

AL creates a multiple-file assembly called MyApp.exe, which contains the assembly manifest. Open the MyApp.exe file in the Ildasm tool to view the assembly manifest. Some of the contents of the assembly manifest are shown in the following graphic.

11. Run the application by typing **MyApp** at the Visual Studio .NET Command Prompt. The output of the application should look as follows:

Hello from Main
Hello, how are you doing!
Goodbye, see you next time!

Review

The questions in this section reinforce key information presented in this chapter. If you are unable to answer a question, review the appropriate lesson, and then try answering the question again. Answers to the questions can be found in Appendix A, "Questions and Answers."

1. What are the development tools and operational systems that .NET provides to build, deploy, and integrate applications?

2. What are the functions of the components of the common language runtime?

3. What are the different types of assemblies?

4. What are the different types of configuration files that the .NET Framework provides?

5. What are application domains?

C H A P T E R   2

Creating and Managing Windows Services

About This Chapter

In this chapter, you will learn about the Windows service programming model, create Windows services in Microsoft Visual Studio .NET, and control the behavior of Windows services. You will also learn to make entries in default event logs, create custom event logs, and record information in custom event logs. In addition you will learn to install, deploy, and debug a Windows service. Finally, you will learn to configure a service dynamically and manage a service manually and programmatically.

Before You Begin

To complete the lessons in this chapter, you

- Must be familiar with the Microsoft .NET Framework and its architecture
- Must have knowledge of programming in Microsoft Visual Basic .NET or Microsoft Visual C#

Lesson 1: Understanding Windows Services

Windows services enable you to perform tasks that execute as different background processes. You can use Windows services to perform tasks, such as monitoring the usage of a database. A Windows service executes in its own process space until a user stops it, or the computer is shut down.

After this lesson, you will be able to

- Describe Windows services
- Differentiate between Windows services and other Visual Studio .NET applications
- Describe the programming model of a Windows service

Estimated lesson time: 30 minutes

Overview of Windows Services

Windows services run as background processes. These applications do not have a user interface, which makes them ideal for tasks that do not require any user interaction. You can install a Windows service on any server or computer that is running Windows 2000, Windows XP, or Windows NT. You can also specify a Windows service to run in the security context of a specific user account that is different from the logged on user account or the default computer account. For example, you can create a Windows service to monitor performance counter data and react to threshold values in a database.

You create Windows services to perform tasks, such as managing network connections and monitoring resource access and utilization. You can also use Windows services to collect and analyze system usage data and log events in the system or custom event log. You can view the list of services running on a computer at any time by opening Administrative Tools from Control Panel and then opening Services. Figure 2.1 displays the Services window.

A Windows service is installed in the registry as an executable object. The Service Control Manager (SCM) manages all the Windows services. The Service Control Manager, which is a remote procedure call (RPC) server, supports the local or remote management of a service. You can create applications that control Windows services through the SCM by using Visual Studio .NET. The .NET Framework provides classes that enable you to create, install, and control Windows services easily.

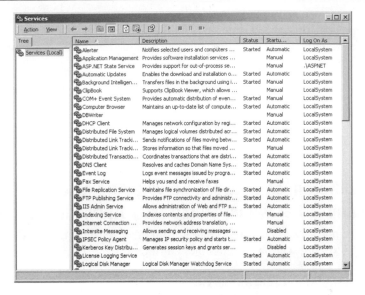

Figure 2.1   The Services window of the Administrative Tools component.

Let's look at the Windows service architecture. The Windows service architecture consists of three components:

- **Service application.**   An application that consists of one or more services that provide the desired functionality
- **Service controller application.**   An application that enables you to control the behavior of a service
- **Service Control Manager.**   A utility that enables you to control the services that are installed on a computer

You can create Windows services by using any .NET language, such as Visual C# or Visual Basic .NET. The System.ServiceProcess namespace of the .NET Framework contains classes that enable you to create, install, implement, and control Windows services. You use the methods of the ServiceBase class to create a Windows service. After you create a Windows service application, you install it by registering the application in the registry of a computer. You use the ServiceInstaller and ServiceProcessInstaller classes to install Windows services. You can view all the registered service applications in the Windows registry under HKEY_LOCAL_MACHINE\SYSTEM\CurrentControlSet\Services. After you install a service, you need to start it. You use the ServiceController class and the SCM to start, stop, pause, and continue a Windows service. The ServiceController class also allows you to execute custom commands on a service.

After you start a Service application on a computer, it can then exist in a running, paused, or stopped state. In addition, a service can be in a pending state. A *pending state* indicates that a command, such as the command to pause a service, was issued but not completed.

Windows services are categorized based on the number of services that run in a process space. You can have one service running in one process space or multiple services sharing a process space. The services that use a single process space are called *Win32OwnProcess services*, whereas the services that share a process with other services are called *Win32ShareProcess services*.

Differences Between Service Applications and Other Visual Studio .NET Applications

Windows services are different from other Visual Studio .NET applications. The following sections discuss these differences.

Installing Windows Services

Unlike other Visual Studio projects, you need to install a service application before the service can run. To register and install the service, you first need to add installation components to a service application. You will learn to install a service application in Lesson 4.

Debugging Windows Services

You cannot debug a service application by pressing the F5 or F11 key like you can with other types of Visual Studio .NET applications. To debug a service application, you need to install and start the service, and then attach a debugger to the process of the service. You will learn to debug a service application in Lesson 5.

Executing Windows Services

In a Windows service, the Run method loads a service into the SCM. You call the Run method from the Main method of a service application. Another difference between executing a Windows service and other Visual Studio .NET applications is that the dialog boxes raised from a Windows service are not visible to the user. In addition, the error messages generated from a Windows service are logged in the event logs. You can specify that Windows services run in their own security context. Therefore, a Windows service can start before a user logs on and continue to run even after the user logs off.

Programming Model of Windows Service Applications

You create Windows service applications by using the classes of the System.ServiceProcess namespace. You use the methods of the classes in this namespace to provide functionality to your service application. Table 2.1 describes some of the classes that you use to create, install, and manage your service applications.

Table 2.1   Some of the Classes of the System.ServiceProcess Namespace

Class	Description
ServiceBase	You override the methods in the ServiceBase class to create a service application. The methods of this class enable you to specify the behavior of your service application.
ServiceProcessInstaller and ServiceInstaller	These classes enable you to define the process of installing and uninstalling your service application.
ServiceController	The methods of this class enable you to manipulate the behavior of your service application. For example, you can use the methods of this class to start and stop the service. You use the methods of this class in the application that you create to manage and control a service.

In addition to the classes of the System.ServiceProcess namespace, you use the classes of the System.Diagnostics namespace to monitor the status and debug the service when it is running. Table 2.2 describes some of the classes of the System.Diagnostics namespace that you can use to monitor your service while it is running.

Table 2.2   Some of the Classes of the System.Diagnostics Namespace

Class	Description
EventLog	The methods of this class allow your service to report its errors in the event log.
PerformanceCounter	The methods of this class allow you to use performance counters that enable you to monitor the resource utilization.
Trace and Debug	The methods of these classes enable you to debug your code and provide you with methods and properties that help you trace the execution of your code.

To create a Windows service, you create a class that extends the System.Service-Process.ServiceBase class. You override the functions of the ServiceBase class to customize the behavior of your service application. Table 2.3 describes the methods of the ServiceBase class that you override to define the functionality of your service application.

Table 2.3   Methods of the ServiceBase Class

Method	Description
OnStart	You override this method to specify the tasks your service performs when it starts, such as initializing database connections, performance counters, event logs, and child threads.
OnPause	You override this method to specify the tasks your service performs when it pauses. For example, you can read the value of a performance counter and write it in an event log. You can also close the database connections that were opened in the OnStart method.
OnStop	You override this method to specify the tasks your service performs when it stops. For example, you can release the system resources and database connections that the service initialized during its execution.
OnContinue	You override this method to specify how your service behaves when it restarts after pausing. For example, you can open the database connections that were closed in the OnPause method.
OnShutDown	You override this method to specify the task that your service performs when the computer it is running on is shut down.
OnCustomCommand	You override this method when you want a service to accept custom commands. A service can respond in a specific way depending on the arguments that are passed with the custom command.
OnPowerEvent	You override this method to specify how your service performs when it receives a power management event such as low battery.

After you create a Windows service by overriding the methods of the ServiceBase class, you use the ServiceProcessInstaller and ServiceInstaller classes to install the service application. As mentioned earlier, each service runs in its own process space. Therefore, before you install a service application, a service process needs to be created and installed. The ServiceProcessInstaller class creates and registers the process in which your service runs, whereas the ServiceInstaller class installs the class that extends the ServiceBase class to implement your service.

After you create and install your service, you can use the ServiceController class to programmatically control the service. Table 2.4 describes the methods of the ServiceController class that you use to control the behavior of a service.

Table 2.4   Methods of the ServiceController Class

Method	Description
Close	Disconnects the instance of the ServiceController class from the service and releases all the resources allocated for the application
Continue	Resumes a service after it is paused
ExecuteCommand	Enables you to execute a custom command on a service
Pause	Pauses the service
Refresh	Refreshes the values of all the properties
Start	Starts the service
Stop	Stops the service and all dependent services

In this lesson, you learned about the classes and methods that enable you to create Windows services easily. In the next lesson, you will learn to create a Windows service.

Lesson 2: Creating Windows Services

In this lesson, you will learn to create a new Windows service, change its default properties, and add functionality to your Windows service.

After this lesson, you will be able to

- Create a blank Windows service application
- Change the default properties of a Windows service application
- Add functionality to a Windows service application

Estimated lesson time: 40 minutes

Creating a Windows Service Application

To create a Windows service application, you need to create a project by using the Windows Service template in Visual Basic .NET or Visual C#. The Windows Service template creates a blank service application for you. It automatically adds code to the Main method of your service application and inserts function headers for the OnStart and OnStop methods. To complete the service application, you just need to override the OnStart and OnStop methods. You can also override other methods of the ServiceBase class, such as OnPause and OnContinue, and change the properties of the service application to customize it to your needs. To create a blank Windows service application, perform the following steps:

1. Start Visual Studio .NET and open a new project.
2. Select Visual Basic Projects or Visual C# Projects from the Project Types pane.
3. Select the Windows Service template from the Templates pane in the New Project dialog box. Figure 2.2 displays the New Project dialog box.

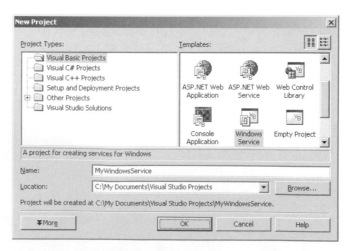

Figure 2.2   The Visual Studio .NET New Project dialog box

4. Change the name of the project to MyWindowsService in the Name text box and click OK. A new .NET solution named MyWindowsService is created. Figure 2.3 displays a Windows service project.

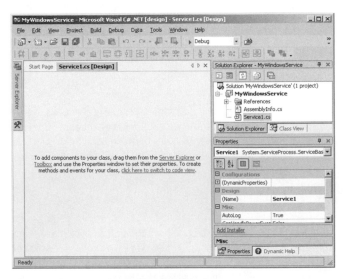

Figure 2.3   A Windows service solution

The Windows Service template includes references to namespaces, such as System.ServiceProcess namespace, and adds certain files in the Windows service project, which are required to create your service. The Windows Service template adds the following files to your Windows service project:

- **AssemblyInfo file (AssemblyInfo.vb in Visual Basic and AssemblyInfo.cs in Visual C#).**   This file describes the assembly and contains version information.

- **Service file (Service1.vb in Visual Basic and Service1.cs in Visual C#).**   This file contains the code for your service application. This includes the code generated by the Windows Service template and the code that you add to customize the service application.

In addition to the AssemblyInfo file and Service file, the Windows Service template adds references to the following .NET Framework namespaces, which you use to customize your service application:

- **System.**   This namespace contains the classes that define the value and reference data types. The classes of this namespace also define events and event handlers, interfaces, and attributes. In addition, this namespace contains methods for exception handling.

- **System.Data.**   This namespace defines the ADO.NET architecture and is used for various database-related tasks. You will learn about ADO.NET in Chapter 5, "Database Programming Using ADO.NET."

- **System.ServiceProcess.** The classes of this namespace allow you to create, install, and run Windows services.
- **System.Xml.** This namespace consists of classes that provide support for processing XML.

The Windows Service template also inserts the following code in the Main method of your service application.

Visual Basic .NET

```
Shared Sub Main()
    Dim ServicesToRun() As System.ServiceProcess.ServiceBase
    ServicesToRun = New System.ServiceProcess.ServiceBase () {New Service1}
    System.ServiceProcess.ServiceBase.Run(ServicesToRun)
End Sub
```

Visual C#

```
static void Main()
{
    System.ServiceProcess.ServiceBase[] ServicesToRun;
    ServicesToRun = new System.ServiceProcess.ServiceBase[]
        { new Service1() };
    System.ServiceProcess.ServiceBase.Run(ServicesToRun);
}
```

Changing the Default Properties of a Windows Service Application

After you open a new Windows service project, you need to specify properties to customize the service application to your requirements. You first need to change the ServiceName and Name properties of the service application. You use the ServiceName property to specify the name that the SCM uses to identify your Windows service. To change the name of the service application, click the Design window and change the ServiceName property to MyWindowsService_VB (MyWindowsService_CSharp in Visual C#) in the Properties window. You also need to change the Name property to MyWindowsService_VB (MyWindowsService_CSharp in Visual C#). The Name property specifies the name of the class that extends the System.ServiceProcess.ServiceBase class in your service application. After you change the Name and ServiceName properties, you also need to change the service name in the Main method. The following code displays the changed code in the Main method.

Visual Basic .NET

```
Shared Sub Main()
    Dim ServicesToRun() As System.ServiceProcess.ServiceBase
    ' Change the name of the instance of the service to match
    ' the ServiceName property
```

```
    ServicesToRun = New System.ServiceProcess.ServiceBase() _
        {New MyWindowsService_VB()}
    System.ServiceProcess.ServiceBase.Run(ServicesToRun)
End Sub
```

Visual C#

```
static void Main()
{
    System.ServiceProcess.ServiceBase[] ServicesToRun;
    /* Change the name of the instance of the service to match
       the ServiceName property */
    ServicesToRun = new System.ServiceProcess.ServiceBase[]
        { new MyWindowsService_CSharp() };
    System.ServiceProcess.ServiceBase.Run(ServicesToRun);
}
```

You can change the following service application properties to customize your service application:

- **AutoLog.**   This property enables your service to make entries in the system event log to report command failures and changes of state. You can set the AutoLog property to False if you want your service application to use custom event logs. You can specify the log to use and the entries to make in the OnContinue, OnPause, or OnStop method of your service application.

- **CanStop.**   This property enables you to specify whether your service can stop after it has been started. You set the CanStop property to False if you do not want a user to stop your service application. If you set the CanStop property to True, the SCM calls the OnStop method when a Stop request is sent to your service.

- **CanShutdown.**   You use this property to specify whether your service should be notified when the system is shutting down. If you set the CanShutdown property to True, the SCM informs your service when the system is shutting down. This allows your service to call the OnShutdown method.

- **CanPauseAndContinue.**   You use this property to specify whether a user can pause and resume your service. If you set the CanPauseAndContinue property to True, you can override the OnPause and OnContinue methods to specify the tasks the service needs to perform when the SCM sends Pause and Continue requests to your service. If you set the CanPauseAndContinue property to False, the SCM does not send a Pause or Continue request to your service. Therefore, the OnPause and OnContinue methods are not called, even if you define them.

- **CanHandlePowerEvent.**   You use this property to specify whether your service can handle changes in the computer power status, such as the standby mode. This property takes a Boolean value.

You can change the properties of a service application by using the Properties window of your service application. To access the Properties window of the service application, right-click the designer pane and choose Properties. The properties for your service application appear. Figure 2.4 displays the Properties window of a service application.

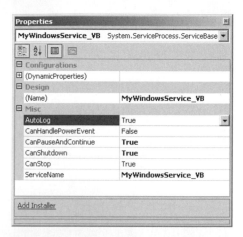

Figure 2.4   The Properties window of a service application

After you change the properties of your service application according to your requirements, you need to change the name of the Service1.vb (Service1.cs in Visual C#) file. To change the name of the Service1.vb file, click Service1.vb (Service1.cs in Visual C#) in Solution Explorer, and then change the File Name property to MyWindowsService.vb (MyWindowsService.cs in Visual C#) in the Properties window.

Adding Functionality to a Service Application

To provide functionality to your service, you override the OnStart and OnStop methods. For example, the following code creates a text file and writes information in it as soon as the service starts.

Visual Basic .NET

```
Protected Overrides Sub OnStart(ByVal args() As String)
    Dim fs As New FileStream("C:\MyWindowsService_VB.txt", _
        FileMode.Append, FileAccess.Write)
    Dim sr As New StreamWriter(fs)
    sr.WriteLine("MyWindowsService_VB started")
    sr.Flush()
End Sub
```

Visual C#

```
protected override void OnStart(string[] args)
{
    FileStream fs = new FileStream(@"c:\MyWindowsService_CS.txt",
        FileMode.OpenOrCreate, FileAccess.Write);
    StreamWriter sr = new StreamWriter(fs);
    sr.WriteLine("MyWindowsService_CS started");
    sr.Flush();
}
```

Note   To create a file, use the methods and properties of the FileStream class. The FileStream class is defined in the System.IO namespace. Therefore, you need to add a reference to the System.IO namespace to create a file.

Visual Basic .NET

```
Protected Overrides Sub OnStop()
    Dim fs As New FileStream("C:\Temp\MyWindowsService_VB.txt", _
        FileMode.Append, FileAccess.Write)
    Dim sr As New StreamWriter(fs)
    sr.WriteLine("MyWindowsService_VB stopped")
    sr.Flush()
    sr.Close()
End Sub
```

Visual C#

```
protected override void OnStop()
{
    FileStream fs = new FileStream("C:\\Temp\\MyWindowsService_CS.txt",
        FileMode.OpenOrCreate, FileAccess.Write);
    StreamWriter sr = new StreamWriter(fs);
    sr.WriteLine("MyWindowsService_CS Stopped");
    sr.Flush();
    sr.Close();
}
```

In addition to the OnStart and OnStop methods, you can define the OnCustom-Command method to increase the functionality of your service. You will learn to define and use this method in Lesson 5. Besides the code that you write, the designer automatically writes the following code for your service application.

Visual Basic .NET

```
Imports System.ServiceProcess

Public Class MyWindowsService_VB
    Inherits System.ServiceProcess.ServiceBase
```

(continued)

```vb
#Region " Component Designer generated code "

Public Sub New()
    MyBase.New()

    ' This call is required by the Component Designer.
    InitializeComponent()

    ' Add any initialization after the InitializeComponent() call

End Sub

' UserService overrides dispose to clean up the component list.
Protected Overloads Overrides Sub Dispose(ByVal disposing As Boolean)
    If disposing Then
        If Not (components Is Nothing) Then
            components.Dispose()
        End If
    End If
    MyBase.Dispose(disposing)
End Sub

' The main entry point for the process
<MTAThread()> _
Shared Sub Main()
    Dim ServicesToRun() As System.ServiceProcess.ServiceBase

    ' More than one NT service may run within the same process. To add
    ' another service to this process, change the following line to
    ' create a second service object. For example,
    '
    ' ServicesToRun = New System.ServiceProcess.ServiceBase () {New
    '    Service1, New MySecondUserService}
    '
    ServicesToRun = New System.ServiceProcess.ServiceBase() {New _
        MyWindowsService_VB()}

    System.ServiceProcess.ServiceBase.Run(ServicesToRun)
End Sub

' Required by the Component Designer
Private components As System.ComponentModel.IContainer

' NOTE: The following procedure is required by the Component Designer
' It can be modified using the Component Designer.
' Do not modify it using the code editor.
<System.Diagnostics.DebuggerStepThrough()> Private Sub _
    InitializeComponent()
```

```vb
        '
        ' MyWindowsService_VB
        '
        Me.ServiceName = "MyWindowsService_VB"

    End Sub

#End Region

Protected Overrides Sub OnStart(ByVal args() As String)
    Dim FS As New FileStream("C:\MyWindowsService_VB.txt", FileMode.Append, _
        FileAccess.Write)
    Dim SR As New StreamWriter(FS)
    SR.WriteLine("MyWindowsService_VB started")
    SR.Flush()
End Sub

Protected Overrides Sub OnStop()
    Dim FS As New FileStream("C:\Temp\MyWindowsService_VB.txt", _
        FileMode.Append, FileAccess.Write)
    Dim SR As New StreamWriter(FS)
    SR.WriteLine("MyWindowsService_VB stopped")
    SR.Flush()
    SR.Close()
End Sub


End Class
```

Visual C#

```csharp
using System;
using System.Collections;
using System.ComponentModel;
using System.Data;
using System.Diagnostics;
using System.ServiceProcess;

namespace MyWindowsService_CSharp
{
    public class MyWindowsService_CSharp : System.ServiceProcess.ServiceBase
    {
        /// <summary>
        /// Required designer variable.
        /// </summary>
        private System.ComponentModel.Container components = null;

        public MyWindowsService_CSharp()
        {
```

(continued)

```csharp
        // This call is required by the Windows.Forms Component Designer.
        InitializeComponent();

        // TODO: Add any initialization after the InitComponent call
    }

    // The main entry point for the process
    static void Main()
    {
        System.ServiceProcess.ServiceBase[] ServicesToRun;

        // More than one user service may run within the same process.
        // To add another service to this process,
        // change the following line to
        // create a second service object. For example,
        //
        //    ServicesToRun = New System.ServiceProcess.ServiceBase[]
        //         {new Service1(), new MySecondUserService()};
        //
        ServicesToRun = new System.ServiceProcess.ServiceBase[] {
            new MyWindowsService_CSharp() };
        System.ServiceProcess.ServiceBase.Run(ServicesToRun);
    }
    /// <summary>
    /// Required method for Designer support - do not modify
    /// the contents of this method with the code editor.
    /// </summary>
    private void InitializeComponent()
    {
        //
        // MyWindowsService_CSharp
        //
        this.ServiceName = "MyWindowsService_CSharp";
    }
    /// <summary>
    /// Clean up any resources being used.
    /// </summary>
    protected override void Dispose( bool disposing )
    {
        if( disposing )
        {
            if (components != null)
            {
                components.Dispose();
            }
        }
        base.Dispose( disposing );
    }
```

```
/// <summary>
/// Set things in motion so your service can do its work.
/// </summary>

protected override void OnStart(string[] args)
{
    FileStream fs = new FileStream(@"c:\MyWindowsService_CS.txt" ,
        FileMode.OpenOrCreate, FileAccess.Write);
    StreamWriter SR = new StreamWriter(fs);
    SR.WriteLine("MyWindowsService_CS started");
    SR.Flush();
}

/// <summary>
/// Stop this service.
/// </summary>
protected override void OnStop()
{
    FileStream fs = new FileStream(
        @"C:\Temp\MyWindowsService_CS.txt", FileMode.OpenOrCreate,
        FileAccess.Write);
    StreamWriter SR = new StreamWriter(fs);
    SR.WriteLine("MyWindowsService_CS Stopped");
    SR.Flush();
    SR.Close();
}
    }
}
```

This completes the creation of the basic structure of your Windows service. After you create the structure of your Windows service, you can further enhance the functionality of your application by enabling it to handle various events and report information. The next lesson talks about handling events and logging information from a Windows service.

Lesson 3: Handling Events and Logging Information from a Windows Service Application

You can customize your Windows service to handle various events, such as a change in the power status of the computer on which the service is running. You can also allow your service to log information, such as a change in the state of the service or errors in the system event logs as well as custom event logs. In addition, you can monitor the performance of your service by using *performance counters*.

After this lesson, you will be able to

- Handle the events of a Windows service
- Log information in event logs
- Create custom event logs
- Use performance counters to monitor performance of a service

Estimated lesson time: 30 minutes

Handling Events of a Windows Service

Like any other Windows application, a Windows service supports events. The events of a Windows service depend on the state of the service. As the state of a service changes, the corresponding event occurs. For example, when a service is paused, its state changes from running to paused, and the Pause event occurs. A Windows service supports four events: Start, Stop, Pause, and Continue.

Start Event

The Start event occurs when you start a service using the SCM. When the Start event occurs, the system locates the .exe file for the target of that event and calls the OnStart method for the service. You use the OnStart method to handle the Start event. You specify the tasks that you want your service to perform when it starts. You can set your service to start when the computer on which it is installed reboots. To do this, use the StartType property of the service. You can specify that your service start automatically, when the computer boots, or manually by a user. You can also disable a service so that a user cannot start it. You use the members of the ServiceStartMode enumeration to define whether a service automatically starts when the computer starts, starts when a user manually starts it, or is disabled. Accordingly, the ServiceStartMode enumeration provides members, which include Automatic, Manual, and Disabled. You can refer to Lesson 2 for examples of how to respond to the Start event.

Stop Event

When you stop a service using the SCM, the Stop event occurs, and the OnStop method for the service application is called. You use the OnStop method to handle the Stop event by specifying the tasks that you want your service to perform when it is stopped. When the Stop event occurs, the SCM checks the value of the CanStop property for your service. If the CanStop property is set to True, the SCM passes the Stop command to the service and calls the OnStop method. If you do not define the OnStop method for your service application, the SCM handles the Stop command. If the value of the CanStop property is set to False, the SCM does not pass the Stop command to the service application. In addition, when you stop a service, all the dependent services also stop.

As with the Start and Stop events, you can also write code to handle the Pause and Continue events. The following sections discuss how to handle the Pause and Continue events. You can refer to Lesson 2 for examples of how to respond to the Stop event.

Pause Event

You use the OnPause method to handle the Pause event by specifying the tasks that you want your service to perform when it is paused. When the service is paused, the SCM checks the value of the CanPauseAndContinue property. If the CanPauseAndContinue property is set to True, the SCM sends a pause request to your service and calls the OnPause method. You use the OnPause method to conserve system resources that are used when the service is running. For example, if you declare certain variables when the service starts, pausing a service allows those variables to remain in memory.

Continue Event

You use the OnContinue method to perform the tasks that you stopped or to stop the tasks that you started when the service was paused. As with the Pause event, the SCM checks the value of the CanPauseAndContinue property when a service is resumed from the paused state. If the CanPauseAndContinue property is set to True, the SCM passes the Continue command to the service and calls the OnContinue method.

Usually, you use these events to track the state of your service by logging information in the event logs. The following sections explain how to log information in event logs when these events occur.

Logging Information in System Event Logs

You can use the event logging feature to log software and hardware events, such as the failure of a service, low-memory conditions, or the pausing of a service. The event logs can then help you determine the type and cause of the error. You use the EventLog component to access the event logs on both local and remote computers and write entries to these logs. In addition, you can use Server Explorer to view a list of the event logs that you can access. There are three types of event logs available by default in which you can log entries.

- **System log.**   Contains messages regarding the events that occur on system components such as device drivers
- **Security log.**   Contains messages regarding security changes
- **Application log.**   Contains messages regarding the events that occur in applications installed on the computer

These event logs log all entries as error messages, warnings, information, success audits, or failure audits. You can view the entries of the various event logs in the Event Viewer window. Figure 2.5 displays the Event Viewer window.

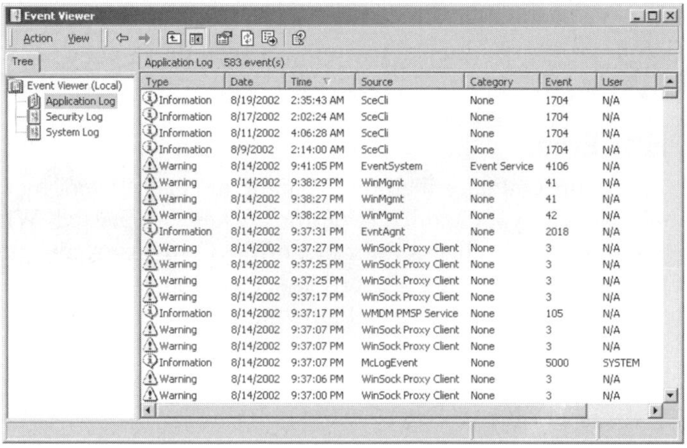

Figure 2.5   The Event Viewer window

You can specify a service application to access the default event logs to log information such as errors, exceptions, and changes in the state of the service application. To enable your service application to access the system event logs and create entries in them, set the AutoLog property of a service application to True.

When you install your service application, the installer for your service application checks the value of the AutoLog property. If the AutoLog property is set to True, the installer of your service application registers your service in the Application log of the computer as a source of events. The service can then automatically log information each time the service is started, stopped, paused, resumed, installed, or uninstalled. In addition, the service can log exceptions, failures, and errors. The following code shows how to log entries into the default event logs.

Visual Basic .NET

```
Protected Overrides Sub OnStart(ByVal args() As String)
    EventLog.WriteEntry("MyWindowsService Started")
End Sub
```

```
Protected Overrides Sub OnStop()
    EventLog.WriteEntry("MyWindowsService Stopped")
End Sub
```

Visual C#

```
protected override void OnStart(string[] args)
{
    // TODO: Add code here to start your service.
    EventLog.WriteEntry("Starting MyWindowsServices");
}

protected override void OnStop()
{
    // TODO: Add code here to perform any tear-down
    // necessary to stop your service.
    EventLog.WriteEntry("Stopping MyWindowsServices");
}
```

Creating Custom Event Logs

In addition to the system event logs, Visual Studio .NET allows you to create custom event logs to log events exclusively for your applications. For example, if you need to save all the log entries that are related to your service, you can create a custom event log. This enables you to store all the log entries related to your service in one place. In addition, these log entries are not lost if default logs are cleared.

You use the CreateEventSource method of the EventLog class to create a custom event log. This method creates a source and enables you to specify the log in which your service will write. To use the CreateEventSource method, add a reference to the System.Diagnostics namespace. To create a custom event log, perform the following steps:

1. Set the AutoLog property of your service application to False.
2. Add an instance of the EventLog component from the Components toolbox in your service application.
3. Specify a value for the Source property and the name of the log file that you want to create in the Log property.

You can also create a custom event log programmatically. The following code shows how to create a custom event log programmatically.

Visual Basic .NET

```
Private EventLog1 as New System.Diagnostics.EventLog
    .
    .
    .
```

(continued)

```vb
Sub CreateEventLog()
    ' Initialize the instance of the EventLog component

    ' Create an event log for your service.
    ' The code also checks if an event log already exists
    ' for your service application
    If Not EventLog1.SourceExists("Transaction Service") Then
        EventLog1.CreateEventSource("Transaction Service", "Transaction Log")
    End If

    ' Specify the event log to use your service application as source
    EventLog1.Source = " Transaction Service"
End Sub
```

Visual C#

```csharp
private System.Diagnostics.EventLog eventLog1;
.
.
.

private void CreateEventLog()
{
    //Initialize the instance of the EventLog component
    eventLog1 = new System.Diagnostics.EventLog();

    /* Create an event log for your service. The code also checks if an
       event log already exists for your service application */
    if (!System.Diagnostics.EventLog.SourceExists("Transaction Service"))
    {
        System.Diagnostics.EventLog.CreateEventSource("Transaction Service",
            "Transaction Log");
    }
    //Specify the event log to use your service application as source
    eventLog1.Source = "Transaction Service";
}
```

You can call the CreateEventLog() method in the OnStart method. After you create a custom event log, you can direct your service to create entries in it. The following code shows how to write entries in a custom event log.

Visual Basic .NET

```vb
Protected Overrides Sub OnStart(ByVal args() As String)
    CreateEventLog()
    EventLog1.WriteEntry("MyWindowsService_VB Started", _
        EventLogEntryType.Information)
End Sub
```

Visual C#

```csharp
protected override void OnStart(string[] args)
{
    CreateEventLog();
    eventLog1.WriteEntry("MyWindowsService_CSharp Started",
        EventLogEntryType.Information);
}
```

You can then use the Event Viewer window to view entries made in the custom event log you created. Figure 2.6 displays the entries in a custom event log.

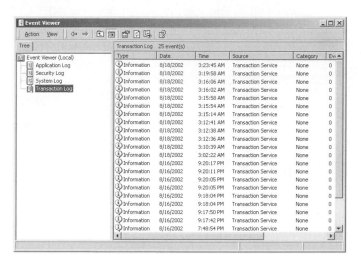

Figure 2.6   Entries in a custom event log

Using Performance Counters

Performance counters allow you to monitor the performance of your applications and help you to identify and remove performance bottlenecks. You can enable your applications to publish performance-related data by using performance counters. For example, you can enable an application to publish data regarding memory utilization, number of active database connections, or number of active threads within a process. You can collect the performance data that you want your application to publish and analyze it to fine-tune your application.

The .NET Framework provides the PerformanceCounter class in the System.Diagnostics namespace. This class allows you to publish, collect, and analyze the performance data of an application. The PerformanceCounter class also allows you to use existing performance counters in your application. In addition, it allows you to use custom performance counters that you create for your applications.

To use existing performance counters in your service application, complete the following steps:

1. Open your Windows service in design view.
2. Open Server Explorer.
3. Expand the Servers node, locate your server, and expand the Performance Counters node.
4. Select a performance counter category and expand it.
5. Locate the performance counter that you want to use. For example, you can use the Global # Of IL Bytes Jitted counter from the .NET CLR Jit category, which specifies the number of bytes JIT-compiled.
6. Drag and drop the counter on the designer as shown here.

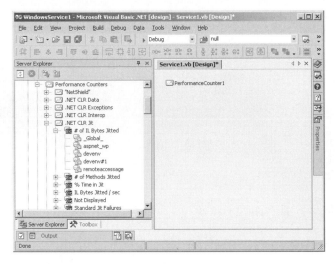

Visual Studio .NET adds the following code to your service class to create an instance of the performance counter that you add to your service application.

Visual Basic .NET

```
Friend WithEvents PerformanceCounter1 As
    System.Diagnostics.PerformanceCounter
<System.Diagnostics.DebuggerStepThrough()> Private Sub InitializeComponent()

    Me.PerformanceCounter1 = New System.Diagnostics.PerformanceCounter()
    CType(Me.PerformanceCounter1, _
        System.ComponentModel.ISupportInitialize).BeginInit()
```

```
Me.PerformanceCounter1.CategoryName = ".NET CLR Jit"
Me.PerformanceCounter1.CounterName = "Total # of IL Bytes Jitted"
Me.PerformanceCounter1.InstanceName = "_Global_"
```

```
End Sub
```

Visual C#

```csharp
private System.Diagnostics.PerformanceCounter performanceCounter1;

private void InitializeComponent()
{
    this.performanceCounter1 = new System.Diagnostics.PerformanceCounter();
    ((System.ComponentModel.ISupportInitialize)
        (this.performanceCounter1)).BeginInit();
    this.performanceCounter1.CategoryName = ".NET CLR Jit";
    this.performanceCounter1.CounterName = "Total # of IL Bytes Jitted";
    this.performanceCounter1.InstanceName = "_Global_";
}
```

Note   By default the designer also adds the MachineName property, which specifies the machine name where the counter is installed. To make the installation of the performance counter machine-independent, you can set the MachineName property of the performance counter to blank in the Properties window. When you set the MachineName property of the performance counter to blank, the designer does not add the code to set the MachineName property.

You can also create custom performance counters. To create a custom performance counter, complete the following steps:

1. Right-click the Performance Counter node in Server Explorer.
2. Choose Create New Category from the shortcut menu.
3. In the Performance Counter Builder window, specify a name for the performance counter category you create.
4. Click New to create a new counter. Specify the Name and Type properties of the counter.

Visual Studio .NET creates a new category of performance counters and adds the performance counter to this category. You can view the custom performance counter in Server Explorer. A custom performance counter, Counter1 is displayed in the following graphic.

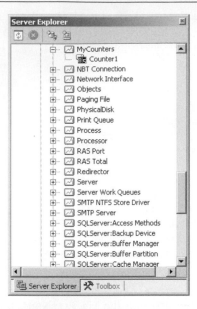

After you create the custom counter, add it to your application by dragging the performance counter from Server Explorer to your application. You can then add code to increment, decrement, or set the value of the performance counter as shown in the following code.

Visual Basic .NET

```
' Increments the value of counter by 1
PerformanceCounter1.Increment()
' Increments the value of counter by 5
PerformanceCounter1.IncrementBy(5)
' Decreases the value of counter by 1
PerformanceCounter1.Decrement()
' Sets the value of counter to 10
PerformanceCounter1.RawValue = 10
' Gets the value of counter
Dim val as Integer = PerformanceCounter1.RawValue
```

Visual C#

```
// Increments the value of counter by 1
performanceCounter1.Increment();
// Increments the value of counter by 5
performanceCounter1.IncrementBy(5);
// Decreases the value of counter by 1
performanceCounter1.Decrement();
// Sets the value of counter to 10
performanceCounter1.RawValue = 10;
// Gets the value of counter
int val = performanceCounter1.RawValue;
```

After you create a service application, add functionality to it, and enable it to handle events and log information, you need to install the service application, and then start it. The next lesson talks about installing and running Windows services on a computer.

Lesson 4: Adding Installers, Specifying Security Context, and Installing and Uninstalling a Windows Service

To start a service on a computer, you need to add installers to the service application and use the Installutil tool to install the service application. Installers install and register your service application on a computer. In addition, installers install and configure the resources, such as performance counters and event logs, that your service uses. Installers also allow you to specify the security context for your service.

After this lesson, you will be able to

- Describe the role of installers in a service application deployment
- Add installers to a Windows service
- Specify the security context for a service application
- Install and uninstall a Windows service application

Estimated lesson time: 30 minutes

Understanding the Role of Installers

The .NET Framework includes installation components, which enable you to install a Windows service and resources, such as custom logs and performance counters, that a service application uses. The installation components automatically install these resources when you install a service and uninstall them when you uninstall the service. You use the general-purpose and predefined installation components to install your services and the components that the services use. In addition, you can create custom installers to install your components.

The general-purpose installation components, or installers, include the Installer classes that enable you to perform tasks such as specifying the location for installing the service application and its resources. Predefined installers include installer components that you can use to install event logs, performance counters, Windows services, and message queues. Whenever you include event logs, performance counters, and message queues in your service application, use the predefined installers to configure these components. You also use the predefined installers to install and configure the custom event logs, performance counters, and message queues that you create in your application. The predefined installer classes that the .NET Framework provides include

- **System.Diagnostics.EventLogInstaller.**   This class allows you to configure the default EventLogs, such as the Application and System logs that your application uses. The System.Diagnostics.EventLogInstaller class also allows you to install and configure custom event logs that you create for your service.

- **System.Diagnostics.PerformanceCounterInstaller.**   This class allows you to configure the performance counters installed on the system. It also allows you to install and configure the custom performance counters that you create for your service.

- **System.ServiceProcess.ServiceInstaller and System.ServiceProcess.ServiceProcessInstaller.**   These two classes allow you to install and configure a Windows service on a computer. You need to include one instance of the System.ServiceProcess.ServiceProcessInstaller class for your service application and one instance of System.ServiceProcess.ServiceInstaller for each service within your service application. The ServiceProcessInstaller class performs the tasks that are common for all the services within a service application, such as writing entries in the system registry, whereas the ServiceInstaller class performs tasks specific to a service. For example, the ServiceInstaller class passes the ServiceName of a service to the installation utility. The installation utility uses the ServiceName to create a registry entry for the service in the HKEY_LOCAL_MACHINE\System\CurrentControlSet\Services registry key.

- **System.Messaging.MessageQueueInstaller.**   This class allows you to configure and install the message queues that your service application uses to send and receive messages.

Adding Installers

To install your service application, you need to create an Installer class, which derives from the System.Configuration.Install.Installer class. The Installer class contains a collection called Installers, which contains the installation components for the resources that your service application uses at run time. You add the EventLogInstallers, PerformanceCounterInstallers, ServiceInstallers, ServiceProcessInstaller, and the MessageQueueInstallers to the Installers collection.

You add installers to your service application project for various components including event logs and performance counters for the service application by using the Visual Studio .NET Component Designer. To add installers for a component, click the Add Installer link in the Properties window. You can also right-click the component for which you want to add an installer, and then choose Add Installer from the shortcut menu. The Add Installer options are shown in Figure 2.7.

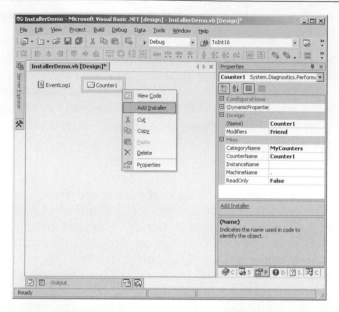

Figure 2.7   Adding installers in the Component Designer

As mentioned earlier, you need one instance of the ServiceProcessInstaller class for a Windows service application and one instance of the ServiceInstaller class for each Windows service in the service application. To add installers for your service application, click the designer window for your service application, and then click the Add Installer link in the Properties window. Visual Studio .NET automatically creates a ProjectInstaller class that includes an instance of the ServiceProcess-Installer class and an instance of the ServiceInstaller class. Figure 2.8 shows the ProjectInstaller class for a Windows service project that includes installers for an event log and a performance counter.

The ProjectInstaller class code created by Visual Studio .NET is shown next. Note that the EventLogInstaller, PerformanceCounterInstaller, ServiceInstaller, and the ServiceProcessInstaller are added to the Installers collection of the ProjectInstaller class.

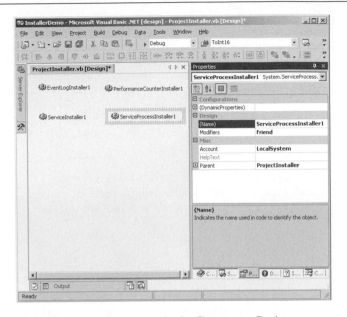

Figure 2.8   Installer classes in the Component Designer

Visual Basic .NET

```vb
Imports System.ComponentModel
Imports System.Configuration.Install

<RunInstaller(True)> Public Class ProjectInstaller
Inherits System.Configuration.Install.Installer

#Region " Component Designer generated code "

    Public Sub New()
        MyBase.New()
        'This call is required by the Component Designer.
        InitializeComponent()
        'Add any initialization after the InitializeComponent() call
    End Sub

    'Installer overrides dispose to clean up the component list.
    Protected Overloads Overrides Sub Dispose(ByVal disposing As Boolean)
        If disposing Then
            If Not (components Is Nothing) Then
                components.Dispose()
            End If
        End If
        MyBase.Dispose(disposing)
    End Sub
```

(continued)

```vb
'Required by the Component Designer
Private components As System.ComponentModel.IContainer

'NOTE: The following procedure is required by the Component Designer
'It can be modified using the Component Designer.
'Do not modify it using the code editor.
Friend WithEvents EventLogInstaller1 As_
    System.Diagnostics.EventLogInstaller
Friend WithEvents ServiceProcessInstaller1 As _
    System.ServiceProcess.ServiceProcessInstaller
Friend WithEvents ServiceInstaller1 As _
    System.ServiceProcess.ServiceInstaller
Friend WithEvents PerformanceCounterInstaller1 As _
    System.Diagnostics.PerformanceCounterInstaller

<System.Diagnostics.DebuggerStepThrough()> Private Sub _
    InitializeComponent()
    Me.EventLogInstaller1 = New System.Diagnostics.EventLogInstaller()
    Me.ServiceProcessInstaller1 = New
    System.ServiceProcess.ServiceProcessInstaller()
    Me.ServiceInstaller1 = New System.ServiceProcess.ServiceInstaller()
    Me.PerformanceCounterInstaller1 = New _
        System.Diagnostics.PerformanceCounterInstaller()
    '
    'EventLogInstaller1
    '
    Me.EventLogInstaller1.Log = "Application"
    Me.EventLogInstaller1.Source = "MyService"
    '
    'ServiceProcessInstaller1
    '
    Me.ServiceProcessInstaller1.Account = _
        System.ServiceProcess.ServiceAccount.LocalSystem
    Me.ServiceProcessInstaller1.Password = Nothing
    Me.ServiceProcessInstaller1.Username = Nothing
    '
    'ServiceInstaller1
    '
    Me.ServiceInstaller1.ServiceName = "MyService"
    '
    'PerformanceCounterInstaller1
    '
    Me.PerformanceCounterInstaller1.CategoryHelp = "None"
    Me.PerformanceCounterInstaller1.CategoryName = "MyCounters"
    Me.PerformanceCounterInstaller1.Counters.AddRange(New _
        System.Diagnostics.CounterCreationData() {New _
        System.Diagnostics.CounterCreationData("MyAppCounter", "", _
        System.Diagnostics.PerformanceCounterType.NumberOfItems32)})
```

```
        '
        'ProjectInstaller
        '
        Me.Installers.AddRange(New System.Configuration.Install.Installer() _
            {Me.EventLogInstaller1, Me.ServiceProcessInstaller1, _
            Me.ServiceInstaller1, Me.PerformanceCounterInstaller1})
    End Sub
#End Region
End Class
```

Visual C#

```csharp
using System;
using System.Collections;
using System.ComponentModel;
using System.Configuration.Install;

namespace InstallerDemoCS
{
    /// <summary>
    /// Summary description for ProjectInstaller.
    /// </summary>
    [RunInstaller(true)]
    public class ProjectInstaller : System.Configuration.Install.Installer
    {
        private System.ServiceProcess.ServiceProcessInstaller
            serviceProcessInstaller1;
        private System.ServiceProcess.ServiceInstaller serviceInstaller1;
        private System.Diagnostics.EventLogInstaller eventLogInstaller1;
        private System.Diagnostics.PerformanceCounterInstaller
            performanceCounterInstaller1;
        /// <summary>
        /// Required designer variable.
        /// </summary>
        private System.ComponentModel.Container components = null;

        public ProjectInstaller()
        {
            // This call is required by the Designer.
            InitializeComponent();

            // TODO: Add any initialization after the InitComponent call
        }

        #region Component Designer generated code
        /// <summary>
        /// Required method for Designer support - do not modify
        /// the contents of this method with the code editor.
        /// </summary>
```

(continued)

```csharp
        private void InitializeComponent()
        {
            this.serviceProcessInstaller1 = new
                System.ServiceProcess.ServiceProcessInstaller();
            this.serviceInstaller1 = new
                System.ServiceProcess.ServiceInstaller();
            this.eventLogInstaller1 = new
                System.Diagnostics.EventLogInstaller();
            this.performanceCounterInstaller1 = new
                System.Diagnostics.PerformanceCounterInstaller();
            //
            // serviceProcessInstaller1
            //
            this.serviceProcessInstaller1.Password = null;
            this.serviceProcessInstaller1.Username = null;
            //
            // serviceInstaller1
            //
            this.serviceInstaller1.ServiceName = "MyService";
            //
            // eventLogInstaller1
            //
            this.eventLogInstaller1.Log = "Application";
            this.eventLogInstaller1.Source = "MyService";
            //
            // performanceCounterInstaller1
            //
            this.performanceCounterInstaller1.CategoryHelp = "None";
            this.performanceCounterInstaller1.CategoryName = "MyCounters";
            this.performanceCounterInstaller1.Counters.AddRange(new
                System.Diagnostics.CounterCreationData[] { new
                System.Diagnostics.CounterCreationData("MyAppCounter",
                "MyAppCounter help",
                System.Diagnostics.PerformanceCounterType.NumberOfItems32
                    )}});
            //
            // ProjectInstaller
            //
            this.Installers.AddRange(new
                System.Configuration.Install.Installer[] {
                this.serviceProcessInstaller1,
                this.serviceInstaller1,
                this.eventLogInstaller1,
                    this.performanceCounterInstaller1}});
        }
        #endregion
    }
}
```

The ProjectInstaller class is marked with the attribute [RunInstaller(true)] in Visual C# and <RunInstaller(True)> in Visual Basic.NET. This requires you to install the assembly containing the ProjectInstaller class by using the Installutil.exe tool. Invoking an installer ensures that all the components are either successfully installed or do not get installed at all. If any component fails to install during the installation process, the installer rolls back the installation process by removing all the components previously installed.

Specifying Security Context for a Service Application

In addition to registering and installing your service application, the installer allows you to specify the security context within which the services in your service application run. This enables you to specify whether the services you install on a computer will run for all users who log in to the computer or for a particular user. You use the Account property of the ServiceProcessInstaller class to specify the security context for your service application. You can set the Account property of the ServiceProcessInstaller class from the Properties window. The right pane of Figure 2.8 displays the properties of the ServiceProcessInstaller class.

You can set the Account property to LocalService, LocalSystem, NetworkService, or User. Table 2.5 describes the values of the Account property.

Table 2.5   Values of the Account Property

Method	Description
LocalService	Enables a service to run in the context of an account that provides extensive local privileges and provides the credentials of the computer to a remote server.
LocalSystem	Enables a service to run in the context of an account that acts as a nonprivileged user on the local computer and provides anonymous credentials to a remote server.
NetworkService	Enables a service to run in the context of an account that acts as a nonprivileged user on the local computer and provides the credentials of the computer to a remote server.
User	Enables a service to run in the context of a user. You need to supply a valid user name and password when you install the service application on a computer.

Installing and Uninstalling a Windows Service

After you add installers to your service application and specify the security context in which the service will run, you are ready to build the service application and install it on a computer. To build a service application, open the Build menu and choose Build Solution.

After you build your service application, Visual Studio .NET creates a .exe file for your service application. You then need to install the .exe file on a computer. The

.NET Framework provides the Installutil.exe tool, which enables you to install a service application. You run this tool from the command prompt. The syntax for using this tool to install a service application is

Installutil <.*exe filename*>

for example, Installutil MyWindowsService.exe.

When you run the Installutil tool, it runs all the installers in your service application. The installers then install your service application and the resources included in the service application according to the properties you have specified. If you specify the Account property of the ServiceProcessInstaller instance in your service application as User, you will be prompted for a user name and password. Figure 2.9 displays the Set Service Login dialog box in which you enter a valid user name and password.

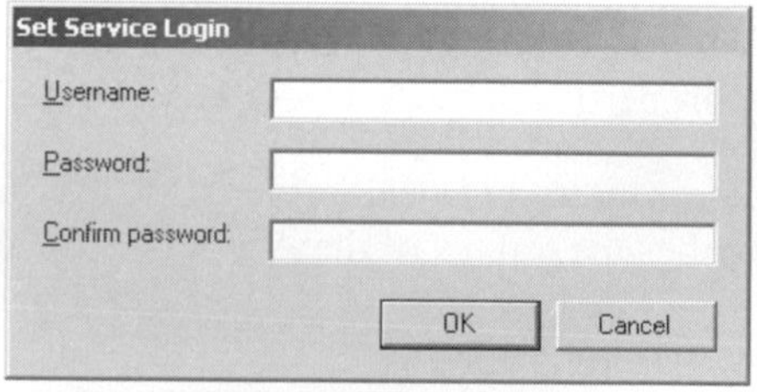

Figure 2.9   The Set Service Login dialog box

After you enter the user name and password of the account, the Installutil tool completes the installation process, and a message is displayed in the Command Prompt window. Figure 2.10 displays the Command Prompt window after a service application is installed on a computer.

The Installutil tool also allows you to uninstall a service application. To uninstall a service application, run the Installutil tool with the /u option. The syntax to uninstall a service application by using the Installutil tool is

Installutil /u <.*exe filename*>

for example, Installutil /u MyWindowsService.exe.

After you successfully install a service, you can manage and control its behavior manually by using the SCM. In addition, you can also manage and control a service programmatically by using the methods of the ServiceController class. You will learn about managing Windows services in the next lesson.

Figure 2.10   The Visual Studio .NET Command Prompt window

Lesson 5: Managing Windows Services

After you create and install a Windows service, you can manage your service by performing tasks such as changing the state of your service. You can manage your services manually by using the SCM or programmatically by using a component of the ServiceController class in an application.

After this lesson, you will be able to

- Use the Service Control Manager to control a service
- Use the ServiceController class to manage a service

Estimated lesson time: 20 minutes

Using the Service Control Manager

You use the SCM to control your service application and perform the following administrative tasks:

- Change the state of a service
- Specify how to start a service
- Specify the recovery actions in case of a service failure
- Specify a user account for a service
- View service dependencies

You access the SCM by using the Services window. To open the Services window, open Control Panel, double-click Administrative Tools, and then double-click Services. Figure 2.11 displays the Services window.

The Services window displays all the installed services. To change the state of a service, click the service, and then use the appropriate button on the toolbar to start, pause, stop, or resume the service.

Note   You can change the state of a service only if the appropriate properties of the service are specified. For example, you can pause and resume a service only if the CanPauseAndContinue property of the service application is set to True.

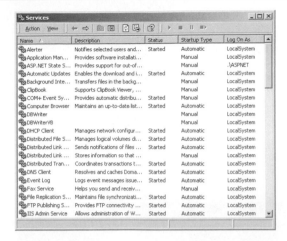

Figure 2.11   A list of services displayed in the Services window

You can also specify how a service starts by changing the startup type of the service. To change the startup type for a service application, complete the following steps:

1. Select a service and click Properties on the toolbar. Figure 2.12 displays the properties dialog box for a service application.

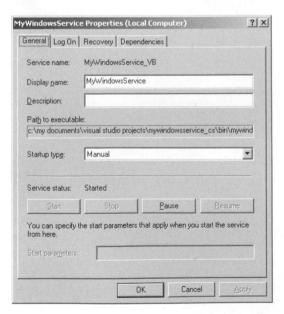

Figure 2.12   The properties dialog box

2. Select the appropriate startup type from the Startup Type drop-down list on the General tab.

3. Click OK to close the properties dialog box.

The SCM also allows you to specify recovery actions in case a service fails. To specify the recovery actions for a service, perform the following steps:

1. Select a service and click Properties on the toolbar. The properties dialog box opens.

2. Select the Recovery tab. Figure 2.13 displays the Recovery tab of the properties dialog box.

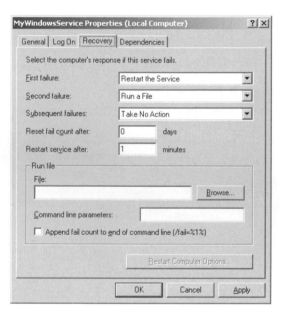

Figure 2.13   The Recovery tab

3. Specify the action that you want to perform at first, second, and subsequent failures of your service. You can specify that the SCM restart the service, run a program, restart the computer, or take no action.

4. Click OK to close the properties dialog box.

You can also use the SCM to specify the account that a service uses to log on to a computer. This enables you to modify the privileges that your service has on a computer. The account you specify also determines how a service interacts with the network. You can specify that a service run in the security context of a LocalSystem account or a user account. To specify the account that a service uses to log on to a computer, complete the following steps:

1. Select a service and click Properties on the toolbar. The properties dialog box opens.

2. Click the Log On tab. Figure 2.14 displays the Log On tab of the properties dialog box.

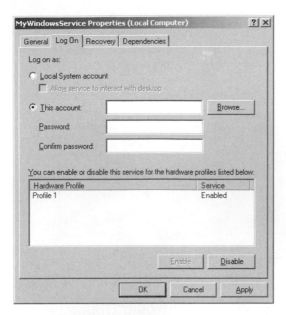

Figure 2.14 The Log On tab

3. Select the Local System Account option if you want to run the service in the security context of a LocalSystem account. Alternatively, you can select This Account and specify the user account you want your service to use. You can also select a user account by browsing all the user accounts in the network.

4. Click OK to close the properties dialog box.

The SCM also allows you to view dependencies of your service. You can view a list of services that depend on your service and the list of services on which your service depends. For example, the Indexing Service in Windows 2000 depends on the Remote Procedure Call (RPC) service. To view the list of service dependencies for your service application, perform the following steps:

1. Select a service and click Properties on the toolbar.

2. Select the Dependencies tab. Figure 2.15 displays the Dependencies tab for the Indexing Service in Windows 2000.

3. Click OK to close the properties dialog box.

In addition to the SCM, you can use the methods of the ServerController class to control a service programmatically.

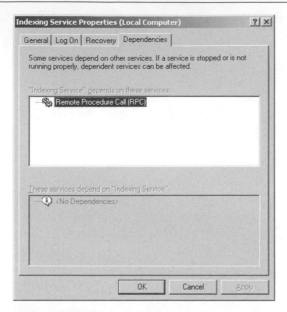

Figure 2.15   The Dependencies tab

Using the ServiceController Class

The ServiceController class enables you to connect and control the Windows services running on a computer. Like the SCM, you can use the methods of the ServiceController class to perform various tasks, such as starting, stopping, pausing, and resuming services. However, unlike the SCM, you can execute custom commands by using the methods of the ServiceController class. You can perform the following tasks by using the ServiceController class:

- View the list of services on a computer
- Start and stop a service
- Pause and resume a service
- Query and retrieve the properties of a service
- Specify a custom command to execute on your service

To control the behavior of a service, you write code to specify the tasks that the service should perform when an event occurs. For example, you can define the OnPause method, which is called when the Pause event is sent to your service application. However, you need to ensure that the corresponding properties for the events that you want to control are set accordingly. For example, if you set the CanPause property for a service to False, you cannot stop the service by using the ServiceController or the Service Control Manager.

To use the methods of the ServiceController class, you create an instance of the ServiceController component. Next, you set the properties for this instance, which enables you to specify both the service to which you want to connect and the computer on which the service is running. You can then use the methods of the Service-Controller class to control the behavior of the service by calling the appropriate methods of the ServiceController class. When you call a method of the Service-Controller class, the instance of the ServiceController component passes a request for actions to the SCM. The SCM then passes the request to the service, and the service application executes the method corresponding to the event.

Note   You should always create a separate application that contains a component of the ServiceController class to control a service application.

Let's first look at creating an instance of the ServiceController component. You can drag an instance of the ServiceController component from the Components tab of the Toolbox and drop it on the form of a Windows application. You then need to specify the name of the service that you want to control and the computer on which the service is running by using the ServiceName and MachineName properties, respectively. Figure 2.16 displays a Windows application with an instance of the ServiceController component.

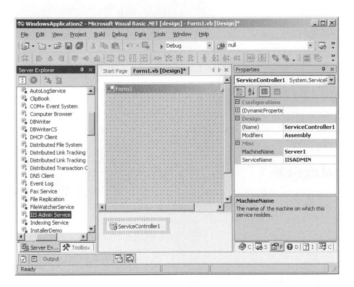

Figure 2.16   A Windows application with an instance of the ServiceController component

You can also add an instance of the ServiceController component from Server Explorer. To add an instance of the ServiceController component from Server Explorer, complete the following steps:

1. In Server Explorer, locate the server on which the service you want to control is running.
2. Expand the Services node for that server, and locate the service you want to control.

3. Right-click the name of the service and choose Add To Designer from the shortcut menu. A ServiceController component appears in your Windows application project, and the component is configured to interact with the service you need to control. Therefore, you do not need to specify the MachineName and ServiceName properties for this instance of the ServiceController component. Figure 2.17 displays the list of services in Server Explorer.

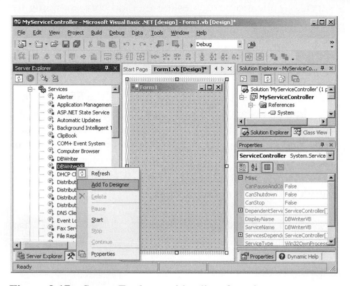

Figure 2.17   Server Explorer with a list of services

You can also create an instance of the ServiceController component programmatically. The following code shows how to create an instance of a ServiceController component in a Windows application.

Visual Basic .NET

```
Dim DBWriterController As System.ServiceProcess.ServiceController
Me.DBWriterController = New System.ServiceProcess.ServiceController()
Me.DBWriterController.MachineName = "NancyD"
Me.DBWriterController.ServiceName = "DBWriterVB"
```

Visual C#

```
private System.ServiceProcess.ServiceController serviceController1;
this.serviceController1 = new System.ServiceProcess.ServiceController();
this.serviceController1.MachineName = " NancyD";
this.serviceController1.ServiceName = " DBWriterCS";
```

After you create an instance of the ServiceController component in your Windows application, you call the methods of the ServiceController class. Table 2.4 in Lesson 1 describes some of the methods of the ServiceController class. Let's now look at controlling a service by using the methods of the ServiceController class.

The following code displays a method that starts a service from a Windows application.

Note   In order for the following applications to run correctly, you need to add a reference to the System.ServiceProcess namespace.

Visual Basic .NET

```
Sub StartService()
    ' Check the current status of the service before you
    ' try to change the current status of the service
    If (DBWriterController.Status = ServiceControllerStatus.Stopped) Then
        DBWriterController.Start()
        MessageBox.Show("Service Started")
    Else
        MessageBox.Show("Service Running")
    End If
End Sub
```

Visual C#

```
private void StartService()
{
    /* Check the current status of the service before you
    try to change the current status of the service */
    if (DBWriterController.Status == ServiceControllerStatus.Stopped)
    {
        DBWriterController.Start();
        MessageBox.Show("Service Started");
    }
    else
    {
        MessageBox.Show("Service Running");
    }
}
```

Similarly, you can use the other methods of the ServiceController class, such as Pause, Continue, and Stop, to control a service. The following code displays a method that pauses a service running on a computer.

Visual Basic .NET

```
Sub PauseService()
    ' Check the current status of the service before you try
    ' to change the current status of the service*/
    If (DBWriterController.Status = ServiceControllerStatus.Running) Then
        ' Check whether you can pause the service
        If (DBWriterController.CanPauseAndContinue = True) Then
            DBWriterController.Pause()
            MessageBox.Show("Service Paused")
```

(continued)

```
        Else
           MessageBox.Show("You Can not Pause the Service")
        End If
    Else
        MessageBox.Show("Service not Running")
    End If
End Sub
```

Visual C#

```
private void PauseService()
{
    /* Check the current status of the service before you try to
       change the current status of the service*/
    if (DBWriterController.Status == ServiceControllerStatus.Running)
    {
        //Check whether you can pause the service
        if(DBWriterController.CanPauseAndContinue==true)
        {
            DBWriterController.Pause();
            MessageBox.Show("Service Paused");
        }
        else
            MessageBox.Show("You Can not Pause the Service");
    }
    else
        MessageBox.Show("Service not Running");
}
```

In addition to the Start, Stop, Pause, and Continue methods, you can use the ExecuteCommand method to run custom commands on your service. To run custom commands on your service application, complete the following steps:

1. Create a method that calls the ServiceController.ExecuteCommand method in the application that you use to control your service application.
2. Override the OnCustomCommand method in your service application to specify the tasks that you want your service application to perform.

The following code shows the RunCommand method, which calls the Service-Controller.ExecuteCommand method. The ServiceController.ExecuteCommand method takes a numeric value as a parameter. This numeric value should be between 128 and 256.

Visual Basic .NET

```
' The method in the controller application that calls ExecuteCommand method
Public Sub RunCommand()
    If Date.Now.Hour <= 12 Then
        MyServiceController.ExecuteCommand(200)
```

```
ElseIf Date.Now.Hour > 12 Then
    MyServiceController.ExecuteCommand(220)
    End If
End Sub
```

Visual C#

```
void RunCommand()
{
    if(System.DateTime.Now.Hour <= 12 )
        MyServiceController.ExecuteCommand(200);
    else
        if(System.DateTime.Now.Hour <= 24 )
            MyServiceController.ExecuteCommand(220);
}
```

The following code shows how to override the OnCustomCommand method. In this method, you can use the If...Then construct to perform various tasks, depending on the value of the parameter passed by the RunCommand method.

Visual Basic .NET

```
Protected Overrides Sub OnCustomCommand(ByVal command As Integer)
    Dim FS As New FileStream("C:\Temp\MyWindowsService_VB.txt", _
        FileMode.Append, FileAccess.Write)
    Dim SR As New StreamWriter(FS)
    If command = 200 Then
        SR.WriteLine("Good Morning")
        SR.Flush()
    ElseIf command = 220 Then
        SR.WriteLine("Good Evening")
        SR.Flush()
    End If
End Sub
```

Visual C#

```
protected override void OnCustomCommand(int command)
{
    FileStream FS = new FileStream(@"c:\Temp\MyWindowsService_CSharp.txt",
        FileMode.OpenOrCreate, FileAccess.Write);
    StreamWriter SR = new StreamWriter(FS);
    if(command == 200)
    {
        SR.WriteLine("Good Morning");
        SR.Flush();
    }
    else
    {
        if (command==220)
```

(continued)

```
            {
                SR.WriteLine("Good Evening");
                SR.Flush();
            }
        }
}
```

The instance of the ServiceController also allows you to retrieve a list of services running on a computer by using the GetServices method. The following code shows how to retrieve the list of services running on a computer.

Visual Basic .NET

```
Imports System.ServiceProcess

Module Module1

    Sub Main()
        Dim MyServiceController As New ServiceController()
        Dim services As ServiceController()
        services = MyServiceController.GetServices()
        Dim enumerator As IEnumerator = services.GetEnumerator
        While enumerator.MoveNext
            Console.WriteLine(CType(enumerator.Current, _
                ServiceController).ServiceName)
        End While
        Console.WriteLine("Press the <Enter> key to exit")
        Console.Read()
    End Sub


End Module
```

Visual C#

```
using System;
using System.ServiceProcess;
using System.Collections;

namespace ConsoleApplication5
{
    /// <summary>
    /// Summary description for Class1.
    /// </summary>
    class Class1
    {
        /// <summary>
        /// The main entry point for the application.
        /// </summary>
        [STAThread]
        static void Main(string[] args)
```

```
        {
            ServiceController MyServiceController = new
                ServiceController();
            ServiceController[] services= ServiceController.GetServices();
            IEnumerator enumerator   = services.GetEnumerator();
            while (enumerator.MoveNext())
            {
                Console.WriteLine(
                    ((ServiceController)enumerator.Current).ServiceName);
            }
            Console.WriteLine("Press <Enter> to exit");
            Console.Read();
        }
    }
}
```

After you create a Windows service, you might need to configure your service application to install it on a computer. You might also need to debug your service once it is installed. You will learn to configure and debug your service application in Lesson 6.

Lesson 6: Configuring and Debugging Windows Services

After you create and install a Windows service, you can change its properties dynamically. The .NET Framework provides dynamic properties for Windows services that enable you to change settings such as AutoLog, CanShutdown, and CanPauseAndContinue without recompiling the code. In addition, you can debug a Windows service to ensure that it performs all the tasks that you want the service application to perform.

After this lesson, you will be able to

- Configure a Windows service dynamically
- Debug a Windows service

Estimated lesson time: 20 minutes

Configuring a Windows Service

Windows services can use resources such as event logs, performance counters, and database connections. You write the code in the Service class to access these resources. If you want to change the event log, performance counter, or the database server that your service uses, you need to change the code and recompile the service application. In addition, you need to uninstall the service and install the new version of the service application. Therefore, the task of maintaining the service becomes difficult if the dependency of a service on external resources changes often.

The .NET Framework provides configuration files that make the maintenance of services a simple task. The configuration files contain property settings, which allow you to dynamically configure a service without recompiling the service application. Each service application has one configuration file. By changing the property settings in the configuration file, you can reconfigure the service application. For example, by changing the database connection property in the configuration file, you can enable your application to connect to a different database. You can define the properties that can be dynamically configured using the Properties window at design time. The following graphics show how you can set the dynamic properties for a performance counter.

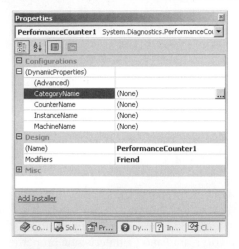

When you configure dynamic properties, Visual Studio .NET adds code to your service application, which enables the service application to read the value of the properties defined in the configuration file at run time. Visual Studio .NET adds the following code when you define dynamic properties for your service application.

Visual Basic .NET

```
Dim configurationAppSettings As System.Configuration.AppSettingsReader = New _
    System.Configuration.AppSettingsReader()

Me.PerformanceCounter1.CategoryName = CType( _
    configurationAppSettings.GetValue( "PerformanceCounter1.CategoryName", _
    GetType(System.String)), String)

Me.PerformanceCounter1.CounterName = CType( _
    configurationAppSettings.GetValue("PerformanceCounter1.CounterName", _
    GetType(System.String)),String)
```

Visual C#

```csharp
System.Configuration.AppSettingsReader configurationAppSettings = new
    System.Configuration.AppSettingsReader();

this.performanceCounter1.CategoryName = ((string)
    (configurationAppSettings.GetValue("performanceCounter1.CategoryName",
    typeof(string))));

this.performanceCounter1.CounterName = ((string)
    (configurationAppSettings.GetValue("performanceCounter1.CounterName",
    typeof(string))));
```

When you configure dynamic properties, Visual Studio .NET creates a configuration file that contains key-value pairs for the properties that you can configure dynamically. The following code shows the configuration file that is created when you configure the CategoryName and CounterName properties of a performance counter as dynamic properties.

XML

```xml
<?xml version="1.0" encoding="Windows-1252"?>
<configuration>
    <appSettings>
        <!-- User application and configured property settings go here.-->
        <!-- Example: <add key="settingName" value="settingValue"/> -->
        <add key="PerformanceCounter1.CategoryName" value=".NET CLR Jit" />
        <add key="PerformanceCounter1.CounterName" value="Total # of IL Bytes
            Jitted" />
    </appSettings>
</configuration>
```

After you specify the dynamic properties of a service application, you simply change the value of the appropriate key in the configuration file to change the value of the dynamic properties.

Debugging a Windows Service

To debug a Windows service, you start the service and then attach a debugger to the process in which the service is running. You cannot debug a service from within Visual Studio .NET by pressing the F5 and F11 keys or by using the Debug menu for two reasons. First, you need to add an installer and install a service application before a service can run. Second, a service runs in a different security context than that of Visual Studio .NET.

After you attach a debugger to a process, you can use all standard debugging features, such as setting breakpoints or stepping into the code, that Visual Studio .NET provides to debug an application. To attach a debugger to a process, complete the following steps:

1. Start your service by using the SCM.
2. Choose Processes from the Debug menu. The Processes dialog box appears.
3. Select Show System Processes. Figure 2.18 displays the Processes dialog box.

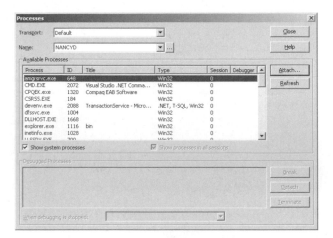

Figure 2.18   The Processes dialog box

4. Select the process for your service application and click Attach. The Attach To Process dialog box appears.
5. Select Common Language Runtime, click OK to specify a debugger, and close the Attach To Process dialog box. Figure 2.19 displays the Attach To Process dialog box.

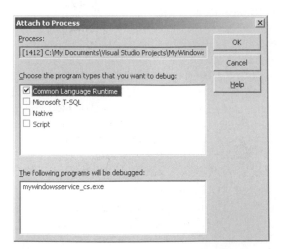

Figure 2.19   The Attach To Process dialog box

After you close the Attach To Process dialog box, your service application enters the debug mode, and the Microsoft development environment is attached to your service application as the debugger. When you attach a debugger to a service application, the processing of the service is suspended. The Processes dialog box displays the attached debuggers for various dialog service applications. Figure 2.20 displays the Processes dialog box.

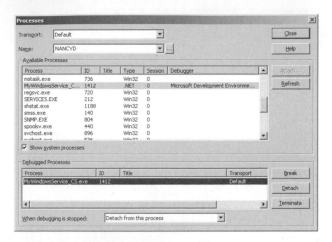

Figure 2.20   The Processes dialog box after you have attached to a process

You can then insert breakpoints in the code of your service application. To debug various methods in your code, you can use the SCM to send stop, pause, and continue commands to your service.

When you attach a debugger to a service application, you only can debug the OnPause, OnContinue, and OnStop methods. You cannot debug the OnStart and Main methods because the service starts before you attach a debugger to your service application. To debug the OnStart and Main methods, you can create a test harness service in your service application to help debug your service. You can install both services, and then start the test harness service to load the service process that contains both services. After the test harness service starts the process, you can use the Debug menu in Visual Studio .NET to attach a debugger to the service process.

Summary

- Windows services enable you to perform tasks that execute in background processes. You can use Windows services to perform tasks such as monitoring the usage of a database. A Windows service executes in its own process and does not have a user interface. You use the methods of the ServiceBase, ServiceProcessInstaller, ServiceInstaller, and ServiceController classes in the System.ServiceProcess namespace to create a Windows service application.

- To create a Windows service, you need to create a project by using the Windows Service template in Visual Basic .NET or Visual C#. The Windows Service template automatically adds code to the Main method of your service application and inserts function headers for the OnStart and OnStop methods. You override the OnStart and OnStop methods to add functionality to your service application. In addition, you can override the OnPause and OnContinue methods, and change the properties of the service application to customize the service according to your needs.

- You can customize your Windows service to handle events for a service. You can also enable your service application to log information, such as a change in the state of the service or errors in the system event logs. In addition, you can create a custom event log to record information about your service. These features of Windows services enable you to define how your service application will run.

- To start a Windows service on a computer, you first need to install the service application. To do so, you need to add installers to the service application and use the Installutil tool to install the service application. Installers install and register your service application on a computer. In addition, installers install and configure the resources, such as performance counters and event logs, that your service uses. Installers also allow you to configure the security context of your service application.

- After you create and install a Windows service, you can monitor and control the behavior of your service. For example, you can change the state of your service. You can also manage your service manually by using the SCM or programmatically by using a component of the ServiceController class in an application.

- After you create and install a Windows service, you can debug a Windows service to ensure that it performs all the tasks that you want the service application to perform. To debug a service application, you start a service and attach a debugger to it. In addition, you can configure certain properties of a service application dynamically. The dynamic properties of service applications enable you to change settings, such as AutoLog, CanShutdown, and CanPauseAndContinue.

Lab: Creating and Managing Windows Services

In this lab, you will create and install Windows services. In addition, you will create client applications to communicate with the service applications. You will also create a Windows application to manage the services running on a local or remote machine. The solutions to the exercises in this lab can be found in the \Solution folder on the Supplemental Course Materials CD-ROM.

Estimated lab time: 60 minutes

Exercise 1: Creating and Installing a Windows Service

In this exercise, you will create and install a Windows service. The Windows service, called TransactionService, consists of a Windows service called DBWriter. When the DBWriter service starts, it creates two files: Transaction.tmp and Customers.db. The client application writes customer records into the Transaction.tmp file. The client application can request that the DBWriter service commit or roll back the customer records written in the Transaction.tmp file. When the client application requests to commit the records, the DBWriter service writes the customer records from the Transaction.tmp file to the Customers.db file. After writing the records in the Customers.db file, the DBWriter removes all the records from the Transaction.tmp file. However, if the client application requests to roll back all the records, the DBWriter removes all the records from the Transaction.tmp file without saving them in the Customers.db file.

The DBWriter service uses a custom event log called Transaction Log to write entries at various execution stages. The DBWriter service also uses a custom performance counter called Ctr1 in the MyCounters category to track the number of committed transactions. When the DBWriter service stops, it deletes the Transaction.tmp file and sets the counter Ctr1 value to 0.

To create the DBWriter Windows service in the TransactionService application, complete the following steps:

1. Start Visual Studio .NET and open the New Project window from the File menu.
2. Select Visual Basic Projects or Visual C# Projects from Project Types.
3. Select the Windows Service template.
4. Type **TransactionService** in the Name field.
5. Change the file names of Service1.vb or Service.cs to DBWriter.vb or DBWriter.cs.

6. In Solution Explorer, right-click DBWriter.vb or DBWriter.cs, and choose View Designer to open the Component Designer.

7. Right-click anywhere in the Component Designer, and choose Properties from the shortcut menu.

8. Change the Name and ServiceName property of the service from Service1 to DBWriter. Set the AutoLog property to False.

9. Right-click the TransactionService project in Solution Explorer, and choose Properties. Set the Startup Object as DBWriter.

Note   This is required only for Visual Basic .NET projects.

---

10. Choose View Code from the shortcut menu by right-clicking in the Component Designer window to view the code of the DBWriter Service class. You will see the following code in the Main method.

Visual Basic .NET

```
ServicesToRun = New System.ServiceProcess.ServiceBase () {New Service1}
```

Visual C#

```
ServicesToRun = new System.ServiceProcess.ServiceBase[] { new Service1() };
```

11. Use the Search and Replace feature to change Service1 to DBWriter.

12. Drag and drop an EventLog component on the Component Designer from the Components toolbox.

13. Type **Transaction Log** for the Log property and **Transaction Service** for the Source property.

14. Right-click the Performance Counters node under the Servers node in Server Explorer and choose Create New Category from the shortcut menu. In the Performance Counter Builder window, type **MyCounters** in the Category Name text box. Click New and change CounterName to Ctr1. Let the type remain as the default of NumberOfItems32. Click OK to create the MyCounters category and the Ctr1 counter.

15. Drag and drop the counter Ctr1 on the Component Designer. Change the MachineName property to **.** (dot) and the ReadOnly property to False.

16. Add the following code to the DBWriter class.

Note   You will use the Imports System.IO or the using System.IO directive for the DBWriter class.

Visual Basic .NET

```
Protected Overrides Sub OnStart(ByVal args() As String)
    ' Create a transaction file and close it
    Dim tfs As FileStream = File.Create("C:\Transaction.tmp")
    tfs.Close()
```

(continued)

```vb
            ' Create Customers.db file if it does not exist
            If Not (File.Exists("C:\Customers.db")) Then
                Dim cfs As FileStream = File.Create("C:\Customers.db")
                cfs.Close()
            End If
            ' Write entry into the custom event log
            EventLog1.WriteEntry("DBWriterVB service started on " + _
                Date.Now.ToString)
        End Sub

        Protected Overrides Sub OnStop()
            ' Delete the Transaction.tmp file
            File.Delete("C:\Transaction.tmp")
            ' Set the performance counter value to 0
            PerformanceCounter1.RawValue = 0
            ' Write entry into the custom event log
            EventLog1.WriteEntry("DBWriterVB service stopped on " + _
                Date.Now.ToString)
        End Sub

        Protected Overrides Sub OnCustomCommand(ByVal command As Integer)
            If command = 201 Then
                Commit()
            ElseIf command = 200 Then
                Rollback()
            End If
        End Sub

        Private Sub Commit()
            ' Create a StreamReader to read data from the Transaction.tmp file
            Dim sr As New StreamReader(New FileStream("C:\Transaction.tmp", _
                FileMode.Open))
            ' Create a StreamWriter to append data to the Customers.db file
            Dim sw As New StreamWriter(New FileStream("C:\Customers.db", _
                FileMode.Append, FileAccess.Write))
            sw.WriteLine(sr.ReadToEnd)
            sw.Flush()
            ' Close the files
            sr.Close()
            sw.Close()
            ' Increment the counter and write entry in the EventLog
            PerformanceCounter1.Increment()
            truncateTransactionFile()
            EventLog1.WriteEntry("DBWriterVB service committed a " & _
                "transaction on " + Date.Now.ToString)
        End Sub
```

```
Private Sub Rollback()
    truncateTransactionFile()
    EventLog1.WriteEntry("DBWriterVB service rolled back a " & _
        "transaction on " + Date.Now.ToString)
End Sub

Private Sub truncateTransactionFile()
    ' Delete data from the Transaction.tmp file
    Dim fs As New FileStream("C:\Transaction.tmp", FileMode.Truncate)
    fs.Flush()
    fs.Close()
End Sub
```

Visual C#

```csharp
protected override void OnStart(string[] args)
{
    // Create a transaction file and close it
    FileStream tfs = File.Create("C:\\Transaction.tmp");
    tfs.Close();
    // Create Customers.db file if it does not exist
    if  (!File.Exists("C:\\Customers.db"))
    {
        FileStream cfs= File.Create("C:\\Customers.db");
        cfs.Close();
    }
    // Write entry into the custom event log
    eventLog1.WriteEntry("DBWriterCS service started on "
        + System.DateTime.Now.ToString());
}

protected override void OnStop()
{
    // Delete the Transaction.tmp file
    File.Delete("C:\\Transaction.tmp");
    // Set the performance couter value to 0
    performanceCounter1.RawValue = 0;
    // Write entry into the custom event log
    eventLog1.WriteEntry("DBWriterCS service stopped on "
        + System.DateTime.Now.ToString());
}

protected override void OnCustomCommand(int command)
{
    if (command == 201)
        Commit();
    else if (command == 200)
        Rollback();
}
```

(continued)

```
private void Commit()
{
    // Create a StreamReader to read data from the Transaction.tmp file
    StreamReader sr = new StreamReader(new FileStream
        ("C:\\Transaction.tmp",
        FileMode.Open));
    // Create a StreamWriter to append data to the Customers.db file
    StreamWriter sw = new StreamWriter(new FileStream("C:\\Customers.db",
        FileMode.Append, FileAccess.Write));
    sw.WriteLine(sr.ReadToEnd());
    sw.Flush();
    //Close the files
    sr.Close();
    sw.Close();
    //Increment the counter and write entry in the EventLog
    performanceCounter1.Increment();
    truncateTransactionFile();
    eventLog1.WriteEntry("DBWriterCS service committed a transaction on "
        + System.DateTime.Now.ToString());
}

private void Rollback()
{
    truncateTransactionFile();
    eventLog1.WriteEntry("DBWriterCS service rolled back a
        transaction on "
        + System.DateTime.Now.ToString());
}

private void truncateTransactionFile()
{
    // Delete data from the Transaction.tmp file
    FileStream fs =new FileStream("C:\\Transaction.tmp",
        FileMode.Truncate);
    fs.Flush();
    fs.Close();
}
```

17. Add installers for the event log, performance counter, and Windows service. Choose Add Installer from the shortcut menu by right-clicking on the component or the Add Installer hyperlink at the bottom of the Properties window of the components.

18. The Component Designer shows the ProjectInstaller class and the EventLog-Installer, PerformanceCounterInstaller, ServiceProcessInstaller, and Service-Installer objects that are added to the ProjectInstaller class.

19. Change the Account property of the ServiceProcessInstaller to LocalSystem.

20. Build the solution to create the TransactionService.exe assembly.

21. Install the assembly by running the following command at the Visual Studio .NET Command Prompt:

    Installutil TransactionService.exe

22. Verify that the DBWriter service is correctly installed, and start it by using the SCM. Open the Event Viewer and verify that the Transaction Log was correctly installed. Verify that the DBWriter service writes correct entries in the Transaction Log.

23. Verify that the DBWriter creates the C:\Customers.db and C:\Transaction.tmp files. Verify that the Transaction.tmp file is deleted when you stop the DBWriter service.

Exercise 2: Creating a Client Application

In this exercise, you will create a Windows application to write records in the Transaction.tmp file and execute custom commands on the DBWriter service.

1. Open the New Project window from the File menu.

2. Select Windows Application from the Templates pane.

3. Type **TransactionClient** in the Name field.

4. Rename Form1.vb or Form1.cs to CustomerForm.vb or CustomerForm.cs in Solution Explorer under the TransactionClient project.

5. Open the CustomerForm in the Component Designer.

6. Change the Name property to CustomerForm and the Text property to Customer Form.

7. Open the Properties window for the TransactionClient project from the shortcut menu by right-clicking the project name in Solution Explorer and set the Startup Object as CustomerForm.

Note   This is required only for Visual Basic .NET projects.

---

8. Right-click References under the TransactionClient project and choose Add Reference. In the Add Reference window, scroll down to select System.ServiceProcess.dll on the .NET tab. Click the Select button. The System.ServiceProcess.dll appears in the Selected Components list. Click OK to add a reference to it.

9. Add labels, text boxes, a main menu, and menu items on the CustomerForm, and set the Text and Font properties so that the form appears as shown in the following graphics.

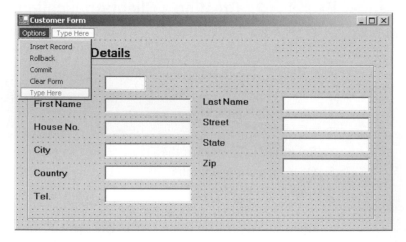

10. Set the Name property of the text boxes to CustId, FName, LName, HouseNo, Street, City, State, Country, Zip, and Tel, respectively. Set the Text property of all the text boxes to blank.

11. Set the Name property of the menu items to InsertRecordMenuItem, Rollback-MenuItem, CommitMenuItem, and ClearFormMenuItem respectively.

12. Add the following code to the CustomerForm class.

Visual Basic .NET

```
Imports System.IO
Imports System.ServiceProcess

Public Class CustomerForm
    Inherits System.Windows.Forms.Form
```

```
' Component Designer Code goes here
.
.
.

Private Sub InsertRecordMenuItem_Click(ByVal sender As System.Object, _
    ByVal e As System.EventArgs) Handles InsertRecordMenuItem.Click
    Dim record As String
    record = "CustomerId: " + CustId.Text + "|FName: " + FName.Text + _
            "|LName: " + LName.Text + "|House No.: " + HouseNo.Text + _
            "|Street: " + Street.Text + "|City: " + City.Text + _
            "|State: " + State.Text + "|Country: " + Country.Text + _
            "|Zip: " + Zip.Text + "|Tel.: " + Tel.Text

    'Write the record in the C:\Transaction.tmp file
    Dim sw As New StreamWriter(New FileStream("C:\Transaction.tmp", _
        FileMode.Append, FileAccess.Write))
    sw.WriteLine(record)
    sw.Flush()
    sw.Close()
End Sub

Private Sub ClearFormMenuItem_Click(ByVal sender As System.Object, _
    ByVal e As System.EventArgs) Handles ClearFormMenuItem.Click
    clear()
End Sub


Private Sub RollbackMenuItem_Click(ByVal sender As System.Object, _
    ByVal e As System.EventArgs) Handles RollbackMenuItem.Click
    ' Roll back all the changes made in the Transaction.tmp file
    Dim sc As New ServiceController("DBWriter")
    sc.ExecuteCommand(200)
    clear()
End Sub


Private Sub CommitMenuItem_Click(ByVal sender As System.Object, _
    ByVal e As System.EventArgs) Handles CommitMenuItem.Click
    ' Commit all the changes made in the Transaction.tmp file
    Dim sc As New ServiceController("DBWriter")
    sc.ExecuteCommand(201)
End Sub

Private Sub clear()
    CustId.Text = ""
    FName.Text = ""
    LName.Text = ""
    HouseNo.Text = ""
```

(continued)

```vb
            Street.Text = ""
            City.Text = ""
            State.Text = ""
            Country.Text = ""
            Zip.Text = ""
            Tel.Text = ""
    End Sub

End Class
```

Visual C#

```csharp
using System.Drawing;
using System.Collections;
using System.ComponentModel;
using System.Windows.Forms;
using System.Data;
using System.IO;
using System.ServiceProcess;

public class CustomerForm : System.Windows.Forms.Form
{

    // Component Designer Code goes here
    .
    .
    .

    private void InsertMenuItem_Click(object sender,
        System.EventArgs e)
    {
        String record;
        record = "CustomerId: " + CustId.Text + "|FName: " +
            FName.Text + "|LName: " + LName.Text +
            "|House No.: " + HouseNo.Text + "|Street: " +
            Street.Text + "|City: " + City.Text + "|State: " +
            State.Text + "|Country: " + Country.Text + "|Zip: " +
            Zip.Text + "|Tel.: " + Tel.Text;

        //Write the record in the C:\Tranasaction.tmp file
        StreamWriter sw =new StreamWriter(new FileStream(
        "C:\\Transaction.tmp", FileMode.Append, FileAccess.Write));
        sw.WriteLine(record);
        sw.Flush();
        sw.Close();
    }
```

```
private void RollbackMenuItem_Click(object sender,
    System.EventArgs e)
{
    // Roll back all the changes made in the Transaction.tmp file
    ServiceController sc = new ServiceController("DBWriterCS");
    sc.ExecuteCommand(200);
    clear();
}

private void CommitMenuItem_Click(object sender,
    System.EventArgs e)
{
    // Commit all the changes made in the Transaction.tmp file
    ServiceController sc = new ServiceController("DBWriterCS");
    sc.ExecuteCommand(201);
}

private void ClearFormMenuItem_Click(object sender,
    System.EventArgs e)
{
    clear();
}

private void clear()
{
    CustId.Text = "";
    FName.Text = "";
    LName.Text = "";
    HouseNo.Text = "";
    Street.Text = "";
    City.Text = "";
    State.Text = "";
    Country.Text = "";
    Zip.Text = "";
    Tel.Text = "";
}
}
```

13. Choose Build Solution from the Build menu.

14. Run the CustomerForm. Be sure that you start the DBWriter service before running the CustomerForm.

15. Create customer records and insert them in the Transaction.tmp file by choosing Insert from the Record menu. View the effect of committing or rolling back the records in the Transaction.tmp file. Verify that only the committed records are written to the Customers.db file.

16. Open the Performance Monitor. Add the Ctr1 counter from the MyCounters category. Ctr1 increases with the number of committed transactions.

17. Open the Event Viewer to view the entries that the DBWriter service writes in the Transaction Log.

Exercise 3: Managing Windows Services

In this exercise, you will create a Windows application to manage Windows services on a computer.

1. Open the New Project window from the File menu.
2. Select Windows Application from the Templates pane.
3. Type **ServiceController** in the Name field.
4. Change Form1.vb or Form1.cs to ServiceControllerForm.vb or Service-ControllerForm.cs in Solution Explorer under the ServiceController project.
5. Open the ServiceControllerForm in the Component Designer.
6. Change the Name property to ServiceControllerForm and the Text property to Service Controller.
7. Open the Properties window for the ServiceController project from the shortcut menu in Solution Explorer and set the Startup Object as ServiceControllerForm.

Note   This is required only for Visual Basic .NET projects.

---

8. Right-click References under the ServiceController project and choose Add Reference.
9. In the Add Reference window, select System.ServiceProcess.dll on the .NET tab.
10. Click Select. The System.ServiceProcess.dll appears in the Selected Components list.
11. Click OK to add a reference to it.
12. Add labels, a text box, a button, a list box, a context menu, and menu items on the ServiceControllerForm, and set the Text and Font properties so that the form appears as displayed in the following graphics.

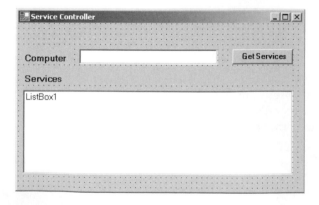

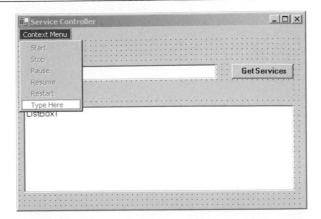

13. Set the Name property of the menu items to StartMenu, StopMenu, Pause-Menu, ResumeMenu, and RestartMenu, respectively. Set the Enabled property of all the menu items to False.

14. Set the Text property of the button to Get Services and the Name property to GetServices_Button.

15. Write the following code for the ServiceControllerForm class.

Visual Basic .NET

```vb
Imports System.ServiceProcess
Public Class ServiceControllerForm
    Inherits System.Windows.Forms.Form

    Private svcs As ServiceProcess.ServiceController()
    Private svcs_enum As Ienumerator

    ' Component Designer generated Code
    .
    .
    .

    Private Sub ServiceControllerForm_Load(ByVal sender As System.Object, _
        ByVal e As System.EventArgs) Handles MyBase.Load
        ListBox1.ContextMenu = ContextMenu1
    End Sub

    Private Sub GetServices_Button_Click(ByVal sender As _
        System.Object, ByVal e As System.EventArgs) Handles _
        GetServices_Button.Click
        ListBox1.Items.Clear()
        If TextBox1.Text.Equals("") Then
            svcs = ServiceProcess.ServiceController.GetServices()
            Label2.Text = "Services on the local machine"
```

(continued)

```vb
        Else
            Try
                svcs = ServiceProcess.ServiceController.GetServices _
                    (TextBox1.Text)
                Label2.Text = "Services on " + TextBox1.Text
            Catch
                MsgBox("Unable to find the computer!")
                TextBox1.Text = ""
                Exit Sub
            End Try
        End If

        svcs_enum = svcs.GetEnumerator
        Dim sc As ServiceProcess.ServiceController

        While svcs_enum.MoveNext
            sc = CType(svcs_enum.Current, ServiceProcess.ServiceController)
            ListBox1.Items.Add(sc.ServiceName)
        End While
    End Sub

    Private Sub StartMenu_Click(ByVal sender As System.Object, _
        ByVal e As System.EventArgs) Handles StartMenu.Click
        Dim sc As ServiceProcess.ServiceController
        sc = svcs.GetValue(ListBox1.SelectedIndex)
        enable_disable_MenuItems(sc)
        Try
            sc.Start()
            sc.WaitForStatus(ServiceProcess.ServiceControllerStatus.Running)
            MsgBox("Service " + sc.ServiceName + " started on " + _
                sc.MachineName + " !")
        Catch
            MsgBox("Unable to start " + sc.ServiceName + " service!")
        End Try
    End Sub

    Private Sub StopMenu_Click(ByVal sender As System.Object, ByVal e As _
        System.EventArgs) Handles StopMenu.Click
        Dim sc As ServiceProcess.ServiceController
        sc = svcs.GetValue(ListBox1.SelectedIndex)
        enable_disable_MenuItems(sc)
        Try
            sc.Stop()
            sc.WaitForStatus(ServiceProcess.ServiceControllerStatus.Stopped)
            MsgBox("Service " + sc.ServiceName + " stopped on " + _
                sc.MachineName + " !")
```

```vb
            Catch
                MsgBox("Unable to stop " + sc.ServiceName + " service!")
            End Try
    End Sub

    Private Sub PauseMenu_Click(ByVal sender As System.Object, ByVal e As _
        System.EventArgs) Handles PauseMenu.Click
        Dim sc As ServiceProcess.ServiceController
        sc = svcs.GetValue(ListBox1.SelectedIndex)
        enable_disable_MenuItems(sc)
        Try
            sc.Pause()
            sc.WaitForStatus(ServiceProcess.ServiceControllerStatus.Paused)
            MsgBox("Service " + sc.ServiceName + " paused on " + _
                sc.MachineName + " !")
        Catch
            MsgBox("Unable to pause " + sc.ServiceName + " service!")
        End Try
    End Sub

    Private Sub ResumeMenu_Click(ByVal sender As System.Object, _
        ByVal e As System.EventArgs) Handles ResumeMenu.Click
        Dim sc As ServiceProcess.ServiceController
        sc = svcs.GetValue(ListBox1.SelectedIndex)
        enable_disable_MenuItems(sc)
        Try
            sc.Continue()
            sc.WaitForStatus(ServiceProcess.ServiceControllerStatus.Running)
            MsgBox("Service " + sc.ServiceName + " resumed on " + _
                sc.MachineName + " !")
        Catch
            MsgBox("Unable to resume " + sc.ServiceName + " service!")
        End Try
    End Sub

    Private Sub RestartMenu_Click(ByVal sender As System.Object, _
        ByVal e As System.EventArgs) Handles RestartMenu.Click
        Dim sc As ServiceProcess.ServiceController
        sc = svcs.GetValue(ListBox1.SelectedIndex)
        enable_disable_MenuItems(sc)
        Try
            sc.Stop()
            sc.WaitForStatus(ServiceProcess.ServiceControllerStatus.Stopped)
            sc.Start()
            sc.WaitForStatus(ServiceProcess.ServiceControllerStatus.Running)
```

(continued)

```vb
            MsgBox("Service " + sc.ServiceName + " restarted on " + _
                sc.MachineName + " !")
        Catch
            MsgBox("Unable to restart " + sc.ServiceName + " service!")
        End Try
    End Sub


    Private Sub ListBox1_MouseDown(ByVal sender As Object, ByVal e As _
        System.Windows.Forms.MouseEventArgs) Handles ListBox1.MouseDown
        If ListBox1.Items.Count <> 0 Then
            Dim top_index As Integer = ListBox1.TopIndex()
        Dim sel_index As Integer = top_index + System.Math.Floor(e.Y / _
            ListBox1.ItemHeight)
            ListBox1.SetSelected(sel_index, True)
        End If
    End Sub


    Private Sub enable_disable_MenuItems(ByVal sc As _
        ServiceProcess.ServiceController)
        If sc.Status = ServiceProcess.ServiceControllerStatus.Stopped Then
            Me.StartMenu.Enabled = True
            Me.StopMenu.Enabled = False
            Me.PauseMenu.Enabled = False
            Me.ResumeMenu.Enabled = False
            Me.RestartMenu.Enabled = False
        ElseIf sc.Status = _
            ServiceProcess.ServiceControllerStatus.Paused Then
            Me.StartMenu.Enabled = False
            Me.StopMenu.Enabled = True
            Me.PauseMenu.Enabled = False
            Me.ResumeMenu.Enabled = True
            Me.RestartMenu.Enabled = True
        ElseIf sc.Status = _
            ServiceProcess.ServiceControllerStatus.Running Then
            Me.StartMenu.Enabled = False
            Me.StopMenu.Enabled = True
            If sc.CanPauseAndContinue Then
                Me.PauseMenu.Enabled = True
                Me.ResumeMenu.Enabled = False
            End If
            Me.RestartMenu.Enabled = True
        End If
    End Sub

    Private Sub ContextMenu1_Popup(ByVal sender As Object, ByVal e As _
        System.EventArgs) Handles ContextMenu1.Popup
```

```
            Dim sc As ServiceProcess.ServiceController
            sc = svcs.GetValue(ListBox1.SelectedIndex)
            enable_disable_MenuItems(sc)
        End Sub
    End Class
```

Visual C#

```csharp
using System;
using System.Drawing;
using System.Collections;
using System.ComponentModel;
using System.Windows.Forms;
using System.Data;
using System.ServiceProcess;

namespace ServiceController
public class ServiceControllerForm : System.Windows.Forms.Form
{
    private void GetServices_Button_Click(object sender,
        System.EventArgs e)
    {
        ListBox1.Items.Clear();
        if (TextBox1.Text.Equals(""))
        {
            svcs = ServiceController.GetServices();
            Label2.Text = "Services on the local machine";
        }
        else
        {
            try
            {
                svcs = ServiceController.GetServices(TextBox1.Text);
                Label2.Text = "Services on " + TextBox1.Text;
            }
            catch
            {
                MessageBox.Show("Unable to find the computer!");
                TextBox1.Text = "";
                return;
            }
        }
        svcs_enum = svcs.GetEnumerator();
        ServiceController sc ;
```

(continued)

```csharp
        while (svcs_enum.MoveNext())
        {
            sc = (ServiceController)svcs_enum.Current;
            ListBox1.Items.Add(sc.ServiceName);
        }
    }

    private void StartMenu_Click(object sender, System.EventArgs e)
    {
        ServiceController sc;
        sc = (ServiceController)svcs.GetValue(ListBox1.SelectedIndex);
        enable_disable_MenuItems(sc);
        try
        {
            sc.Start();
            sc.WaitForStatus(ServiceControllerStatus.Running);
            MessageBox.Show("Service " + sc.ServiceName + " started on "
                + sc.MachineName + " !");
        }
        catch
        {
            MessageBox.Show("Unable to start " + sc.ServiceName +
            " service!");
        }
    }

    private void StopMenu_Click(object sender, System.EventArgs e)
    {
        ServiceController sc;
        sc = (ServiceController)svcs.GetValue(ListBox1.SelectedIndex);
        enable_disable_MenuItems(sc);
        try
        {
            sc.Stop();
            sc.WaitForStatus(ServiceControllerStatus.Stopped);
            MessageBox.Show("Service " + sc.ServiceName + " stopped on " +
                sc.MachineName + " !");
        }
        catch
        {
            MessageBox.Show("Unable to stop " + sc.ServiceName +
                " service!");
        }
    }

    private void PauseMenu_Click(object sender, System.EventArgs e)
    {
        ServiceController sc ;
        sc = (ServiceController)svcs.GetValue(ListBox1.SelectedIndex);
        enable_disable_MenuItems(sc);
```

```
        try
        {
            sc.Pause();
            sc.WaitForStatus(ServiceControllerStatus.Paused);
            MessageBox.Show("Service " + sc.ServiceName + " paused on " +
                sc.MachineName + " !");
        }
        catch
        {
            MessageBox.Show("Unable to pause " + sc.ServiceName +
                " service!");
        }
    }

    private void ResumeMenu_Click(object sender, System.EventArgs e)
    {
        ServiceController sc ;
        sc = (ServiceController)svcs.GetValue(ListBox1.SelectedIndex);
        enable_disable_MenuItems(sc);
        try
        {
            sc.Continue();
            sc.WaitForStatus(ServiceControllerStatus.Running);
            MessageBox.Show("Service " + sc.ServiceName + " resumed on " +
                sc.MachineName + " !");
        }
        catch
        {
            MessageBox.Show("Unable to resume " + sc.ServiceName +
                " service!");
        }
    }

    private void RestartMenu_Click(object sender, System.EventArgs e)
    {
        ServiceController sc ;
        sc = (ServiceController)svcs.GetValue(ListBox1.SelectedIndex);
        enable_disable_MenuItems(sc);
        try
        {
            sc.Stop();
            sc.WaitForStatus(ServiceControllerStatus.Stopped);
            sc.Start();
            sc.WaitForStatus(ServiceControllerStatus.Running);
            MessageBox.Show("Service " + sc.ServiceName +
                " restarted on " + sc.MachineName + " !");
        }
```

(continued)

```csharp
    catch
    {
        MessageBox.Show("Unable to restart " + sc.ServiceName +
            " service!");
    }
}

private void ListBox1_MouseDown(object sender,
    System.Windows.Forms.MouseEventArgs  e)
{
    if (ListBox1.Items.Count != 0)
    {
        int top_index = ListBox1.TopIndex ;
        int sel_index = top_index + (int)System.Math.Floor(e.Y /
            ListBox1.ItemHeight);
        ListBox1.SetSelected(sel_index, true);
    }
}

private void enable_disable_MenuItems( ServiceController sc  )
{
    if (sc.Status == ServiceControllerStatus.Stopped)
    {
        this.StartMenu.Enabled = true;
        this.StopMenu.Enabled = false;
        this.PauseMenu.Enabled = false;
        this.ResumeMenu.Enabled = false;
        this.RestartMenu.Enabled = false;
    }
    else if (sc.Status == ServiceControllerStatus.Paused)
    {
        this.StartMenu.Enabled = false;
        this.StopMenu.Enabled = true;
        this.PauseMenu.Enabled = false;
        this.ResumeMenu.Enabled = true;
        this.RestartMenu.Enabled = true;
    }
    else if (sc.Status == ServiceControllerStatus.Running)
    {
        this.StartMenu.Enabled = false;
        this.StopMenu.Enabled = true;
        if (sc.CanPauseAndContinue)
        {
            this.PauseMenu.Enabled = true;
            this.ResumeMenu.Enabled = false;
        }
        this.RestartMenu.Enabled = true;
    }
}
```

```
private void ContextMenu1_Popup(object sender, System.EventArgs e)
{
  ServiceController sc ;
  sc = (ServiceController)svcs.GetValue(ListBox1.SelectedIndex);
  enable_disable_MenuItems(sc);
}

private void ServiceControllerForm_Load(object sender,
    System.EventArgs e)
{
    this.ContextMenu=this.ContextMenu1;
}
}
```

16. Choose Build Solution from the Build menu.

17. Run the application. Click Get Services to obtain the list of services on the local computer. Use the application's shortcut menu to manage the services.

18. Type the name (not the IP address) of a network computer, and click Get Services to obtain the list of services on the remote computer. Manage the services using the shortcut menu on the ListBox.

Review

The questions in this section reinforce key information presented in this chapter. If you are unable to answer a question, review the appropriate lesson, and then try answering the question again. Answers to the questions can be found in Appendix A, "Questions and Answers."

1. What are the states of a service application?

2. What are the different types of Windows services?

3. What are the tasks that you perform to create a Windows service?

4. How do you add functionality to a service application?

5. Write code to specify that a service application create an entry in the file named C:\Temp\ServiceStartStatus.log every time the service application starts.

6. How do you log custom information in the default event logs?

7. Why do you need to include installers in your service application?

8. Why do you need to add instances of both the ServiceProcessInstaller and ServiceInstaller classes to install your service application?

9. How do you specify the security context of a user account within which a service application runs?

10. What administrative tasks can you perform on your service using the SCM?

11. What are the steps to run custom commands on your service application?

12. What are the steps to attach a debugger to your service application?

C H A P T E R   3

Creating and Consuming Serviced Components

About This Chapter

The .NET Framework enables you to create components called *serviced compo-nents*, to access COM+ services, such as automatic transaction management, object pooling, and just-in-time (JIT) activation. These components share their context with COM+ applications, enabling them to access COM+ services. In this chapter, you will learn about the basics of the COM+ programming model, create and regis-ter serviced components, utilize COM+ services, and manage serviced components using the Component Services tool. In addition, you will learn to restrict access to serviced components only to authentic users by defining roles and security levels.

Before You Begin

To complete the lessons in this chapter, you

- Must have knowledge of basic programming in Microsoft Visual Basic .NET and Microsoft Visual C#
- Must have a basic knowledge of COM+
- Must have Microsoft SQL Server 2000 installed on your computer to complete Exercise 3 of the Lab

Tip   A free evaluation copy of Microsoft SQL Server 2000 is available for download online from the Microsoft Web site at *http://www.microsoft.com/sql*.

Lesson 1: Overview of COM+ Programming

COM+ provides the infrastructure to create and deploy distributed multitier applications. In addition, it provides services that allow you to create highly secure and
scalable applications. In this lesson, you will learn the COM+ programming model
and the services that COM+ provides to applications.

After this lesson, you will be able to

- Identify the advantages of the COM+ programming model
- Understand COM+ services

Estimated lesson time: 30 minutes

Evolution of COM+

The Component Object Model (COM) programming model introduced a
component-based approach to software development. The component-based
approach of COM allowed you to create small, logical, reusable, and stand-alone
modules that you could integrate into a single application. However, you could not
deploy COM components over networks. Microsoft extended the COM programming model and developed the distributed COM (DCOM) programming model to
overcome this limitation of the COM programming model. The DCOM programming model enabled you to deploy COM components over networks and distribute
applications easily across platforms. In addition, the DCOM programming model
allowed you to create two-tier client/server applications.

The two-tier architecture consists of a client tier and a database tier. The client tier
consists of applications that provide the user interface and code for business logic
and data access, whereas the database tier provides data to the applications on the
client tier. This architecture allows you to distribute the processing load across multiple computers. However, the two-tier architecture has the following limitations:

- A client application cannot share the code for business logic and data access
  with another client application. This restricts the reusability of code across multiple client applications.
- Any change made to the business logic requires you to make corresponding
  changes in the client code and recompile and redeploy the application.
- Each client application requires a separate connection to a database server. This
  restricts the number of clients that can simultaneously connect to a database
  server.

■   You need to configure a driver on each client computer for every database server to which the client applications connect. Therefore, in a large organization with a heterogeneous database environment and multiple client computers, maintaining applications is time-consuming and expensive.

The two-tier application architecture is shown in Figure 3.1.

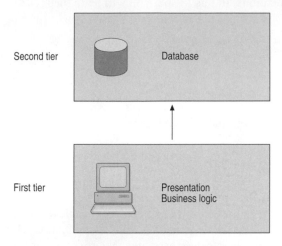

Figure 3.1   The two-tier application architecture

The two-tier architecture did facilitate the sharing of resources and data; however, this approach also had a few drawbacks. The client computer was overburdened with the responsibility of performing all processing functions while the server merely acted as a traffic controller, facilitating the movement of data to and from the client and server computer. The availability of resources was, therefore, always a problem and the performance of the application suffered. Multiple data requests from the database increased network traffic, causing bottlenecks that ultimately led to decreased application performance. To add to the performance degradation, the two-tier architecture gave rise to maintenance issues, because any changes made to the application necessitated considerable changes to the complete application architecture.

Microsoft introduced Windows Distributed interNet Applications (Windows DNA) architecture that overcomes the shortcomings of the two-tier system. The Windows DNA architecture enables you to implement a three-tier application architecture, which enables you to maintain the business logic and data access code in separate components called business objects. The separation of client applications from the business logic and data access code eliminates the need for recompiling and redeploying client applications after making modifications to the code. In addition, business components enable client applications to share the business logic and data access code. Figure 3.2 shows the components of a three-tier architecture.

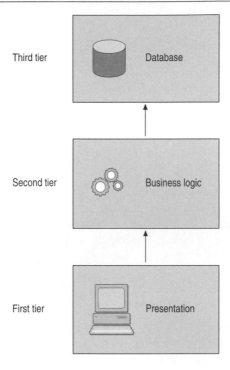

Figure 3.2   The three-tier architecture

Windows DNA provides the following infrastructure and services that enable you to create and deploy applications based on the three-tier architecture.

- **Presentation Services.**   These services support HTML, DHTML, scripting languages, and the Win32 API that you use to develop client applications such as Windows applications and Web applications.
- **Application Services.**   These services provide the infrastructure, such as automatic transaction management and message queue management, to the business objects. These services also include Microsoft Internet Information Server (IIS), component services (COM+), and Microsoft Message Queuing services (MSMQ).
- **Data Services.**   These services include ActiveX Data Object (ADO) and OLE DB, which allow business objects and client applications to access a database server.
- **System Services.**   These services allow applications to securely communicate with each other within a network. These include directory, networking, security, and communication services.

Component Services of COM+

Application services include COM+ services, which allow you to create and deploy business components in a three-tier application architecture. COM+ services provide you with a standard set of frequently required services, which enable you to focus on developing the business components of an application. COM+ services include transactions, queued components (QC), security, loosely coupled events (LCE), JIT activation, and object pooling. The following sections describe these services in detail.

Transactions

Transactions group a set of tasks into a single execution unit. Each transaction begins with a specific task and ends when all the tasks in the group successfully complete. If any of the tasks fails, the transaction fails. Therefore, a transaction has only two results: success or failure. Incomplete steps result in the failure of the transaction.

When you create COM+ components, they can automatically participate in transactions. COM+ components do not need explicit code to specify the start and end of a transaction.

After a COM+ component creates an object, it is activated with the BeginTransaction method that the COM+ model provides. The operations that form a part of the transactions are then performed, after which, the object is deactivated using the CommitTransaction or AbortTransaction method, depending on the success or failure of the transaction. The AbortTransaction method reverses the transaction by using the RollbackTransaction method.

The properties of transaction-supported applications are atomicity, concurrency, isolation, and durability (ACID), as described next:

- **Atomicity.**   This property of a transaction ensures that a transaction is a success as a single atomic unit. An unsuccessful transaction results in the failure of all the tasks that form a part of that transaction. For example, at an ATM counter, the availability of funds in an account ensures the completion or success of a withdrawal operation. Alternatively, insufficient funds lead to the failure of the transaction or withdrawal operation. In case of a failed task, the entire transaction rolls back to the previous menu, prompting the user for an alternative transaction.

- **Consistency.**   During a transaction, the data is modified by multiple tasks. The consistency property tracks the modifications made to the data during a transaction. This ensures that in case of a transaction failure, the data is restored to its original state. For example, the deposit and withdrawals made to an account are maintained consistently in the supporting database at all times.

- **Isolation.**   This property of a transaction ensures that when concurrent transactions access the same data, changes made to the data by one transaction are
  not visible to the other transactions unless the transactions are complete. For
  example, credit and debit events within an account can occur in parallel, but the
  balance available to the customer is the updated balance that is obtained at the
  end of a completed transaction.
- **Durability.**   This property of a transaction ensures data recovery in all situations. The updates made to the data during a transaction are maintained in case
  of system failure.

Queued Components

The Queued Component service of COM+ is based on the MSMQ model. MSMQ
is a middle-tier service that enables the asynchronous delivery of messages to
named queues. The MSMQ system arranges the method calls in a queue and executes them automatically when the component is available. You can, therefore, use
queued components to execute client methods even after the component is unavailable or offline, ensuring the continuous running of a distributed application.

You can programmatically configure a COM+ component to read or write to the
message queues using an attribute. After the COM+ component is deployed, you
can enable or disable it to read or write to message queues using the Component
Services tool.

Security

COM+ provides a role-based security service that reduces the complexity of the
administration issues in middle-tier components. The role-based security implementation in COM+ is of two types: declarative and programmatic. The security
settings that you can configure without using an explicit programming interface are
known as *declarative security* settings. There are situations, such as the exchange
of sensitive data across networks, that require a temporary increase in security
implementation. Security implementation in these situations can occur only
through a programming interface and is known as *programmatic security*. The
primary areas for security implementation are authentication and access control.

Loosely Coupled Events

COM+ enables an application to produce notifications about the change in its state
by using events. The notifications provide information about applications or components without revealing their identity. Applications that send notifications are
called *publishers*, whereas those that receive notifications are called *subscribers*.
COM+ events are loosely coupled events in which the publishers send notifications
about the events to an event store. The subscribers search the event store for the
event information they require.

JIT Activation

The JIT activation service ensures that the client application has references to objects as long as it requires them. This ensures that a client application does not use the valuable memory resources of the server to save the object references.

A COM+ component exists in three states: exists and activated, exists and not activated, and nonexistent. When the client initiates a COM+ object, it actually obtains a reference to a context object, not the component object. A reference to the component object is made available only after the client makes a method call to the component. A COM+ component can remain deactivated even if the client still holds a reference to the component because an object is instantiated only after a client makes a method call on the object. The object is deactivated and released after the return of the method call. Subsequent calls for a deactivated object result in its reactivation. Therefore, to a client, it appears to be working on the same object, but COM+ actually creates multiple instances of the same class.

Object Pooling

COM+ provides an automated service for configuring a component so that it can maintain ready-to-use and active object instances in a pool to process client requests. To configure and monitor the pool, you specify characteristics such as the pool size and the creation request time-out values. The COM+ object pooling service is responsible for managing the pool and ensuring the activation and reuse of the pool objects according to the configured specifications.

The pool objects are not destroyed even after their release from the client application. COM+ retains the destroyed object in the pool for recycling to ensure its availability on the receipt of a request from the same or any other client. The object pool adds to the scalability of an application by providing the means for recycling COM+ objects. Object pooling is, therefore, a resource saver that cuts down the costs of creating new instances of the same object time and again. Table 3.1 shows a list of available COM+ services.

Table 3.1   An Overview of COM+ Services

COM+ services	Used to
Automatic transaction processing	Apply declarative transaction-processing features
XA Interoperability	Support the X/Open transaction-processing model
Synchronization (Activity)	Manage concurrency
Shared properties	Share a state among multiple objects within a server process
Role-based security	Apply role-based security permissions
Queued components	Provide asynchronous message queuing
Object pooling	Provide a pool of ready-made objects

Table 3.1   An Overview of COM+ Services *(continued)*

COM+ services	Used to
Object construction	Pass a persistent string value to a class instance on the construction of the instance
Loosely coupled events	Manage object-based events
Just-in-time activation	Activate an object on a method call and deactivate the object after the call returns
Compensating resource managers (CRMs)	Apply atomicity and durability properties to nontransactional resources
COM transaction integrator (COMTI)	Encapsulates access to IBM's CICS and IMS applications in automation objects

Lesson 2: Understanding, Creating, and Registering Serviced Components

The .NET Framework allows you to build serviced components that can use COM+ services. These components run within the managed execution environment of the .NET Framework and share their context with COM+ applications. In this lesson, you will learn how to create and register a serviced component for accessing the built-in COM+ services.

After this lesson, you will be able to

- Understand the tasks to be executed before adding a .NET component to a COM+ application
- Create a serviced component
- Register a serviced component with COM+ using manual, dynamic, and programmatic registration procedures

Estimated lesson time: 40 minutes

Developing a Serviced Component

The .NET Framework allows you to build components using .NET languages and deploy them as COM+ applications. These components can utilize COM+ services, such as automatic transaction management and object pooling, by sharing their context with COM+ applications. The .NET namespace that contains the types necessary to use COM+ services is called System.EnterpriseServices. The serviced components derive from the System.EnterpriseServices.ServicedComponent class.

To create a serviced component, you define a class that derives from the ServicedComponent class. For example, the following code shows the Account class, which is derived from the System.EnterpriseServices.ServicedComponent class.

Visual Basic .NET

```
Imports System.EnterpriseServices
Public Class Account
    Inherits ServicedComponent

    Shared Sub Main()
    End Sub
End Class
```

Visual C#

```
using System.EnterpriseServices;
public class Account : ServicedComponent
{
    static void Main()
    {}
}
```

Service-Related Attributes of a Serviced Component

A serviced component can utilize COM+ services by using service-related attributes in the System.EnterpriseServices namespace. Some of these attributes have default values. Knowing the default values of these attributes helps you identify the attributes that you should use for your serviced component. The different usages of the service-related attributes are:

- **Attribute scope.**   This attribute specifies whether an attribute applies to a method, a class, or an entire assembly.
- **Unconfigured default value.**   This attribute specifies the value that COM+ assigns to the field when the attribute is omitted from the code.
- **Configured default value.**   This attribute specifies the value that COM+ assigns to a field when you apply an attribute but omit the attribute value.

In the following code, JustInTimeActivationAttribute is applied to the Account class without any value assigned to the attribute. In such a case, COM+ assigns a value of True to JustInTimeActivationAttribute.

Visual Basic .NET

```
Imports System.EnterpriseServices
<JustInTimeActivation()> Public Class Account
    Inherits ServicedComponent
    Shared Sub Main()
    End Sub
End Class
```

Visual C#

```
using System.EnterpriseServices;
[JustInTimeActivation]
public class Account : ServicedComponent
{
    static void Main()
    {}
}
```

However, if JustInTimeActivationAttribute is omitted from the code completely, COM+ assigns a default value of False to JustInTimeActivationAttribute.

Service-Related Attributes

The .NET Framework provides the following service-related attributes to configure serviced components:

- **ApplicationAccessControlAttribute.** This attribute allows you to configure security for serviced components. The scope of this attribute is the assembly. The unconfigured default value of ApplicationAccessControlAttribute is False and the configured default value is True.

- **ApplicationActivationAttribute.** This attribute defines whether a serviced component runs in the system process or in the process of the creator. The scope of this attribute is the assembly. ApplicationActivationAttribute has no configured default value, and the unconfigured default value is Library.

- **ApplicationIDAttribute.** This attribute specifies the globally unique identifier (GUID) of the application that contains serviced components. The scope of this attribute is assembly. ApplicationIDAttribute has no configured default value, and the unconfigured default value is the generated GUID.

- **ApplicationNameAttribute.** This attribute specifies the name of the COM+ application that hosts the serviced components. The scope of this attribute is the assembly. ApplicationNameAttribute has no configured default value, and the unconfigured default value is the assembly name.

- **ApplicationQueuingAttribute.** This attribute defines whether the serviced component can read messages from message queues. The scope of this attribute is the assembly, and it has no configured or unconfigured default value.

- **AutoCompleteAttribute.** This attribute is applied to the methods of a serviced component class to specify whether the method automatically calls SetComplete or SetAbort. If the method returns normally, it calls SetComplete; otherwise, it calls SetAbort automatically. The unconfigured default value of AutoCompleteAttribute is False, and the configured default value is True.

- **ComponentAccessControlAttribute.** This attribute is applied to a class and enables security checking on the method calls. The unconfigured default value of ComponentAccessControlAttribute is False, and the configured default value is True.

- **COMTIIntrinsicsAttribute.** This attribute applies to a serviced component class and enables you to pass the context properties from the COM transaction integrator (COMTI) to the COM+ context. COMTI is a set of tools and services that allows you to wrap mainframe transactions and business components as COM components. The unconfigured default value of COMTIIntrinsicAttribute is False, and the configured default value is True.

- **ConstructionEnabledAttribute.** This attribute allows you to specify the initialization information externally so that you do not have to hard code the configuration information that is located inside a class. The scope of this attribute is the class. The unconfigured default value is False, and the configured default value is True.

- **DescriptionAttribute.**   This attribute is an informational attribute describing the assembly, class, method, or interface to which it is applied. It has no default unconfigured or configured value.

- **EventClassAttribute.**   This attribute applies to a class and specifies the class as an event class. An event class does not handle the method calls itself; instead, the method calls are diverted to the event class subscribers. There are no default configured or unconfigured values for this attribute.

- **EventTrackingEnabledAttribute.**   This attribute enables event tracking for a class to which it is applied. The unconfigured default value of EventTrackingEnabledAttribute is False, and the configured default value is True.

- **TransactionsAttribute.**   This attribute specifies the type of transaction that is available for the class to which it is applied. The unconfigured default value for this attribute is False. The configured default value of TransactionsAttribute is TransactionOption.Required, TransactionIsolationLevel.Serializable, and Timeout. Lesson 3 discusses TransactionAttribute in detail.

- **JustInTimeActivationAttribute.**   This attribute applies to a class and enables JIT activation for the object to which it applies. JIT activation allows you to create an object as nonactive and context only. The object is activated only when a method is called on it. After the method call returns, the object is deactivated. If you have configured JIT activation with this attribute, do not turn off JIT activation using the Component Services tool. The unconfigured default value of JustInTimeActivationAttribute is False, and the configured default value is True.

- **ObjectPoolingAttribute.**   This attribute allows you to enable and configure object pooling for the class to which it is applied. If object pooling is enabled, the object is not created from scratch when a client requires the object. COM+ maintains a pool of objects for which object pooling is enabled. When a client requires an object, the object is activated from the pool. The object is returned to the pool when the client finishes working with the object. The unconfigured default value of ObjectPoolingAttribute is False, and the configured default value is True.

- **LoadBalancingSupportedAttribute.**   This attribute determines whether the component participates in load balancing if the component load balancing service is installed and enabled on the server. This attribute applies to a class. The unconfigured default value of LoadBalancingSupportedAttribute is False, and the configured default value is True.

- **MustRunInClientContextAttribute.**   This attribute is applied to a class and enables the objects of the class to be created in the context of the creator. The unconfigured default value of MustRunInClientContextAttribute is False, and the configured default value is True.

- **PrivateComponentAttribute.**   This attribute applies to a class and makes the objects of the class accessible only within the application. PrivateComponent-Attribute has no unconfigured default value, and the configured default value is Private.

- **SecureMethodAttribute.**   This attribute applies to an assembly, a class, or a method. Applying this attribute ensures secure calls to a method or to the methods within a class or assembly. SecureMethodAttribute has no configured or unconfigured default value.

- **SecurityRoleAttribute.**   This attribute allows you to add security roles to an application and associate the security roles with components. You can apply this attribute to an assembly, a class, or a method. SecurityRoleAttribute has no configured or unconfigured default value.

The following code shows how to use some of the attributes to configure a serviced component.

Visual Basic .NET

```
Imports System.Reflection
Imports System
Imports System.EnterpriseServices

<Assembly: ApplicationName("MyServicedComponents")>
<Assembly: AssemblyDescription("This app contains serviced components")>

<ObjectPooling(MinPoolSize:=1, MaxPoolSize:=5, CreationTimeout:=20000), _
    Transaction(TransactionOption.Supported)> _
Public Class Account
    Inherits System.EnterpriseServices.ServicedComponent

    <AutoComplete()> _
    Public Sub Debit()
    End Sub

    <AutoComplete()> _
    Public Sub Credit()
    End Sub

End Class
```

Visual C#

```
using System;
using System.Reflection ;
using System.EnterpriseServices;

[assembly: ApplicationName("MyServicedComponents")]
[assembly: AssemblyDescription("This app contains serviced components")]
```

```
[ObjectPooling(MinPoolSize=1, MaxPoolSize=5, CreationTimeout=20000),
    Transaction(TransactionOption.Supported)]
public class Account : System.EnterpriseServices.ServicedComponent
{

    [AutoComplete]
    public void Debit()
    {
    }

    [AutoComplete]
    public void credit()
    {
    }
}
```

After you create a serviced component, you need to host it in a COM+ application. To host a serviced component in a COM+ application, perform the following tasks:

- Assign a strong name to the assembly.
- Register the assembly in the Windows registry.
- Register and install the type library definitions in a COM+ application.

Assigning a Strong Name to the Assembly

You use AssemblyKeyFileAttribute to assign a strong name to an assembly. The following code illustrates the use of AssemblyKeyFileAttribute to assign a strong name to an assembly.

Visual Basic .NET

```
Imports System.Reflection
<Assembly: AssemblyKeyFile("MyKey.snk")>
Public Class Account
    Inherits System.EnterpriseServices.ServicedComponent
End Class
```

Visual C#

```
using System.Reflection;
[assembly: AssemblyKeyFile("MyKey.snk")]
public class Account : System.EnterpriseServices.ServicedComponent
{
}
```

You use the Strong Name Tool, Sn.exe, to create a file containing the public key information. The Strong Name Tool is described in Chapter 1, "Understanding the .NET Framework."

Registering a Serviced Component

You can register a serviced component manually, dynamically, or programmatically. During the process of registration, the serviced components are added to a COM+ application and configured according to the attributes used. When you configure a serviced component, you apply attributes to increase the flexibility of the component. COM+ applies default attributes to the components that are not configured with explicit values. You can apply the following attributes to serviced components so that they can access COM+ services:

- Application identity attribute
- Application activation type attribute
- Description attribute

Application Identity Attribute

The ApplicationName or ApplicationID attribute identifies a COM+ application. The ApplicationID or GUID is unique and can be provided along with the application name. The application name is assigned to a COM+ application by using the assembly-level ApplicationName attribute. The application ID is assigned by using the ApplicationID attribute that is derived from the System.EnterpriseServices namespace. The application ID serves as an index for all application searches made during the registration process. The application name is a readable identifier that you do not use for assembly- and application-level references.

The application name for unidentified applications is generated during the registration process by using the full name of the assembly. The following code shows how to assign an application name and ID to a COM+ application.

Visual Basic .NET

```
Imports System.EnterpriseServices
<Assembly: ApplicationName("MyServicedComponents")>
<Assembly: ApplicationID("8fb2d46f-efc8-4643-bcd0-4e5bfa6a174c")>
Public Class Account
    Inherits ServicedComponent
    Shared Sub Main()
    End Sub
End Class
```

Visual C#

```
using System.EnterpriseServices;
[assembly: ApplicationName("MyServicedComponents")]
[assembly: ApplicationID("8fb2d46f-efc8-4643-bcd0-4e5bfa6a174c")]
public class Account : ServicedComponent
{
    static void Main()
    {}
}
```

Activation Type Attribute

You use the activation type to specify whether the serviced component you create is created in the library of the caller process or in a new process of the server. If the activation type of an application is set to Server, the dependent assemblies must be added to the Global Assembly Cache (GAC), and the parameters of the component must be marked as serializable to avoid exceptions. You use the ApplicationActivation attribute to specify the activation type of a COM+ application.

When you do not specify the ApplicationActivation attribute for an application, the default activation type of the .NET library is used as the activation type of the application. The following code shows how to specify the activation type for a COM+ serviced component.

Visual Basic .NET

```
Imports System.EnterpriseServices
<Assembly: ApplicationName("MyServicedComponents")>
<Assembly: ApplicationID("8fb2d46f-efc8-4643-bcd0-4e5bfa6a174c")>
<Assembly: ApplicationActivation(ActivationOption.Server)>
Public Class Account
    Inherits ServicedComponent
    Shared Sub Main()
    End Sub
End Class
```

Visual C#

```
using System.EnterpriseServices;
[assembly: ApplicationName("MyServicedComponents")]
[assembly: ApplicationID("8fb2d46f-efc8-4643-bcd0-4e5bfa6a174c")]
[assembly: ApplicationActivation(ActivationOption.Server)]
public class Account : ServicedComponent
{
    static void Main()
    {}
}
```

Description Information

You use the Description attribute to add a descriptive field specifying the assembly, class, interface, and method used in a particular component. You can specify the Description attribute in the Description field of the General Properties tab in the Component Services tool. The Component Services tool is described in Lesson 4. The following code demonstrates the method that you use to specify the description information for a COM+ serviced component.

Visual Basic .NET

```
Imports System.EnterpriseServices
Imports System.Reflection
<Assembly: ApplicationName("MyServicedComponents")>
```

(continued)

```
<Assembly: ApplicationID("8fb2d46f-efc8-4643-bcd0-4e5bfa6a174c")>
<Assembly: ApplicationActivation(ActivationOption.Server)>
<Assembly: AssemblyDescription("This app contains serviced components")>
Public Class Account
    Inherits ServicedComponent
    Shared Sub Main()
    End Sub
End Class
```

Visual C#

```
using System.EnterpriseServices;
using System.Reflection;

[assembly: ApplicationName("MyServicedComponents")]
[assembly: ApplicationID("8fb2d46f-efc8-4643-bcd0-4e5bfa6a174c")]
[assembly: ApplicationActivation(ActivationOption.Server)]
[assembly: AssemblyDescription("This app contains serviced components ")]
public class Account : ServicedComponent
{
    static void Main()
    {}
}
```

COM+ services use the following three types of registrations for a serviced component:

- Manual registration
- Dynamic registration
- Programmatic registration

Manual Registration

You use the .NET Framework services installation tool, RegSvcs.exe, to manually register an assembly that contains a serviced component. This command-line tool accepts the name of the file with the assembly metadata information as the parameter during registration. Table 3.2 lists various options that you can use with the RegSvcs.exe tool.

You should use manual registration for design-time testing to learn about the types of errors that may occur during the execution of the application. The RegSvcs.exe tool performs the following tasks during the manual registration of an assembly:

- Loads the assembly
- Registers the assembly
- Generates the type library
- Calls the LoadTypeLibrary method to register the type library
- Installs the type library into the specified COM+ application
- Configures the class

Table 3.2   RegSvcs Options

Option	Usage
/appname	Explicitly specify the name of the single DLL assembly attribute as a command-line parameter.
	To add the serviced components of MyFirstAssembly.dll to the COM+ application MyFirstApp, type the following at the command prompt:
	RegSvcs.exe /appname:MyFirstApp MyFirstAssembly.dll
/c	Create an application in a particular assembly.
	To create an application called MyFirstApp in MyFirstAssembly.dll, type the following at the command prompt:
	RegSvcs.exe /c MyFirstApp MyFirstAssembly.dll
/fc	Locate a COM+ application with a name and create it if not found.
	To locate an application called MyFirstApp in MyFirstAssembly.dll, type the following at the command prompt:
	RegSvcs.exe /fc MyFirstApp MyFirstAssembly.dll
/reconfig	Reconfigure an existing assembly version.
	To reconfigure the version of MyFirstAssembly.dll, type the following at the command prompt:
	RegSvcs.exe /reconfig /fc MyFirstApp MyFirstAssembly.dll

Table 3.3 lists some of the errors that can occur while manually registering an application.

Table 3.3   Manual Registration Errors

Encountered error	Output
The assembly fails to load	Displays an error message describing the reason for failure.
The type registration fails	Generates incorrect assembly specifications resulting in a TypeLoadException.
The generation of the type library fails	Generates incorrect assembly specifications resulting in a TypeLoadException.
The call to the LoadTypeLibrary fails	Generates a TypeLoadException.
Regasm.exe used for the assembly registration fails to locate the specified application	Displays the "One of the objects could not be found" error message.
Service attribute mismatch detected during the registration process	Displays an error message describing the reason for the conflict of service attributes. Often, modifying one of the specified service attributes solves an attribute conflict.

Dynamic Registration

Dynamic registration copies the assembly with the serviced components into the COM+ applications directory. The common language runtime creates an instance of the serviced component after the first call and subsequently registers the assembly and the type library, and configures the COM+ catalog accordingly. Assemblies that are registered dynamically need not be placed in the GAC. You use dynamic registration only when a managed client creates the serviced component. Managed clients, such as ASP.NET, can use dynamic registration to make calls to unregistered serviced components. On the other hand, for COM clients you should register the service components manually by using the command-line utility, RegScvs.exe.

Dynamic registration is useful for those serviced components that are configured according to the attributes in the assembly.

Programmatic Registration

You can register an assembly programmatically by creating an instance of the RegistrationHelper class. The RegistrationHelper class implements the IRegistrationHelper interface and cannot be inherited. The definition for the RegistrationHelper class follows:

Visual Basic .NET

```
<Guid("")>
NotInheritable Public Class RegistrationHelper
    Inherits MarshalByRefObject
    Implements IRegistrationHelper
```

Visual C#

```
[Guid("")]
public sealed class RegistrationHelper : MarshalByRefObject,
    IRegistrationHelper
```

The following code creates a serviced component for a bank transaction. The code consists of a client and a server. The Account class is derived from the Serviced-Component class to ensure that the contexts of Account objects are hosted in COM+. The following attributes are used in the serviced component example:

- ApplicationNameAttribute is used to specify the name of the COM+ application during the installation of the components in the assembly.
- AssemblyKeyFileAttribute is used to provide the COM+ catalog with information regarding the location of the strong name.
- TransactionAttribute is used to set the transaction to Required. This is similar to using the COM+ Explorer to set the transaction support on a COM+ component.
- AutoCompleteAttribute is used in the Post method. It ensures that the runtime automatically calls the SetAbort method if an exception is generated during the

execution of the method. The runtime calls the SetComplete function if no exceptions occur.

The following is the code for the server component.

Visual Basic .NET

```
Imports System.EnterpriseServices
Imports System.Runtime.CompilerServices
Imports System.Reflection

' Specify a name for the COM+ application.
<Assembly: ApplicationName("MyServicedComponents")>
' Specify a strong name for the assembly.
<Assembly: AssemblyKeyFile("MyKey.snk")>

<Transaction(TransactionOption.Required)> _
Public Class Account
    Inherits ServicedComponent

    <AutoComplete()> _
    Public Sub Post(accountNum As Integer, amount As Double)
        ' Calls SetAbort if an exception occurs
        ' Calls SetComplete automatically if no exception is generated.
    End Sub
End Class
```

Visual C#

```
using System.EnterpriseServices;
using System.Runtime.CompilerServices;
using System.Reflection;

// Specify a name for the COM+ application.
[assembly: ApplicationName("MyServicedComponents")]
// Specify a strong name for the assembly.
[assembly: AssemblyKeyFile("MyKey.snk")]

[Transaction(TransactionOption.Required)]
public class Account : ServicedComponent
{
    [AutoComplete]
    public bool Post(int accountNum, double amount)
    {
        // Calls SetAbort if an exception occurs
        // Calls SetComplete automatically if no exception is Generated.
        return false;
    }
}
```

The following is the code for the client component.

Visual Basic .NET

```
Public Class Client
    Shared Sub Main()
        Dim Account As New Account()
        ' Post money into the account.
        Account.Post(5, 100)
    End Sub
End Class
```

Visual C#

```
public class Client
{
    public static int Main()
    {
        Account act = new Account();
        // Post money into the account.
        act.Post(5, 100);
        return 0;
    }
}
```

Run the following commands at the command prompt to compile the server and the client.

Visual Basic .NET

```
sn -k MyKey.snk
vbc /t:library /r:System.EnterpriseServices.dll Account.vb
vbc /t:library /r:System.EnterpriseServices.dll Client.vb
```

Visual C#

```
sn -k MyKey.snk
csc /t:library /r:System.EnterpriseServices.dll Account.cs
csc /t:library /r:System.EnterpriseServices.dll Client.cs
```

Lesson 3: Utilizing COM+ Services

In this lesson, you will learn how to configure serviced components to consume COM+ services by applying certain attributes.

After this lesson, you will be able to

Identify the attributes that you add to a serviced component to

- Initiate transactions in an application
- Initiate JIT activation in an application
- Support loosely coupled events
- Implement object pooling
- Access message queues
- Support object construction

Estimated lesson time: 45 minutes

Enabling COM+ Transactions

An online shopping site uses an e-commerce model to facilitate shopping on the Web. The entire operation of online shopping includes tasks such as choosing the items for purchase, filling in the shopping requisition, and specifying the mode of payment. If a customer chooses to pay using a credit card, the task of verifying card credentials is added to the entire shopping operation. The successful completion of each task leads to the initiation of the next task. If a single task in the series fails, the entire operation fails. You do not get the delivery of the selected items in the shopping cart, and the online store does not get your money.

You can relate the preceding example to a transaction that consists of a series of operations, each connected to the other to form a single unit. The success of a transaction depends upon the success of all tasks that make up the transaction. COM+ uses the transaction model to perform application-based tasks.

At the end of its execution, a transaction exists in one of the following states:

- **Committed.**   Indicates the successful execution of all the tasks in a transaction.
- **Disable commit.**   Indicates that the component has not finished its task, and the transactional updates are in an inconsistent state.

- **Enable commit.**   Indicates that the task of the object is not finished, but its transactional updates are in a consistent state.
- **Aborted.**   Indicates the unsuccessful execution of one of the tasks of the transaction, which resulted in the failure of the transaction.

A transaction processing system consists of:

- **Transaction manager (TM).**   The TM is the conductor of the transactions. It is responsible for ensuring that all parties in the transaction are notified of the outcome (commit or rollback). The TM also coordinates the recovery of one or more of the systems from failure. The Microsoft Distributed Transaction Coordinator (MSDTC) is the transaction manager in a COM+ environment.
- **Resource manager.**   The Resource Manager manages the ACID properties of a particular resource. In other words, a resource manager is a server resource that is responsible for coordination between various tasks of a transaction. Microsoft Message Queue (MSMQ) is often used as a COM+ resource manager.
- **Transaction Processing Monitor (TP Monitor).**   The TP Monitor is an environment present between the clients and the server resources to manage transactions, manage resources, provide load balancing and fault tolerance.
- **Resource dispensers.**   The resource dispenser forms part of the COM+ programming model and run-time environment. Application components use resource dispensers to access shared information. Resource dispensers can also be used to load the auxiliary components.

You use the transaction attributes to enable the serviced components to participate in a transaction. The transaction attributes determine whether the serviced components participate in a new or an existing transaction.

Transaction Attributes

Transaction attributes specify the requirements of a transaction. As a declarative property, the transaction attribute automatically manages transactions, depending on the specified requirements. COM+ transaction attributes can have the following values:

- **Required.**   This attribute enables you to create a transactional object from a COM+ component. On activation, the transactional object along with the Required attribute detects the transactional status of the caller. If the caller has a transaction, the new object is included in the current transaction. If the caller does not have a transaction, COM+ initiates a transaction with the new object as the root object of the transaction.
- **RequiresNew.**   This attribute ensures that an object created from the COM+ component participates in a new transaction as the root of the transaction. The transactional status of the caller is ignored.

- **Disabled.** This attribute specifies that the components do not access a resource manager. When you disable the transaction attribute, COM+ ignores the transactional requirements of the component to determine the context placement of the object. The object can, therefore, share the caller context of the transaction. You should disable the transaction attribute when you move a COM component to COM+ to maintain the same transactional behavior as a COM+ component.

- **Supported.** This attribute ensures that an object created from the COM+ component participates in an existing transaction. You can use this attribute when you want an object to share the transaction of the caller without initiating a transaction of its own.

- **Not Supported.** This attribute ensures that an object created from the COM+ component does not participate in a transaction. The transactional status of the caller is ignored. You can use this attribute when you do not want the object to share the transaction of the caller or initiate a transaction of its own. Not Supported is the default attribute for all components.

Dependencies of the Transaction Attribute

Table 3.4 lists the characteristics and effects of the COM+ transaction attributes.

Table 3.4   Characteristics of the COM+ Transaction Attribute Values

Transaction attribute	Start a new transaction	Use a client's transaction	Transaction root
Required	Maybe	Yes, if client has an existing transaction	Yes, if client does not have an existing a transaction
Requires New	Yes	Maybe	Maybe
Disabled	Never	Maybe	Never
Not Supported	Never	Never	Never
Supported	Never	Yes, if client has an existing transaction	Never

Setting the Transaction Time-Out

You can specify the time-out value for each class that requires a transaction to resolve conflicts that arise from mismatched time-out specifications. For example, you have a conflicting time-out setup if your component contains a short transaction time within long running batch stored procedures. When the time-out value of a transaction is not specified, the transaction initiates with the default systemwide time-out value. You use the Component Services tool to set the systemwide time-out value. The Component Services tool is explained in Lesson 4.

The transaction time-out value is an integer that is measured in seconds. The following code sets the transaction time-out value to 25 seconds.

Visual Basic .NET

```
<Transaction(TransactionOption.Required, Isolation := _
    TransactionIsolationLevel.Serializable, Timeout := 25)>
```

Visual C#

```
[Transaction(TransactionOption.Required, Isolation=
    TransactionIsolationLevel.Serializable, Timeout=25)]
```

Enabling JIT Activation

You can use the JIT activation service to create an object that is a nonactive, context-only object. The nonactive state of the object is maintained until a client invokes a method on the object, after which, the run time creates the full object. COM+ deactivates the object when the method call returns, but leaves the context in memory. The deactivated object subsequently releases all resources such as locks on expensive data stores. To enable JIT activation, you can use JustInTimeActivationAttribute for a class that derives from the System.EnterpriseServices.ServicedComponent class.

JIT activation is automatically set to True on the classes that are configured for automatic transactions. The following code shows how to use the JustInTime-ActivationAttribute class.

Visual Basic .NET

```
<JustInTimeActivation()> _
Public Class Account
    Inherits ServicedComponent
```

Visual C#

```
[JustInTimeActivation]
public class Account : ServicedComponent
```

Using the Loosely Coupled Events Service

You can make late-bound event or method calls to the publishers and subscribers within an event system. The event system provides the publisher and the subscriber with information as and when it is made available. This technique saves the task of repeatedly polling the server for information.

You can use the loosely coupled event service by adding an event class and an event sink. Both the event class and the event sink should be directly or indirectly derived from the System.EnterpriseServices.ServicedComponent class. The following example illustrates the use of an event interface (IEvent), an event class, an event sink, and a publisher to add support for the loosely coupled service of COM+.

Visual Basic .NET

```
Imports System
Imports System.IO
Imports System.Reflection
```

```vbnet
Imports System.EnterpriseServices
Imports System.Runtime.InteropServices
Imports System.Windows.Forms

<Assembly: ApplicationName("DemoLCE")>
<Assembly: ApplicationActivation(ActivationOption.Library)>
<Assembly: AssemblyKeyFile("DemoLCESvr.snk")>

Namespace DemoLCE
    Public Interface IEvent
        Sub EvntMethod(mess As String)
    End Interface

    <EventClass()> _
    Public Class LCEClass
        Inherits ServicedComponent
        Implements IEvent

        Public Sub EvntMethod(mess As String) _
            Implements IEvent.EvntMethod
        End Sub
    End Class

    Public Class LCEEvntSink
        Inherits ServicedComponent
        Implements IEvent

        Public Sub EvntMethod(mess As String) _
            Implements IEvent.EvntMethod
            MessageBox.Show(mess, "Event sink")
        End Sub
    End Class
End Namespace
```

Visual C#

```csharp
using System;
using System.IO;
using System.Reflection;
using System.EnterpriseServices;
using System.Runtime.InteropServices;
using System.Windows.Forms;

[assembly: ApplicationName("DemoLCE")]
[assembly: ApplicationActivation(ActivationOption.Library)]
[assembly: AssemblyKeyFile("DemoSvrLCE.snk")]

namespace DemoLCE
{
    public interface IEvent
```

(continued)

```
    {
        void EvntMethod(string mess);
    }

    [EventClass]
    public class LCEClass : ServicedComponent, IEvent
    {
        public void EvntMethod(string mess){}
    }

    public class LCESink : ServicedComponent, IEvent
    {
        public void EvntMethod(string mess)
        {
            MessageBox.Show(mess, "Event sink");
        }
    }
}
```

The following is the code for a Windows application that contains a button control named FireEventButton. The EvntMethod method is called by the event handling code of the FireEventButton.Click event.

Visual Basic .NET

```
Public Class LCEClient
    Inherits System.Windows.Forms.Form

    Protected Sub FireEventButton_Click(Mysender As Object, _
        e As System.EventArgs) _
        Handles FireEventButton.Click
        Dim MyEvent As IEvent = CType(New LCEClass(),IEvent)
        MyEvent.EvntMethod("This is a welcome message for events")
    End Sub
End class
```

Visual C#

```
public class LCEClient : System.Windows.Forms.Form
{
    protected void FireEventButton_Click(object Mysender, System.EventArgs e)
    {
        IEvent MyEvent = (IEvent) new LCEClass();
        MyEvent.EvntMethod("This is a welcome message for events ");
    }
}
```

In the above code samples, LCEClass is the event class, LCESink is the subscriber of the event class, and LCEClient is the publisher class. LCEClient calls the EvntMethod method on the LCEClass object. Since LCEClass is an event class, the

EvntMethod implementation of LCEClass is not invoked. Instead, the implementation of EvntMethod in the LCESink class is invoked.

Note   You can create event subscriptions using the Component Services tool. To subscribe to an event, expand the node containing your component in the Component Services tool. Right-click on the Subscriptions node and select New, Subscription.

Using the Object Pooling Service

You can use object pooling to save the resources that are used during object creation. In a normal, nonpooled environment, objects are created at each method call. However, when object pooling is enabled, a pool of objects is created. The object is extracted from the pool on activation. Similarly, on deactivation, the object is returned to the pool for later use. To configure object pooling, you apply ObjectPoolingAttribute to a class that is derived from the System.EnterpriseServices.ServicedComponent class.

The following code illustrates the use of the ObjectPoolingAttribute class.

Visual Basic .NET

```
<ObjectPooling(MinPoolSize := 1, MaxPoolSize := 10, _
    CreationTimeout := 25000)> _
Public Class MyPooledObject
    Inherits ServicedComponent
End Class
```

Visual C#

```
[ObjectPooling(Enabled=true, MinPoolSize=1, MaxPoolSize=10,
    CreationTimeout=25000)]
public class MyPooledObject : ServicedComponent
{}
```

Using the Queued Components Service

You can use queued components to invoke and execute COM+ components asynchronously. To use the queued components service, you need to apply the ApplicationQueuingAttribute class, which is derived from the System.Enterprise-Services.ServicedComponent class. The ApplicationQueuingAttribute class uses the MaxListenerThreads attribute to specify the maximum number of queued components listener threads. The MaxListenerThreads attribute can hold values from 0 to 1000. The following code illustrates the use of the ApplicationQueuingAttribute class to set the MaxListenerThreads attribute to 35.

Visual Basic .NET

```
<Assembly:ApplicationQueuingAttribute(QueueListenerEnabled := true, _
    MaxListenerThreads :=  35 )>
```

Visual C#

```
[assembly:ApplicationQueuingAttribute(QueueListenerEnabled = true,
    MaxListenerThreads =  35 )]
```

Using Object Construction

You often need to write configuration-related information within a class in your component. You can use COM+ object construction to eliminate this tedious task. You can use object construction to initialize the configuration information externally. To configure object construction, you apply ConstructionEnabledAttribute to a class that is derived from the System.EnterpriseServices.ServicedComponent class. The following code shows the implementation of the System.Enterprise-Services.ConstructionEnabledAttribute class. When a serviced component is created COM+ passes a default value of Hello to the object.

Visual Basic .NET

```
<ConstructionEnabled([Default]:="Hello")>
```

Visual C#

```
[ConstructionEnabled(Default="Hello")]
```

In this lesson, you learned how to enable a serviced component to utilize COM+ services by using various service related attributes. You can also configure a serviced component by using the Component Services tool. Using the Component Services tool, you can change the properties, such as transaction, activation, JIT activation, object pooling, and object construction, of a serviced component. The next lesson discusses how to configure a serviced component using the Component Services tool.

Lesson 4: Managing Serviced Components Using the Component Services Tool

The Component Services tool allows you to configure the properties of a COM+ application. In this lesson, you will learn how to manage serviced components using the Component Services tool.

After this lesson, you will be able to

- Understand the capabilities of the Component Services tool
- Configure and manage serviced components by using the Component Services tool

Estimated lesson time: 30 minutes

Component Services Tool

The Component Services tool is a Microsoft Management Console (MMC) snap-in tool that allows you to create, configure, and maintain COM+ applications. You can also use this tool to view system events and manage the system services. In addition, the Component Services tool helps you manage distributed transactions. You can use the Component Services tool to perform the following tasks:

- Configure the system for component services. Some of the system settings that you can configure include transaction time-out, log information, and protocols.
- Install and configure COM+ applications for client- or server-side deployment.
- Configure various services such as queued components, load balancing, security, and transaction processing. You can configure queued components to request services from another component. Load balancing helps to define the participating computers and components, monitor computer activity, and handle exceptions. The transaction-related tasks of the Component Services tool include viewing transaction statistics and resolving their states.

To open the Component Services tool, complete the following steps:

1. Open Control Panel.
2. Double-click Administrative Tools to open the Administrative Tools window.
3. Click Component Services to open the Component Services window.

Note   Most of the components described in this section are common to both Microsoft Windows 2000 and Windows XP. Those components that are specific only to Windows XP are noted as such.

The Component Services snap-in administrative tool is shown in Figure 3.3.

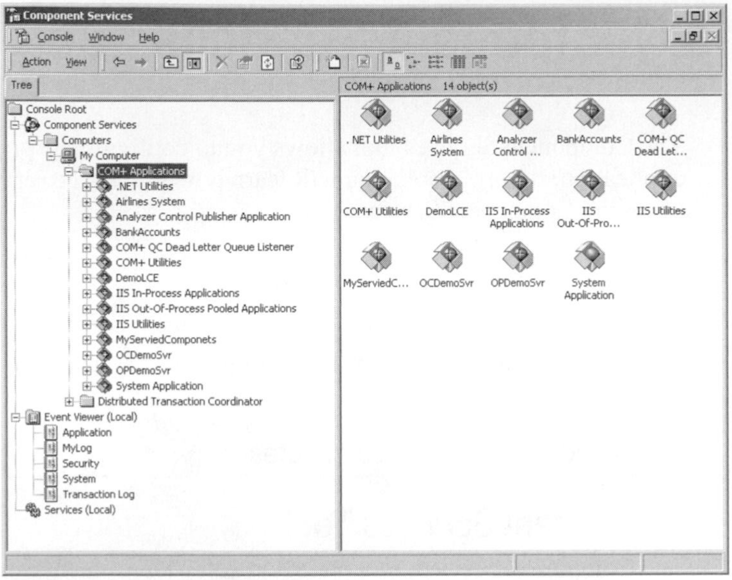

Figure 3.3   The Component Services snap-in administrative tool

The left pane of the Component Services snap-in administrative tool displays a console tree that you can expand to view the component services, the local event viewer, and the available services. You can expand the entries in the left pane of the console to view the applications, components, and security roles of a COM+ application. The nodes appearing in the console tree of the Component Services snap-in include:

- **My Computer and other computers.**   This node of the console tree includes My Computer and all the other computers that have been added by the administrator. My Computer corresponds to the local computer that hosts the Component Services administrative tool and includes the COM+ Applications and Distributed Transaction Coordinator nodes.

- **COM+ Applications.**   This node is a part of My Computer and corresponds to the COM+ applications installed on the computer. You can view the properties of the application by right-clicking on the application in the Component Services tool and selecting Properties from the shortcut menu. The properties dialog box of a COM+ application is shown in Figure 3.4.

- **DCOM Config (Windows XP).**   This node provides access to the DCOM configuration tool. In Windows 2000 this tool was only accessible by running Dcomcnfg.exe from the command line. In Windows XP, DCOM configuration is now possible via the Component Services tool.

- **Running Processes (Windows XP).**   This node was added to the Windows XP release to display a list of all COM+ application processes that are currently running.

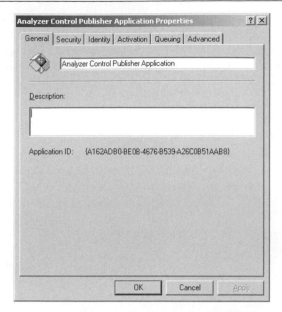

Figure 3.4   The properties dialog box of a COM+ application

- **Components.**   This node includes the components that are installed in a particular COM+ application. You can use the properties dialog box to change the properties of the installed COM+ components.

- **Roles.**   This node corresponds to the roles available for a COM+ application. The properties dialog box can be used to change the properties of the COM+ component roles. The My Computer, COM+ Applications, Components, and Roles nodes of the Component Services snap-in are shown in Figure 3.5.

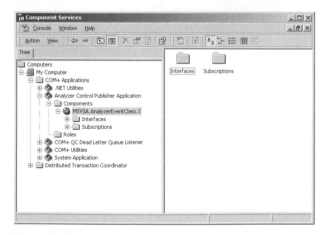

Figure 3.5   The Component Services snap-in

- **Legacy Components (Windows XP)**   This node displays a list of objects that are unconfigured for COM+, but wish to take advantage of the object pooling services offered by COM+. This is possible for objects that were not written specifically with object pooling in mind. These components have to be non-transactional.

- **Interfaces.**   This node corresponds to the interfaces available in a COM+ component. The properties dialog box can be used to change the properties of the interfaces that are associated with a COM+ component.

- **Methods.**   This node corresponds to the methods available from the listed interfaces. The properties dialog box can be used to change the properties of the methods that are associated with the interfaces of a COM+ component. The contents of the Interfaces node are shown in Figure 3.6.

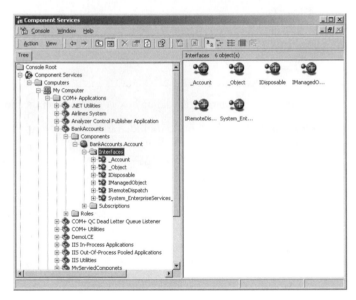

Figure 3.6   The Interfaces node displaying the methods of the Component Services snap-in administrative tool

- **Distributed Transaction Coordinator.**   This node includes the Transaction List node, which contains the list of the current transactions of the computer, and the Transaction Statistics node, which displays transaction-specific information. The Distributed Transaction Coordinator node is shown in Figure 3.7.

You can use the Component Services tool to configure various properties of COM+ applications and components. At the application level, you use the Component

Figure 3.7   The Distributed Transaction Coordinator node

Services tool to configure properties such as security, identity, activation, and queuing. You can also configure the properties of a COM+ application for advanced functionality such as server process shutdown and debugging. At the component level, you use the Component Services tool to configure properties such as transactions, security, activation, and concurrency. You can also configure the properties of a COM+ component for advanced functionality such as queuing and implementation of loosely coupled events services.

Configuring Activation Using the Component Services Tool

At the application level, you configure the activation of a COM+ application by specifying whether it is a library or server application. The options available for activation at the application level are shown in Figure 3.8.

Note   In Windows XP, you will see two additional tabs titled Dump and Pooling & Recycling.

At the component level, you configure the activation of a COM+ component by specifying the attributes for object pooling, object construction, JIT activation, and support for events. The options available for activation at the component level are shown in Figure 3.9.

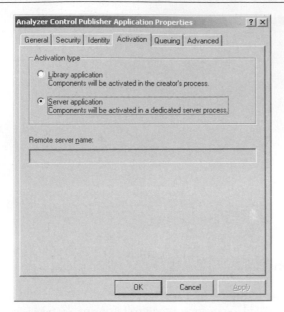

Figure 3.8   The options for activation at the application level

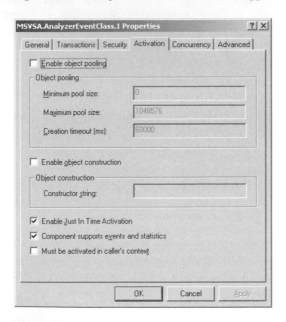

Figure 3.9   The options for activation at the component level

Configuring Transactions
Using the Component Services Tool

The automatic transaction processing in COM+ allows you to modify the transaction behavior according to application requirements.

Setting the Attribute for Transaction Support

You can set transaction attributes manually by using the Component Services administrative tool. To set the attribute value of a transaction using the Component Services administrative tool, complete the following steps:

1. In the console tree of the Component Services tool, right-click the component that you want to configure and click Properties.
2. In the component properties dialog box, select the Transactions tab.
3. Select the appropriate option for transaction support. The default value for all components is Not Supported.
4. Click OK.

You should perform these steps for all components. The options that are available for specifying transaction support at the component level are shown in Figure 3.10.

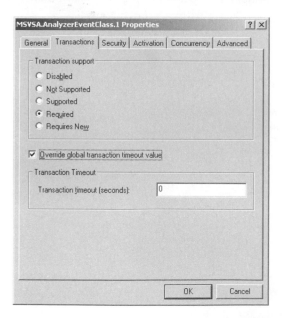

Figure 3.10   The options for transaction support at the component level

Setting the Transaction Time-Out

You can manually set the time-out for transactions by using the Component Services administrative tool. To configure the time-out value for individual components or at the local computer level, complete the following steps:

1. In the console tree of the Component Services tool, right-click the component that you want to configure and click Properties.
2. In the component properties dialog box, select the Transactions tab.
3. Select the check box labeled Override Global Transaction Timeout Value.
4. Under Transaction Timeout, enter the transaction time-out in seconds. The default time-out value is 0 seconds, which means that the component will never cause the transaction to time out.
5. Click OK.

Similarly, perform the following steps to set the transaction time-out for the local computer by using the Component Services administrative tool.

1. In the console tree of the Component Services tool, right-click the local computer that you want to configure and click Properties.
2. In the My Computer Properties dialog box, select the Options tab.
3. Under Transaction Timeout, enter the transaction time-out value in seconds. The default time-out value is 60 seconds.
4. Click OK.

The option available for specifying the transaction time-out at the local computer level is shown in Figure 3.11.

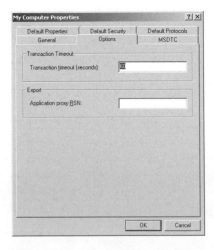

Figure 3.11   The option for transaction time-out at the local computer level

Configuring Security Using the Component Services Tool

You can use the Component Services tool to execute all security-based tasks in COM+ applications. The following tasks are associated with the security services in COM+:

- Configuring role-based security
- Setting the authentication level
- Setting the impersonation level

Configuring Role-Based Security

Before executing the tasks for configuring role-based security in your COM+ application, define the roles in the design phase. A *role* is a group of users who are assigned permissions to a COM+ component or an application. You also associate the defined roles with the components, methods, and interfaces of the application. To configure role-based security, complete the following steps:

1. Enable access checks at the application level.
2. Set the security level for access checks.
3. Enable access checks at the component level.
4. Define roles for an application.
5. Assign roles to components, interfaces, or methods.

Enabling Access Checks at the Application Level

Access checks at the application level can be configured to enable process access checks or full role-based security checks. The security level of the application as well as enabling or disabling of access checking for the application components determines the type of access check. To enable access checks for an application, complete the following steps:

1. In the console tree of the Component Services tool, right-click the COM+ application for which you want to enable access checks.
2. Click Properties.
3. In the application properties dialog box, select the Security tab.
4. Select the Enforce Access Checks For This Application check box.
5. Click OK.

Figure 3.12 shows the Security tab of the BankAccounts Properties dialog box with its security options set to enable access checks at the application level.

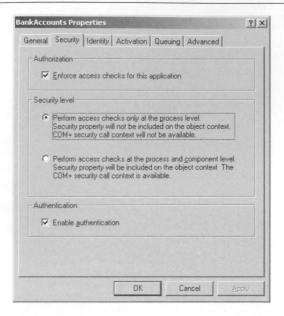

Figure 3.12   The options to enable access checks at the application level

Setting a Security Level for Access Checks

To select a security level for a COM+ application in the properties dialog box, under Security Level on the Security tab, select one of the following options:

- **Perform Access Checks Only At The Process Level. Security Property Will Not Be Included On The Object Context. COM+ Security Call Context Will Not Be Available.**   Select this option to indicate that users in roles are assigned to the application and will be added to the process security descriptor. Selecting this option has the following effects:
  - Fine-grained role checking is turned off at the component, method, and interface levels. In this case, the security checks are performed only at the application level.
  - The security property is not included in the context for any objects running within the application.
  - The security call context is not made available. Therefore, the programmatic security that relies on security call context information does not function.
- **Perform Access Checks At The Process And Component Level. Security Property Will Be Included On The Object Context. The COM+ Security Call Context Is Available.**   Select this option to indicate that process-level

security descriptor checks and full role-based security checks will be performed. Selecting this option will have the following effects:

■ The access check at the component level is enabled for role checking in particular components.

■ The security property is included on the context for any objects that are running within the application.

■ The security call context is available and programmatic role-based security is enabled.

Figure 3.13 shows the BankAccounts Properties dialog box with its security options set to provide security for access checks at the process and component levels.

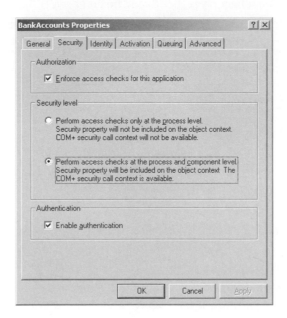

Figure 3.13   The options to set a security level for access checks at the process and component levels

When the application is restarted, security is automatically checked at the specified level, and only valid users that are assigned roles applicable for the application are granted access to the application.

Enabling Access Checks at the Component Level

The components of your application that do not require security checks should be disabled for role checks to improve performance. Similarly, if you are debugging, you can disable security to concentrate on other application functionality.

Each time you install a component, component level access checks are enabled by default. At this level of security check, an application level access check should be enabled, and the security level should be set to perform access checks at the process and component levels. To enable or disable access checks at the component level, complete the following steps:

1. In the console tree of the Component Services tool, locate the COM+ application that contains the component for which you want to disable or enable role checks.
2. Expand the COM+ application in the tree to view the components in the Components folder.
3. Open the component properties dialog box and select the Security tab.
4. Select Enforce Component Level Access Checks to enforce component level checks.
5. Click OK.

Note   The new setting takes effect when the application is restarted.

Defining Roles for an Application

The security privileges of an application define the security policy of the application. To define the security privileges of an application, define the role for the application and assign it to specific resources. To add a role to an application, complete the following steps:

1. In the console tree of the Component Services tool, locate the COM+ application to which you want to add the role.
2. Expand the tree to view the folders for the application.
3. Right-click the Roles folder for the application.
4. Point to New and click Role.
5. In the Role dialog box, enter the name of the new role.
6. Click OK.

Figure 3.14 shows the Role dialog box for defining roles for an application.

Figure 3.14   The Role dialog box

Note   After you add roles to the application, assign the roles to appropriate components, interfaces, and methods. If this is not done and role-based security is enabled for the application, all calls to the application will fail.

Assigning Roles to Components, Interfaces, or Methods

You can explicitly assign a role to an item within a COM+ application to ensure that the member users of the role can access the application. To assign roles to a component, method, or interface, complete the following steps:

1. In the console tree of the Component Services tool, locate the COM+ application for which the role is defined.
2. Expand the tree to view the components, interfaces, or methods of the application, depending on whom you are assigning the role.
3. Right-click the item to which you want to assign the role and click Properties.
4. In the properties dialog box, select the Security tab.
5. In the Roles Explicitly Set For Selected Item(s) list box, select the roles that you want to assign to the item.
6. Click OK.

Setting the Authentication Level

Setting the authentication level of an application means that you define the degree of authentication to be performed when clients call into the application. Higher authentication levels provide greater security and data integrity. To select an authentication level for a server application, complete the following steps:

1. Open the properties dialog box of the application for which you are setting authentication and select the Security tab.
2. In the Authentication Level For Calls drop-down list box, select the appropriate level and then click OK. The following are the ordered levels from lowest to highest security:
    - **None.**   No authentication occurs.
    - **Connect.**   Authenticates credentials only when the connection is made.
    - **Call.**   Authenticates credentials at the beginning of every call.
    - **Packet.**   Authenticates credentials and verifies that all call data is received. This is the default setting for COM+ server applications.
    - **Packet Integrity.**   Authenticates credentials and verifies that no call data is modified in transit.
    - **Packet Privacy.**   Authenticates credentials and encrypts the packet, including the data and the identity and signature of the sender.

Setting the Impersonation Level

Setting the impersonation level for an application is the same as defining the authority of the application by allowing another application to use its identity. The impersonation level can be set for server applications only. To select an impersonation level, complete the following steps:

1. Open the properties dialog box of the COM+ application for which you are setting the authentication and select the Security tab.

2. In the Impersonation Level drop-down list, select the appropriate level and then click OK. The following are the ordered levels from lowest to highest security:

   - **Anonymous.**   The client is unknown to the server. The server can impersonate the client without carrying information about the client in an impersonation token.

   - **Identify.**   The server can obtain the client's identity and impersonate the client to conduct access control list (ACL) checks.

   - **Impersonate.**   The server can impersonate the client and act on its behalf within restrictions. If the server is on the same computer as the client, it can access network resources like the client. However, if the server is on a different computer, it can only access resources on the same computer as the server. This is the default setting for COM+ server applications.

   - **Delegate.**   The server can impersonate the client acting on its behalf regardless of whether it is on the same computer as the client. During impersonation, the client's credentials can be passed to any number of computers.

Lesson 5: Implementing Security for Serviced Components

Security checks are an important aspect of component-based application development because they restrict access to sensitive application data. The security checks for COM+ are performed across process boundaries. Therefore, security checks are initiated in situations in which a call from the client in one process crosses the process boundary. In this lesson, you will learn about the various levels of security checks performed by COM+.

After this lesson, you will be able to

- Identify the various levels of security implementations for serviced components
- Differentiate between role-based security, authentication, impersonation, and delegation
- Use application programming interfaces (APIs) to implement security in serviced components

Estimated lesson time: 30 minutes

Implementation of Security in Serviced Components

An important objective of application development is to secure applications by protecting them from malicious and nonauthenticated users. You can secure your applications either programmatically by using the security APIs or manually by using the Component Services tool. You programmatically configure security for situations that require explicit security implementation to match application requirements. The choice of implementing programmatic or manual security depends upon factors such as application design, performance requirements, and mode of data access. COM+ allows you to secure your serviced components by implementing:

- Role-based security
- Client authentication
- Client impersonation and delegation

Role-Based Security

Role-based security is an automatic, flexible, and configurable security model provided by COM+ to enforce access control for COM+ applications. Role-based security is an important feature of the COM+ application security that helps you to create role-based authorization policies for an application so that access to application resources is restricted to selected users or roles. A role comprises a list or category of users who share the same security privileges. When you assign a role to an application resource, all the members of that role automatically gain permission to access that particular application resource.

You can use this mechanism of security implementation as a framework for imposing a rigid and intrinsic security check from within the application code. Role-based security facilitates the retrieval of information about all the callers of a particular component. As a result, you can use this information to establish the identity of the callers during auditing and logging procedures.

Role-based security implementation in serviced components is of the following two types:

- **Declarative role-based security.**   Enables you to declare and assign roles to application resources. You can assign roles to the entire application, a specific component, a specific interface, or a specific method of an interface. Roles are inherited and are therefore implicitly assigned to every interface and method exposed by a role-assigned component. Declarative role-based security is implemented by using the Component Services administrative tool or the Administrative software development kit (SDK) functions to configure the security properties of an application or component.

- **Programmatic role-based security.**   Although a declarative role is used to implement method level security in components and interfaces, you might often need to implement security checks in the methods programmatically. Programmatic role-based security enables you to add security logic into components to perform role checks in code. You can verify the security permissions of a user or determine if a caller belongs to a specified role by using the security APIs. You can use the declarative role-based security with programmatic role-based security to ensure a higher level of security checks in applications. When you implement the role-based security, it ensures that you have programmatic access to information about the callers of the component.

The level of effectiveness of role-based security depends on the way the roles are designed. You should consider the following factors when designing roles in a particular application:

- The suitability of roles depends upon the characteristics of users and the accessed data. As a result, roles should reflect the characteristics of the user or data according to their implementation in a particular environment. For example, at the organizational level, you can use the designation of the employees to assign role-based security in applications. Roles can be mapped to the employee designations to enforce business rules, such as limiting the transfer of money to certain profiles or allowing specific profiles to access sensitive data. However, the complexity and effectiveness of the role design in the preceding example increases when employees hold multiple profiles. In such cases, the role is designed based on the innate characteristics of the accessed data instead of the characteristics of the user profile.

- The effective implementation of role-based security depends upon the complexity and scalability of the role-based authorization policy. During application deployment, the system administrator can easily interpret a simple policy, ensuring that the correct users are assigned the correct roles according to the security policy. A policy is not effective if administrators make mistakes when assigning roles to users. For example, an intrinsic role-based policy with multiple users and roles or a policy with ambiguous role criteria can create problems if the security policy is not designed well.

The performance of an application depends upon the number of roles assigned to the application. As the number of roles increases, COM+ takes more time to look for the caller membership in the roles, which results in the degradation of application performance. You can use the following guidelines to resolve issues that arise because of complex role designs.

- Role names should be self-descriptive so that you can easily identify and map users and roles.
- Role-based policies should be simple and define few roles.
- The role-based policy should be well documented for easy interpretation by the administrator.
- The description field of the role should provide a detailed description of the role. The administrator can misinterpret a generic role description.
- The roles should be populated with Microsoft Windows user groups, which ensures the scalability of roles. Roles that are populated with individual users are difficult to delete and modify.

Component Level Security Checks in Applications

Security checks are performed at application boundaries. When two components that are a part of the same application call each other, security checks are not performed. However, when two applications share the same process and the component in one application calls a component in the other application, the calls cross the application boundaries. In such situations, security checks are performed to ensure that only authorized users can access the application or component resources. Therefore, you can implement security checks by placing components in separate COM+ applications. The decision about implementing security checks on a call to a component depends upon the security property of the object context.

In server applications, security access checks are implemented at the component level where checks are role-based. Therefore, you can assign roles to components, interfaces, and methods by using the authorization policy. Component level security should be used to implement role-based security. Component level security should also be used when you use programmatic role-based security. Security call context information and security context properties provide vital information regarding the security implementation in a component. The security call context information is available in the component level security implementations and is used to retrieve information about the upstream callers who make calls to components.

Implementing Component Security Programmatically

Role-based security is implemented at the component level to retrieve information about all callers of a particular component. You can use the System.Enterprise-Services.SecurityCallContext class to access security call context information programmatically. Security call context is carried across boundaries, and security checks are therefore implemented for calls between the components that reside outside their security boundaries. Similarly, calls between processes and applications carry security call context information. You can use the call context information for caller-related details during auditing and logging.

Security Call Context Information

When implementing security programmatically, you can use the System.Enterprise-Services.SecurityCallContext class to access information about the caller and verify the role membership in certain sections of code.

SecurityCallContextClass provides a description of the chain of callers that constitute the current method call. SecurityCallContextClass consists of member classes that define its properties and methods. The properties of SecurityCallContextClass are

- **SecurityCallContext.Callers property.**   Enables you to retrieve the SecurityCallers object describing the caller.
- **SecurityCallContext.CurrentCall property.**   Enables you to retrieve the SecurityCallContext object describing the security call context.
- **SecurityCallContext.DirectCaller property.**   Enables you to retrieve the SecurityIdentity object describing the direct caller of this method.
- **SecurityCallContext.IsSecurityEnabled property.**   This property is used to determine whether the security checks of the current context are enabled.
- **SecurityCallContext.MinAuthenticationLevel property.**   Enables you to retrieve the MinAuthenticationValue from the ISecurityCallContext collection in COM+.
- **SecurityCallContext.NumCallers property.**   Enables you to retrieve the NumCallers value from the ISecurityCallContext collection in COM+.
- **SecurityCallContext.OriginalCaller property.**   Enables you to retrieve the SecurityIdentity object describing the original caller.

The following are the methods of the SecurityCallContext class:

- **Object.IsCallerInRole.**   This method verifies whether the direct caller is a member of a specified role. This method accepts a role as the parameter to validate the direct caller as a member of the specified role. After the verification, the Object.IsCallerInRole method returns a True value if the direct caller is a member of the specified role or a False value if the direct caller is not a member of the specified role.

- **Object.IsUserInRole.**   This method verifies that a specified user is in the specified role. This method accepts two parameters, user and role, to accept the name of the specified user and the role. After the verification, the Object.IsCallerInRole method returns a True value if the direct caller is a member of the specified role or a False value if the direct caller is not a member of the specified role.

Enabling Role-Based Security in Components

You can use the IsSecurityEnabled method of the SecurityCallContext object to determine if security is enabled in the current object. You can call the IsSecurityEnabled method before using the IsCallerInRole method to check the role membership because IsCallerInRole returns a True value when security is disabled. The following example illustrates the use of the IsSecurityEnabled method to determine whether the security checks are enabled in the current context. If security is enabled, the code also checks whether the caller is a member of a particular role.

Visual Basic .NET

```
Dim scc As SecurityCallContext
Dim SecEn As Boolean
scc = SecurityCallContext.CurrentCall
SecEn = scc.IsSecurityEnabled()
If SecEn Then
    If scc.IsCallerInRole("Managers") Then
        ' Do some task
    End If
End If
```

Visual C#

```
SecurityCallContext scc;
bool SecEn;
scc = SecurityCallContext.CurrentCall();
SecEn = scc.IsSecurityEnabled();
if (SecEn)
{
    if (scc.IsCallerInRole("Managers"))
    {
        // Do some task
    }
}
```

SecurityCallers Collection

The SecurityCallers collection represents callers that can be retrieved by using an index between 0 and NumCallers minus 1. A SecurityIdentity object represents each caller. Table 3.5 lists the collections of properties available from the Security-Identity object.

Table 3.5   SecurityIdentity Properties

Property	Contains information about
AccountName	The account name of the caller.
AuthenticationService	The authentication service used. For example, Kerberos or Secure Sockets Layer (SSL).
AuthenticationLevel	The authentication level used. This level represents the level of protection during object communication.
ImpersonationLevel	The level of impersonation set by the client. This level represents the amount of authority granted to the server by the client.

You can programmatically add roles to an application and associate the roles with components by applying the SecurityRoleAttribute attribute to a class. Security-RoleAttribute is derived from the System.EnterpriseServices.ServicedComponent class. When you apply SecurityRoleAttribute to a component, this attribute ensures that the role exists in the application configuration and associates the target component with the role.

You can use the SetEveryoneAccess property to set a value specifying whether to add the Everyone users group as a user. If the SetEveryoneAccess property is set to True, the role Everyone is added as a member. The default value of this property is False, which means there are no users assigned to the role. The following code illustrates the use of the SecurityRole attribute and the SetEveryoneAccess property.

Visual Basic .NET

```
<SecurityRole("Authorized Users", True|False)>
Public Class MyClass
    .
    .
    .

End Class
```

Visual C#

```
[SecurityRole("Authorized Users", true|false)]
public class MyClass
{
    .
    .
    .

}
```

Inspecting Role Memberships

You can call the IsCallerInRole method of the SecurityCallContext class to determine the role membership of an object caller or direct caller. This functionality ensures that a certain block of code is not executed unless the caller is a member of a particular role. For example, you can use the SecurityCallContext.IsCallerInRole method to restrict access to certain bank information to bank managers only. The following example illustrates the use of the IsCallerInRole method of the SecurityCallContext class to verify the membership of a caller in a particular role.

Visual Basic .NET

```
Dim scc as SecurityCallContext
scc = SecurityCallContext.CurrentCall
If (scc.IsCallerInRole("BankManagers")) Then
    ' Continue with the transaction.
Else
    ' Display an error message.
End If
```

Visual C#

```
SecurityCallContext scc;
scc = SecurityCallContext.CurrentCall;

if (scc.IsCallerInRole("BankManagers"))
    // Continue with the transaction.
else
    // Display an error message.
```

Interoperability Between COM+ Security Services and the .NET Framework

The .NET Framework allows managed applications to interoperate with existing COM+ applications. This support for interoperability also extends to the security services. The security in COM+ 1.0 applications is managed and configured by the security context and the Component Services tool, respectively. Tools such as Tlbexp.exe help to make the .NET Framework objects visible to the COM+ 1.0 objects. The Tlbexp.exe tool generates a type library for the public interface and registers the objects, which are also part of the creation and registration of serviced components. After registration, the .NET Framework objects are visible to the COM+ 1.0 administrative utility and can be configured for the implementation of role-based security.

The security interoperability between COM+ 1.0 applications and the .NET Framework exhibits some limitations. The COM+ 1.0 properties are not transmitted across process boundaries, computer boundaries, or into the newly created execution threads of managed code. Therefore, you can implement COM+ 1.0 security services only in the managed code of Windows 2000 systems.

Summary

- COM+ is an extension of the COM programming model. COM+ is based on the Windows DNA architecture and provides a set of services that make application development easy. The built-in services of COM+ handle tasks related to the technological infrastructure so that the developer is able to concentrate on solving application level business problems.

- A .NET component that uses available component services of COM+ is called a serviced component. You create a serviced component by defining a class that derives from the ServicedComponent base class.

- A serviced component can access the component services of COM+ after you register the serviced component. You can register serviced components manually, dynamically, or programmatically. You can then manage and configure serviced components using the Component Services tool.

- You need to complete a few steps to run a .NET component under COM+ services. You have to create a class that derives from the System.Enterprise-Services.ServicedComponent class. The System.EnterpriseServices.Serviced-Component base class gives you the appropriate methods and properties to interact with COM+ services.

- You can configure a COM+ application and its components programmatically by adding attributes to your code. You can directly modify the properties of a COM+ application and its components by using the Component Services administrative tool.

- When you have many users making calls to components that run under COM+, you need to verify that only specific people have access to component resources. COM+ allows you to define roles and assign users to those roles. After defining roles, you can assign those roles to components. Assigning roles to components determines which role can run a certain component. You can apply the same role to determine the methods on the components that can be run.

Lab: Creating, Configuring, and Managing Serviced Components

In this lab, you will create a serviced component and a client of the serviced component. You will also manage the serviced component using the Component Services tool. The solutions to the exercises in this lab can be found in the \Solution folder on the Supplemental Course Materials CD-ROM.

Estimated lab time: 60 minutes

Exercise 1: Creating a Serviced Component

In this exercise, you will create a serviced component called Account that inherits from the ServicedComponent class. The Account class is a simulation of a bank account. It has attributes to store values for an account ID and account balance. The Account class also provides methods to transfer amounts from one account to another. The Account class transfers money from one account to another according to the following rule:

> If money is transferred from account A to account B, the remaining balance in account A after the transaction should not be below 5000, and the new balance in account B should not exceed 25000. A transfer is successful only when both conditions are satisfied.

The Account class also provides methods to obtain the balance of an account as well as obtain the IDs of all accounts. The Account class accesses a Microsoft SQL Server database to save and manipulate the account information. You will create an Accounts table in the Northwind database by running a script.

The Account component will be configured to use automatic transaction processing, object pooling, JIT activation, object construction, and role-based security services.

Note   This exercise contains code to perform database operations. The functionality of these statements is explained using in-line comments in the code. Accessing a database using ADO.NET is covered in detail in Chapter 5, "Database Programming Using ADO.NET," and Chapter 6, "Accessing and Manipulating XML Data." In this exercise, you need to focus on the code segments and the attributes that are used to define the behavior of the serviced component.

To create the Account class, open Visual Studio .NET and complete the following steps:

1. From the File menu, choose New Project.
2. Select Visual Basic Projects or Visual C# Projects from the Project Types pane, and select Class Library from the Templates pane.

3. Type **BankAccounts** in the Name field and click OK.

4. In Solution Explorer, delete Class1.vb or Class1.cs from the BankAccounts project.

5. From the shortcut menu of the project in Server Explorer or from the File menu, choose Add New Item.

6. Select Class from the Templates pane, type **Account.vb** or **Account.cs** in the Name field, and click Open.

7. Right-click the BankAccounts project, and select Add Reference from the shortcut menu. Select System.EnterpriseServices and System.Windows.Forms.dll (for Visual C# code only) from the .NET tab in the Add Reference dialog box. Click OK to add the references to the BankAccounts project.

8. Modify the code for the Account class as shown in the following code.

Visual Basic .NET

```
' Account
Imports System.EnterpriseServices
Imports System
Imports System.Reflection
Imports System.Data
Imports System.Data.SqlClient

<Assembly: AssemblyKeyFile("..\..\MyKey.snk")>

<Transaction(TransactionOption.Required), ObjectPooling(MinPoolSize:=1, _
    MaxPoolSize:=5), JustInTimeActivation(True), _
    SecurityRole("Authorized Users", False), _
    ConstructionEnabled([Default]:= _
    "server=localhost; integrated security=sspi; database=Northwind")> _
Public Class Account
    Inherits ServicedComponent
    ' Member that stores the connection string value
    Private connectionString As String

    Protected Overrides Sub Construct(ByVal constructString As String)
        ' Called after constructor
        ' connectionString can be configured from the Activation tab
        ' in the Properties window of the Account component
        connectionString = constructString
    End Sub

    ' Method to create an account
    ' AutoComplete ensures that transaction is committed when the
    ' method returns normally, else the transaction is rolled back
    <AutoComplete()> _
    Public Sub createAccount(ByVal id As Integer, ByVal amt As Integer)
```

```vb
        ' Create the connection object to the database server
        Dim conn As New SqlConnection(connectionString)
        ' SQL Statement to be executed
        Dim stmt As String = "insert into accounts values(" & id & "," & _
            amt & ")"
        ' SQL command to be executed over the connection
        ' SQL command encapsulates the SQL Statement
        Dim command As New SqlCommand(stmt, conn)
        ' Open the connection before executing the command
        conn.Open()
        ' Execute the command
        command.ExecuteNonQuery()
        ' Close the connection
        conn.Close()
End Sub

' Method to transfer the amount from one account to another
' AutoComplete ensures that transaction is committed when the
' method returns normally, else the transaction is rolled back
<AutoComplete()> _
Public Sub transferMoney(ByVal fromAccount As Integer, _
    ByVal toAccount _
    As Integer, ByVal amt As Integer)
    ' Create a connection to the database server
    Dim conn As New SqlConnection(connectionString)
    ' Update the balance in the account from which the balance is
    ' transferred
    Dim stmt As String = "update accounts set bal=bal-" & amt & _
        " where id =" & fromAccount
    Dim command As New SqlCommand(stmt, conn)
    conn.Open()
    command.ExecuteNonQuery()

    ' Update the balance in the account to which the balance is
    ' transferred
    stmt = "update accounts set bal=bal+" & amt & " where id =" & _
        toAccount
    command = New SqlCommand(stmt, conn)
    command.ExecuteNonQuery()

    ' Retrieve the new balances
    Dim fromBal As Integer = getBal(fromAccount)
    Dim toBal As Integer = getBal(toAccount)

    ' Ensure that fromBal>=5000 and toBal<=25000
    If fromBal >= 5000 And toBal <= 25000 Then
        MsgBox("Money Transferred successfully!")
        conn.Close()
```

(continued)

```vb
            Else
                'if any of the condition is not fulfilled
                'close the connection and throw an Exception
                conn.Close()
                Throw New Exception("Can not transfer money!")
                ' This aborts the transaction
            End If
            ' Method returns normally and transaction is committed automatically
        End Sub

        ' Method to get balance in an account
        Public Function getBal(ByVal id As Integer) As Integer
            ' Create connection object to the database server
            Dim conn As New SqlConnection(connectionString)
            Dim stmt As String = "select bal from accounts where id=" & id
            ' Create the command object to execute over the connection
            Dim Command As New SqlCommand(stmt, conn)
            ' Open the connection
            conn.Open()
            ' Execute a query that returns only one scalar value
            ' and assign the value to an int variable
            getBal = CType(Command.ExecuteScalar(), Integer)
            ' close the connection
            conn.Close()
        End Function

        ' Method to get the ids of all accounts in the Accounts table
        Public Function getAccountIds() As ArrayList
            Dim conn As New SqlConnection(connectionString)
            Dim stmt As String = "select id from accounts "
            Dim Command As New SqlCommand(stmt, conn)
            conn.Open()
            '   ExecuteReader method returns a SQLDataReader
            '   that allows you to sequentially read data from a table
            Dim dr As SqlClient.SqlDataReader = Command.ExecuteReader
            ' Create an ArrayList object to store id values
            Dim ids As New ArrayList()
            ' Add values to the ArrayList object
            While dr.Read
                ids.Add(dr.GetValue(0))
            End While
            conn.Close()
            Return ids
        End Function
End Class
```

Visual C#

```csharp
using System;
using System.Reflection;
using System.Data;
```

```csharp
using System.Data.SqlClient;
using System.EnterpriseServices;
using System.Collections;
using System.Windows.Forms;

[assembly: AssemblyKeyFile("..\\..\\MyKey.snk")]
// Delete the AssemblyKeyFile attribute from the AssemblyInfo.cs file
// that Visual Studio .NET creates automatically
namespace BankAccounts
{
    [Transaction(TransactionOption.Required), ObjectPooling(MinPoolSize =1,
        MaxPoolSize =5),
        JustInTimeActivation(true), SecurityRole("Authorized Users", false),
        ConstructionEnabled(Default =
        "server=localhost; integrated security=sspi; database=Northwind")]
    public class Account : ServicedComponent
    {
        // Member that stores the connection string value
        private String connectionString;

        public Account()
        {
        }

        protected override void Construct(string constructString)
        {
            // Called after constructor.
            // connectionString can be configured from the Activation tab
            // in the Properties window of the Account component
            connectionString=constructString;
        }

        // Method to create an account
        // AutoComplete ensures that transaction is committed when the
        // method returns normally, else the transaction is rolled back
        [AutoComplete()]
        public void createAccount(int id ,int amt)
        {
            // Create the connection object to the database server
            SqlConnection conn = new SqlConnection(connectionString);
            // SQL Statement to be executed
            string stmt = "insert into accounts values(" + id + "," +
                amt + ")";
            // SQL command to be executed over the connection
            // SQL command encapsulates the SQL Statement
            SqlCommand command = new SqlCommand(stmt, conn);
            // Open the connection before executing the command
            conn.Open();
```

(continued)

```
    // Execute the command
    command.ExecuteNonQuery();
    // Close the connection
    conn.Close();
}


// Method to transfer the amount from one account to another
// AutoComplete ensures that transaction is committed when the
// method returns normally, else the transaction is rolled back
[AutoComplete()]
public void transferMoney(int fromAccount, int toAccount, int amt)
{
    // Create a connection to the database server
    SqlConnection conn =new SqlConnection(connectionString);

    // Update the balance in the account from which the balance is
    // transferred
    string stmt  = "update accounts set bal=bal-" + amt +
        " where id =" + fromAccount;
    SqlCommand command = new SqlCommand(stmt, conn);
    conn.Open();
    command.ExecuteNonQuery();

    // Update the balance in the account to which the balance is
    //transferred
    stmt = "update accounts set bal=bal+" + amt +
        " where id =" + toAccount;
    command = new SqlCommand(stmt, conn);
    command.ExecuteNonQuery();

    // Retrieve the new balances in the accounts involved in the
    // transfer
    int fromBal  = getBal(fromAccount);
    int toBal  = getBal(toAccount);

    // Ensure that fromBal>=5000 and toBal<=25000
    if (fromBal >= 5000 && toBal <= 25000)
    {
        MessageBox.Show ("Money Transferred successfully!");
        conn.Close();
    }

    else
    {
        // if any of the condition is not fulfilled
        // close the connection and throw an Exception
        conn.Close();
        throw new Exception("Can not transfer money!");
```

```
        // This aborts the transaction
    }

    // Method returns normally and transaction is committed
    // automatically
}

// Method to get balance in an account
public int getBal(int id )
{
    // Create connection object to the database server
    SqlConnection  conn = new SqlConnection(connectionString);
    string stmt  = "select bal from accounts where id=" + id;
    // Create the command object to execute over the connection
    SqlCommand Command = new SqlCommand(stmt, conn);
    // Open the connection
    conn.Open();
    // Execute a query that returns only one scalar value
    // and assign the value to an int variable
    int bal=(int)Command.ExecuteScalar();
    // close the connection
    conn.Close();
    return  bal;
}

// Method to get the ids of all accounts in the Accounts table
public ArrayList getAccountIds()
{
    SqlConnection conn = new SqlConnection(connectionString);
    string stmt = "select id from accounts ";
    SqlCommand Command = new SqlCommand(stmt, conn);
    conn.Open();
    // ExecuteReader method returns a SQLDataReader
    // that allows you to sequentially read data from a table
    SqlDataReader dr = Command.ExecuteReader();
    // Create an ArrayList object to store id values
    ArrayList ids= new ArrayList();
    // Add values to the ArrayList object
    while (dr.Read())
    {
        ids.Add(dr.GetValue(0));
    }

    conn.Close();
    return ids;
    }
  }
}
```

> **Note**   Before compiling the code, you need to create the MyKey.snk file using the Sn.exe tool and save it in the application's folder.

9. From the Build menu, choose Build Project to build your project.

Exercise 2: Creating the Client Application

In this exercise, you will create a Windows application that you will use to communicate with the Account component you created in the previous exercise. To create the client application, complete the following steps:

1. From the File menu, choose New Project.
2. Select Visual Basic Projects or Visual C# Projects from the Project Types pane and select Windows Application from the Templates pane.
3. Type **TransactionApp** in the Name field and click OK.
4. Change the name of Form1.vb or Form1.cs to TransactionForm.vb or TransactionForm.cs.
5. In the design view, change the Name property of Form1 to TransactionForm and the Text property to Transaction Form.
6. Add labels, text boxes, combo boxes, buttons, and group boxes to the TransactionForm, and set Text properties so that the form looks as shown here.

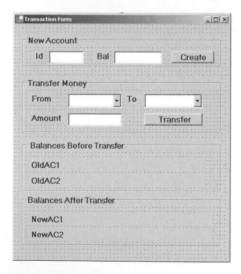

7. Set the Name properties of the buttons to createbtn and transferbtn.
8. Set the Name properties of the combo boxes to fromcbx and tocbx.
9. Set the Name properties of the labels having the Text properties OldAC1, OldAC2, NewAC1, and NewAC2 to OldAC1, OldAC2, NewAC1, and NewAC2, respectively.

10. Add the following code to the TransactionForm class.

Visual Basic .NET

```vbnet
Imports System.Data
Imports System.Data.SqlClient
Imports System.Collections

Public Class TransactionForm
    Inherits System.Windows.Forms.Form

    Private account As BankAccounts.Account

    Private Sub createbtn_Click(ByVal sender As System.Object, ByVal e _
        As System.EventArgs) Handles createbtn.Click
        Try
            account.createAccount(CInt(Idtbx.Text), CInt(baltbx.Text))
            load_Combos()
            MsgBox("Account created successfully!")
        Catch ex As Exception
            MsgBox(ex.Message)
        End Try
    End Sub

    Private Sub TransactionForm_Load(ByVal sender As System.Object, _
        ByVal e As System.EventArgs) Handles MyBase.Load
        account = New BankAccounts.Account()
        load_Combos()
    End Sub

    Private Sub load_Combos()
        fromcbx.Items.Clear()
        tocbx.Items.Clear()
        Dim accounts As ArrayList = account.getAccountIds()

        If accounts.Count <> 0 Then
            Dim enumerator As IEnumerator = accounts.GetEnumerator
            While enumerator.MoveNext
                fromcbx.Items.Add(enumerator.Current())
                tocbx.Items.Add(enumerator.Current())
            End While

            fromcbx.SelectedItem = fromcbx.Items.Item(0)
            tocbx.SelectedItem = fromcbx.Items.Item(0)
        End If
    End Sub
```

(continued)

```vb
    Private Sub transferbtn_Click(ByVal sender As System.Object, ByVal e _
        As System.EventArgs) Handles transferbtn.Click
        Try
            showOldBalances()
            account.transferMoney(CInt(fromcbx.Items.Item( _
                fromcbx.SelectedIndex)), CInt(tocbx.Items.Item( _
                tocbx.SelectedIndex)), CInt(amounttbx.Text))
        Catch ex As Exception
            MsgBox(ex.Message)
        Finally
            showNewBalances()
            amounttbx.Text = ""
        End Try

    End Sub

    Private Sub showOldBalances()
        Try
            OldAC1.Text = "Account Id: " & fromcbx.Items.Item( _
                fromcbx.SelectedIndex) & "          Balance " & _
                account.getBal(CInt(fromcbx.Items.Item( _
                fromcbx.SelectedIndex)) ).ToString
            OldAC2.Text = "Account Id: " & tocbx.Items.Item( _
                tocbx.SelectedIndex) & "          Balance " & _
                account.getBal(CInt(tocbx.Items.Item( _
                tocbx.SelectedIndex))).ToString
        Catch
        End Try
    End Sub

    Private Sub showNewBalances()
        Try
            NewAC1.Text = "Account Id: " & fromcbx.Items.Item( _
                fromcbx.SelectedIndex) & "          Balance " & _
                account.getBal(CInt(fromcbx.Items.Item( _
                fromcbx.SelectedIndex))).ToString
            NewAC2.Text = "Account Id: " & tocbx.Items.Item( _
                tocbx.SelectedIndex) & "          Balance " & _
                account.getBal(CInt(tocbx.Items.Item( _
                tocbx.SelectedIndex))).ToString
        Catch
        End Try
    End Sub

    Private Sub fromcbx_SelectedIndexChanged(ByVal sender As System.Object, _
        ByVal e As System.EventArgs) Handles fromcbx.SelectedIndexChanged
        showOldBalances()
        clearNewBalances()
```

```
        End Sub

        Private Sub tocbx_SelectedIndexChanged(ByVal sender As System.Object, _
            ByVal e As System.EventArgs) Handles tocbx.SelectedIndexChanged
            showOldBalances()
            clearNewBalances()
        End Sub

        Public Sub clearNewBalances()
            NewAC1.Text = ""
            NewAC2.Text = ""
        End Sub
End Class
```

Visual C#

```csharp
using System;
using System.Drawing;
using System.Collections;
using System.ComponentModel;
using System.Windows.Forms;
using System.Data;
using BankAccounts;

namespace TransactionApp
{
    public class TransactionForm : System.Windows.Forms.Form
    {
        private BankAccounts.Account account;

        private void createbtn_Click(object sender, System.EventArgs e)
        {
            try
            {
                account.createAccount(Convert.ToInt32(Idtbx.Text),
                    Convert.ToInt32(baltbx.Text));
                load_Combos();
                MessageBox.Show ("Account created successfully!");
            }
            catch (Exception ex)
            {
                MessageBox.Show (ex.Message);
            }
        }

        private void transferbtn_Click(object sender, System.EventArgs e)
        {
            try
```

(continued)

```
        {
            showOldBalances();
            account.transferMoney(Convert.ToInt32(
                fromcbx.SelectedItem.ToString() ),Convert.ToInt32(
                tocbx.SelectedItem.ToString()), Convert.ToInt32(
                amounttbx.Text));
        }
        catch (Exception ex)
        {
            MessageBox.Show(ex.Message);
        }
        finally
        {
            showNewBalances();
            amounttbx.Text = "";
        }
    }

    private void showOldBalances()
    {
        try
        {
            OldAC1.Text = "Account Id: " +
                fromcbx.SelectedItem.ToString()
                + "          Balance " + account.getBal(Convert.ToInt32(
                fromcbx.SelectedItem.ToString())).ToString();
            OldAC2.Text = "Account Id: " +
                tocbx.SelectedItem.ToString() +
                "          Balance " + account.getBal(Convert.ToInt32(
                tocbx.SelectedItem.ToString())).ToString();
        }
        catch{}
    }

    private void showNewBalances()
    {
        try
        {
            NewAC1.Text = "Account Id: " +
                fromcbx.SelectedItem.ToString() +
                "          Balance " + account.getBal(Convert.ToInt32(
                fromcbx.SelectedItem.ToString() )).ToString();
            NewAC2.Text = "Account Id: " +
                tocbx.SelectedItem.ToString() +
                "          Balance " + account.getBal(Convert.ToInt32(
                tocbx.SelectedItem.ToString() )).ToString();
        }
        catch{}
    }
```

```csharp
private void fromcbx_SelectedIndexChanged(object sender,
    System.EventArgs e)
{

    showOldBalances();
    clearNewBalances();
}

private void tocbx_SelectedIndexChanged(object sender,
    System.EventArgs e)
{
    showOldBalances();
    clearNewBalances();
}

public void clearNewBalances()
{
    NewAC1.Text = "";
    NewAC2.Text = "";
}

private void TransactionForm_Load(object sender,
    System.EventArgs e)
{

    account = new BankAccounts.Account();
    load_Combos();
}

private void load_Combos()
{
    fromcbx.Items.Clear();
    tocbx.Items.Clear();
    ArrayList accounts  = account.getAccountIds();
    if (accounts.Count != 0)
    {
        IEnumerator enumerator  = accounts.GetEnumerator();
        while (enumerator.MoveNext())
        {
            fromcbx.Items.Add(enumerator.Current );
            tocbx.Items.Add(enumerator.Current);
        }
        fromcbx.SelectedIndex=0;
        tocbx.SelectedIndex =0;
    }
}
    }
}
```

11. Right-click on the TransactionApp project, and select Add Reference from the shortcut menu to open the Add Reference dialog box. From the Projects tab, add a reference to the BankAccounts project. Also, for the C# project, add a reference to System.EnterpriseServices from the .NET tab.

12. From the Build menu, choose Build Project to build the project.

Before running the application, you need to create the Accounts table in the Northwind database, which we will do in Exercise 3.

Note   The next exercise requires access to Microsoft SQL Server.

Exercise 3: Creating the Accounts Table

From the Start menu, locate Microsoft SQL Server and open Query Analyzer. Connect to a SQL server using the Connect To SQL Server dialog box. The Connect To SQL Server dialog box and the Query Analyzer window are shown here.

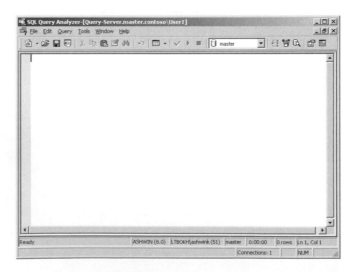

Select the Northwind database from the list of databases. Execute the following script to create the Accounts table.

SQL Script

```
if exists (select * from dbo.sysobjects where id = object_id(
N'[dbo].[Accounts]') and OBJECTPROPERTY(id, N'IsUserTable') = 1)
drop table [dbo].[Accounts]
GO

if not exists (select * from dbo.sysobjects where id = object_id(
N'[dbo].[Accounts]') and OBJECTPROPERTY(id, N'IsUserTable') = 1)
 BEGIN
CREATE TABLE [dbo].[Accounts] (
    [id] [int] NOT NULL ,
    [bal] [int] NULL
) ON [PRIMARY]
END

GO

ALTER TABLE [dbo].[Accounts] WITH NOCHECK ADD
    CONSTRAINT [PK_Accounts] PRIMARY KEY  CLUSTERED
    (
        [id]
    )  ON [PRIMARY]
GO
```

Exercise 4: Configuring Serviced Components Using the Component Services Tool

In this exercise, you will dynamically register the Accounts component and configure it using the Component Services tool.

1. Run the TransactionApp application in Visual Studio .NET.

2. The TransactionForm_Load method creates an instance of the BankAccounts.Account object and calls the load_Combos() method. The load_Combos() method calls the getAccountIds() method, and the dynamic registration of the Account object starts.

3. Create the accounts and transfer an amount from one account to another. See what happens when you enter a duplicate account ID. Also, verify that if money is transferred from account A to account B, the remaining balance in account A after the transaction is not below 5000, and the new balance in account B does not exceed 25000.

4. From the Administrative Tools folder, open the Component Services tool. Under Component Services, locate the BankAccounts application.

5. Right-click the BankAccounts application and choose Properties from the shortcut menu. Select the Security tab, and then select the Enforce Access Checks For This Application check box. Select the Perform Process Checks At The Process And Component Level option. Click OK.

6. Under the BankAccounts application, expand the Components node, and view the properties for the BankAccount.Account component. Examine properties such as transaction, object pooling, and object construction. What is the default value of the constructor string?

7. On the Security tab of the BankAccounts.Account Properties dialog box, select the Enforce Component Level Access Checks option. What role is created for the BankAccounts application?

8. Add users to the Authorized Users role. These users will have access to the BankAccount.Account component.

9. Run TransactionApp.exe using a user account that is not included in the Authorized Users role. What error do you receive?

Review

The questions in this section reinforce key information presented in this chapter. If you are unable to answer a question, review the appropriate lesson, and then try answering the question again. Answers to the questions can be found in Appendix A, "Questions and Answers."

1. How is COM+ related to the DNA architecture?

2. Briefly explain the use of the following COM+ services:
   - JIT activation
   - Queued components
   - Object pooling

3. What is a serviced component?

4. Which class do you need to define when creating serviced components?

5. How do you assign a name and ID to a COM+ application?

6. What is the importance of the activation type attribute in the registration of a serviced component?

7. Which tool is used to add a strong name to an assembly?

8. Which procedures can be used to register serviced components?

9. How do you configure a serviced component for implementation of role-based security at the interface level?

10. The following is the code for a transaction component. Add the appropriate attribute to the Public class to have the component participate in a transaction. In addition, add the appropriate attribute to continue with the transaction or abort the transaction based on the occurrence of exceptions.

Visual Basic .NET

```
Imports System.EnterpriseServices
Imports System.Reflection

' Providing a name for the COM+ application
<Assembly: ApplicationNameAttribute("MyFirstComPlusExample")>

' Providing a strong-name for the assembly
<Assembly: AssemblyKeyFileAttribute("bin/MyFirstComPlusExample.snk")>

 Public Class MyFirstCOMPlusServices
    Inherits ServicedComponent

    Public Sub New()
        MyBase.New()
    End Sub

    Public Function DoTransaction() _
     As String
        Return "SUCCESSFUL"
    End Function
End Class
```

Visual C#

```
using System.EnterpriseServices;
using System.Reflection;

//Providing a name for the COM+ application
[assembly: ApplicationNameAttribute("MyFirstComPlusExample")]

//Providing a strong-name for the assembly
[assembly: AssemblyKeyFileAttribute("bin/MyFirstComPlusExample.snk")]

public class MyFirstCOMPlusServices :ServicedComponent
{

    public  MyFirstCOMPlusServices()
    {
    }

    public string DoTransaction()
```

```
        {
            return "SUCCESSFUL";
        }
}
```

11. Write the code for implementing role-based security at the component level. In the code, add a new method to a class called IsSeniorLecturer to check whether the user is a member of the role IsSeniorLecturer.

C H A P T E R   4

Creating and Consuming .NET Remoting Objects

About This Chapter

Distributed applications help to establish communication between objects running in different processes located on the same computer or located on computers at different geographic locations. The .NET Framework provides a set of classes and methods that allow you to establish a connection and communicate between objects with ease.

With earlier programming infrastructures, creating a distributed application required an in-depth knowledge of the transmission protocols used in the communication process. Using the .NET Framework, you can establish communication between objects without having to know about the protocols or about the encoding and decoding mechanisms involved in the development of a distributed application. In this chapter, you will learn to create, configure, and secure .NET Remoting objects by using the classes that the .NET Framework provides.

Before You Begin

To complete the lessons in this chapter, you

- Must have knowledge of basic programming in Microsoft Visual Basic .NET and Microsoft Visual C#
- Must have a basic knowledge of distributed programming

Lesson 1: Understanding .NET Remoting

You can use .NET Remoting to enable communication between different applications regardless of whether they reside on the same computer or on different computers. These computers can be part of the same network or part of networks in different geographic locations across the world. In addition, these computers can run different operating systems and still communicate with each other using .NET Remoting.

After this lesson, you will be able to

- Explain .NET Remoting
- Identify various methods of accessing objects across remoting boundaries
- Describe the .NET Remoting architecture
- Identify remotable and nonremotable objects

Estimated lesson time: 35 minutes

Overview of .NET Remoting

Consider the following example: You have created a pocket PC application using Visual C# running on Microsoft Windows CE to access the latest sales data from a Microsoft Windows 2000 Server computer that is not part of the same network. A server component that exports this data to the pocket PC application is created using Microsoft Visual Basic 6.0. This server component retrieves relevant data from a Microsoft SQL Server 2000 database. This is a very common scenario today where you can access information anytime, anywhere, on any device. In this scenario, the applications can easily communicate with one another using the .NET Remoting classes provided by the .NET Framework.

The .NET Remoting system provides a number of services to activate objects, control the lifetime of each object, and transport messages to and from remote objects using communication channels. *Communication channels* are the objects that transport messages between the remote objects. Communication channels are covered in detail in Lesson 3. Any message that is sent along a communication channel is encoded and decoded using native .NET serialization formatters, such as binary and SOAP. *Serialization formatters* are the objects that help you to encode and decode messages that are sent to or received from a remote object. Two kinds of encoding are possible for all messages: binary and XML encoding. Applications in which performance is critical use binary encoding. In cases where interoperability with other remoting systems is essential, XML encoding is the preferred choice.

The .NET Remoting system enables you to perform communication between different objects in different application domains or processes using different transportation protocols, such as HTTP and TCP/IP; serialization formats, such as binary or SOAP; object lifetime schemes; and modes of object creation.

Accessing Objects Across Remoting Boundaries

The .NET Remoting system allows clients to call methods on objects across remoting boundaries. Remoting boundaries include application domains, processes, and computers. An application domain, as discussed in Chapter 1, "Understanding the .NET Framework," is the boundary within which an application runs. More than one application domain can run in a single process. Communication between objects across the remoting boundaries requires

- A server object that exposes the functionality to callers outside its boundary
- A client that makes calls to the server object
- A transportation mechanism to pass the calls from one end to the other

To access objects and call methods on them, you need pointers or references to those objects. However, accessing objects across remoting boundaries is difficult because addresses are process dependent. Addresses in one process do not have any meaning in a different process. To handle this problem, you can use a copy of the server object in the client application. The client can then call a method on the local copy of the server object.

When you are copying objects to the client process, make sure that the objects do not contain a large number of methods, and that the objects are not large in size. Extremely large objects with many methods can be poor choices for copying or passing by value to other processes because the client requires only the values returned by one or a few methods of the server object. Copying an entire server object to the client process is a waste of client resources, which include bandwidth, memory, and processing time. In addition, many server objects expose public functionality but require private data on the server for internal execution.

Warning   When you copy server objects, you might enable malicious clients to examine internal server data, creating the potential for security problems.

It is also inadvisable to copy objects, such as a FileInfo object, to the client process because a FileInfo object contains a reference to an operating system file, which has a unique address in the memory of the server process. You can copy this address along with the object, but the address is process-specific and will not work in another process. In this situation, you pass the server object as a reference to the client application. The client application uses this reference to call methods on the server object. The remoting system handles the method call and sends it to the server object. After the method is executed, the result is returned to the client application.

The .NET Remoting Architecture

To communicate between server objects and clients in .NET Remoting, you need to use object references of the server object in the client application. When you create an instance of the remote object using the *new* keyword, your client receives a reference to the server object. After obtaining the object reference, the client can call methods on the server object as if the object resides in the client's process and does not run on a separate computer.

.NET Remoting uses proxy objects to allow the use of the server object in the client process. When you create an instance of the remote object type in the client application, .NET Remoting creates a proxy object and sends it to the client application. This proxy object contains references to all the methods and properties of the server object. When you call a method that is on that proxy object, the remoting system receives the call, routes it to the server process, invokes the server object, and returns the return value to the client proxy, which returns the result to the client application. Figure 4.1 shows how a client communicates with a remote object.

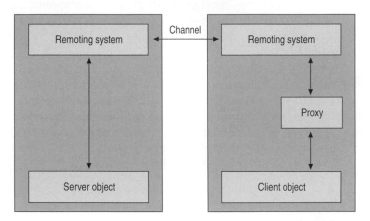

Figure 4.1   Communication between a client and a remote object

To create a remoting system to perform the preceding operations, you need to learn network programming and know about a wide array of protocols, such as TCP/IP and HTTP, and about serialization format specifications. However, in .NET Remoting, a combination of technologies performs the low-level tasks, such as opening a network connection, formatting messages, writing messages into streams, and sending bytes to the receiving application. This combination of technologies is known as the *transport channel*.

To understand the role of channels in .NET Remoting, consider the following example: You have an application running on one computer, and you want to use the functionality exposed by a type that is available on another computer. If you properly configure both the client and server objects, the client application only has to create a new instance of the server class.

The remoting system creates a proxy object that represents the class in the server and returns a reference of the proxy object to the client object. When a client calls any method on the remote object, the remoting system handles the method call, checks the type information, and sends the call over the channel to the server process. A listening channel receives the request from the client application and forwards it to the server remoting system. The server remoting system creates or locates the requested object and calls it. After the call is processed, the server remoting system creates a response message, and the server channel sends it to the client channel. The client remoting system then returns the result of the call to the client object through the proxy object. The role of channels is explained in detail in Lesson 3.

Remotable and Nonremotable Objects

In distributed applications, there are two categories of objects: remotable and nonremotable. Nonremotable objects do not provide the remoting system with a method to either copy them or use them in another application domain. Therefore, you can access these objects only in their own application domain. Remotable objects can either be accessed outside their application domain or context using a proxy or copied and passed outside their application domain or context. This implies that some remotable objects are passed by reference and some are passed by value. For example, if you have a large object with a number of methods, your best option is to make the object nonremotable. Then, create a remotable object that is small in size that can be published or copied to the client application. Use the remotable object to direct the call to the larger nonremotable object.

There are two types of remotable objects:

- **Marshal-by-value objects.**   These objects are copied and passed by value out of the application domain.
- **Marshal-by-reference objects.**   The clients that use these objects need a proxy to access the object remotely.

Marshal-by-Value Objects

Marshal-by-value objects should implement the ISerializable interface or should be marked with the SerializableAttribute attribute so that the remoting system can serialize these objects automatically. When the client calls a method on marshal-by-value objects, the remoting system creates a copy of these objects and passes the copy to the client application domain. After the client application receives the copy, the copy in the client application domain handles any method call. In addition, when marshal-by-value objects are passed as arguments, a copy of the object is passed to the method.

To improve performance and reduce processing time, move the complete state of the object and its functionality to the target application domain. Using marshal-by-value objects reduces time- and resource-consuming trips across network, process, and application domain boundaries. You also use marshal-by-value objects directly from within the original application domain of the object. In this case, access is efficient because marshaling does not take place.

Marshal-by-Reference Objects

Marshal-by-reference objects are remotable objects that extend the System.Marshal-ByRefObject class. When a client creates an instance of a marshal-by-reference object in its own application domain, the .NET Remoting infrastructure creates a proxy object in the caller application domain that represents the marshal-by-reference object and returns a reference of that proxy to the caller. The client then makes method calls to the proxy object. The remoting system marshals those calls, returns them to the server application domain, and invokes the call on the actual object.

Note   If the client is in the same application domain as the marshal-by-reference object, the infrastructure returns a direct reference to the marshal-by-reference object, avoiding the overhead of marshaling.

Before you create a distributed application, you should know the following:

- You can call an object created in a specific domain directly from that domain.
- If you need to call an object from a process outside its own application domain, you should publish the object. When you *publish* an object, you either copy the object to another application domain or create a proxy of the object in another application domain.
- If the size of the object is large or if it contains a large number of methods, the object can not be efficiently published or consumed across domain boundaries. Therefore, you must decide which type of object you want to publish based on the requirement of your application.

In this lesson, you learned about the basics of .NET Remoting, passing objects between processes, and the .NET Remoting architecture. In addition, you learned about remotable and nonremotable objects. You also learned about the marshal-by-value and marshal-by-reference objects.

In the next lesson, you will learn to create and activate objects. In addition, you will learn about the lifetimes of objects. You will also learn to control objects.

Lesson 2: Implementing Server-Activated and Client-Activated Objects

In the previous lesson, you learned about .NET Remoting and its architecture. As mentioned earlier, in .NET Remoting, there are server and client processes. To communicate with the server process, you use references of the server objects in the client application. In this lesson, you will learn how to create the server and client objects. You will also learn how to activate these objects and control the lease of these objects.

After this lesson, you will be able to

- Identify server- and client-activated objects
- Perform various modes of activation
- Control the lifetime leases of objects

Estimated lesson time: 40 minutes

Understanding Remote Object Activation

When you develop an object, you need not track the creation of the object. You only need to ensure that the object responds to the method calls. However, when you develop a remote object, you need to track the creation and initialization of the object because the way a remote object behaves depends on how the object is created and activated. You have to be aware of how remote objects are activated. You need to specify to the remoting system what type of activation is required on the objects before the remoting system provides these objects to the clients.

In the next two sections, you will learn about the two types of activation modes in the .NET Remoting system: server activation and client activation.

Server Activation

In server activation, objects are created on the server when you call a method in the server class. However, objects are not created when you use the *new* keyword to create an instance of the server class.

Consider the following example: The Social Security office has a service component that enables organizations, such as banks and apartment offices, to check the validity of a particular social security number (SSN). Clients connect to this service and provide the SSN of a person for validation. The service validates the number and returns the appropriate personal information. In this scenario, clients are always connected to the server at the Social Security office. The service is activated only when a method call arrives from the clients asking for the validation of an SSN. This is known as server activation. The following code displays server activation of objects.

Visual Basic .NET

```
Imports System.Runtime.Remoting
Public Class SSNServer
    Inherits MarshalByRefObject
    Public Function ValidateSSN(Byval number as Long) As String
        ' Return the address
        Dim address As String

        ' Do some work here to validate the SSN
        Return address
    End Function
End Class
```

Visual C#

```
using System;
using System.Runtime.Remoting;
namespace SSNComponentCSharp
{
    public class SSNServer : MarshalByRefObject
    {
        public SSNServer()
        {
        }
        public String ValidateSSN(long number)
        {
            // Return the address
            String address;

            // Do some work here to validate the SSN
            return address;
        }
    }
}
```

The preceding code displays a sample server object that takes a value of the long type value as a parameter and returns the corresponding address. The following code illustrates how to call the ValidateSSN method. Because this is in server-activation mode, the object is created only when you call the ValidateSSN method, not when you create an instance of the class.

Visual Basic .NET

```
Dim serverInstance as New SSNServer()
' Remote Object on the server is created in the next line
Console.WriteLine(serverInstance.ValidateSSN(242990307))
```

Visual C#

```
SSNServer serverInstance = new SSNServer();
// Remote Object on the server is created in the next line
Console.WriteLine(serverInstance.ValidateSSN(242990307));
```

You can create a server-activated object as a Singleton or SingleCall object based on the requirements of your remote application. Singleton objects can have only one instance regardless of the number of clients they have. These objects also have a default lifetime. Therefore, if you create a server object as a Singleton object, a single instance of the server object manages all the clients. When you declare an object as a SingleCall object, the remoting system creates an object each time a client method invokes a remote object. To register a server object as a Singleton object, you specify the type of the object as WellKnownObjectMode.Singleton. The following code shows how to specify an object as WellKnownObject-Mode.Singleton.

Visual Basic .NET

```
Imports System.Runtime.Remoting
Public Class SSNServer
    Inherits MarshalByRefObject
    Sub New()
        RemotingConfiguration.ApplicationName = "testService"
        RemotingConfiguration.RegisterWellKnownServiceType( _
            GetType(testService), "MyUri", _
            WellKnownObjectMode.Singleton)
        Console.WriteLine("Press Enter to Stop")
        Console.ReadLine()
    End Sub
End Class
Class testService
    'Service Component
End Class
```

Visual C#

```
using System;
using System.Runtime.Remoting;
using System.Runtime.Remoting.Channels;
using System.Runtime.Remoting.Channels.Tcp;

namespace SSNComponentCSharp
{
    public class SSNServer
    {
        public SSNServer()
        {
            RemotingConfiguration.ApplicationName = "testService";
            RemotingConfiguration.RegisterWellKnownServiceType(
                typeof(testService),
```

```
            "MyUri",WellKnownObjectMode.Singleton);
            Console.WriteLine("Press enter to stop.");
            Console.ReadLine();
        }
    }
}

class testService : MarshalByRefObject
{
    // Service Object Registered in the SSNServer class above.
}
```

Note   You need to add a reference to System.Runtime.Remoting to use the classes in the System.Runtime.Remoting.Channels.Tcp namespace.

To register a server object as a SingleCall object, you specify the type of the object as WellKnownObjectMode.SingleCall. The following code shows how to specify the type of an object as WellKnownObjectMode.SingleCall.

Visual Basic .NET

```
Imports System.Runtime.Remoting
Public Class SSNServer
    Inherits MarshalByRefObject
    Sub New()
        RemotingConfiguration.ApplicationName = "testService"
        RemotingConfiguration.RegisterWellKnownServiceType( _
            GetType(testService), "MyUri", _
            WellKnownObjectMode.SingleCall)
        Console.WriteLine("Press Enter to Stop")
        Console.ReadLine()
    End Sub
End Class
Class testService
    'Service Component
End Class
```

Visual C#

```
using System;
using System.Runtime.Remoting;
using System.Runtime.Remoting.Channels;
using System.Runtime.Remoting.Channels.Tcp;

namespace SSNComponentCSharp
{
    public class SSNServer
    {
        public SSNServer()
        {
```

(continued)

```
                    RemotingConfiguration.ApplicationName = "testService";
                    RemotingConfiguration.RegisterWellKnownServiceType(
                        typeof(testService),
                        "MyUri",WellKnownObjectMode.SingleCall);
                    Console.WriteLine("Press enter to stop.");
                    Console.ReadLine();
                }
            }
        }

        class testService : MarshalByRefObject
        {
            // Service Object Registered in the SSNServer class above.
        }
```

Client Activation

Client-activated objects are created on the server when you create an instance using the *new* keyword. For example, you can create a chat application that allows users to communicate with other users over an intranet. When a user logs on, a new instance of the chat server object is created. The default constructor of the chat server object contains the code to locate users who are currently online and displays it to the user who logs in. In this case, the remote object on the server will be created when you create the instance using the *new* keyword.

The client application domain defines the lifetimes of client-activated objects. These objects are present in the client application domain. In client activation, when the client tries to create an instance of the server object, a connection is made to the server, and the client proxy is created. The proxy object is created using an object reference, which is obtained after the remote object is created on the server. When a client creates a client-activated instance, the instance of the remote object serves a particular client until its lease expires and the garbage collector recycles its memory. The *lease* controls the time a remote object remains in memory. If a client creates two new instances of a remote object, each reference to the remote object invokes only the particular instance in the server application.

In COM, clients hold an object in memory by maintaining a reference to it. When the last COM client releases its last reference to an object, the object deletes itself. Client activation enables you to control the lifetime of the server object without maintaining references or constantly pinging to confirm the continued existence of the server or the client.

Client-activated objects use lifetime leases to determine the duration of their existence. When a client creates an object, it specifies a default duration for which the object should exist. If the remote object reaches the end of its default lifetime duration, the object contacts the client and asks whether it should continue to exist and for how long. If the client is not currently available, a default time limit is specified for which the server object waits while trying to contact the client before marking itself available for garbage collection. The client might even request an indefinite default lifetime, preventing the remote object from being recycled until the server application domain is torn down.

Note   The difference between a client-activated indefinite lifetime and a server-activated indefinite lifetime is that an indefinite server-activated object serves all client requests for that type, whereas the client-activated instances serve only the client and the references that are responsible for their creation.

Remoting Tasks

After learning about server- and client-activated objects, you can now turn your attention to the basic remoting tasks that are essential for establishing communication between a client and a remote object. You perform the following remoting tasks to publish any service outside the service domain:

- Identify the application domain that will host the service
- Identify the activation mode: server activation or client activation
- Identify and create a channel and a port
- Identify how the client application obtains the metadata information about the service

The host application domain can be a Windows Services, console application, Windows Forms application, or an XML Web service that use ASP.NET. After choosing an application domain for your service, you identify the activation mode for the service.

Once you have specified the activation mode and other relevant information such as the application name and the endpoints for the remoting system, you then configure your system using the configuration file. To configure a remote system, call the Configure method of the RemotingConfiguration class. The following code shows how to call the Configure method of the RemotingConfiguration class.

Visual Basic .NET

```
RemotingConfiguration.Configure("configuration.config")
```

Visual C#

```
RemotingConfiguration.Configure("configuration.config");
```

In the preceding code snippet, the Configuration.config file contains information on configuring the remoting system. You can also configure the remoting system programmatically. When you configure the remoting system programmatically, you do not require the configuration file.

Next, create the appropriate channel, TcpChannel or HttpChannel, and register it using the RegisterChannel method of the RemotingConfiguration class. If you use the configuration file to configure the remoting system, you can create the appropriate channel by simply loading the configuration file using the Remoting-Configuration.Configure method.

Finally, publish the service so that it is accessible from outside the domain. This enables the server application to function.

Using Lifetime Leases

The lifetime of a marshal-by-reference object is the duration for which the object resides in memory. A marshal-by-reference object stays in memory forever regardless of the type of the object. In other words, all marshal-by-reference server-activated and client-activated objects have a lifetime of their own. These objects are released from memory after the lifetime expires and the object is marked for garbage collection. The GC then removes the objects from memory.

The .NET Remoting system deletes an object only when it is marked as ready for garbage collection. The lifetime lease manager of the server application domain is responsible for determining the objects that are ready for garbage collection. However, a sponsor object can request a new lease for a particular object by registering itself with the lease manager.

Whenever a marshal-by-reference object is remoted outside an application domain, a lifetime lease is created for that object. Each application domain contains a *lease manager* that administers the leases in its domain. The lease manager periodically reviews the leases for expiration. If a lease expires, the lease manager goes through its list of sponsors for that object and asks if any of them want to renew the lease. If none of the sponsors renew the lease, the lease manager removes the lease. The object is then deleted, and garbage collection reclaims the object memory. The lifetime of an object can therefore be much longer than its lifetime lease.

Initializing Lifetime Leases

To initialize a lifetime lease, you override the InitializeLifetimeService function of the MarshalByRefObject class. The following is the syntax used to override the InitializeLifetimeService function.

Visual Basic .NET

```
Imports System.Runtime.Remoting.Lifetime
Public Class MyLifetimeControlObject
    Inherits MarshalByRefObject
    Public Overrides Function InitializeLifetimeService() As [Object]
        Dim lease As ILease = CType(MyBase.InitializeLifetimeService(), _
            ILease)
        If lease.CurrentState = LeaseState.Initial Then
            lease.InitialLeaseTime = TimeSpan.FromMinutes(2)
            lease.SponsorshipTimeout = TimeSpan.FromMinutes(3)
            lease.RenewOnCallTime = TimeSpan.FromSeconds(3)
```

```
            End If
            Return lease
        End Function
End Class
```

Visual C#

```csharp
using System;
using System.Runtime;
using System.Runtime.Remoting;
using System.Runtime.Remoting.Lifetime;

public class MyLifetimeControlObject: MarshalByRefObject
{
    public override object InitializeLifetimeService()
    {
        ILease lease = (ILease)base.InitializeLifetimeService();
        if (lease.CurrentState == LeaseState.Initial)
        {
            lease.InitialLeaseTime = TimeSpan.FromMinutes(2);
            lease.SponsorshipTimeout = TimeSpan.FromMinutes(3);
            lease.RenewOnCallTime = TimeSpan.FromSeconds(3);
        }
        return lease;
    }
}
```

Renewing Lifetime Leases

After you create a lifetime lease for an object, you can only change the Current-LeaseTime property of the lease object. The CurrentLeaseTime property returns the amount of time remaining on the lease. These are the two ways to renew a lease:

- A client application calls the ILease.Renew method.
- A sponsor renews the lease.

The following code shows how to renew a lease using a client application.

Visual Basic .NET

```vbnet
Dim obj As New RemoteType()
Dim lease As ILease = CType(RemotingServices.GetLifetimeService(obj), _
    ILease)
Dim expireTime As TimeSpan = lease.Renew(TimeSpan.FromSeconds(30))
```

Visual C#

```csharp
RemoteType obj = new RemoteType();
ILease lease = (ILease)RemotingServices.GetLifetimeService(obj);
TimeSpan expireTime = lease.Renew(TimeSpan.FromSeconds(30));
```

When you publish remote objects, you should know the members of the remote objects that are published. Clients can only access those members that the remote object publishes.

Scope of Publication

The .NET Remoting system exposes the functionality of server objects to client applications assuming that the objects are contained locally in the client application. However, there are some exceptions to the objects that are exported remotely. Table 4.1 provides details about various objects and how the .NET Remoting system manages these objects.

Table 4.1   Scope of Publication

Objects	Description
Static members	You cannot export static members, such as fields and methods, remotely. .NET Remoting needs instance members to enable communication between the client and server objects.
Instance fields and accessors	The .NET Remoting system checks whether the object that you use is exported as a proxy object. If it is a proxy object, the client can directly access instance fields through the proxy. If the exported object is not a proxy, the proxy object provides instance accessors to the client.
Private members	You cannot export private members of a remote object.
Delegates	Delegates are marshal-by-value objects. The object in delegates can be a remotable object, such as a serializable object, a MarshalByRef object, or a ContextBound object.
Overriding methods on an object	To enhance performance, the virtual methods on an object always execute locally in the application domain in which they are called.

In addition to the objects listed in Table 4.1, calls to Equals() and ToString() methods are executed in the remote object provided that these methods are overridden in the remote object. However, calls to GetHashCode() and MemberwiseClone() methods are executed locally.

In this lesson, you learned about server- and client-activated objects. You also learned to create Singleton and SingleCall objects, and to establish a connection between server and client applications. In addition, you identified the objects that cannot be exported as remote objects. You also learned about lifetime leases and how to initialize and renew the lifetime leases of objects. Finally, you learned about the scope of publication.

Lesson 3: Transporting Messages Across Application Domains Using Channels

Channels are the objects that remote objects use to communicate with each other. In this lesson, you will learn about the role of channels in transporting messages between remote objects. You will also learn how to use and configure channels.

After this lesson, you will be able to

- Describe channels and their role in transporting messages between remote objects
- Describe different types of channels
- Define the format in which messages are transported over a channel

Estimated lesson time: 60 minutes

Understanding Channels

Channels enable an application that is running in one application domain, process, or computer to send messages to an application running in a different application domain, process, or computer. In addition, channels allow applications to send and receive messages using various protocols, such as TCP and HTTP.

Channels work as message carriers between remoting boundaries, such as contexts, application domains, processes, and computers. A channel listens for messages at one remoting boundary and sends messages to another remoting boundary. The remoting boundaries at the end of channels constitute the channel endpoints. Before one remote object sends a message to another remote object, a channel converts the message into an appropriate format such as the XML or binary format. Before sending the message, the channel performs the necessary conversions.

Channel Interfaces

The .NET Framework provides the System.Runtime.Remoting.Channels namespace, which includes the interfaces and classes that you use to work with channels. All channels implement the IChannel interface. The IChannel interface provides properties such as ChannelName and ChannelPriority, which uniquely identify a channel and define the channel priority, respectively.

Depending on whether you use a channel to receive or send messages, channels are categorized as receiver or server and sender or client channels. A receiver or server channel implements the IChannelReceiver interface, and a sender or client channel implements the IChannelSender interface. The IChannelReceiver interface specifies methods, such as StartListening and StopListening, that must be implemented by a receiver channel class. The IChannelSender interface specifies a method, CreateMessageSink, which must be implemented by a sender or client channel class. The CreateMessageSink method creates and returns a message sink that the channel object uses to deliver messages to a remote object located at a specific URL. You will learn about sinks later in this lesson.

The HttpServerChannel and TcpServerChannel classes implement the IChannel-Receiver interface, whereas the HttpClientChannel and TcpClientChannel classes implement the IChannelSender interface. A channel can also implement the IChannelSender and IChannelReceiver interfaces, which enable the channel to send as well as receive messages. The HttpChannel and TcpChannel classes implement the IChannelSender and IChannelReceiver interfaces, which enable objects of these classes to send and receive messages. Table 4.2 shows various interfaces and their members that are implemented by the channel classes.

Table 4.2   Channel Interfaces

Channel	Description
Public properties of IChannel interface	
ChannelName	This property gets the name of the channel.
ChannelPriority	This property gets the priority of the channel. A higher number indicates a higher priority. The client channel with a higher priority gets the first chance to connect to a remote object. On the other hand, the priority in the case of server channels indicates the order in which the clients will use channels while connecting to the server objects.
Public methods of IChannel interface	
Parse	This method returns the Uniform Resource Identifier (URI) of the current channel and the object URI as an out parameter.
Public properties of IChannelReceiver interface	
ChannelData	This property gets the channel-specific data, which includes information about the object being remoted.
Public methods of IChannelReceiver interface	
StartListening	This method instructs a channel to start listening for client requests.
StopListening	This method instructs a channel to stop listening for client requests.
GetUrlsForUri	This method returns an array of all the URLs for a URI.
Public methods of IChannelSender interface	
CreateMessageSink	This method returns a message sink object that delivers messages to a specific URL or a channel data object.

Registering a Channel

Before one remote object sends messages to another remote object, you need to register a client channel with the remoting system. Similarly, to enable a remote component to receive messages, you need to register a server channel with the remoting infrastructure. To register channels with the remoting infrastructure, you use the ChannelServices class. The ChannelServices class provides static methods that enable you to register channels, resolve URLs, and discover remote objects using the object URLs. The RegisterChannel static method of the ChannelServices class allows you to register a channel with the remoting infrastructure. The following code shows how to register a TcpServerChannel method to listen at port 8010.

Visual Basic .NET

```
Dim channel as New TcpServerChannel(8010)
ChannelServices.RegisterChannel(channel)
```

Visual C#

```
TcpServerChannel channel = new TcpServerChannel(8010);
ChannelServices.RegisterChannel(channel);
```

After you register a channel on the client and server computers, the remote objects can call methods on each other. The next section explains how remote objects use channels to communicate across remoting boundaries.

Selecting Channels for Remoting

When a client object calls a method on a remote object, channels carry the parameters and other call-related information to the remote object. A client can use any of the channels registered on the client computer to call a method on the remote object. In addition, you can customize an existing channel or create a channel that uses a different transport protocol. You should apply the following rules when selecting channels for remote objects:

- A client cannot call a method on a remote object unless you register at least one client channel, such as TcpClientChannel or HttpClientChannel, with the remoting system on the client computer. In addition, you should register a server channel, such as TcpServerChannel or HttpServerChannel, before registering a remote object.
- You must register a server channel on the client computer if a remote object calls back a method on the client.
- Channel names within an application domain cannot be the same. However, an application domain can contain multiple channels of the same type. For example, an application domain can have more than one TcpChannel object registered

with the remoting system. The ChannelName property of these channels should uniquely identify these channels.

- Two channels registered with the remoting system on a computer cannot listen on the same port.

When a client calls a remote object, the remoting infrastructure creates a message that contains parameters and other call-related information. The process by which the parameters and call-related information are bundled into a message is known as *marshaling*. The remoting infrastructure sends the message to a RealProxy object. The RealProxy object, in turn, forwards the message to a message sink. A *message sink* is an object that allows a client to establish a connection with the channel registered by the remote object and forwards the messages to the channel. When the channel in the application domain of the remote object receives the message, the remoting system on the server unmarshals the message and forwards the call along with parameters and other call-related information to an appropriate remote object.

Note   When the remoting system creates a RealProxy object, the remoting system also creates a message sink object by calling the IChannelSender.CreateMessage-Sink method on the selected channel.

During the communication between a client and the remote object, the message payload that contains the marshaled parameters and call-related information is transported.

The channel that carries the message payload can use various transport protocols, such as HTTP and TCP. Depending on the transport protocols used, channels are divided into two namespaces: System.Runtime.Remoting.Channels.Http and System.Runtime.Remoting.Channels.Tcp.

HTTP Channels

The System.Runtime.Remoting.Channels.Http namespace provides channel classes that use the HTTP protocol to transport messages between remote objects. The System.Runtime.Remoting.Channels.Http namespace provides classes, such as HttpClientChannel, HttpServerChannel, and HttpChannel. You can use the HttpClientChannel class to transport messages from a client to a remote object. To create an HttpClientChannel object and register it with the remoting system, use the following code.

Visual Basic .NET

```
ChannelServices.RegisterChannel(New HttpClientChannel())
```

Visual C#

```
ChannelServices.RegisterChannel(new HttpClientChannel());
```

Note The constructor for the HttpClientChannel object does not require you to pass the port number because the remoting system automatically allocates an available port to the channel.

The HttpServerChannel allows a remote object to listen to the remote calls from clients. You must register the HttpServerChannel object at a specific port. The following code shows how to create and register an HttpServerChannel object to listen at port 8080.

Visual Basic .NET

```
Dim channel as New HttpServerChannel(8080)
ChannelServices.RegisterChannel(channel)
```

Visual C#

```
HttpServerChannel channel=new HttpServerChannel(8080);
ChannelServices.RegisterChannel(channel);
```

Note You pass the port number as an argument to the HttpServerChannel constructor that determines the port at which the server channel listens for the remote calls. Specifying a port that is already in use causes an exception to be thrown. Therefore, if you are not sure which port number to specify, pass 0 as an argument to the constructor. The remoting system allocates an available port to the server channel.

You can use the HttpChannel class to transport messages to and from remote objects. The following code shows how to create and register an HttpChannel object to listen at port 8010.

Visual Basic .NET

```
Dim channel as New HttpChannel(8010)
ChannelServices.RegisterChannel(channel)
```

Visual C#

```
HttpChannel channel = new HttpChannel(8010);
ChannelServices.RegisterChannel(channel);
```

Table 4.3 shows the constructor methods of various HTTP channel classes.

Note The constructor methods in Visual Basic.NET are identified with the New name, whereas in Visual C# the constructors have the same name as that of the class.

Table 4.3   Constructors of HTTP Channel Classes

Constructor	Description
HttpChannel class	
New() or HttpChannel()	The default constructor initializes all the fields. The HttpChannel class functions as a client channel when you use the default constructor to create it.
New(*port*) or HttpChannel(*port*)	This constructor allows the HttpChannel object to function as a client channel as well as a server channel. *Port* specifies the port at which the HttpChannel object listens to remote calls.
New(*properties,* *clientchannelsinkprovider,* *serverchannelsinkprovider*) or HttpChannel(*properties,* *clientchannelsinkprovider,* *serverchannelsinkprovider*)	*Properties* is an IDictionary object that contains a collection of channel properties in key-value pairs. *Clientchannelsinkprovider* is an IClientChannel-SinkProvider object that creates the client channel sinks through which messages flow. *Serverchannelsink-provider* is an IServerChannelSinkProvider object that creates server channel sinks through which the messages flow. (Channel sinks are described in Lesson 3.)
HttpClientChannel class	
New() or HttpClientChannel()	This constructor initializes a new instance of the HttpClientChannel class with default values.
New(*properties,* *clientchannelsinkprovider*) or HttpClientChannel(*properties,* *clientchannelsinkprovider*)	This constructor initializes the HttpClientChannel class and sets the properties according to the key-value pairs in the *properties* object. *Clientchannelsinkprovider* is the IClientChannelSinkProvider object that the HttpClientChannel object uses to create a client channel sink. The messages sent by the client channel pass through a chain of client channel sinks.
New(*name,* *clientchannelsinkprovider*) or HttpClientChannel(*name,* *clientchannelsinkprovider*)	This constructor initializes the HttpClientChannel object and sets its ChannelName property to *name*. *Clientchannelsinkprovider* is the IClientChannel-SinkProvider object that the HttpClientChannel object uses to create a client channel sink. The messages sent by the client channel pass through a chain of client channel sinks.
HttpServerChannel class	
New() or HttpServerChannel()	This constructor initializes the HttpServerChannel object with the default values.
New(*port*) or HttpServerChannel(*port*)	This constructor initializes the HttpServerChannel object to listen at the specified *port*.

Table 4.3   Constructors of HTTP Channel Classes *(continued)*

Constructor	Description
New(*name*, *port*) or HttpServerChannel(*name*, *port*)	This constructor initializes the HttpServerChannel object with the ChannelName property set to *name* and sets the *port* at which the channel listens for the remote method calls.
New(*properties*, *serverchannelsinkprovider*) or HttpServerChannel(*properties*, *serverchannelsinkprovider*)	This constructor initializes the HttpServerChannel object and sets the properties according to the key-value pairs in the *properties* object. *Serverchannelsinkprovider* is the IServerChannelSinkProvider object that the HttpServerChannel object uses to create a server channel sink. The messages received by the server channel pass through a chain of server channel sinks.

You use HTTP channels when interoperability between remote components is the main objective. HTTP channels use the SoapFormatter class to serialize messages into the XML format using the SOAP protocol before sending the message payload across the channel. The interoperability of SOAP messages allows a client to call methods on a remote object that might not be using the .NET Framework. However, if performance is the main objective, use channels that allow you to transport messages in the binary format. The System.Runtime.Remoting.Channels.Tcp namespace provides channel classes that enable you to transport messages to and from remote objects. The next section discusses the classes provided by the System.Runtime.Remoting.Channels.Tcp namespace.

Note   *Serialization* is a process by which the state of an object is stored on a disk or transported across a wire. *Deserialization* involves recreating an object by reading the persisted state information of the object from a disk or across a wire.

TCP Channels

TCP channels allow you to transport messages across application domains using the TCP protocol. The TCP channels use the BinaryFormatter class to serialize messages into a binary stream before a client sends them to a remote object. In addition, the BinaryFormatter class deserializes the binary payload before delivering it to the remote object. The TCP channel classes that you can use include TcpClientChannel, TcpServerChannel, and TcpChannel. The TcpClientChannel class allows a client to send messages to a remote object, whereas the TcpServer-Channel class allows a remote object to receive messages from clients. The TcpChannel class allows you to transport messages to and from a remote object. You register a TCP channel the same way in which you register an HTTP channel. The following code shows how to register TCP channels.

Visual Basic .NET

```
ChannelServices.RegisterChannel(New TcpClientChannel())
```

(continued)

```
Dim channel as New TcpServerChannel(8070)
ChannelServices.RegisterChannel(channel)

Dim tcpchannel as New TcpChannel(8010)
ChannelServices.RegisterChannel(tcpchannel)
```

Visual C#

```
ChannelServices.RegisterChannel(new TcpClientChannel());

TcpServerChannel channel=new TcpServerChannel(8070);
ChannelServices.RegisterChannel(channel);

TcpChannel tcpchannel = new TcpChannel(8010);
ChannelServices.RegisterChannel(tcpchannel);
```

Table 4.4 shows the constructor methods of various TCP channel classes.

Table 4.4   Constructors of TCP Channel Classes

Constructor	Description
TcpChannel class	
New() or TcpChannel()	The default constructor initializes all the fields. When you use the default constructor, the TcpChannel class functions as the client channel.
New(*port*) or TcpChannel(*port*)	This constructor allows the TcpChannel object to function as a client channel as well as a server channel. The *port* number specifies the port at which the TcpChannel object listens to remote calls.
New(*properties,* *clientchannelsinkprovider,* *serverchannelsinkprovider*) or TcpChannel(*properties,* *clientchannelsinkprovider,* *serverchannelsinkprovider*)	*Properties* are IDictionary objects that contains a collection of channel properties in key-value pairs. *Clientchannelsinkprovider* is an IClientChannelSink-Provider object that creates the client channel sinks through which messages flow. *Serverchannelsink-provider* is an IServerChannelSinkProvider object that creates server channel sinks through which messages flow.
TcpClientChannel class	
New() or TcpClientChannel()	This constructor initializes the TcpClientChannel object with default values.
New(*properties,* *clientchannelsinkprovider*) or TcpClientChannel(*properties,* *clientchannelsinkprovider*)	This constructor initializes the TcpClientChannel object and sets the properties according to the key-value pairs in the *properties* object. *Clientchannelsinkprovider* is the IClientChannelSinkProvider object that the TcpClientChannel object uses to create a client channel sink. The messages sent by the client channel pass a chain of client channel sinks.

Table 4.4   Constructors of TCP Channel Classes *(continued)*

Constructor	Description
New(*name*, *clientchannelsinkprovider*) or TcpClientChannel(*name*, *clientchannelsinkprovider*)	This constructor initializes the TcpClientChannel object and sets its ChannelName property to *name*. *Clientchannelsinkprovider* is the IClientChannelSink-Provider object that the TcpClientChannel object uses to create a client channel sink. The messages sent by the client channel pass through a chain of client channel sinks.
TcpServerChannel class	
New(*port*) or TcpServerChannel(*port*)	This constructor initializes the TcpServerChannel object to listen to a specified port.
New(*name*, *port*) or TcpServerChannel(*name*, *port*)	This constructor initializes the TcpServerChannel object with the ChannelName property set to *name* and sets the port at which the channel listens for remote method calls.
New(*properties*, *serverchannelsinkprovider*) or TcpServerChannel(*properties*, *serverchannelsinkprovider*)	This constructor initializes the TcpServerChannel object and sets the properties according to the key-value pairs in the *properties* object. *Serverchannelsinkprovider* is the IServerChannelSinkProvider object that the TcpServerChannel object uses to create a server channel sink. The messages that the server channel receives are routed through a chain of server channel sinks.

Note   There is no default constructor for the TcpServerChannel class.

If a remote object uses a TcpChannel or TcpServerChannel object to receive messages from clients, the clients can call the methods on the remote object only if they use either a TcpChannel or TcpClientChannel object. If clients use an HttpClientChannel or HttpChannel object to connect to a remote object that uses a TcpChannel or TcpServerChannel object, an exception is thrown. The client sees the error message, "The underlying connection was closed: An unexpected error occurred on a receive."

The decision of selecting HTTP or TCP channels depends on different features of these two types of channels. Table 4.5 shows and compares the features of HTTP and TCP channels.

Whether you select HTTP or TCP channels for your remote applications, channels perform tasks that are independent of the channel type. The messages that channels send to or receive from remote objects pass through a chain of objects called channel sinks. The channel sink objects perform tasks such as formatting, transporting, and stack building. In the next section, you will learn about channel sinks and sink chains and understand their role in remoting.

Table 4.5   Features of HTTP and TCP Channels

HTTP channels	TCP channels
Transport messages to and from remote objects using the HTTP protocol.	Transport messages to and from remote objects using the TCP protocol.
Use the SoapFormatter class to serialize and deserialize messages.	Use the BinaryFormatter class to serialize and deserialize messages.
Create two connections by default to connect to a given server. You can configure this channel by changing the clientConnectionLimit attribute in an application configuration file.	Create as many connections as the number of client threads making the requests. The socket connections are closed if the connections remain inactive for 15–20 seconds.
Generate and consume the Channel-DataStore for object references.	Generate and consume the ChannelDataStore for object references.

Sinks and Sink Chains

Channels connect objects across remoting boundaries by allowing them to send messages to each other. The messages carried by channels pass through a chain of channel sinks. A *channel sink* performs certain functions on the message before forwarding the message to the next channel sink in the chain. Within the channel sink chain, you can access the message that is routed to or coming from a remote object. Within a channel sink chain, you can perform tasks, such as logging, applying filters, encrypting the message, and imposing security restrictions. Figure 4.2 shows channel sink chains on the client and on the server.

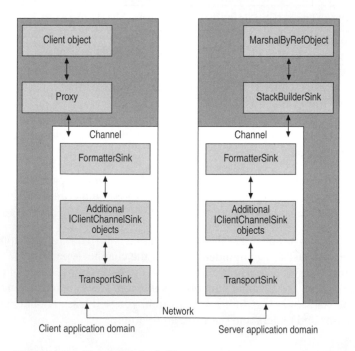

Figure 4.2   Channel sink chains

You use channel sink providers to create channel sink chains. These include objects that implement the IClientChannelSinkProvider, IClientFormatterSinkProvider, or IServerChannelSinkProvider interfaces. When you activate a remote object, the remoting system retrieves the channel sink provider from the current channel and calls the CreateSink method on the channel sink provider to create the first channel in the chain. The first channel sink on a client must be a formatter sink that serializes the message into a stream. The last sink on the channel sink chain should be a transport sink that sends the stream over the network wire.

The following code shows how to create a channel sink chain.

Visual Basic .NET

```
private Function CreateSinkChain() As IClientChannelSinkProvider
    Dim chain As New FormatterSinkProvider_1
    Dim sink As IClientChannelSinkProvider
    sink = chain
    sink.Next = New FormatterSinkProvider_2
    sink = sink.Next
    return chain
End Function
```

Visual C#

```
private IClientChannelSinkProvider CreateSinkChain()
{
    IClientChannelSinkProvider chain = new FormatterSinkProvider_1();
    IClientChannelSinkProvider sink = chain;
    sink.Next = new FormatterSinkProvider_2();
    sink = sink.Next;
    return chain;
}
```

Note The FormatterSinkProvider_1 and FormatterSinkProvider_2 classes in the above code are the classes that you create to create custom formatters.

In this lesson, you learned about channels that enable clients to send messages to remote objects. Channels also transport information about events that might occur in client or server objects. .NET Remoting allows you to do event-based programming for your remote applications. In the next lesson, you will learn how to implement event-based programming for your remoting applications.

Lesson 4: Implementing Events and Delegates

The .NET Framework enables you to implement event handling and delegates in the remoting applications that you create. This allows you to enhance the functionality of your remoting applications.

After this lesson, you will be able to

- Describe events and delegates
- Implement events and delegates in remoting applications

Estimated lesson time: 30 minutes

Understanding Events and Delegates

You usually associate event-based programming with applications that provide a graphical user interface (GUI). In such applications, an event is triggered when an action, such as a mouse click, occurs on an interface element. The information about the event is sent to another object, which responds to the event by performing a task. The object that raises an event is called the *event sender* or *event source*. The object that receives and responds to the event is called the *event receiver* or *event sink*.

You can use the event-based programming model for non-GUI applications, such as .NET Remoting applications. An event in such an application occurs when the state of the application changes. The event-based programming model for non-GUI applications also consists of a sender and a receiver. However, in the communication between the sender and the receiver, the sender does not know which object or method will receive the event. To ensure smooth communication between two objects, the .NET Framework provides a special type called delegates.

A *delegate* is a class that holds a reference to the method that is called when an event is fired. Unlike other classes of the .NET Framework, the delegate class has a signature. The delegate class can hold references only to the methods that match its signature. The following code shows how to declare an event delegate.

Visual Basic .NET

```
Public Delegate Sub RetirementHandler(sender As Object, _
    e As RetireEventArgs)
```

Visual C#

```
public delegate void RetirementHandler(object sender, RetireEventArgs e);
```

After you declare an event delegate, you can define a method to which the event delegate points. The signature of that method should match the signature of the event delegate. The following code shows the method to which the event delegate points.

Visual Basic .NET

```
Public Class Action
    ' RetireEvent has the same signature as RetirementHandler.
    Public Sub RetireEvent(sender As Object, e As RetireEventArgs)

End Sub
```

Visual C#

```
public class Action
{
    // RetireEvent has the same signature as RetirementHandler.
    public void RetireEvent (object sender, RetireEventArgs e)
    {}
}
```

You then create an instance of the delegate and store the address of the method whose reference the delegate holds.

Visual Basic .NET

```
Dim a As New Action()
Dim handler As RetirementHandler = AddressOf a.RetireEvent
```

Visual C#

```
Action a = new Action();
NewEventHandler handler = new RetirementHandler(a.RetireEvent);
```

Event delegates are multicasted. Therefore, you can define an event delegate to hold a reference to multiple event handling methods. The next section discusses implementing events and delegates in a remoting application.

Implementing Events and Delegates in Remoting Applications

Events and delegates enable you to enhance the functionality of your remoting application. You can use delegates to implement callback functions, event programming, and asynchronous programming in your remoting applications. Events use delegates to enable callback functions to the client in remoting applications. This enables the client and the remote application to function as domain servers. Therefore, you need to design a server/server application instead of designing a client/server application.

Note   A *callback* function is a reference to a method that you pass to another method. When the second method calls the referenced method, it actually calls back the first method.

When you implement events and delegates in remoting applications, you should ensure that:

■   The delegates you pass to the server for callback functions are delegates to instance members because you cannot call static members remotely.

■   You register a channel to listen for the callback function.

Delegates enable the methods, which handle events, to be abstract. Events invoke all the delegates that are registered to listen to that type of event. The delegates are similar to callback functions; the only difference between a delegate and a callback function is that a client must register the delegate with the event. You must perform the following tasks to enable delegates to listen for events in the remoting application:

1. Define an event and the extension to the EventArgs class that the event passes to a delegate.

2. Define a delegate that wraps an event-handler method of the signature required by the event.

3. Define a method that handles the event.

4. Initialize a delegate that wraps the event-handler method.

5. Add the delegate to the event.

The following code shows how to implement events and delegates in a remoting application.

Visual Basic .NET

```vb
' Implement an EventArgs class
Public Class RetirementEventArgs
    Inherits EventArgs

    Private ret_age as Integer

    Public Sub New(ByVal age as Integer)
        ret_age = age
    End Sub

    Public ReadOnly Property RetirementAge() as Integer
        Get
            Return ret_age
        End Get
    End Property
End Class
```

```vb
' Define Delegate to handle the RetirementEvent
Public Delegate Sub RetirementEventHandler(ByVal sender As Object, ByVal _
    e as RetirementEventArgs)

' Implement a class that raises the retirement event
Public Class Employee
    Inherits MarshalByRefObject

    Public Event retirement as RetirementEventHandler
    Public Sub Retire()
        Dim e as New RetirementEventArgs(58)
        RaiseEvent retirement(Me ,e)
    End Sub
End class


' Implement class that handles the retirement event
Public Class HR
    Public Shared Sub Main()
        Dim emp as New Employee()
        Dim hr as New HR()
        AddHandler emp.retirement, AddressOf hr.RetirementHandler

    End Sub

Public Shared Sub RetirementHandler(ByVal sender as Object, ByVal e as _
    RetirementEventArgs)
    Console.writeline("Retirement Age is " & Cint(e.RetirementAge))
    End Sub
End Class
```

Visual C#

```csharp
using System;
// Implement an EventArgs class
public class RetirementEventArgs : EventArgs
{
    private int ret_age;

    public RetirementEventArgs(int age)
{
    ret_age = age;
}

public int RetirementAge
{
    get
    {
        return ret_age;
    }
}
```

(continued)

```csharp
}

//Define Delegate to handle the RetirementEvent
public delegate void RetirementEventHandler(Object sender,
    RetirementEventArgs e);

//Implement a class that raises the retirement event
public class Employee : MarshalByRefObject
{
    public event RetirementEventHandler retirement;

    public void Submit()
    {
        RetirementEventArgs e = new RetirementEventArgs(58);
        retirement(this, e);
    }
}

// Implement class that handles the retirement event
public class HR
{
    public static void Main()
    {
        Employee emp = new Employee();
        HR hr = new HR();
        emp.retirement+= new RetirementEventHandler(hr.RetirementHandler);
    }

    public void RetirementHandler(Object sender, RetirementEventArgs e)
    {
        Console.WriteLine("Retirement Age is " + (int)e.RetirementAge);
    }
}
```

Besides implementing event-based programming in your remoting applications, you can also implement asynchronous programming.

Lesson 5: Implementing Asynchronous Methods

.NET asynchronous programming enables you to call and execute a method while the program, which calls the methods, continues to execute. This enables methods to continue executing without waiting for the called methods to finish execution, which increases the speed of applications. .NET Remoting supports asynchronous programming. Asynchronous programming in a remoting scenario is similar to asynchronous programming in a single application domain or context. Therefore, you can make calls to remote methods on servers while the application continues to execute on the client computer.

After this lesson, you will be able to

- Describe asynchronous programming
- Implement asynchronous programming in remoting applications

Estimated lesson time: 30 minutes

Asynchronous Methods

In .NET asynchronous programming, a call is made to a class method while the calling program continues to execute. This happens until either the specified callback is made or until blocking, polling, or waiting for the call to complete. You can use .NET asynchronous programming to:

- Perform file IO, stream IO, and socket IO
- Create networking applications (HTTP, TCP)
- Define remoting channels (HTTP, TCP) and proxies
- Develop XML Web services using ASP.NET
- Create ASP.NET Web Forms
- Create message queues over Microsoft Message Queuing (MSMQ)
- Define asynchronous delegates

In .NET asynchronous programming, the server splits an asynchronous operation into two tasks. The first task takes inputs from the client and starts the asynchronous operation. In addition, this task takes an AsyncCallback delegate, which is called when the asynchronous operation completes. The second task supplies the results of the asynchronous operation to the client. The first task returns a waitable object that implements the IAsyncResult interface. The client uses the IAsyncResult interface to determine the status of the asynchronous operation. The server uses the waitable object until it is returned to the client to maintain any state associated with the asynchronous operation. The client then supplies the waitable object to the second task to obtain the results of the asynchronous operation. You implement asynchronous programming in the following ways:

- **Use callbacks.**   You supply the callback delegate when you begin asynchronous calls.
- **Poll completed.**   You poll the IAsyncResult.IsCompleted property to determine the completion of asynchronous calls.
- **BeginInvoke, EndInvoke.**   You use these methods when you need to complete the operation prematurely.
- **BeginInvoke, WaitHandle, EndInvoke.**   You use these methods to wait on IAsyncResult.

You use asynchronous delegates to call a method asynchronously. The common language runtime uses multithreading to implement asynchronous method calls. When you call a delegate synchronously, the Invoke method calls the target method on the thread on which the caller method is running. If the compiler supports asynchronous delegates, it generates the Invoke method and the BeginInvoke and EndInvoke methods.

When the BeginInvoke method is called, the common language runtime queues the request and immediately returns to the called method. The target method is later called on a thread from the thread pool. The original thread, which submitted the request, continues executing the target method. If a callback is specified on the BeginInvoke method, it is called when the target method returns. In the callback, the EndInvoke method obtains the return value and the in/out parameters. If the callback is not specified on the BeginInvoke method, you can use the EndInvoke method on the original thread that submitted a request.

Implementing Asynchronous Methods in Remoting Applications

Implementing asynchronous programming in remoting applications is similar to implementing asynchronous programming in a single application domain or context. You just need to configure asynchronous method calls according to the requirements of .NET Remoting. When implementing asynchronous programming in a .NET Remoting application, you must remember that:

- The caller decides whether a particular remote call is asynchronous.
- Remote types do not have to support asynchronous behavior by their clients.
- You need to complete type safety.
- You must use the System.Threading objects appropriately to wait or synchronize your methods.

To implement asynchronous programming in a remoting application, complete the following steps:

1. Create an instance of an object that can receive a remote call to a method.
2. Wrap that instance method with an AsyncDelegate method.
3. Wrap the remote method with another delegate.
4. Call the BeginInvoke method on the second delegate, passing any arguments, the AsyncDelegate method, and some object to hold the state.
5. Wait for the server object to call your callback method.

The following code shows how to call methods asynchronously in a .NET Remoting application.

Visual Basic .NET

```
' Create an instance of the class that can receive remote calls
Dim remoteObj as New MyRemoteObject()

' Create delegate to a method that is executed when async method
' finishes execution.
Dim remoteMethod as New AsyncCallback(AddressOf remoteObj.CallBackMethod)

' Define a delegate to a method
Delegate Sub MyAsyncDelegate()

' Create a delegate to the method that will be executed asynchronously
Dim remoteDel As New MyAsyncDelegate(AddressOf obj.LongCall)

' Begin the invocation of the asynchronous method.
remoteDel.BeginInvoke(remoteMethod,nothing)
```

Visual C#

```
// Create an instance of the class that can receive remote calls
MyRemoteObject remoteObj = new MyRemoteObject();

// Create delegate to a method that is executed when async method
// finishes execution.
AsyncCallback remoteMethod = new AsyncCallback(remoteObj.CallBackMethod);

// Create a delegate to the method that will be executed asynchronously
MyAsyncDelegate remoteDel = new MyAsyncDelegate(obj.LongCall);

// Begin the invocation of the asynchronous method.
remoteDel.BeginInvoke(remoteMethod,nothing);
```

Lesson 6: Configuring and Securing .NET Remoting Objects

The .NET Framework allows you to configure remote applications programmatically by calling configuration methods inside the application. In addition, the .NET Framework allows you to configure the remote application by adding the remoting configuration section in the application configuration file. You can use role-based security to secure remote applications. In addition, you can secure the remote components hosted in ASP.NET by using Secure Sockets Layer (SSL) and the security features of Internet Information Services (IIS).

After this lesson, you will be able to

- Describe how to configure remoting applications
- Configure secure remote objects
- Describe the security options for remote objects

Estimated lesson time: 30 minutes

Remote Object Configuration

The .NET Framework allows you to configure remote objects programmatically or manually. You can programmatically configure your remote objects when you do not want to change the properties of remote objects after they are created and compiled. However, to change the properties of remote objects dynamically without recompiling code, you use the application configuration file. To configure remote objects programmatically or manually, you have to provide certain information to the remoting system. This information enables a client to call your objects remotely. The information that you need to provide includes

- The activation type for the remote object
- The channels that the remote object will use to receive messages from clients
- The URL of the remote object
- The type metadata that describes the type of your remote object

The .NET Framework provides the RemotingConfiguration class in the System.Runtime.Remoting namespace that allows you to configure your remote components programmatically. The following code shows how you can set the activation type and application name for your remote object.

Visual Basic .NET

```
ChannelServices.RegisterChannel(New TcpChannel(8020))
Dim myservice As New WellKnownServiceTypeEntry(GetType(MyService), _
```

```
    "TcpService", WellKnownObjectMode.SingleCall)
RemotingConfiguration.ApplicationName = "TcpService"
RemotingConfiguration.RegisterWellKnownServiceType(myservice)
```

Visual C#

```
ChannelServices.RegisterChannel(new TcpChannel(8020));
WellKnownServiceTypeEntry myservice =
    new WellKnownServiceTypeEntry(typeof(MyService),"TcpService",
    WellKnownObjectMode.SingleCall);
RemotingConfiguration.ApplicationName = " TcpService";
RemotingConfiguration.RegisterWellKnownServiceType(myservice);
```

Alternatively, you can configure remote objects by adding the remoting configuration section to the application configuration file. The following code shows the remoting configuration section of an application configuration file for server-activated and client-activated objects.

XML

```
<configuration>
    <system.runtime.remoting>
        <application>
            <service>
                <wellknown
                    mode = "SingleCall"
                    type = "MyRemoteClass,RemoteAssembly"
                    objectUri = "MyApp.rem"
                />
                <activated
                    type="ClientActivatedType, TypeAssembly"
                />
            </service>
        </application>
    </system.runtime.remoting>
</configuration>
```

Table 4.6 on the next page describes the configuration attributes.

You can configure the settings for your remote objects in the Machine.config file or in the application configuration file. You need to call the RemotingConfiguration.Configure(*configfilename*) method in your code to load the settings from the application configuration file. However, you need to remember that the .NET Framework always loads the settings from the Machine.config file before loading settings from the application configuration file. Therefore, you should not call the RemotingConfiguration.Configure() method on the Machine.config file because some of the settings might already exist in memory. The following code shows how to load settings from an application configuration file called MyApp.exe.config.

Visual Basic .NET

```
RemotingConfiguration.Configure("MyApp.exe.config")
```

Visual C#

```
RemotingConfiguration.Configure("MyApp.exe.config");
```

Table 4.6   Configuration Attributes

Element	Description
<application>	This element contains information about the remote objects that are exposed or consumed by an application.
<service>	This element contains the objects that are exposed by an application. The <service> element can occur one or more times in the <application> element.
<wellknown>	This element contains information about server-activated objects exposed by the application. The <wellknown> element can occur one or more times in the <service> element. The <wellknown> element has three required attributes: mode, type, and objectUri. Mode can be Singleton or SingleCall. Type specifies the type name and the name of the assembly that contains the type implementation. ObjectUri specifies the endpoint for the URI of an object.
<activated>	This element contains information about the client-activated objects that are exposed by the application. The <activated> element can occur one or more times in the <service> element. This element consists of one attribute, type, which specifies the type of the object and the assembly that implements the remote object type.

Securing .NET Remoting Objects

You can use code-access security to secure remote objects. This enables you to control the resources that a remote object can access on a computer. When you enable code-access security, a remote object receives permissions depending on its security group. Table 4.7 shows the permissions of a remote object in different security zones.

Table 4.7   Code-Access Security for Remote Objects

Security zone	Access to channel and type?	Access to channel sink chain?
Everything	Yes	Yes
Full Trust (Local Machine)	Yes	Yes
LocalIntranet	Yes	No
Internet	No	No
Nothing	No	No

If you host remote objects in IIS, you can use the security feature of IIS and SSL to secure remote objects. IIS hosting provides SSL, which allows you to secure messages sent to or received from remote objects. In addition, you can use Integrated Windows Authentication or Kerberos to secure the remote objects hosted in IIS. Therefore, whenever you have a choice between using the HttpChannel and the TcpChannel class, you should use the HttpChannel class and host your remote objects in IIS.

Summary

- You use .NET Remoting to enable communication between different applications residing on the same computer or on different computers. These computers can be part of the same network or part of networks in different geographic locations across the world. In addition, .NET Remoting enables computers running different operating systems to communicate with each other.

- You develop a remoting application by creating client and server objects and activating them. You then use references of the server objects in the client application to enable communication between the client and the server.

- Channels enable a client object running in an application domain, process, or computer to send messages to another object running in a different application domain, process, or computer. In addition, channels allow applications to send and receive messages using various protocols, such as TCP and HTTP.

- Events and delegates enable you to enhance the functionality of your remoting application. You can use delegates to implement callback functions, event programming, and asynchronous programming in your remoting applications.

- You can implement asynchronous programming to make calls to remote methods on servers while the application continues to execute on the client computer.

- You can configure remoting applications programmatically by calling configuration methods inside the application or by adding the remoting configuration section into the application configuration file.

- You can secure your remoting application by implementing role-based security. In addition, you can secure the remote components hosted in ASP.NET by using SSL and the security features of IIS.

Lab: Creating and Consuming .NET Remoting Objects

In this lab, you will create a chat application that uses .NET Remoting. The chat application allows users to send messages to all the other users who are currently logged on. The chat application consists of a ChatCoordinator class, a Server class, and a Client class. The ChatCoordinator class inherits from the MarshalByRefObject class and is the remotable object in the chat application. The Client objects call methods on the ChatCoordinator object to send messages to other Client objects. The Server class is a console application that configures the ChatCoordinator object by using the settings in a .config file. The ChatCoordinator object and the Client objects use event-based messaging. The chat application consists of the SubmitEventArgs class, which inherits from the EventArgs class. The ChatCoordinator object is the source of the SubmitEventArgs event whereas the Client objects are the reciever or the sink of the SubmitEventArgs event. The solutions to the exercises in this lab can be found in the \Solution folder on the Supplemental Course Materials CD-ROM.

Estimated lab time: 90 minutes

Exercise 1: Create the ChatCoordinator.dll Library

In this exercise, you will create the ChatCoordinator.dll library. The ChatCoordinator.dll library consists of ChatCoordinator and SubmitEventArgs classes. To create the ChatCoordinator.dll library, perform the following steps:

1. Open Notepad and type the following code.

    Visual Basic .NET

```vb
Imports System
Imports System.Runtime.Remoting
Imports System.Collections

<Serializable()> _
Public Class SubmitEventArgs
    Inherits EventArgs
    Private message As String = Nothing
    Private username As String = Nothing
    Public Sub New(ByVal contribution As String, ByVal contributor _
        As String)
        Me.message = contribution
        Me.username = contributor
    End Sub 'New

    Public ReadOnly Property Contribution() As String
        Get
```

(continued)

```vb
                Return message
            End Get
        End Property


        Public ReadOnly Property Contributor() As String
            Get
                Return username
            End Get
        End Property
    End Class 'SubmitEventArgs


    Public Delegate Sub SubmissionEventHandler(ByVal sender As Object, _
        ByVal submitArgs As SubmitEventArgs)


    Public Class ChatCoordinator
        Inherits MarshalByRefObject
        Public Sub New()
            Console.WriteLine("ChatCoordinator created. Instance: " & _
                Me.GetHashCode().ToString())
        End Sub 'New
        Public Overrides Function InitializeLifetimeService() As Object
            Return Nothing
        End Function 'InitializeLifetimeService


        Public Event Submission As SubmissionEventHandler


        Public Sub Submit(ByVal contribution As String, ByVal contributor _
            As String)
            Console.WriteLine("{0} says: {1}.", contributor, contribution)
            Dim e As New SubmitEventArgs(contribution, contributor)
            RaiseEvent Submission(Me, e)
        End Sub 'Submit
    End Class 'ChatCoordinator
```

Visual C#

```csharp
using System;
using System.Runtime.Remoting;
using System.Collections;


[Serializable]
public class SubmitEventArgs : EventArgs{

    private string _string = null;
    private string _alias = null;

    public SubmitEventArgs(string contribution, string contributor)
    {
        this._string = contribution;
        this._alias = contributor;
    }
```

```
        public string Contribution
        {
            get{ return _string; }
        }

        public string Contributor
        {
            get { return _alias; }
        }
    }
    public delegate void SubmissionEventHandler(object sender,
        SubmitEventArgs submitArgs);


    public class ChatCoordinator : MarshalByRefObject
    {

        public ChatCoordinator()
        {
            Console.WriteLine("ChatCoordinator created. Instance: " +
                this.GetHashCode().ToString());
        }


        public override object InitializeLifetimeService()
        {
            return null;
        }

        public event SubmissionEventHandler Submission;

        public void Submit(string contribution, string contributor)
        {
            Console.WriteLine("{0} sent: {1}.", contributor, contribution);
            SubmitEventArgs e = new SubmitEventArgs(contribution,
                contributor);

            if (Submission != null)
            {
                Console.WriteLine("Broadcasting...");
                Submission(this, e);
            }
        }
    }
}
```

2. Save the file as ChatCoordinator.vb or ChatCoordinator.cs.

3. Open the Visual Studio .NET Command Prompt. Type **vbc /t:library ChatCoordinator.vb** to compile the code in ChatCoordinator.vb or type **csc /t:library ChatCoordinator.cs** to compile the code in ChatCoordinator.cs.

Exercise 2: Create a Configuration File for Configuring the ChatCoordinator Object

In this exercise, you will create a configuration file to specify the settings for the ChatCoordinator remotable object that you created in the previous exercise. To create the configuration file, perform the following steps:

1. Open Notepad and type the following code.

   XML

   ```xml
   <configuration>
       <system.runtime.remoting>
           <application>
           <service>
               <wellknown
                   mode="Singleton"
                   type="ChatCoordinator, ChatCoordinator"
                   objectUri="Chat"
               />
           </service>
           <channels>
           <channel
               ref="http"
               port="8080"
           />
           </channels>
       </application>
       </system.runtime.remoting>
   </configuration>
   ```

2. Save the file as Central.config.

Exercise 3: Create a Console Application to Activate the ChatCoordinator Object

In this exercise, you will create a console application to activate the ChatCoordinator object by using the remote configuration settings defined in the Central.config file. To create the console application, perform the following steps:

1. Open Notepad and type the following code.

   Visual Basic .NET

   ```vbnet
   Imports System
   Imports System.Diagnostics
   Imports System.Runtime.Remoting
   Imports System.Runtime.Remoting.Channels

   Public Class Server
       Public Shared Sub Main()
   ```

```
            RemotingConfiguration.Configure("Central.config")
            Console.WriteLine("The host application is currently " & _
                "running. Press Enter to exit.")
            Console.ReadLine()
        End Sub 'Main
    End Class 'ServerProcess
```

Visual C#

```csharp
using System;
using System.Runtime.Remoting;

public class Server
{
    public static void Main(string[] Args)
    {
        RemotingConfiguration.Configure("Central.config");
        Console.WriteLine("The host application is currently " +
            "running. Press Enter to exit.");
        Console.ReadLine();
    }
}
```

2. Save the file as Server.vb or Server.cs.

3. Compile the code in the Server.vb file by typing **vbc /r:ChatCoordinator.dll Server.vb** or compile it in the Server.cs file by typing **csc /r:ChatCoordinator.dll Server.cs** at the Visual Studio .NET Command Prompt.

Exercise 4: Create a Chat Client

In this exercise, you will create a console-based chat client application. The chat client application consists of the ChatClient class, which calls methods on the ChatCoordinator remotable object. The ChatClient class contains a Run method and a SubmissionReceiver method. The Run method configures the client object. The configuration values are specified in the Client.config file. To create the chat client application, perform the following steps:

1. Open Notepad and type the following code.

Visual Basic .NET

```vbnet
Imports System
Imports System.Runtime.Remoting
Imports System.Runtime.Remoting.Channels
Imports Microsoft.VisualBasic

Public Class ChatClient
        Inherits MarshalByRefObject

    Public Overrides Function InitializeLifetimeService() As Object
        Return Nothing
```

(continued)

```
        End Function

        Private username As String = Nothing

        Public Sub New(ByVal [alias] As String)
            Me.username = [alias]
        End Sub

        Public Sub Run()
            RemotingConfiguration.Configure("Client.config")
            Dim chatcenter As New ChatCoordinator()
            AddHandler chatcenter.Submission, AddressOf Me.SubmissionReceiver
            Dim userInput As String = ""
            While True
                Console.WriteLine("Press 0 (zero) and ENTER to Exit:")
                userInput = Console.ReadLine()
                If userInput = "0" Then Exit While
                chatcenter.Submit(userInput, username)
            End While
            RemoveHandler chatcenter.Submission, AddressOf _
                Me.SubmissionReceiver
        End Sub

        Public Sub SubmissionReceiver(ByVal sender As Object, ByVal args As _
            SubmitEventArgs)
            If args.Contributor = username Then
                Console.WriteLine("Your message was broadcast.")
            Else
                Console.WriteLine(args.Contributor & " says:" & _
                    args.Contribution)
            End If
        End Sub 'SubmissionReceiver

        Public Shared Sub Main()
            Dim Args() As String = Environment.GetCommandLineArgs()
            If Args.Length <> 2 Then
                Console.WriteLine("You need to type an alias.")
                Return
            End If
            Dim client As New ChatClient(Args(1))
            client.Run()
        End Sub 'Main
End Class 'ChatClient
```

Visual C#

```
using System;
using System.Runtime.Remoting;
using System.Runtime.Remoting.Channels;
using System.Runtime.Remoting.Channels.Http;
```

```csharp
public class ChatClient : MarshalByRefObject
{
    private string username = null;
    public override object InitializeLifetimeService()
    {
        return null;
    }

    public ChatClient(string alias)
    {
        this.username = alias;
    }

    public void Run()
    {
        RemotingConfiguration.Configure("Client.config");
        ChatCoordinator chatcenter = new ChatCoordinator();
        chatcenter.Submission += new
            SubmissionEventHandler(this.SubmissionReceiver);
        String keyState = "";
        while (true)
        {
            Console.WriteLine("Press 0 (zero) and ENTER to Exit:\r\n");
            keyState = Console.ReadLine();
            if (String.Compare(keyState,"0", true) == 0)
                break;
            chatcenter.Submit(keyState, username);
        }

        chatcenter.Submission -= new
            SubmissionEventHandler(this.SubmissionReceiver);
    }

    public void SubmissionReceiver(object sender, SubmitEventArgs args)
    {
        if (String.Compare(args.Contributor, username, true) == 0)
        {
            Console.WriteLine("Your message was broadcast.");
        }
        else
            Console.WriteLine(args.Contributor
                + " says: " + args.Contribution);
    }

    public static void Main(string[] Args)
    {
        if (Args.Length != 1)
        {
            Console.WriteLine("You need to type an alias.");
            return;
```

(continued)

```
        }

        ChatClient client = new ChatClient(Args[0]);
        client.Run();
    }
}
```

2. Save the file as Client.vb or Client.cs.

3. Compile the code in Client.vb by typing **vbc /r:ChatCoordinator.dll Client.vb** or compile it in Client.cs by typing **csc /r:ChatCoordinator.dll Client.cs** at the Visual Studio .NET Command Prompt.

Exercise 5: Create a Configuration File to Configure the ChatClient Object

In this exercise, you will create a Client.config file to specify the settings to configure the ChatClient object. To create the Client.config file, perform the following steps:

1. Open Notepad and type the following code.

XML

```xml
<configuration>
    <system.runtime.remoting>
        <application>
        <client>
        <wellknown
            type="ChatCoordinator, ChatCoordinator"
            url="http://localhost:8080/Chat"
        />
        </client>
        <channels>
        <channel
            ref="http"
            port="0"
        />
        </channels>
        </application>
    </system.runtime.remoting>
</configuration>
```

2. Save the file as Client.config.

Exercise 6: Executing the Chat Application

In this exercise, you will run the chat application that you created in the previous exercises. To run the chat application, perform the following steps:

1. Open the Visual Studio .NET Command Prompt to the directory where you saved the Server.exe, ChatCoordinator.dll, and Server.config files.

2. Type **Server** at the command prompt. The output of the Server command is shown here.

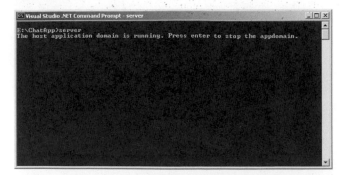

3. Open another Visual Studio .NET Command Prompt to the directory where you saved the Client.exe, ChatCoordinator.dll, and Client.config files.

4. Type **Client** *UserName* at the command prompt. The output of typing *Client User1* is shown here.

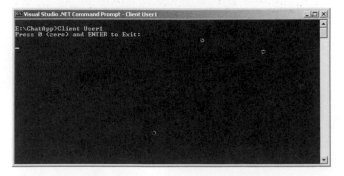

5. Open a few more Visual Studio .NET Command Prompts to the directory where you saved the Client.exe, ChatCoordinator.dll, and Client.config files.

6. Type **Client** *UserName* at the command prompt, using different user names.

7. Send messages from the client applications. Some of the messages that User1 sends to and receives from other users are shown here.

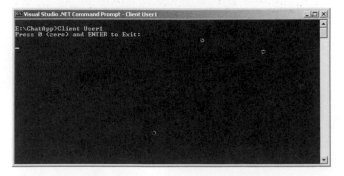

The messages that User2 receives from and sends to other users are shown here.

Review

The questions in this section reinforce key information presented in this chapter. If you are unable to answer a question, review the appropriate lesson, and then try answering the question again. Answers to the questions can be found in Appendix A, "Questions and Answers."

1. What are the requirements to enable communication between objects across remoting boundaries?

2. Describe the two types of remotable objects.

3. Describe the two types of activation modes of the .NET Remoting system.

4. How can you renew lifetime leases of objects?

5. What are channels?

6. List the tasks you need to perform to publish a service outside the service domain.

7. Why do you use delegates in your remoting applications?

8. What steps do you perform to implement asynchronous programming in a remoting application?

9. What information do you need to provide to the .NET Remoting system to configure remote objects?

C H A P T E R 5

Database Programming Using ADO.NET

About This Chapter

In this chapter, you will learn about ADO.NET as well as the architecture and benefits of ADO.NET. You will learn about the .NET data providers and how to use them as well. You will also learn how to create and use ADO.NET DataSet and DataView objects. In addition, you will learn how to manage and control data using DataReader and DataAdapter objects.

Before You Begin

To complete the lessons in this chapter, you

- Must have knowledge of programming in Microsoft Visual Basic .NET or Microsoft Visual C#
- Must have a working knowledge of database programming
- Must know how to connect to a database using Visual Basic .NET or Visual C#

Lesson 1: Understanding ADO.NET

In today's world, any distributed business solution that you create will probably be required to access data from various data sources within the organization. The .NET Framework enables you to create datacentric applications that enable you to access data from various data sources in a heterogeneous environment using ADO.NET. The components of ADO.NET enable you to create distributed, data-sharing applications.

After this lesson, you will be able to

- Describe ADO.NET
- Describe the architecture of ADO.NET
- Describe the benefits of ADO.NET
- List the differences between ADO and ADO.NET

Estimated lesson time: 45 minutes

Overview of ADO.NET

ADO.NET enables datacentric applications to connect to various data sources and retrieve, manipulate, and update data. ADO.NET uses XML to transfer data across applications and data sources. This enables you to use ADO.NET to access data from data sources that expose data via OLE DB or ODBC or from the data sources that providers are available for. The .NET Framework includes SQL Server .NET Data Provider to access Microsoft SQL Server (version 7.0 and later) and OLE DB .NET Data Provider to access database servers that use OLE DB to expose data. In addition, you can also download ODBC .NET Data Provider and Oracle .NET Data Provider from *http://msdn.microsoft.com/downloads*. In traditional database applications, clients establish a connection to a database and keep the connection open until the application completes execution. Open database connections require system resources. For example, multiple open connections make the database server slow to respond to client calls because most databases can only maintain a small number of concurrent connections. Similarly, applications that require an open database connection are difficult to scale.

One of the advantages of ADO.NET is that it supports disconnected architecture. Using a disconnected architecture, applications connect to a database server only to retrieve or update the data. This enables you to reduce the number of open connections to various database servers. ADO.NET also provides a common data representation that enables you to access data from multiple and various types of data sources and have it appear as one entity.

ADO.NET allows you to use data commands to execute SQL statements or stored procedures from a client application. These data commands enable you to execute SQL statements on a database server easily and quickly. For example, to retrieve a set of rows from a database, you establish a connection to the database, create a data command, specify the SQL SELECT statement to retrieve the required records, and call the execute method of the command. The command object returns the set of rows, which you can process immediately or store in an ADO.NET DataSet for processing at a later time.

An ADO.NET *DataSet* is a cache of records that you retrieve from a data source, such as a database or an XML file. A DataSet contains records from one or more tables. In addition, a DataSet contains information regarding the relationships between tables. DataSets enable you to process data whenever a user needs to access and process data. You can also use DataSets without a data source to manage data from an application or from an XML file. In addition, DataSets enable you to remain disconnected from the database. Another advantage of DataSets is that components can exchange DataSets. For example, a business object in the middle tier can create and populate a DataSet and then pass it to another component in the application, which then processes the DataSet.

When you create a datacentric application using ADO.NET, data moves between various objects. The data first moves from a data source to a DataSet and then to components, such as controls, in a form. ADO.NET uses XML to transfer data between various components of an application. The ADO.NET data APIs automatically create the XML files of the data in a DataSet and send them to other components.

The application you create accesses a data source by using a .NET data provider. A .NET *data provider* enables you to connect to a data source and execute commands to retrieve results and manipulate data. The .NET Framework provides two data providers: OLE DB .NET and SQL Server .NET. You use the OLE DB .NET data provider to connect to and access an OLE DB data source, whereas the SQL Server .NET data provider enables you to connect to and access a SQL Server database. These data providers are an important part of the ADO.NET architecture.

The classes of ADO.NET are defined in the System.Data namespace. This namespace defines classes, such as DataSet and DataTable, which constitute the ADO.NET architecture. Therefore, you add a reference to the System.Data namespace in your application when you want to use ADO.NET. The next section discusses the ADO.NET architecture.

ADO.NET Architecture

ADO.NET enables data transfer between components, such as data sources, DataSets, and the applications that request data. Together, all of these components constitute the ADO.NET architecture. Figure 5.1 displays the ADO.NET architecture.

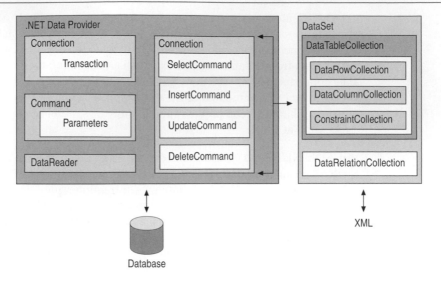

Figure 5.1   The ADO.NET architecture

In addition to the data source, the ADO.NET architecture includes data providers and DataSets.

Data Sources

A *data source* is a database server for which the .NET Framework provides a data provider or an XML file. To access a data source, you create a connection to the data source using the data providers of ADO.NET. The ADO.NET data providers enable you to establish a connection with a data source and perform other tasks, such as executing SQL commands on data sources. You will learn more about data providers later in this lesson.

.NET DataSets

The datacentric applications that you create usually need to access data from multiple tables. In addition, you might need to process data from multiple tables as one entity. For example, an organization might need to access the names of all its customers and the quantity of each product supplied to them.

ADO.NET DataSets are designed to store data in disconnected and distributed data environments. ADO.NET DataSets enable you to store data from multiple data sources. The DataSet stores data in a collection of tables. In addition, DataSets store relationships between tables. A DataSet is the data source for the application that requests data. The application can access and manipulate records in the DataSet without having to repeatedly connect to the database.

The functionality of DataSets is defined in the DataSet class. The DataSet class consists of a collection of one or more DataTable objects that represent tables. You will learn about DataSets in Lesson 3.

.NET Data Providers

.NET data providers enable an application to connect to a data source, execute commands, and retrieve results. A .NET data provider consists of the Connection, Command, DataReader, and DataAdapter objects, which you use to perform such tasks as connecting to a database and executing SQL commands. Table 5.1 describes the function of each object.

Table 5.1   Components of a .NET Data Provider

Object	Description
Connection	This object enables you to establish and manage a connection to a database.
Command	This object enables you to execute SQL commands and retrieve results from a database. The Command object also enables you to perform other tasks, such as updating the records of the database.
DataReader	This object enables you to read data in a sequential manner. The DataReader retrieves a read-only, forward-only data stream from the database. However, the DataReader object allows you to store only one row of data in memory at any point in time.
DataAdapter	This object enables a database and a DataSet to communicate with each other. You use the DataAdapter object to transfer data between a data source and a DataSet. In addition, the DataAdapter object can transfer data between a DataSet and some other applications, such as Microsoft Exchange Server.

Visual Studio .NET and the .NET Framework include two ADO.NET data providers: an OLE DB .NET data provider and a SQL Server .NET data provider.

The OLE DB .NET data provider enables you to connect to the OLE DB data sources, whereas the SQL Server .NET data provider enables you to connect to SQL Server 7.0 and later databases. The System.Data namespace contains two namespaces: System.Data.OleDb and System.Data.SqlClient. These namespaces contain classes for the OLE DB .NET and SQL Server .NET data providers, respectively. Therefore, to use a data provider in your application, you add a reference to the appropriate namespace. The classes of each data provider contain methods that enable you to perform the following tasks:

- Create a connection with a database
- Execute SQL statements or stored procedures on a database
- Read data rows from a database in forward-only mode
- Transfer data between a database and a DataSet
- Display errors and warning messages returned by a database
- Handle exceptions when a database returns an error or warning
- Execute Transact-SQL statements on a database

XML

XML is an important component of the ADO.NET architecture. ADO.NET uses XML internally to store and transfer data. You need not explicitly convert data to the XML format or the XML format to data. XML is integrated with ADO.NET as DataSets. The structure of the DataSet, including table definitions, columns, data types, and constraints, is defined by using an XML schema. You can serialize the data within a DataSet as XML. Similarly, you can serialize the structure of the DataSet as an XML schema.

The components of the ADO.NET architecture listed in Table 5.1 enable you to access data and perform operations on data sources easily.

Benefits of ADO.NET

ADO.NET provides many benefits that will help you create datacentric applications. The following sections discuss the benefits of ADO.NET.

Interoperability

Interoperability is one of the key benefits provided by ADO.NET. Because ADO.NET uses XML to exchange data, any component that understands XML can receive data from ADO.NET. For example, you can transfer data between ADO.NET and an application that is running on any platform. The integration of XML and ADO.NET allows ADO.NET to operate easily with the applications that support XML.

Maintainability

Applications created using ADO.NET are easier to manage and scale than applications created using ADO. For example, after developing an application, you might need to change its architecture to improve its speed or increase the number of people who can access the application. Consider the example of an e-commerce site. As the e-commerce site becomes popular, the number of hits on the site increases. If the number of hits increases, you might need to change the architecture of the application and increase the number of tiers. However, increasing the number of tiers in a deployed application is a difficult and time-consuming task. In addition, problems might occur during data exchange or data transfer between the tiers. ADO.NET enables you to easily increase tiers in a deployed application because ADO.NET uses XML to transfer data between tiers. This enables the objects in new tiers to exchange data seamlessly.

Programmability

ADO.NET simplifies programming for various tasks, such as executing SQL commands. This enables you to increase productivity and minimize the number of errors. For example, you can use the ADO.NET data commands to execute SQL statements or stored procedures. The actual task of building and executing a SQL statement is abstract and performed by ADO.NET. In addition, the ADO.NET data classes enable you to use typed programming to write code. Typed programming allows automatic statement completion. Therefore, it becomes easy to write code. In addition, typed programming increases the safety of the code and reduces the number of compilation errors.

Performance

ADO disconnected recordsets use COM marshaling to transfer data between applications. This requires data type conversion in order for COM to recognize the data types, and the conversion diminishes the performance of an application. Alternatively, ADO.NET uses XML to transfer data. Therefore, the requirement to convert the data type does not exist, which increases the performance of an application.

Scalability

With the increase in data and the change in the business models of organizations, the demand for data has increased rapidly. Consider a Web site that sells sporting goods. When a prospective buyer wants to view product information, the information is available in the Products database. If several prospective customers accessing the Web site simultaneously want to view information about the same product, the demand for data from the Products database increases. ADO.NET enables your applications to scale according to requirements because it uses disconnected architecture. This enables you to reduce the open connections to the database and results in optimum usage of resources.

The features of ADO.NET discussed in the preceding sections provide greater benefits than ADO. The following section explains the basic differences between ADO and ADO.NET.

Differences Between ADO and ADO.NET

ADO and ADO.NET have various differences, such as differences in architecture, data representation, and methods of sharing data between applications.

In-Memory Representations of Data

ADO uses a recordset to represent data that is retrieved from tables in memory, whereas ADO.NET uses DataSets. A recordset usually contains data from a single table. To store data from multiple tables, you use a JOIN query. The JOIN query retrieves the data from multiple tables as a single result table. Alternatively, ADO.NET uses a DataSet to represent data in memory. As mentioned earlier, a DataSet can store data from multiple tables and multiple sources. In addition, a DataSet can also contain relationships between tables and the constraints on a table. Therefore, a DataSet can represent the structure of a database.

ADO provides a read-only navigation on recordsets, which allows you to navigate sequentially through the rows of the recordset. However, in ADO.NET, rows are represented as collections. Therefore, you can access records using the primary key index. In addition, you can also filter and sort results.

Minimized Open Connections

In ADO.NET, you only connect to a database to retrieve and update records. You can retrieve records from a database, copy them into a DataSet, and then disconnect from the database. Although a recordset can provide disconnected data access in ADO, ADO was primarily designed for connected scenarios.

In ADO.NET, you communicate with the database using a DataAdapter or a DataReader that makes calls to an OLE DB provider or to the APIs provided by the data source.

Sharing Data Between Applications

You use COM marshaling in ADO to transfer a disconnected recordset from one component to another. In ADO.NET, you transfer a DataSet using an XML stream. XML provides the following advantages over COM marshaling when transferring data:

- **Richer data types.**   COM marshaling can only convert data types that are defined by the COM standard. In an XML-based data transfer, restrictions on data types do not exist. You can use XML-based data transfer to transfer any data that is serializable.

- **Bypassing firewalls.**   A firewall does not allow system-level requests, such as COM marshaling. Therefore, a recordset cannot bypass a firewall. However, because firewalls allow HTML text to pass and ADO.NET uses XML to transfer DataSets, you can send an ADO.NET DataSet through a firewall.

Lesson 2: Understanding .NET Data Providers

In the previous lesson, you learned about ADO.NET and its components. In addition, you learned about the architecture and the benefits of ADO.NET. You also learned about the differences between ADO and ADO.NET.

In this lesson, you will learn how to connect to a data source and perform database operations such as querying, inserting, updating, and deleting data. You will also learn about data providers, such as SQL and OLE DB, which allow you to connect to various data sources. In addition, you will learn to connect to a data source using DataAdapter and Connection objects. You will also learn how to manipulate data using a Command object and how to populate the DataSet object with data. Finally, you will learn to use the DataReader object to read forward-only and read-only streams of data.

After this lesson, you will be able to

- Connect to a data source using the Connection object
- Manipulate data using data commands
- Populate DataSet objects
- Use DataReader objects to retrieve read-only and forward-only data
- Identify the instances in which to use DataSet and DataReader objects

Estimated lesson time: 120 minutes

Overview of .NET Data Providers

.NET data providers form the interface between the application and the data source. The data providers that the .NET Framework provides allow you to connect to a data source, execute commands, and retrieve results. You can either directly work with the data retrieved by a data provider or store it in an ADO.NET DataSet object. DataSets allow you to store and manipulate data from multiple data sources. In addition, you can use a DataSet to transfer data between different tiers. The .NET Framework provides the OLE DB .NET data provider to access data from OLE DB and SQL Server .NET data provider to access data from Micorosoft SQL Server (version 7.0 or later). Though you can use the OLE DB .NET data provider to access data from SQL Server, you should use the SQL Server .NET data provider to access data from SQL Server (version 7.0 or later). The SQL Server .NET data provider makes native calls to SQL Server and therefore is more efficient than the OLE DB .NET data provider. You can also download the ODBC .NET data provider and the .NET data provider for Oracle to access data from an ODBC data source and Oracle database server, respectively.

A .NET data provider consist of these four core objects:

- **Connection.**   This object provides a connection to a data source.
- **Command.**   This object executes a command against a data source.
- **DataReader.**   This object provides a read-only, forward-only stream of data from a data source.
- **DataAdapter.**   This object populates a DataSet and resolves updates with the data source.

Once you identify the data source, the next step is to connect to the data source. In this lesson, you will only be using SQL Server data sources and both the OLE DB .NET and SQL Server .NET data providers to connect to the data source. The .NET Framework provides the Connection object to connect to different data sources. There are two Connection objects: OleDbConnection and SqlConnection.

The OleDbConnection Class

The OleDbConnection class allows you to create a connection with a data source. When you want to manipulate data from a data source, you must create a connection to the data source. To make a connection to a data source, you provide the OleDbConnection class information about the data source such as the name of the database, the source computer, the data provider, the user name, and the password. The syntax for creating a connection using the OleDbConnection class is shown in the following code.

Visual Basic .NET

```
Imports System.Data.OleDb
Dim Connection As New OleDbConnection()
' Set the ConnectionString property
connection.ConnectionString = _
    "Provider=Microsoft.Jet.OLEDB.4.0;Password=;User ID=Admin; " & _
    "Data Source=E:\Authors.mdb"
' Open the Connection
connection.Open()
```

Visual C#

```
using System.Data.OleDb;
OleDbConnection connection = new OleDbConnection();
connection.ConnectionString =
    "Provider=Microsoft.Jet.OLEDB.4.0;Password=;User ID=Admin; " +
    "Data Source=E:\Authors.mdb"
connection.Open();
```

In the preceding code snippet, the ConnectionString property of the OleDbConnection class enables you to specify the information required by the .NET Framework to connect to the Authors database. In the second line of code where the

ConnectionString property is set, the Provider is Microsoft.Jet.OLEDB.4.0 and the data source refers to the Microsoft Access database file named Authors.mdb. The user ID and password are the credentials required to access the Authors database. To use the OleDbConnection class, you import the OleDb namespace that contains the OleDbConnection class. The OleDb namespace is available in the System.Data namespace.

The SqlConnection Class

The following code shows how to use the SqlConnection class to connect to the Northwind database.

Visual Basic .NET

```
Imports System.Data.SqlClient
Dim connection As New SqlConnection()
' Set the ConnectionString property
connection.ConnectionString = "Data Source=" & _
    "localhost;user id=sa;pwd=;Initial Catalog=Northwind"
' Open the Connection
connection.Open()
```

Visual C#

```
using System.Data.SqlClient;
SqlConnection connection = new SqlConnection();
connection.ConnectionString =
    "Data Source=localhost;user id=sa;pwd=;Initial Catalog=Northwind";
connection.Open();
```

The preceding code snippet is similar to the code that uses the OleDbConnection class. The only difference is that you do not need to provide the Provider attribute in the ConnectionString property. To use the SqlConnection class, you need to import the SqlClient namespace that contains the SqlConnection class. The SqlClient namespace is available in the System.Data namespace.

The OleDbCommand Class

In the previous sections, you learned how to use the Connection objects to connect to a particular database. In this section, you will learn how to use the Command objects in the .NET Framework to execute a command against a data source. There are two types of Command objects: OleDbCommand and SqlCommand.

The OleDbCommand class represents a SQL statement or a stored procedure that you want to execute against a data source. For example, you can use the OleDbCommand object to execute a batch insert or a batch update against a data source. The syntax for creating an OleDbCommand object is provided in the following code.

Visual Basic .NET

```
Dim myCommand as New OleDbCommand()
Dim myConnection as New OleDbConnection()
Dim mySQL as String = "Select COUNT(ProductID) from Products"

myConnection.ConnectionString = "Provider=SQLOLEDB.1;data source=" & _
    "localhost;user id=sa;pwd=;Initial Catalog=Northwind"
myConnection.Open()
myCommand.Connection = myConnection

myCommand.CommandText = mySQL.Trim();

Console.WriteLine(myCommand.ExecuteScalar().ToString())
```

Visual C#

```
OleDbCommand myCommand = new OleDbCommand();
OleDbConnection myConnection = new OleDbConnection();
string mySQL = "Select COUNT(ProductID) from Products";

myConnection.ConnectionString = "Provider=SQLOLEDB.1;data source=" +
    "localhost;user id=sa;pwd=;Initial Catalog=Northwind";
myConnection.Open();
myCommand.Connection = myConnection;

myCommand.CommandText = mySQL.Trim();

Console.WriteLine(myCommand.ExecuteScalar().ToString());
```

In the preceding code, an OleDbCommand object is declared. After you initialize the OleDbConnection object, you set the Connection property of the OleDbCommand object to specify which Connection object to use. Next, the OleDbCommand object requires a SQL statement. This SQL statement specifies the command to be executed against the specified data source. The SQL statement can be a SELECT statement, an INSERT statement, an UPDATE statement, or a DELETE statement. A SELECT statement is specified in the string variable mySQL. This SELECT statement is executed against the data source, and the count of ProductID is retrieved from the Products table of the Northwind database. The CommandText property of the OleDbCommand object is set to the string variable mySQL. The CommandText property represents the SQL statement or a stored procedure that will be executed against a data source.

After you specify the Connection and CommandText properties of the OleDb-Command object, you execute the specified command against the selected data source. To do this, you use the ExecuteScalar, ExecuteReader, or ExecuteNonQuery method. Each of these methods is discussed in detail in the following sections.

The ExecuteScalar Method

The ExecuteScalar method executes a SQL statement against a specified data source and returns a single value. The single value represents the value in the first row and the first column. In addition, the rest of the values are ignored. The ExecuteScalar method is commonly used to execute aggregate functions on a table. For example, if you want to retrieve the number of employees residing in the ZIP code 28273, you need to use the COUNT function. The SQL statement might look like this:

SELECT COUNT(*) from Employees where Zip = 28273

This SQL statement returns just one value that is part of a single row and single column.

The ExecuteReader Method

The ExecuteReader method executes a SQL statement or a stored procedure against the available data source and returns an OleDbDataReader object. You will learn about the OleDbDataReader object later in this lesson. The following code snippet shows how to use the ExecuteReader method to retrieve an OleDbDataReader object.

Visual Basic .NET

```
Dim myCommand as New OleDbCommand()
Dim myConnection as New OleDbConnection()
Dim mySQL as String = "Select * from Products"

myConnection.ConnectionString = "Provider=SQLOLEDB.1;data source=" & _
    "localhost;user id=sa;pwd=;Initial Catalog=Northwind"
myConnection.Open()
myCommand.Connection = myConnection

myCommand.CommandText = mySQL

Dim myReader as OleDbDataReader
myReader = myCommand.ExecuteReader()

Console.WriteLine(myReader.FieldCount.ToString())
```

Visual C#

```
OleDbCommand myCommand = new OleDbCommand();
OleDbConnection myConnection = new OleDbConnection();
string mySQL = "Select * from Products";

myConnection.ConnectionString = "Provider=SQLOLEDB.1;data source=" +
    "localhost;user id=sa;pwd=;Initial Catalog=Northwind";
myConnection.Open();
myCommand.Connection = myConnection;

myCommand.CommandText = mySQL.Trim();
```

(continued)

```
OleDbDataReader myReader;
myReader = myCommand.ExecuteReader();

Console.WriteLine(myReader.FieldCount.ToString());
```

The ExecuteReader method is used to return an OleDbDataReader object that contains a read-only, forward-only copy of the data from the data source. The OleDb-DataReader object is covered in greater detail later in this lesson.

The ExecuteNonQuery Method

The ExecuteNonQuery method is used to execute INSERT, UPDATE, or DELETE statements. The ExecuteNonQuery method executes these three statements against the data source and returns an integer value specifying the number of rows affected by the INSERT, UPDATE, or DELETE statements. The following code snippet shows how to use the ExecuteNonQuery method.

Visual Basic .NET

```
Dim myCommand as New OleDbCommand()
Dim myConnection as New OleDbConnection()
Dim mySQL as String = "INSERT INTO PRODUCTS VALUES (..)"

myConnection.ConnectionString = "Provider=SQLOLEDB.1;data source=" & _
    "localhost;user id=sa;pwd=;Initial Catalog=Northwind"
myConnection.Open()
myCommand.Connection = myConnection

myCommand.CommandText = mySQL

dim NoOfRows = myCommand.ExecuteNonQuery()

Console.WriteLine("({0}) rows affected.",NoOfRows)
```

Visual C#

```
OleDbCommand myCommand = new OleDbCommand();
OleDbConnection myConnection = new OleDbConnection();
string mySQL = "INSERT INTO PRODUCTS VALUES(..)";

myConnection.ConnectionString = "Provider=SQLOLEDB.1;data " +
    "source=localhost;user id=sa;pwd=;Initial Catalog=Northwind";
myConnection.Open();

myCommand.Connection = myConnection;

myCommand.CommandText = mySQL.Trim();
int NoOfRows = 0;
NoOfRows = myCommand.ExecuteNonQuery();
Console.WriteLine("({0}) rows affected.", NoOfRows);
```

The SqlCommand Class

The SqlCommand class represents a SQL statement or stored procedure that you want to execute against a SQL Server data source. For example, to execute a batch insert or a batch update against a SQL Server data source, you use the SqlCommand object. The syntax for creating a SqlCommand object is shown in the following code.

Visual Basic .NET

```
Dim myCommand As New SqlCommand()
Dim myConnection As New SqlConnection()
Dim mySQL As String = "Select COUNT(ProductID) from Products"

myConnection.ConnectionString = "data source=" & _
    "localhost;user id=sa;pwd=;Initial Catalog=Northwind"
myConnection.Open()
myCommand.Connection = myConnection

myCommand.CommandText = mySQL

Console.WriteLine(myCommand.ExecuteScalar().ToString())
```

Visual C#

```
SqlCommand myCommand = new SqlCommand();
SqlConnection myConnection = new SqlConnection();
string mySQL = "Select COUNT(ProductID) from Products";

myConnection.ConnectionString = "data source=localhost;user id=sa; " +
    "pwd=;Initial Catalog=Northwind";
myConnection.Open();

myCommand.Connection = myConnection;

myCommand.CommandText = mySQL.Trim();

Console.WriteLine(myCommand.ExecuteScalar().ToString());
```

The usage of the SqlCommand object is very similar to the usage of the OleDb-Command object. However, you need not specify the name of the provider in the ConnectionString property.

The SqlCommand object consists of four Execute methods: ExecuteScalar, ExecuteReader, ExecuteNonQuery, and ExecuteXMLReader. The syntax and functionality of these methods are identical to the syntax and functionality of the OleDbCommand object.

Using Data Adapters

A data adapter forms an interface between the application and the data source for retrieving and saving data. The OleDbDataAdapter object represents a connection and a set of command objects that helps populate a DataSet object. You will learn about the DataSet object in the next lesson.

You use the OleDbDataAdapter object to fill the DataSet object with data. When a DataSet object is filled, the primary key information available on the table is not implicitly imported to the DataSet object. Therefore, when you populate a DataSet, you have to import the information explicitly to the DataSet. To use the OleDbDataAdapter object for filling the DataSet, you specify properties such as which Command and Connection objects to use. The OleDbDataAdapter object consists of four properties that you use to specify Command objects: Select-Command, InsertCommand, UpdateCommand, and DeleteCommand.

These properties are discussed in more detail in the following sections.

The SelectCommand Property

You use the SelectCommand property to set the SQL statement or a stored procedure that selects data from the data source. You can set the SelectCommand property of an existing OleDbCommand object, or you can set the CommandText property of the default Command object that is created when you use the Select-Command object. When a SelectCommand property does not return any rows, no table is added to the DataSet and no exception is thrown.

The InsertCommand Property

You use the InsertCommand property to set the SQL statement or a stored procedure that inserts data into the data source. You can set the InsertCommand property to an existing OleDbCommand object, or you can set the CommandText property of the default Command object that is created when you use the InsertCommand object. The InsertCommand property returns an integer value that specifies the number of rows affected by the corresponding insert operation.

The UpdateCommand Property

You use the UpdateCommand property to set the SQL statement or a stored procedure that updates data in the data source. You can set the UpdateCommand property to an existing OleDbCommand object, or you can set the CommandText property of the default Command object that is created when you use the UpdateCommand object. When you execute an UpdateCommand object, it returns the number of rows affected by the update operation.

The DeleteCommand Property

You use the DeleteCommand property to set the SQL statement or a stored procedure that deletes data from the data source. You can set the DeleteCommand property to an existing OleDbCommand object, or you can set the CommandText property of the default Command object that is created when you use the Delete-Command object. When you execute a DeleteCommand property, it returns the number of rows affected by the delete operation.

The following code snippet shows how to use the SelectCommand, Insert-Command, UpdateCommand, and DeleteCommand properties.

Visual Basic .NET

```
Dim myAdapter As New OleDbDataAdapter()
Dim myCommand As New OleDbCommand()
Dim myConnection As New OleDbConnection()
Dim mySQL As String = "Select * from Products"

myConnection.ConnectionString = "Provider=sqloledb.1;data source=" & _
    "localhost;user id=sa;pwd=;Initial Catalog=Northwind"
myConnection.Open()
myCommand.Connection = myConnection
myCommand.CommandText = mySQL
myAdapter.SelectCommand = myCommand

Dim myDataSet As New DataSet()
myAdapter.Fill(myDataSet, "Products")
Dim myRow As DataRow
For Each myRow In myDataSet.Tables(0).Rows
    Console.WriteLine(myRow("productid"))
Next

mySQL = "INSERT INTO PRODUCTS(PRODUCTNAME) VALUES('Nuts')"
myCommand.CommandText = mySQL
myAdapter.InsertCommand = myCommand
Dim count As Integer
count = myAdapter.InsertCommand.ExecuteNonQuery()
Console.WriteLine("({0}) rows affected", count)

mySQL = "Update PRODUCTS Set PRODUCTNAME = 'Caps' WHERE PRODUCTID = 78"
myCommand.CommandText = mySQL
myAdapter.UpdateCommand = myCommand
count = myAdapter.UpdateCommand.ExecuteNonQuery()
Console.WriteLine("({0}) rows affected", count)

mySQL = "DELETE FROM PRODUCTS WHERE PRODUCTID = 78"
myCommand.CommandText = mySQL
myAdapter.DeleteCommand = myCommand
count = myAdapter.DeleteCommand.ExecuteNonQuery()
Console.WriteLine("({0}) rows affected", count)
```

Visual C# .NET

```
string mySQL = "Select * from Products";

OleDbDataAdapter myAdapter = new OleDbDataAdapter();

OleDbCommand myCommand = new OleDbCommand();
OleDbConnection myConnection = new OleDbConnection();

myConnection.ConnectionString =
    "Provider=SQLOLEDB.1;data source=localhost;" +
```

(continued)

```
                  "user id=sa;pwd=;Initial Catalog=Northwind";
myConnection.Open();

myCommand.Connection = myConnection;
myCommand.CommandText = mySQL.Trim();

myAdapter.SelectCommand = myCommand;

DataSet myDataSet = new DataSet();
myAdapter.Fill(myDataSet, "Products");

foreach(DataRow myRow in myDataSet.Tables[0].Rows)
{
    Console.WriteLine(myRow[0]);
}

mySQL = "INSERT INTO PRODUCTS(PRODUCTNAME) VALUES('Nuts')";
myCommand.CommandText = mySQL;
myAdapter.InsertCommand = myCommand;
int count;
count = myAdapter.InsertCommand.ExecuteNonQuery();
Console.WriteLine("({0}) rows affected", count);

mySQL = "Update PRODUCTS Set PRODUCTNAME = 'Caps' WHERE PRODUCTID = 78";
myCommand.CommandText = mySQL;
myAdapter.UpdateCommand = myCommand;
count = myAdapter.UpdateCommand.ExecuteNonQuery();
Console.WriteLine("({0}) rows affected", count);

mySQL = "DELETE FROM PRODUCTS WHERE PRODUCTID = 78";
myCommand.CommandText = mySQL;
myAdapter.DeleteCommand = myCommand;
count = myAdapter.DeleteCommand.ExecuteNonQuery();
Console.WriteLine("({0}) rows affected", count);
```

The implementation of the SqlDataAdapter class is similar to the OleDbDataAdapter class. If you are using the SqlDataAdapter class, then you need to use the corresponding Command and Connection objects. The Command and Connection objects that are used in conjunction with the SqlDataAdapter class are the SqlCommand and SqlConnection objects, respectively.

The DataReader Class

The DataReader class provides read-only and forward-only access to data from a data source. The DataReader object reduces the system overhead at any given time because only one row of data exists in memory. To fetch the next record, the DataReader object reconnects to the data source and retrieves the data. You can create a DataReader object by executing the ExecuteReader() method of the Command object. As discussed in the previous sections, the ExecuteReader() method of the Command object returns an object of the type DataReader. There are two data readers: the SqlDataReader class and the OleDbDataReader class. The following sections discuss these two data readers in detail.

The SqlDataReader Class

The SqlDataReader class allows you to read the read-only, forward-only data from a SQL Server database. To create a SqlDataReader object, you execute the ExecuteReader() method of the SqlCommand class. You need to call the Open() method on the connection object that the SqlCommand object uses before calling ExecuteReader(). You close the SqlDataReader object by using the Close() method to release the SqlConnection object. The following code shows how to implement the SqlDataReader class.

Visual Basic .NET

```
Dim myString As String
myString = "data source=localhost; Initial Catalog=Northwind; " & _
    "user id=sa; pwd=;"
Dim mySQL As String = "SELECT lastname, firstname FROM Employees"
Dim myConnection As New SqlConnection(myString)
Dim myCommand As New SqlCommand()
myCommand.CommandText = mySQL
myCommand.Connection = myConnection
myConnection.Open()
Dim myReader As SqlDataReader
myReader = myCommand.ExecuteReader()
' Always call Read before accessing data.
While myReader.Read()
    Console.WriteLine((myReader.GetString(0) & ", " & _
        myReader.GetString(1)))
End While
' Always call Close when done reading.
myReader.Close()
' Close the connection when done with it.
myConnection.Close()
```

Visual C#

```
string myString;
myString = "data source=localhost; Initial Catalog=Northwind;" +
    "user id=sa;pwd=;";
string mySQL = "SELECT lastname, firstname FROM Employees";
SqlConnection myConnection = new SqlConnection(myString);
SqlCommand myCommand = new SqlCommand();
myCommand.CommandText = mySQL;
myCommand.Connection = myConnection;
myConnection.Open();
SqlDataReader myReader;
myReader = myCommand.ExecuteReader();
```

(continued)

```
while (myReader.Read())
{
    Console.WriteLine((myReader.GetString(0) + ", " +
        myReader.GetString(1)));
}

myReader.Close();
myConnection.Close();
```

In the code, the SqlDataReader object is initialized to the object returned by the ExecuteReader() method. You use the Read() method of the SqlDataReader object to read a row from the data source. Observe that the DataReader object has just one row at any given time. You call the Read() method of the SqlDataReader object to fetch subsequent rows. After reading from the SqlDataReader object, you close the SqlDataReader object. After closing the SqlDataReader object, you can call the IsClosed() method and the RecordsAffected property.

The IsClosed() Method

The IsClosed() method of the SqlDataReader class returns a value indicating whether the SqlDataReader is closed.

The RecordsAffected Property

The RecordsAffected property of the class returns the number of rows that are changed, inserted, or deleted by the current database operation performed by Transact-SQL statements. The RecordsAffected property always calls the Close() method before returning the affected rows to ensure an accurate return of values.

The OleDbDataReader Class

The OleDbDataReader class provides read-only and forward-only access to data from any data source. To create an OleDbDataReader object, you execute the ExecuteReader() method of the OleDbCommand class. If the OleDbDataReader object is being used, the associated OleDbConnection provides the required data for the OleDbDataReader object. During this period, no other operation can use the OleDbConnection object to retrieve or send data from or to the data source. You close the OleDbDataReader object by using the Close() method to release the OleDbConnection object.

Creating Data Access Components
Using the Data Adapter Configuration Wizard

In the previous section, you learned how to create data access components programmatically. Now you will learn how to create data access components using the Data Adapter Configuration Wizard. To use the wizard, perform the following steps:

1. Start Visual Studio .NET and open a new project.
2. Select Visual Basic Projects or Visual C# Projects from the Project Types pane.
3. Select Windows Application from the Templates pane in the New Project dialog box.
4. Specify the name of the project in the Name box and click OK.
5. Open the Toolbox. From the Data tab drag a SqlDataAdapter object onto the Windows form. The Data Adapter Configuration Wizard's welcome screen appears. Click Next to continue.
6. On the Choose Your Data Connection page, click New Connection.
7. In the Data Link Properties dialog box, specify the appropriate credentials for SQL Server. Select the Northwind database from the list. If the server name is left blank, the default server is chosen. The default server is the database running on the local machine. Figure 5.2 displays the Data Connection page with the data connection information. Click Next.

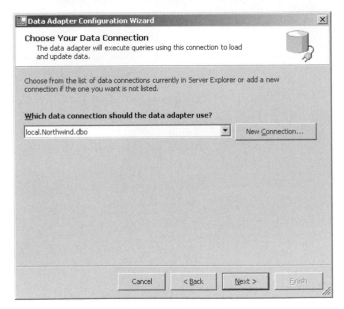

Figure 5.2 Choose Your Data Connection page

8. On the Choose A Query Type page, shown in Figure 5.3, ensure that the Use SQL Statements option is selected, and click Next.

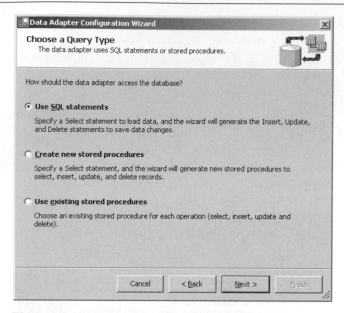

Figure 5.3   Choose A Query Type page

9. On the Generate The SQL Statements page, click the Query Builder button.

10. Select the Customers table from the Add Table dialog box and click Add. Click Close to close the Add Table dialog box. In the Query Builder window, select All Columns to select all the columns of the Customers table. Figure 5.4 shows the Query Builder window with the Customers table.

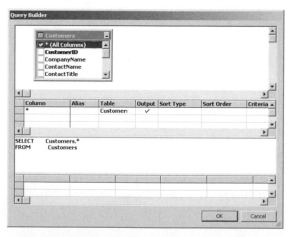

Figure 5.4   Query Builder window with the Customers table

11. Click OK. Figure 5.5 shows the Generate The SQL Statements page with the query generated by the Query Builder.

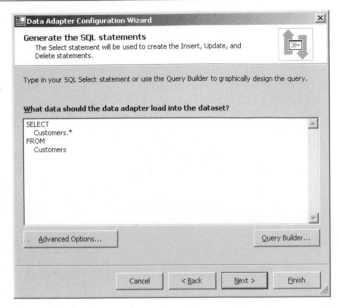

Figure 5.5   Generate The SQL Statements page showing the query generated by the Query Builder

12. Click the Advanced Options button and ensure that all three check boxes are selected in the Advanced SQL Generation Options dialog box shown in Figure 5.6.

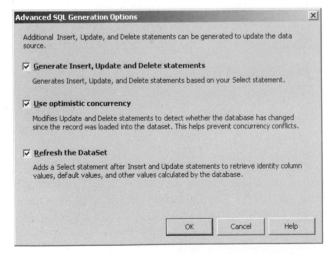

Figure 5.6   Advanced SQL Generation Options dialog box

13. Click Next, and then click Finish on the View Wizard Results page.

14. As shown in Figure 5.7, two objects, SqlDataAdapter1 and SqlConnection1, have been added to the Form1 Windows form.

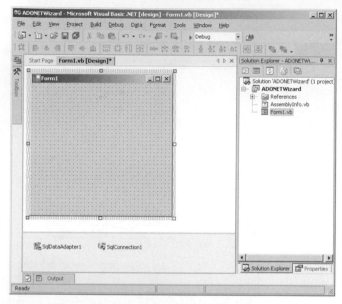

Figure 5.7   Form1 in Design view

15. Right-click the SqlDataAdapter1 object and choose Generate Dataset.

16. In the Generate Dataset dialog box, click OK.

17. The DataSet11 object is added to the Windows form.

18. In the Load event of the Windows form, type the following code.

Visual Basic .NET

```
SqlDataAdapter1.Fill(DataSet11)
```

Visual C#

```
SqlDataAdapter.Fill(DataSet11);
```

As you have just seen, there is very little code that you need to write when you configure a data adapter using the Data Adapter Configuration Wizard. In addition, Visual Studio .NET makes it very simple to create typed DataSets. DataSets are covered in detail in the next lesson.

Lesson 3: Working with DataSets

As described in Lesson 1, an ADO.NET DataSet provides a disconnected view of a data source. ADO.NET DataSets enable you to store data from multiple data sources. You can create relationships between the tables in a DataSet, even though relationships might not exist between tables in the data sources. In addition, you can create different data views from the data contained within the DataSets. In this lesson, you will learn to create an ADO.NET DataSet as well as add and manipulate tables in an ADO.NET DataSet. In addition, you will learn to work with ADO.NET DataSet events.

After this lesson, you will be able to

- Describe an ADO.NET DataSet
- Create an ADO.NET DataSet
- Manipulate an ADO.NET DataSet
- Manage ADO.NET DataSet events

Estimated lesson time: 60 minutes

Understanding ADO.NET DataSets

ADO.NET DataSets support in-memory, disconnected data architecture. You establish a connection to a data source, retrieve records from a DataSet, and then close the connection. This enables you to work with the data without requiring you to connect to the database. In-memory, disconnected data enables you to minimize the number of live connections to a database. In addition, disconnected data architecture reduces the number of round trips to a database server and allows the database server to fulfill other requests. The in-memory, disconnected architecture provides quick access to data because the DataSet is present in the memory of a client computer, and all data operations, such as updating tables, occur at the client level.

An ADO.NET DataSet is a collection of tables and information about the relationships between tables. Each table further consists of collections of rows, columns, and constraints. You can access these components using the properties and collections of a DataSet. You use the following classes to work with DataSets in ADO.NET:

- **DataSet class.**   This class includes the Tables collection of the tables in a DataSet. In addition, the DataSet class contains the Relations collection that represents the relationships between the tables in a DataSet.
- **DataTable class.**   This class includes the Rows and Columns collections that represent rows and columns. In addition, the DataTable class contains the ChildRelations and ParentRelations collections that represent relationships between tables.

- **DataRow class.** This class includes the RowState property. The RowState property indicates whether a row has changed after loading the data table from a database. The RowState property can take the following values: Deleted, Modified, New, and Unchanged.

A DataTable also contains the Constraints collection. The Constraints collection allows DataSets to implement all constraints including the constraints at the database level. When you modify the data of a table in a DataSet, the DataSet implements all the constraints at the client level. Therefore, when a DataSet connects to a database to perform an update operation, data is updated quickly; the round trip from the database server to the client is avoided. Figure 5.8 displays the structure of an ADO.NET DataSet.

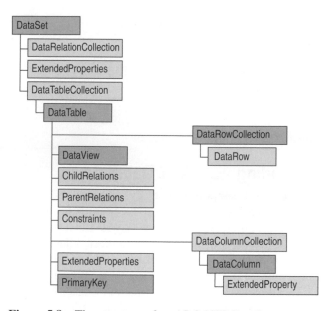

Figure 5.8   The structure of an ADO.NET DataSet

Creating ADO.NET DataSets

You can create an ADO.NET DataSet by creating an object of the DataSet class that is present in the System.Data namespace. When you create an object of the DataSet class by calling the DataSet constructor, you can optionally pass the name of the DataSet as an argument to the constructor. The following code shows how to create a DataSet named Employees.

Visual Basic .NET

```
' Create a new instance of DataSet class
Dim EmployeeDS As new DataSet("Employees")
```

Visual C#

```csharp
//Create a new instance of the DataSet class
DataSet EmployeeDS = new DataSet("Employees");
```

After you create a DataSet, you can populate the DataSet by adding tables to the DataSet. To add tables to a DataSet, you create DataTable objects and add them to a DataSet. The following code shows how to add tables to a DataSet.

Visual Basic .NET

```vb
Dim EmployeeDS As new DataSet("Employees")
Dim EmpTable As DataTable = EmployeeDS.Tables.Add("Employees")
```

Visual C#

```csharp
DataSet EmployeeDS = new DataSet("Employees");
DataTable EmpTable = EmployeeDS.Tables.Add("Employees");
```

Adding Columns to a Table in a DataSet

After you add a table to a DataSet, you add columns to the table according to your requirements. The following code shows how to populate a table with columns.

Visual Basic .NET

```vb
Dim EmployeeDS As new DataSet("Employees")
Dim EmpTable As DataTable = EmployeeDS.Tables.Add("Employees")

' Add columns to the dataset
EmpTable.Columns.Add("EmployeeID", Type.GetType("System.String"))
EmpTable.Columns.Add("LastName", Type.GetType("System.String"))
EmpTable.Columns.Add("FirstName", Type.GetType("System.String"))
```

Visual C#

```csharp
DataSet EmployeeDS = new DataSet("Employees");
DataTable EmpTable = EmployeeDS.Tables.Add("Employees");

//Add columns to the dataset
EmpTable.Columns.Add("EmployeeID", Type.GetType("System.String"));
EmpTable.Columns.Add("LastName", Type.GetType("System.String"));
EmpTable.Columns.Add("FirstName", Type.GetType("System.String"));
```

Setting Constraints on a Table in a DataSet

When you add columns to a DataSet, you set constraints, such as a primary key, on the columns by using the PrimaryKey and Unique properties of the Data-Column object. The following code shows how to add the primary key constraint on a column.

Visual Basic .NET

```
Dim EmployeeDS As new DataSet("Employees")
Dim EmpTable As DataTable = EmployeeDS.Tables.Add("Employees")

' Specifying an identifier for the primary key column
Dim pkCol As DataColumn = EmpTable.Columns.Add("EmployeeID", _
    Type.GetType("System.String"))
EmpTable.Columns.Add("LastName", Type.GetType("System.String"))
EmpTable.Columns.Add("FirstName", Type.GetType("System.String"))

' Specifying the EmployeeID column as the primary key
EmpTable.PrimaryKey = New DataColumn() {pkCol}
```

Visual C#

```
DataSet EmployeeDS = new DataSet("Employee");
DataTable EmpTable = EmployeeDS.Tables.Add("Employees");

// Specifying an identifier for the primary key column
DataColumn pkCol = EmpTable.Columns.Add("EmployeeID",
    Type.GetType("System.String"));
EmpTable.Columns.Add("LastName", Type.GetType("System.String"));
EmpTable.Columns.Add("FirstName", Type.GetType("System.String"));

// Specifying the EmployeeID column as the primary key
EmpTable.PrimaryKey = new DataColumn[] {pkCol};
```

Creating Relationships Between the Tables in a DataSet

As mentioned earlier, a DataSet object can contain multiple tables. You can also create relationships between the tables in aDataSet. You can use various methods of the DataRelation object to create and manage relationships between the tables in a DataSet.

To create a relationship between two tables in a DataSet, you use the Add method of the DataRelation object. The Add method takes a name for the relationship being created, and the DataColumn references of the columns that you want to define as the parent and child columns in the relationship. The following code shows how to create relationships between two tables in a DataSet.

Visual Basic .NET

```
EmployeeDS.Relations.Add("Employees_Territories", _
    EmployeeDS.Tables("Employees").Columns("EmployeeID"), _
    EmployeeDS.Tables("EmployeeTerritories").Columns("EmployeeID"))
```

Visual C#

```
EmployeeDS.Relations.Add("Employees_Territories ",
    EmployeeDS.Tables["Employees"].Columns["EmployeeID"],
    EmployeeDS.Tables["EmployeeTerritories"].Columns["EmployeeID"]);
```

Note   When you create a relationship between tables, a UniqueConstraint is added to the parent table, and a ForeignKeyConstraint is added to the child table by default.

Manipulating an ADO.NET DataSet

After you create and populate a DataSet, you can manipulate it by performing tasks such as merging DataSet contents and copying the contents of one DataSet to another DataSet. Each of these tasks is explained in the following sections.

Merging the Contents of DataSets

You can merge the contents of a DataSet, DataTable, or DataRow object with another DataSet, DataTable, or DataRow object. When you merge the contents of two DataSets, the data in a DataSet is added to another DataSet. However, you must remember certain rules before you merge the contents of two DataSets. The following sections describe these rules.

Check Primary Keys

When you merge the contents of DataSets, the table receiving the new data or schema ensures data integrity by checking the primary key values. The table receiving the new data matches the primary key values of its existing rows with those of the rows from the incoming table. The data in the existing rows is modified only if the columns from the incoming schema match those of the existing schema. In addition, the new rows containing primary key values that do not match any existing rows are added to the existing table. However, if the table receiving new data does not have a primary key, new rows from the incoming data are added to the table. If the incoming and existing tables have primary keys on different columns, an exception is thrown, and the DataSet raises the MergeFailed event. An exception is also thrown when the incoming and existing tables contain columns that have the same name but different data types.

Preserve Changes

When you merge a DataSet, DataTable, or DataRow object with a DataSet, you can specify whether to preserve the changes in the existing DataSet and how to manage the new schema elements in the incoming data. You use the PreserveChanges property to specify whether to preserve the changes in the existing DataSet. If the PreserveChanges property is set to True, the existing values in the table receiving data are not overwritten with the incoming values. However, if the PreserveChanges flag is set to False, the existing values are overwritten by the incoming values in the current row version of the existing row.

Apply Constraints

When you merge the contents of two DataSets, constraints are not checked when the Merge method is executed. After you add the data to a receiving table, constraints are enforced on the current values in the DataSet. Therefore, you need to ensure that you can handle the exceptions in your code.

You use the Merge method of a DataSet object to combine the contents of a DataSet, DataTable, or DataRow object with another DataSet, DataTable, or DataRow object.

Visual Basic .NET

```
Dim DBConn As SqlConnection = New SqlConnection("server=localhost; " & _
    "integrated security=sspi; Database=Northwind")

Dim EmpDA As SqlDataAdapter = New SqlDataAdapter("SELECT " & _
    "EmployeeID, FirstName FROM Employees", DBConn)

DBConn.Open()

Dim EmpDS As DataSet = New DataSet()
EmpDA.FillSchema(EmpDS, SchemaType.Source, "Employees")
EmpDA.Fill(EmpDS, "Employees")

Dim TerDS As DataSet = New DataSet()
TerDS.ReadXml("Territories.xml", XmlReadMode.ReadSchema)
TerDS.AcceptChanges()

DBConn.Close()

EmpDS.Merge(TerDS, True, MissingSchemaAction.AddWithKey)
```

Visual C#

```
SqlConnection DBConn = new SqlConnection("server=localhost; " +
    "integrated security=sspi; Database=Northwind");

SqlDataAdapter EmpDA = new SqlDataAdapter("SELECT EmployeeID, " +
    "FirstName FROM Employees", DBConn);

DBConn.Open();

DataSet EmpDS = new DataSet();
EmpDA.FillSchema(EmpDS, SchemaType.Source, "Employees");
EmpDA.Fill(EmpDS, "Employees");

DataSet TerDS = new DataSet();
TerDS.ReadXml("Territories.xml", XmlReadMode.ReadSchema);
```

```
TerDS.AcceptChanges();

DBConn.Close();

EmpDS.Merge(TerDS, true, MissingSchemaAction.AddWithKey);
```

Copying DataSet Contents

Sometimes, you might need to work with data without affecting the original data in a DataSet. Alternatively, you might have to create a subset of the data present in a DataSet. In such cases, you can create a copy of an existing DataSet instead of connecting to the database server and creating a new DataSet.

ADO.NET allows you to create a copy of a DataSet. You can also create a DataSet that is a subset of an existing DataSet. ADO.NET enables you to:

- Create an exact copy of a DataSet including the schema, data, row state information, and row version.
- Create a DataSet that contains the schema of an existing DataSet containing only the modified rows. You can specify that the copy contain all the modified rows or only the rows with the specified DataRowState.
- Copy only the schema or relational structure of a DataSet but not any rows from the original DataSet.

The following code shows how to create an exact copy of a DataSet.

Visual Basic .NET

```
Dim EmployeeDS As new DataSet("Employees")
Dim copyDS As DataSet = EmployeeDS.Copy()
```

Visual C#

```
DataSet EmployeeDS = new DataSet("Employees");
DataSet copyDS = EmployeeDS.Copy();
```

As mentioned earlier, you can also create a copy of a DataSet object that includes only the schema and the modified data. To create a copy of a DataSet that contains only the modified records, you use the GetChanges method of the DataSet object. The GetChanges method also allows you to retrieve the rows with specified row states. The following code shows how to create a copy of a DataSet object that contains only changed records.

Visual Basic .NET

```
Dim changeDS As DataSet = EmployeeDS.GetChanges()
```

Visual C#

```
DataSet changeDS = EmployeeDS.GetChanges();
```

ADO.NET also allows you to copy only the schema of an existing DataSet object. You use the Clone method to create a copy of the schema of a DataSet. The following code shows how to use the Clone method to copy the schema of a DataSet.

Visual Basic .NET

```
Dim changeDS As DataSet = EmployeeDS.Clone()
```

Visual C#

```
DataSet changeDS = EmployeeDS.Clone();
```

After you populate a DataSet, you can view the data in various ways by creating a data view.

Creating Data Views

Like a database, a DataSet also allows you to create various views of data. For example, you might want to view a subset of all the records in a DataSet that fulfill a certain criterion. An ADO.NET DataView object provides you with a dynamic view of a single set of data. You can then sort and filter the data per your requirements. However, unlike database views, you cannot treat a DataView object as a table. In addition, you cannot create a view of joined tables by using a data view. You also cannot exclude columns that are present in the source table or append columns that are not present in the source table.

You use an object of the DataView class to create a data view on a DataSet. You can create a DataView object by using the DataView constructor. When you create an instance of the DataView class, you can invoke the default constructor of the DataView class and pass a table name as an argument. The following code shows how to create a DataView object using the DataView constructor.

Visual Basic .NET

```
Dim EmployeeDV As DataView = New DataView( _
    EmployeeDS.Tables("Employees"), "Country = 'USA'", "City", _
    DataViewRowState.CurrentRows)
```

Visual C#

```
DataView EmployeeDV = new DataView(EmployeeDS.Tables["Employees"],
    "Country = 'USA'", "City", DataViewRowState.CurrentRows);
```

In the above code example, the DataView object named EmployeeDV contains the current rows from the Employees table of the EmployeeDS DataSet. Only the records that match the condition Country ='USA' are stored in the DataView object. In addition, the records in the EmployeeDV DataView object are sorted based on the values in the City column.

The following code shows how to set the Sort and RowFilter properties after creating a DataView object.

Visual Basic .NET

```
Dim EmployeeDV As DataView = New DataView(EmployeeDS.Tables( _
    "Employees"))
EmployeeDV.Sort = "City"
EmployeeDV.RowFilter = "Country='USA'"
```

Visual C#

```
DataView EmployeeDV = new DataView(EmployeeDS.Tables["Employees"]);
EmployeeDV.Sort = "City";
EmployeeDV.RowFilter = "Country='USA'";
```

Handling ADO.NET DataSet Events

ADO.NET supports event-driven programming, which enables you to capture changes and react to them properly. The ADO.NET DataSet provides the Merge-Failed event, which is raised when a conflict occurs when merging the contents of two DataSets. For example, when merging the contents of two DataSets, if the incoming and existing tables contain a column with the same name but different data type, an exception is thrown, and the MergeFailed event is raised. You pass the MergeFailedEventArgs parameter to the MergeFailed event. MergeFailedEvent-Args has a Conflict property that identifies the conflict between the two DataSet objects, and a Table property that identifies the name of the table in conflict. You can then use these properties to resolve the conflict. The following code shows how to add the MergeFailed event to an event handler.

Visual Basic .NET

```
Dim EmployeeDS As DataSet = New DataSet()

AddHandler EmployeeDS.MergeFailed, New MergeFailedEventHandler( _
    AddressOf DataSetMergeFailed)

Private Shared Sub DataSetMergeFailed(sender As Object, args As _
    MergeFailedEventArgs)
    Console.WriteLine("Merge failed for table " & args.Table.TableName)
    Console.WriteLine("Conflict = " & args.Conflict)
End Sub
```

Visual C#

```
DataSet EmployeeDS = new DataSet();

EmployeeDS.MergeFailed += new MergeFailedEventHandler
    (DataSetMergeFailed);

private static void DataSetMergeFailed(object sender,
    MergeFailedEventArgs args)
{
    Console.WriteLine("Merge failed for table " + args.Table.TableName);
    Console.WriteLine("Conflict = " + args.Conflict);
}
```

In addition to the MergeFailed event, ADO.NET provides certain events for the DataTable object. As with the MergeFailed event, you can write event-handling code for each of these events. These events correspond to changes in a column or row of a table. Table 5.2 describes the events of the DataTable object.

Table 5.2   Events of the DataTable Object

Event	Description
ColumnChanged	This event occurs when you successfully insert a value in a column.
ColumnChanging	This event occurs when you submit a value for a column.
RowChanged	This event occurs after you edit a row in the table.
RowChanging	This event occurs when a row in the table is changing.
RowDeleted	This event occurs after you mark a row in the table as Deleted.
RowDeleting	This event occurs before you mark a row in the table as Deleted.

Creating a Typed ADO.NET DataSet

Unlike an untyped DataSet that does not have an XML schema associated with it, a *strongly typed* DataSet does have an XML schema associated with it. In addition to the late-bound access to values through weakly typed variables, the strongly typed DataSets allow you to access tables and columns using user-friendly names and strongly typed variables.

A typed DataSet is a class that derives from a DataSet. The strongly typed DataSet inherits all the methods, events, and properties of a DataSet. In addition, a typed DataSet provides you with strongly typed methods, events, and properties. Therefore, you can access tables and columns by their names instead of using collection-based methods. This feature of strongly typed DataSets improves the readability of your code and allows the Visual Studio .NET code editor to provide the IntelliSense technology, which automatically completes the statements as you type. The IntelliSense technology increases the quality of your code because it corrects type mismatch errors at compile time rather than at run time.

You create a strongly typed DataSet using the command-line utility XSD.exe. The following command creates a strongly typed DataSet:

    xsd.exe /d /l:CS XSDSchemaFileName.xsd /n:XSDSchema.Namespace

Summary

- ADO.NET enables datacentric applications to connect to various data sources and retrieve, manipulate, and update data. ADO.NET uses XML to transfer data across applications and data sources. This enables you to use ADO.NET to access any data source including SQL Server and other database servers that use OLE DB to expose data.

- .NET data providers form the interface between the application and the data source. The data providers that the .NET Framework provides allow you to connect to various data sources such as SQL Server 7.*x* or later and OLE DB.

- A data adapter forms an interface between the application and the data source for retrieving and saving data. The OleDbDataAdapter object represents a connection and a set of Command objects that help populate a DataSet object.

- An ADO.NET DataReader allows you to read the read-only, forward-only data from a data source. To create a DataReader object, you execute the Execute-Reader() method of the appropriate class.

- ADO.NET DataSets provide a disconnected view of a data source. ADO.NET DataSets enable you to store data from multiple data sources. You can create relationships between the tables in a DataSet, even though the relationships might not exist between the tables in the data sources. In addition, you can create different data views from the data contained within the DataSets.

- An ADO.NET DataSet is a collection of tables and information about the relationships between tables. Each table further consists of collections of rows, columns, and constraints.

Lab: Creating and Using Data Access Components

In this lab, you will create data access components that enable you to build a robust and scalable distributed data access solution. You will create serviced components, remotable objects, a Windows service, and a remote client that will let you access and modify a database from any remote computer. The solutions to the exercises in this lab can be found in the \Solution folder on the Supplemental Course Materials CD-ROM.

The lab simulates an airline reservation system that enables you to view flight information and make flight reservations from a local or remote computer. The reservation system consists of:

- An airline database that contains two tables, Flights and Bookings, which store information about flight reservations

- Two business objects, Flights and Bookings, hosted as serviced components, which provide access to the airline database

- A remotable component, FlightBookings, which allows remote clients to access business objects

- A Windows service, RemoteAccessAgent, which configures the remotable component and makes it available to remote clients

Estimated lab time: 30 minutes

Exercise 1: Creating the Airline Database

In this exercise, you will create an airline database and the Flights and Bookings tables. To create the airline database, perform the following steps:

1. Open Server Explorer in Visual Studio .NET.

2. Expand the Servers node and locate the SQL Servers node.

3. Under the SQL Servers node, right-click your SQL Server, and select New Database from the shortcut menu to create a database.

4. In the Create Database dialog box, type **Airline** in the New Database Name box. Specify the required authentication level and click OK to create the Airline database.

5. From the Programs menu, choose Microsoft SQL Server, and then click Query Analyzer. Provide the required authentication information to connect to your database server.

6. Select the Airline database from the list of databases in the Query Analyzer.

7. Execute the following script.

SQL Script

```
if exists (select * from dbo.sysobjects where id =
object_id(N'[dbo].[FK_Bookings_Flights1]') and
OBJECTPROPERTY(id, N'IsForeignKey') = 1)

ALTER TABLE [dbo].[Bookings] DROP CONSTRAINT FK_Bookings_Flights1
GO

if exists (select * from dbo.sysobjects where id =
object_id(N'[dbo].[UPDATE_FLIGHTS]') and
OBJECTPROPERTY(id, N'IsTrigger') = 1)
drop trigger [dbo].[UPDATE_FLIGHTS]
GO

if exists (select * from dbo.sysobjects where id =
object_id(N'[dbo].[UPDATE_FLIGHTS_ON_DELETED]') and
OBJECTPROPERTY(id, N'IsTrigger') = 1)
drop trigger [dbo].[UPDATE_FLIGHTS_ON_DELETED]
GO

if exists (select * from dbo.sysobjects where id =
object_id(N'[dbo].[Bookings]') and OBJECTPROPERTY(id,
N'IsUserTable') = 1)
drop table [dbo].[Bookings]
GO

if exists (select * from dbo.sysobjects where id =
object_id(N'[dbo].[Flights]') and OBJECTPROPERTY(id, N'IsUserTable') = 1)
drop table [dbo].[Flights]
GO

if not exists (select * from dbo.sysobjects where id =
object_id(N'[dbo].[Bookings]') and OBJECTPROPERTY(id,
N'IsUserTable') = 1)
BEGIN
CREATE TABLE [dbo].[Bookings] (
    [Flight_No] [char] (5) COLLATE SQL_Latin1_General_CP1_CI_AS NOT NULL,
    [Flight_Date] [datetime] NOT NULL ,
    [Seat_No] [char] (10) COLLATE SQL_Latin1_General_CP1_CI_AS NOT NULL,
    [Passenger_Name] [varchar] (50) COLLATE SQL_Latin1_General_CP1_CI_AS
        NOT NULL ,
    [Age] [int] NULL ,
    [Fare_Charged] [int] NOT NULL
) ON [PRIMARY]
END

GO
```

(continued)

```
if not exists (select * from dbo.sysobjects where id =
object_id(N'[dbo].[Flights]') and OBJECTPROPERTY(id, N'IsUserTable') = 1)
 BEGIN
CREATE TABLE [dbo].[Flights] (
    [Flight_No] [char] (5) COLLATE SQL_Latin1_General_CP1_CI_AS NOT NULL,
    [Carrier] [varchar] (50) COLLATE SQL_Latin1_General_CP1_CI_AS
        NOT NULL ,
    [From_City] [varchar] (50) COLLATE SQL_Latin1_General_CP1_CI_AS
        NOT NULL ,
    [To_City] [varchar] (50) COLLATE SQL_Latin1_General_CP1_CI_AS
        NOT NULL ,
    [Capacity] [int] NOT NULL ,
    [Seats_Booked] [int] NOT NULL ,
    [Flight_Date] [datetime] NOT NULL ,
    [Fare] [int] NOT NULL
) ON [PRIMARY]
END

GO

ALTER TABLE [dbo].[Bookings] WITH NOCHECK ADD
    CONSTRAINT [PK_Bookings] PRIMARY KEY CLUSTERED
    (
        [Flight_No],
        [Flight_Date],
        [Seat_No]
    )  ON [PRIMARY]
GO

ALTER TABLE [dbo].[Flights] WITH NOCHECK ADD
    CONSTRAINT [PK_Flights] PRIMARY KEY CLUSTERED
    (
        [Flight_No],
        [Flight_Date]
    )  ON [PRIMARY]
GO

ALTER TABLE [dbo].[Flights] WITH NOCHECK ADD
    CONSTRAINT [CK_Flights] CHECK ([Seats_Booked] <= [Capacity])
GO

ALTER TABLE [dbo].[Bookings] ADD
    CONSTRAINT [FK_Bookings_Flights1] FOREIGN KEY
    (
        [Flight_No],
        [Flight_Date]
    ) REFERENCES [dbo].[Flights] (
        [Flight_No],
        [Flight_Date]
```

```
        )
GO

SET QUOTED_IDENTIFIER ON
GO
SET ANSI_NULLS ON
GO

CREATE TRIGGER UPDATE_FLIGHTS_ON_INSERT
ON BOOKINGS
AFTER INSERT
AS
BEGIN
    UPDATE FLIGHTS
    SET Seats_Booked=Seats_Booked+1
    From inserted
    where flights.flight_no = inserted.flight_no
    and flights.flight_date=inserted.flight_date
END

GO
SET QUOTED_IDENTIFIER OFF
GO
SET ANSI_NULLS ON
GO

SET QUOTED_IDENTIFIER ON
GO
SET ANSI_NULLS ON
GO

CREATE TRIGGER UPDATE_FLIGHTS_ON_DELETE
ON BOOKINGS
AFTER DELETE
AS
BEGIN
    UPDATE FLIGHTS
    SET Seats_Booked=Seats_Booked-1
    From deleted
    where flights.flight_no = deleted.flight_no
    and flights.flight_date=deleted.flight_date
END

GO
SET QUOTED_IDENTIFIER OFF
GO
SET ANSI_NULLS ON
GO
```

8. Expand the Tables node under the Airline database in Server Explorer to verify that the Flights and Bookings tables are created in the Airline database.

Exercise 2: Creating Data Access Components

In this exercise, you will create two components that allow you to access and modify the data in the Airline database using ADO.NET. These two components also use the COM+ component services for automatic transaction management, object construction, and just-in-time activation. To create data access components, perform the following steps:

1. Open Visual Studio .NET.
2. From the File menu, click New Project.
3. Select Class Library from the Templates pane. Type **BusinessComponents** in the Name field.
4. Change the name of the Class1.vb or Class1.cs file to Flights.vb or Flights.cs. In the Solution Explorer, right-click the Flights.vb or Flights.cs file, and from the shortcut menu choose View Code to see the code. Replace the code with the following code.

Visual Basic .NET

```
Imports System.EnterpriseServices
Imports System.Data.SqlClient
Imports System.Reflection

<Assembly: ApplicationName("Airlines System")>
<Assembly: AssemblyKeyFile("..\\..\\MyKey.snk")>

<Transaction(TransactionOption.RequiresNew), _
    ConstructionEnabled([Default]:="server=localhost; " & _
    "integrated security=sspi; database=Airline"), _
    JustInTimeActivation(True)> _
Public Class Flights
    Inherits ServicedComponent
    Private connectionString As String
    Private flights_data As DataTable
    Private DataAdapter As SqlDataAdapter
    Private connection As SqlConnection

    Protected Overrides Sub Construct(ByVal constructString As String)
        ' Called after constructor
        ' connectionString can be configured from the Activation tab
        ' in the Properties window of the Account component
        connectionString = constructString
        initialize()
    End Sub
```

```
Private Sub initialize()
    ' Initialize the connection
    connection = New SqlConnection(connectionString)
    DataAdapter = New SqlDataAdapter("select * from flights", _
        connectionString)
    Dim commandbuilder As New SqlCommandBuilder(DataAdapter)
    DataAdapter.MissingSchemaAction = MissingSchemaAction.AddWithKey
    flights_data = New DataTable("Flights")
    DataAdapter.Fill(flights_data)
End Sub

Public Function getFlightsInfo() As DataTable
    Return flights_data
End Function

<AutoComplete()> _
Public Function update(ByVal new_dt As DataTable) As DataTable
    DataAdapter.Update(new_dt)
    flights_data = Nothing
    DataAdapter.MissingSchemaAction = MissingSchemaAction.AddWithKey
    flights_data = New DataTable("Flights")
    DataAdapter.Fill(flights_data)
    Return flights_data
End Function
End Class
```

Visual C#

```
using System.EnterpriseServices;
using System.Data.SqlClient;
using System.Reflection;
using System.Data;

[assembly: ApplicationName("Airlines System")]
[assembly: AssemblyKeyFile("..\\..\\MyKey.snk")]

[Transaction(TransactionOption.RequiresNew),
    ConstructionEnabled(Default =
    "server=localhost; integrated security=sspi; database=Airline"),
    JustInTimeActivation(true)]
public class Flights : ServicedComponent
{
    private string connectionstring  ;
    private DataTable flights_data ;
    private SqlDataAdapter DataAdapter ;
    private SqlConnection connection ;

    protected override void Construct(string constructstring  )
    {
        // Called after constructor
```

(continued)

```csharp
    // connectionstring can be configured from the Activation tab
    // in the Properties window of the Account component
    connectionstring = constructstring;
    initialize();
}

private void initialize()
{
    // Initialize the connection
    connection = new SqlConnection(connectionstring);
    DataAdapter = new SqlDataAdapter("select * from flights",
        connectionstring);
    SqlCommandBuilder commandbuilder = new SqlCommandBuilder(
        DataAdapter);
    DataAdapter.MissingSchemaAction = MissingSchemaAction.AddWithKey;
    DataTable flights_data = new DataTable("Flights");
    DataAdapter.Fill(flights_data);
}

public  DataTable getFlightsInfo()
{
    return flights_data;
}

[AutoComplete()]
public DataTable update(DataTable new_dt  )
{
    DataAdapter.Update(new_dt);
    flights_data = null;
    DataAdapter.MissingSchemaAction = MissingSchemaAction.AddWithKey;
    flights_data = new DataTable("Flights");
    DataAdapter.Fill(flights_data);
    return flights_data;
}
}
```

5. Delete the AssemblyInfo.vb or AssemblyInfo.cs file from the BusinessComponents project.

6. From the File menu, click Add New Item.

7. Select Class from the Templates pane, and type **Bookings.vb** or **Bookings.cs** in the Name field.

8. Replace the code of the Bookings class with the following code.

Visual Basic .NET

```vbnet
Imports System.EnterpriseServices
Imports System.Data.SqlClient
Imports System.Reflection
```

```vb
<Transaction(TransactionOption.RequiresNew), _
    ConstructionEnabled([Default]:="server=localhost; integrated " & _
    "security=sspi; database=Airline"), _
    JustInTimeActivation(True)> _
Public Class Bookings
    Inherits ServicedComponent
    Private connectionString As String
    Private bookings_data As DataTable
    Private DataAdapter As SqlDataAdapter
    Private connection As SqlConnection

    Protected Overrides Sub Construct(ByVal constructString As String)
        ' Called after constructor
        ' connectionString can be configured from the Activation tab
        ' in the Properties window of the Account component
        connectionString = constructString
        initialize()
    End Sub

    Private Sub initialize()
        ' Initialize the connection
        connection = New SqlConnection(connectionString)
        DataAdapter = New SqlDataAdapter("select * from bookings", _
            connectionString)
        Dim commandbuilder As New SqlCommandBuilder(DataAdapter)
        DataAdapter.MissingSchemaAction = MissingSchemaAction.AddWithKey
        bookings_data = New DataTable("Bookings")
        DataAdapter.Fill(bookings_data)
    End Sub

    Public Function getBookingsInfo() As DataTable
        Return bookings_data
    End Function

    <AutoComplete()> _
    Public Function update(ByVal new_dt As DataTable) As DataTable
        DataAdapter.Update(new_dt)
        bookings_data = Nothing
        DataAdapter.MissingSchemaAction = MissingSchemaAction.AddWithKey
        bookings_data = New DataTable("Bookings")
        DataAdapter.Fill(bookings_data)
        Return bookings_data
    End Function
End Class
```

Visual C#

```csharp
using System.EnterpriseServices;
using System.Data.SqlClient;
```

(continued)

```csharp
using System.Reflection;
using System.Data;

[Transaction(TransactionOption.RequiresNew ),
    ConstructionEnabled(Default =
    "server=localhost; integrated security=sspi; database=Airline"),
    JustInTimeActivation(true)]
public class Bookings : ServicedComponent
{
    private string connectionstring ;
    private DataTable bookings_data  ;
    private SqlDataAdapter DataAdapter;
    private SqlConnection connection ;

    protected override void Construct(string constructstring  )
    {
        // Called after constructor
        // connectionstring can be configured from the Activation tab
        // in the Properties window of the Account component
        connectionstring = constructstring;
        initialize();
    }

    private void initialize()
    {
        // Initialize the connection
        connection = new SqlConnection(connectionstring);
        DataAdapter = new SqlDataAdapter("select * from bookings",
            connectionstring);
        SqlCommandBuilder commandbuilder = new SqlCommandBuilder(
            DataAdapter);
        DataAdapter.MissingSchemaAction = MissingSchemaAction.AddWithKey;
        bookings_data = new DataTable("Bookings");
        DataAdapter.Fill(bookings_data);
    }

    public DataTable getBookingsInfo()
    {
        return bookings_data;
    }

    [AutoComplete()]
    public DataTable update(DataTable new_dt  )
    {
        DataAdapter.Update(new_dt);
        bookings_data = null;
        DataAdapter.MissingSchemaAction = MissingSchemaAction.AddWithKey;
        bookings_data = new DataTable("Bookings");
```

```
DataAdapter.Fill(bookings_data);
return bookings_data;
    }
}
```

9. Expand the BusinessComponents project in the Solution Explorer. Right-click
    References and choose Add Reference from the shortcut menu to open the Add
    Reference dialog box. On the .NET tab, add a reference to System.Enterprise-
    Services.

10. Create a strong name key file by typing the following command at the Visual
    Studio .NET command prompt:

    sn –k MyKey.snk

11. From the Build menu, choose Build Solution to build the solution.

Exercise 3: Creating a Remote Data Access Component

In this exercise, you will create a .NET remotable component called FlightBookings, which allows remote clients to access the data provided by the Flights and
Bookings components. The FlightBookings object creates a DataSet object by
using the DataTables object provided by the Flights and Bookings objects. Remote
clients call methods on the FlightBookings object, which in turn calls methods on
the Flights and Bookings objects, to retrieve and modify the data on flight bookings. To create the FlightBookings component, perform the following steps:

1. From the File menu, point to Add Project, and then click Add New Project to
    add a new project to the solution.

2. Select Class Library from the Templates pane. Type **RemoteAccessCompo-
    nents** in the Name field.

3. Change the name of the Class1.vb or Class1.cs file to FlightBookings.vb or
    FlightBookings.cs.

4. Right-click the RemoteAccessComponents project in the Solution Explorer,
    and select Add Reference from the shortcut menu to open the Add Reference
    dialog box. On the .NET tab, add a reference to System.Runtime.Remoting. On
    the Projects tab shown in Figure 5.9, add a reference to BusinessComponents.

5. In the Solution Explorer, right-click the FlightBookings.vb or FlightBook-
    ings.cs file to open the shortcut menu, and then choose View Code to see the
    code. Replace the code with the following code.

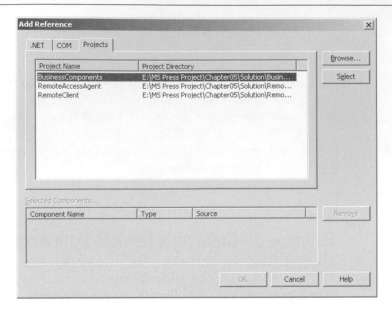

Figure 5.9   Add Reference dialog box

Visual Basic .NET

```vb
Imports System.Runtime.Remoting
Imports System.Runtime.Remoting.Channels
Imports System.Runtime.Remoting.Channels.Tcp

Public Class FlightBookings
    Inherits MarshalByRefObject

    Private flt_bkgs As DataSet
    Private flights As BusinessComponents.Flights
    Private bookings As BusinessComponents.Bookings

    Public Sub New()
        flt_bkgs = New DataSet("Flight Bookings")
        flights = New BusinessComponents.Flights()
        bookings = New BusinessComponents.Bookings()
        flt_bkgs.Tables.Add(flights.getFlightsInfo)
        flt_bkgs.Tables.Add(bookings.getBookingsInfo)
        Dim dr As New DataRelation("Flight Bookings", _
            flt_bkgs.Tables(0).Columns(0), _
            flt_bkgs.Tables(1).Columns(0))
        flt_bkgs.Relations.Add(dr)
    End Sub

    Public Function getInfo() As DataSet
        Return flt_bkgs
    End Function
```

```
        Public Function update(ByVal ds As DataSet) As DataSet
            flights.update(ds.Tables(0))
            bookings.update(ds.Tables(1))
            flt_bkgs = New DataSet("Flight Bookings")
            flt_bkgs.Tables.Add(flights.getFlightsInfo)
            flt_bkgs.Tables.Add(bookings.getBookingsInfo)
            Dim dr As New DataRelation("Flight Bookings", _
                flt_bkgs.Tables(0).Columns(0), flt_bkgs.Tables(1).Columns(0))
            flt_bkgs.Relations.Add(dr)
            Return flt_bkgs
        End Function
    End Class
End Class
```

Visual C#

```
using System.Runtime.Remoting;
using System.Runtime.Remoting.Channels;
using System.Runtime.Remoting.Channels.Tcp;
using System.Data;
using System;
using BusinessComponents;

public class FlightBookings : MarshalByRefObject
{
    private DataSet flt_bkgs ;
    private Flights flights ;
    private Bookings bookings ;

    public  FlightBookings()
    {
        flt_bkgs = new DataSet("Flight Bookings");
        flights = new Flights();
        bookings = new Bookings();
        flt_bkgs.Tables.Add(flights.getFlightsInfo());
        flt_bkgs.Tables.Add(bookings.getBookingsInfo());
        DataRelation dr = new DataRelation("Flight Bookings",
            flt_bkgs.Tables[0].Columns[0],
            flt_bkgs.Tables[1].Columns[0]);
        flt_bkgs.Relations.Add(dr);
    }

    public DataSet getInfo()
    {
        return flt_bkgs;
    }

    public DataSet update(DataSet ds  )
    {
        flights.update(ds.Tables[0]);
        bookings.update(ds.Tables[1]);
        flt_bkgs = new DataSet("Flight Bookings");
```

(continued)

```
flt_bkgs.Tables.Add(flights.getFlightsInfo());
flt_bkgs.Tables.Add(bookings.getBookingsInfo());
DataRelation dr = new DataRelation("Flight Bookings",
    flt_bkgs.Tables[0].Columns[0],
    flt_bkgs.Tables[1].Columns[0]);
flt_bkgs.Relations.Add(dr);
return flt_bkgs;
    }
}
```

6. From the Build menu, choose Build Solution to build the solution.

Exercise 4: Creating a Windows Service to Host the Remote Data Access Component

In this exercise, you will create a Windows service application to configure and host the FlightBookings component that you created in the previous exercise. To create the Windows Service application, perform the following steps:

1. From the File menu, point to Add Project, and then click Add New Project to add a new project to the solution. Select Windows Service from the Templates pane. Type **RemoteAccessAgent** in the Name field.

2. Change the name of the Service1.vb or Service1.cs file to RemoteAccess-Agent.vb or RemoteAccessAgent.cs.

3. Right-click the RemoteAccessAgent.vb or RemoteAccessAgent.cs file and choose View Designer from the shortcut menu. Right-click in the Design window to open the Properties window of the Windows service. Change the Name and ServiceName properties of the Windows service to RemoteAccessAgent.

4. In the Solution Explorer, right-click the RemoteAccessAgent.vb or RemoteAccess-Agent.cs file to open the shortcut menu, and then choose View Code. Locate the following line of code and replace *Service1* with **RemoteAccessAgent**.

Note   You will need to expand the region containing the Designer Generated code in Visual Basic .NET to locate the given line of code.

Visual Basic .NET
```
ServicesToRun = New System.ServiceProcess.ServiceBase() {New Service1()}
```

Visual C#
```
ServicesToRun = new System.ServiceProcess.ServiceBase[] { new Service1() };
```

5. Right-click the RemoteAccessAgent project in the Solution Explorer, and select Add Reference from the shortcut menu to open the Add Reference dialog box. On the .NET tab, add a reference to System.Runtime.Remoting. On the Projects tab, add a reference to RemoteAccessComponents.

6. Replace the code for the OnStart method, add references to the appropriate namespaces, and declare the private variable, as shown in the following code.

Visual Basic .NET

```
Imports System.ServiceProcess
Imports System.Runtime.Remoting
Imports System.Runtime.Remoting.Channels
Imports System.Runtime.Remoting.Channels.Tcp

Public Class RemoteAccessAgent
    Inherits System.ServiceProcess.ServiceBase
    Private channel As TcpChannel
    ' Designer Generated code
    .
    .
    .

    Protected Overrides Sub OnStart(ByVal args() As String)
        channel = New TcpChannel(7000)
        ChannelServices.RegisterChannel(channel)
        RemotingConfiguration.ApplicationName = _
            "Remote Flight System Access"
        RemotingConfiguration.RegisterWellKnownServiceType( _
            GetType(RemoteAccessComponents.FlightBookings), _
            "RemoteDataAccessServer", WellKnownObjectMode.Singleton)
    End Sub
End Class
```

Visual C#

```
using System;
using System.Collections;
using System.ComponentModel;
using System.Data;
using System.Diagnostics;
using System.ServiceProcess;
using System.Runtime.Remoting;
using System.Runtime.Remoting.Channels;
using System.Runtime.Remoting.Channels.Tcp;
using RemoteAccessComponents;

namespace RemoteAccessAgent
{
    public class RemoteAccessAgent : System.ServiceProcess.ServiceBase
    {
        private TcpChannel channel ;
// Designer Generated code
    .
    .
    .

        protected override void OnStart(string[] args)
        {
```

(continued)

```
                        // TODO: Add code here to start your service.
                        channel = new TcpChannel(7000);
                        ChannelServices.RegisterChannel(channel);
                        RemotingConfiguration.ApplicationName =
                            "Remote Flight System Access";
                        RemotingConfiguration.RegisterWellKnownServiceType(
                            Type.GetType("FlightBookings"), "RemoteDataAccessServer",
                            WellKnownObjectMode.Singleton);
                    }
                }
            }
```

7. Add installers to the RemoteAccessAgent service.

Note   To review how to add installers, see Lesson 4 in Chapter 2, "Creating and Managing Windows Services."

---

8. For a Visual Basic .NET project, change the startup object for the project. In the Solution Explorer, right-click the RemoteAccessAgent project and choose Properties from the shortcut menu. Then select RemoteAccessAgent from the Startup Object list.

9. From the Build menu, choose Build Solution to build the solution.

Exercise 5: Creating a Remote Client Application

In this exercise, you will create a Windows application that allows you to access the FlightBookings component from a local or remote computer. To create the client application, perform the following steps:

1. From the File menu, point to Add Project, and then click Add New Project to add a new project to the solution. Select Windows Application from the Templates pane. Type **RemoteClient** in the Name field.

2. From the Windows Forms Toolbox, add a DataGrid control and a Button control to Form1. Change the Text property of Form1 to Flight Bookings and the Text property of Button1 to Save, so that the form appears as shown here.

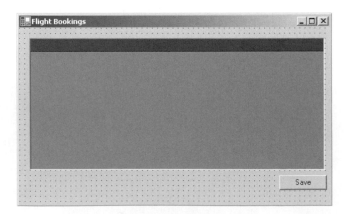

3. Right-click the RemoteClient project in the Solution Explorer, and select Add Reference from the shortcut menu to open the Add Reference dialog box. On the .NET tab, add a reference to System.Runtime.Remoting. On the Projects tab, add a reference to RemoteAccessComponents.

4. Right-click on the Form1.vb or Form1.cs file and choose View Code from the shortcut menu to see the code. Replace the code with the following code.

Visual Basic .NET

```
Imports System.Data
Imports System.Reflection
Imports System.Runtime.Remoting
Imports System.Runtime.Remoting.Channels
Imports System.Runtime.Remoting.Channels.Tcp
Imports RemoteAccessComponents

Public Class Form1
    Inherits System.Windows.Forms.Form
    Private flight_Bookings As FlightBookings
    Private ds As DataSet
    .
    .
    .

    Private Sub Form1_Load(ByVal sender As System.Object, _
        ByVal e As System.EventArgs) Handles MyBase.Load
        Try
            ds = New DataSet()
            ChannelServices.RegisterChannel(New TcpChannel())
            RemotingConfiguration.RegisterWellKnownClientType( _
                GetType(FlightBookings), _
                "tcp://localhost:7000/RemoteDataAccessServer")
            flight_Bookings = New RemoteAccessComponents.FlightBookings()
            ds = flight_Bookings.getInfo
            DataGrid1.DataSource = ds
        Catch ex As Exception
            MsgBox(ex.Message)
        End Try
    End Sub

    Private Sub Button1_Click(ByVal sender As System.Object, _
        ByVal e As System.EventArgs) Handles Button1.Click
        Try
            Dim ds1 As DataSet = flight_Bookings.update(ds)
            ds = ds1
            DataGrid1.DataSource = ds
            DataGrid1.DataMember = ds.Tables(0).TableName
        Catch ex As Exception
            MsgBox(ex.Message)
```

(continued)

```
            End Try
        End Sub
End Class
```

Visual C#

```csharp
using System;
using System.Drawing;
using System.Collections;
using System.ComponentModel;
using System.Windows.Forms;
using System.Data;
using System.Runtime.Remoting;
using System.Runtime.Remoting.Channels;
using System.Runtime.Remoting.Channels.Tcp;
using RemoteAccessComponents;

namespace RemoteClient
{
    /// <summary>
    /// Summary description for Form1.
    /// </summary>
    public class Form1 : System.Windows.Forms.Form
    {
        internal System.Windows.Forms.Button Button1;
        internal System.Windows.Forms.DataGrid DataGrid1;

        private FlightBookings flight_Bookings  ;
        private DataSet ds ;
        .
        .
        .


        private void Button1_Click(object sender, System.EventArgs e)
        {
            try
            {
                DataSet ds1 = flight_Bookings.update(ds);
                ds = ds1;
                DataGrid1.DataSource = ds;
                DataGrid1.DataMember = ds.Tables[0].TableName;
            }
            catch (Exception ex )
            {
                MessageBox.Show(ex.Message);
            }
        }
```

```
private void Form1_Load(object sender, System.EventArgs e)
{
    try
    {
        ds = new DataSet();
        ChannelServices.RegisterChannel(new TcpChannel());
        RemotingConfiguration.RegisterWellKnownClientType(
            typeof(FlightBookings),
            "tcp://localhost:7000/RemoteDataAccessServer");
        flight_Bookings = new
            RemoteAccessComponents.FlightBookings();
        ds = flight_Bookings.getInfo();
        DataGrid1.DataSource = ds;
    }
    catch (Exception ex )
    {
        MessageBox.Show(ex.Message);
    }
}
```

5. From the Build menu, choose Build Solution to build the solution.

6. Using the Installutil tool, install the RemoteAccessAgent service. To install the RemoteAccessAgent service, type the following command at the Visual Studio .NET command prompt:

Installutil RemoteAccessAgent.exe

7. From the service control panel, start the RemoteAccessAgent service.

8. Execute the RemoteClient.exe file to run the Windows application. Initially, the application shows an empty DataGrid with a + sign on the left. Click the + sign to show the two links for displaying either flights or bookings as shown here.

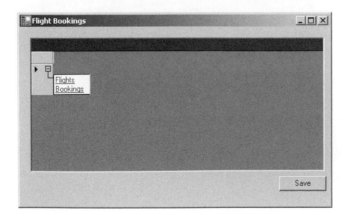

The next figure shows the Flight Bookings screen, which is displayed after clicking Flights in the previous screen. You can expand a row and click the Flight Bookings link to view the Flight Booking details for a particular flight.

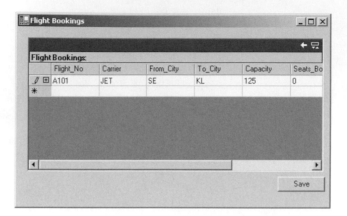

9. Test the application by creating, deleting, and modifying the records.

Note   The Flight_No and Flight_Date columns of the Flights table constitute the composite primary key. The check constraint on the Flights table ensures that Seats_Booked <= Capacity. The Flight_No, Seat_No, and Flight_Date columns constitute the composite primary key for the Bookings table. The Flight_No and Flight_Date columns of the Bookings table reference the respective columns in the Flights table.

Review

The questions in this section reinforce key information presented in this chapter. If you are unable to answer a question, review the appropriate lesson, and then try answering the question again. Answers to the questions can be found in Appendix A, "Questions and Answers."

1. What are the components of an ADO.NET data provider?

2. What tasks do the data providers enable you to perform?

3. What are the options you need to specify when you set the ConnectionString property of a SqlConnection object?

4. Which method of the Command object is best suited for when you are using aggregate functions such as COUNT, MAX, and MIN in a SELECT statement?

5. Which object holds read-only and forward-only data that you retrieve from a data source?

6. How do you create relationships between two tables in a DataSet?

7. What events are exposed by the DataTable object?

C H A P T E R   6

Accessing and Manipulating XML Data

About This Chapter

XML is central to data exchange between applications in the .NET Framework. You need to know the XML Document Object Model (DOM) and how to access XML data in your applications. In this lesson you will learn how to read and write data from XML documents, perform queries on XML documents, and validate XML documents with XML Schema. In addition, you will also learn to populate a DataSet with data from an XML file and write data from a DataSet into an XML file.

Before You Begin

To complete the lessons in this chapter, you

- Must have knowledge of programming in Microsoft Visual Basic .NET or Microsoft Visual C#
- Must have a working knowledge of XML

Lesson 1: Understanding the XML Document Object Model

You need to know the XML Document Object Model (XML DOM) to work with XML data in your applications. In this lesson, you will learn about the XML DOM and what constitutes a well-formed XML document. You will also learn how to use the objects available in the XML DOM to read and write XML data. Finally, you will learn how to create an XML Parser in Visual Studio .NET.

After this lesson, you will be able to

- Describe the XML Document Object Model
- Use the XML Document Object Model to read and write XML data
- Create an XML Parser in Visual Studio .NET

Estimated lesson time: 30 minutes

Overview of the XML Document Object Model

To enable disparate systems to communicate with each other, you require a standard that is understandable by all systems. Therefore, the obvious choice is a standard that is text-based. Because most systems understand text-based data, XML is the preferred standard of communication. XML files conform to the standards developed by the World Wide Web Consortium (W3C). Let's take a look at a well-formed XML document.

XML Document

```
<?xml version= "1.0"?>
    <employees>
        <employee>
            <FirstName>John</FirstName>
            <LastName>Doe</LastName>
            <DateOfBirth>08/09/1968</DateOfBirth>
            <DateOfJoining>04/01/1992</DateOfJoining>
            <Address>2010 Stanley Dr., Charlotte, NC 28273</Address>
            <Basic>2100</Basic>
            <Designation>Associate Consultant</Designation>
            <LeaveBalance>12</LeaveBalance>
        </employee>
        <employee>
            <FirstName>Luis</FirstName>
            <LastName>Bonifaz</LastName>
            <DateOfBirth>01/12/1972</DateOfBirth>
            <DateOfJoining>06/01/2000</DateOfJoining>
```

```
        <Address>7862 Freepoint Pkwy, Tampa, FL 33624</Address>
        <Basic>1400</Basic>
        <Designation>Developer</Designation>
        <LeaveBalance>4</LeaveBalance>
      </employee>
  </employees>
```

The preceding XML code contains information about two employees and is a well-formed XML document. A well-formed XML document contains an end tag for every begin tag. For example, for every <employee> tag, a </employee> tag should be present. A well-formed XML document can have an associated document type definition (DTD) or an XML Schema that describes the data and the relationship between the data within an XML document. DTDs define the grammar for a class of XML documents. DTDs have a syntax that is different from the syntax of XML. XML Schema, on the other hand, is an XML document that describes the elements and attributes of an XML document and can include type information. You use DTDs or XML Schema to describe and validate XML documents. Validating XML documents is discussed in detail in Lesson 5.

To read XML documents, your application should be able to decipher the way in which XML documents are formed. The XML Document Object Model allows you to read, manipulate, and modify an XML document programatically.

The XML Document Object Model

The XML Document Object Model (XML DOM) class is a representation of the XML document in memory. The DOM class lets you read, write, and manipulate an XML document. The .NET Framework provides classes, which enable you to navigate through an XML document and obtain relevant information. Every XML document consists of parent and child nodes. In the XML document presented earlier, <employees> is the parent node. The immediate child node of the <employees> tag is the <employee> node. The <employee> node has many child nodes. When nodes are in the same level, such as the <FirstName> and <LastName> nodes in the example document, they are known as siblings.

The XML DOM contains different types of nodes. Table 6.1 lists the most commonly used nodes and their descriptions.

Table 6.1   Nodes in the XML DOM

DOM node type	Description
Document	This node type is the container for all the nodes and is also known as the *document root*.
DocumentType	This node type represents the <!DOCTYPE> node.
Element	This node type represents element nodes.

(continued)

Table 6.1   Nodes in the XML DOM *(continued)*

DOM node type	Description
Attribute	This node type represents the attributes of an element node.
Comment	This node type represents comment nodes.
Text	This node type represents the text that belongs to a particular node or to an attribute.

You can also use Simple API for XML (SAX) to read data from XML documents. Unlike DOM, SAX does not load the entire XML document into memory. Rather, the SAX parser reads the contents sequentially and generates events as it reads the XML document. Because SAX does not load the XML document into memory, it is good for reading large XML documents. However, one of the limitations of SAX is that it does not maintain any data structures that are required to perform complex searches. In addition, you cannot use SAX when you want to modify the XML document.

Another way in which you can work with XML documents is by using the XmlReader class of the .NET Framework. The XmlReader class provides read-only, forward-only access to XML documents. Unlike XML DOM, the XmlReader class does not load the XML document into memory.

Before you learn about various objects that you use to read and edit an XML document using the XML DOM, you should learn how the XML document is structured in memory. The root node is the document node and is represented by the XmlDocument object. The XmlDocument object is derived from the XmlNode class. The XmlDocument object is used to perform tasks such as loading and saving XML documents. The XmlDocument object consists of the Load, LoadXml, and Save methods, which enable you to load and save XML documents. In addition, you can use the XmlDocument object to access all the nodes in the document.

The following code snippet shows how to load an XML document into the XML DOM.

Visual Basic .NET

```
Imports System
Imports System.IO
Imports System.Xml

Module Module1
    Sub Main()
        Dim myDocument As New XmlDocument()
        myDocument.Load("emp.xml")
        Console.WriteLine(myDocument.InnerXml.ToString)
        Console.ReadLine()
    End Sub
End Module
```

Visual C#

```csharp
using System;
using System.IO;
using System.Xml;

namespace CSharp_XMLSample
{
    class Class1
    {
        [STAThread]
        static void Main(string[] args)
        {
            XmlDocument myDocument = new XmlDocument();
            myDocument.Load("emp.xml");
            Console.WriteLine(myDocument.InnerXml.ToString());
            Console.ReadLine();
        }
    }
}
```

This code snippet uses the XmlDocument object and loads the XML document into the variable myDocument. There are two ways of loading the XML document into a variable. You can use the Load method and specify the file name as the parameter. Alternatively, you can use the LoadXml method and specify the XML data as the parameter. The following code snippet shows the usage of the LoadXml method.

Visual Basic .NET

```vbnet
Imports System
Imports System.IO
Imports System.Xml

Module Module1
    Sub Main()
        Dim myDocument As New XmlDocument()
        myDocument.LoadXml("<employees>" & _
            "<employee>" & _
            "<FirstName>John</FirstName>" & _
            "<LastName>Doe</LastName>" & _

            .
            .
            .

            "</employee>" & _

            .
            .
            .

            "</employees>")
        Console.WriteLine(myDocument.InnerXml.ToString)
        Console.ReadLine()
```

(continued)

```
        End Sub
End Module
```

Visual C#

```csharp
using System;
using System.IO;
using System.Xml;

namespace CSharp_XMLSample
{
    class Class1
    {
        [STAThread]
        static void Main(string[] args)
        {
            XmlDocument myDocument = new XmlDocument();
            myDocument.LoadXml("<employees>" +
                "<employee>" +
                "<FirstName>John</FirstName>" +
                "<LastName>Doe</LastName>" +
                .
                .
                .

                "</employee>" +

                .
                .
                .

                "</employees>");
            Console.WriteLine(myDocument.InnerXml.ToString());
            Console.ReadLine();
        }
    }
}
```

You can also use the XmlDocument object to write XML data. To write XML data, you can use the Save method. The following code snippet shows the usage of the Save method.

Visual Basic .NET

```vb
Imports System
Imports System.IO
Imports System.Xml

Module Module1
    Sub Main()
        Dim myDocument As New XmlDocument()
        Dim xmlData As String
        xmlData = "<employees>" & _
```

```
                            "<employee>" & _
                            "<FirstName>John</FirstName>" & _
                            "<LastName>Doe</LastName>" & _
                            .

                            .

                            .

                            "</employee>" & _
                            .

                            .

                            .

                            "</employees>"
                myDocument.LoadXml(xmlData)
                myDocument.Save("newemp.xml")
                Console.WriteLine(myDocument.InnerXml.ToString)
                Console.ReadLine()
            End Sub
        End Module
```

Visual C#

```csharp
using System;
using System.IO;
using System.Xml;

namespace CSharp_XMLSample
{
    class Class1
    {
        [STAThread]
        static void Main(string[] args)
        {
            XmlDocument myDocument = new XmlDocument();
            string xmlData = "<employees>" +
                "<employee>" +
                "<FirstName>John</FirstName>" +
                "<LastName>Doe</LastName>" +
                .

                .

                .

                "</employee>" +
                .

                .

                .

                "</employees>";
            myDocument.LoadXml(xmlData);
            myDocument.Save("newEmp.xml");
            Console.WriteLine(myDocument.InnerXml.ToString());
            Console.ReadLine();
```

(continued)

```
        }
    }
}
```

Creating an XML Parser

In the previous topic, you learned how to load and save XML documents. In this topic, we will go one step ahead and create an XML parser that reads an XML document and displays the contents in a console window. The following piece of code shows how to create an XML parser.

Visual Basic .NET

```vb
Imports System
Imports System.IO
Imports System.Xml

Module Module1
    Sub Main()
        Dim myDocument As New XmlDocument()
        Dim xmlData As String
        myDocument.Load("emp.xml")
        Dim node1 As XmlNode
        Dim i As Integer
        Dim count As Integer
        count = 0
        i = 1
        node1 = myDocument.ChildNodes(1)
        For Each node1 In node1.ChildNodes
            Console.WriteLine(vbCrLf)
            Console.WriteLine("The elements under node number: {0}", i)
            Console.WriteLine("----------------------------------------")
            Dim node2 As XmlNode
            For Each node2 In node1.ChildNodes
                Console.WriteLine( _
                myDocument.DocumentElement.FirstChild.ChildNodes _
                (count).Name + ": " + node2.FirstChild.Value)
                count = count + 1
            Next
            i = i + 1
            count = 0
        Next
        Console.WriteLine(vbCrLf)
        Console.WriteLine("Press <Enter> to quit...")
        Console.ReadLine()
    End Sub
End Module
```

Visual C#

```csharp
using System;
using System.IO;
```

```csharp
using System.Xml;

namespace CSharp_XMLSample
{
    class Class1
    {
        [STAThread]
        static void Main(string[] args)
        {
            try
            {
                XmlDocument myDocument = new XmlDocument();
                string xmlData;
                myDocument.Load("emp.xml");
                int i;
                int count;
                count = 0;
                i = 1;
                XmlNode node = myDocument.ChildNodes[1];
                foreach (XmlNode node1 in node.ChildNodes)
                {
                    Console.WriteLine("\n");

                    Console.WriteLine(
                        "The elements under node number: {0}", i);
                    Console.WriteLine(
                        "------------------------------------------");
                    foreach (XmlNode node2 in node1.ChildNodes)
                    {
                        Console.WriteLine(
                            myDocument.DocumentElement.FirstChild.ChildNodes

                            [count].Name + ": " +
                            node2.FirstChild.Value);
                        count = count + 1;
                    }
                    i = i + 1;
                    count = 0;
                }
                Console.WriteLine("\n");
                Console.WriteLine("Press <Enter> to quit...");
                Console.ReadLine();
            }
            catch (Exception e)
            {
                Console.WriteLine(e.Message);
                Console.ReadLine();
            }
        }
    }
}
```

Lesson 2: Working with XmlReader and XmlWriter

The System.Xml namespace provides the XmlReader and XmlWriter classes that enable you to parse and write XML data from streams or XML documents. These are abstract base classes that you can extend to create your own customized classes. In this lesson, you will learn about the functionalities that are provided by the XmlReader and XmlWriter classes. In addition, you will also learn to use the classes that implement the XmlReader and XmlWriter classes.

After this lesson, you will be able to

- Describe the XmlReader and XmlWriter classes
- Use various XmlReader and XmlWriter classes

Estimated lesson time: 30 minutes

Overview of XmlReader

The XmlReader class allows you to access XML data from a stream or XML document. This class provides fast, non-cacheable, read-only, and forward-only access to XML data. The XmlReader class is an abstract class and provides methods that are implemented by the derived classes to provide access to the elements and attributes of XML data. You use XmlReader classes to determine various factors such as the depth of a node in an XML document, whether the node has attributes, the number of attributes in a node, and the value of an attribute. The XmlTextReader class is one of the derived classes of the XmlReader class and implements the methods defined by the XmlReader class. You can use the XmlTextReader class to read XML data. However, the XmlTextReader class does not enable you to access or validate the document type definition (DTD) or schema information. The XmlValidatingReader class, which is another derived class of the XmlReader class, enables you to read XML data as well as supporting DTD and schema validation. The XmlValidatingReader class is described in detail in Lesson 5.

Reading XML Using XmlTextReader

The XmlTextReader class is used when you require fast access to XML data but don't need support for DTD or schema validation. The XmlTextReader class should be used when you don't need to read the entire document into memory via the DOM. Some of the more commonly used properties and methods of the XmlTextReader class are shown in Table 6.2.

Table 6.2   Commonly Used XmlTextReader Members

Members	Description
Properties	
AttributeCount	Gets an Integer value specifying the number of attributes on the current node
Depth	Gets an Integer value specifying the depth of the current node in an XML document
HasAttributes	Gets a Boolean value specifying whether a node has attributes
HasValue	Gets a Boolean value specifying whether the current node can have a value
IsEmptyElement	Gets a Boolean value indicating whether the current node is empty
Item	Gets the value of an attribute as String
Value	Gets the text value of the current node
Methods	
IsStartElement	Checks if the element is the start element
MoveToElement	Moves to the element that contains the current attribute node
MoveToFirstAttribute	Moves to the first attribute
MoveToNextAttribute	Moves to the next attribute
Read	Reads the next node from the stream
ReadAttributeValue	Reads the attribute value and parses it into one or more nodes
ReadString	Reads the content of an element or text node in text
ReadStartElement	Checks if the current node is an element and moves the reader to the next node
ReadEndElement	Checks if the current node is an end tag and moves the reader to the next node
Skip	Skips the children of the current node

You can initialize an XmlTextReader object to read data from an XML document as shown in the following code.

Visual Basic .NET

```
Dim textReader as New XmlTextReader("Emp.xml")
```

Visual C#

```
XmlTextReader textReader = new XmlTextReader("Emp.xml");
```

You can also initialize an XmlTextReader object to read data from a stream as shown in the following code.

Visual Basic .NET

```vbnet
Dim stream as New System.IO.StringReader(  _
    "<?xml version= ""1.0""?>" & _
    "<employees>" & _
    "    <employee>" & _
    "        <FirstName>John</FirstName>" & _
    "        <LastName>Doe</LastName>" & _
    "        <DateOfBirth>08/09/1968</DateOfBirth>" & _
    "        <DateOfJoining>04/01/1992</DateOfJoining>" & _
    "        <Address>2010 Stanley Dr., Charlotte, NC 28273</Address>"& _
    "        <Basic>2100</Basic>" & _
    "        <Designation>Associate Consultant</Designation>" & _
    "        <LeaveBalance>12</LeaveBalance>" & _
    "    </employee>" & _
    "</employees>")

Dim textReader as New XmlTextReader(stream)
```

Visual C#

```csharp
System.IO.StringReader stream ;
stream = new System.IO.StringReader("<?xml version= \"1.0\"?>" +
    "<employees>" +
    "    <employee>" +
    "        <FirstName>John</FirstName>" +
    "        <LastName>Doe</LastName>" +
    "        <DateOfBirth>08/09/1968</DateOfBirth>" +
    "        <DateOfJoining>04/01/1992</DateOfJoining>" +
    "        <Address>2010 Stanley Dr., Charlotte, NC 28273</Address>" +
    "        <Basic>2100</Basic>" +
    "        <Designation>Associate Consultant</Designation>" +
    "        <LeaveBalance>12</LeaveBalance>" +
    "    </employee>" +
    "</employees>");

XmlTextReader textReader = new XmlTextReader(stream);
```

The following code shows how to read data using the XmlTextReader class.

Visual Basic .NET

```vbnet
Dim reader As New XmlTextReader("E:\emp.xml")
While reader.Read()
    Select Case reader.NodeType
    Case XmlNodeType.Element
        Console.Write("<" + reader.Name)
```

```
        While (reader.MoveToNextAttribute())
            Console.Write(" " & reader.Name & "='" & _
                reader.Value & "'")
        End While
        Console.Write(">")
        If reader.HasAttributes Then
        While reader.MoveToNextAttribute
            Console.Write(" " & reader.Value & " ")
        End While
        End If
    Case XmlNodeType.Text
        Console.Write(reader.Value)
    Case XmlNodeType.EndElement
        Console.WriteLine(("</" & reader.Name & ">"))
    End Select
End While
```

Visual C#

```csharp
XmlTextReader reader =new XmlTextReader(@"E:\emp.xml");
    while (reader.Read())
    {
        switch (reader.NodeType)
        {
            case XmlNodeType.Element:
                Console.Write("<" + reader.Name);
                while (reader.MoveToNextAttribute())
                {
                    Console.Write(" " + reader.Name + "='" +
                        reader.Value + "'");
                }
                Console.Write(">");
                if (reader.HasAttributes )
                {
                    while (reader.MoveToNextAttribute())
                        Console.Write(" " + reader.Value + " ");
                }
                break;
            case XmlNodeType.Text:
                Console.Write(reader.Value);
                break;
            case XmlNodeType.EndElement:
                Console.WriteLine(("</" + reader.Name + ">"));
                break;
        }
    }
```

Now you will learn how to write XML data using XmlWriter.

Overview of XmlWriter

The XmlWriter class is an abstract class that enables you to create XML streams and write data to well-formed XML documents. XmlWriter is used to perform tasks such as writing multiple documents into one output stream, writing valid names and tokens into the stream, encoding binary data and writing text output, managing output, and flushing and closing the output stream. The XmlTextWriter class, which is a derived class of XmlWriter, provides properties and methods that you use to write XML data to a file, stream, console, or other types of output. Some of the more commonly used properties and methods of the XmlTextWriter class are shown in Table 6.3.

Table 6.3   Commonly Used XmlTextWriter Members

Members	Description
Properties	
BaseStream	Gets the stream to which XmlTextWriter writes the output
Formatting	Specifies the formatting of the output, which can be Indented or None. If the Formatting is Indented, the child elements are indented using the Indentaion and IndentChar properties.
Indentation	Specifies the number of the IndentChars to use when writing the child elements.
IndentChar	Gets or sets the indenting character when formatting is set to Formatting.Indented.
WriteState	Gets the state of the writer. The valid values for WriteState include Start, Element, Attribute, Content, Prolog, and Closed.
Methods	
WriteStartDocument	Writes the following XML declaration to the start of the document: <?xml version="1.0" ?>
WriteStartElement	Writes the start tag of a specified element
WriteElementString	Writes an element containing a string value
WriteStartAttribute	Writes the start of an attribute
WriteAttributeString	Writes the value of a given attribute
WriteEndAttribute	Writes the end of an attribute
WriteEndElement	Writes the end tag of an element

Writing XML Using XmlTextWriter

The following code shows how to use XmlTextWriter to write XML to a file.

Visual Basic .NET

```
Dim textWriter As New XmlTextWriter("e:\Emp.xml", _
    System.Text.Encoding.UTF8)
textWriter.Formatting = Formatting.Indented
textWriter.WriteStartDocument(False)
textWriter.WriteDocType("Employees", Nothing, Nothing, Nothing)
textWriter.WriteComment("This file represents a fragment of Employees" & _
    "database")
textWriter.WriteStartElement("Employees")
textWriter.WriteStartElement("Employee", Nothing)
textWriter.WriteElementString("FirstName", "John")
textWriter.WriteElementString("LastName", "Doe")
textWriter.WriteElementString("DateOfBirth", "08/09/1968")
textWriter.WriteElementString("DateOfJoining", "04/01/1992")
textWriter.WriteEndElement()
textWriter.WriteEndElement()

' Write the XML to file and close the textWriter
textWriter.Flush()
textWriter.Close()
Console.WriteLine("Press <Enter> to exit.")
Console.Read()
```

Visual C#

```
XmlTextWriter textWriter=new XmlTextWriter(@"e:\Emp.xml",
    System.Text.Encoding.UTF8);
textWriter.Formatting = Formatting.Indented;
textWriter.WriteStartDocument(false);
textWriter.WriteDocType("Employees", null, null, null);
textWriter.WriteComment("This file represents a fragment of Employees" +
    "database");
textWriter.WriteStartElement("Employees");
textWriter.WriteStartElement("Employee", null);
textWriter.WriteElementString("FirstName","John");
textWriter.WriteElementString("LastName","Doe");
textWriter.WriteElementString("DateOfBirth","08/09/1968");
textWriter.WriteElementString("DateOfJoining","04/01/1992");
textWriter.WriteEndElement();
textWriter.WriteEndElement();

//Write the XML to file and close the textWriter
textWriter.Flush();
textWriter.Close();
Console.WriteLine("Press <Enter> to exit.");
Console.Read();
```

Lesson 3: Working with XPathNavigator

In the previous lesson, you learned how to use XmlWriter and XmlReader to create and read XML documents. In an XML document, you use XML Path Language (XPath) to access a node or a set of nodes. The XPathNavigator class of the .NET Framework contains the methods that you use to perform XPath queries on an XML document. In this lesson, you will learn about the methods of the XPathNavigator class. In addition, you will learn how to perform XPath queries on an XML document.

After this lesson, you will be able to
- Describe the XPathNavigator class
- Use the methods of the XPathNavigator class to perform XPath queries

Estimated lesson time: 20 minutes

Understanding the XPathNavigator Class

After you create an XML document, you might need to access a value from a certain node. XPath enables you to access a node or a set of nodes in an XML document. In addition, XPath enables you to create expressions that can manipulate strings, numbers, and Boolean values. XPath treats an XML document as a tree containing different types of nodes, which include elements, attributes, and text. You can create XPath expressions that identify these nodes in an XML document based on their type, name, and value. In addition, an XPath expression can identify the relationship between the nodes in a document. The XPath implementation recognizes several node types in an XML document, such as Root, Element, Attribute, Namespace, Text, ProcessingInstruction, Comment, SignificantWhitespace, Whitespace, and All.

The XPathNavigator class, based on the data model described in the XPath 1.0 recommendation (located at *http://www.w3.org/TR/xpath*), lets you perform XPath queries on any data source, such as an XML document, a database, or a DataSet. The XPathNavigator class is defined in the System.Xml.XPath namespace. Table 6.4 describes the classes of the System.Xml.XPath namespace that enable you to perform an XPath query on an XML document.

Table 6.4   Classes and Interfaces of the System.Xml.XPath Namespace

Classes and interfaces	Description
Classes	
XPathNavigator	This class allows you to define a read-only, random access cursor on a data store.
XPathNodeIterator	This class enables you to iterate a set of nodes that you select by calling an XPath method.
XPathExpression	This class encapsulates a compiled XPath expression. An XPathExpression object is returned when you call the Compile method. The Select, Evaluate, and Matches methods use this class.
XPathDocument	This class provides a read-only cache for a fast and highly optimized processing of XML documents using XSLT.
XPathException	This is the exception that is thrown when an error occurs during the processing of an XPath expression.
Interface	
IXPathNavigable	This interface enables you to create an XPathNavigator class. The classes that implement this interface enable you to create navigators using the CreateNavigator method.

To create an XPathNavigator object for an XML document, you use the Create-Navigator method of the XmlNode and XPathDocument classes, which implement the IXPathNavigable interface. The CreateNavigator method returns an XPath-Navigator object. You can then use the XPathNavigator object to perform XPath queries. You can use XPathNavigator to select a set of nodes from any data store that implements the IXPathNavigable interface. A data store is the source of data, which may be a file, a database, an XmlDocument object, or a DataSet object. You can also create your own implementation of the XPathNavigator class that can query over other data stores.

The XPathNavigator object reads data from an XML document by using a cursor that enables forward and backward navigation within the nodes. In addition, XPathNavigator provides random access to nodes. However, because the cursor that the XPathNavigator object uses is read-only, you cannot edit an XML document by using the XPathNavigator object.

Performing XPath Queries

Before you can perform XPath queries, you must select a set of nodes to perform XPath queries against. You use the Select method of the XPathNavigator object to select the set of nodes from any store that implements the IXPathNavigable interface. The Select method returns an object of the XPathNodeIterator class. You can then use the object of the XPathNodeIterator class to iterate through the selected nodes. In addition to the Select method, the SelectChildren, SelectAncestors,

SelectDescendents, and Evaluate methods also return an XPathNodeIterator object. After you have an XPathNodeIterator object, you can navigate within the selected set of nodes. The following code displays how to create an XPathNavigator object on an XML document, select a set of nodes by using the Select method, and iterate through the set of nodes. In this example, we are using the XML document created in Lesson 1. Figure 6.1 shows the nodes that are returned as a result of executing the Select method.

Visual Basic .NET

```vbnet
Imports System.Xml
Imports System.Xml.XPath

Dim Doc As XPathDocument = New XPathDocument("emp.xml")
Dim Navigator As XPathNavigator
Navigator = Doc.CreateNavigator()
Dim Iterator As XPathNodeIterator = Navigator.Select("/employees/employee")
While Iterator.MoveNext()
    Console.WriteLine(Iterator.Current.Name)
    Console.WriteLine(Iterator.Current.Value)
End While
```

Visual C#

```csharp
using System.Xml;
using System.Xml.XPath;

XPathDocument Doc = new XPathDocument("emp.xml");
XPathNavigator navigator = Doc.CreateNavigator();
XPathNodeIterator iterator = navigator.Select("/employees/employee");
while (iterator.MoveNext())
{
    Console.WriteLine(iterator.Current.Name);
    Console.WriteLine(iterator.Current.Value);
}
```

Figure 6.1   Nodes returned by the sample XPathNavigator object's Select method

The nodes returned by the Select method have the following characteristics:

- The node set is a virtual tree of nodes.
- The Attribute and Namespace nodes are not a part of the tree navigation methods.

In addition to the Select method, the XPathNavigator class provides some additional methods for optimal performance. These methods enable you to retrieve nodes faster than retrieving nodes using the corresponding XPath query. The optimized methods are SelectChildren, SelectAncestors, SelectDescendants, and IsDescendant.

All the methods, except IsDescendant, return an XPathNodeIterator object. Calling these methods does not affect the state or position of the XPathNavigator object.

After you select a set of nodes, you can navigate the nodes randomly by using the XPathNavigator object, which provides various methods for navigation. Table 6.5 describes the methods that you use to navigate a set of selected nodes.

Table 6.5   Navigation Methods of the XPathNavigator Object

Methods	Description
MoveTo	This method enables you to move the XPathNavigator object to another node and make it the current position. The MoveTo method returns a Boolean value to indicate the success or failure of the movement.
MoveToNext	This method enables you to move the XPathNavigator object to the next sibling of the current node.
MoveToPrevious	This method enables you to move the XPathNavigator object to the previous sibling of the current node.
MoveToFirst	This method enables you to move the XPathNavigator object to the first sibling of the current node.
MoveToFirstChild	This method enables you to move the XPathNavigator object to the first child of the current node. You can use the MoveToFirstChild method only when the current node is the root node or is a node that has child nodes.
MoveToParent	This method enables you to move the XPathNavigator object to the parent node of the current node. You cannot call the MoveToParent method when the root node is the current node because the root node does not have a parent node.

(continued)

Table 6.5   **Navigation Methods of the XPathNavigator Object** *(continued)*

Methods	Description
MoveToRoot	This method enables you to move the XPathNavigator object to the root node.
MoveToId	This method enables you to move the XPathNavigator object to the node that has an ID attribute. You need to specify the ID of the node to which you want the XPathNavigator to move.

In addition to selecting a set of nodes from an XML node, you can use the Evaluate method to evaluate XPath expressions. The Evaluate method takes an XPath expression, evaluates it, and returns a typed result. You can use this method to perform calculations. However, you should compile an XPath expression before you pass it to the Evaluate method by calling the Compile method on the XPathNavigator object. The Compile method converts the string representing the XPath expression into an XPathExpression object. Compiling allows you to cache an XPath expression object and improve the performace. The following code shows how to use the Evaluate method. Figure 6.2 shows the result of summing the <Basic> nodes in Emp.xml by using the Evaluate method.

Visual Basic .NET

```
Dim XPathDocument As XmlDocument = New XmlDocument()
XPathDocument.Load("emp.xml")
Dim Navigator As XPathNavigator = XPathDocument.CreateNavigator()
Dim XPathExpr As XPathExpression = Navigator.Compile("sum(//Basic/text())")
Console.WriteLine(Navigator.Evaluate(XPathExpr))
```

Visual C#

```
XmlDocument XPathDocument = new XmlDocument();
XPathDocument.Load("emp.xml");
XPathNavigator navigator = XPathDocument.CreateNavigator();
XPathExpression XPathExpr = navigator.Compile("sum(//Basic/text())");
Console.WriteLine(navigator.Evaluate(XPathExpr));
```

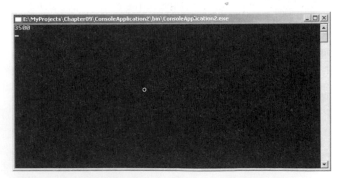

Figure 6.2   The result of using the Compile and Evalute methods of the XPathNavigator object

Lesson 4: Understanding the XML Schema Object Model

In the previous lesson, you learned about XPathNavigator and how to access a particular element and its attributes. You also learned about various XPath classes and how to query a particular XML document using the XPath classes. In this lesson, you will learn about the XML Schema Object Model. You will also learn about the System.Xml.Schema namespace. Finally, you will learn how to create an XML Schema and validate an XML file against an XML Schema.

After this lesson, you will be able to

- Describe the XML Schema Object Model
- Use the System.Xml.Schema namespace
- Create an XML Schema definition file and use it to validate an existing XML file

Estimated lesson time: 30 minutes

Overview of the XML Schema Object Model

The structure of XML documents is based on rules that are also known as *grammar*. These rules are specified in an XML Schema definition (XSD) file, which is also known as an XML Schema. An XSD file contains the definitions of elements, attributes, and data types. Any XML file that is created can be validated against an XML Schema.

You use XML Schema to create and validate the structure of XML documents. XML Schema provides a way to define the structure of XML documents. To specify the structure of an XML document, you specify the following:

- Names of elements that you can use in documents
- The structure and types of elements to be valid for that specific schema

A schema is an XML file and has an .xsd file name extension. The XSD file uses valid XML objects to describe the contents of a target XML document. These XML objects include elements and attributes, which are declared in the XSD file using element and attribute elements. The structure of the XML document is created using simpleType and complexType elements. A *simpleType* element is defined using the built-in data types or existing simple types and cannot contain elements or attributes. A *complexType* definition can consist of elements and attributes. An XSD file defining the elements, attributes, and data types of the employees XML document created in Lesson 1 is shown next.

Employees.xsd File

```xml
<?xml version="1.0" ?>
<xs:schema id="employees" targetNamespace=http://tempuri.org/emp1.xsd
    xmlns:mstns="http://tempuri.org/emp1.xsd"
    xmlns="http://tempuri.org/emp1.xsd"
    xmlns:xs="http://www.w3.org/2001/XMLSchema"
    xmlns:msdata="urn:schemas-microsoft-com:xml-msdata"
    attributeFormDefault="qualified" elementFormDefault="qualified">
<xs:element name="employees" msdata:IsDataSet="true"
    msdata:EnforceConstraints="False">
<xs:complexType>
<xs:choice maxOccurs="unbounded">
    <xs:element name="employee">
    <xs:complexType>
        <xs:sequence>
            <xs:element name="FirstName" type="xs:string" />
            <xs:element name="LastName" type="xs:string" />
            <xs:element name="DateOfBirth" type="xs:date" />
            <xs:element name="DateOfJoining" type="xs:date" />
            <xs:element name="Address" type="xs:string" />
            <xs:element name="Basic" type="xs:integer" />
            <xs:element name="Designation" type="xs:string" />
            <xs:element name="LeaveBalance" type="xs:int" />
        </xs:sequence>
    </xs:complexType>
</xs:element>
</xs:choice>
</xs:complexType>
</xs:element>
</xs:schema>
```

The Schema Object Model (SOM) consists of a set of classes that enable you to read the schema definition from a file. In addition, you can use the classes in the SOM to create the schema definition files programmatically. These SOM classes are part of the System.Xml.Schema namespace. When you create a schema using the classes in the System.Xml.Schema namespace, the schema resides in memory. You need to validate and compile the schema before writing it to a file.

The SOM provides the following features:

- You can load valid XSD schemas from files, and also save valid XSD schemas to files.
- You can create in-memory schemas using strongly typed classes.
- You can cache and retrieve schemas by using the XmlSchemaCollection class.
- You can validate XML instance documents against the schemas by using the XmlValidatingReader class.
- You can build editors to create and maintain schemas.

You can use the XmlSchema class to build a schema programmatically. After you create a schema definition file, you can use the SOM to edit these files. The way in which you edit schema definition files using the SOM is similar to the way in which you edit XML documents using the DOM.

To validate any XSD file that you create, you can use the Compile method of the XmlSchema class. You use the Compile method to verify whether the schema is semantically correct. For example, the Compile method checks that the XML Schema structure is correct, verifies that the constraints are correctly applied, and ensures that the types are derived correctly. While performing validation, a validation callback is used if the parser gives a warning or an error. The ValidationEventHandler event for the Compile method is raised for the semantic validation checking of XML Schema. In addition to building schemas, you can load schemas from a file using the XmlSchema.Read method. The ValidationEventHandler event is raised when any syntactic or semantic validation errors occur during a read operation with the XmlSchema.Read method. You can use the SOM to read and write XSD language schemas from files or other sources using the XmlTextReader, XmlTextWriter, and XmlSchema classes.

The following code example illustrates reading XML Schema from a file, Employees.xsd, displaying the file to the console, and then writing the schema to a new file, New.xsd.

Visual Basic .NET

```
Imports System.IO
Imports System
Imports System.Xml
Imports System.Xml.Schema
Imports System.Text

Class ReadWriteSample
    Public Shared Sub Main()
        Try
            Dim reader As New XmlTextReader("Employees.xsd")
            Dim myschema As XmlSchema = XmlSchema.Read(reader, Nothing)
            myschema.Write(Console.Out)
            Console.WriteLine("Press <Enter> to exit.")
            Console.Read()
            Dim file As New FileStream("New.xsd", FileMode.Create, _
                FileAccess.ReadWrite)
            Dim xwriter As New XmlTextWriter(file, New UTF8Encoding())
            xwriter.Formatting = Formatting.Indented
            myschema.Write(xwriter)
        Catch e As Exception
            Console.WriteLine(e)
        End Try
    End Sub
End Class
```

Visual C#

```csharp
using System.IO;
using System;
using System.Xml;
using System.Xml.Schema;
using System.Text;

class ReadWriteSample
{
    public static void Main()
    {
        try
        {
            XmlTextReader reader = new XmlTextReader ("Employees.xsd");
            XmlSchema myschema = XmlSchema.Read(reader, null);
            myschema.Write(Console.Out);
            Console.WriteLine("Press <Enter> to exit.");
            Console.Read();
            FileStream file = new FileStream ("New.xsd",
                FileMode.Create, FileAccess.ReadWrite);
            XmlTextWriter xwriter = new XmlTextWriter (file,
                new UTF8Encoding());
            xwriter.Formatting = Formatting.Indented;
            myschema.Write (xwriter);
        }
        catch(Exception e)
        {
            Console.WriteLine(e);
        }
    }
}
```

Lesson 5: Validating an XML Document

In the previous lesson, you learned about the SOM and its features that enable you to create in-memory schemas. In this lesson, you will learn about XML validation and how to use XmlValidatingReader to validate an XML document.

After this lesson, you will be able to

- Describe the functions of XmlValidatingReader
- Validate XML documents using XmlValidatingReader
- Read XML fragments using XmlValidatingReader

Estimated lesson time: 30 minutes

Understanding XML Validation

You should ensure that the XML document that you create is well formed. Any XML parser can read a well-formed XML document; therefore, you can display the XML document anywhere. You should also ensure that the XML document matches its schema or conforms to the constraints defined by its DTD. For example, if you specify the age of an employee to be between 18 and 60 years in the schema of your XML document, the actual data in your XML document must conform to the condition or it will be considered invalid.

You can ensure the validation of XML documents by using the XmlValidating-Reader class. The XmlValidatingReader class is a derived class of the XmlReader class and adds validation support to the XmlTextReader class. The XmlValidating-Reader class provides the DTD, XML-Data Reduced (XDR), and XSD schema validation services that allow you to validate an XML document or a fragment of an XML document. The XmlValidatingReader class takes XmlTextReader as the input and applies the properties that you specify in the XmlTextReader class.

Note   The XDR schema can be used to create XML views of relational data. For example, Microsoft SQL Server 2000 allows you to obtain the result of a query in the form of an XML document, which can be validated against an XDR schema.

The following code shows how to use the XmlValidatingReader class to add validation support to the XmlTextReader class.

Visual Basic .NET

```
Dim Reader as XmlTextReader = new XmlTextReader("emp.xml")
Dim Validater as XmlValidatingReader = new XmlValidatingReader(Reader)
```

Visual C#

```
XmlTextReader Reader = new XmlTextReader("emp.xml");
XmlValidatingReader Validater = new XmlValidatingReader(Reader);
```

Validating XML Documents Using XmlValidatingReader

To validate an XML document, you first load XmlValidatingReader for an XML document by using the Load method. The following code shows how to load XmlValidatingReader to validate an XML document.

Visual Basic .NET

```
Dim XMLDoc as XmlDocument = new XmlDocument()
Dim Reader as XmlTextReader = new XmlTextReader("emp.xml")
Dim Validater as XmlValidatingReader = new XmlValidatingReader(Reader)
XMLDoc.Load(Validater)
```

Visual C#

```
XmlDocument XMLDoc = new XmlDocument();
XmlTextReader Reader = new XmlTextReader("emp.xml");
XmlValidatingReader Validater = new XmlValidatingReader(Reader);
XMLDoc.Load(Validater);
```

XmlValidatingReader Validation Types

After you load XmlValidatingReader for an XML document, you use the ValidationType property to specify the type of validations that you want to perform on that document. The default value of ValidationType is Auto. The other values for this property can be DTD, Schema, XDR, and None. Table 6.6 describes the validations performed by XmlValidatingReader when you set the ValidationType property to Auto.

Table 6.6   Validations Performed by ValidationType.Auto

Validation type	Validation
No DTD or no schema	Parses the XML without validation.
DTD	Performs DTD validation on the document, expands the default attributes and entities, and loads and parses the general entities only if they are expanded.
XML Schema (reference or inline)	Performs XSD validation, validates the schema, expands the default attributes, and supplies the type information.
XDR schema (reference or inline)	Performs XDR schema validation, validates the schema, expands the default attributes, and supplies the type information.
DTD, XML Schema, or XDR schema (reference or inline)	Performs DTD/XML Schema/XDR validation according to the first occurrence of the validation type. The DTD validation always takes precedence.

If you set ValidationType to XDR, XmlValidatingReader validates the document according to XDR schemas, including inline schemas. Table 6.7 displays the validations that are performed when you set the ValidationType property to XDR.

Table 6.7   Validations Performed by ValidationType.XDR

Validation type	Validation
No DTD or schema	Returns a final warning that no validation has occurred.
DTD	Throws XmlException indicating mixed validation types.
XML Schema (reference or inline)	Throws XmlException indicating mixed validation types.
XDR schema (reference or inline)	Performs XDR validation, validates a schema, expands the default attributes from the schema, and supplies Type information.
DTD, XML Schema, or XDR schema (reference or inline)	Performs XDR validation, expands the default attributes schema, and supplies Type information. If XmlValidatingReader finds a DTD or XML Schema, XmlException is thrown indicating mixed validation types.

If you set the ValidationType property to Schema, XmlValidatingReader validates the document according to the XML Schema, including inline schemas. Table 6.8 displays the validations that are performed when you set the ValidationType property to Schema.

Table 6.8   Validations Performed by ValidationType.Schema

Validation type	Validation
No DTD or schema	Returns a "No schema found" warning for each element.
DTD	Throws XmlException indicating mixed validation types.
XML Schema (reference or inline)	Performs XML Schema validation, validates a schema, expands the default attributes, and supplies Type information.
XDR schema (reference or inline)	Throws an XmlException indicating mixed validation types
DTD, XML Schema, or XDR schema (reference or inline)	Performs XML Schema validation, expands the default attributes, and supplies Type information. If the XmlValidatingReader finds a DTD or XML Schema, XmlException is thrown indicating mixed validation types.

You can also set the ValidationType property to None. The None value creates a nonvalidating parser that complies with the World Wide Web Consortium XML 1.0 recommendation (located at *http://www.w3.org/TR/2000/REC-xml-20001006*). This enables you to report the default attributes and resolve the general entities. The None value does not throw any validation errors. Table 6.9 displays the validations that are performed when you set the ValidationType property to None.

Table 6.9　Validations Performed by ValidationType.None

Validation type	Validation
No DTD or schema	Parses the XML without performing any validation and does not throw any exception or supply any information.
DTD	Creates an XML 1.0–compliant nonvalidating parser, does not perform any DTD validation, and expands the default attributes and entities in the DTD. However, no type information is supplied.
XML Schema (reference or inline)	Parses XML without performing any validation, does not throw any exception or supply any information, and expands the default attributes and entities in the schema.
XDR schema (reference or inline)	Parses the XML without performing any validation, does not throw any exception or supply any information, and does not expand the default attributes and entities in the schema.
DTD, XML Schema, or XDR schema (reference or inline)	Creates an XML 1.0–compliant nonvalidating parser, parses the XML without performing any validation, does not throw any exception or supply any information, and expands the default attributes and entities in the DTD.

Performing Validation Against DTD Using XmlValidatingReader

DTD uses a formal language to describe the structure and syntax of an XML document. In addition, DTD specifies the content and values in an XML document. The XML document that you create can either have inline DTD or a reference to an external DTD file. When you load XmlValidatingReader to validate an XML document against its DTD, XmlValidatingReader uses the DTD defined in the DOCTYPE declaration of the XML document.

The following code displays how to create an XmlValidatingReader class that takes an XML document as the input and validates it against an external DTD file, Emp.dtd. All severity types and error messages are displayed. Figure 6.3 shows the results of validating the Emp.xml file using an external DTD file.

Visual Basic .NET

```
Imports System
Imports System.IO
Imports System.Xml
Imports System.Xml.Schema

public class DTDValidation

    public shared sub Main()
        Dim Reader As XmlTextReader = new XmlTextReader("emp.xml")
```

```
        Dim Validater As XmlValidatingReader
        Validater = new XmlValidatingReader(Reader)
        Validater.ValidationType = ValidationType.DTD
        AddHandler Validater.ValidationEventHandler, AddressOf _
            ValidationCallback
        while(Reader.Read())
        end while
        Console.WriteLine("Validation finished")
    end sub

    public shared sub ValidationCallBack (sender As object, args As _
        ValidationEventArgs)
        Console.WriteLine("Validation Error")
        Console.WriteLine("Severity:{0}", args.Severity)
        Console.WriteLine("Message:{0}", args.Message)
    end sub
end class
```

Visual C#

```csharp
using System;
using System.IO;
using System.Xml;
using System.Xml.Schema;

class DTDValidation
{
    public static void Main()
    {
        XmlTextReader Reader = new XmlTextReader("emp.xml");
        XmlValidatingReader validater = new XmlValidatingReader(Reader);
        validater.ValidationType = ValidationType.DTD;
        validater.ValidationEventHandler += new ValidationEventHandler
            (ValidationHandler);
        while(validater.Read());
        Console.WriteLine("Validation finished");
    }

    public static void ValidationHandler(object sender,
        ValidationEventArgs args)
    {
        Console.WriteLine("Validation Error");
        Console.WriteLine("\tSeverity:{0}", args.Severity);
        Console.WriteLine("\tMessage  :{0}", args.Message);
    }
}
```

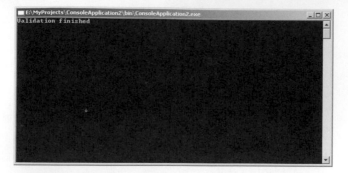

Figure 6.3   The results of validating Emp.xml with an external DTD

To enable validation against a DTD, you need to add the following line in the Emp.xml file:

XML

```
<?xml version = "1.0"?>
<!DOCTYPE employees SYSTEM "emp.dtd">
    <employees>
        <employee>
            .
            .
            .

        </employee>
    </employees>
```

DTD

```
<!ELEMENT employees (employee)*>
<!ELEMENT employee (FirstName, LastName, DateOfBirth, DateOfJoining, Address,
    Basic, Designation, LeaveBalance)>
<!ELEMENT FirstName (#PCDATA)>
<!ELEMENT LastName (#PCDATA)>
<!ELEMENT DateOfBirth (#PCDATA)>
<!ELEMENT DateOfJoining (#PCDATA)>
<!ELEMENT Address (#PCDATA)>
<!ELEMENT Basic (#PCDATA)>
<!ELEMENT Designation (#PCDATA)>
<!ELEMENT LeaveBalance (#PCDATA)>
```

Reading XML Fragments Using XmlValidatingReader

You can use XmlValidatingReader to read XML fragments. XmlValidatingReader parses a string as an XML fragment. This enables you to bypass the root-level rules of an XML document. The value that you pass to the XmlNodeType parameter of XmlValidatingReader determines how you parse an XML string. Table 6.10 describes how each type of XML fragment is parsed when XmlValidatingReader reads the XML fragment.

Table 6.10   Parsing of XML Fragments

Type	Parsed as
Element	Any valid element content, including a combination of elements, comments, processing instructions, CDATA, and text.
Attribute	The value of an attribute.
Document	Entire XML document. This type enforces the root-level rules.

The following code shows how to use XmlValidatingReader to read an XML fragment and display its values. Figure 6-4 shows the results of reading an XML fragment.

Visual Basic .NET

```
Imports System
Imports System.Xml

Module Module1
Public Class XMLFragment
    Public Overloads Shared Sub Main(ByVal args() As [String])
        Dim Reader As New XmlValidatingReader( _
            "<FirstName>John</FirstName>" & _
            "<LastName>Doe</LastName>" & _
            "<DateOfBirth>08/09/1968</DateOfBirth>" & _
            "<Address>2010 Stanley Dr., Charlotte, NC 28273</Address>" & _
            "<Basic>2100</Basic>" & _
            "<Designation>Associate Consultant</Designation>", _
            XmlNodeType.Element, Nothing)
        While Reader.Read()
        Console.WriteLine("NodeType: {0} NodeName: {1} NodeValue: " & _
            "{2}", Reader.NodeType, Reader.Name, Reader.Value)
        End While
        Console.WriteLine("Press <Enter> to exit.")
        Console.Read()
    End Sub
End Class
End Module
```

Visual C#

```
using System;
using System.Xml;

public class XMLFragment
{
    public static void Main (String[] args)
    {
        XmlValidatingReader reader = new XmlValidatingReader (
```

(continued)

```
                           "<FirstName>John</FirstName>" +
                           "<LastName>Doe</LastName>" +
                           "<DateOfBirth>08/09/1968</DateOfBirth>" +
                           "<DateOfJoining>04/01/1992</DateOfJoining>" +
                           "<Address>2010 Stanley Dr., Charlotte, NC 28273</Address>" +
                           "<Basic>2100</Basic>" +
                           "<Designation>Associate Consultant</Designation>",
                            XmlNodeType.Element, null);
                while(reader.Read())
                    Console.WriteLine("NodeType: {0} NodeName: {1}" +
                        "NodeValue: {2}", reader.NodeType, reader.Name,
                        reader.Value);
                Console.WriteLine("Press <Enter> to exit.");
                Console.Read();
            }
        }
```

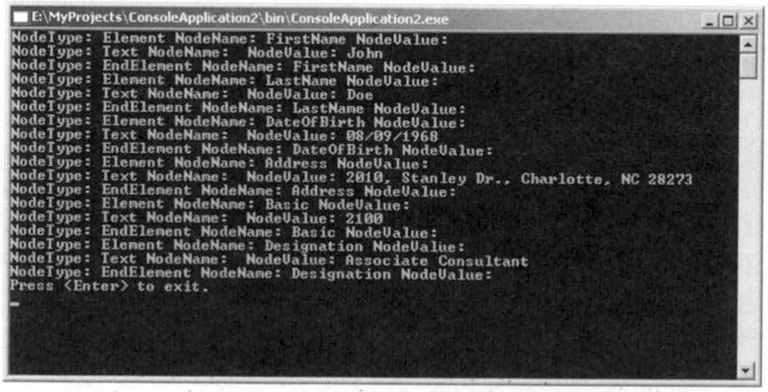

Figure 6.4   The values from an XML fragment

Note   You cannot parse a fragment if the ValidationType property is set to DTD. This is because, to perform validation, a DTD requires that an entire XML document be loaded.

Lesson 6: Working with XML and DataSets

In the previous lesson, you learned how to validate an XML document using XML Schema. You also learned about the XmlValidationReader class. In this lesson, you will learn how to populate a DataSet with data from an XML document. In addition, you will learn how to write XML documents using data from a data source. You will also learn about various methods of the DataSet class that enable you to work with XML data.

After this lesson, you will be able to

- Populate a DataSet from an XML file
- Create XML documents using a DataSet

Estimated lesson time: 30 minutes

Overview of XML and DataSets

A *DataSet* stores data that is obtained from a data source. This data source can be any source, such as a relational database or an XML document. A DataSet can either be typed or untyped. A *typed* DataSet is a class that is derived from a DataSet class and has an associated XML Schema. On the other hand, an *untyped* DataSet does not have an XML Schema associated with it. In a typed DataSet, you can make changes to the XSD file, which are reflected in the underlying DataSet. XML Schema is similar to the typed DataSet representation because both are available as XSD files in the XML designer. However, a typed DataSet has an associated class file and a predefined root node. When you load an XML document into a DataSet, XML Schema validates the data that is fetched from the XML document. The XML Schema contains all the information about the relational structure, such as tables, constraints, and relations, that is necessary to validate an XML document. This information is stored in the XSD file. The .NET Framework uses the XSD files to generate the data for the DataSet object.

A DataSet object contains methods that enable you to work with XML data. Table 6.11 shows these methods and their descriptions.

Table 6.11   XML Related Methods of a DataSet Object

Method	Description
GetXml	This method enables you to retrieve the XML representation of the data stored in a DataSet in a string variable.
GetXmlSchema	This method enables you to retrieve the XSD schema for the XML representation of the data stored in the DataSet.

(continued)

Table 6.11   XML Related Methods of a DataSet Object *(continued)*

Method	Description
InferXmlSchema	This method enables you to infer the structure of data in the DataSet by using the schema provided in the TextReader, XMLReader, or Stream object.
ReadXml	This method reads the XML data and schema into the DataSet.
ReadXmlSchema	This method enables you to read XML Schema into the DataSet.
WriteXml	This method enables you to write the data of the DataSet into an XML file.
WriteXmlSchema	This method enables you to write the data in the DataSet into an XML Schema.

Working with XML Files and DataSets

You can use ADO.NET to transfer data between XML files and DataSet objects. ADO.NET enables you to write DataSet data as XML data and XML Schema to a file. ADO.NET also enables you to view XML Schema and the XML document.

Populating a DataSet with Data from a Data Source

To fill the DataSet with data obtained from a data source, you use the Fill() method of a DataAdapter class. Consider the following example. You want to populate your DataSet with the contents of the Products table in the Northwind Traders database. To do so, you first connect to the SQL Server database using either the OleDbConnection or SqlConnection class. Then, you use the Fill() method of the SqlDataAdapter or OleDbDataAdapter class to populate the DataSet, as shown in the following code snippet.

Visual Basic .NET

```vb
Try
    Dim RowCount As Integer
    Dim myConnection As SqlConnection
    myConnection = New System.Data.SqlClient.SqlConnection( _
        "user id=sa;password=;initial catalog=Northwind; " & _
        "data source=localhost")
    myConnection.Open()
    Dim AdapObj As SqlDataAdapter = New SqlDataAdapter("Select * from " & _
        "Products", myConnection)
    Dim myDataSet As New DataSet()
    AdapObj.Fill(myDataSet, "ProdTable")
    RowCount = myDataSet.Tables("ProdTable").Rows.Count
    Console.WriteLine(RowCount.ToString)
    Console.ReadLine()
Catch e As Exception
    Console.WriteLine(e.Message.ToString)
    Console.ReadLine()
End Try
```

Visual C#

```csharp
try
{
    int RowCount;
    SqlConnection myConnection;
    myConnection = new System.Data.SqlClient.SqlConnection(
        "user id=sa;password=;initial catalog=Northwind; " +
        "data source=localhost");
    myConnection.Open();
    SqlDataAdapter AdapObj = new SqlDataAdapter("Select * from Products",
        myConnection);
    DataSet myDataSet = new DataSet();
    AdapObj.Fill(myDataSet, "ProdTable");
    RowCount = myDataSet.Tables["ProdTable"].Rows.Count;
    Console.WriteLine(RowCount.ToString());
    Console.ReadLine();
}
catch(Exception e)
{
    Console.WriteLine(e.Message.ToString());
    Console.ReadLine();
}
```

In the preceding code, the Fill() method of the AdapObj data adapter object is called to populate the DataSet named ProdTable by using myDataSet as the DataSet object.

Writing XML Data from a DataSet

You can use the methods available in the DataSet class to write the XML representation of the data in the DataSet into an XML file. The .NET Framework enables you to write XML data with or without XML Schema. When you write the DataSet data as XML data, the latest data of the DataSet is written. However, ADO.NET enables you to write the DataSet data as a DiffGram, which means that both the original and current versions of the rows are included.

DiffGrams

A DataSet uses a DiffGram to store and preserve all versions of the data that it contains. A DiffGram is in the XML format. You use a DiffGram to differentiate between the original and current versions of data. When you write a DataSet as a DiffGram, the DiffGram is populated with all the information that you require to re-create the contents of the DataSet. These contents include the current and original values of rows and the error information and order of the rows. However, the DiffGram format is not populated with the information to re-create XML Schema. A DataSet also uses the DiffGram format to serialize data for transmission across the network. Now you will learn how to read from an XML file and write to an XML file.

GetXml() and WriteXml() Methods

You use the GetXml() method to write the XML representation of a DataSet, as shown in the following code snippet.

Visual Basic .NET

```
Dim XmlData As String
XmlData = AuthorsDataSet.GetXml()
```

Visual C#

```
String XmlData;
XmlData = AuthorsDataSet.GetXml();
```

As you can see in the preceding code, the GetXml() method returns the XML representation of a DataSet as a string. However, if you want to write the XML representation of the DataSet to XmlWriter, a stream, or a file, you use the WriteXml() method. The WriteXml() method takes two parameters. The first parameter is mandatory and specifies the destination of XML output. The second parameter is optional and specifies how the XML output is written. This second parameter of the WriteXml() method can take any one of the following three values:

- IgnoreSchema, which is the default option and enables you to write the current contents of the DataSet (without the schema) as XML data
- WriteSchema, which enables you to write the current contents of the DataSet and the schema as XML data
- DiffGram, which enables you to write the DataSet as a DiffGram

XmlWriteMode.WriteSchema is the second parameter of the WriteXml() method and enables you to write the current contents of the DataSet as well as XML Schema.

Consider the following code.

Visual Basic .NET

```
Dim myConnection As SqlConnection
myConnection = New SqlConnection("user id=sa;pwd=;initial " & _
    "catalog=Northwind;data source=localhost;")
myConnection.Open()
Dim AdapObj As SqlDataAdapter = New SqlDataAdapter("Select * from " & _
    "Products", myConnection)
Dim DstObj As DataSet = New DataSet()
AdapObj.Fill(DstObj, "ProdTable")
DstObj.WriteXml("Products.xml", XmlWriteMode.WriteSchema)
```

Visual C#

```
SqlConnection myConnection;
myConnection = new SqlConnection("user id=sa;pwd=;initial " +
    "catalog=Northwind;data source=localhost;");
```

```
myConnection.Open();
SqlDataAdapter AdapObj = new SqlDataAdapter("Select * from Products",
    myConnection);
DataSet DstObj = new DataSet();
AdapObj.Fill(DstObj, "ProdTable");
DstObj.WriteXml("Products.xml", XmlWriteMode.WriteSchema);
```

In this code, the DataSet object DstObj is created. You use the Fill() method to populate this DataSet object. Then, you use the WriteXml() method to write the contents of the DataSet in an XML file called Products.xml. Instead of specifying an XML file in the WriteXml() method, you can also pass a System.IO.StreamWriter object, as shown in the following code.

Visual Basic .NET

```
Dim XmlStream As System.IO.StreamWriter
XmlStream = New System.IO.StreamWriter("Authors.xml")
AuthorsDataSet.WriteXml(XmlStream, XmlWriteMode.WriteSchema)
```

Visual C#

```
System.IO.StreamWriter XmlStream;
XmlStream = new System.IO.StreamWriter("Authors.xml");
AuthorsDataSet.WriteXml(XmlStream, XmlWriteMode.WriteSchema);
```

Populating a DataSet with XML Data

The .NET Framework provides flexibility in choosing the information to be loaded in the DataSet from XML. You use the ReadXml() method of the DataSet object to read and load a DataSet from an XML document or stream. In addition, the ReadXml() method reads XML data from a file, stream, or XMLReader object. This method takes two arguments, the source of XML data and an XMLReadMode argument. Although you have to provide the source of XML data, the XMLReadMode argument is optional. You can use the following options for the XmlReadMode argument:

- **Auto.**   This option examines the XML document or string and selects the options in a specific order. This option chooses a DiffGram if the XML is a DiffGram. The Auto option chooses ReadSchema if either the XML contains an inline schema or the DataSet contains a schema. However, if the XML does not contain an inline schema or if the DataSet does not contain a schema, the InferSchema option is used.

Note   For best results, use the appropriate XMLReadMode option if you know the format of the data that is being read.

- **ReadSchema.**   This option reads the inline schema and loads the schema and data into the DataSet. If the DataSet already contains a schema, new tables from the inline schema are added to the existing DataSet. For the inline schema tables that already exist in the DataSet, an exception is thrown.

- **Fragment.**   This option continues to read an XML fragment until the end of the stream is reached. The fragments that match the DataSet are appended to appropriate tables. However, the fragments that do not match the DataSet are discarded.

- **IgnoreSchema.**   This option ignores the inline schema and writes the data to the existing DataSet schema. This option discards any data that does not match the existing schema. However, if the DataSet does not have an existing schema, no data is loaded.

Note   If the XML data is in the DiffGram format, the IgnoreSchema option functions like the DiffGram option.

- **InferSchema.**   This option ignores the inline schema and interprets the schema as defined by the structure of the XML data before loading the data into a DataSet. The new tables are added to the existing schema of the DataSet. However, an exception is thrown if the inferred tables already exist in the DataSet schema. In addition, an exception is thrown if the inferred columns already exist in the schema tables.

- **DiffGram.**   This option reads a DiffGram and then adds the data to the schema. If the unique identifier values match, the DiffGram option merges the new rows with the existing rows.

Summary

- Because most systems understand text-based data, XML is the preferred standard of communication. XML files conform to the standards developed by the W3C.

- The XML DOM class is a representation of the XML document in memory. The DOM class allows you to read, write, and manipulate an XML document. The DOM includes a set of libraries that contain classes, which enable you to navigate through an XML document and obtain relevant information. Every XML document consists of parent and child nodes.

- The System.Xml namespace provides the XmlReader and XmlWriter classes that enable you to parse and write XML data from streams or XML documents. These are abstract classes. You can extend these classes to create your own customized classes.

- The XmlReader class enables you to access XML data from a stream or XML document. This class provides fast, non-cacheable, read-only, and forward-only access to XML data.

- The XmlWriter class is an abstract class that enables you to create XML streams and write data in well-formed XML documents. You use XmlWriter to perform tasks such as writing multiple documents into one output stream, writing valid names and tokens into the stream, encoding binary data and writing text output, managing output, and flushing and closing the output stream.

- In an XML document, you use XPath to access a node or a set of nodes. The XPathNavigator class of the .NET Framework contains the methods that you use to perform XPath queries on an XML document.

- You use the Select method of the XPathNavigator object to select the set of nodes from any store that implements the IXPathNavigable interface. The Select method returns an object of the XPathNodeIterator class. You can then use the object of the XPathNodeIterator class to iterate through the selected nodes.

- The structure of valid XML documents is specified by XSD files.

- The SOM consists of a set of classes that enable you to read the schema definition from a file. In addition, you can use the classes in the SOM to create the schema definition files programmatically. These SOM classes are part of the System.Xml.Schema namespace.

- You can ensure the validation of XML documents by using the XmlValidatingReader class. The XmlValidatingReader class provides the DTD, XML-Data Reduced (XDR), and XSD schema validation services that enable you to validate an XML document or a fragment of an XML document.

- When you load an XML document into a DataSet, XML Schema validates the data that is fetched from the XML document. The XML Schema contains all the information about the relational structure, such as tables, constraints, and relations that are necessary to validate an XML document. This information is stored in an XSD file. The .NET Framework uses XSD files to generate the relational structure for the DataSet object.

Lab: Accessing and Manipulating XML Data

In this lab, you will create a Windows application that enables you to access and manipulate a product catalog, which is stored in the Products.xml file. The application provides a relational as well as an XML view of the product information. Both the relational and the XML views are synchronized with each other. You can add, modify, and delete the product information either using the relational view or using the XML view. Any change made in the relational view is also reflected in the XML view and vice versa. In addition, the application enables you to perform XPath queries. The solutions to the exercises in this lab can be found in the \Solution folder on the Supplemental Course Materials CD-ROM.

Estimated lab time: 90 minutes

Exercise 1: Creating the Product Catalog

In this exercise, you will create a product catalog by creating the Products.xml file. The Products.xml file contains the ID, name, and price information of various products.The application that you will create in the next exercise will use the Products.xml file to read and write product information. To create the Products.xml file, perform the following steps:

1. Open Notepad and type the following XML code.

XML
```
<?xml version="1.0" standalone="yes"?>
<products>
    <product>
        <id>100</id>
        <name>Football</name>
        <price>50</price>
    </product>
    <product>
        <id>101</id>
        <name>Baseball</name>
        <price>15</price>
    </product>
    <product>
        <id>102</id>
        <name>Bat</name>
        <price>45</price>
    </product>
    <product>
        <id>103</id>
        <name>Ball</name>
        <price>10</price>
    </product>
```

(continued)

```
<product>
    <id>104</id>
    <name>Glove</name>
    <price>25</price>
</product>
<product>
    <id>105</id>
    <name>Helmet</name>
    <price>75</price>
</product>
</products>
```

2. Save the file as Products.xml.

Exercise 2: Creating the Product Catalog Windows Application

In this exercise, you will create a Windows application that will enable you to view and modify the product information stored in the Products.xml file. The application uses DataSet and XmlDataDocument objects to store the relational and XML views of the product catalog in memory, respectively. The relational view of the products information is displayed in a data grid, whereas the XML view is displayed in a text box.

When the application starts, the form's Load event reads the product information from the Products.xml file and creates a DataSet object. The form's Load event also creates an XmlDataDocument object, which is synchronized with the DataSet object. You can add, delete, or modify product information either in the data grid or the text box that displays the XML view. Because the XmlDataDocument is synchronized with the DataSet object, any change made in the data grid is automatically reflected in the text box displaying the XML view and vice versa. In addition, you can also search products based on ID or name attribute values. Figure 6.5 shows the interface of the Product Catalog Windows application.

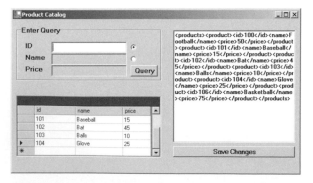

Figure 6.5   The user interface for the Product Catalog application

To create the Product Catalog Windows application, perform the following steps:

1. Open Visual Studio .NET.
2. From the File menu, point to New and choose Project to open the New Project dialog box.
3. Select Visual Basic Projects or Visual C# Projects from the Project Types pane and Windows Application from the Templates pane. Type **VBProduct Catalog** or **CSProduct Catalog** in the Name box.
4. In the design view, right-click on Form1 and select View Code from the short-cut menu to open the code view.
5. In the code view, replace the code with the following code.

Visual Basic .NET

```
Imports System.IO
Imports System.Xml
Imports System.Xml.XPath

Public Class ProductCatalog
    Inherits System.Windows.Forms.Form
    Private xml_data As XmlDataDocument
    Private relational_data As DataSet


#Region " Windows Form Designer generated code "

    Public Sub New()
        MyBase.New()

        'This call is required by the Windows Form Designer.
        InitializeComponent()

        'Add any initialization after the InitializeComponent() call

    End Sub

    'Form overrides dispose to clean up the component list.
    Protected Overloads Overrides Sub Dispose(ByVal disposing As Boolean)
        If disposing Then
            If Not (components Is Nothing) Then
                components.Dispose()
            End If
        End If
        MyBase.Dispose(disposing)
    End Sub

    'Required by the Windows Form Designer
    Private components As System.ComponentModel.IContainer

    'NOTE: The following procedure is required by the Windows Form
    'Designer. It can be modified using the Windows Form Designer.
```

(continued)

```
'Do not modify it using the code editor.
Friend WithEvents Label1 As System.Windows.Forms.Label
Friend WithEvents Label2 As System.Windows.Forms.Label
Friend WithEvents Label3 As System.Windows.Forms.Label
Friend WithEvents GroupBox1 As System.Windows.Forms.GroupBox
Friend WithEvents RadioButton1 As System.Windows.Forms.RadioButton
Friend WithEvents RadioButton2 As System.Windows.Forms.RadioButton
Friend WithEvents Button1 As System.Windows.Forms.Button
Friend WithEvents DataGrid1 As System.Windows.Forms.DataGrid
Friend WithEvents Id_TxtBx As System.Windows.Forms.TextBox
Friend WithEvents Name_TxtBx As System.Windows.Forms.TextBox
Friend WithEvents Price_TxtBx As System.Windows.Forms.TextBox
Friend WithEvents Xml_TxtBx As System.Windows.Forms.TextBox
Friend WithEvents Button2 As System.Windows.Forms.Button
<System.Diagnostics.DebuggerStepThrough()> _
Private Sub InitializeComponent()
    Me.Label1 = New System.Windows.Forms.Label()
    Me.Label2 = New System.Windows.Forms.Label()
    Me.Label3 = New System.Windows.Forms.Label()
    Me.Id_TxtBx = New System.Windows.Forms.TextBox()
    Me.Name_TxtBx = New System.Windows.Forms.TextBox()
    Me.Price_TxtBx = New System.Windows.Forms.TextBox()
    Me.GroupBox1 = New System.Windows.Forms.GroupBox()
    Me.Button1 = New System.Windows.Forms.Button()
    Me.RadioButton2 = New System.Windows.Forms.RadioButton()
    Me.RadioButton1 = New System.Windows.Forms.RadioButton()
    Me.DataGrid1 = New System.Windows.Forms.DataGrid()
    Me.Xml_TxtBx = New System.Windows.Forms.TextBox()
    Me.Button2 = New System.Windows.Forms.Button()
    Me.GroupBox1.SuspendLayout()
    CType(Me.DataGrid1, _
        System.ComponentModel.ISupportInitialize).BeginInit()
    Me.SuspendLayout()
    '
    'Label1
    '
    Me.Label1.Font = New System.Drawing.Font( _
        "Microsoft Sans Serif", 10.0!, _
        System.Drawing.FontStyle.Bold, _
        System.Drawing.GraphicsUnit.Point, CType(0, Byte))
    Me.Label1.Location = New System.Drawing.Point(24, 40)
    Me.Label1.Name = "Label1"
    Me.Label1.Size = New System.Drawing.Size(56, 23)
    Me.Label1.TabIndex = 0
    Me.Label1.Text = "ID"
    '
    'Label2
    '
    Me.Label2.Font = New System.Drawing.Font( _
        "Microsoft Sans Serif", 10.0!, _
        System.Drawing.FontStyle.Bold, _
```

```
            System.Drawing.GraphicsUnit.Point, CType(0, Byte))
        Me.Label2.Location = New System.Drawing.Point(24, 64)
        Me.Label2.Name = "Label2"
        Me.Label2.Size = New System.Drawing.Size(56, 23)
        Me.Label2.TabIndex = 1
        Me.Label2.Text = "Name"
        '
        'Label3
        '
        Me.Label3.Font = New System.Drawing.Font( _
            "Microsoft Sans Serif", 10.0!, _
            System.Drawing.FontStyle.Bold, _
            System.Drawing.GraphicsUnit.Point, CType(0, Byte))
        Me.Label3.Location = New System.Drawing.Point(24, 88)
        Me.Label3.Name = "Label3"
        Me.Label3.Size = New System.Drawing.Size(56, 23)
        Me.Label3.TabIndex = 2
        Me.Label3.Text = "Price"
        '
        'Id_TxtBx
        '
        Me.Id_TxtBx.Font = New System.Drawing.Font( _
            "Microsoft Sans Serif", 10.0!, _
            System.Drawing.FontStyle.Bold, _
            System.Drawing.GraphicsUnit.Point, CType(0, Byte))
        Me.Id_TxtBx.Location = New System.Drawing.Point(80, 40)
        Me.Id_TxtBx.Name = "Id_TxtBx"
        Me.Id_TxtBx.Size = New System.Drawing.Size(160, 23)
        Me.Id_TxtBx.TabIndex = 3
        Me.Id_TxtBx.Text = ""
        '
        'Name_TxtBx
        '
        Me.Name_TxtBx.Font = New System.Drawing.Font( _
            "Microsoft Sans Serif", 10.0!, _
            System.Drawing.FontStyle.Bold, _
            System.Drawing.GraphicsUnit.Point, CType(0, Byte))
        Me.Name_TxtBx.Location = New System.Drawing.Point(80, 64)
        Me.Name_TxtBx.Name = "Name_TxtBx"
        Me.Name_TxtBx.Size = New System.Drawing.Size(160, 23)
        Me.Name_TxtBx.TabIndex = 4
        Me.Name_TxtBx.Text = ""
        '
        'Price_TxtBx
        '
        Me.Price_TxtBx.Font = New System.Drawing.Font( _
            "Microsoft Sans Serif", 10.0!, _
            System.Drawing.FontStyle.Bold, _
            System.Drawing.GraphicsUnit.Point, CType(0, Byte))
```

(continued)

```
Me.Price_TxtBx.Location = New System.Drawing.Point(80, 88)
Me.Price_TxtBx.Name = "Price_TxtBx"
Me.Price_TxtBx.ReadOnly = True
Me.Price_TxtBx.Size = New System.Drawing.Size(160, 23)
Me.Price_TxtBx.TabIndex = 5
Me.Price_TxtBx.Text = ""
'
'GroupBox1
'
Me.GroupBox1.Controls.AddRange(New _
    System.Windows.Forms.Control() _
    {Me.Button1, Me.RadioButton2, Me.RadioButton1})
Me.GroupBox1.Font = New System.Drawing.Font( _
    "Microsoft Sans Serif", 10.0!, _
    System.Drawing.FontStyle.Bold, _
    System.Drawing.GraphicsUnit.Point, CType(0, Byte))
Me.GroupBox1.Location = New System.Drawing.Point(8, 8)
Me.GroupBox1.Name = "GroupBox1"
Me.GroupBox1.Size = New System.Drawing.Size(304, 112)
Me.GroupBox1.TabIndex = 6
Me.GroupBox1.TabStop = False
Me.GroupBox1.Text = "Enter Query"
'
'Button1
'
Me.Button1.Location = New System.Drawing.Point(240, 80)
Me.Button1.Name = "Button1"
Me.Button1.Size = New System.Drawing.Size(56, 23)
Me.Button1.TabIndex = 2
Me.Button1.Text = "Query"
'
'RadioButton2
'
Me.RadioButton2.Location = New System.Drawing.Point(240, 56)
Me.RadioButton2.Name = "RadioButton2"
Me.RadioButton2.Size = New System.Drawing.Size(16, 24)
Me.RadioButton2.TabIndex = 1
'
'RadioButton1
'
Me.RadioButton1.Checked = True
Me.RadioButton1.Location = New System.Drawing.Point(240, 32)
Me.RadioButton1.Name = "RadioButton1"
Me.RadioButton1.Size = New System.Drawing.Size(16, 24)
Me.RadioButton1.TabIndex = 0
Me.RadioButton1.TabStop = True
'
'DataGrid1
'
```

```
Me.DataGrid1.DataMember = ""
Me.DataGrid1.HeaderForeColor = _
    System.Drawing.SystemColors.ControlText
Me.DataGrid1.Location = New System.Drawing.Point(8, 152)
Me.DataGrid1.Name = "DataGrid1"
Me.DataGrid1.PreferredColumnWidth = 101
Me.DataGrid1.Size = New System.Drawing.Size(303, 128)
Me.DataGrid1.TabIndex = 7
'
'Xml_TxtBx
'
Me.Xml_TxtBx.Font = New System.Drawing.Font( _
    "Microsoft Sans Serif", 8.25!, _
    System.Drawing.FontStyle.Bold, _
    System.Drawing.GraphicsUnit.Point, CType(0, Byte))
Me.Xml_TxtBx.Location = New System.Drawing.Point(336, 16)
Me.Xml_TxtBx.Multiline = True
Me.Xml_TxtBx.Name = "Xml_TxtBx"
Me.Xml_TxtBx.Size = New System.Drawing.Size(256, 232)
Me.Xml_TxtBx.TabIndex = 8
Me.Xml_TxtBx.Text = ""
'
'Button2
'
Me.Button2.Font = New System.Drawing.Font( _
    "Microsoft Sans Serif", 10.0!, _
    System.Drawing.FontStyle.Bold, _
    System.Drawing.GraphicsUnit.Point, CType(0, Byte))
Me.Button2.Location = New System.Drawing.Point(336, 256)
Me.Button2.Name = "Button2"
Me.Button2.Size = New System.Drawing.Size(256, 23)
Me.Button2.TabIndex = 3
Me.Button2.Text = "Save Changes"
'
'ProductCatalog
'
Me.AutoScaleBaseSize = New System.Drawing.Size(5, 13)
Me.ClientSize = New System.Drawing.Size(600, 317)
Me.Controls.AddRange(New System.Windows.Forms.Control() _
    {Me.Xml_TxtBx, Me.DataGrid1, Me.Price_TxtBx, Me.Name_TxtBx, _
        Me.Id_TxtBx, Me.Label3, Me.Label2, Me.Label1, _
        Me.GroupBox1, Me.Button2})
Me.MaximizeBox = False
Me.MaximumSize = New System.Drawing.Size(608, 344)
Me.MinimizeBox = False
Me.MinimumSize = New System.Drawing.Size(608, 344)
Me.Name = "ProductCatalog"
Me.Text = "Product Catalog"
Me.GroupBox1.ResumeLayout(False)
```

(continued)

```vb
            CType(Me.DataGrid1, _
                System.ComponentModel.ISupportInitialize).EndInit()
            Me.ResumeLayout(False)


        End Sub

    #End Region

        Private Sub ProductCatalog_Load(ByVal sender As System.Object, _
            ByVal e As System.EventArgs) Handles MyBase.Load
            ' Load products data into the DataSet object
            relational_data = New DataSet()
            relational_data.ReadXml("..\products.xml")

            ' Display the data in DataGrid1
            DataGrid1.DataSource = relational_data.Tables(0)

            ' Synchronize the DataSet with the XmlDataDocument object.
            ' Any change made in the DataSet object is automatically made
            ' in the XmlDataDocument object.
            xml_data = New XmlDataDocument(relational_data)

            ' Show the XML view in the Xml_TxtBx textbox
            Xml_TxtBx.Text = xml_data.InnerXml.ToString
        End Sub

        Private Sub Button2_Click(ByVal sender As System.Object, _
            ByVal e As System.EventArgs) Handles Button2.Click
            ' Read the XML data from the Xml_TxtBx into the DataSet object
            Dim xml_reader As New XmlTextReader(New _
                StringReader(Xml_TxtBx.Text))
            relational_data = New DataSet()
            relational_data.ReadXml(xml_reader)

            ' Create a new XmlDataDocument object
            xml_data = New XmlDataDocument(relational_data)

            ' Save the changes in the products.xml file
            relational_data.WriteXml("..\products.xml")

            ' Show the data in the DataGrid
            DataGrid1.DataSource = xml_data.DataSet.Tables(0)

        End Sub


        Private Sub DataGrid1_CurrentCellChanged(ByVal sender As Object, _
            ByVal e As System.EventArgs) Handles DataGrid1.CurrentCellChanged
            Xml_TxtBx.Text = xml_data.InnerXml.ToString
```

```
End Sub

Private Sub RadioButton1_CheckedChanged(ByVal sender As _
    System.Object, ByVal e As System.EventArgs) _
    Handles RadioButton1.CheckedChanged
    Id_TxtBx.ReadOnly = False
    Name_TxtBx.ReadOnly = True
    Id_TxtBx.Focus()
End Sub

Private Sub RadioButton2_CheckedChanged(ByVal sender As _
    System.Object, ByVal e As System.EventArgs) Handles _
    RadioButton2.CheckedChanged
    Id_TxtBx.ReadOnly = True
    Name_TxtBx.ReadOnly = False
    Name_TxtBx.Focus()
End Sub

Private Sub Button1_Click(ByVal sender As System.Object, _
    ByVal e As System.EventArgs) Handles Button1.Click
    If Button1.Text.Equals("Query") Then
        If RadioButton1.Checked Then
            ' Create an XPathNavigator object
            Dim navigator As XPathNavigator
            navigator = xml_data.CreateNavigator()

            ' Create and compile an XPathExpression
            Dim expr As XPathExpression
            Try
                expr = navigator.Compile("descendant::product[id=" & _
                    Id_TxtBx.Text & "]")
                ' Call the Select method on the XPathNavigator object
                ' and store the reference to XPathNodeIterator object
                ' returned by the Select method
                Dim iterator As XPathNodeIterator
                iterator = navigator.Select(expr)

                ' Navigate to get the value of id, name, and price
                iterator.MoveNext()
                Dim nav2 As XPathNavigator = iterator.Current.Clone()
                nav2.MoveToFirstChild()
                Id_TxtBx.Text = nav2.Value
                nav2.MoveToNext()
                Name_TxtBx.Text = nav2.Value
                nav2.MoveToNext()
                Price_TxtBx.Text = nav2.Value
            Catch ex As Exception
                MsgBox("Enter a valid product id")
            End Try
```

(continued)

```vb
        ElseIf RadioButton2.Checked Then
            ' Create an XPathNavigator object
            Dim navigator As XPathNavigator
            navigator = xml_data.CreateNavigator()

            ' Create and compile an XPathExpression
            Dim expr As XPathExpression
            Try
                expr = navigator.Compile( _
                    "descendant::product[name='" & _
                    Name_TxtBx.Text & "']")
                ' Call the Select method on the XPathNavigator object
                ' and store the reference to XPathNodeIterator object
                ' returned by the Select method
                Dim iterator As XPathNodeIterator
                iterator = navigator.Select(expr)

                ' Navigate to get the value of id, name, and price
                iterator.MoveNext()
                Dim nav2 As XPathNavigator = iterator.Current.Clone()
                nav2.MoveToFirstChild()
                Id_TxtBx.Text = nav2.Value
                nav2.MoveToNext()
                Name_TxtBx.Text = nav2.Value
                nav2.MoveToNext()
                Price_TxtBx.Text = nav2.Value
            Catch ex As Exception
                MsgBox("Enter a valid product name, which is " & _
                    "case sensitive.")
            End Try
        End If
        Button1.Text = "Clear"
        GroupBox1.Text = "Clear Query"
    Else
        Id_TxtBx.Text = ""
        Name_TxtBx.Text = ""
        Price_TxtBx.Text = ""
        Button1.Text = "Query"
        GroupBox1.Text = "Enter Query"
    End If
End Sub

End Class
```

Visual C#

```csharp
using System;
using System.IO;
using System.Xml;
using System.Xml.XPath;
```

```
using System.Drawing;
using System.Collections;
using System.ComponentModel;
using System.Windows.Forms;
using System.Data;

namespace CSProduct_Catalog
{
    /// <summary>
    /// Summary description for Form1.
    /// </summary>
    public class ProductCatalog : System.Windows.Forms.Form
    {
        internal System.Windows.Forms.DataGrid DataGrid1;
        internal System.Windows.Forms.TextBox Xml_TxtBx;
        internal System.Windows.Forms.TextBox Price_TxtBx;
        internal System.Windows.Forms.TextBox Name_TxtBx;
        internal System.Windows.Forms.TextBox Id_TxtBx;
        internal System.Windows.Forms.Label Label3;
        internal System.Windows.Forms.Label Label2;
        internal System.Windows.Forms.Label Label1;
        internal System.Windows.Forms.GroupBox GroupBox1;
        internal System.Windows.Forms.Button Button1;
        internal System.Windows.Forms.RadioButton RadioButton2;
        internal System.Windows.Forms.RadioButton RadioButton1;
        internal System.Windows.Forms.Button Button2;
        private XmlDataDocument xml_data ;
        private DataSet relational_data;

        /// <summary>
        /// Required designer variable.
        /// </summary>
        private System.ComponentModel.Container components = null;

        public ProductCatalog()
        {
            //
            // Required for Windows Form Designer support
            //
            InitializeComponent();

            //
            // TODO: Add any constructor code after InitializeComponent
            // call
        }

        /// <summary>
        /// Clean up any resources being used.
        /// </summary>
        protected override void Dispose( bool disposing )
```

(continued)

```
    {
        if( disposing )
        {
            if (components != null)
            {
                components.Dispose();
            }
        }
        base.Dispose( disposing );
    }

    #region Windows Form Designer generated code
    /// <summary>
    /// Required method for Designer support - do not modify
    /// the contents of this method with the code editor.
    /// </summary>
    private void InitializeComponent()
    {
        this.DataGrid1 = new System.Windows.Forms.DataGrid();
        this.Xml_TxtBx = new System.Windows.Forms.TextBox();
        this.Price_TxtBx = new System.Windows.Forms.TextBox();
        this.Name_TxtBx = new System.Windows.Forms.TextBox();
        this.Id_TxtBx = new System.Windows.Forms.TextBox();
        this.Label3 = new System.Windows.Forms.Label();
        this.Label2 = new System.Windows.Forms.Label();
        this.Label1 = new System.Windows.Forms.Label();
        this.GroupBox1 = new System.Windows.Forms.GroupBox();
        this.Button1 = new System.Windows.Forms.Button();
        this.RadioButton2 = new System.Windows.Forms.RadioButton();
        this.RadioButton1 = new System.Windows.Forms.RadioButton();
        this.Button2 = new System.Windows.Forms.Button();
        ((System.ComponentModel.ISupportInitialize)
            (this.DataGrid1)).BeginInit();
        this.GroupBox1.SuspendLayout();
        this.SuspendLayout();
        //
        // DataGrid1
        //
        this.DataGrid1.DataMember = "";
        this.DataGrid1.HeaderForeColor =
            System.Drawing.SystemColors.ControlText;
        this.DataGrid1.Location = new System.Drawing.Point(8, 158);
        this.DataGrid1.Name = "DataGrid1";
        this.DataGrid1.PreferredColumnWidth = 101;
        this.DataGrid1.Size = new System.Drawing.Size(303, 128);
        this.DataGrid1.TabIndex = 17;
        this.DataGrid1.CurrentCellChanged  += new
            System.EventHandler(this.DataGrid1_CurrentCellChanged);
        //
```

```
// Xml_TxtBx
//
this.Xml_TxtBx.Font = new System.Drawing.Font(
    "Microsoft Sans Serif", 8.25F,
    System.Drawing.FontStyle.Bold,
    System.Drawing.GraphicsUnit.Point, ((System.Byte)(0)));
this.Xml_TxtBx.Location = new System.Drawing.Point(336, 22);
this.Xml_TxtBx.Multiline = true;
this.Xml_TxtBx.Name = "Xml_TxtBx";
this.Xml_TxtBx.Size = new System.Drawing.Size(256, 232);
this.Xml_TxtBx.TabIndex = 18;
this.Xml_TxtBx.Text = "";
//
// Price_TxtBx
//
this.Price_TxtBx.Font = new System.Drawing.Font(
    "Microsoft Sans Serif", 10F,
    System.Drawing.FontStyle.Bold,
    System.Drawing.GraphicsUnit.Point, ((System.Byte)(0)));
this.Price_TxtBx.Location = new System.Drawing.Point(80, 94);
this.Price_TxtBx.Name = "Price_TxtBx";
this.Price_TxtBx.ReadOnly = true;
this.Price_TxtBx.Size = new System.Drawing.Size(160, 23);
this.Price_TxtBx.TabIndex = 15;
this.Price_TxtBx.Text = "";
//
// Name_TxtBx
//
this.Name_TxtBx.Font = new System.Drawing.Font(
    "Microsoft Sans Serif", 10F,
    System.Drawing.FontStyle.Bold,
    System.Drawing.GraphicsUnit.Point, ((System.Byte)(0)));
this.Name_TxtBx.Location = new System.Drawing.Point(80, 70);
this.Name_TxtBx.Name = "Name_TxtBx";
this.Name_TxtBx.Size = new System.Drawing.Size(160, 23);
this.Name_TxtBx.TabIndex = 14;
this.Name_TxtBx.Text = "";
//
// Id_TxtBx
//
this.Id_TxtBx.Font = new System.Drawing.Font(
    "Microsoft Sans Serif", 10F,
    System.Drawing.FontStyle.Bold,
    System.Drawing.GraphicsUnit.Point, ((System.Byte)(0)));
this.Id_TxtBx.Location = new System.Drawing.Point(80, 46);
this.Id_TxtBx.Name = "Id_TxtBx";
this.Id_TxtBx.Size = new System.Drawing.Size(160, 23);
this.Id_TxtBx.TabIndex = 13;
this.Id_TxtBx.Text = "";
```

(continued)

```csharp
//
// Label3
//
this.Label3.Font = new System.Drawing.Font(
    "Microsoft Sans Serif", 10F,
    System.Drawing.FontStyle.Bold,
    System.Drawing.GraphicsUnit.Point, ((System.Byte)(0)));
this.Label3.Location = new System.Drawing.Point(24, 94);
this.Label3.Name = "Label3";
this.Label3.Size = new System.Drawing.Size(56, 23);
this.Label3.TabIndex = 11;
this.Label3.Text = "Price";
//
// Label2
//
this.Label2.Font = new System.Drawing.Font(
    "Microsoft Sans Serif", 10F,
    System.Drawing.FontStyle.Bold,
    System.Drawing.GraphicsUnit.Point, ((System.Byte)(0)));
this.Label2.Location = new System.Drawing.Point(24, 70);
this.Label2.Name = "Label2";
this.Label2.Size = new System.Drawing.Size(56, 23);
this.Label2.TabIndex = 10;
this.Label2.Text = "Name";
//
// Label1
//
this.Label1.Font = new System.Drawing.Font(
    "Microsoft Sans Serif", 10F,
    System.Drawing.FontStyle.Bold,
    System.Drawing.GraphicsUnit.Point, ((System.Byte)(0)));
this.Label1.Location = new System.Drawing.Point(24, 46);
this.Label1.Name = "Label1";
this.Label1.Size = new System.Drawing.Size(56, 23);
this.Label1.TabIndex = 9;
this.Label1.Text = "ID";
//
// GroupBox1
//
this.GroupBox1.Controls.AddRange(new
    System.Windows.Forms.Control[]
    { this.Button1,
      this.RadioButton2,
      this.RadioButton1});
this.GroupBox1.Font = new System.Drawing.Font(
    "Microsoft Sans Serif", 10F,
    System.Drawing.FontStyle.Bold,
    System.Drawing.GraphicsUnit.Point, ((System.Byte)(0)));
this.GroupBox1.Location = new System.Drawing.Point(8, 14);
```

```
this.GroupBox1.Name = "GroupBox1";
this.GroupBox1.Size = new System.Drawing.Size(304, 112);
this.GroupBox1.TabIndex = 16;
this.GroupBox1.TabStop = false;
this.GroupBox1.Text = "Enter Query";
//
// Button1
//
this.Button1.Location = new System.Drawing.Point(240, 80);
this.Button1.Name = "Button1";
this.Button1.Size = new System.Drawing.Size(56, 23);
this.Button1.TabIndex = 2;
this.Button1.Text = "Query";
this.Button1.Click += new
    System.EventHandler(this.Button1_Click);
//
// RadioButton2
//
this.RadioButton2.Location = new
    System.Drawing.Point(240, 56);
this.RadioButton2.Name = "RadioButton2";
this.RadioButton2.Size = new System.Drawing.Size(16, 24);
this.RadioButton2.TabIndex = 1;
this.RadioButton2.CheckedChanged += new
    System.EventHandler(this.RadioButton2_CheckedChanged);
//
// RadioButton1
//
this.RadioButton1.Checked = true;
this.RadioButton1.Location = new
    System.Drawing.Point(240, 32);
this.RadioButton1.Name = "RadioButton1";
this.RadioButton1.Size = new System.Drawing.Size(16, 24);
this.RadioButton1.TabIndex = 0;
this.RadioButton1.TabStop = true;
this.RadioButton1.CheckedChanged += new
    System.EventHandler(this.RadioButton1_CheckedChanged);
//
// Button2
//
this.Button2.Font = new System.Drawing.Font(
    "Microsoft Sans Serif", 10F,
    System.Drawing.FontStyle.Bold,
    System.Drawing.GraphicsUnit.Point, ((System.Byte)(0)));
this.Button2.Location = new System.Drawing.Point(336, 262);
this.Button2.Name = "Button2";
this.Button2.Size = new System.Drawing.Size(256, 23);
this.Button2.TabIndex = 12;
this.Button2.Text = "Save Changes";
```

(continued)

```csharp
        this.Button2.Click += new
            System.EventHandler(this.Button2_Click);
        //
        // ProductCatalog
        //
        this.AutoScaleBaseSize = new System.Drawing.Size(5, 13);
        this.ClientSize = new System.Drawing.Size(600, 317);
        this.Controls.AddRange(new System.Windows.Forms.Control[] {

            this.DataGrid1,
            this.Xml_TxtBx,
            this.Price_TxtBx,

            this.Name_TxtBx,
            this.Id_TxtBx,
            this.Label3,

            this.Label2,
            this.Label1,
            this.GroupBox1,

            this.Button2});
        this.MaximumSize = new System.Drawing.Size(608, 344);
        this.MinimumSize = new System.Drawing.Size(608, 344);
        this.Name = "ProductCatalog";
        this.Text = "Product Catalog";
        this.Load += new System.EventHandler(
            this.ProductCatalog_Load);
        ((System.ComponentModel.ISupportInitialize)
            (this.DataGrid1)).EndInit();
        this.GroupBox1.ResumeLayout(false);
        this.ResumeLayout(false);

    }
    #endregion

    /// <summary>
    /// The main entry point for the application.
    /// </summary>
    [STAThread]
    static void Main()
    {
        Application.Run(new ProductCatalog());
    }

    private void ProductCatalog_Load(object sender,
        System.EventArgs e)
    {
        // Load products data into the DataSet object
```

```
relational_data = new DataSet();
relational_data.ReadXml(@"..\..\products.xml");

// Display the data in DataGrid1
DataGrid1.DataSource = relational_data.Tables[0];

// Synchronize the DataSet with the XmlDataDocument object.
// Any change made in the DataSet object is automatically
// made in the XmlDataDocument object.
xml_data = new XmlDataDocument(relational_data);

// Show the XML view in the Xml_TxtBx textbox
Xml_TxtBx.Text = xml_data.InnerXml.ToString();
}

private void Button2_Click(object sender, System.EventArgs e)
{
    // Read the XML data from the Xml_TxtBx into the DataSet
    // object
    XmlTextReader xml_reader = new XmlTextReader(new
            StringReader(Xml_TxtBx.Text));
    relational_data = new DataSet();
    relational_data.ReadXml(xml_reader);

    // Create a new XmlDataDocument object
    xml_data = new XmlDataDocument(relational_data);

    // Save the changes in the products.xml file
    relational_data.WriteXml(@"..\..\products.xml");

    // Show the data in the DataGrid
    DataGrid1.DataSource = xml_data.DataSet.Tables[0];

}

private void RadioButton1_CheckedChanged(object sender,
    System.EventArgs e)
{

    Id_TxtBx.ReadOnly = false;
    Name_TxtBx.ReadOnly = true;
    Id_TxtBx.Focus();
}

private void RadioButton2_CheckedChanged(object sender,
    System.EventArgs e)
{

    Id_TxtBx.ReadOnly = true;
    Name_TxtBx.ReadOnly = false;
    Name_TxtBx.Focus();
```

(continued)

```
        }

        private void Button1_Click(object sender, System.EventArgs e)
        {
            if (Button1.Text.Equals("Query")){
                if (RadioButton1.Checked)
                {
                    // Create an XPathNavigator object
                    XPathNavigator navigator;
                    navigator = xml_data.CreateNavigator();

                    // Create and compile an XPathExpression
                    XPathExpression expr;
                    try
                    {
                        expr = navigator.Compile(
                            "descendant::product[id=" +
                            Id_TxtBx.Text + "]");
                        // Call the Select method on the XPathNavigator
                        // object and store the reference to the
                        // XPathNodeIterator object returned by the
                        // Select method
                        XPathNodeIterator iterator;
                        iterator = navigator.Select(expr);

                        // Navigate to get the value of id, name,
                        // and price
                        iterator.MoveNext();
                        XPathNavigator nav2 = iterator.Current.Clone();
                        nav2.MoveToFirstChild();
                        Id_TxtBx.Text = nav2.Value;
                        nav2.MoveToNext();
                        Name_TxtBx.Text = nav2.Value;
                        nav2.MoveToNext();
                        Price_TxtBx.Text = nav2.Value;
                    }
                    catch (Exception ex)
                    {
                        MessageBox.Show("Enter a valid product id");
                    }
                }

                else if (RadioButton2.Checked)
                {
                    // Create an XPathNavigator object
                    XPathNavigator navigator;
                    navigator = xml_data.CreateNavigator();

                    // Create and compile an XPathExpression
                    XPathExpression expr;
```

```
                                try
                                {
                                    expr = navigator.Compile(
                                        "descendant::product[name='" +
                                        Name_TxtBx.Text + "']");
                                    // Call the Select method on the XPathNavigator
                                    // object and store the reference to the
                                    // XPathNodeIterator object returned by the
                                    // Select method
                                    XPathNodeIterator iterator;
                                    iterator = navigator.Select(expr);

                                    // Navigate to get the value of id, name,
                                    // and price
                                    iterator.MoveNext();
                                    XPathNavigator nav2 = iterator.Current.Clone();
                                    nav2.MoveToFirstChild();
                                    Id_TxtBx.Text = nav2.Value;
                                    nav2.MoveToNext();
                                    Name_TxtBx.Text = nav2.Value;
                                    nav2.MoveToNext();
                                    Price_TxtBx.Text = nav2.Value;
                                }
                                catch (Exception ex)
                                {
                                    MessageBox.Show("Enter a valid product name, " +
                                        "which is case sensitive.");
                                }
                            }
                            Button1.Text = "Clear";
                            GroupBox1.Text = "Clear Query";
                        }
                        else
                        {
                            Id_TxtBx.Text = "";
                            Name_TxtBx.Text = "";
                            Price_TxtBx.Text = "";
                            Button1.Text = "Query";
                            GroupBox1.Text = "Enter Query";
                        }
                    }

    private void DataGrid1_CurrentCellChanged(object sender,
        System.EventArgs e)
    {
        Xml_TxtBx.Text = xml_data.InnerXml.ToString();
    }
    }
}
```

Switch to design view to see the effect of the code that you have just added. The interface of the ProductCatalog form is shown next.

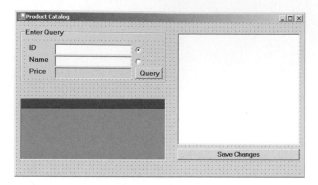

6. Using Windows Explorer, place the Products.xml file that you created in the previous exercise in the VBProduct Catalog or CSProduct Catalog folder.

7. In the Solution Explorer, right-click the VBProduct Catalog or CSProduct Catalog project. From the shortcut menu, choose Add, then Add Existing Item. In the Add Existing Item dialog box, locate the Products.xml file that you created in the previous exercise and click Open to include the Products.xml file in the project.

8. For a Visual Basic .NET project, change the startup object for the project. In the Solution Explorer, right-click the VBProduct Catalog project and choose Properties from the shortcut menu to open the properties dialog box. Select ProductCatalog from the Startup Object drop-down list.

9. Click Build Solution from the Build menu to build your solution.

Exercise 3: Running the Product Catalog Application

In this exercise, you will run the Product Catalog application that you created in Exercise 2. You will perform queries and add, modify, and delete product information using the data grid as well as the text box that displays the product information in XML format. In addition, you will save the changes to the Products.xml file. To work with the Product Catalog application, perform the following steps:

1. Press F5 to start the application in debug mode. The application loads the data from the Products.xml file and displays it in the data grid and text box objects.

2. You can query the product information either by providing the ID or the name of a product and clicking the Query button inside the Enter Query group box. To perform queries based on the product ID, select the radio button next to the ID box, type a valid product ID in the ID text box, and click the Query button. The following graphic shows the result of a query performed for ID = 104.

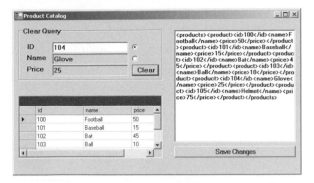

3. To perform another query, click the Clear button.

4. To perform a query based on product name, select the radio button next to the Name box. Type **Ball** in the Name box and click the Query button. The following graphic shows the result of a query performed for Name = Ball.

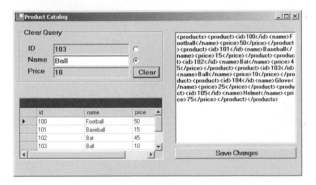

5. To add a new product using the data grid, scroll down the data grid, enter the values for Product ID, Name, and Price in an empty row, and navigate out of the new row. Note that the new product information is also displayed in the box displaying the XML view of the data. The following graphic shows a new record with Product ID = 106, Name = Basketball, and Price = 75 being added in the data grid.

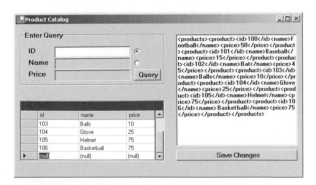

6. Delete and modify some records in the data grid and see the corresponding changes in the XML view.

7. To save the changes in the Products.xml file, click the Save Changes button.

8. To add a new product using the XML view, add the appropriate XML fragment. For example, the following graphic shows how to add a product with ID = 107, Name = Shoes, and Price = 45.

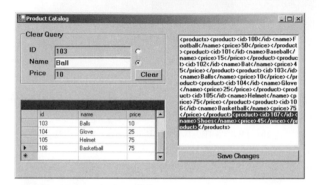

Click the Save Changes button to display the changes in the data grid. Clicking the Save Changes button also saves the product information in the Products.xml file.

9. Modify and delete the records in the XML view. Click the Save Changes button to display the changes in the data grid and save those changes in the Products.xml file.

Review

The questions in this section reinforce key information presented in this chapter. If you are unable to answer a question, review the appropriate lesson, and then try answering the question again. Answers to the questions can be found in Appendix A, "Questions and Answers."

1. Which method will you use to load the contents of an XML file into an XmlDocument object?

2. Which method will you use to write the contents of the XmlDocument object into an XML file?

3. How do you read the contents of an XML document using XmlTextReader?

4. Which class do you use to write data to an XML file?

5. How does XPathNavigator read data from an XML document?

6. Which methods of the XPathNavigator class do you use to navigate within the nodes selected from an XML document?

7. What objects are used to create the structure of an XML document within a schema?

8. Which event is raised for validating the semantics of the XML Schema?

9. How can you ensure your XML document is valid?

10. How can you read fragments of an XML document?

11. Which method enables you to retrieve the XSD schema for the XML representation of the data stored in the DataSet?

12. Which method of the DataSet class enables you to write the contents of a DataSet into an XML file?

Creating and Consuming XML Web Services

About This Chapter

The XML Web services programming model enables you to build highly scalable, loosely coupled, distributed applications using standard Web protocols such as HTTP, XML, and SOAP. In this chapter you will learn about the XML Web services programming model and learn to create, deploy, and consume XML Web services.

Before You Begin

To complete the lessons in this chapter, you

- Must have knowledge of programming in Microsoft Visual Basic .NET or Microsoft Visual C#
- Must have knowledge of XML

Lesson 1: Understanding XML Web Services

XML Web services are program components that allow you to build scalable, loosely coupled, platform-independent applications. XML Web services enable disparate applications to exchange messages using standard protocols such as HTTP, XML, XSD, SOAP, and Web Services Description Language (WSDL). In this lesson, you will learn about the Web services programming model and various components that constitute the Web services infrastructure.

After this lesson, you will be able to

- Describe XML Web services
- Describe various infrastructure elements of XML Web services
- Describe the life cycle of an XML Web service

Estimated lesson time: 30 minutes

Overview of XML Web Services

An XML Web service is a component that implements program logic and provides functionality for disparate applications. These applications use standard protocols, such as HTTP, XML, and SOAP, to access the functionality. XML Web services use XML-based messaging to send and receive data, which enables heterogeneous applications to interoperate with each other. You can use XML Web services to integrate applications that are written in different programming languages and deployed on different platforms. In addition, you can deploy XML Web services within an intranet as well as on the Internet. While the Internet brings users closer to organizations, XML Web services allow organizations to integrate their applications.

One important feature of the XML Web services–based computing model is that a client need not know the language in which XML Web services are implemented. The client just needs to know the location of an XML Web service and the methods that the client can call on the service.

Some examples will help you understand the contexts in which you can implement XML Web services–based solutions. In its simplest form, an XML Web service can consist of specific programming logic to provide functionality, such as income tax calculation. An XML Web service that computes income tax requires a client application to provide information such as income, savings, and investments made during the year. Client applications can call a method on the service and provide the necessary information as arguments to the method call. The data related to the method call and to the arguments is sent to the Web service in XML format using the SOAP protocol over the HTTP transport. Another example in which you can use XML Web services is application integration. You can enable a payroll application written in one language, such as COBOL, to send data to a component that is written in another language, such as Visual Basic, using an XML Web service.

XML Web Services Infrastructure

One of the important features of the XML Web services–based computing model is that both clients and XML Web services are unaware of the implementation details of each other. The XML Web services infrastructure provides several components that enable client applications to locate and consume XML Web services. These components include the following:

- **XML Web services directories.**   These directories provide a central place to store published information about XML Web services. These directories might also be XML Web services that allow you to search for information about other XML Web services programmatically. The Universal Description, Discovery, and Integration (UDDI) specifications define the guidelines for publishing information about XML Web services. The XML schemas associated with UDDI define four types of information that you must publish to make your XML Web service accessible. This information includes business information, service information, binding information, and service specifications. Microsoft provides one such directory service, which is located at *http://uddi.microsoft.com*.

- **XML Web services discovery.**   Using this process, clients locate the documents that describe an XML Web service using WSDL. The discovery process enables clients to know about the presence of an XML Web service and about the location of a particular XML Web service.

- **XML Web services description.**   This component provides information that enables you to know which operations to perform on an XML Web service. The XML Web service description is an XML document that specifies the format of messages that an XML Web service can understand. For example, the description document specifies the SOAP message schemas that you use when invoking methods on an XML Web service.

- **XML Web service wire formats.**   To enable communication between disparate systems, XML Web services use open wire formats. Open wire formats are the protocols that can be understood by any system that is capable of supporting common Web standards, such as HTTP and SOAP. The HTTP-GET and HTTP-POST protocols are the standard Web protocols that allow you to send parameters as name-value pairs. The HTTP-GET protocol allows you to send URL-encoded parameters as name-value pairs to an XML Web service. The HTTP-GET protocol requires you to append the parameter name-value pairs to the URL of the XML Web service. You can also use the HTTP-POST protocol to URL-encode and pass parameters to the XML Web service as name-value pairs. However, the parameters are passed inside the actual request message and not appended to the URL of the XML Web service.

The SOAP protocol allows you to exchange structured and typed information between the applications on the Internet. The SOAP protocol consists of four parts. The first part is mandatory and defines the envelope that contains the message. The SOAP envelope is the basic unit of exchange between the processors of SOAP messages. The second part defines the optional data encoding rules that you use to encode application-specific data types. The third part defines the request/response pattern of message exchanges between XML Web services. The fourth part, which is optional, defines the bindings between the SOAP and HTTP protocols.

Figure 7.1 shows how various components of the XML Web services infrastructure enable clients to locate and call methods on XML Web services.

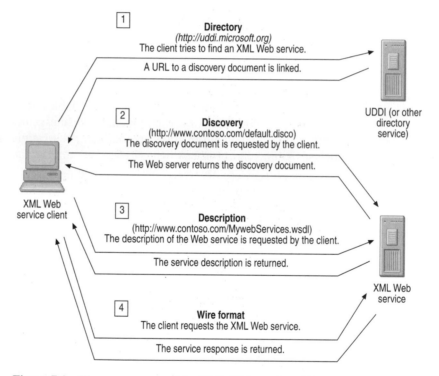

Figure 7.1   The components of the XML Web services infrastructure

When a client accesses a UDDI service to locate an XML Web service, the UDDI service returns a URL to the discovery document of the XML Web service. A discovery document is a .disco file, which contains the link to the resources that describe an XML Web service. A discovery file is an XML document that enables programmatic discovery of an XML Web service. After the client receives the URL to the discovery document, the client requests a server, which returns the discovery document to the client. The contents of a sample discovery document are shown in the following code.

XML

```xml
<?xml version="1.0" ?>
<disco:discovery xmlns:disco="http://schemas.xmlsoap.org/disco"
    xmlns:wsdl="http://schemas.xmlsoap.org/disco/wsdl">
    <wsdl:contractRef ref="http://www.contoso.com/MyWebService.asmx?WSDL"/>
</disco:discovery>
```

The client uses the information in the discovery document and requests a server to return the service description of an XML Web service. The service description is a .wsdl file and enables a client to interact with an XML Web service.

Now you will look at the process involved when a client invokes methods on an XML Web service.

Communication Between the Client and the XML Web Service

The process of communication between a client and an XML Web service is similar to a remote procedure call (RPC). The client uses a proxy object of the XML Web service on the local computer to call methods on the XML Web service. Figure 7.2 shows the process of communication between a client and an XML Web service.

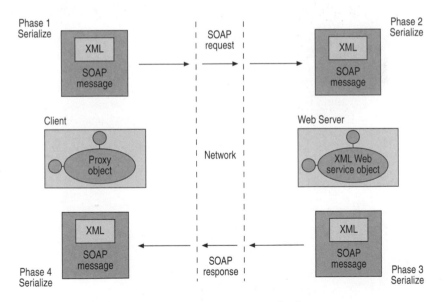

Figure 7.2   Client and XML Web service communication

As shown in Figure 7.2, the interaction between a client and an XML Web service consists of several phases. The following tasks are performed during these phases:

1. The client creates an object of the XML Web service proxy class on the same computer on which the client resides.
2. The client calls a method on the proxy object.
3. The XML Web services infrastructure on the client system serializes the method call and arguments into a SOAP message and sends it to the XML Web service over the network.
4. The infrastructure on the server on which the XML Web service resides deserializes the SOAP message and creates an instance of the XML Web service. The infrastructure then calls the method with the arguments on the XML Web service.
5. The XML Web service executes the method and returns the value with any out parameters to the infrastructure.
6. The infrastructure serializes the return value and any out parameters into a SOAP message and sends them to the client over the network.
7. The infrastructure on the client computer deserializes the SOAP message containing the return value and any out parameters and sends them to the proxy object.
8. The proxy object sends the return value and any out parameters to the client.

To build XML Web services that the clients can consume, you use the ASP.NET infrastructure, which is an integral part of the .NET Framework. Visual Studio .NET provides tools to build, deploy, and publish your XML Web services using ASP.NET. In the next lesson, you will learn how to create XML Web services using Visual Studio .NET.

Lesson 2: Creating XML Web Services

In the previous lesson, you learned about XML Web services and various components of the XML Web services infrastructure. You also learned about the architecture of XML Web services. In this lesson, you will learn how to create XML Web services using Visual Studio .NET. In addition, you will learn about various files that are created when you create an XML Web service.

After this lesson, you will be able to

- Create an XML Web service using Visual Studio .NET
- Identify the files that are created when you create an XML Web service using Visual Studio .NET

Estimated lesson time: 60 minutes

Creating an XML Web Service

Creating an XML Web service is similar to creating a Component Object Model (COM) component that provides application logic to a client application. You create an XML Web service to provide specific functionality to client applications over the Web. To create an XML Web service, you first choose a programming language in which you want to create the service and create a class that inherits from System.Web.Services.WebService. Next, you require an infrastructure that makes the XML Web service available for client applications to use over the Internet. Visual Studio .NET provides you with tools that help you build, deploy, and consume an XML Web service.

You'll now learn how to create an XML Web service. In this lesson, you'll take a sample travel service and process it through various stages in the life cycle of an XML Web service. This sample XML Web service enables users to create their appointments in a Scheduler application and send e-mail notification to the person they are to meet. To provide this functionality to client applications, you need to create an XML Web service for creating appointments and sending notification by e-mail.

The TravelService XML Web service, however, is not user-interface driven or interactive. The XML Web service provides the application logic and is integrated with a Scheduler application. The Scheduler application allows users to create and maintain appointments. The application schedules travel reservations based on the appointment details provided by users. The Scheduler application acts as the client for the XML Web service and can be a Windows application or an ASP.NET Web application. You will learn to create a client application in the next lesson.

The Visual Studio .NET IDE provides you with the environment needed to create projects for distributed desktop applications, Web applications, and XML Web services. To create an XML Web service, perform the following steps:

1. Open the Visual Studio .NET IDE. Start a project to create an application or a service by pointing to New on the File menu and choosing Project to open the New Project dialog box.

2. In the New Project dialog box, select Visual Basic Projects in the Project Types pane. In the Templates pane, select ASP.NET Web Service. In the Location box, type the name and location of the XML Web service as **http://localhost/TravelService**, and click OK. Figure 7.3 shows the New Project dialog box.

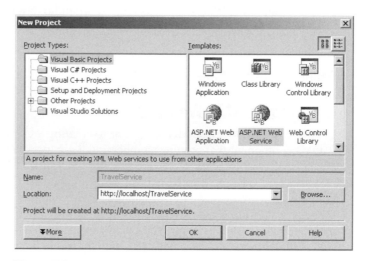

Figure 7.3 The New Project dialog box

3. The Create New Web message box appears while a Web folder with the specified name is being created. Figure 7.4 shows the Create New Web message box.

Figure 7.4 The Create New Web message box

When you create the ASP.NET Web service project, the default page is displayed in design mode, and an .asmx file is created. After creating an XML Web service project, you write the code to provide functionality to the XML Web service. This code is stored in a file associated with the .asmx.cs or

.asmx.vb file and is known as the code-behind file. The code-behind file depends on the language that you use to create the XML Web service. For a Visual C# project, the code-behind file is a .cs file. For a Visual Basic .NET project, the code-behind file is a .vb file.

4. Rename the Service1.asmx file in the Solution Explorer as TravelService.asmx.

5. To add functionality to the XML Web service, select the Solution Explorer tab, right-click the TravelService.asmx file, and choose View Code. The window in which you write the code for the service appears. Figure 7.5 shows the startup screen of the TravelService XML Web service.

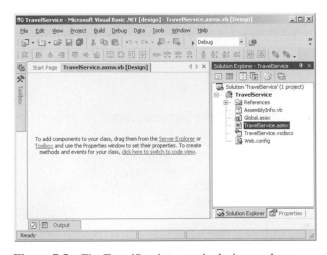

Figure 7.5   The TravelService page in design mode

For each XML Web service that you create, the following files are created by Visual Studio .NET:

- AssemblyInfo.cs or AssemblyInfo.vb
- Global.asax
- Global.asax.cs or Global.asax.vb
- Service1.asmx
- Service1.asmx.cs or Service1.asmx.vb
- Service1.vsdisco
- Web.config

AssemblyInfo File

An assembly is the functional unit for sharing and reuse in the common language runtime. For more information about assemblies and configuration, refer to Chapter 1, "Understanding the .NET Framework." The AssemblyInfo file consists of general information about the assemblies in the project. To modify the assembly information, such as the version number, you change the attributes in the AssemblyInfo file.

Web.config File

This file contains configuration information, such as the debug mode and the authentication mode for a Web project. It also includes information about whether to display custom errors for a Web project. You can also use the Web.config file to store custom configuration information for your XML Web service.

Global.asax and Global.asax.cs or Global.asax.vb Files

These files enable you to manage application-level and session-level events. These files reside in the root directory of an ASP.NET Web application or ASP.NET Web service. The Global.asax.cs or Global.asax.vb class file is a hidden, dependent file of Global.asax, which contains the code for handling application events such as the Application_OnError event.

Service1.asmx and the Service1.asmx.cs or Service1.asmx.vb Files

These two files make up a single XML Web service. The Service1.asmx file contains the XML Web service–processing directive and serves as the addressable entry point for the XML Web service. The Service1.asmx.cs or Service1.asmx.vb class file is a hidden, dependent file of WebService.asmx and contains the code-behind class for the XML Web service.

WebService.vsdisco

The .vsdisco file is also known as the discovery file. This file is an XML-based file that contains links or URLs to resources providing discovery information for an XML Web service.

Before you create the TravelService XML Web service, you need to create a database, BookingDetails, consisting of the following tables:

- **AppointmentDetails.**   This table stores the details of all appointments.
- **ContactPersonDetails.**   This table stores the details of the person to be met at a particular destination.
- **FlightDetails.**   This table stores the details of preferred airlines and classes of users.
- **MyDetails.**   This table stores the personal details and preferences of users.
- **TravelDetails.**   This table stores travel details, such as destination, flight time, and date.

Figure 7.6 displays the BookingDetails database schema.

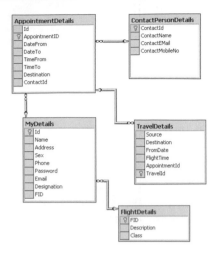

Figure 7.6 The BookingDetails database schema

To create the BookingDetails database and the tables, perform the following steps:

1. From the Start menu, locate the Microsoft SQL Server folder and open Enterprise Manager.
2. Expand your SQL Server node and locate the Databases node. Right-click the Databases node and choose New Database from the shortcut menu.
3. In the Database Properties dialog box, type **BookingDetails** in the Name field, and click OK to create the BookingDetails database.
4. Open Query Analyzer. Provide the required authentication information to connect to your database server.
5. Select the BookingDetails database from the list of databases in Query Analyzer.
6. Execute the following script.

SQL Script

```
if exists (select * from dbo.sysobjects where id = object_id(
N'[dbo].[FK_TravelDetails_AppointmentDetails]') and OBJECTPROPERTY(id,
N'IsForeignKey') = 1)
ALTER TABLE [dbo].[TravelDetails] DROP CONSTRAINT
FK_TravelDetails_AppointmentDetails
GO

if exists (select * from dbo.sysobjects where id = object_id(
N'[dbo].[FK_AppointmentDetails_ContactPersonDetails]') and OBJECTPROPERTY(
```

(continued)

```
id, N'IsForeignKey') = 1)
ALTER TABLE [dbo].[AppointmentDetails] DROP CONSTRAINT
FK_AppointmentDetails_ContactPersonDetails
GO

if exists (select * from dbo.sysobjects where id = object_id(
N'[dbo].[FK_AppointmentDetails_MyPersonalDetails]') and OBJECTPROPERTY(id,
N'IsForeignKey') = 1)
ALTER TABLE [dbo].[AppointmentDetails] DROP CONSTRAINT
FK_AppointmentDetails_MyPersonalDetails
GO

if exists (select * from dbo.sysobjects where id = object_id(
N'[dbo].[AppointmentDetails]') and OBJECTPROPERTY(id, N'IsUserTable') = 1)
drop table [dbo].[AppointmentDetails]
GO

if exists (select * from dbo.sysobjects where id = object_id(
N'[dbo].[ContactPersonDetails]') and OBJECTPROPERTY(id, N'IsUserTable')
= 1)
drop table [dbo].[ContactPersonDetails]
GO

if exists (select * from dbo.sysobjects where id = object_id(
N'[dbo].[FlightDetails]') and OBJECTPROPERTY(id, N'IsUserTable') = 1)
drop table [dbo].[FlightDetails]
GO

if exists (select * from dbo.sysobjects where id = object_id(
N'[dbo].[MyPersonalDetails]') and OBJECTPROPERTY(id, N'IsUserTable') = 1)
drop table [dbo].[MyPersonalDetails]
GO

if exists (select * from dbo.sysobjects where id = object_id(
N'[dbo].[TravelDetails]') and OBJECTPROPERTY(id, N'IsUserTable') = 1)
drop table [dbo].[TravelDetails]
GO

if not exists (select * from dbo.sysobjects where id = object_id(
N'[dbo].[AppointmentDetails]') and OBJECTPROPERTY(id, N'IsUserTable') = 1)
 BEGIN
CREATE TABLE [dbo].[AppointmentDetails] (
    [ID] [int] NOT NULL ,
    [AppointmentID] [int] NOT NULL ,
    [DateFrom] [char] (10) COLLATE SQL_Latin1_General_CP1_CI_AS NOT NULL,
    [DateTo] [char] (10) COLLATE SQL_Latin1_General_CP1_CI_AS NOT NULL,
    [TimeFrom] [char] (10) COLLATE SQL_Latin1_General_CP1_CI_AS NOT NULL,
    [TimeTo] [char] (10) COLLATE SQL_Latin1_General_CP1_CI_AS NOT NULL,
    [Destination] [char] (20) COLLATE SQL_Latin1_General_CP1_CI_AS
```

```
        NOT NULL ,
        [ContactID] [int] NOT NULL
) ON [PRIMARY]
END


GO


if not exists (select * from dbo.sysobjects where id = object_id(
N'[dbo].[ContactPersonDetails]') and OBJECTPROPERTY(id, N'IsUserTable')
= 1)
 BEGIN
CREATE TABLE [dbo].[ContactPersonDetails] (
    [ContactID] [int] NOT NULL ,
    [ContactName] [char] (20) COLLATE SQL_Latin1_General_CP1_CI_AS
        NOT NULL ,
    [ContactEmail] [char] (20) COLLATE SQL_Latin1_General_CP1_CI_AS
        NOT NULL ,
    [ContactMobileNo] [char] (10) COLLATE SQL_Latin1_General_CP1_CI_AS
        NOT NULL
) ON [PRIMARY]
END


GO


if not exists (select * from dbo.sysobjects where id = object_id(
N'[dbo].[FlightDetails]') and OBJECTPROPERTY(id, N'IsUserTable') = 1)
 BEGIN
CREATE TABLE [dbo].[FlightDetails] (
    [FlightID] [int] NOT NULL ,
    [Description] [char] (20) COLLATE SQL_Latin1_General_CP1_CI_AS
        NOT NULL ,
    [Class] [char] (5) COLLATE SQL_Latin1_General_CP1_CI_AS NOT NULL
) ON [PRIMARY]
END


GO


if not exists (select * from dbo.sysobjects where id = object_id(
N'[dbo].[MyPersonalDetails]') and OBJECTPROPERTY(id, N'IsUserTable') = 1)
 BEGIN
CREATE TABLE [dbo].[MyPersonalDetails] (
    [ID] [int] NOT NULL ,
    [Name] [char] (20) COLLATE SQL_Latin1_General_CP1_CI_AS NOT NULL,
    [Address] [char] (40) COLLATE SQL_Latin1_General_CP1_CI_AS NOT NULL,
    [Sex] [char] (1) COLLATE SQL_Latin1_General_CP1_CI_AS NOT NULL,
    [Phone] [char] (10) COLLATE SQL_Latin1_General_CP1_CI_AS NOT NULL,
    [Password] [char] (8) COLLATE SQL_Latin1_General_CP1_CI_AS NOT NULL,
    [Email] [char] (20) COLLATE SQL_Latin1_General_CP1_CI_AS NOT NULL,
    [Designation] [char] (20) COLLATE SQL_Latin1_General_CP1_CI_AS
```

(continued)

```
        NOT NULL,
    [FlightID] [int] NOT NULL
) ON [PRIMARY]
END


GO


if not exists (select * from dbo.sysobjects where id = object_id(
N'[dbo].[TravelDetails]') and OBJECTPROPERTY(id, N'IsUserTable') = 1)
 BEGIN
CREATE TABLE [dbo].[TravelDetails] (
    [TravelID] [int] NOT NULL ,
    [Source] [char] (20) COLLATE SQL_Latin1_General_CP1_CI_AS NOT NULL,
    [Destination] [char] (20) COLLATE SQL_Latin1_General_CP1_CI_AS
        NOT NULL,
    [FromDate] [char] (10) COLLATE SQL_Latin1_General_CP1_CI_AS NOT NULL,
    [FlightTime] [char] (10) COLLATE SQL_Latin1_General_CP1_CI_AS
        NOT NULL,
    [AppointmentID] [int] NOT NULL
) ON [PRIMARY]
END


GO


ALTER TABLE [dbo].[AppointmentDetails] WITH NOCHECK ADD
    CONSTRAINT [PK_AppointmentDetails] PRIMARY KEY CLUSTERED
    (
        [AppointmentID]
    )  ON [PRIMARY]
GO


ALTER TABLE [dbo].[ContactPersonDetails] WITH NOCHECK ADD
    CONSTRAINT [PK_ContactPersonDetails] PRIMARY KEY CLUSTERED
    (
        [ContactID]
    )  ON [PRIMARY]
GO


ALTER TABLE [dbo].[FlightDetails] WITH NOCHECK ADD
    CONSTRAINT [PK_FlightDetails] PRIMARY KEY CLUSTERED
    (
        [FlightID]
    )  ON [PRIMARY]
GO


ALTER TABLE [dbo].[MyPersonalDetails] WITH NOCHECK ADD
    CONSTRAINT [PK_MyPersonalDetails] PRIMARY KEY CLUSTERED
    (
        [ID]
```

```
        )  ON [PRIMARY]
GO

ALTER TABLE [dbo].[TravelDetails] WITH NOCHECK ADD
    CONSTRAINT [PK_TravelDetails] PRIMARY KEY CLUSTERED
    (
        [TravelID]
    )  ON [PRIMARY]
GO

ALTER TABLE [dbo].[AppointmentDetails] ADD
    CONSTRAINT [FK_AppointmentDetails_ContactPersonDetails] FOREIGN KEY
    (
        [ContactID]
    ) REFERENCES [dbo].[ContactPersonDetails] (
        [ContactID]
    ),
    CONSTRAINT [FK_AppointmentDetails_MyPersonalDetails] FOREIGN KEY
    (
        [ID]
    ) REFERENCES [dbo].[MyPersonalDetails] (
        [ID]
    )
GO

ALTER TABLE [dbo].[TravelDetails] ADD
    CONSTRAINT [FK_TravelDetails_AppointmentDetails] FOREIGN KEY
    (
        [AppointmentID]
    ) REFERENCES [dbo].[AppointmentDetails] (
        [AppointmentID]
    )
GO
```

After you create the database and the tables, you provide the relevant functionality to the XML Web service. To enable client applications to access and use the XML Web service, you expose the functionality of the XML Web service by creating Web methods. Web methods are independent functional units that perform certain predefined operations in an XML Web service. You use the <WebMethod> attribute in Visual Basic .NET or the [WebMethod] attribute in Visual C# to declare a Web method, depending on the language you choose to develop your XML Web service. The following code snippet shows a sample Web method:

Visual Basic .NET

```
<WebMethod()> Public Function HelloWorld() As String
    HelloWorld = "Hello World"
End Function
```

Visual C#

```
[WebMethod]
public string HelloWorld()
{
    return "Hello World";
}
```

The TravelService XML Web service consists of two Web methods, MakeReservations and SendMessage. The MakeReservations Web method is exposed to client applications for the TravelService XML Web service. The SendMessage Web method is used to send e-mail notifications to the specified e-mail address. The signature of the MakeReservations Web method is shown here.

Visual Basic .NET

```
<WebMethod()> _
Public Function MakeReservations(ByVal DateFrom As String, _
    ByVal TimeFrom As String, ByVal TimeTo As String, _
    ByVal Destination As String, ByVal ContactId As String) As String

End Function
```

Visual C#

```
[WebMethod]
public string MakeReservations(string DateFrom, string TimeFrom,
    string TimeTo, string Destination, string ContactId)
{

}
```

The MakeReservations Web method performs three major tasks:

- Populates the DataSet
- Creates a reservation
- Sends an e-mail notification

Populating the DataSet

The code for populating the DataSet initializes the OleDbConnection object and creates a connection with the server through the object. To accomplish this task, the connection string is declared according to server specifications. An object of the DataSet class is created to retrieve the contents from the AppointmentDetails table. Finally, an OleDbDataAdapter object is created to execute a query and populate the DataSet.

Visual Basic .NET

```
Imports System.Data
Imports System.Data.OleDB
```

```
Public Class MyWebService

    <WebMethod()> _
    Public Function MakeReservations(ByVal ID As Integer, ByVal _
        DateFrom As String, ByVal DateTo As String, ByVal TimeFrom As _
        String, ByVal TimeTo As String, ByVal Destination As String, _
        ByVal ContactId As String) As String
        Dim sqlStatement As String = ""
        Try

            Dim strConnectionString As String
            strConnectionString = "Provider=SQLOLEDB.1; Data Source=" & _
                "localhost;uid=sa;pwd=;Initial Catalog=BookingDetails;"
            Dim conADOConnect As New OleDbConnection(strConnectionString)
            conADOConnect.Open()
            Dim dsID As New DataSet()
            Dim comADOCommand As New OleDbCommand()
            comADOCommand.Connection = conADOConnect
            comADOCommand.CommandText = "Select * from AppointmentDetails"
            Dim adosc As New OleDbDataAdapter()
            adosc.SelectCommand = comADOCommand
            adosc.Fill(dsID, "AppointmentDetails")
            Dim dview As New DataView(dsID.Tables("AppointmentDetails"))
            dview.RowStateFilter = DataViewRowState.CurrentRows
            ' Code for creating the reservation
            .
            .
            .


        Catch e As Exception
            MakeReservations = e.Message
        End Try
    End Function

End Class
```

Visual C#

```
using System.Data.OleDb;

public class MyWebService
{
    [WebMethod]
    public string MakeReservations(int ID, string DateFrom, string
    DateTo, string TimeFrom, string TimeTo, string Destination, int
    ContactId)
    {
        String sqlStatement = "";
        try
        {
            String strConnectionString = "";
            strConnectionString = "Provider= SQLOLEDB.1; Data Source=" +
```

(continued)

```
                    "localhost; uid=sa; pwd=; Initial Catalog=Booker;";
                OleDbConnection conADOConnect = new OleDbConnection(
                    strConnectionString);
                conADOConnect.Open();
                DataSet dsID = new DataSet();
                OleDbCommand comAdoCommand = new OleDbCommand();
                comAdoCommand.Connection = conADOConnect;
                comAdoCommand.CommandText =
                    "Select * from AppointmentDetails";
                OleDbDataAdapter adosc = new OleDbDataAdapter();
                adosc.SelectCommand = comAdoCommand;
                adosc.Fill(dsID,"AppointmentDetails");
                DataView dview = new
                    DataView(dsID.Tables["AppointmentDetails"]);
                dview.RowStateFilter = DataViewRowState.CurrentRows;

                // Code for creating the reservation
                .
                .
                .
            }
        catch(Exception e)
        {
            return e.ToString ();
        }
    }
}
```

Creating a Reservation

After populating the DataSet, the next step is to create a reservation (or appointment). The code for this task calculates the last value of the AppointmentID field and increments it by 1. The AppointmentID field is a primary key field, and you cannot insert duplicate or null values into the field. The following shows the code for creating the reservation.

Visual Basic .NET

```
' Code for creating the reservation


Dim conid As Integer = 0
Dim drview As DataRowView
For Each drview In dview
    conid = Int32.Parse(drview("AppointmentId").ToString())
Next
If conid > 0 Then
    conid = conid + 1
Else
```

```
        conid = 1
End If
Dim adcConnection As New OleDbConnection(strConnectionString)
adcConnection.Open()
sqlStatement = "Insert into AppointmentDetails values(ID," + _
    conid + ",'" + DateFrom + "','" + DateTo + "','" + TimeFrom + _
    "','" + TimeTo + "','" + Destination + "'," + ContactId + ")"
conid = conid + 1
Dim cSQLStatement As New OleDbCommand(sqlStatement, adcConnection)
cSQLStatement.CommandText = sqlStatement
cSQLStatement.ExecuteNonQuery()
```

Visual C#

```
// Code for creating the reservation
//

int conid=0;
foreach(DataRowView drview in dview)
{
    conid = Int32.Parse(drview["AppointmentId"].ToString());
}
if(conid>0)
{
    conid++;
}
else
{
    conid = 1;
}
OleDbConnection adcConnection = new OleDbConnection(strConnectionString);
adcConnection.Open();
sqlStatement = "Insert into AppointmentDetails values(" + ID + "," +
    conid + ",'" + DateFrom + "','" + DateTo + "','" + TimeFrom + "','" +
    TimeTo + "','" + Destination + "'," + ContactId + ")";
conid++;
OleDbCommand cSQLStatement = new OleDbCommand(sqlStatement,adcConnection);
cSQLStatement.CommandText = sqlStatement;
cSQLStatement.ExecuteNonQuery();
```

Sending an E-Mail Notification

The final task of the MakeReservations Web method is to send a notification
through e-mail to the user and to the contact person about the appointment and
travel details. In the code for making reservations, a Web reference to another XML
Web service is created. You will learn how to add a Web reference in Lesson 4. The
other XML Web service is the MailSender service that sends e-mail notifications.
Finally, an object of the XML Web service is created, and then the Web method
SendMessage, exposed by the XML Web service, is called.

Note   Make sure that you include the required assemblies for the MailSender service to execute properly. You should include the System.Text.RegularExpressions and System.Web.Mail namespaces. In addition, please note that this entire piece of code is part of the MakeReservations Web method.

Visual Basic .NET

```
'Sending mail
SendMessage("johnd@mymail.com", "susanj@mail.com", _
    "Appointment Booking Confirmation", _
    "Your appointment has been confirmed.", 1)
MakeReservations = "Appointment created successfully."
```

Visual C#

```
/* Sending mail */
SendMessage("johnd@mymail.com", "susanj@mail.com",
    "Appointment Booking Confirmation",
    "Your appointment has been confirmed.", 1);
return "Appointment created successfully.";
```

Similarly, the TravelService XML Web service contains a Web method that sends e-mail notifications to users whenever you make a reservation for them.

The SendMessage Web method sends a message to each recipient in a distribution list. The method accepts the e-mail address of the sender; a list of recipients; and the subject, content, and format of the message. Each recipient address is delimited by using a comma, a semicolon, or a tab separator. The message can be either in plain text or in the HTML format, as shown in the following code.

Visual Basic .NET

```
<WebMethod()> Public Function SendMessage(ByVal from As String, _
    ByVal recipients As String, ByVal subject As String, _
    ByVal body As String, ByVal format As Integer) As String
    Dim retValue As String = ""
        Try
            Dim aryRecipients As String()
            Dim Separators As Char() = New Char(2) {",", ";", "\t"}
            aryRecipients = recipients.Split(Separators)
            Dim recipient As String
            For Each recipient In aryRecipients
                If recipient <> "" And recipient <> Nothing Then
                retValue = SendMail(from, recipient, subject, body, _
                    format)
                End If
            Next
        Catch e As Exception
            retValue = "Error"
```

```
                    Throw New Exception(e.ToString())
            End Try
        SendMessage = retValue
End Function
```

Visual C#

```csharp
public string SendMessage(string from, string recipients, string
    subject,string body,int format)
{
    string retValue = "";
    try
    {
        string[] aryRecipients;
        char[] Separators = new Char[] {',', ';', '\t'};
        aryRecipients = recipients.Split(Separators);
        foreach (string recipient in aryRecipients)
        {
            if ((recipient != "") && (recipient != null))
            {
                retValue = SendMail(from, recipient, subject, body,
                    format);
            }
        }
    }
    catch(Exception e)
    {
        retValue = "Error";
        throw new Exception(e.ToString());
    }
    return retValue;
}
```

The <WebMethod> or [WebMethod] directive informs other applications that they can access the SendMessage method. The WebMethod attribute is covered in detail in Chapter 8, "Advanced XML Web Services Programming." The SendMessage method consists of the following parameters:

- *From* represents the e-mail ID of the sender. It is a String data type.
- *Recipients* represent e-mail IDs of recipients. It is a String data type.
- *Subject* represents the subject of the mail message. It is a String data type.
- *Body* represents the content of the message. It is a String data type.
- *Format* represents the format of the composed message. It is an integer data type that can take two values, 0 for plain text and 1 for HTML.

The SendMessage method splits the list of recipient addresses into individual addresses and calls the SendMail method to send the message to each address.

Consider the following code to see how you use the SendMail method to send e-mail messages.

Visual Basic .NET

```
Protected Function SendMail(ByVal fromID As String, ByVal toID As _
    String, ByVal subject As String, ByVal body As String, ByVal format _
    As Integer) As String
    Dim strErrorMessage As String
    If ValidateEmail(toID) Then
        Try
            Dim objMessage As New MailMessage()
            objMessage.From = fromID
            objMessage.To = toID
            objMessage.Subject = subject
            objMessage.Body = body
            If format = 0 Then
                objMessage.BodyFormat = MailFormat.Text
            Else
                objMessage.BodyFormat = MailFormat.Html
            End If
            SmtpMail.Send(objMessage)
            SendMail = "Sent"
        Catch e As Exception
        If e.Message.ToString = "Could_not_access_cdo_newmail_object" Then
            strErrorMessage = "Failed. Mail server was not " & _
            "available. Please try again later."
        Else
            strErrorMessage = "Failed.  " + e.ToString() + "."
            SendMail = strErrorMessage
        End If
        End Try
    Else
        strErrorMessage = "Failed. The address was poorly formed."
        SendMail = strErrorMessage
    End If
End Function
```

Visual C#

```
protected string SendMail(string from, string to, string subject,
    string body, int format)
{
    string strErrorMessage = null;
    if (ValidateEmail(to))
    {
        try
        {
            MailMessage objMessage = new MailMessage();
            objMessage.From = from;
```

```
        objMessage.To = to;
        objMessage.Subject = subject;
        objMessage.Body = body;
        if (format == 0)
        {
          objMessage.BodyFormat = MailFormat.Text;
        }
        else
        {
          objMessage.BodyFormat = MailFormat.Html;
        }
        SmtpMail.Send(objMessage);
        return "Sent";
      }
      catch (Exception e)
      {
        if (e.Message== "Could_not_access_cdo_newmail_object")
        {
            strErrorMessage = "Failed. Mail server was not " +
                "available. Please try again later.";
        }
        else
        {
            strErrorMessage = "Failed.   " + e.ToString() + ".";
        }
        return strErrorMessage;
      }
    }
    else
    {
      strErrorMessage = "Failed. The address was poorly formed.";
      return strErrorMessage;
    }
}
```

The SendMail method uses the MailMessage class to compose and send messages. To use the properties and methods of the MailMessage class, you need to create an object of the MailMessage class. In the above code, the object of the MailMessage class is named objMessage.

Visual Basic .NET

```
Public Function ValidateEmail(ByVal email As String) As Boolean
    Dim blnValidated As Boolean = False
    If Regex.IsMatch(email, "@") Then
        blnValidated = True
    End If
    Return blnValidated
End Function
```

Visual C#

```
public bool ValidateEmail(string email)
{
    bool blnValidated = false;
    if (Regex.IsMatch(email,"@"))
    {
        blnValidated = true;
    }
    return blnValidated;
}
```

Before creating an object of the MailMessage class, you need to check whether or not the recipient's e-mail address is in the correct format. In the above code, the ValidateEmail method verifies the addresses for the correct format.

The ValidateEmail method checks whether the recipient's e-mail address is valid, by checking if it contains the @ symbol. This verification is done using the IsMatch method of the Regex class. The ValidateEmail method returns True if the e-mail address of the recipient contains the @ symbol, otherwise, it returns False.

The MailMessage class that the SendMail method instantiates consists of the following parameters:

- The From, To, Subject, and Body properties of objMessage are set to the values passed to the SendMail method by the SendMessage Web method.
- The BodyFormat property of objMessage is set to MailFormat.Text or MailFormat.HTML depending on the value passed to the SendMail method.
- The composed message is sent using the Send method of the SmtpMail class.
- The Send method of the SmtpMail class accepts an object of the MailMessage class as a parameter.

Once the above-mentioned Web methods are created, you can build your ASP.NET Web service project.

Building and Executing an ASP.NET Web Service Project

To build an ASP.NET Web service project, select Build Solution from the Build menu. In order to execute the ASP.NET Web service project, select Start from the Debug menu.

Lesson 3: Deploying and Discovering XML Web Services

In the last lesson, you learned how to create XML Web services. After you create an XML Web service, you need to deploy the XML Web service to a Web server to make it available to the applications that want to use the XML Web service. When you deploy an XML Web service, you publish the discovery .disco file. The discovery file for an XML Web service contains information such as the location of Web services. Each client that needs to access your XML Web service uses this file to locate the Web service. In this lesson, you will learn about the tasks that you need to perform when you deploy and publish an XML Web service. In addition, you will learn about the XML Web services discovery mechanism and how to configure discovery information about your XML Web service.

After this lesson, you will be able to

- Deploy an XML Web service by copying the Web service files to the Web server
- Describe the items that you publish when you deploy an XML Web service
- Describe the discovery mechanism of XML Web services
- Configure discovery information for an XML Web service

Estimated lesson time: 40 minutes

Publishing an XML Web Service

When you deploy an XML Web service on a Web server, the service is published on the Web and becomes accessible to client applications. You can deploy an XML Web service on a Web server in two ways. You can either create a Web setup project or copy the XML Web service files to the Web server. You will learn how to create a Web setup project in Chapter 10, "Deploying XML Web Services and Server Components." You will now deploy an XML Web service by copying the XML Web service files to the Web server.

To deploy your XML Web service on a Web server, perform the following steps:

1. Copy the files for your XML Web service application to the Inetpub\Wwwroot folder. You only need to copy the .asmx, Web.config, and Global.asax files to the application folder and the .dll file to the \bin folder. Figure 7.7 displays the directory structure of a deployed XML Web service.

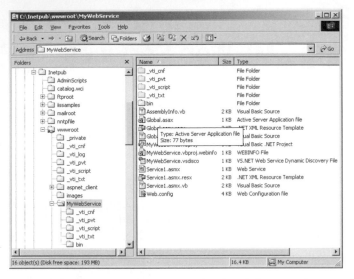

Figure 7.7   The directory structure of a virtual directory that contains an XML Web service

2. Open Internet Services Manager from the Administrative Tools folder.

3. Expand the Default Web Site node.

4. Right-click the Web service folder you copied in the Inetpub\Wwwroot folder, and choose Properties from the shortcut menu to open the MyWebService Properties dialog box, shown in Figure 7.8.

Figure 7.8   The MyWebService Properties dialog box

5. Click the Create button in the MyWebService Properties dialog box to configure the virtual folder as the root of your Web service application.

After you configure your Web service application, your Web service is ready to be used by client applications. You can then right-click the .asmx file in the right pane of Internet Services Manager and select Browse from the shortcut menu to view the description of your Web service, shown in Figure 7.9.

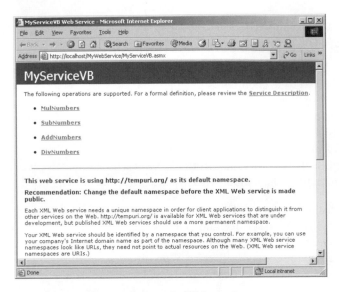

Figure 7.9   The description of a Web service

Items Published with a Web Service

When you deploy an XML Web service, the following components of the Web service are published on the Web:

- **The Web application directory.**   This component is the root directory for your XML Web service. All the XML Web service files are present in this directory or the subdirectories that you may create. You need to configure the Web application directory as an IIS Web application.

- **The <WebService>.asmx file.**   This file is the base URL for the clients who access your XML Web service.

- **The <WebService>.disco file.**   This is an optional file that describes the discovery mechanism for your XML Web service. You will learn more about the discovery mechanism in the next lesson.

- **The Web.config file.**   This file is optional. You include it to override the default configuration settings of your XML Web service. You can use the configuration file to customize the system or store configuration information for your application.

- **The \Bin directory.**   This directory contains binary files for the XML Web service. If you do not define your XML Web service class in the same file as the .asmx file, the assembly containing the class should be present in the \Bin directory.

After you deploy XML Web services to a Web server, applications can locate the XML Web services by using a discovery mechanism.

Understanding the XML Web Services Discovery Mechanism

The XML Web service discovery mechanism enables a client application to locate or discover the documents that describe an XML Web service. The XML Web service discovery mechanism returns a service description document to a client. The service description document is written in Web Services Description Language (WSDL) and contains information about the capabilities of an XML Web service, its location, and how to interact with it. In the XML Web service discovery process, files, such as service descriptions, XSD schemas, or discovery documents, which contain the details of an XML Web service, are downloaded to the client computer.

A .disco file, or discovery document, contains links to other resources that describe your XML Web service and enables clients to discover an XML Web service. The discovery document contains information regarding other XML Web services that reside on the same or different Web server. The following code displays the contents of a discovery document.

XML

```
<?xml version="1.0" encoding="utf-8"?>
<discovery xmlns:xsd="http://www.w3.org/2001/XMLSchema"
    xmlns:xsi="http://www.w3.org/2001/XMLSchema-instance"
    xmlns="http://schemas.xmlsoap.org/disco/">
<discoveryRef ref="/Folder/Default.disco"/>
<contractRef ref="http://Nancyd/mywebservice/Service1.asmx?wsdl"
    docRef="http://Nancyd/mywebservice/Service1.asmx"
    xmlns="http://schemas.xmlsoap.org/disco/scl/" />
<soap address="http://Nancyd/mywebservice/Service1.asmx"
    xmlns:q1="http://tempuri.org/" binding="q1:Service1Soap"
    xmlns="http://schemas.xmlsoap.org/disco/soap/" />
</discovery>
```

You can add multiple references of service descriptions within a <discovery> element. You can specify service description references in a discovery document by adding a <contractRef> element with the http://schemas.xmlsoap.org/disco/scl/ XML namespace. Similarly, you can specify references to other discovery documents and XSD schemas by adding <discoveryRef> and <schemaRef> elements, respectively. If you add an XSD schema reference, you need to specify the XML namespace http://schemas.xmlsoap.org/disco/schema. For all referenced documents, you specify the location of the document by using the ref attribute.

Configuring Discovery Information for a Web Service

At design time, the discovery process helps the client application of a Web service learn about details, such as the location and capabilities of the Web service. The discovery mechanism also enables the client to find out how to interact with the XML Web service.

A client application can programmatically discover an XML Web service if you publish a .disco file for your XML Web service. The XML Web services you create using ASP.NET automatically generate a discovery document. In addition, a discovery document is automatically generated for an XML Web service when you access it using a URL with ?DISCO in the query string. For example, if the URL for an XML Web service is http://www.contoso.com/getprice.asmx, a discovery document is automatically generated with http://www.contoso.com/getprice.asmx?DISCO as the URL. To configure discovery information for an XML Web service, perform the following steps:

1. Create an XML document and insert the `<?xml version="1.0" ?>` tag in the first line.

2. Add a <discovery> element, such as:

   ```
   <discovery xmlns="http://schemas.xmlsoap.org/disco/">
   </discovery>
   ```

3. Add references to service descriptions, XSD schemas, and other discovery documents within the <discovery> element as displayed in the following code:

   ```
   <?xml version="1.0"?>
   <discovery xmlns="http://schemas.xmlsoap.org/disco/">
   <discoveryRef ref="/Folder/Default.disco"/>
   <contractRef ref="http://NancyD/MyWebService.asmx?WSDL"
       docRef="Service.htm"
       xmlns="http://schemas.xmlsoap.org/disco/scl/"/>
   <schemaRef ref="Schema.xsd"
       xmlns="http://schemas.xmlsoap.org/disco/schema/"/>
   </discovery>
   ```

4. Deploy the discovery document to a Web server.

   After you specify the discovery information for your XML Web service and publish the discovery file, users can browse the discovery file to locate your XML Web service.

In addition to .disco files, Visual Studio .NET creates a .vsdisco file, which enables dynamic discovery of Web services. Dynamic discovery enables a client application to iteratively search through the folders on a Web server to locate all XML Web services available on the Web server. The .vsdisco file is an XML-based file with <dynamicDiscovery> as the root node instead of the <discovery> node in a

.disco document. This node contains one or more <exclude> nodes. The <exclude> node contains a path attribute, which contains the relative path to a subfolder that the dynamic discovery process will exclude. The following code displays a sample .vsdisco file.

XML

```
<?xml version="1.0" encoding="utf-8" ?>
<dynamicDiscovery xmlns="urn:schemas-dynamicdiscovery:disco.2000-03-17">
    <exclude path="_vti_cnf" />
    <exclude path="_vti_pvt" />
    <exclude path="_vti_log" />
    <exclude path="_vti_script" />
    <exclude path="_vti_txt" />
    <exclude path="Web References" />
</dynamicDiscovery>
```

After a client application discovers a Web service, the client application can access and use all the exposed methods of a Web service. The process of using an exposed method of a Web service is known as consuming a Web service. You will learn about consuming a Web service in the next lesson.

Lesson 4: Consuming an XML Web Service

In the previous lesson, you learned about the XML Web service discovery mechanism and how to configure discovery information for an XML Web service. After a client application discovers an XML Web service, the client application can access the services provided by it. This is known as consuming a Web service. In this lesson, you will learn about consuming an XML Web service. In addition, you will learn how to access the services provided by an XML Web service.

After this lesson, you will be able to

- Understand how to consume an XML Web service
- Consume the services exposed by an XML Web service

Estimated lesson time: 30 minutes

Consuming an XML Web Service

After you create an XML Web service and publish it, any application having permission to access the Web service can access your XML Web service and consume its services. The application that consumes a Web service is known as the Web service client. A Web service client can be a component, service, or desktop application. In fact, the most common Web service clients that consume Web services are Web applications and Web services.

To access an XML Web service from a client application, you need to perform the following tasks:

- Add a Web reference to the XML Web service in the client application by discovering the XML Web service that you want to consume.
- Generate a proxy class for the XML Web service.
- Create an object of the XML Web service proxy class in the client application.
- Access the XML Web service by using a proxy object.

Now you will look at these tasks in detail.

Adding a Web Reference

To use the services of an XML Web service, you first locate the XML Web service using the discovery mechanism. To use an XML Web service created by another programmer, you should know the location of the XML Web service and whether the Web service fulfills your requirement. If you don't know where the service is, you can search for it via UDDI. To make it easy to discover an XML Web service, Visual Studio .NET provides a Web reference for each XML Web service that you use in a project. A Web reference is the local representation of an XML Web service in your project.

You can add a Web reference to your project by using the Add Web Reference dialog box. This dialog box enables you to browse your local server, the Microsoft UDDI Directory, and the Web to locate a Web service. The Add Web Reference dialog box uses the Web service discovery mechanism to locate XML Web services on the Web sites that you provide. The Add Web Reference dialog box requests the URL for the description of XML Web services on the site and displays it. After you select an XML Web service, you click Add Reference to add a Web reference in your project.

Generating a Proxy Class

When you click the Add Reference button in the Add Web Reference dialog box, Visual Studio .NET downloads the service description to the local computer and generates a proxy class for the Web service. The proxy class of an XML Web service contains instructions for calling each XML Web service method. In addition, the proxy class marshals arguments between an XML Web service and the client application. Visual Studio .NET uses WSDL to create the proxy class. The proxy class is described in the .wsdl file. After you add a Web reference to an XML Web service and generate a proxy class, you add a reference to the proxy class and create an object of the proxy class in the client application.

However, if you are unable to locate an XML Web service by using the Add Web Reference dialog box, you can use the WSDL tool, WSDL.exe, to generate a proxy class manually for the XML Web service. The WSDL tool can take a WSDL contract, an XSD schema, or a .DiscoMap document as a parameter and generate a proxy class.

You execute the WSDL tool from the command prompt. The syntax to execute the WSDL tool from the command prompt is

Wsdl [*options*] {*URL\Path*}

The Table 7.1 shows some options that you can use with the Wsdl command.

The following command creates a .wsdl file and a client proxy class, WebService.cs in Visual C# for the Web service located at the specified URL.

Wsdl http://hostserver/MyApp/WebService.asmx?wsdl

You can change the language of the output file WebService.cs by using the /language switch. The syntax to generate a proxy class in Visual Basic .NET is

Wsdl /language:VB http://hostserver/MyApp/WebService.asmx?wsdl

---

Tip   After you create the source code for the proxy class, you compile it into the assembly of the current project, which is a stand-alone assembly, or you can compile the proxy class into its own assembly and install it in the global assembly cache for global use.

Table 7.1   Some Options of the Wsdl Command

Option	Description
/baseurl:*baseurl*	Specifies the base URL to use when calculating the URL fragment. The tool calculates the URL fragment by converting the relative URL from the *baseurl* argument to the URL in the WSDL document. You must specify the /appsettingurlkey option with this option.
/d[omain]:*domain*	Specifies the domain name to use when connecting to a server that requires authentication.
/l[anguage]:*language*	Specifies the language to use for the generated proxy class. You can specify CS (C#; default), VB (Visual Basic), or JS (JScript) as the language argument.
/n[amespace]:*namespace*	Specifies the namespace for the generated proxy or template. The default namespace is the global namespace.
/o[ut]:*filename*	Specifies the file in which to save the generated proxy code. The tool derives the default file name from the XML Web service name. The tool saves generated datasets in different files.
/protocol:*protocol*	Specifies the protocol to implement. You can specify SOAP (default), HttpGet, HttpPost, or a custom protocol specified in the configuration file.
/?	Displays command syntax and options for the tool.
/proxy:*URL*	Specifies the URL of the proxy server to use for HTTP requests. The default is to use the system proxy setting.

Creating an Object of the Proxy Class

The proxy class that is generated by adding a reference to an XML Web service is defined in its own namespace. You need to include the proxy class namespace in your client application before you can create an object of the proxy class. After you include the proxy class namespace in your client application, you create an object of the proxy class by using the *new* operator. The object of the proxy class allows you to invoke the exposed methods of an XML Web service and access the results like any other method of a component.

Accessing the Web Service Using a Proxy Object

The object of the proxy class converts the method calls on an XML Web service to a request message and the response message to a return value, which you can access in the client application.

After you create an object of the proxy class, you can easily write code against an XML Web service. Visual Studio .NET provides IntelliSense and type safety when you use an object of the proxy class to access the methods of a Web service.

Consuming the Methods Exposed by a Web Service

Previously you learned about the process of consuming an XML Web service. Now you will look at consuming an XML Web service by using a sample XML Web service, which contains four Web methods that allow you to perform simple arithmetic operations, such as addition, subtraction, multiplication, and division of two integers. All these Web methods take the two integers as parameters. The following code shows a sample XML Web service.

Visual Basic .NET

```
Imports System.Web.Services

<WebService(Namespace:="http://tempuri.org/")> _
Public Class MyServiceVB
    Inherits System.Web.Services.WebService

    <WebMethod()> Public Function AddNumbers(ByVal Num1 As Integer, _
        ByVal Num2 As Integer) As Integer
        AddNumbers = Num1 + Num2
    End Function
    <WebMethod()> Public Function SubNumbers(ByVal Num1 As Integer, _
        ByVal Num2 As Integer) As Integer
        SubNumbers = Num1 - Num2
    End Function
    <WebMethod()> Public Function MulNumbers(ByVal Num1 As Integer, _
        ByVal Num2 As Integer) As Integer
        MulNumbers = Num1 * Num2
    End Function
    <WebMethod()> Public Function DivNumbers(ByVal Num1 As Integer, _
        ByVal Num2 As Integer) As Integer
        DivNumbers = Num1 / Num2
    End Function
End Class
```

Visual C#

```
using System;
using System.Collections;
using System.ComponentModel;
using System.Data;
using System.Diagnostics;
using System.Web;
using System.Web.Services;
```

```
namespace MyWebServiceCS
{
    public class MyServiceCS : System.Web.Services.WebService
    {
        public MyServiceCS()
        {
        }

        [WebMethod]
        public int AddNumbers(int num1, int num2)
        {
            return (num1+num2);
        }
        [WebMethod]
        public int SubNumbers(int num1, int num2)
        {
            return (num1-num2);
        }
        [WebMethod]
        public int MulNumbers(int num1, int num2)
        {
            return (num1*num2);
        }
        [WebMethod]
        public int DivNumbers(int num1, int num2)
        {
            return (num1/num2);
        }

    }
}
```

The first task in consuming an XML Web service is to add a Web reference to
the client application by using the Add Web Reference dialog box. To open the
Add Web Reference dialog box, perform the following steps.

1. Right-click the References node in the Solution Explorer window, as shown in Figure 7.10.

Figure 7.10   The Solution Explorer window

2. Choose Add Web Reference from the shortcut menu. The Add Web Reference dialog box opens, as shown in Figure 7.11.

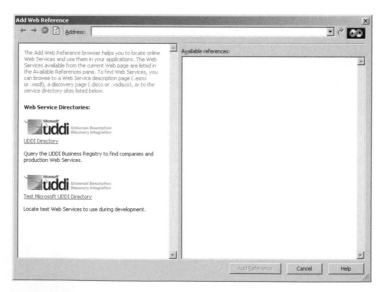

Figure 7.11   The Add Web Reference dialog box

3. In the Address bar of the Add Web Reference dialog box, specify the path of the XML Web service that you want to use. When the Add Web Reference dialog box discovers the XML Web service that you are looking for, it displays information regarding the XML Web service. The information also includes details about the methods that the XML Web service exposes. Figure 7.12 shows the details of an XML Web service in the Add Web Reference dialog box.

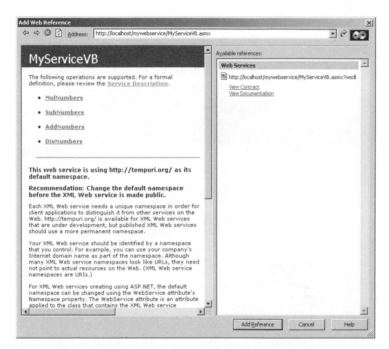

Figure 7.12   Details of a Web service displayed in the Add Web Reference dialog box

You can also view details, such as the method parameters, for each method exposed by the XML Web service by clicking a method in the Add Web Reference dialog box. You can also test an XML Web service by using this dialog box before you use it in the application. To test an exposed method of an XML Web service, perform the following steps:

1. Click a method from the list of methods in the Add Web Reference dialog box. Figure 7.13 displays the page generated automatically by Visual Studio .NET to test an exposed method of an XML Web service.

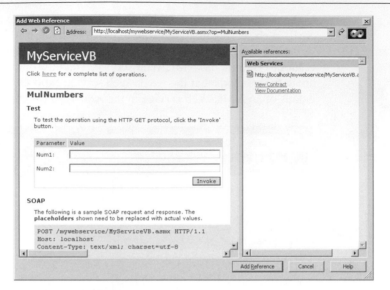

Figure 7.13   Testing an exposed method of an XML Web service

2. Enter the appropriate parameters for the method and click Invoke. The result of the test is displayed in an Internet Explorer window, as shown in Figure 7.14.

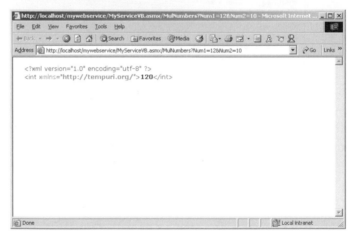

Figure 7.14   The results of testing an exposed method of an XML Web service

In addition, the Add Web Reference dialog box enables you to view the SOAP request and response, the HTTP-GET request and response, and the HTTP-POST request and response for an XML Web service method. The following code snippets display the SOAP request and response, the HTTP-GET request and response, and the HTTP-POST request and response for an exposed method of an XML Web service.

SOAP

```
POST /mywebserviceCS/MyServiceCS.asmx HTTP/1.1
Host: localhost
Content-Type: text/xml; charset=utf-8
Content-Length: length
SOAPAction: "http://tempuri.org/MulNumbers"

<?xml version="1.0" encoding="utf-8"?>
<soap:Envelope xmlns:xsi="http://www.w3.org/2001/XMLSchema-
    instance" xmlns:xsd="http://www.w3.org/2001/XMLSchema"
    xmlns:soap="http://schemas.xmlsoap.org/soap/envelope/">
    <soap:Body>
        <MulNumbers xmlns="http://tempuri.org/">
            <num1>int</num1>
            <num2>int</num2>
        </MulNumbers>
    </soap:Body>
</soap:Envelope>

HTTP/1.1 200 OK
Content-Type: text/xml; charset=utf-8
Content-Length: length

<?xml version="1.0" encoding="utf-8"?>
<soap:Envelope xmlns:xsi="http://www.w3.org/2001/XMLSchema-
    instance" xmlns:xsd="http://www.w3.org/2001/XMLSchema"
    xmlns:soap="http://schemas.xmlsoap.org/soap/envelope/">
    <soap:Body>
        <MulNumbersResponse xmlns="http://tempuri.org/">
            <MulNumbersResult>int</MulNumbersResult>
        </MulNumbersResponse>
    </soap:Body>
</soap:Envelope>
```

Note The SOAP protocol allows applications to exchange structured and typed information on the Web using XML-based standards. When a client application communicates with an XML Web service using SOAP, the data that is exchanged between the client application and the XML Web service follows a standard format. The format consists of data that is encoded in an XML document. The XML document consists of a root Envelope element, which in turn consists of a mandatory Body element. The Body element contains the data specific to the message. The Envelope element can contain an optional Header element which contains additional information not directly related to the message. Each child element of the Header element is called a SOAP header.

HTTP-GET

```
GET /mywebserviceCS/MyServiceCS.asmx/MulNumbers?num1=string&num2=
     string HTTP/1.1
Host: localhost
HTTP/1.1 200 OK
Content-Type: text/xml; charset=utf-8
Content-Length: length

<?xml version="1.0" encoding="utf-8"?>
<int xmlns="http://tempuri.org/">int</int>
```

HTTP-POST

```
POST /mywebserviceCS/MyServiceCS.asmx/MulNumbers HTTP/1.1
Host: localhost
Content-Type: application/x-www-form-urlencoded
Content-Length: length
num1=string&num2=string
HTTP/1.1 200 OK
Content-Type: text/xml; charset=utf-8
Content-Length: length
<?xml version="1.0" encoding="utf-8"?>
<int xmlns="http://tempuri.org/">int</int>
```

3. Finally, click the Add Reference button to add a reference to the XML Web service to your client application. Visual Studio .NET adds a Web References node, which has the same name as the computer that provides the XML Web service, to your client application. You can rename the Web reference to change the namespace in which the proxy class is created. When you click Add Reference, Visual Studio .NET includes a Web reference and adds the following files to your client application:

   - .wsdl
   - .disco
   - .map

   Figure 7.15 displays a Web References node.

The .wsdl file contains the proxy class generated by Visual Studio .NET. As described earlier, the proxy class contains instructions for calling XML Web service methods. In addition, the proxy class marshals arguments between an XML Web service and a client application. To view the .wsdl file that Visual Studio .NET creates, expand the Web References node under your project in the Solution Explorer. Under the Web References node, locate the localhost node. This node

Figure 7.15   A Web References node in a client application

contains the namespace that contains the proxy class created by Visual Studio
.NET. The localhost node contains the .wsdl, .disco, and Reference.map files. You
can change the default localhost namespace by right-clicking localhost and clicking Rename on the shortcut menu.

After you create the proxy class, you need to create an object of the proxy class to
access the exposed methods of an XML Web service. To reference a proxy class in
your code, you need to give the fully qualified name of the proxy class. That is, if
your application is in the MyApps namespace, and the proxy class, MyWebService,
is in the WebServices namespace, then in Visual Basic .NET, you must refer to the
MyWebService class as WebServices.MyWebService. However, in Visual C#, you
must refer to the MyWebService class as MyApps.WebServices.MyWebService.
The following code displays how to create an object of the proxy class.

Visual Basic .NET

```
Private VBService As New WebServices.MyWebServiceVB()
```

Visual C#

```
private MyApps.WebServices.MyWebServiceCS CSService = new
    MyApps.WebServices.MyWebServiceCS();
```

Finally, you can access the exposed methods of an XML Web service by using the
proxy class object. Figure 7.16 displays the interface of a client application, which
consumes the methods exposed by the XML Web service.

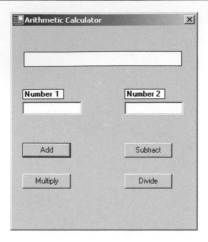

Figure 7.16   The client application interface

The following code displays the code that the client application uses to access the exposed methods of an XML Web service. In the following code, the exposed methods of the XML Web service are called inside the button-click event handling codes of the client interface.

Visual Basic .NET

```
Private Sub BtnAdd_Click(ByVal sender As System.Object, ByVal e As _
    System.EventArgs) Handles BtnAdd.Click
    Dim Result as Integer = VBService.AddNumbers(Val(TxtNum1.Text), _
        Val(TxtNum2.Text))
    LblResult.Text = Result.ToString
End Sub

Private Sub BtnSub_Click(ByVal sender As System.Object, ByVal e As _
    System.EventArgs) Handles BtnSub.Click
    Dim Result as Integer = VBService.SubNumbers(Val(TxtNum1.Text), _
        Val(TxtNum2.Text))
    LblResult.Text = Result.ToString
End Sub

Private Sub BtnMul_Click(ByVal sender As System.Object, ByVal e As _
    System.EventArgs) Handles BtnMul.Click
    Dim Result as Integer= VBService.MulNumbers(Val(TxtNum1.Text), _
        Val(TxtNum2.Text))
    LblResult.Text = Result.ToString
End Sub

Private Sub BtnDiv_Click(ByVal sender As System.Object, ByVal e As _
    System.EventArgs) Handles BtnDiv.Click
```

```
        Dim Result as Integer = VBService.DivNumbers(Val(TxtNum1.Text), _
            Val(TxtNum2.Text))
        LblResult.Text = Result.ToString
End Sub
```

Visual C#

```csharp
private void BtnAdd_Click(object sender, System.EventArgs e)
{
    int result = CSService.AddNumbers(Int32.Parse(TxtNum1.Text),
        Int32.Parse(TxtNum2.Text));
    LblResult.Text= result.ToString();
}


private void BtnSub_Click(object sender, System.EventArgs e)
{
    int result = CSService.SubNumbers(Int32.Parse(TxtNum1.Text),
        Int32.Parse(TxtNum2.Text));
    LblResult.Text= result.ToString();
}


private void BtnMul_Click(object sender, System.EventArgs e)
{
    int result = CSService.MulNumbers(Int32.Parse(TxtNum1.Text),
        Int32.Parse(TxtNum2.Text));
    LblResult.Text= result.ToString();
}


private void BtnDiv_Click(object sender, System.EventArgs e)
{
    int result = CSService.DivNumbers(Int32.Parse(TxtNum1.Text),
        Int32.Parse(TxtNum2.Text));
    LblResult.Text= result.ToString();
}
```

When a client application consumes an XML Web service, the client application calls Web methods on the XML Web service and passes arguments if the Web methods require them. The Web methods can also return a value to the client. The arguments that clients send to an XML Web service and the values the XML Web service returns are transported over the network. Before the objects or values can be transported over the network, they need to be converted into a format that can be transported. The process by which the objects and values are converted into a format suitable for transportation is called serialization.

Serialization

Serialization is the process by which objects or values are converted into a format that can be persisted or transported. Serialization allows you to save the state of objects from memory to a storage medium such as files. You can also use serialization to transport objects and values across the network. To read the state of the objects or values that you persist or transport using serialization, you use another process called *deserialization*. Deserialization is complementary to serialization. The .NET Framework supports two types of serialization, binary serialization and XML serialization.

Binary serialization converts the state of an object by writing the public and private fields, name of the class, and the assembly containing the class into a stream of bytes. To make your objects serializable, you need to mark the class with the Serializable attribute as shown in the following code.

Visual Basic .NET

```
<Serializable()> _
Public Class MySerializableClass
    Public n1 as Integer
    Public s1 as String
    ' Implement the class
End Class
```

Visual C#

```
[Serializable()]
public class MySerializableClass {
    public int n1;
    public string s1;
    // Implement the class
}
```

It is important to note that the Serializable attribute is not inheritable. That is, if another class, MyDerivedClass, derives from the class MySerializableClass in the previous code, the MyDerivedClass class does not become serializable. You need to explicitly mark MyDerivedClass with the Serializable attribute to make it serializable. The following code shows how to serialize an object of MySerializableClass.

Visual Basic .NET

```
Imports System.IO
Imports System.Runtime.Serialization.Formatters.Binary

Public Class SerializeDemo
    Public Shared Sub Main()
        Dim obj as New MySerializableClass()
        obj.n1 = 10
        obj.s1 = "Hello"
        Dim stream As New FileStream("MyFile.dat", FileMode.Create)
        Dim formatter As New BinaryFormatter()
        formatter.Serialize(stream, obj)
```

```
        End Sub
End Class
```

Visual C#

```
using System;
using System.IO;
using System.Runtime.Serialization.Formatters.Binary;

public class SerializeDemo
{
    [STAThread]
    static void Main(string[] args)
    {
        MySerializableClass obj = new MySerializableClass();
        obj.n1 = 10;
        obj.s1 = "Hello";
        FileStream stream = new FileStream("MyFile.dat",
            FileMode.Create);
        BinaryFormatter formatter = new BinaryFormatter();
        formatter.Serialize(stream, obj);
    }
}
```

XML serialization converts the public fields and properties of an object, parameters, and return values of methods into an XML stream that conforms to a specific XML schema definition document (XSD). To create the classes that can be serialized using XML serialization, you use the XML Schema Definition tool (XSD.exe). To serialize and deserialize objects you use the XmlSerializer class. XML Web services created using ASP.NET use the XmlSerializer class to create XML streams that pass the data between Web service applications. The following code shows how to use XmlSerializer to serialize an object of MySerializableClass.

Visual Basic .NET

```
Imports System.IO
Imports System.Xml.Serialization

Public Class SerializeDemo
    Public Shared Sub Main()
        Dim obj As New MySerializableClass()
        obj.n1 = 10
        obj.s1 = "Hello"
        Dim stream As New FileStream("MyFile.xml", FileMode.Create)
        Dim formatter As New XmlSerializer(GetType(MySerializableClass))
        formatter.Serialize(stream, obj)
    End Sub
End Class
```

Visual C#

```csharp
using System;
using System.IO;
using System.Xml.Serialization;
using System.Reflection;

public class SerializeDemo
{
    [STAThread]
    static void Main(string[] args)
    {
        MySerializableClass obj = new MySerializableClass();
        obj.n1 = 10;
        obj.s1 = "Hello";
        FileStream stream = new FileStream("MyFile.xml",
            FileMode.Create);
        XmlSerializer formatter = new XmlSerializer(obj.GetType());
        formatter.Serialize(stream, obj);
    }
}
```

Summary

- XML Web services are program components that allow you to build scalable, loosely coupled, platform-independent applications. XML Web services enable disparate applications to exchange messages using standard protocols such as HTTP, XML, XSD, SOAP, and WSDL.

- You create an XML Web service to provide specific functionality to client applications over the Web. The Visual Studio .NET IDE provides you with the environment needed to create projects for distributed desktop applications, Web applications, and XML Web services.

- After you create an XML Web service, you need to deploy the XML Web service to a Web server to make it available to the applications that want to use the XML Web service. You can deploy an XML Web service to a Web server by copying the XML Web service files to the Web server.

- The XML Web service discovery mechanism enables a client application to locate or discover the documents that describe an XML Web service. The XML Web service discovery mechanism returns a service description document to a client. The service description document is written in WSDL and contains information about the capabilities of the XML Web service, its location, and how to interact with it.

- After you create an XML Web service and publish it, any application having permission to access it can access your XML Web service and consume its services. The application that consumes a Web service is known as the Web service client. A Web service client can be a component, service, or desktop application.

Lab: Creating and Consuming XML Web Services

In this lab, you will create an XML Web service that enables you to build a loosely coupled, distributed, data access solution. The lab simulates an airline reservation system that allows you to view flight information and make flight reservations from a local or remote computer. The system consists of the following:

- An airline database that contains two tables, Flights and Bookings, to store information about flight reservations
- An XML Web service that provides flight information to clients
- A Windows client application that consumes the XML Web service

Note   You have already created the database structure for the airline database in Chapter 5, "Database Programming Using ADO.NET."

The solutions to the exercises in this lab can be found in the \Solution folder on the Supplemental Course Materials CD-ROM.

Estimated lab time: 50 minutes

Exercise 1: Creating an XML Web Service

In this exercise, you will create an XML Web service that enables client applications to access and modify information about flight bookings in the airline database. To create the XML Web service, perform the following steps:

1. Open Visual Studio .NET.
2. Choose New Project from the File menu. The New Project dialog box opens.
3. Select ASP.NET Web Service from the Templates pane. Type **http://localhost/ AirlineServices** in the Location field.
4. Delete the Service1.asmx file. Right-click the AirlineServices project, point to Add on the shortcut menu, then choose Add Web Service to open the Add New Item dialog box.
5. In the Add New Item dialog box, type **FlightBooking.asmx** and click Open.
6. Open the code view for the FlightBooking.asmx file.
7. Type the following code for the FlightBooking class.

Visual Basic .NET

```
Imports System.Web.Services
Imports System.Data
Imports System.Data.SqlClient
```

```vbnet
<WebService(Namespace := "http://tempuri.org/")> _
Public Class FlightBooking
    Inherits System.Web.Services.WebService

    Private flights_data As DataTable
    Private dataadapter As SqlDataAdapter
    Private connection As SqlConnection
    Private bookings_data As DataTable
    Private dataadapter1 As SqlDataAdapter
    Private flt_bkgs As DataSet

#Region " Web Services Designer Generated Code "

    Public Sub New()
        MyBase.New()
        ' Initialize the SQL connection
        connection = New SqlConnection("server=localhost;user id=sa;" & _
            "password=;initial catalog=Airline")

        ' Create a DataTable to store flights info
        dataadapter = New SqlDataAdapter("select * from flights", _
            connection)
        Dim commandbuilder As New SqlCommandBuilder(dataadapter)
        dataadapter.MissingSchemaAction = MissingSchemaAction.AddWithKey
        flights_data = New DataTable("Flights")
        dataadapter.Fill(flights_data)

        ' Create a DataTable to store bookings info
        dataadapter1 = New SqlDataAdapter("select * from bookings", _
            connection)
        Dim commandbuilder1 As New SqlCommandBuilder(dataadapter1)
        dataadapter.MissingSchemaAction = MissingSchemaAction.AddWithKey
        bookings_data = New DataTable("Bookings")
        dataadapter1.Fill(bookings_data)

        ' Initialize a DataSet to store flights booking information
        flt_bkgs = New DataSet("Flight Bookings")
        flt_bkgs.Tables.Add(flights_data)
        flt_bkgs.Tables.Add(bookings_data)
        Dim dr As New DataRelation("Flight Bookings", _
            flt_bkgs.Tables(0).Columns(0), flt_bkgs.Tables(1).Columns(0))
        flt_bkgs.Relations.Add(dr)

        'This call is required by the Web Services Designer.
        InitializeComponent()

        'Add your own initialization code after the InitializeComponent()
        'call
```

(continued)

```vb
    End Sub

    'Required by the Web Services Designer
    Private components As System.ComponentModel.IContainer

    'NOTE: The following procedure is required by the Web Services
    'Designer. It can be modified using the Web Services Designer.
    'Do not modify it using the code editor.
    <System.Diagnostics.DebuggerStepThrough()> _
        Private Sub InitializeComponent()

    End Sub

    Protected Overloads Overrides Sub Dispose(ByVal disposing As _
        Boolean)
        'CODEGEN: This procedure is required by the Web Services Designer
        'Do not modify it using the code editor.
        If disposing Then
            If Not (components Is Nothing) Then
                components.Dispose()
            End If
        End If
        MyBase.Dispose(disposing)
    End Sub

#End Region

    <WebMethod()> _
    Public Function getInfo() As DataSet
        Return flt_bkgs
    End Function

    <WebMethod()> _
    Public Function update(ByVal ds As DataSet) As DataSet
        ' Update the database tables
        dataadapter.Update(ds.Tables(0))
        dataadapter1.Update(ds.Tables(1))

        ' Update the flights_data DataTable
        flights_data = Nothing
        dataadapter.MissingSchemaAction = MissingSchemaAction.AddWithKey
        flights_data = New DataTable("Flights")
        dataadapter.Fill(flights_data)

        ' Update the bookings_data DataTable
        bookings_data = Nothing
        dataadapter1.MissingSchemaAction = MissingSchemaAction.AddWithKey
        bookings_data = New DataTable("Bookings")
        dataadapter1.Fill(bookings_data)
```

```
        ' Update the flt_bkgs DataSet
        flt_bkgs = New DataSet("Flight Bookings")
        flt_bkgs.Tables.Add(flights_data)
        flt_bkgs.Tables.Add(bookings_data)
        Dim dr As New DataRelation("Flight Bookings", _
            flt_bkgs.Tables(0).Columns(0), flt_bkgs.Tables(1).Columns(0))
        flt_bkgs.Relations.Add(dr)

        ' Return the updated DataSet
        Return flt_bkgs
    End Function
End Class
```

Visual C#

```csharp
using System;
using System.Collections;
using System.ComponentModel;
using System.Data;
using System.Diagnostics;
using System.Web;
using System.Web.Services;
using System.Data.SqlClient;

namespace CSAirlineServices
{
    /// <summary>
    /// Summary description for FlightBooking.
    /// </summary>
    public class FlightBooking : System.Web.Services.WebService
    {
        private DataTable flights_data ;
        private SqlDataAdapter dataadapter ;
        private SqlConnection connection  ;
        private DataTable bookings_data  ;
        private SqlDataAdapter dataadapter1  ;
        private DataSet flt_bkgs   ;

        public FlightBooking()
        {
            // Initialize the SQL connection
            connection = new SqlConnection("server=localhost; " +
                "user id=sa;password=;initial catalog=Airline");

            // Create a DataTable to store flights info
            dataadapter = new SqlDataAdapter("select * from flights",
                connection);
            SqlCommandBuilder commandbuilder = new
                SqlCommandBuilder(dataadapter);
            dataadapter.MissingSchemaAction =
```

(continued)

```
            MissingSchemaAction.AddWithKey;
        flights_data = new DataTable("Flights");
        dataadapter.Fill(flights_data);

        // Create a DataTable to store bookings info
        dataadapter1 = new SqlDataAdapter("select * from bookings",
            connection);
        SqlCommandBuilder commandbuilder1 = new
            SqlCommandBuilder(dataadapter1);
        dataadapter.MissingSchemaAction =
            MissingSchemaAction.AddWithKey;
        bookings_data = new DataTable("Bookings");
        dataadapter1.Fill(bookings_data);

        // Initialize a DataSet to store flights booking information
        flt_bkgs = new DataSet("Flight Bookings");
        flt_bkgs.Tables.Add(flights_data);
        flt_bkgs.Tables.Add(bookings_data);
        DataRelation dr = new DataRelation("Flight Bookings",
            flt_bkgs.Tables[0].Columns[0],
            flt_bkgs.Tables[1].Columns[0]);
        flt_bkgs.Relations.Add(dr);

        //CODEGEN: This call is required by the ASP.NET Web Services
        //Designer
        InitializeComponent();
    }

    #region Component Designer generated code

    //Required by the Web Services Designer
    private IContainer components = null;

    /// <summary>
    /// Required method for Designer support - do not modify
    /// the contents of this method with the code editor.
    /// </summary>
    private void InitializeComponent()
    {
    }

    /// <summary>
    /// Clean up any resources being used.
    /// </summary>
    protected override void Dispose( bool disposing )
    {
        if(disposing && components != null)
        {
```

```
                components.Dispose();
            }
            base.Dispose(disposing);
        }

        #endregion

        [WebMethod()]
        public DataSet getInfo()
        {
            return flt_bkgs;
        }

        [WebMethod()]
        public DataSet update(DataSet ds  )
        {
            // Update the data base tables
            dataadapter.Update(ds.Tables[0]);
            dataadapter1.Update(ds.Tables[1]);

            // Update the flights_data DataTable
            flights_data = null;
            dataadapter.MissingSchemaAction =
                MissingSchemaAction.AddWithKey;
            flights_data = new DataTable("Flights");
            dataadapter.Fill(flights_data);

            // Update the bookings_data DataTable
            bookings_data = null;
            dataadapter1.MissingSchemaAction =
                MissingSchemaAction.AddWithKey;
            bookings_data = new DataTable("Bookings");
            dataadapter1.Fill(bookings_data);

            // Update the flt_bkgs DataSet
            flt_bkgs = new DataSet("Flight Bookings");
            flt_bkgs.Tables.Add(flights_data);
            flt_bkgs.Tables.Add(bookings_data);
            DataRelation dr = new DataRelation("Flight Bookings",
                flt_bkgs.Tables[0].Columns[0],
                flt_bkgs.Tables[1].Columns[0]);
            flt_bkgs.Relations.Add(dr);

            // return the updated DataSet
            return flt_bkgs;
        }
    }
}
```

8. Choose Build Solution from the Build menu.

9. Right-click the FlightBooking.asmx file in the Solution Explorer and select View In Browser from the shortcut menu. The service description page is displayed as shown next.

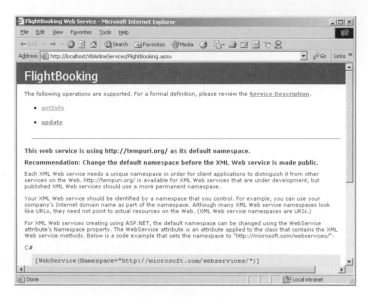

10. Click the GetInfo hyperlink. On the page that is displayed, click the Invoke button to test the GetInfo method. If the method returns successfully, the XML output is displayed, as shown next.

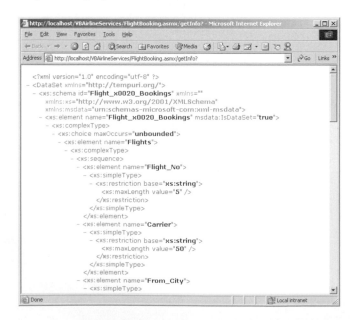

Exercise 2: Creating a Windows Client Application

In this exercise, you will create a Windows application that enables you to access the FlightBookings Web service. To create a client application, follow these steps:

1. From the File menu, point to Add Project, and then choose New Project to add a new project to the solution.

2. Select Windows Application from the Templates pane and type **AirlineBooking** in the Name field and click OK.

3. Add a DataGrid control and a Button control to the form from the Windows Forms Toolbox. Change the Text property of the form to Flight Bookings and the Text property of the Button to Save so that the form appears as shown next.

4. In the AirlineBooking project, right-click References, and choose Add Web Reference from the shortcut menu to open the Add Web Reference dialog box. Type **http://localhost/AirlineServices/FlightBooking.asmx** in the Address box, and press Enter. Click the Add Reference button to add a Web reference to the project.

5. Right-click the Form1.vb or Form1.cs file in the Solution Explorer, and choose View Code from the shortcut menu to see the code. Replace it with the following code.

Visual Basic .NET

```
Public Class Form1
    Inherits System.Windows.Forms.Form
    Private service As localhost.FlightBooking
    Private ds As DataSet

#Region " Windows Form Designer generated code "

    Public Sub New()
        MyBase.New()
```

(continued)

```vb
    'This call is required by the Windows Form Designer.
    InitializeComponent()

    'Add any initialization after the InitializeComponent() call

End Sub

'Form overrides dispose to clean up the component list.
Protected Overloads Overrides Sub Dispose(ByVal disposing As Boolean)
    If disposing Then
        If Not (components Is Nothing) Then
            components.Dispose()
        End If
    End If
    MyBase.Dispose(disposing)
End Sub

'Required by the Windows Form Designer
Private components As System.ComponentModel.IContainer

Friend WithEvents DataGrid1 As System.Windows.Forms.DataGrid
Friend WithEvents Button1 As System.Windows.Forms.Button
<System.Diagnostics.DebuggerStepThrough()> _
    Private Sub InitializeComponent()
    Me.DataGrid1 = New System.Windows.Forms.DataGrid()
    Me.Button1 = New System.Windows.Forms.Button()
    CType(Me.DataGrid1, _
        System.ComponentModel.ISupportInitialize).BeginInit()
    Me.SuspendLayout()
    '
    'DataGrid1
    '
    Me.DataGrid1.DataMember = ""
    Me.DataGrid1.HeaderForeColor = _
        System.Drawing.SystemColors.ControlText
    Me.DataGrid1.Location = New System.Drawing.Point(16, 24)
    Me.DataGrid1.Name = "DataGrid1"
    Me.DataGrid1.Size = New System.Drawing.Size(504, 232)
    Me.DataGrid1.TabIndex = 0
    '
    'Button1
    '
    Me.Button1.Location = New System.Drawing.Point(440, 264)
    Me.Button1.Name = "Button1"
    Me.Button1.TabIndex = 1
    Me.Button1.Text = "Save"
    '
    'Form1
```

```vb
                                '
            Me.AutoScaleBaseSize = New System.Drawing.Size(5, 13)
            Me.ClientSize = New System.Drawing.Size(544, 309)
            Me.Controls.AddRange(New System.Windows.Forms.Control() _
                {Me.Button1, Me.DataGrid1})
            Me.Name = "Form1"
            Me.Text = "Flight Bookings"
            CType(Me.DataGrid1, _
                System.ComponentModel.ISupportInitialize).EndInit()
            Me.ResumeLayout(False)

        End Sub

#End Region

    Private Sub Form1_Load(ByVal sender As System.Object, ByVal e As _
        System.EventArgs) Handles MyBase.Load
        service = New localhost.FlightBooking()
        ds = service.getInfo
        DataGrid1.DataSource = ds
    End Sub

    Private Sub Button1_Click(ByVal sender As System.Object, ByVal e As _
        System.EventArgs) Handles Button1.Click
        Try
            Dim ds1 As DataSet = service.update(ds)
            ds = ds1
            DataGrid1.DataSource = ds
            DataGrid1.DataMember = ds.Tables(0).TableName
        Catch ex As Exception
            MsgBox(ex.Message)
        End Try
    End Sub
End Class
```

Visual C#

```csharp
using System;
using System.Drawing;
using System.Collections;
using System.ComponentModel;
using System.Windows.Forms;
using System.Data;

namespace AirlineBooking
{
    /// <summary>
    /// Summary description for Form1.
    /// </summary>
```

(continued)

```csharp
public class Form1 : System.Windows.Forms.Form
{
    internal System.Windows.Forms.Button Button1;
    internal System.Windows.Forms.DataGrid DataGrid1;
    /// <summary>
    /// Required designer variable.
    /// </summary>
    private System.ComponentModel.Container components = null;
    private localhost.FlightBooking service ;
    private DataSet ds ;

    public Form1()
    {

        //
        // Required for Windows Form Designer support
        //
        InitializeComponent();
    }

    /// <summary>
    /// Clean up any resources being used.
    /// </summary>
    protected override void Dispose( bool disposing )
    {
        if( disposing )
        {
            if (components != null)
            {
                components.Dispose();
            }
        }
        base.Dispose( disposing );
    }

    #region Windows Form Designer generated code
    /// <summary>
    /// Required method for Designer support - do not modify
    /// the contents of this method with the code editor.
    /// </summary>
    private void InitializeComponent()
    {
        this.Button1 = new System.Windows.Forms.Button();
        this.DataGrid1 = new System.Windows.Forms.DataGrid();
        ((System.ComponentModel.ISupportInitialize)
            (this.DataGrid1)).BeginInit();
        this.SuspendLayout();
        //
        // Button1
        //
```

```
this.Button1.Location = new System.Drawing.Point(432, 256);
this.Button1.Name = "Button1";
this.Button1.TabIndex = 3;
this.Button1.Text = "Save";
this.Button1.Click += new
    System.EventHandler(this.Button1_Click);
//
// DataGrid1
//
this.DataGrid1.DataMember = "";
this.DataGrid1.HeaderForeColor =
    System.Drawing.SystemColors.ControlText;
this.DataGrid1.Location = new System.Drawing.Point(8, 16);
this.DataGrid1.Name = "DataGrid1";
this.DataGrid1.Size = new System.Drawing.Size(504, 232);
this.DataGrid1.TabIndex = 2;
//
// Form1
//
this.AutoScaleBaseSize = new System.Drawing.Size(5, 13);
this.ClientSize = new System.Drawing.Size(520, 285);
this.Controls.AddRange(new System.Windows.Forms.Control[]
    {this.Button1,
     this.DataGrid1});
this.Name = "Form1";
this.Text = "Flight Bookings";
this.Load += new System.EventHandler(this.Form1_Load);
((System.ComponentModel.ISupportInitialize)
    (this.DataGrid1)).EndInit();
this.ResumeLayout(false);
}
#endregion

/// <summary>
/// The main entry point for the application.
/// </summary>
[STAThread]
static void Main()
{
    Application.Run(new Form1());
}

private void Button1_Click(object sender, System.EventArgs e)
{
    try
    {
        DataSet ds1 = service.update(ds);
        ds = ds1;
        DataGrid1.DataSource = ds;
        DataGrid1.DataMember = ds.Tables[0].TableName;
```

(continued)

```
        }
        catch (Exception ex )
        {
            MessageBox.Show(ex.Message);
        }
    }

    private void Form1_Load(object sender, System.EventArgs e)
    {
        service = new localhost.FlightBooking();
        ds = service.getInfo();
        DataGrid1.DataSource = ds;
    }
    }
}
```

6. Choose Build Solution from the Build menu.

7. Run the Windows application. Test the application by creating, deleting, and modifying records.

Note   The Flight_No and Flight_Date columns of the Flights table constitute the composite primary key. The check constraint on the Flights table ensures that Seats_Booked <= Capacity.

The Flight_No, Seat_No, and Flight_Date columns constitute the composite primary key for the Bookings table. The Flight_No and Flight_Date columns of the Bookings table reference the respective columns in the Flights table.

Review

The questions in this section reinforce key information presented in this chapter. If you are unable to answer a question, review the appropriate lesson, and then try answering the question again. Answers to the questions can be found in Appendix A, "Questions and Answers."

1. What is an XML Web service?

2. What are the components of the XML Web service infrastructure?

3. What are the steps to deploy a Web service?

4. What are the components that are published when you deploy a Web service?

5. What does the .disco file contain?

6. What are the steps to configure discovery information for an XML Web service?

7. What tasks do you need to perform to consume a Web service in a client application?

8. Which attribute is used to create a Web method?

9. Which file contains configuration information, such as debug mode?

10. Which file allows you to handle application-level events?

C H A P T E R   8

Advanced XML Web Services Programming

About This Chapter

XML Web services enable client applications to call Web methods using standard
Internet protocols such as HTTP, XML, and SOAP. A Web method is a method of
an XML Web service that is decorated with the WebMethod attribute. The Web-
Method attribute has properties that you can use to modify the behavior of Web
methods. XML Web services also enable you to call the Web methods asynchronously. In addition, you can use SOAP extensions to access and modify the SOAP
messages that the XML Web services send to and receive from client applications.
In this chapter, you will learn to use properties of the WebMethod attribute to modify the behavior of Web methods, use asynchronous versions of Web methods, and
use SOAP extensions to access and modify the SOAP messages. In addition, you
will learn to configure and secure XML Web services.

Before You Begin

To complete the lessons in this chapter, you

■ Must have knowledge of XML Web services

Lesson 1: Controlling the Characteristics of a Web Method Using Attributes

In the previous chapter, you learned that XML Web services use XML messaging to enable data exchange and remote invocation of methods. This process allows you to move data through firewalls and between heterogeneous systems. Therefore, client applications that are created in any language and running in any environment can access XML Web services.

When you create an XML Web service, you can use the properties of the Web-Method attribute to define the behavior of the methods exposed by the Web service. In this lesson, you will learn how to buffer and cache responses, specify a description, and enable the methods exposed by a Web service to participate as the root object of a transaction.

After this lesson, you will be able to

- List the properties of a Web method
- Buffer the responses for a Web method
- Cache the responses of a Web method
- Specify a description for a Web method
- Enable a Web method to participate as the root object of a transaction
- Enable the session state for a Web method
- Use an alias to identify overloaded Web methods

Estimated lesson time: 30 minutes

Attributes of a Web Method

You supply the WebMethod attribute to any method that you want to expose as a method of an XML Web service. The WebMethod attribute enables a client application to use standard Internet protocols to access the method. The WebMethod attribute provides the following properties that enable you to customize and control the behavior of the methods that you expose in your Web service:

- **BufferResponse.**   This Boolean property specifies whether the response of a Web method is buffered in memory.
- **CacheDuration.**   This integer property specifies the number of seconds the response of a Web method is cached in memory.

- **Description.**   This string property describes a Web method.
- **EnableSession.**   This Boolean property specifies whether the session state is enabled for a Web method. If the session state is enabled, the Web method can access the HttpSessionState object of ASP.NET.
- **MessageName.**   This property is used to give an alias name to a Web method.
- **TransactionOption.**   This property specifies the transaction support for a Web method.

You'll next look at how to use these properties to customize and control the behavior of the methods exposed in a Web service.

Buffering Responses for a Web Method

You buffer responses for a Web method to improve the performance of an application by reducing communication between the worker process and the IIS process. To buffer responses for a Web method, you use the BufferResponse property of the WebMethod attribute. When you set the BufferResponse property to True, ASP.NET buffers all the responses before communicating them to the client. If you set the BufferResponse property to False, ASP.NET buffers the responses in chunks of 16 KB each. The default value of the BufferResponse property is True. The following Microsoft Visual Basic .NET and Microsoft Visual C# code samples show how to use the BufferResponse property.

Visual Basic .NET

```
Public Class Service1
    Inherits System.Web.Services.WebService
    <WebMethod(BufferResponse:=False)> _
    Public Function AddNumbers(ByVal Num1 As Integer, _
        ByVal Num2 As Integer) As Integer
        AddNumbers = Num1 + Num2
    End Function
End Class
```

Visual C#

```
public class Service1 : System.Web.Services.WebService
{
    [WebMethod (BufferResponse=false)]
    public int AddNumbers(int num1, int num2)
    {
        return (num1+num2);
    }
}
```

Caching the Results for a Web Method

The CacheDuration property of the WebMethod attribute enables you to cache the results for a Web method. ASP.NET caches the results for each unique parameter set for the duration that you specify as the value of this property. The default value of the CacheDuration property is zero. The following code sets the CacheDuration property of the AddNumbers Web method to 60 seconds.

Visual Basic .NET

```
Public Class Service1
    Inherits System.Web.Services.WebService
    <WebMethod(CacheDuration:=60)> Public Function AddNumbers(ByVal Num1 _
        As Integer, ByVal Num2 As Integer) As Integer
        AddNumbers = Num1 + Num2
    End Function
End Class
```

Visual C#

```
public class Service1 : System.Web.Services.WebService
{
    [WebMethod(CacheDuration=60)]
    public int AddNumbers(int num1, int num2)
    {
        return (num1+num2);
    }
}
```

Specifying a Description for a Web Method

The Description property enables you to specify a description for a Web method. The description that you specify using the Description property appears on the Service help page. The Description property takes a string as an input value. The following code displays how to use the Description property.

Visual Basic .NET

```
Public Class Service1
    Inherits System.Web.Services.WebService
    <WebMethod(Description:="Takes two integer values and returns " & _
        "their sum.")> Public Function AddNumbers(ByVal Num1 As Integer, _
        ByVal Num2 As Integer) As Integer
        AddNumbers = Num1 + Num2
    End Function
End Class
```

Visual C#

```
public class Service1 : System.Web.Services.WebService
{
```

```
[WebMethod(Description="Takes two integer values and returns " +
"their sum.")]
public int AddNumbers(int num1, int num2)
{
    return (num1+num2);
}
}
```

Enabling a Session State for a Web Method

You can configure a Web method to maintain the state of objects across sessions. The EnableSession property of the WebMethod attribute allows you to enable the session state for a Web method. If you set the EnableSession property to True, the XML Web service accesses the session state collection directly from the Http-Context.Current.Session session or the WebService.Session property if it is inherited from the WebService base class. The default value of the EnableSession property is False. The following code displays how to enable the session state for a Web method.

Visual Basic .NET

```
Public Class Service1
    Inherits System.Web.Services.WebService
    <WebMethod(EnableSession:=True)> _
    Public Function ConvertPounds(ByVal kgs As Double) _
        As Double
        Session("Conversions") = Session("Conversions") + 1
        ConvertPounds = (kgs * .45)
    End Function
    <WebMethod(EnableSession:=True)> _
    Public Function GetNumberOfConversions() As Integer
        GetNumberOfConversions = Session("Conversions")
    End Function
End Class
```

Visual C#

```
public class Service1 : System.Web.Services.WebService
{
    [WebMethod(EnableSession=true)]
    public double ConvertPounds (double kgs)
    {
        Session["Conversions"] = (int) Session["Conversions"] + 1;
        return (kgs * .45);
    }
    [WebMethod(EnableSession=true)]
    public int GetNumberOfConversions()
    {
        return (int) Session["Conversions"];
    }
}
```

Identifying Overloaded Web Methods Using an Alias

You can use the MessageName property of the WebMethod attribute to uniquely identify overloaded Web methods. The MessageName property enables you to use an alias to uniquely identify Web methods in an XML Web service. When you specify a value for the MessageName property, the SOAP messages use this value as the method name instead of the actual method name. The following code sample displays how to use the MessageName property.

Visual Basic .NET

```
Public Class Service1
    Inherits System.Web.Services.WebService
    <WebMethod(MessageName:="AddIntegers")> _
    Public Function AddNumbers(ByVal Num1 As Integer, _
        ByVal Num2 As Integer) As Integer
        AddNumbers = Num1 + Num2
    End Function

    <WebMethod(MessageName:="AddLongs")> _
    Public Function AddNumbers(ByVal Num1 As Long, _
        ByVal Num2 As Long) As Long
        AddNumbers = Num1 + Num2
    End Function

End Class
```

Visual C#

```
public class Service1 : System.Web.Services.WebService
{
    [WebMethod(MessageName="AddIntegers")]
    public int AddNumbers(int num1, int num2)
    {
        return (num1+num2);
    }
    [WebMethod(MessageName="AddLongs")]
    public long AddNumbers(long num1, long num2)
    {
        return (num1+num2);
    }

}
```

Enabling a Web Method to Participate as the Root Object of a Transaction

You can use a Web method to support transactions and enable a Web method to participate as the root object of a transaction. You can use this property to specify whether you want the Web method to participate in a transaction or not. The

TransactionOption property can take the following values: Disabled, NotSupported, Supported, Required, and RequiresNew. To support transactions and enable a Web method to participate as the root object of a transaction, you can set Transaction-Option to Required or RequiresNew. On the other hand, to disable transaction support for a Web method, you can set TransactionOption to Disabled, NotSupported, or Supported.

To enable Web methods to support transactions, you need to add a reference to the System.EnterpriseServices.dll file and include the System.EnterpriseServices name-space in addition to setting a value for the TransactionOption property. This name-space contains the methods and properties that expose the distributed transaction model in COM+ services. The ContextUtil class of the System.Enterprise-Services namespace enables you to control a transaction using the SetAbort or SetComplete method. You need to perform the following tasks to enable transactions in a Web method:

- Add a reference to the System.EnterpriseServices.dll by using the Solution Explorer.
- Include the System.EnterpriseServices namespace in the XML Web service.
- Set the TransactionOption property to an appropriate value. The following code displays how to set the value of the TransactionOption property.

Visual Basic .NET

```
Public Class Service1
    Inherits System.Web.Services.WebService
    <WebMethod(TransactionOption:=TransactionOption.RequiresNew)> _
    Public Function DoSomethingTransactional() As String
        'The transaction was successful...
        ContextUtil.SetComplete
        DoSomethingTransactional = ContextUtil.TransactionId.ToString()
    End Function
End Class
```

Visual C#

```
public class Service1 : System.Web.Services.WebService
{
    [WebMethod(TransactionOption=TransactionOption.RequiresNew)]
    public string DoSomethingTransactional()
    {
        // The transaction was successful...
        ContextUtil.SetComplete();
        return ContextUtil.TransactionId.ToString();
    }
}
```

For more information on the Transaction attribute, refer to Chapter 3, "Creating and Consuming Serviced Components."

Lesson 2: Creating Asynchronous Methods

Asynchronous programming allows a program to call a method on an object and return immediately without waiting for the method to return. Asynchronous programming is useful when the method called by a program on an object takes significant time to execute, and you do not want the program to wait for the method to return. In this lesson, you will learn how to implement asynchronous programming in XML Web services.

After this lesson, you will be able to

- Describe asynchronous programming architecture
- Use asynchronous programming in XML Web services

Estimated lesson time: 45 minutes

Overview of Asynchronous Programming

Asynchronous programming allows a program to call methods on a managed object and continue execution until either the managed object calls a specified callback or until blocking, waiting, or polling for the call is completed. You can implement asynchronous programming by using the following options:

- **Callbacks.**   You use callbacks to specify the method that is called when the asynchronous method returns. You specify a callback delegate when you begin a call to an asynchronous method.
- **Poll Completed.**   When you use this option, the program repeatedly polls the IAsyncResult.IsCompleted property of the asynchronous method to check whether the method has finished execution.
- **BeginInvoke, EndInvoke.**   When you use this option, a client that makes asynchronous calls block execution until the synchronous method completes execution.
- **BeginInvoke, WaitHandle, EndInvoke.**   When you use this option, the client tries to complete the operation by calling a block until the operation completes. However, the client can use a time-out to wake up periodically.

.NET asynchronous programming consists of two logical parts. In the first part, a server object takes the input from the client and begins the asynchronous operation. The server can also take a callback delegate from the client that is called when the server returns the asynchronous call. In addition, the server returns an object that implements the IAsyncResult interface, which the client uses to determine the status of the asynchronous operation. In the second part, the server returns the result of the asynchronous operation to the client. The server utilizes the IAsyncResult object that it returned to the client to maintain the state of the asynchronous operation. The client returns the IAsyncResult object to the server to obtain the result of the asynchronous operation.

The following code shows the design pattern of a method that clients can call asynchronously.

Visual Basic .NET

```
Public Class Server
    ' A method that can be called asynchronously
    Public Function AsyncMethod() As Object
        ' Perform a long running task
        .
        .
        .

    End Function

    Public Function BeginAsyncMethod(ByVal callback AsyncCallback, _
    ByVal asyncState As Object) As IAsyncResult
        .
        .
        .

    End Function

    Public Function EndAsyncMethod (ByVal asyncResult As IAsyncResult) _
        As Object
        .
        .
        .
    End Function

End Class
```

Visual C#

```
public class Server
{
    // A method that can be called asynchronously
    public object AsyncMethod()
    {
        .
        .
        .
    }

    public IAsyncResult BeginAsyncMethod (AsyncCallback callback, object
```

(continued)

```
                    asyncState)
        {
             .
             .
             .
        }
        public object EndAsyncMethod (IAsyncResult asyncResult)
        {
             .
             .
             .
        }
}
```

In the preceding code, Begin and End methods exist for AsyncMethod that you can call asynchronously. BeginAsyncMethod returns an IAsyncResult object to the client. The client uses the IAsyncResult object to determine the state of the asynchronous execution. EndAsyncMethod returns the result of the asynchronous call to the client.

The following code shows how a client calls AsyncMethod on the server object asynchronously.

Visual Basic .NET

```
Public Class Client
    Public svr As Server
    Public Sub callbackMethod(IAsyncResult result)
        svr.EndAsyncMethod(result)
    End Sub
    Public Shared Sub Main()
        svr = New Server()
        Dim stateobj As New Object()
        Dim cb As New AsyncCallback(Me.callbackMethod)
        svr.BeginAsyncMethod(cb, stateobj)
    End Sub
End Class
```

Visual C#

```
public class Client
{
    public Server svr;

    public void callbackMethod(IAsyncResult asyncResult)
    {
        svr.EndAsyncMethod(result)
    }
    [STAThread]
    static void Main(string[] args)
```

```
    {
        svr = new Server();
        object stateobj = new object();
        Callback cb = new AsyncCallback(this.callbackMethod);
        svr.BeginAsyncMethod(cb, stateobj);
    }
}
```

In the preceding code, the client calls the BeginAsyncMethod() method on the server object and passes a callback reference. After the asynchronous execution, the server object calls callbackMethod() on the client using the callback reference. The callbackMethod() method of the client, in turn, calls EndAsyncMethod() on the server object, which returns the result to the client.

The client can also synchronously call AsyncMethod on the object of the Server class. If the client needs to call the AsyncMethod synchronously, the client uses the object reference to call the method directly, as shown in the following code.

Visual Basic .NET

```
Dim svr as New Server()
svr.AsyncMethod()
```

Visual C#

```
Server svr = new Server();
svr.AsyncMethod();
```

Therefore, it is the client that decides whether a method is to be executed synchronously or asynchronously.

Using Asynchronous Programming in XML Web Services

You use the WSDL tool to create the Begin and End methods for the Web methods of XML Web services. After you create the synchronous and asynchronous versions of Web methods, clients can execute either, depending on their requirements. To create the asynchronous versions of exposed methods, type one of the following commands at the Visual Studio .NET Command Prompt.

wsdl http://server/MyApp/Service1.asmx
or
wsdl /language:VB http://server/MyApp/Service1.asmx

Note   When you compile a Web service in Visual Studio .NET, Visual Studio .NET creates both the synchronous and the asynchronous versions of a Web method.

The preceding commands create a Service1.cs or Service1.vb file, which contains the Begin and End methods for all the Web methods exposed in Service1.

The following code shows a Web service with a Web method, Factorial, which calculates the factorial of a number. Before the Factorial method returns the result, it creates a thread and sleeps the thread for 10 seconds. This increases the time that the Factorial method takes to execute.

Visual Basic .NET

```vbnet
Imports System.Web.Services

<WebService(Namespace:="http://tempuri.org/")> _
Public Class Service1
    Inherits System.Web.Services.WebService
    <WebMethod()> Public Function Factorial(ByVal n As Integer) As Double
        Dim n1 As Double = 1
        Dim result As Double = 1
        While n1 <= n
            result = result * n1
            n1 = n1 + 1
        End While
        Dim t As New Threading.Thread(AddressOf longtask)
        t.Start()
        t.Sleep(10000)
        t.Abort()
        Return result
    End Function

    Private Sub longtask()
        While True
        End While
    End Sub

End Class
```

Visual C#

```csharp
public class Service1 : System.Web.Services.WebService
    {

        [WebMethod()]
        public Double Factorial(int n   )
        {
            double  n1 = 1;
            double result = 1;
            while (n1 <= n)
            {
                result = result * n1;
```

```
            n1 = n1 + 1;
        }

        System.Threading.Thread.Sleep(10000);

        return result;
    }

    private void longtask()
    {
        while (true){}
    }
  }
}
```

Visual Studio .NET creates synchronous as well as asynchronous versions of a Web method when you build an XML Web service, which you can call in your client applications. However, if you develop Web services using command line compilers, you need to generate the asynchronous versions of methods using the WSDL tool. The following is the code of a Windows application that calls the Factorial method of the Service1 Web service both synchronously and asynchronously.

Visual Basic .NET

```vb
Public Class Form1
    Inherits System.Windows.Forms.Form
    Private svcs As localhost.Service1
    Private Sub Button1_Click(ByVal sender As System.Object, ByVal e As _
        System.EventArgs) Handles Button1.Click
        MsgBox(svcs.Factorial(20).ToString)
    End Sub

    Private Sub Button2_Click(ByVal sender As System.Object, ByVal e As _
        System.EventArgs) Handles Button2.Click
        Dim cb As New AsyncCallback(AddressOf Form1.callback)
        Dim ar As IAsyncResult = svcs.BeginFactorial(20, cb, svcs)
    End Sub

    Public Shared Sub callback(ByVal ar As IAsyncResult)
        Dim svcs As localhost.Service1
        svcs = CType(ar.AsyncState, localhost.Service1)
        Dim result As Double = svcs.EndFactorial(ar)
        MsgBox(result.ToString)
    End Sub
```

(continued)

```vb
        Private Sub Form1_Load(ByVal sender As System.Object, ByVal e As _
            System.EventArgs) Handles MyBase.Load
            svcs = New localhost.Service1()
        End Sub
    End Class
```

Visual C#

```csharp
using System;
using System.Drawing;
using System.Collections;
using System.ComponentModel;
using System.Windows.Forms;
using System.Data;

namespace WindowsApplication2
{
    /// <summary>
    /// Summary description for Form1.
    /// </summary>
    public class Form1 : System.Windows.Forms.Form
    {
        internal System.Windows.Forms.Button Button2;
        internal System.Windows.Forms.Button Button1;
        /// <summary>
        /// Required designer variable.
        /// </summary>
        private System.ComponentModel.Container components = null;
        private  localhost.Service1 svcs;

        private void Button1_Click(object sender, System.EventArgs e)
        {
            MessageBox.Show(svcs.Factorial(20).ToString());
        }

        private void Button2_Click(object sender, System.EventArgs e)
        {
            AsyncCallback cb = new AsyncCallback(callback);
            IAsyncResult ar = svcs.BeginFactorial(20, cb, svcs);
        }

        private void Form1_Load(object sender, System.EventArgs e)
        {
            svcs = new localhost.Service1();
        }

        public static void callback(IAsyncResult  ar )
        {
            localhost.Service1 svcs;
```

```
            svcs = (localhost.Service1)ar.AsyncState;
            double result = svcs.EndFactorial(ar);
            MessageBox.Show(result.ToString());
        }

    }
}
```

Lesson 3: Using SOAP Extensions

SOAP extensions enable you to access and modify SOAP messages that XML Web services send to and receive from clients. In this lesson, you will learn about SOAP extensions. You will also learn how to build a SOAP extension and execute it using an XML Web service.

After this lesson, you will be able to

- Identify SOAP extensions
- Create SOAP extensions
- Execute SOAP extensions with XML Web services

Estimated lesson time: 40 minutes

Overview of SOAP Extensions

An XML Web service sends and receives data from clients in the form of SOAP messages. These SOAP messages can consist of information about a certain operation or about the result of an operation. Whenever a client requires information from the server that hosts the XML Web service, the client sends a SOAP request to the server. The SOAP request should be in compliance with a format that the XML Web service understands. The XML Web service processes the SOAP request and sends a response to the client. The client receives the SOAP response, interprets it, and performs a specified operation. If you need to access and modify the SOAP messages that are exchanged between an XML Web service and its clients, you can use SOAP extensions. SOAP extensions enable you to access and modify the SOAP messages that are exchanged between the client and the XML Web service. For example, you can use SOAP extensions to validate the SOAP message before it reaches the XML Web service and change the SOAP message after validation so that the XML Web service receives a valid SOAP request. You can also implement an encryption or compression algorithm that can be executed within an existing XML Web service by using SOAP extensions.

When a client calls a Web method from the server, the request is serialized into a SOAP message and sent over the network as a SOAP request. The SOAP request is deserialized at the server side. The server then composes a SOAP message, serializes it, and sends it over the network as a SOAP response. The SOAP response is deserialized at the client side before the SOAP message is received by the client application. Therefore, serialization and deserialization occur both at the client side and the server side. You can use the SOAP extension to perform various operations, such as validating and modifying SOAP messages before and after the serialization and deserialization phases. Encrypting and decrypting the SOAP messages in these two phases on both the client and server sides is an example of a SOAP extension. The encryption takes place only after ASP.NET serializes the SOAP messages. The decryption of these messages occurs before ASP.NET deserializes the messages at the server side. The phases in which the SOAP extension validates and modifies a SOAP message are defined in the SoapMessageStage enumeration. Table 8.1 displays various stages that are available in the SoapMessageStage enumeration.

Table 8.1   Members of the SoapMessageStage Enumeration

Member	Description
AfterDeserialize	This member represents the stage just after a SoapMessage is deserialized from a SOAP message into an object.
AfterSerialize	This member represents the stage just after a SoapMessage is serialized but before the SOAP message is sent over the wire.
BeforeDeserialize	This member represents the stage just before a SoapMessage is deserialized from the SOAP message that is sent over the network.
BeforeSerialize	This member represents the stage just before a SoapMessage is serialized.

When a SOAP extension modifies a SOAP message, the modification should be made at both the client side and the server side. This is necessary because the decryption has to occur before deserialization, if a SOAP extension encrypts a SOAP message after serialization. Otherwise, the ASP.NET infrastructure is unable to deserialize the SOAP message. Therefore, any changes that you make to the SOAP message at the client side must be made at the server side and those made at the server side should be made at the client side.

Building SOAP Extensions

To build a SOAP extension, you need to perform the following tasks:

- Create a class that inherits from the SoapExtension class.
- Save a reference to the Stream class that represents future SOAP messages.
- Initialize SOAP extension–specific data.
- Process the SOAP messages during the relevant SoapMessageStage stages.
- Configure the SOAP extension to run with specific XML Web service methods.

Creating a Class That Inherits from the SoapExtension Class

To provide the functionality of a SOAP extension to your class, you derive your class from the System.Web.Services.Protocols.SoapExtension class. For example, if the SOAP extension you are designing is an encryption SOAP extension, your class should implement the encryption algorithm.

Saving a Reference to the Stream Class
That Represents Future SOAP Messages

Before you modify a SOAP message, you should obtain a reference to the stream of data that represents the contents of the message. Next, you override the Chain-Stream method to modify the contents of the SOAP message. The ChainStream method provides access to the SOAP request or response message contained in a memory buffer. A reference to the stream containing the SOAP request or response is passed to the ChainStream method as a parameter before any SoapMessageStage stage starts. This object of the Stream class refers to the XML of the SOAP message after the SOAP extensions execute and modify the message. Therefore, a SOAP extension should save this reference in a member variable for access during the SoapMessageStage stage when a SOAP extension inspects or modifies the SOAP message.

You should not modify the Stream object that is passed into the ChainStream method by using a SOAP extension. Instead, you should create an instance of a Stream object, save the instance in a private member variable, copy the contents of the SOAP message to the private Stream object, and return the instance to the calling program from the ChainStream method. As the SOAP extension executes during each SoapMessageStage and modifies the SOAP message, a SOAP extension should read from the Stream object passed into ChainStream and write to the Stream object that the ChainStream method returns. Therefore, you must save both the Stream references within the ChainStream method. Figure 8.1 shows the stages of how a SOAP extension modifies a SOAP message.

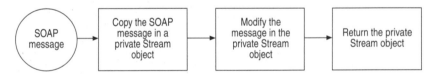

Figure 8.1   Modification of SOAP message using SOAP extensions

The following example demonstrates a common implementation of the Chain-Stream method.

Visual Basic .NET

```
Imports System.Web.Services
Imports System.Web.Services.Protocols

Public Class TraceExtension
    Inherits SoapExtension
        .
        .
        .

    Public Overrides Function ChainStream(defaultStream As Stream) _
        As Stream
```

```
         ' Save the passed Stream in a member variable
         existingStream = defaultStream
         ' Create a new instance of a Stream and save that in a member
         ' variable.
         newStream = New MemoryStream()
         Return newStream
      End Function
End Class
```

Visual C#

```
using System.Web.Services;
using System.Web.Services.Protocols;

public class TraceExtension : SoapExtension
{
    public override Stream ChainStream(Stream defaultStream)
    {
        // Save the passed stream in a member variable
        existingStream = defaultStream;
        // Create a new instance of a Stream and save that in a
        // member variable
        newStream = new MemoryStream();
        return newStream;
    }
}
```

Initializing SOAP Extension–Specific Data

You can use a SOAP extension to create and initialize internal data, based on the XML Web service or service method to which it is applied. For example, you can create and initialize a file that the SOAP extension can use to log the SOAP message that is sent to and from an XML Web service method. The class deriving from SoapExtension uses two methods to initialize data, GetInitializer and Initialize. The GetInitializer method is called only the first time you access an XML Web service or service method. If you use an attribute to configure the SOAP extension, the ASP.NET infrastructure calls the GetInitializer method for every XML Web service method. If you configure the SOAP extension in a configuration file, the ASP.NET infrastructure calls the GetInitializer method only the first time you access the XML Web service. The ASP.NET infrastructure caches the data that a SOAP extension returns from the GetInitializer method. The cached data is passed to a SOAP extension whenever the SOAP extension runs with the XML Web service or service method in the Initialize method.

Processing SOAP Messages

In the class derived from the SoapExtension class, the implementation of the SoapExtension.ProcessMessage method is the most important stage. ASP.NET calls this method several times at every stage in the SoapMessageStage enumeration. Whenever the SoapExtension.ProcessMessage method is called, a SoapMessage object or a class deriving from it is passed to the method with information about the SOAP message at that particular stage. If the SOAP extension is executing with an XML Web service, a SoapServerMessage is passed as the parameter. If the SOAP extension is running with an XML Web service client, a SoapClientMessage is passed as the parameter.

The following code is the ProcessStage method of a SOAP extension that traces a call to an XML Web service. During the trace, if parameters are serialized into XML in the SoapMessageStage, the XML is written to a file.

Visual Basic .NET

```
Public Overrides Sub ProcessMessage(message As SoapMessage)
    Select Case message.Stage
        Case SoapMessageStage.BeforeSerialize
        Case SoapMessageStage.AfterSerialize
            ' Write the SOAP message out to a file.
            WriteOutput(message)
        Case SoapMessageStage.BeforeDeserialize
            ' Write the SOAP message out to a file.
            WriteInput(message)
        Case SoapMessageStage.AfterDeserialize
        Case Else
            Throw New Exception("invalid stage")
    End Select
End Sub
```

Visual C#

```
public override void ProcessMessage(SoapMessage message)
{
    switch (message.Stage)
    {
        case SoapMessageStage.BeforeSerialize:
            break;
        case SoapMessageStage.AfterSerialize:
            // Write the SOAP message out to a file.
            WriteOutput( message );
            break;
        case SoapMessageStage.BeforeDeserialize:
            // Write the SOAP message out to a file.
            WriteInput( message );
            break;
        case SoapMessageStage.AfterDeserialize:
            break;
        default:
            throw new Exception("invalid stage");
    }
}
```

Configuring SOAP Extensions to Execute Using XML Web Service Methods

You can configure a SOAP extension to run using a custom attribute or by modifying a configuration file. To use a custom attribute, apply it to each XML Web service method that you want the SOAP extension to run with. When you use a configuration file, the SOAP extension runs with all the XML Web services that are within the scope of the configuration file.

To use a custom attribute, derive a class from SoapExtensionAttribute. SoapExtensionAttribute has two properties, ExtensionType and Priority. A SOAP extension should return the type of the extension in the ExtensionType property. The Priority property represents the relative priority of the SOAP extension, which is described later in this lesson.

To specify that a SOAP extension should run with all the XML Web services within the scope of a configuration file, you add entries to the appropriate Web.config file. You must add a <soapExtensionTypes> XML element to the webServices section of the configuration file. Within the <soapExtensionTypes> XML element, you add the <add> XML elements for each SOAP extension that you want to run with every XML Web service within the scope of the configuration file. Table 8.2 lists the properties of the <add> XML element.

Table 8.2   Properties of the <add> XML Element

Property	Description
Type	Indicates the type of the SOAP extension
Priority	Indicates the priority of a SOAP extension within a group
Group	Indicates the group a SOAP extension belongs to

SOAP extensions have a priority assigned to them that dictates the relative order of execution when multiple SOAP extensions are configured to run with an XML Web service method. The higher the priority of a SOAP extension, the closer it executes to the SOAP message that is being sent or received over the network. SOAP extensions belong to one of three priority groups. Within each group, the Priority property distinguishes each member. The lower the Priority property, the higher the relative priority, with 0 being the highest.

The three relative priority groups for SOAP extensions are

- SOAP extensions configured using an attribute
- SOAP extensions specified in the configuration file with a Group setting of 0
- SOAP extensions specified in the configuration file with a Group setting of 1.

SOAP extensions configured using an attribute are members of the medium group. SOAP extensions configured using a configuration file with a Group setting of 0 have the highest relative priority. Those with a Group setting of 1 have the lowest relative priority.

The following code is a configuration file that specifies that the MyLog.LogExtn SOAP extension runs within the relative priority group 0 and has a priority of 1.

XML

```
<configuration>
    <system.web>
        <webServices>
            <soapExtensionTypes>
                <add type="MyLog.LogExtn, MyLog" Priority="1"
                    Group="0"/>
            </soapExtensionTypes>
        </webServices>
    </system.web>
</configuration>
```

Lesson 4: Configuring and Securing a Web Service

In the previous lesson, you learned how to enhance the functionality of a Web service by implementing SOAP extensions. You also learned how to use Visual Studio .NET to configure your Web service by using the Web.config file. In this lesson, you will learn about various elements of the Web.config file and how to use these elements to configure and secure a Web service.

After this lesson, you will be able to

- Identify the structure of the Web.config file
- Use the elements of the Web.config file to configure a Web service
- Secure a Web service

Estimated lesson time: 30 minutes

Understanding the Structure of the Web.config File

The configuration files are XML-based files, which you can use to change the settings of your applications without recompiling them. The common language runtime uses the settings specified in the application configuration file to dynamically configure an application. You use the Web.config file, which is the application configuration file for the ASP.NET Web applications and services, to specify the configuration settings for your XML Web services. The Web.config file enables you to define configuration settings when your Web service is deployed. The features of the Web.config file include the following:

- Multiple configuration files can exist in various Web application folders on a Web server. Each Web.config file applies configuration settings to its own Web application folder and to all the child folders. The Web.config files in the child folders can contain configuration information that is in addition to the configuration information inherited from the parent folder.

- At run time, the common language runtime uses the configuration information in the Web.config files in a hierarchical structure to create a collection of configuration settings for each unique URL. The resulting configuration settings are then cached for all subsequent requests made to a resource.

- The common language runtime can automatically detect changes made to Web.config files and apply the new settings to a Web service. In addition, hierarchical configuration settings are automatically recalculated and cached again when you make modifications to a Web.config file in the hierarchy.

- The Web.config file is extensible. Therefore, you can define new configuration parameters and write configuration section handlers to process them.

- The Web server prevents direct access to the Web.config file. The Web server returns the HTTP access error 403 to any browser that tries to request a configuration file directly.

The Web.config file for each Web service is present in the Web folder of the Web service. The following code displays a sample Web.config file.

XML

```
<?xml version="1.0" encoding="utf-8" ?>
<configuration>
    <system.web>
        <compilation defaultLanguage="vb" debug="true" />
        <customErrors mode="RemoteOnly" />
        <authentication mode="Windows" />
        <authorization>
            <allow users="*" /> <!-- Allow all users -->
        </authorization>
        <trace enabled="false" requestLimit="10" pageOutput="false"
            traceMode="SortByTime" localOnly="true" />
        <sessionState
            mode="InProc"
            stateConnectionString="tcpip=127.0.0.1:42424"
            sqlConnectionString="data source=127.0.0.1;user id=sa;pwd="
            cookieless="false"
            timeout="20"
        />
        <globalization requestEncoding="utf-8" responseEncoding="utf-8" />
    </system.web>
</configuration>
```

Using the Elements of the Web.config File to Configure a Web Service

As you learned in the previous topic, a Web.config file contains nested XML tags with attributes that specify configuration settings. All the attributes of the configuration settings are present within the <configuration> and </configuration> root tags. You use the following attributes to configure a Web service:

- **<compilation />.**   You use this tag to specify the compilation language and whether you want to debug the Web service. You can set the debug attribute to True to insert debugging symbols (.pdb information) into the compiled page. For example, the `<compilation defaultLanguage="vb" debug="true" />` tag sets the default language to VB and enables debugging of the XML Web Service.

- **<customErrors />.**   You use this tag to manage custom error messages. You can set the mode attribute to On or RemoteOnly to enable custom error messages, and Off to disable error messages, as in the tag `<customErrors mode="RemoteOnly" />`.

- **<authentication />.**   You use this tag to specify the authentication policies of the application. You can set the mode attribute to Windows, Forms, Passport, or None. The Web service uses the authentication policy that you specified to authenticate users, as in the tag `<authentication mode="Windows" />`.

- **<authorization />.**   You use this tag to set the authorization policies of your Web service. You can allow or deny access to your Web service. You can set the users attribute to * and ? wildcards to allow everyone and anonymous or unauthenticated users, respectively, as in the tag `<allow users="*" />`.

- **<trace />.**   You use this tag to enable application-level tracing of the Web service. This enables trace log output for every page within an application. You can set the enabled attribute to True to enable application trace logging, as in the tag `<trace enabled="false" />`.

- **<globalization />.**   You use this tag to specify globalization settings for a Web service, as in the tag `<globalization requestEncoding="utf-8" responseEncoding="utf-8" />`.

You can also specify the settings in a Web.config file to configure security for your Web service. The next topic explores how to secure a Web service.

Securing a Web Service

You can secure a Web service by using the <authentication /> and <authorization /> tags of the Web.config file.

Authentication

An XML Web service implements authentication policies by using authentication providers, which are in addition to the IIS authentication schemes. You can specify the following authentication providers in your Web service:

- **Windows.**   This is the default authentication mode. When you specify the authentication mode as Windows, the authentication process relies upon IIS to perform the required authentication of a client. After IIS authenticates a client, IIS passes a security token to the Web service. The following code shows how to use Windows authentication:

  `<authentication mode="Windows" />`

- **Forms.**   You can use this authentication mode to ensure that a Web service collects credentials using an HTML log-in form directly from the client. The client submits credentials to your Web service for authentication. When the Web service authenticates the client, it issues a cookie to the client. The client uses this cookie to access the Web service. If a request for a protected service does not contain the cookie, the client is redirected to the HTML log-in page specified in the configuration file. The following code displays how to use Forms authentication:

```
<authentication mode="Forms">
    <forms forms="Sales" loginUrl="/login.aspx" />
</authentication>
```

- **Passport.**   This authentication provider is a centralized authentication service. The Passport authentication mode enables a single logon and profile services for member sites. Passport is a forms-based authentication service in which member sites register with the Passport service. The Passport service grants a site-specific key. The Passport logon server uses this key to encrypt and decrypt the query strings that are passed between the member site and the Passport logon server. The following code displays how to use Passport authentication:

  ```
  <authentication mode="Passport" />
  ```

- **None.**   You use this authentication provider if you do not want to authenticate users or if you want to use custom authentication code. The following code displays how to use None:

  ```
  <authentication mode="None" />
  ```

In addition to authentication modes, you can secure the Web service by specifying specific users and roles that can access the Web service.

Authorization

You can use the <authorization /> tag to specify the users and roles that can access your Web service. This tag enables you to implement both positive and negative authorization assertions. You use this tag to allow or deny access to your Web service based on specific users or roles.

To specify roles and users who can access your Web service, you place a list of users and roles in the <allow> or <deny> elements of the <authorization> tags in the Web.config file. The following code displays how to allow and deny permissions to specific users and roles:

```
<authorization>
    <deny users="Nancy"/>
    <allow role="Administrator" />
</authorization>
```

In addition to specific roles and users, you can use the * and ? wildcards to allow or deny permission to all and anonymous identities, respectively. The following code displays how to deny access to all users except one:

```
<authorization>
    <allow users="Nancy" />
    <deny users="*" />
</authorization>
```

Summary

- The WebMethod attribute enables a client application to use the standard Internet protocols to access the methods of an XML Web service. The Web-Method attribute provides properties, such as BufferResponse, CacheDuration, Description, EnableSession, MessageName, and TransactionOption, which enable you to customize and control the behavior of the methods that you expose in your Web service.

- Asynchronous programming allows a program to call a method on an object and return immediately without waiting for the method to return. Asynchronous programming is useful when the method called by a program on an object takes significant time to execute and you do not want the program to wait for the method to return.

- SOAP extensions enable you to access and modify the SOAP messages that are exchanged between the client and the XML Web service. For example, you can use SOAP extensions to validate the SOAP message before it reaches the XML Web service and change the SOAP message after validation so that the XML Web service receives a valid SOAP request. You can also implement an encryption or compression algorithm that can be executed within an existing XML Web service by using SOAP extensions.

- You use the Web.config file, which is the application configuration file for the ASP.NET Web applications and services, to specify the configuration settings for your XML Web services.

Lab: Implementing Transactions, Asynchronous Methods, and SOAP Extensions

In this lab, you will create XML Web services and modify the behavior of Web methods using the properties of the WebMethod attribute. You will create Web methods to participate in transactions. You will also use SOAP extensions to log information about the SOAP messages that are exchanged between an XML Web service and a client application. In addition, you will use the asynchronous versions of a Web method in a client application. The solutions to the exercises in this lab can be found in the \Solution folder on the Supplemental Course Materials CD-ROM.

Estimated lab time: 120 minutes

Exercise 1: Creating the LabTest Database and Authors Table

In this exercise, you will create the LabTest database and the Authors table. You will use the LabTest database and Authors table in Exercise 2.

To create the LabTest database, perform the following tasks:

1. From the Start menu, locate the Microsoft SQL Server folder and open Enterprise Manager.

2. Expand your SQL Server node and locate the Databases node. Right-click the Databases node and choose New Database from the shortcut menu, as shown here.

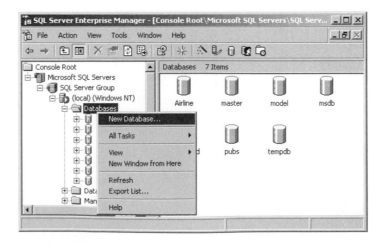

3. In the Database Properties dialog box, type **LabTest** in the Name field and click OK to create the LabTest database, as shown here.

4. From the Start menu, locate the Microsoft SQL Server folder and open Query Analyzer. Provide the required authentication information to connect to your database server.

5. Select the LabTest database from the list of databases in Query Analyzer.

6. Execute the following script.

SQL Script

```
if exists (select * from dbo.sysobjects where id = object_id(
N'[dbo].[Authors]') and OBJECTPROPERTY(id, N'IsUserTable') = 1)
drop table [dbo].[Authors]
GO

if not exists (select * from dbo.sysobjects where id = object_id(
N'[dbo].[Authors]') and OBJECTPROPERTY(id, N'IsUserTable') = 1)
 BEGIN
CREATE TABLE [dbo].[Authors] (
    [au_id] [int] NOT NULL ,
    [au_lname] [char] (20) COLLATE SQL_Latin1_General_CP1_CI_AS NOT NULL,
    [au_fname] [char] (20) COLLATE SQL_Latin1_General_CP1_CI_AS NOT NULL,
    [Phone] [char] (10) COLLATE SQL_Latin1_General_CP1_CI_AS NULL,
    [Address] [char] (40) COLLATE SQL_Latin1_General_CP1_CI_AS NULL,
    [State] [char] (10) COLLATE SQL_Latin1_General_CP1_CI_AS NULL,
    [Zip] [char] (10) COLLATE SQL_Latin1_General_CP1_CI_AS NULL
) ON [PRIMARY]
END

GO

ALTER TABLE [dbo].[Authors] WITH NOCHECK ADD
```

(continued)

```
                    CONSTRAINT [PK_Authors] PRIMARY KEY CLUSTERED
                    (
                        [au_id]
                    ) ON [PRIMARY]
        GO
```

7. View the Tables node in the LabTest database in Enterprise Manager to verify
   that the Authors table has been created in the LabTest database.

Exercise 2: Implementing the Transaction Property of the WebMethod Attribute

In this exercise, you will create a Web method that shows how to implement the
Transaction property of the <WebMethod> or [WebMethod] attribute.

To create an XML Web service, perform the following steps:

1. Open Visual Studio .NET.
2. Open the New Project dialog box from the File menu.
3. Select ASP.NET Web Service from the Templates pane. Type **http://localhost/
   VBTransEx** or **http://localhost/CSTransEx** in the Location text box.
4. Change the name of the Service1.asmx file to TransEx.asmx. Right-click the
   TransEx.asmx file in the Solution Explorer, and select View Code from the
   shortcut menu to see the code. Add a Web method called DeleteAuthor by adding the following code to the Web service.

Visual Basic .NET

```
<WebMethod(False, TransactionOption.RequiresNew)> _
    Public Function DeleteAuthor(ByVal lastName As String) As Integer
    Dim deleteCmdSQL As String = "DELETE FROM authors WHERE " & _
        "au_lname='" + lastName + "'"
    Dim exceptionCausingCmdSQL As String = "DELETE FROM author " & _
        "WHERE " + "au_lname='" + lastName + "'"
    Dim sqlConn As New SqlConnection("user id=sa;pwd=;initial " & _
        "catalog=" + "LabTest;data source=localhost")
    Dim deleteCmd As New SqlCommand(deleteCmdSQL, sqlConn)
    Dim exceptionCausingCmd As New SqlCommand( _
        exceptionCausingCmdSQL, sqlConn)

    deleteCmd.Connection.Open()
    deleteCmd.ExecuteNonQuery()

    Dim Result As Integer = 0
    Result = exceptionCausingCmd.ExecuteNonQuery()
    sqlConn.Close()
    Return Result
End Function
```

Visual C#

```csharp
[WebMethod(TransactionOption=TransactionOption.RequiresNew)]
public int DeleteAuthor(string lastName)
{
    String deleteCmdSQL = "DELETE FROM authors WHERE au_lname='" +
        lastName + "'" ;
    String exceptionCausingCmdSQL = "DELETE FROM author WHERE au_lname='"
        + lastName + "'" ;
    SqlConnection sqlConn = new SqlConnection("user id=sa;pwd=;initial " +
        "catalog=LabTest;data source=localhost");
    SqlCommand deleteCmd = new SqlCommand(deleteCmdSQL,sqlConn);
    SqlCommand exceptionCausingCmd = new SqlCommand(
        exceptionCausingCmdSQL,sqlConn);
    // This command executes without an exception. This command deletes a
    // row from the Authors table.
    deleteCmd.Connection.Open();
    deleteCmd.ExecuteNonQuery();

    // This command throws an exception as the table author doesn't exist.
    // Therefore, the first command is automatically rolled back.  Since
    // the XML Web service method is participating in a transaction, and
    // an exception occurs, ASP.NET automatically aborts the transaction.
    // The deleteCmd that executed without an exception is rolled back.

    int Result=0;
    Result = exceptionCausingCmd.ExecuteNonQuery();
    sqlConn.Close();
    return Result;
}
```

5. Right-click References and choose Add Reference from the shortcut menu to open the Add Reference dialog box. Form the .NET tab, double-click System.EnterpriseServices and click OK to add reference to the System.EnterpriseServices namespace.

6. Add the following namespaces at the top of the Web service code:

Visual Basic .NET

```vbnet
Imports System.EnterpriseServices
Imports System.Data.SqlClient
```

Visual C#

```csharp
using System.EnterpriseServices;
using System.Data.SqlClient;
```

7. From the Build menu, choose Build Solution to build the Web service project.

Exercise 3: Implementing a SOAP Extension in an XML Web Service

In this exercise, you will create an XML Web service that enables you to implement the SOAP extension attribute for a Web method.

To create an XML Web service, perform the following tasks:

1. Open Visual Studio .NET.
2. From the File menu, choose New Project to open the New Project dialog box.
3. Select ASP.NET Web Service from the Templates pane. Type **http://localhost/ VBSoapEx** or **http://localhost/CSSoapEx** in the Location field.
4. Change the name of the Service1.asmx file to SoapEx.asmx. Right-click the SoapEx.asmx file, and choose View Code from the shortcut menu to see the code. Replace it with the following code.

Visual Basic .NET

```
Imports System
Imports System.Web.Services
Imports System.Web.Services.Protocols
Imports System.IO


<WebService(Namespace:="http://tempuri.org/")> _
Public Class SoapEx
    Inherits System.Web.Services.WebService

#Region " Web Services Designer Generated Code "

    Public Sub New()
        MyBase.New()

        'This call is required by the Web Services Designer.
        InitializeComponent()

    End Sub


    'Required by the Web Services Designer
    Private components As System.ComponentModel.IContainer

    'NOTE: The following procedure is required by the Web Services
    'Designer. It can be modified using the Web Services Designer.
    'Do not modify it using the code editor.
    <System.Diagnostics.DebuggerStepThrough()> _
    Private Sub InitializeComponent()
        components = New System.ComponentModel.Container()
    End Sub

    Protected Overloads Overrides Sub Dispose(ByVal disposing As Boolean)
        'CODEGEN: This procedure is required by the Web Services Designer
```

```
                            'Do not modify it using the code editor.
                            If disposing Then
                                If Not (components Is Nothing) Then
                                    components.Dispose()
                                End If
                            End If
                            MyBase.Dispose(disposing)
                        End Sub

#End Region

    <WebMethod(), TraceExtensionAttribute()> _
    Public Function SoapTest(ByVal message As String) As String
        SoapTest = "Hey, I got this message from you: " & message
    End Function

End Class

Public Class TraceExtension
    Inherits SoapExtension

    Private oldStream As Stream
    Private newStream As Stream
    Private m_filename As String

    ' Save the Stream representing the SOAP request or SOAP response into
    ' a local memory buffer.
    Public Overrides Function ChainStream(ByVal stream As Stream) _
        As Stream
        oldStream = stream
        newStream = New MemoryStream()
        Return newStream
    End Function

    ' When the SOAP extension is accessed for the first time, the XML Web
    ' service method it is applied to is accessed to store the file
    ' name passed in, using the corresponding SoapExtensionAttribute.
    Public Overloads Overrides Function GetInitializer(ByVal methodInfo _
        As LogicalMethodInfo, ByVal attribute As _
        SoapExtensionAttribute) As Object
        Return CType(attribute, TraceExtensionAttribute).Filename
    End Function

    ' The SOAP extension was configured to run using a configuration file
    ' instead of an attribute applied to a specific XML Web service
    ' method.  Return a file name based on the class implementing the Web
    ' service's type.
    Public Overloads Overrides Function GetInitializer(ByVal _
        WebServiceType As Type) As Object
        ' Return a file name to log the trace information to, based on the
        ' type.
```

(continued)

```vb
            Return WebServiceType.GetType().ToString() & ".log"
    End Function


    ' Receive the file name stored by GetInitializer and store it in a
    ' member variable for this specific instance.
    Public Overrides Sub Initialize(ByVal initializer As Object)
        m_filename = CStr(initializer)
    End Sub


    ' If the SoapMessageStage is such that the SoapRequest or SoapResponse
    ' is still in the SOAP format to be sent or received over the network,
    ' save it out to file.
    Public Overrides Sub ProcessMessage(ByVal message As SoapMessage)
        Select Case message.Stage
            Case SoapMessageStage.BeforeSerialize
            Case SoapMessageStage.AfterSerialize
                WriteOutput(message)
            Case SoapMessageStage.BeforeDeserialize
                WriteInput(message)
            Case SoapMessageStage.AfterDeserialize
            Case Else
                Throw New Exception("invalid stage")
        End Select
    End Sub


    ' Write the SOAP message out to a file.
    Public Sub WriteOutput(ByVal message As SoapMessage)
        newStream.Position = 0
        Dim fs As New FileStream(m_filename, FileMode.Append, _
            FileAccess.Write)
        Dim w As New StreamWriter(fs)
        w.WriteLine("-----Response at " + DateTime.Now.ToString())
        w.Flush()
        Copy(newStream, fs)
        w.Close()
        newStream.Position = 0
        Copy(newStream, oldStream)
    End Sub


    ' Write the SOAP message out to a file.
    Public Sub WriteInput(ByVal message As SoapMessage)
        Copy(oldStream, newStream)
        Dim fs As New FileStream(m_filename, FileMode.Append, _
            FileAccess.Write)
        Dim w As New StreamWriter(fs)
        w.WriteLine("----- Request at " + DateTime.Now.ToString())
        w.Flush()
        newStream.Position = 0
        Copy(newStream, fs)
        w.Close()
        newStream.Position = 0
    End Sub
```

```vb
    Sub Copy(ByVal fromStream As Stream, ByVal toStream As Stream)
        Dim reader As New StreamReader(fromStream)
        Dim writer As New StreamWriter(toStream)
        writer.WriteLine(reader.ReadToEnd())
        writer.Flush()
    End Sub
End Class

' Create a SoapExtensionAttribute for our SOAP extension that can be
' applied to an XML Web service method.
<AttributeUsage(AttributeTargets.Method)> _
Public Class TraceExtensionAttribute
    Inherits SoapExtensionAttribute

    Private m_filename As String = "c:\log.txt"
    Private m_priority As Integer

    Sub New()
        m_filename = "c:\\mylogVB.txt"
    End Sub

    Public Overrides ReadOnly Property ExtensionType() As Type
        Get
            Return GetType(TraceExtension)
        End Get
    End Property

    Public Overrides Property Priority() As Integer
        Get
            Return m_priority
        End Get
        Set(ByVal Value As Integer)
            m_priority = Value
        End Set
    End Property

    Public Property Filename() As String
        Get
            Return m_filename
        End Get
        Set(ByVal Value As String)
            m_filename = Value
        End Set
    End Property
End Class
```

Visual C#

```csharp
using System;
using System.Collections;
using System.ComponentModel;
```

(continued)

```csharp
using System.Data;
using System.Diagnostics;
using System.Web;
using System.Web.Services;
using System.Web.Services.Protocols;
using System.Net;
using System.IO;

namespace SoapEx
{
    /// <summary>
    /// Summary description for Service1.
    /// </summary>
    public class SoapEx : System.Web.Services.WebService
    {
        public SoapEx()
        {
            InitializeComponent();
        }

        #region Component Designer generated code

        //Required by the Web Services Designer
        private IContainer components = null;

        /// <summary>
        /// Required method for Designer support - do not modify
        /// the contents of this method with the code editor.
        /// </summary>
        private void InitializeComponent()
        {
        }

        /// <summary>
        /// Clean up any resources being used.
        /// </summary>
        protected override void Dispose( bool disposing )
        {
            if(disposing && components != null)
            {
                components.Dispose();
            }
            base.Dispose(disposing);
        }

        #endregion

        [WebMethod]
        [TraceExtensionAttribute]
        public string SoapExtensionTest(string message)
        {
```

```
            return "Hey, I got this message from you: " + message;
        }
    }

public class TraceExtension : SoapExtension
{
    Stream oldStream;
    Stream newStream;
    string filename;

    // Save the Stream representing the SOAP request or SOAP response
    // into a local memory buffer.
    public override Stream ChainStream( Stream stream )
    {
        oldStream = stream;
        newStream = new MemoryStream();
        return newStream;
    }

    // When the SOAP extension is accessed for the first time, the
    // XML Web service method it is applied to is accessed to store
    // the file name passed in, using the corresponding
    // SoapExtensionAttribute.
    public override object GetInitializer(LogicalMethodInfo
        methodInfo, SoapExtensionAttribute attribute)
    {
        return ((TraceExtensionAttribute) attribute).Filename;
    }

    // The SOAP extension was configured to run using a configuration
    // file instead of an attribute applied to a specific XML Web
    // service method.
    public override object GetInitializer(Type WebServiceType)
    {
        // Return a file name to log the trace information to, based
        // on the type.
        return WebServiceType.GetType().ToString() + ".log";
    }

    // Receive the file name stored by GetInitializer and store it in
    // a member variable for this specific instance.
    public override void Initialize(object initializer)
    {
        filename = (string) initializer;
    }

    //  If the SoapMessageStage is such that the SoapRequest or
    //  SoapResponse is still in the SOAP format to be sent or
    //  received, save it out to a file.
    public override void ProcessMessage(SoapMessage message)
    {
```

(continued)

```csharp
            switch (message.Stage)
            {
                case SoapMessageStage.BeforeSerialize:
                    break;
                case SoapMessageStage.AfterSerialize:
                    WriteOutput(message);
                    break;
                case SoapMessageStage.BeforeDeserialize:
                    WriteInput(message);
                    break;
                case SoapMessageStage.AfterDeserialize:
                    break;
                default:
                    throw new Exception("invalid stage");
            }
        }

        public void WriteOutput(SoapMessage message)
        {
            newStream.Position = 0;
            FileStream fs = new FileStream(filename, FileMode.Append,
                FileAccess.Write);
            StreamWriter w = new StreamWriter(fs);

            string soapString = (message is SoapServerMessage) ?
                "SoapResponse" : "SoapRequest";
            w.WriteLine("-----" + soapString + " at " + DateTime.Now);
            w.Flush();
            Copy(newStream, fs);
            w.Close();
            newStream.Position = 0;
            Copy(newStream, oldStream);
        }

        public void WriteInput(SoapMessage message)
        {
            Copy(oldStream, newStream);
            FileStream fs = new FileStream(filename, FileMode.Append,
                FileAccess.Write);
            StreamWriter w = new StreamWriter(fs);

            string soapString = (message is SoapServerMessage) ?
                "SoapRequest" : "SoapResponse";
            w.WriteLine("-----" + soapString + " at " + DateTime.Now);
            w.Flush();
            newStream.Position = 0;
            Copy(newStream, fs);
            w.Close();
            newStream.Position = 0;
        }
```

```
            void Copy(Stream from, Stream to)
            {
                TextReader reader = new StreamReader(from);
                TextWriter writer = new StreamWriter(to);
                writer.WriteLine(reader.ReadToEnd());
                writer.Flush();
            }
        }

        // Create a SoapExtensionAttribute for the SOAP extension that can be
        // applied to an XML Web service method.
        [AttributeUsage(AttributeTargets.Method)]
        public class TraceExtensionAttribute : SoapExtensionAttribute
        {

            private string filename = "c:\\log.txt";
            private int priority;

            public TraceExtensionAttribute()
            {
                filename = "c:\\mylog.txt";
            }

            public override Type ExtensionType
            {
                get { return typeof(TraceExtension); }
            }

            public override int Priority
            {
                get { return priority; }
                set { priority = value; }
            }

            public string Filename
            {
                get
                {
                    return filename;
                }
                set
                {
                    filename = value;
                }
            }
        }
    }
}
```

5. From the Build menu, choose Build Solution to build the Web service project.

Exercise 4: Creating the XML Web Service Client

In this exercise, you will create the XML Web service client, which is a Windows application. This client calls a method that implements the SOAP extension attribute of the XML Web service.

To create a Windows application, perform the following steps:

1. Open Visual Studio. NET.
2. Choose New Project from the File menu to open the New Project dialog box.
3. Select Windows Application from the Templates pane. Type **SoapExClientVB** or **SoapExClientCS** in the Name field.
4. Change the name of the Form1.vb or Form1.cs file to SoapExClient.vb or SoapExClient.cs. Right-click the SoapExClient.vb or SoapExClient.cs file, and choose View Code from the shortcut menu to see the code. Replace it with the following code.

Visual Basic .NET

```
Public Class SoapExClient
    Inherits System.Windows.Forms.Form

#Region " Windows Form Designer generated code "

    Public Sub New()
        MyBase.New()

        'This call is required by the Windows Form Designer.
        InitializeComponent()

    End Sub

    'Form overrides dispose to clean up the component list.
    Protected Overloads Overrides Sub Dispose(ByVal disposing As Boolean)
        If disposing Then
            If Not (components Is Nothing) Then
                components.Dispose()
            End If
        End If
        MyBase.Dispose(disposing)
    End Sub

    'Required by the Windows Form Designer
    Private components As System.ComponentModel.IContainer

    'NOTE: The following procedure is required by the Windows Form
    'Designer. It can be modified using the Windows Form Designer.
    'Do not modify it using the code editor.
    Friend WithEvents btnLog As System.Windows.Forms.Button
    <System.Diagnostics.DebuggerStepThrough()> _
```

```vb
        Private Sub InitializeComponent()
            Me.btnLog = New System.Windows.Forms.Button()
            Me.SuspendLayout()
            '
            'btnLog
            '
            Me.btnLog.Location = New System.Drawing.Point(48, 24)
            Me.btnLog.Name = "btnLog"
            Me.btnLog.Size = New System.Drawing.Size(120, 23)
            Me.btnLog.TabIndex = 0
            Me.btnLog.Text = "Log SOAP Data"
            '
            'SoapExClientVB
            '
            Me.AutoScaleBaseSize = New System.Drawing.Size(5, 13)
            Me.ClientSize = New System.Drawing.Size(216, 77)
            Me.Controls.AddRange(New System.Windows.Forms.Control() _
                {Me.btnLog})
            Me.Name = "SoapExClientVB"
            Me.Text = "Soap Extension Client"
            Me.ResumeLayout(False)

        End Sub

#End Region

    Private Sub btnLog_Click(ByVal sender As System.Object, ByVal e As _
        System.EventArgs) Handles btnLog.Click
        Dim ws As New localhost.SoapEx()
        Dim s As String
        s = ws.SoapTest("Message from the client message")
        MessageBox.Show(s)
    End Sub
End Class
```

Visual C#

```csharp
using System;
using System.Drawing;
using System.Collections;
using System.ComponentModel;
using System.Windows.Forms;
using System.Data;

namespace SoapExClient
{
    /// <summary>
    /// Summary description for Form1.
    /// </summary>
    public class SoapExClient : System.Windows.Forms.Form
    {
        private System.Windows.Forms.Button btnLog;
```

(continued)

```csharp
/// <summary>
/// Required designer variable.
/// </summary>
private System.ComponentModel.Container components = null;

public SoapExClient()
{
    InitializeComponent();

}

/// <summary>
/// Clean up any resources being used.
/// </summary>
protected override void Dispose( bool disposing )
{
    if( disposing )
    {
        if (components != null)
        {
            components.Dispose();
        }
    }
    base.Dispose( disposing );
}

#region Windows Form Designer generated code
/// <summary>
/// Required method for Designer support - do not modify
/// the contents of this method with the code editor.
/// </summary>
private void InitializeComponent()
{
    this.btnLog = new System.Windows.Forms.Button();
    this.SuspendLayout();
    //
    // btnLog
    //
    this.btnLog.Location = new System.Drawing.Point(48, 32);
    this.btnLog.Name = "btnLog";
    this.btnLog.Size = new System.Drawing.Size(136, 23);
    this.btnLog.TabIndex = 0;
    this.btnLog.Text = "Log Soap Data";
    this.btnLog.Click += new
        System.EventHandler(this.btnLog_Click);
    //
    // SoapExClient
    //
    this.AutoScaleBaseSize = new System.Drawing.Size(5, 13);
    this.ClientSize = new System.Drawing.Size(248, 93);
    this.Controls.AddRange(new System.Windows.Forms.Control[] {
```

```
                              this.btnLog});
                   this.Name = "SoapExClient";
                   this.Text = "Soap Extension Client";
                   this.ResumeLayout(false);


         }
         #endregion

         /// <summary>
         /// The main entry point for the application.
         /// </summary>
         [STAThread]
         static void Main()
         {
             Application.Run(new SoapExClient());
         }

         private void btnLog_Click(object sender, System.EventArgs e)
         {
             localhost.SoapEx ws = new localhost.SoapEx();
             string s = ws.SoapExtensionTest("How are you?");
             MessageBox.Show(s);
         }
     }
}
```

Note   You will need to change the Startup Object for Visual Basic project. To change the Startup Object, right-click the SoapExClientVB project, and click Properties to open the properties dialog box. Select SoapExClient from the Startup Object list.

5. Add a Web reference to the SoapEx Web service. To add the Web reference, right-click References under the SoapExClientVB or SoapExClientCS project and choose Add Web Reference from the shortcut menu. In the Add Web Reference dialog box, type **http://localhost/VBSoapEx/SoapEx.asmx** or **http://localhost/CSSoapEx/SoapEx.asmx** and press Enter. Click Add Reference after the Web service is displayed under Available References.

6. From the Build menu, click Build Solution to build the project.

7. Press F5 to run the application.

Exercise 5: Calling Web Methods Asynchronously

In this exercise, you will use synchronous as well as asynchronous methods of a Web service.

1. Open Visual Studio. NET.

2. Create an ASP.NET Web service project. Type **http://localhost/VBDataService** or **http://localhost/CSDataService** in the Location field.

3.　Type the following code for the Service1 Web service class.

Visual Basic .NET

```
Imports System.Web.Services
Imports System.Data.SqlClient
Imports System.Xml

<WebService(Namespace := "http://tempuri.org/")> _
Public Class Service1
    Inherits System.Web.Services.WebService

#Region " Web Services Designer Generated Code "

    Public Sub New()
        MyBase.New()

        'This call is required by the Web Services Designer.
        InitializeComponent()

    End Sub

    'Required by the Web Services Designer
    Private components As System.ComponentModel.IContainer

    'NOTE: The following procedure is required by the Web Services
    'Designer. It can be modified using the Web Services Designer.
    'Do not modify it using the code editor.
    <System.Diagnostics.DebuggerStepThrough()> _
    Private Sub InitializeComponent()
    components = New System.ComponentModel.Container()
    End Sub

    Protected Overloads Overrides Sub Dispose(ByVal disposing As Boolean)
        'CODEGEN: This procedure is required by the Web Services Designer
        'Do not modify it using the code editor.
        If disposing Then
            If Not (components Is Nothing) Then
                components.Dispose()
            End If
        End If
        MyBase.Dispose(disposing)
    End Sub

#End Region

    <WebMethod()> _
    Public Function getData() As DataSet
        Dim ds As New DataSet()
        Dim xmlreader As New XmlTextReader("C:\temp\Products.xml")
```

```vb
        ds.ReadXml(xmlreader)
        xmlreader.Close()
        System.Threading.Thread.Sleep(3000)
        Return ds
    End Function

    <WebMethod()> _
    Public Sub setData(ByVal ds As DataSet)
        Dim xmlwriter As New XmlTextWriter("c:\temp\Products.xml", _
            System.Text.Encoding.UTF8)
        ds.WriteXml(xmlwriter, XmlWriteMode.WriteSchema)
        xmlwriter.Close()
        System.Threading.Thread.Sleep(3000)
    End Sub

End Class
```

Visual C#

```csharp
using System;
using System.Collections;
using System.ComponentModel;
using System.Data;
using System.Diagnostics;
using System.Web;
using System.Web.Services;
using System.Xml;

namespace CSDataService
{
    /// <summary>
    /// Summary description for Service1.
    /// </summary>
    public class Service1 : System.Web.Services.WebService
    {
        public Service1()
        {
            InitializeComponent();
        }

        #region Component Designer generated code

        //Required by the Web Services Designer
        private IContainer components = null;

        /// <summary>
        /// Required method for Designer support - do not modify
        /// the contents of this method with the code editor.
        /// </summary>
        private void InitializeComponent()
```

(continued)

```csharp
        {
        }

        /// <summary>
        /// Clean up any resources being used.
        /// </summary>
        protected override void Dispose( bool disposing )
        {
            if(disposing && components != null)
            {
                components.Dispose();
            }
            base.Dispose(disposing);
        }

        #endregion


        [WebMethod()]
        public DataSet getData()
        {
            DataSet  ds = new DataSet();
            XmlTextReader xmlreader = new XmlTextReader
                (@"C:\temp\Products.xml");
            ds.ReadXml(xmlreader);
            xmlreader.Close();
            System.Threading.Thread.Sleep(3000);
            return ds;
        }

        [WebMethod()]
        public void setData(DataSet ds )
        {
            XmlTextWriter xmlwriter = new XmlTextWriter
                (@"C:\temp\Products.xml", System.Text.Encoding.UTF8);
            ds.WriteXml(xmlwriter, XmlWriteMode.WriteSchema);
            xmlwriter.Close();
            System.Threading.Thread.Sleep(3000);
        }
    }
}
```

4. Select Build Solution from the Build menu.
5. Create a Windows application, called VBApplication or CSApplication, and add the following code for the Form1 class.

Visual Basic .NET

```vbnet
Public Class Form1
    Inherits System.Windows.Forms.Form
```

```vbnet
        Private svcs As localhost.Service1
        Private ds As DataSet

#Region " Windows Form Designer generated code "
    Public Sub New()
        MyBase.New()
        'This call is required by the Windows Form Designer.
        InitializeComponent()
        'Add any initialization after the InitializeComponent() call
    End Sub

    'Form overrides dispose to clean up the component list.
    Protected Overloads Overrides Sub Dispose(ByVal disposing As Boolean)
        If disposing Then
            If Not (components Is Nothing) Then
                components.Dispose()
            End If
        End If
        MyBase.Dispose(disposing)
    End Sub

    'Required by the Windows Form Designer
    Private components As System.ComponentModel.IContainer

    'NOTE: This procedure is required by the Windows Form Designer
    'It can be modified using the Windows Form Designer.
    'Do not modify it using the code editor.
    Friend WithEvents DataGrid1 As System.Windows.Forms.DataGrid
    Friend WithEvents TextBox1 As System.Windows.Forms.TextBox
    Friend WithEvents getDataSync_Button As System.Windows.Forms.Button
    Friend WithEvents getDataAsync_Button As System.Windows.Forms.Button
    Friend WithEvents setDataAsync_Button As System.Windows.Forms.Button
    Friend WithEvents setDataSync_Button As System.Windows.Forms.Button
<System.Diagnostics.DebuggerStepThrough()> Private Sub InitializeComponent()
        Me.getDataSync_Button = New System.Windows.Forms.Button()
        Me.getDataAsync_Button = New System.Windows.Forms.Button()
        Me.DataGrid1 = New System.Windows.Forms.DataGrid()
        Me.TextBox1 = New System.Windows.Forms.TextBox()
        Me.setDataAsync_Button = New System.Windows.Forms.Button()
        Me.setDataSync_Button = New System.Windows.Forms.Button()
CType(Me.DataGrid1, System.ComponentModel.ISupportInitialize).BeginInit()
        Me.SuspendLayout()
        '
        'getDataSync_Button
        '
        Me.getDataSync_Button.Location = New System.Drawing.Point(8, 24)
        Me.getDataSync_Button.Name = "getDataSync_Button"
        Me.getDataSync_Button.Size = New System.Drawing.Size(160, 23)
```

(continued)

```vb
Me.getDataSync_Button.TabIndex = 0
Me.getDataSync_Button.Text = "getData Synchronously"
'
'getDataAsync_Button
'
Me.getDataAsync_Button.Location = _
    New System.Drawing.Point(192, 24)
Me.getDataAsync_Button.Name = "getDataAsync_Button"
Me.getDataAsync_Button.Size = New System.Drawing.Size(160, 23)
Me.getDataAsync_Button.TabIndex = 1
Me.getDataAsync_Button.Text = "getData Asynchronously"
'
'DataGrid1
'
Me.DataGrid1.DataMember = ""
Me.DataGrid1.HeaderForeColor = _
    System.Drawing.SystemColors.ControlText
Me.DataGrid1.Location = New System.Drawing.Point(8, 72)
Me.DataGrid1.Name = "DataGrid1"
Me.DataGrid1.Size = New System.Drawing.Size(232, 168)
Me.DataGrid1.TabIndex = 2
'
'TextBox1
'
Me.TextBox1.Location = New System.Drawing.Point(248, 72)
Me.TextBox1.Multiline = True
Me.TextBox1.Name = "TextBox1"
Me.TextBox1.Size = New System.Drawing.Size(100, 168)
Me.TextBox1.TabIndex = 3
Me.TextBox1.Text = ""
'
'setDataAsync_Button
'
Me.setDataAsync_Button.Location = _
    New System.Drawing.Point(196, 272)
Me.setDataAsync_Button.Name = "setDataAsync_Button"
Me.setDataAsync_Button.Size = New System.Drawing.Size(160, 23)
Me.setDataAsync_Button.TabIndex = 5
Me.setDataAsync_Button.Text = "setData Asynchronously"
'
'setDataSync_Button
'
Me.setDataSync_Button.Location = New System.Drawing.Point(12, 272)
Me.setDataSync_Button.Name = "setDataSync_Button"
Me.setDataSync_Button.Size = New System.Drawing.Size(160, 23)
Me.setDataSync_Button.TabIndex = 4
Me.setDataSync_Button.Text = "setData Synchronously"
```

```
        '
        'Form1
        '
        Me.AutoScaleBaseSize = New System.Drawing.Size(5, 13)
        Me.ClientSize = New System.Drawing.Size(368, 309)
        Me.Controls.AddRange(New System.Windows.Forms.Control() _
        {Me.setDataAsync_Button, Me.setDataSync_Button, Me.TextBox1, _
        Me.DataGrid1, Me.getDataAsync_Button, Me.getDataSync_Button})
        Me.Name = "Form1"
        Me.Text = "Form1"
CType(Me.DataGrid1, System.ComponentModel.ISupportInitialize).EndInit()
        Me.ResumeLayout(False)

    End Sub

#End Region

    Private Sub Form1_Load(ByVal sender As System.Object, _
    ByVal e As System.EventArgs) Handles MyBase.Load
        svcs = New localhost.Service1()
        ds = New DataSet()
    End Sub

    Private Sub getDataSync_Button_Click(ByVal sender As System.Object, _
    ByVal e As System.EventArgs) Handles getDataSync_Button.Click
        DataGrid1.DataSource = Nothing
        DataGrid1.Refresh()
        ds = svcs.getData
        DataGrid1.DataSource = ds
    End Sub

    Private Sub getDataAsync_Button_Click(ByVal sender As System.Object, _
    ByVal e As System.EventArgs) Handles getDataAsync_Button.Click
        DataGrid1.DataSource = Nothing
        ds = Nothing
        Dim cb As New AsyncCallback(AddressOf Me.callback1)
        Dim ar As IAsyncResult = svcs.BegingetData(cb, svcs)
    End Sub

    Private Sub setDataSync_Button_Click(ByVal sender As System.Object, _
    ByVal e As System.EventArgs) Handles setDataSync_Button.Click
        svcs.setData(ds)
    End Sub

    Private Sub setDataAsync_Button_Click(ByVal sender As System.Object, _
    ByVal e As System.EventArgs) Handles setDataAsync_Button.Click
        Dim cb As New AsyncCallback(AddressOf Me.callback2)
        Dim ar As IAsyncResult = svcs.BeginsetData(ds, cb, svcs)
    End Sub
```

(continued)

```
        Public Sub callback1(ByVal ar As IAsyncResult)
            ds = svcs.EndgetData(ar)
            MsgBox("Data Received Asynchronously." & _
            "Click the DataGrid to display the data!")
        End Sub

        Public Sub callback2(ByVal ar As IAsyncResult)
            MsgBox("Changes applied successfully!")
        End Sub

        Private Sub DataGrid1_Click(ByVal sender As Object, _
        ByVal e As System.EventArgs) Handles DataGrid1.Click
            DataGrid1.DataSource = ds
        End Sub
    End Class
```

Visual C#

```csharp
using System;
using System.Drawing;
using System.Collections;
using System.ComponentModel;
using System.Windows.Forms;
using System.Data;

namespace CSApplication
{
    /// <summary>
    /// Summary description for Form1.
    /// </summary>
    public class Form1 : System.Windows.Forms.Form
    {
    internal System.Windows.Forms.Button setDataAsync_Button;
    internal System.Windows.Forms.Button setDataSync_Button;
    internal System.Windows.Forms.TextBox TextBox1;
    internal System.Windows.Forms.DataGrid DataGrid1;
    internal System.Windows.Forms.Button getDataAsync_Button;
    internal System.Windows.Forms.Button getDataSync_Button;
    /// <summary>
    /// Required designer variable.
    /// </summary>
    private System.ComponentModel.Container components = null;
    private localhost.Service1 svcs;
    private DataSet ds;

    public Form1()
    {
    InitializeComponent();
```

```
        }

        /// <summary>
        /// Clean up any resources being used.
        /// </summary>
        protected override void Dispose( bool disposing )
        {
            if( disposing )
            {
                if (components != null)
                {
                    components.Dispose();
                }
            }
            base.Dispose( disposing );
        }

        #region Windows Form Designer generated code
        /// <summary>
        /// Required method for Designer support - do not modify
        /// the contents of this method with the code editor.
        /// </summary>
        private void InitializeComponent()
        {
            this.setDataAsync_Button = new System.Windows.Forms.Button();
            this.setDataSync_Button = new System.Windows.Forms.Button();
            this.TextBox1 = new System.Windows.Forms.TextBox();
            this.DataGrid1 = new System.Windows.Forms.DataGrid();
            this.getDataAsync_Button = new System.Windows.Forms.Button();
            this.getDataSync_Button = new System.Windows.Forms.Button();
            ((System.ComponentModel.ISupportInitialize)
                (this.DataGrid1)).BeginInit();
            this.SuspendLayout();
            //
            // setDataAsync_Button
            //
            this.setDataAsync_Button.Location =
                new System.Drawing.Point(210, 279);
            this.setDataAsync_Button.Name = "setDataAsync_Button";
            this.setDataAsync_Button.Size = new System.Drawing.Size(160, 23);
            this.setDataAsync_Button.TabIndex = 11;
            this.setDataAsync_Button.Text = "setData Asynchronously";
            this.setDataAsync_Button.Click +=
                new System.EventHandler(this.setDataAsync_Button_Click);
            //
            // setDataSync_Button
            //
            this.setDataSync_Button.Location = new System.Drawing.Point
                (26, 279);
```

(continued)

```csharp
this.setDataSync_Button.Name = "setDataSync_Button";
this.setDataSync_Button.Size = new System.Drawing.Size(160, 23);
this.setDataSync_Button.TabIndex = 10;
this.setDataSync_Button.Text = "setData Synchronously";
this.setDataSync_Button.Click +=
    new System.EventHandler(this.setDataSync_Button_Click);
//
// TextBox1
//
this.TextBox1.Location = new System.Drawing.Point(262, 79);
this.TextBox1.Multiline = true;
this.TextBox1.Name = "TextBox1";
this.TextBox1.Size = new System.Drawing.Size(100, 168);
this.TextBox1.TabIndex = 9;
this.TextBox1.Text = "";
//
// DataGrid1
//
this.DataGrid1.DataMember = "";
this.DataGrid1.HeaderForeColor =
    System.Drawing.SystemColors.ControlText;
this.DataGrid1.Location = new System.Drawing.Point(22, 79);
this.DataGrid1.Name = "DataGrid1";
this.DataGrid1.Size = new System.Drawing.Size(232, 168);
this.DataGrid1.TabIndex = 8;
this.DataGrid1.Click  +=
    new System.EventHandler(this.DataGrid1_Click);
//
// getDataAsync_Button
//
this.getDataAsync_Button.Location =
    new System.Drawing.Point(206, 31);
this.getDataAsync_Button.Name = "getDataAsync_Button";
this.getDataAsync_Button.Size = new System.Drawing.Size(160, 23);
this.getDataAsync_Button.TabIndex = 7;
this.getDataAsync_Button.Text = "getData Asynchronously";
this.getDataAsync_Button.Click +=
    new System.EventHandler(this.getDataAsync_Button_Click);
//
// getDataSync_Button
//
this.getDataSync_Button.Location =
    new System.Drawing.Point(22, 31);
this.getDataSync_Button.Name = "getDataSync_Button";
this.getDataSync_Button.Size = new System.Drawing.Size(160, 23);
this.getDataSync_Button.TabIndex = 6;
this.getDataSync_Button.Text = "getData Synchronously";
this.getDataSync_Button.Click +=
    new System.EventHandler(this.getDataSync_Button_Click);
```

```
//
// Form1
//
this.AutoScaleBaseSize = new System.Drawing.Size(5, 13);
this.ClientSize = new System.Drawing.Size(392, 333);
this.Controls.AddRange(new System.Windows.Forms.Control[] {
        this.setDataAsync_Button,
        this.setDataSync_Button,
        this.TextBox1,
        this.DataGrid1,
        this.getDataAsync_Button,
        this.getDataSync_Button});
this.Name = "Form1";
this.Text = "Form1";
this.Load += new System.EventHandler(this.Form1_Load);
((System.ComponentModel.ISupportInitialize)(this.DataGrid1)).EndInit();
this.ResumeLayout(false);
}
#endregion

/// <summary>
/// The main entry point for the application.
/// </summary>
[STAThread]
static void Main()
{
    Application.Run(new Form1());
}
private void Form1_Load(object sender, System.EventArgs e)
{
    svcs = new localhost.Service1();
    ds = new DataSet();
}
private void getDataSync_Button_Click
            (object sender, System.EventArgs e)
{
    DataGrid1.DataSource = null;
    DataGrid1.Refresh();
    ds=svcs.getData();
    DataGrid1.DataSource = ds;
}
private void getDataAsync_Button_Click
            (object sender, System.EventArgs e)
{
    DataGrid1.DataSource = null;
    ds = null;
    AsyncCallback cb = new AsyncCallback(this.callback1);
    IAsyncResult ar   = svcs.BegingetData(cb, svcs);
}
```

(continued)

```
                private void setDataSync_Button_Click
                            (object sender, System.EventArgs e)
                {
                    svcs.setData(ds);
                }
                private void setDataAsync_Button_Click
                            (object sender, System.EventArgs e)
                {
                    AsyncCallback cb = new AsyncCallback( this.callback2);
                    IAsyncResult ar   = svcs.BeginsetData(ds, cb, svcs);
                }
                public void callback1(IAsyncResult ar  )
                {
                    ds   = (DataSet)svcs.EndgetData(ar);
                    MessageBox.Show("Data Received Asynchronously. " +
                        "Click the DataGrid to display the data!");
                }
                public void callback2(IAsyncResult ar  )
                {
                    MessageBox.Show("Changes applied successfully!");
                }
                private void DataGrid1_Click(Object sender, System.EventArgs e)
                {
                    DataGrid1.DataSource = ds;
                }
            }
        }
```

6. Add a Web reference to the http://localhost/VBDataService/Service1.asmx
    or http://localhost/CSDataService/Service1.asmx Web service. To add the Web
    reference, right-click References under the VBApplication or CSApplication
    project and choose Add Web Reference from the shortcut menu. In the Add
    Web Reference dialog box, type **http://localhost/VBDataService/
    Service1.asmx** or **http://localhost/CSDataService/Service1.asmx** and press
    Enter. Click Add Reference after the Web service is displayed under Available
    References.

Note   When you build the service project, Visual Studio .NET creates the synchronous as well as asynchronous versions of the Web methods.

---

7. Select Build Solution from the the Build menu.
8. From the File menu, choose Add New Item to open the Add New Item dialog
    box.
9. Select XML File from the Templates pane, and type **Products.xml** in the Name
    text box. Then add the following code to the Products.xml file.

XML

```
<?xml version="1.0" encoding="utf-8"?>
<Product_cf5 xmlns="http://tempuri.org/Products.xsd">
```

```
<Product>
    <id>1000</id>
    <name>FootBall</name>
    <price>50</price>
</Product>
<Product>
    <id>1001</id>
    <name>BaseBall</name>
    <price>12</price>
</Product>
<Product>
    <id>1002</id>
    <name>Glove</name>
    <price>15</price>
</Product>
<Product>
    <id>1003</id>
    <name>Shoes</name>
    <price>55</price>
</Product>
</Product_cf5 >
```

10. Save the Products.xml file in the C:\temp folder.

11. Run the Windows application. Click the GetData Synchronously button on Form1, and try to work with the interface. You will not be able to interact with the interface until the getData() method of Service1 returns. The interface of the Windows application is shown here.

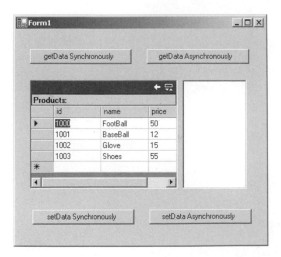

12. Change the product information in the data grid, and click the SetData Synchronously button. Try to work with the interface. You will not be able to interact with the interface until the setData() method of Service1 returns.

13. Now modify the product info in the data grid, and click the SetData Asynchronously button. You can interact with the user interface while the setData() method of the Web service executes asynchronously.

14. Similarly, try executing the getData() method asynchronously by clicking the GetData Asynchronously button. You can interact with the user interface even before the getData() method finishes executing.

Review

The questions in this section reinforce key information presented in this chapter. If you are unable to answer a question, review the appropriate lesson, and then try answering the question again. Answers to the questions can be found in Appendix A, "Questions and Answers."

1. Which property of the WebMethod attribute allows you to maintain the state of objects across sessions in a Web method?

2. What steps do you need to perform to enable transactions in a Web method?

3. When should you use asynchronous programming?

4. Explain how you implement asynchronous programming using callbacks.

5. Which method do you call for the first time when you access an XML Web service or service method with which the SOAP extension is configured to execute?

6. What are the different properties of the <add> XML element?

7. Which element in the Web.config file do you use to manage custom error messages?

8. How can you ensure that only authorized users access your Web service?

C H A P T E R   9

Testing and Debugging XML Web Services

About This Chapter

Testing and debugging is an important task that you perform during the application development life cycle. The Microsoft .NET Framework provides tools that enable you to test and debug your applications before deploying them. In addition, the .NET Framework provides classes that enable you to monitor the application performance and troubleshoot the errors that might occur after the application is deployed. In this chapter, you will learn to develop test plans for your .NET applications. You will also learn to use the debug tools and Trace classes to perform code instrumentation.

Before You Begin

To complete the lessons in this chapter, you

- Must have knowledge of basic programming in Microsoft Visual Basic .NET and Microsoft Visual C#
- Must have completed the previous chapters in this book

Lesson 1: Designing Unit Test Plans

In previous chapters, you learned how to create various types of applications such as Windows services, XML Web services, and console applications. In this lesson, you will learn about testing and why a testing phase should be implemented as part of the software development life cycle. In addition, you will learn about various types of testing.

After this lesson, you will be able to

- Identify the importance of testing your software
- Identify different types of testing
- Develop a test plan

Estimated lesson time: 25 minutes

Overview of the Testing Process

When you develop an application, in addition to meeting the requirements of a customer, you must ensure that the application is defect-free. Therefore, you need to perform various levels of testing on the application. Testing accomplishes a number of tasks, such as checking whether the desired functionality is implemented. However, the most important aspect that testing measures is the quality of the application that you are developing.

For a long time, creating error-free applications has been a high-priority task for many organizations. In fact, organizations implement the testing phase as part of their application development life cycle. The following factors contribute to the importance of testing:

- Testing reduces the cost of developing an application. The cost of rectifying an error after an application has been created is much more than the cost of implementing a thorough testing process as part of the development life cycle.
- Testing ensures that your application performs as specified. In most cases, if testing is not implemented, you cannot actually predict the output of a certain operation. Suppose you create an application that updates a SQL Server database every evening using the data in a DataSet. If you do not test this application, the transaction might not always be successful. To avoid such occurrences, you should test the application thoroughly using various test data. This ensures that your application performs the operations as specified and expected.
- Testing reduces the total cost of ownership. If a software application functions exactly as described in the documentation, users require fewer hours of training and less support from product experts.

- Testing develops customer loyalty and word-of-mouth market share. You are more likely to build a strong customer base with high-quality, bug-free software, which only thorough testing can provide.

To ensure that your application is free of defects and bugs, you can subject your applications to the following types of testing:

- **Requirements testing.**   You perform requirements testing to verify whether your application meets the requirements as specified in the software specification.
- **Usability testing.**   You perform usability testing to test the usability and ease of use of your application. During usability testing, you perform checks to ensure that all the information that users require is provided by the application. In addition, you also perform tests to ensure that the user interface is easily navigable.
- **Unit testing.**   During unit testing, you take the smallest unit of an application and test it to ensure that it functions as expected. The various units that constitute your application are tested separately before they are integrated into modules. To perform unit testing, you create drivers and stubs. A *driver* is a program that simulates a calling unit and a *stub* is program that simulates the called unit.
- **Integration testing.**   During integration testing, you combine the units that have already been tested into a component and test the interface that combines the two units. After successfully testing various units, you combine them into components, test the components, and integrate them into modules. The various modules are then tested and integrated into an application.
- **Regression testing.**   You perform regression testing to ensure that any change made to code that has already been tested does not keep the code from running properly. You perform regression testing by performing the existing tests on the modified code or by creating new tests for the modified code, if necessary.

Organizing the Testing Effort

The earlier you incorporate testing into an application's development process, the better your chances for producing a defect-free application. You need to organize your testing effort carefully so that it is efficient and effective.

It is advisable to develop an application in modules. The modular format enables you to plan for testing the modules separately. This ensures that when the individual modules are arranged in the final application, the entire application is error-free.

The testing process involves testing module interaction and not module execution. Planning is crucial to a successful testing effort because it sets expectations about the outcome of the application's development life cycle. You should also consider the cost, schedule, and performance of the application in test plans. This increases the probability of a successful, effective, and efficient testing process.

Requirements-Based Testing

The first phase of the software development life cycle involves gathering and analyzing requirements. The requirements phase provides the application's necessary features. Requirements also provide the basis for all types of testing. Based on the descriptions in the requirement specification, testing identifies defects that create, cause, or allow unpredictable behavior in the software. Therefore, the test team should also be involved in the specification-writing process.

You should design your test cases while writing the requirements specifications. A *test case* consists of sample data and its corresponding output, which is calculated manually. To design test cases, you need to analyze each specification and determine how well the requirement supports the development of test cases. Developing a test case ensures that you critically analyze the requirement specifications.

Developing a Test Plan

A test plan outlines the entire testing process and includes the individual test cases. A test case includes sample data that is included in the application. The sample data is passed to the application, and the output is verified.

To develop a reliable test plan, you must systematically explore the program to ensure that you cover all the modules thoroughly. A formal test plan establishes a testing process that does not depend upon accidental, random testing.

Approaches to Develop Test Plans

There are two common approaches to testing, the waterfall approach and the evolutionary approach.

Waterfall Approach

The *waterfall* approach to application development and testing consists of various phases, which cover requirements analysis, design and specifications requirements, coding, final testing, and release. Before you begin working on a phase, the work in the preceding phase must have been completed. To the testing team, this means waiting for a final specification and then following the pattern set by the development team. A significant disadvantage of this approach is that it eliminates the opportunity for testing to identify problems early in the process; therefore, this approach is best suited for small projects of limited complexity.

Evolutionary Approach

In the *evolutionary* approach, you develop a modular piece or unit of an application, test it, fix it, and then add another small piece that adds functionality. You then test the two units as an integrated component, increasing the complexity as you proceed. Some of the advantages to this approach are

- You have low-cost opportunities to reappraise requirements and refine the design, as you understand the application better.

- You constantly deliver a working, useful product. If you add functionality in priority order, you can stop development at any time.

- Rather than developing one lengthy test plan, you can start with small, modular pieces of the final test plan. In the interim period, you can use the smaller pieces of the plan to locate bugs.

- You can add new sections to the test plan, explore new areas, and use each part of the plan.

Lesson 2: Overview of Visual Studio .NET Debugging Tools

In the previous lesson, you learned how to design and implement unit test plans. When you test your application by using the test data, you might receive certain errors or bugs in your application. Microsoft Visual Studio .NET provides tools that enable you to locate and identify these bugs and errors in your application. In this lesson, you will learn about the Visual Studio .NET debugging tools and how to use them.

After this lesson, you will be able to

- Describe the Visual Studio .NET debugging process
- Debug Visual Studio .NET applications by using the DbgClr tool
- Debug Visual Studio .NET applications by using the CorDbg tool

Estimated lesson time: 60 minutes

Introduction to the Visual Studio .NET Debugging Process

When you compile and execute the source code for a Visual Studio .NET application, a .NET Framework–compatible compiler compiles the source code to MSIL code. Then, the MSIL code is compiled to native code, which runs on a computer.

However, when you debug a Visual Studio .NET application, the debugger first maps the native code to MSIL, and then maps the MSIL code to source code by using a programmer database (PDB) file. Therefore, to debug a Visual Studio .NET application, you need to create accurate mapping information at each stage in the compilation process. Whenever you enable debugging in a Visual Studio .NET application, you must create a PDB file that maps MSIL to source code. You must also instruct the JIT compiler to map information between MSIL and native code. Visual Studio .NET does all this for you when you set the build configuration to debug.

Visual Studio .NET provides debugging tools, such as DbgClr and CorDbg, to help you locate and remove errors and bugs. The DbgClr tool is a GUI-based tool and the default debugger for Visual Studio .NET.

Alternatively, CorDbg is a command-line debugging tool, which you can run from the command line. Next you'll look at how to debug Visual Studio .NET applications by using these tools.

Debugging Visual Studio .NET Applications Using the DbgClr Tool

To start debugging an application, you choose Start from the Debug menu of Visual Studio .NET, as shown in Figure 9.1.

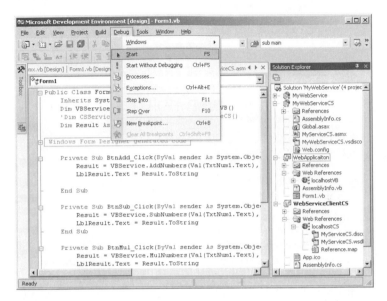

Figure 9.1   The Debug menu

When you choose Start, the application starts and continues to execute until it reaches a breakpoint. When the application reaches a breakpoint, execution of the code is paused and the application enters break mode. In break mode, you can examine values by moving the cursor over an object. In addition, you can modify variables. Figure 9.2 displays a Visual C# application in break mode.

You can also choose the Step Into or Step Over command from the Debug menu. When you choose Step Into or Step Over, the application starts and then enters the breakpoint at the first line of the code. Press the F11 key to continue line-by-line execution of code.

Tip   If your Visual Studio .NET solution contains more than one project, you can select which project is launched first by setting a project as the startup project. To set a project as the startup project, right-click the project and select Set As Startup Project.

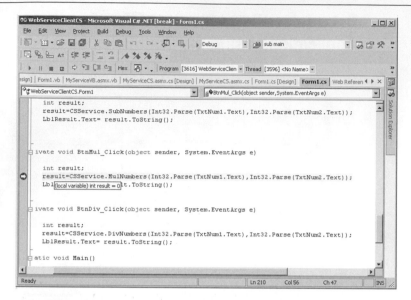

Figure 9.2   A Visual C# application in break mode

In addition to entering breakpoints and viewing the values of variables, the Visual Studio .NET debugger provides various windows and dialog boxes to help you inspect and modify an application. Next you'll look at how you can use these windows and dialog boxes to debug a Visual Studio .NET application.

Watch Window

You can use the Watch window, shown in Figure 9.3, to evaluate variables and expressions and maintain the results. To open the Watch window when an application is in break mode, from the Debug menu, point to Windows and choose Watch. You can also use the Watch window to edit the value of a variable or register. However, you cannot edit the values of constant variables.

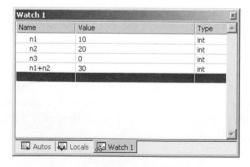

Figure 9.3   The Watch window

To evaluate variables and expressions in the Watch window, perform the following steps:

1. Start the debugger.
2. Double-click an empty row in the Name column in the Watch window.
3. Enter a variable, register, or expression in the row and press Enter. Its value appears in the Value column.

Call Stack Window

You can use the Call Stack window, shown in Figure 9.4, to view the function or procedure calls that are currently on the stack. To open the Call Stack window when an application is in break mode, from the Debug menu, point to Windows and choose Call Stack.

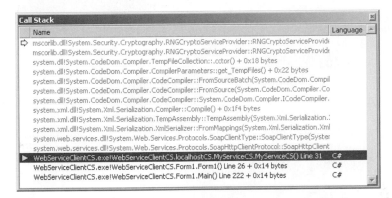

Figure 9.4   The Call Stack window

The Call Stack window displays the name of each function and the language in which it is written. In addition to the function name, the Call Stack window displays optional information, such as module name; line number; byte offset; and parameter names, types, and values. To select which information is displayed in the Call Stack window, right-click in the Call Stack window and choose the appropriate information type.

Locals Window

The Locals window, shown in Figure 9.5, displays variables that are local to the current context. To open the Locals window when the application is in break mode, point to Windows on the Debug menu and choose Locals.

You can also change the values of variables in the Locals window. To change the value of a variable, double-click the value that you want to change and type the new value. However, when you change float values, minor inaccuracies might occur due to decimal-to-binary conversion of fractional components.

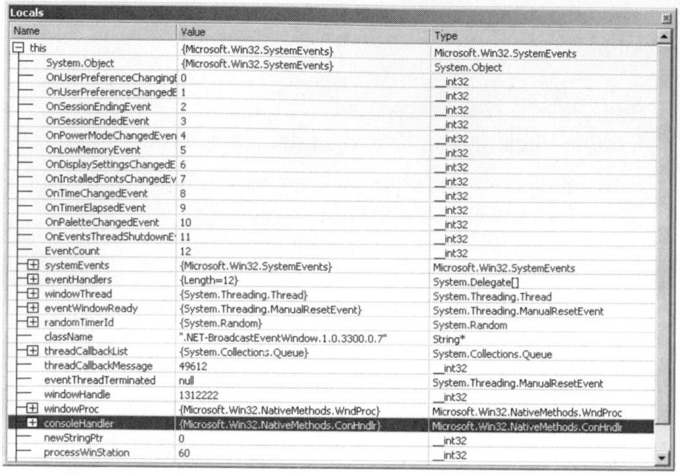

Figure 9.5   The Locals window

Autos Window

You can use the Autos window, shown in Figure 9.6, to view the variables used in the current statement and in the previous statement. However, when you are debugging a Visual Basic .NET application, the Autos window displays variables in the current statement and in the three next and previous statements. When the application is in break mode, you can open the Autos window from the Debug menu by pointing to Windows and clicking Autos.

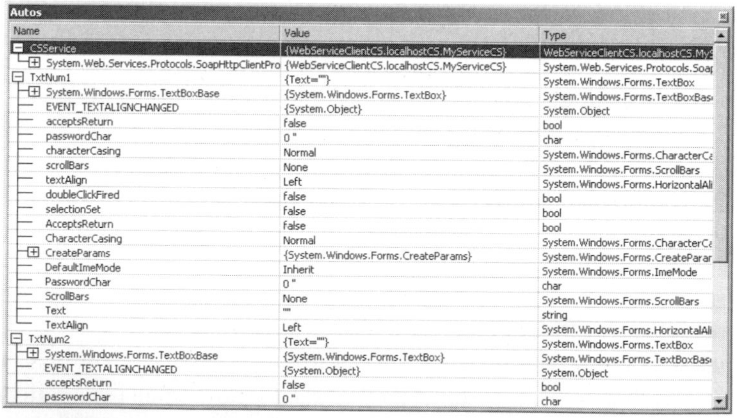

Figure 9.6   The Autos window

Breakpoints Window

Breakpoints are the locations in code where the debugger pauses the execution of a program. When your program and debugger reach a breakpoint, they are said to be in a *break mode*. These are the four types of breakpoints that you can set:

- **Function breakpoint.**   Causes a program to break when execution reaches a specified location in a function.

- **File breakpoint.**   Causes a program to break when execution reaches a specified location within a file.

- **Address breakpoint.**   Causes a program to break when execution reaches a specified memory address.

- **Data breakpoint.**   Causes a program to break when the value of a variable changes.

You can set, enable, disable, edit, or delete breakpoints in the source window, Disassembly window, or the Breakpoints window. To set a breakpoint in the source window, identify the function statement where you want to set the breakpoint and click on the grey margin on the left. Alternatively, you can use the New Breakpoint option from the Debug menu to create a breakpoint.

You can use the Breakpoints window, shown in Figure 9.7, to list all the breakpoints in your Visual Studio .NET application and to display their properties. In addition, you can use the Breakpoints window to delete and set new breakpoints. You can also enable or disable breakpoints and edit the properties of a breakpoint. To open the Breakpoints window, from the Debug menu, point to Windows and choose Breakpoints.

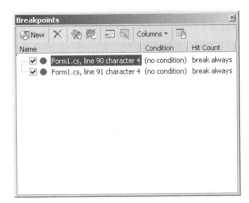

Figure 9.7   The Breakpoints window

The Breakpoints window displays the following three columns by default:

- **Name.**   A descriptive name for the breakpoint, created by the debugger based on the location or other properties of the breakpoint. The Name column enables you to distinguish between breakpoints and select a breakpoint. A check box appears before the name. You can use this check box to enable or disable the breakpoint.

- **Condition.**   An optional property that determines whether the program breaks when a breakpoint is reached. The condition can be any valid expression recognized by the debugger. The debugger evaluates the condition and breaks execution only if the condition is satisfied.

- **Hit Count.**   A property that determines whether your program breaks when the breakpoint is reached. If this property is not set and if the expression shown in the Condition column is satisfied, then the debugger stops each time the breakpoint is hit. The hit count notifies the debugger to break on the nth time when the breakpoint is reached, on every multiple of n hits, or on the nth hit and every time after that.

You can also choose to display the following columns in the Breakpoints window by using the Columns tool from the toolbar:

- **Language.**   Displays the language of the program being debugged.
- **Function.**   Displays the name of the function that contains the current breakpoint.
- **File.**   Displays the name of the file that contains the code of the application being debugged.
- **Address.**   Displays the memory address of the breakpoint.
- **Data.**   Displays the data breakpoint.
- **Program.**   Displays the name of the program being debugged.

Besides the DbgClr debugger you can use the command-line tool, CorDbg, to debug a .NET application.

Debugging .NET Applications Using the CorDbg Tool

In addition to the GUI-based debugging tool DbgClr, the .NET Framework includes a command-line debugging tool, CorDbg.exe, to debug your applications from a command prompt. Unlike DbgClr, CorDbg does not compile applications. Therefore, to use CorDbg you first need to build the application so that it includes the appropriate /debug switch. CorDbg uses the run-time Debug API to debug applications. CorDbg lets you perform the following tasks:

- Start, stop, and resume a running process
- Attach and detach the debugger to applications
- Step into and over source and native code
- Show source-code lines
- Set the value of a variable
- Set the next statement to a new line
- Set or display breakpoints

When you debug an application by using CorDbg, the application is debugged in a new CorDbg session. To start a CorDbg session, you need to type **cordbg** at the Visual Studio .NET Command Prompt. Figure 9.9 displays the CorDbg command prompt.

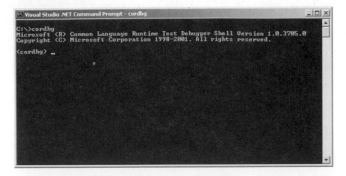

Figure 9.8   The CorDbg command prompt

After the CorDbg command prompt appears, you can specify the application that you want to debug. You can also directly open an application in a CorDbg session by specifying the application file name with the CorDbg command. For example, you can type **cordbg MyConsoleApp.exe** at the Visual Studio .NET Command Prompt. After you start the CorDbg session for an application, you can use additional CorDbg commands to perform such debugging tasks as setting breakpoints, stepping into code, and viewing the values of variables. Table 9.1 describes the commonly used CorDbg commands.

Table 9.1   Commonly Used CorDbg Commands

Command	Description
a *<pid>*	You use this command to attach the debugger to a running application. You need to specify the Process ID (*pid*) of the application you want to debug.
b [[*file:*] *line number*] | [[*class::*] *function* [*:offset*]]	You use this command to set and display breakpoints in an application. If you do not specify any arguments, CorDbg displays a list of current breakpoints. You can set a breakpoint at a line number in the current source file.
con [*number of times to continue*]	You use this command to continue the program. If you do not specify an argument, the program continues once. However, if you specify an argument, the program continues the specified number of times.
del [*breakpoint id*]	You use this command to delete breakpoints. If you do not specify any arguments, all current breakpoints are deleted. However, you can specify the *breakpoint id* of the breakpoints you want to delete, as arguments.
de	You use this command to detach the debugger from the current process.

(continued)

Table 9.1   Commonly Used CorDbg Commands *(continued)*

Command	Description
d [*number of frames*]	You use this command to move the stack frame pointer down the stack toward frames called by the current frame for inspection purposes. If you do not specify an argument, the stack frame pointer moves down one frame. However, you can specify the number of frames you want the pointer to move as an argument to the command.
ex	You can use this command to stop the current process and exit CorDbg.
l [mod|cl|fu]	You can use this command to display the list of modules, classes, and global functions that are currently loaded. You can specify mod, cl, or fu to display the list of modules, classes, and global functions, respectively.
n [*number of lines*]	You use this command to step the program to the next line of the source code. If you do not specify an argument, CorDbg steps one source line. However, you can specify the number of lines you want to step as an argument.
o [*count*]	You use this command to step the program out of the current function. If you do not specify an argument, CorDbg performs a step out once for the current function. However, you can specify the number of times you want CorDbg to perform a step out.
p [*variable name*]	You use this command to display the value of local variables along with their values. You specify the variable name whose value you want to examine as an argument. However, if you do not specify an argument, the tool displays all local variables and their values.
set *variable value*	You use this command to set the value of a variable. This command takes a variable name and the value as parameter.
s [*count*]	You use this command to step the program to the next line in the source code. You can specify the number of lines you want to step as an argument. However, if you do not specify an argument, the program steps to the next line.

Though you would use the Visual Studio .NET debugger to debug your applications most of the time, you can use the CorDbg tool to learn how to use the debugging services of the common language runtime. The CorDbg tool uses the run-time Debug API to provide debugging services and the source code for the CorDbg tool is shipped with Visual Studio .NET. You can examine the source code to learn how to use the Debug API.

Debugging XML Web Services in Visual Studio .NET

You can debug XML Web services during development or after the XML Web services are deployed. To debug an XML Web service during development, you need to perform the following steps:

1. From the Visual Studio .NET File menu, point to New, and click Project to open the New Project dialog box.

2. In the New Project dialog box, select Visual Basic Projects or Visual C# Projects from the Project Types pane. Select ASP.NET Web Service from the Templates pane.

3. Right-click in the Designer window, and choose View Code from the shortcut menu to open the Code View window.

4. Type the following code for your XML Web service to perform simple arithmetic operations.

Visual Basic .NET

```
Public Class MathService
    Inherits System.Web.Services.WebService
' Web Services Designer Generated Code Goes Here
    .
    .
    .

    <WebMethod()> Public Function add(ByVal n1 As Integer, _
        ByVal n2 As Integer) As Integer
        Return n1 + n2
    End Function

    <WebMethod()> Public Function subtract(ByVal n1 As Integer, _
        ByVal n2 As Integer) As Integer
        Return n1 - n2
    End Function

    <WebMethod()> Public Function multiply(ByVal n1 As Integer, _
        ByVal n2 As Integer) As Integer
        Return n1 * n2
    End Function

    <WebMethod()> Public Function divide(ByVal n1 As Integer, _
    ByVal n2 As Integer) As Double
        Return n1 / n2
    End Function
End Class
```

Visual C#

```csharp
public class MathService : System.Web.Services.WebService
    {
        public MathService()
        {
            //CODEGEN: This call is required by the ASP.NET Web Services
            //Designer
            InitializeComponent();
        }
        // Component Generated Code Goes Here
        .
        .
        .

        [WebMethod()] public int add(int n1 ,int  n2 )
        {
            return n1 + n2;
        }

        [WebMethod()] public int subtract(int n1 ,int  n2 )
        {
            return n1 - n2;
        }

        [WebMethod()] public int multiply(int n1 ,int  n2 )
        {
            return n1 * n2;
        }

        [WebMethod()] public double divide(int n1 ,int  n2 )
        {
            return n1 / n2;
        }
    }
```

5. From the Build menu, choose Build Solution to compile the XML Web service.

6. In the Code View window, set a breakpoint on the following code line.

Visual Basic .NET

```vbnet
<WebMethod()> Public Function divide(ByVal n1 As Integer, _
    ByVal n2 As Integer) As Double
```

Visual C#

```csharp
[WebMethod()] public double divide(int n1 ,int  n2 )
```

7. From the Debug menu, choose Start. Internet Explorer displays the Web methods of the XML Web service, as shown next.

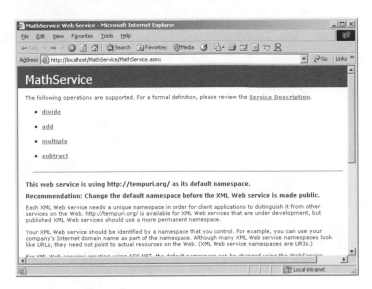

8. Click the Divide link. A new page is displayed where you can test the divide method.

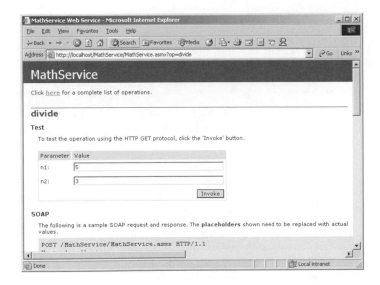

9. Type the values for the n1 and n2 parameters, and click the Invoke button. The debugger breaks the execution at the breakpoint, as shown here for Visual Basic .NET.

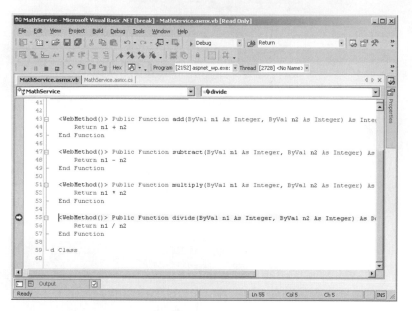

10. From the Debug menu, point to Windows, Watch, and then click Watch1. In the Watch1 window, type the expression **n1/n2** in the Name column, and press Enter. The result of the expression is displayed in the Value column.

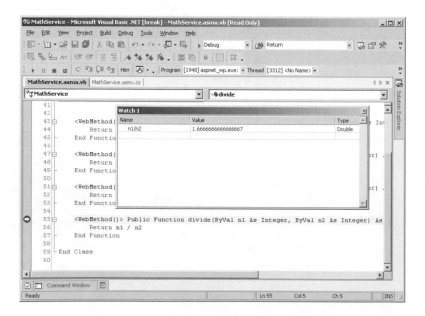

11. You can also use the other debug windows, such as Locals and Autos, to view the variables and their values.

12. To stop debugging, choose Stop Debugging from the Debug menu.

You can also debug an XML Web service after it has been deployed. To debug a deployed XML Web service, you need to perform the following steps:

1. Open the XML Web service in Internet Explorer by entering the URL for the .asmx file, such as http://localhost/MathService/MathService.asmx.

2. From the Debug menu in Visual Studio .NET, choose Processes to open the Processes dialog box.

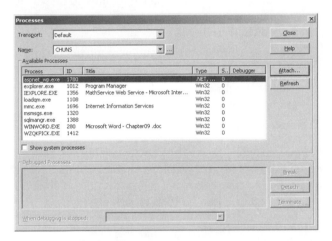

3. Select aspnet_wp.exe from the Process list and click the Attach button, which opens the Attach To Process dialog box, shown here.

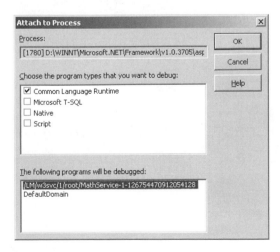

4. In the Attach To Process dialog box, select Common Language Runtime as the program type to debug and select the program that you want to debug, in this case MathService. Click OK, and then click the Close button to close the Processes dialog box.

5. From the File menu in Visual Studio .NET, point to Open, and click File. In the Open File dialog box, select the code-behind file, such as the MathService.asmx.vb or MathService.asmx.cs file, located in the Inetpub\Wwwroot\MathService folder.

6. Set breakpoint(s) in the code. In the MathService example, set a breakpoint on the line containing the divide method.

7. In Internet Explorer, click the Divide link to display a new page where you can pass parameters to the divide method. Pass the values for the n1 and n2 parameters, and click the Invoke button.

   The debugger breaks the execution at the breakpoint set on the line containing the divide method.

8. Use debug windows such as Autos, Locals, and Watch to examine the variables and their values.

9. To stop debugging, choose Stop Debugging from the Debug menu.

Whether you debug an XML Web service during development or after the XML Web service is deployed, you must enable debugging for the Web service using the Web.config file. The following segment of the Web.config file shows how to enable debugging for an XML Web service.

XML (Visual Basic .NET)

```
<?xml version="1.0" encoding="utf-8" ?>
<configuration>
    <system.web>
        <compilation defaultLanguage="vb" debug="true" />
    </system.web>
</configuration>
```

XML (Visual C#)

```
<?xml version="1.0" encoding="utf-8" ?>
<configuration>
    <system.web>
        <compilation defaultLanguage="c#" debug="true" />
    </system.web>
</configuration>
```

Lesson 3: Code Instrumentation

Code instrumentation refers to the task of including code in programs to monitor the performance of .NET applications. You use code instrumentation to display messages or write to event logs in case of a failure during the execution of an application at run time. In this lesson, you will learn how to use code instrumentation to monitor the execution of applications at run time. In addition you will also learn how to write error-handling code in your applications.

After this lesson, you will be able to

- Describe code instrumentation
- Use tracing to monitor applications
- Use trace switches to filter tracing messages
- Use exception handling

Estimated lesson time: 35 minutes

Overview of Code Instrumentation

When you build .NET applications using Visual Studio .NET or command line compilers, you can compile applications into a debug build or a release build. You use the debug build option to troubleshoot logical errors during the application development phase. When you compile an application into a debug build, the compiler creates debug symbols for the application. These debug symbols allow the common language runtime to map native code to source code. However, when you compile applications into a release build, the compiler does not create debug symbols. Therefore, you cannot debug an application that you created using the release build option.

Code instrumentation enables you to monitor and examine an application while developing it or after deploying it. Code instrumentation includes the following tasks:

- **Debugging.**   This process enables you to troubleshoot programming and logical errors in code. You use debugging tools, such as Cordbg.exe or DbgClr.exe, to debug applications. These tools are described in Lesson 2.
- **Tracing.**   Using this procedure, you can collect information about code execution at run time. You use tracing information to troubleshoot an application after it is deployed.
- **Writing to performance counters and event logs.**   With counters and logs you can collect and analyze performance-related data to monitor the performance of applications. Event logs enable you to log information about the events that occur during the execution of an application. Performance counters and event logs are described in Chapter 2, "Creating and Managing Windows Services."

Using Tracing to Instrument Code

You use tracing to monitor the execution of applications while they are running. You can include trace instrumentation in a .NET application while you are developing the application. Tracing enables you to record information in various log files about the errors that might occur at run time. You can analyze these log files to find the cause of errors.

During application development, the Trace and Debug classes of the .NET Framework enable you to monitor and examine an application. This enables you to enhance the efficiency of an application. While creating an application, you can use the output methods of the Debug class to display messages in the Output window of the Visual Studio IDE, as shown in Figure 9.9.

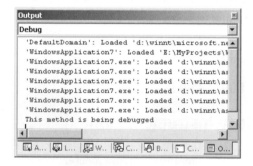

Figure 9.9   The Output window

However, you cannot use the Debug class to monitor your application if you used the release build option to compile the application. In such a case, you use the Trace class instead. You also use the Trace class to implement tracing in your code.

There are three phases in tracing code:

- **Instrumentation.**   In this phase, you add trace instructions to the application.
- **Tracing.**   In this phase, you execute tracing instructions and write trace information to the specified target.
- **Analysis.**   In this phase, you analyze tracing information to identify the cause of bugs and errors in an application.

You use listeners to collect the output of tracing. A *listener* accepts the output generated by tracing and writes the output to devices, such as windows, event logs, or log files. When you create a trace listener, you add it to the Trace.Listeners collection. This enables a listener to receive the output generated by tracing. There are three different types of listeners that you can use in applications:

- **TextWriterTraceListener.**   This listener enables you to write messages to an object of the TextWriter class. You can write a message to output targets such as files, consoles, or any other Stream objects.

- **EventLogTraceListener.**   This listener enables you to write messages to event logs.
- **DefaultTraceListener.**   This listener enables you to send debug messages to the Output window of Visual Studio .NET or to a message box. Default-TraceListener is automatically added to the Trace.Listeners collection.

You use specific methods to write the output to trace listeners. Table 9.2 describes the trace methods that you use to write the output of trace instrumentation.

Table 9.2   Trace Methods

Method	Description
Assert	This method produces an output only if the condition that you specify as an argument in the Assert statement is False. This method returns the specified text string. If you do not specify any text string, it returns the Call Stack.
Fail	This method returns the specified text string. If you do not specify any text string, it returns the Call Stack.
Write	This method writes the specified text string to the target output.
WriteIf	This method produces an output only if the condition that you specify in the WriteIf statement is True. This method returns the specified text string.
WriteLine	This method returns the specified text string and a carriage return.
WriteLineIf	This method produces an output only if the condition that you specify in the WriteLineIf statement is True. This method returns the specified text string and a carriage return.

Tracing usually generates a lot of information that might not be useful for the users of the application. You require tracing information only when you need to trouble-shoot an application. You use trace switches to enable, disable, and filter tracing output in an application. You can configure trace switches using the .config file. You should disable tracing when users are working with applications. When users report problems and you want to troubleshoot an application, you should stop the application, enable tracing using the .config file, and restart the application to gather tracing information.

You use the BooleanSwitch and the TraceSwitch classes to create switch objects in your code. You use the BooleanSwitch class if you want to allow or disallow trace messages to appear in the target output. The TraceSwitch class allows you to define your own debugging messages and associate them with different trace levels defined by the properties that include the TraceSwitch.Off, TraceSwitch.TraceError, TraceSwitch.TraceWarning, TraceSwitch.TraceInfo, and TraceSwitch.Trace-Verbose properties. By default, the BooleanSwitch class is disabled, indicated by an integer value of 0, and the TraceSwitch property is set to TraceSwitch.Off. Table 9.3 shows various properties of the TraceSwitch class and the messages that are sent to the target output.

Table 9.3   TraceSwitch Properties

Enumerated value	Integer value	Type of message displayed
Off	0	None
Error	1	Only error messages
Warning	2	Warning and error messages
Info	3	Informational, warning, and error messages
Verbose	4	Verbose, informational, warning, and error messages

To add tracing code to your Windows application, perform the following tasks:

1. Identify the type of tracing output for your Windows application after you deploy the application. The following code shows how to use TextWriter-TraceListener in your application.

Visual Basic .NET

```
' Create a text file to write messages to
Dim traceLog as New System.IO.FileStream("C:\traceLog.txt", _
    IO.FileMode.OpenOrCreate)
' Create a TextWriterTraceListener
Dim traceListener As New TextWriterTraceListener(traceLog)
' Add the traceListener to the Trace.Listeners collection
Trace.Listeners.Add(traceListener)
```

Visual C#

```
// Create a text file to write messages to
System.IO.FileStream traceLog = new System.IO.FileStream(
    "C:\\traceLog.txt", System.IO.FileMode.OpenOrCreate);
// Create a TextWriterTraceListener
TextWriterTraceListener traceListener = new
    TextWriterTraceListener(traceLog);
// Add the traceListener to the Trace.Listeners collection
Trace.Listeners.Add(traceListener);
```

2. Create TraceSwitch objects in your application. The following code shows how to add trace switches to your application.

Visual Basic .NET

```
Dim Switch1 As New BooleanSwitch("DataSwitch", "Data Access module")
Dim Switch2 as New TraceSwitch("GeneralSwitch", "Entire application")
```

Visual C#

```
BooleanSwitch Switch1 = new BooleanSwitch("DataSwitch ",
    "Data Access module");
TraceSwitch Switch2 = new TraceSwitch("GeneralSwitch ",
    "Entire application");
```

3. Configure TraceSwitch. From the Project menu, choose Add New Item.

4. For Visual Basic .NET projects, in the Add New Item dialog box, choose Application Configuration File. The application configuration file is created and opened. This is an XML document whose root element is <configuration>. For Visual C# projects, in the Add New Item dialog box, choose XML File. Name this file app.config. In the XML editor, after the XML declaration, add the following XML:

```
<configuration>
</configuration>
```

This file should reside in the main project directory.

5. Between the <configuration> and </configuration> tags, add the appropriate XML to configure switches. The following example shows a BooleanSwitch named DataSwitch and a TraceSwitch named GeneralSwitch.

```
<system.diagnostics>
<switches>
    <add name="DataSwitch" value="0" />
    <add name="GeneralSwitch" value="0" />
</switches>
</system.diagnostics>
```

In this configuration, both switches are off.

6. Compile and deploy the application.

7. Use the .config file to turn on tracing if users report a problem with the application at run time.

Exception Handling

One of the ways you can handle errors at run time is by writing error-handling code within your programs. The .NET Framework provides a structured exception-handling mechanism for this purpose. Exception handling enables you to prevent a program from stopping abnormally when an error occurs at run time. With the structured exception-handling mechanism that the .NET Framework provides, you can identify the cause of a run-time error and take appropriate action. For example, an attempt to read from a nonexistent file causes a run-time error, which stops the program abnormally. However, with exception handling you can take appropriate actions, such as asking a user to provide a valid file name.

To implement exception handling, you use a try…catch block. Any code that is expected to cause a run-time error should be enclosed or written within a try...catch block. The following code shows the use of the try…catch block.

Visual Basic .NET

```
Imports System.IO

Module Module1
```

(continued)

```vb
    Sub Main()
        Console.WriteLine("Enter the file to read")
        Dim fn As String
        fn = Console.ReadLine()
        readFile(fn)
        Console.WriteLine("Press any key to exit")
        Console.Read()
    End Sub

    Private Sub readFile(ByVal file As String)
        Try
            Dim stream As New StreamReader(file)
            ' If the file does not exist, the above
            ' statement will cause an exception
            ' and the following statements between the Try and Catch
            ' block will not be executed and the control will move to
            ' the catch block.
            Dim data As String = stream.ReadToEnd()
            Console.WriteLine(data)
        Catch e As Exception
            ' Take appropriate action.
            ' Ask the user to give a correct file name.
            Console.WriteLine("Please enter the correct file name")
            Dim f As String
            f = Console.ReadLine()
            readFile(f)
        End Try
    End Sub
End Module
```

Visual C#

```csharp
using System;
using System.IO;

class Class1
{
    [STAThread]
    static void Main(string[] args)
    {
        Console.WriteLine("Enter the file to read");
        String fn ;
        fn = Console.ReadLine();
        readFile(fn);
        Console.WriteLine("Press any key to exit");
        Console.Read();
    }

    private static void readFile(String file  )
    {
        try
```

```
        {
            StreamReader stream = new StreamReader(file);
            // If the file does not exist, the above
            // statement will cause an exception
            // and the following statements between the try and catch
            // block will not be executed and the control will
            // move to the catch block.
            String data  = stream.ReadToEnd();
            Console.WriteLine(data);
        }
        catch (Exception e  )
        {
            // Take appropriate action.
            // Ask the user to give a correct file name.
            Console.WriteLine("Please enter the correct file name");
            String f ;
            f = Console.ReadLine();
            readFile(f);
        }
    }
}
```

The previous examples use a single catch block to handle exceptions. However, you can use multiple catch blocks to handle exceptions of different types. For example, you can use a catch block to handle IOException exceptions, and a catch block to handle arithmetic exceptions. In addition to the catch blocks, you can also use a finally block, which is executed at the end of a try...catch block. The following code shows how to use multiple catch blocks along with a finally block.

Visual Basic .NET

```
Imports System.IO

Module Module1

    Sub Main()
        Console.WriteLine("Enter the file to read")
        Dim fn As String
        fn = Console.ReadLine()
        readFile(fn)
        Console.WriteLine("Press any key to exit")
        Console.Read()
    End Sub

    Private Sub readFile(ByVal file As String)
        Try
            Dim stream As New StreamReader(file)
            ' If the file does not exist, the above
            ' statement will cause an IOException
            ' and the following statements between Try and Catch
```

(continued)

```vbnet
            ' will not be executed and the control will move to the
            ' catch block that handles IOException.
            Dim data As String = stream.ReadToEnd()
            Console.WriteLine(data)

            Console.WriteLine("File successfully read")
            Console.WriteLine()
            Console.WriteLine("Enter value for n1")
            ' The following statements can cause ArithmeticException.
            ' If the ArithmeticException occurs the control will go to
            ' the Catch block that handles ArithmeticException.
            Dim n1 As Integer = CInt(Console.ReadLine())
            Console.WriteLine("Enter value for n2")
            Dim n2 As Integer = CInt(Console.ReadLine())
            Dim result As Double = n1 / n2
            Console.WriteLine("Result of n1/n2 is " & result.ToString)

        Catch IO_e As IOException
            ' Handle IOException.
            ' Ask the user to give a correct file name.
            Console.WriteLine("Please enter the correct file name")
            Dim f As String
            f = Console.ReadLine()
            readFile(f)

        Catch Ar_e As ArithmeticException
            Console.WriteLine("Arithmetic Exception " & Ar_e.Message)
        Catch e As Exception
            Console.WriteLine("Error: " & e.Message)
        Finally
            Console.WriteLine("readFile() method executed")
        End Try

    End Sub

End Module
```

Visual C#

```csharp
using System;
using System.IO;

class Class1
{

    [STAThread]
    static void Main(string[] args)
    {
        Console.WriteLine("Enter the file to read");
        String fn ;
```

```
        fn = Console.ReadLine();
        readFile(fn);
        Console.WriteLine("Press any key to exit");
        Console.Read();
}

    private static void readFile(String file  )
{

    try
    {
        StreamReader stream = new StreamReader(file);
        // If the file does not exist, the above
        // statement will cause an IOException
        // and the following statements between try and catch
        // will not be executed and the control will move to the
        // catch block that handles IOException.
        String data  = stream.ReadToEnd();
        Console.WriteLine(data);
        Console.WriteLine("File successfully read");
        Console.WriteLine();
        Console.WriteLine("Enter value for n1");
        // The following statements can cause ArithmeticException.
        // If the ArithmeticException occurs the control will go to
        // the catch block that handles ArithmeticException.
        int n1   = int.Parse(Console.ReadLine());
        Console.WriteLine("Enter value for n2");
        int n2   =int.Parse(Console.ReadLine());
        int result  = n1 / n2;
        Console.WriteLine("Result of n1/n2 is " +
            result.ToString());
        }
    catch (IOException IO_e  )
    {
        // Handle IOException.
        // Ask the user to give a correct file name.
        Console.WriteLine("Please enter the correct file name");
        String f ;
        f = Console.ReadLine();
        readFile(f);
    }
    catch (ArithmeticException Ar_e)
    {
        Console.WriteLine("Arithmetic Exception " + Ar_e.Message);
    }
    catch (Exception e)
    {
        Console.WriteLine("Error: " + e.Message);
    }
    finally
    {
```

(continued)

```
                        Console.WriteLine("readFile() method executed");
            }
        }
    }
```

When an exception occurs inside a try block, it is handled by the corresponding catch block if one is there, otherwise, the generic catch block (the one that takes an Exception object as an argument) handles the exception. The generic catch block can handle all the exceptions and must be the last in the sequence of different catch blocks. Whether an exception occurs or not, the code inside the finally block is always executed.

Lesson 4: Creating and Testing Multicultural Satellite Assemblies and Test Data

In the previous lesson, you learned how to debug applications and use tracing to instrument your code. In this lesson, you will learn to use multicultural satellite assemblies.

After this lesson, you will be able to

- Create satellite assemblies
- Install satellite assemblies

Estimated lesson time: 30 minutes

Overview of Satellite Assemblies

When you are creating applications for global users, you need to perform two tasks: globalization and localization. Globalization is the process of enabling your application to accept, process, and display various types of scripts, data formats, and languages. At the end of the globalization process, the language of the user interface is changed. *Localization* is the process of changing the language of the user interface and separating culture-specific data from the application. The data that is specific to a particular culture is stored separately in assemblies called satellite assemblies. Though the satellite assemblies are part of the same application, they are not compiled into the main assembly. This ensures that when you need to add cultures to your application, you need not make any changes to the source code of the application but only to the set of resources that are available. To be used worldwide, your application should contain culture-specific information such as language, fonts, colors, styles, and number and date formats.

If you address the globalization and localization issues during the design phase of the application, the quality of the localized applications increases. In addition, you can decrease the amount of time and money spent to localize your application later.

Culture-specific data is stored in resource files. To create and implement culture-specific applications, the .NET Framework uses the hub-and-spoke model. You also use this model to package and deploy the resources files. In the hub-and-spoke model, the hub is the main assembly that contains the non-localized executable code and the resources for a single, global culture. This culture is called the default or neutral culture. If an application cannot find the culture specified by the user, it uses the default culture. For example, suppose that you are developing an Internet banking application for customers worldwide. You open a branch in Tokyo and want to extend your Internet banking application to support the Japanese culture and language. If your application is unable to locate the culture-specific data, the application will use the default culture-specific information. This is essential for the application to continue functioning and remain online.

The spokes of the hub-and-spoke model connect the main assembly to satellite assemblies that contain resources for all the cultures you want your application to provide. These satellite assemblies do not contain any executable code.

The hub-and-spoke model offers several advantages:

- You can add new resources to the application after deploying it. Developing new culture-specific data requires significant time and money. Therefore, you can release the base application with a default culture and create additional cultures later.
- You can update the satellite assemblies of an application without recompiling the main assembly.
- When a user requests a particular culture, the application has to use only the resources for the requested culture. This reduces the time and load on the system.

The hub-and-spoke model also has some disadvantages:

- You have to manage more than one resource because more than one culture exists.
- The initial cost of testing an application increases because you have to test several configurations. In other words, you need to test each culture-specific version separately. Although you test the functionality of the main assembly separately, the tests for culture-specific versions include language tests, data format tests, color and style issues, and font issues.

Creating Satellite Assemblies

To create satellite assemblies, you first create resource files. The resource files can be text, .resx, or .resources files. Among these three types, you can compile and create only .resources files into a satellite assembly.

You create a .resources file by using the ResourceWriter class, as shown in the following code sample.

Visual Basic .NET

```
Imports System
Imports System.Resources
```

```
Public Class ResourceApplication

    Public Shared Sub Main()
        ' Create a resource writer.
        Dim myResourceWriter As IResourceWriter
        myResourceWriter = new ResourceWriter("myStrings.resources")
        ' Add resources to the file.
        myResourceWriter.AddResource("First", "Mercury")
        myResourceWriter.AddResource("Second", "Venus")
        myResourceWriter.AddResource("Third", "Earth")
        myResourceWriter.AddResource("Fourth", "Mars")
        myResourceWriter.AddResource("Fifth", "Jupiter")
        myResourceWriter.AddResource("Sixth", "Saturn")
        myResourceWriter.AddResource("Seventh", "Uranus")
        myResourceWriter.AddResource("Eighth", "Neptune")
        myResourceWriter.AddResource("Ninth", "Pluto")
        ' Close the ResourceWriter.
        myResourceWriter.Close()
    End Sub
End Class
```

Visual C#

```
using System;
using System.Resources;

class MainApp
{
    public static void Main()
    {
        // Create a resource writer.
        IResourceWriter myResourceWriter = new ResourceWriter
            ("myStrings.resources");
        // Add resources to the file.
        myResourceWriter.AddResource("First", "Mercury");
        myResourceWriter.AddResource("Second", "Venus");
        myResourceWriter.AddResource("Third", "Earth");
        myResourceWriter.AddResource("Fourth", "Mars");
        myResourceWriter.AddResource("Fifth", "Jupiter");
        myResourceWriter.AddResource("Sixth", "Saturn");
        myResourceWriter.AddResource("Seventh", "Uranus");
        myResourceWriter.AddResource("Eighth", "Neptune");
        myResourceWriter.AddResource("Ninth", "Pluto");
        // Close the ResourceWriter.
        rw.Close();
    }
}
```

If you have text files as resource files, you can use the ResGen.exe tool to convert .txt files to .resources files. The following command reads the name/value pairs from the strings.txt file and creates a binary resource file named myResources.resource.

```
ResGen strings.txt myResources.resource
```

After creating a .resources file, you can compile it into a satellite assembly by using Al.exe, the Assembly Linker (AL) tool. The AL tool creates satellite assemblies from the .resources files that you specify. Satellite assemblies cannot contain any executable code but only resources.

The following command shows you how to use the AL tool to generate a satellite assembly.

```
al /t:lib /embed:myResource.resources /culture:de /out:MyRes.resources.dll
```

Table 9.4 describes the various options used in the preceding example.

Table 9.4   Some of the Options of the AL Tool

Option	Description
/t:lib	This option specifies that your satellite assembly should be compiled into a library. Satellite assemblies must be saved as library files because they do not contain any executable code.
/embed:[resource]:*file*, [,*name*][,private]]	This option specifies the name of the file that contains information about the requested culture.
/culture:*culturename*	This option specifies the culture of the resource that is to be compiled.
/out:*filename*	This option specifies the name of the output satellite assembly.

Compiling Satellite Assemblies with Strong Names

To install satellite assemblies into the global assembly cache, the satellite assemblies must have strong names. Strong-named assemblies are signed using a valid public/private key pair.

While creating an application, you cannot access the final public/private key pair of an assembly. If you want to install a satellite assembly into the global assembly cache, you use the delayed signing technique. This technique for signing an assembly ensures that you reserve space in the file for the strong name signature at build time. The actual signing is delayed until a later date when the final public/private key pair is available.

Installing a Satellite Assembly

If your application is unable to locate the required information about the culture, the common language runtime searches the global assembly cache. To ensure that your application will run properly, you need to install the satellite assembly in the global assembly cache. If you compile your satellite assembly using strong names, you can install the satellite assembly in the global assembly cache. To install the satellite assembly into the global assembly cache, you use the global assembly cache tool, Gacutil.exe. The following command shows you how to install MyRes.resources.dll into the global assembly cache.

```
Gacutil.exe /i:MyRes.resources.dll
```

The /i option specifies that the global assembly cache tool can install MyRes.resources.dll into the global assembly cache.

Retrieving Data from the Resource Files

Once you have written the data into resource files, you need to retrieve them based on the culture specified. The ResourceManager class enables you to retrieve data from the satellite assemblies. The following code shows you how to retrieve data from the resource files.

Visual Basic .NET

```
Thread.CurrentThread.CurrentUICulture = New CultureInfo("", False)
Dim MyResMgr As ResourceManager
MyResMgr = ResourceManager.CreateFileBasedResourceManager( _
    "myResources", "E:\Chapter 9\Resources", Nothing)
MessageBox.Show(MyResMgr.GetString("First"))
```

Visual C#

```
Thread.CurrentThread.CurrentUICulture = new CultureInfo("", false);
ResourceManager MyResMgr;
MyResMgr = ResourceManager.CreateFileBasedResourceManager("myResources",
    "E:\\Chapter 9\\Resources", null);
MessageBox.Show(MyResMgr.GetString("First"));
```

As you can see in this code snippet, you use the ResourceManager class to retrieve data from the MyResources.resources file. The ResourceManager class contains the CreateFileBasedResourceManager method that takes three parameters—the name of the .resources file as a string, the path where the resource file resides as a string, and the resource type. In the preceding code, MyResources is the name of the .resources file. The MyResources.resources file in this example would be found in the E:\Chapter 9\Resources folder. However, if the satellite assembly containing the resources is installed in the global assembly cache, you must use the constructor method of the ResourceManager class, as shown in the following code.

Visual Basic .NET

```
Dim private rm As ResourceManager
rm = New ResourceManager("MyResource ", Me.GetType().Assembly)
Console.Writeline(rm.GetString("Name"))
```

Visual C#

```
private ResourceManager rm;
rm = new ResourceManager("MyResource", this.GetType().Assembly);
Console.Writeline(rm.GetString("Name"));
```

The above code uses the ResourceManager.GetString method to retrieve and display a string resource.

Summary

- Testing accomplishes a number of tasks, such as checking whether the desired functionality is implemented. The most important aspect that testing measures is the quality of the application that you are developing.

- Visual Studio .NET provides tools such as CorDbg.exe and DbgClr.exe that enable you to locate and remove bugs and errors from your application.

- Code instrumentation refers to the task of including code in programs to monitor the performance of .NET applications. You use code instrumentation to display messages or write to event logs in case of a failure during the execution of an application at run time.

- Satellite assemblies store data that is specific to a particular culture. They ensure that when you need to add cultures to your application, you need not make any changes to the source code of the application but only to the set of resources that are available.

Lab: Tracing and Debugging

In this lab, you will create a console application that accesses the BookingDetails database and retrieves data. The application also contains trace listeners that write information about a successful or unsuccessful transaction to a log file. You will also debug the XML Web service that you created and deployed in the lab in Chapter 7, "Creating and Consuming XML Web Services." The solutions to the exercises in this lab can be found in the \Solution folder on the Supplemental Course Materials CD-ROM.

Estimated lab time: 70 minutes

Exercise 1: Implementing Tracing

In this exercise, you will create a console application that enables you to read data from a database. You populate a DataSet and write information to a log file using a trace listener. To create the console application, perform the following steps:

1. Open Visual Studio .NET.
2. Open the File menu, point to New, and click Project to open the New Project dialog box.
3. Select Console Application from the Templates pane. In the Name box, type **TraceExampleVB** for a Visual Basic .NET project or **TraceExampleCS** for a Visual C# project.
4. Change the name of the Module1.vb or Module1.cs file to TraceExample.vb or TraceExample.cs. In the Code View window, replace the existing code with the following code.

Visual Basic .NET

```
Imports System
Imports System.Data.SqlClient
Imports System.Data

Module TraceExample
    Sub Main()
        Dim mySwitch As New TraceSwitch("General", "Entire application")
        mySwitch.Level = TraceLevel.Verbose

        Dim traceLog As New System.IO.FileStream("C:\mytraceVB.log", _
            IO.FileMode.OpenOrCreate)
        Dim myTraceListener As New TextWriterTraceListener(traceLog)
```

```
        Try
            Trace.Listeners.Add(myTraceListener)

            Dim conn As New SqlConnection()
            Dim com As New SqlCommand()
            Dim adap As New SqlDataAdapter()
            Dim dataset1 As New DataSet()

            conn.ConnectionString = "data source=localhost;user " & _
                "id=sa;pwd=;initial catalog=Airline"
            conn.Open()

            com.Connection = conn
            com.CommandText = "Select * from Flights"

            adap.SelectCommand = com
            adap.Fill(dataset1, "Flight")

            Dim dr As DataRow
            For Each dr In dataset1.Tables("Flight").Rows
                Console.WriteLine(dr(0) & "      " & dr(1))
                myTraceListener.WriteLine( _
                    "DataRow Successfully Retrieved.")
                Trace.Flush()
                myTraceListener.Flush()
            Next

            Console.ReadLine()
        Catch e As Exception
            Console.WriteLine("Error Occured. Please check the " & _
                "mytrace.log file.")
            myTraceListener.WriteLine("*******************************")
            myTraceListener.WriteLine(e.GetBaseException().ToString())
            Trace.Flush()
            myTraceListener.Flush()
            Console.ReadLine()
        End Try
    End Sub
End Module
```

Visual C#

```
using System;
using System.Data;
using System.Data.SqlClient;
using System.Diagnostics;
using System.IO;

namespace TraceExampleCS
```

(continued)

```
{
    /// <summary>
    /// Summary description for Class1.
    /// </summary>
    class Class1
    {
        /// <summary>
        /// The main entry point for the application.
        /// </summary>
        [STAThread]
        static void Main(string[] args)
        {
            //
            // TODO: Add code to start application here
            //

            TraceSwitch mySwitch = new TraceSwitch("General",
                "Entire application");
            mySwitch.Level = TraceLevel.Verbose;

            System.IO.FileStream traceLog = new System.IO.FileStream(
                "C:\\mytraceCS.log", FileMode.Append);
            TextWriterTraceListener myTraceListener = new
                TextWriterTraceListener(traceLog);

            try
            {
                Trace.Listeners.Add(myTraceListener);

                SqlConnection conn = new SqlConnection();
                SqlCommand com = new SqlCommand();
                SqlDataAdapter adap = new SqlDataAdapter();
                DataSet dataset1 = new DataSet();

                conn.ConnectionString = "data source=localhost;user " +
                    "id=sa;pwd=;initial catalog=Airline";
                conn.Open();

                com.Connection = conn;
                com.CommandText = "Select * from Flights";

                adap.SelectCommand = com;
                adap.Fill(dataset1, "Flight");

                foreach(DataRow dr in dataset1.Tables["Flight"].Rows)
                {
```

```
                Console.WriteLine(dr[0] + "        " + dr[1]);
                myTraceListener.WriteLine("DataRow Successfully" +
                    " Retrieved.");
                Trace.Flush();
                myTraceListener.Flush();
            }

            Console.ReadLine();
        }
        catch(Exception e)
        {
            Console.WriteLine("Error Occured. Please check the " +
                "mytrace.log file.");
            myTraceListener.WriteLine("**************************" +
                "****************************");
            myTraceListener.WriteLine(e.GetBaseException().ToString());
            Trace.Flush();
            myTraceListener.Flush();
            Console.ReadLine();
        }
    }
  }
}
```

When you execute this code, the MytraceVB.log or MytraceCS.log file is generated. A portion of the log is shown next.

Exercise 2: Debugging a Deployed XML Web Service

In this exercise, you will debug the FlightBooking Web service that you created and deployed in Chapter 7. To debug the FlightBooking Web service, perform the following steps:

1. Open the FlightBooking Web service in Internet Explorer by entering the URL **http://localhost/AirlineServices/FlightBooking.asmx**. The methods of the FlightBooking Web service are shown here.

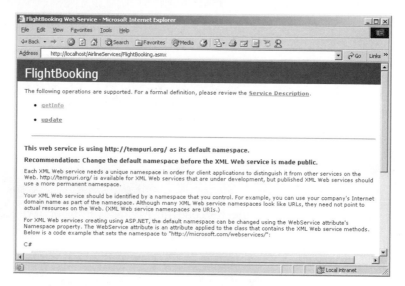

2. From the Debug menu in Visual Studio .NET, choose Processes to open the Processes dialog box, shown next.

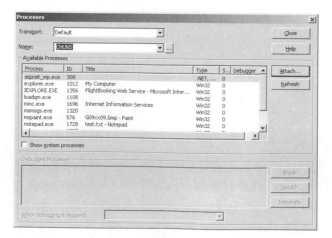

3. Select aspnet_wp.exe from the Process list, and click Attach to open the Attach To Process dialog box.

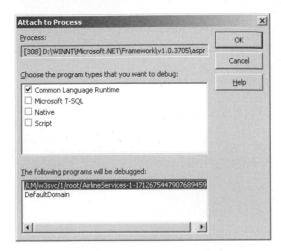

4. In the Attach To Process dialog box, select Common Language Runtime as the program type. Click OK, and then click Close to close the Processes dialog box.

5. Open the File menu in Visual Studio .NET, point to Open, and then click File. In the Open File dialog box, select the code-behind file, the FlightBooking.asmx.vb or FlightBooking.asmx.cs file, located in the Inetpub\Wwwroot\AirlineServices folder.

6. Set a breakpoint on the line containing the getInfo method, as shown here.

Visual Basic .NET

```
<WebMethod()> _
Public Function getInfo() As DataSet
```

Visual C#

```
[WebMethod()]

public DataSet getInfo()
```

7. In Internet Explorer, click the hyperlink for the getInfo method. This displays a new page from which you can invoke the getInfo method. Click the Invoke button to invoke the getInfo method.

The debugger breaks the execution at the breakpoint set on the line containing the getInfo method.

8. Use the debug windows such as Autos, Locals, and Watch to see the variables and their values.

9. To stop debugging, choose Stop Debugging from the Debug menu.

Review

The questions in this section reinforce key information presented in this chapter. If you are unable to answer a question, review the appropriate lesson, and then try answering the question again. Answers to the questions can be found in Appendix A, "Questions and Answers."

1. What are the different approaches to testing?

2. Explain the waterfall approach.

3. Explain the evolutionary approach.

4. How does the Visual Studio .NET debugger work?

5. What are the main windows and dialog boxes that you use to debug a Visual Studio .NET application?

6. What is code instrumentation?

7. How do you implement code instrumentation?

8. Which tool do you need to use to convert .txt files to .resources files?

9. Which tool do you need to use to compile the .resources files into satellite assemblies?

Deploying XML Web Services and Windows Services

About This Chapter

The .NET Framework provides features and tools that enable you to easily package and distribute a variety of applications to a number of users. In this chapter, you will learn about the .NET deployment features. In addition, you will learn how to deploy various types of applications using Microsoft Visual Studio .NET and the .NET Framework tools.

Before You Begin

To complete the lessons in this chapter, you

- Must have read the preceding chapters in this book
- Must have access to a Web server

Lesson 1: Understanding .NET Deployment Features

In the previous chapters, you learned how to develop applications, such as Windows services, XML Web services, and serviced components using the .NET Framework. In addition, you learned how to debug and test your applications using debugging tools and code instrumentation.

Once you ensure that your application is free from all bugs and errors, you need to distribute your applications to users by deploying the application on various computers. In this lesson, you will learn about various deployment features of the .NET Framework.

After this lesson, you will be able to

- Describe .NET deployment
- Describe the packaging and distribution options
- Describe deployment scenarios

Estimated lesson time: 30 minutes

Understanding .NET Deployment

The .NET Framework provides various features and tools that you can use to deploy applications. These features and tools enable you to deploy different types of applications to a large number of users. In addition, you can install new versions of applications on target computers without adversely affecting the older versions of your applications. The .NET Framework provides various packaging and distribution options that make it easy to deploy applications. The features of .NET deployment include

- **No-impact applications.**   This feature isolates an application and removes DLL conflicts. By default, components do not affect other applications.
- **Private components.**   The components are deployed to the application directory and are visible only to the containing application. Because components are private by default, they have no impact on other applications.
- **Controlled code sharing.**   Because components are private by default, multiple applications cannot share components. You need to explicitly make the components available for sharing by assigning a strong name to an assembly containing the components and installing the assembly in the global assembly cache.
- **Side-by-side versioning.**   This feature enables you to deploy multiple versions of a component or an application. You can specify the version of

components that your application must use, and the common language runtime will enforce the versioning policy.

- **Xcopy deployment.** Self-described and self-contained components and applications can be deployed without registry entries or dependencies. You can deploy an application by copying the application files to the installation directory on a target computer.

- **On the fly updates.** Administrators can use hosts, such as ASP.NET, to update program DLLs, even on remote computers. This feature enables you to update an application without stopping it.

- **Integration with Microsoft Windows Installer.** You can create Windows Installer packages and use their features, such as advertisement, publishing, repair, and install-on-demand, to deploy your application.

- **Enterprise deployment.** This feature allows you to easily distribute software in an enterprise network. You can use the software installation feature of Active Directory, which can automatically install applications on network computers. You can configure Active Directory to install applications when a computer boots up for the first time in the network or when a user logs on to a network computer. You can also create setup programs and deploy them on a network share. Users can install applications on their computers by running the setup programs from the network share.

- **Downloading and caching.** Incremental downloads keep downloads small, and components can be isolated for use only by the application for zero-impact deployment.

- **Partially trusted code.** Identity is based on the code rather than the user. The administrator sets policies, and no certificate dialog boxes appear.

As mentioned in Chapter 1, "Understanding the .NET Framework," *assemblies* are the units of application development in the .NET Framework. Assemblies enable you to implement version control, reusability, and security permissions. In addition, assemblies provide the common language runtime with the information it requires concerning type implementations. Therefore, assemblies are the fundamental units for deploying Visual Studio .NET applications. The following sections explain how versioning is implemented for assemblies.

Maintaining Assembly Versions

The details about the versions of assemblies that use the common language runtime are maintained at the assembly level. An assembly manifest contains the specific version of an assembly and the versions of dependent assemblies. Each assembly maintains version information in two ways. An assembly uses an identification number and an informational version.

Each assembly uses an identification number to enforce the version policy. This identification number includes the version number, name, and cultural information about the assembly. The common language runtime considers assemblies that have different version numbers to be different assemblies. This version number is a four-part number. The format of the version number is

<major version>.<minor version>.<build number>.<revision>

For example, in version 1.4.1123.0, the number 1 represents the major version, 4 represents the minor version, 1123 represents the build number, and 0 represents the revision number. The version number is stored in the assembly manifest along with other identity information, including the assembly name and public key, and information regarding the relationships and identities of other assemblies referenced in the application. When you build an assembly, the development tool stores dependency information for each referenced assembly in the assembly manifest. The following code shows the attribute that you use to specify the version of an assembly:

Visual Basic .NET

```
<assembly:AssemblyVersionAttribute("1.2.*")>
```

Visual C#

```
[assembly:AssemblyVersionAttribute("1.2.*")]
```

The AssemblyVersionAttribute attribute takes a string argument that represents the version number. In the preceding code, only the major and minor versions are specified and a wildcard is used for build and revision numbers. The language compiler automatically generates the build and the revision numbers.

In addition to version numbers, an assembly uses a string that represents additional version information. You use this version string for additional information only. For example, an informational version string can be *Common Language Runtime Version 1.0.*

Assembly versioning enables you to implement side-by-side execution of assemblies, which is discussed in the next section.

Side-by-Side Execution

Side-by-side execution enables you to run multiple versions of the same assembly simultaneously. The common language runtime provides the infrastructure that allows multiple versions of the same assembly to run on the same computer. You can also run multiple versions of the same assembly within the same process.

Side-by-side execution provides flexibility and makes assemblies compatible with earlier versions of the assembly. Simultaneous storage and execution of multiple versions of the same assembly also provide greater flexibility to deploy applications. Assemblies can display side-by-side execution on the same computer in the same process.

Side-by-Side Execution on the Same Computer

When assemblies execute simultaneously on the same computer, multiple versions of one application run on one computer at the same time. For example, consider an application that uses a file at a specific location for a cache. The application must either manage multiple versions of the application accessing the file at the same time, or the application must remove the dependency on the specific location and allow each version to have its own cache.

Side-by-Side Execution in the Same Process

When assemblies execute simultaneously within the same process, a single application with multiple dependencies runs multiple versions of the same component. Therefore, to execute simultaneously in the same process, multiple versions of an assembly cannot depend only on the resources within a process.

Packaging and Distribution Options

The .NET Framework provides various options to package and distribute the applications that you create in Visual Studio .NET. These packaging and distribution options allow you to deploy an application in various scenarios. You can package a Visual Studio .NET application as

- **Assemblies.**   This option allows you to deploy the .dll or .exe file as it was built.
- **Cabinet (.cab) files.**   This option allows you to compress the executable code files into .cab files. This reduces the time needed to distribute or download the application.
- **Microsoft Windows Installer packages.**   This option allows you to create .msi files. You can use the .msi files with Microsoft Windows Installer 2.0. You can also use other installers to package the .msi files.

Once you have packaged the Visual Studio .NET application, you can distribute the application. The .NET Framework allows you to distribute an application in the following ways:

- **Xcopy or FTP.**   The common language runtime applications are self-describing and do not require registry entries. Therefore, you can use Xcopy or FTP to copy the application to an appropriate directory on the target computer. You can then run the application from that directory.
- **Code download.**   You can download the code to a folder on a computer and run the application from that folder. This option allows you to easily distribute your application over the Internet or an intranet.
- **Windows Installer 2.0.**   You can use this option to install, repair, or remove the .NET Framework assemblies that are located in the global assembly cache and in private directories. This is the simplest method for an end user to install a Visual Studio .NET application.

Deployment Scenarios

As mentioned earlier, you can deploy a Visual Studio .NET application for multiple users using various methods. Multiple deployment requirements exist for deploying common language runtime applications. You package and deploy applications depending on these requirements. The following are the most common deployment methods:

- Using Windows Installer
- Downloading .cab files
- Using Microsoft Internet Explorer

The following sections discuss these scenarios in detail.

Deploying an Application Using Windows Installer

To deploy a Windows Forms application, you package the application as an .msi file and then use Windows Installer to distribute the application. If you use Windows Installer to distribute a Windows Forms application, you can use Windows Installer and Windows 2000 Application Management tools to package, distribute, and deploy the application. For example, you can use the Add/Remove Programs option in Control Panel to install or remove the application.

You use Windows Installer to install assemblies in the global assembly cache or to an isolated location for a particular application. In addition, Windows Installer enables you to perform the following tasks when you deploy a Windows Forms application.

- Install, repair, and remove assemblies that are located in the global assembly cache.
- Install, repair, and remove assemblies located in isolated locations for particular applications.
- Roll back unsuccessful installations, repair, or removal of assemblies.
- Perform install-on-demand of strong-named assemblies in the global assembly cache.
- Patch assemblies.
- Display shortcuts that point to assemblies.

Deploying an Application by Downloading .cab Files

You can compress a file or directory and create .cab files by using the Win32 Software Development Kit compression tool or the Visual Studio .NET deployment tool. You can then deploy the .cab file by downloading the file. However, you must remember the following when creating .cab files.

- You can insert only one assembly into a single .cab file.

- You must name the .cab file as the file in the assembly that contains the assembly manifest. For example, if the file containing the manifest is named AppClass.dll, you must name the .cab file AppClass.cab.

After you create .cab files, you can reference them by using the <codeBase> tag in a configuration file to specify their location.

Deploying an Application Using Internet Explorer

You can use Internet Explorer to download Web-based applications. A Web-based application can download both .exe and .dll files. The Web page from which you download the application provides information such as which assemblies to download, their location, and the location of the configuration file that provides additional information.

Lesson 2: .NET Deployment Options and Setup Programs

In the previous lesson, you learned about the deployment features of the .NET Framework. You also learned about different packaging and distribution options to deploy your applications. In this lesson, you will learn how to deploy Windows services, serviced components, .NET Remoting objects, and XML Web services using Visual Studio .NET Setup programs.

After completing this lesson, you will be able to

- Identify various types of Visual Studio .NET deployment projects
- Deploy Windows services
- Deploy serviced components
- Deploy .NET Remoting objects
- Deploy XML Web services

Estimated lesson time: 40 minutes

Overview of .NET Deployment Projects

Visual Studio .NET consists of four types of project templates that you can use to deploy different types of projects. The four types of deployment projects are named Setup Project, Web Setup Project, Cab Project, and Merge Module Project.

Creating Installation Files Using Setup Projects

To distribute an application, you create installation files. Setup projects allow you to create these installation files to distribute an application. The resulting Windows Installer (.msi) file contains the application, any dependent files, information about the application such as registry entries, and instructions for installation. When you distribute the .msi file and execute it on the target computer, all the necessary files for installation are included and installed on the target computer.

Note   If the installation fails for any reason, such as an incompatible operating system on the target computer, the installation process is rolled back.

There are two types of Setup projects in Visual Studio .NET: Setup and Web Setup. The only difference between Setup and Web Setup projects is the location in which the installer is deployed. Setup projects install files into the file system of a target computer, whereas Web Setup projects install files into the virtual directory of a Web server. In the next section, you will learn how to deploy a Windows service using a Setup project, and then you will learn how to deploy an XML Web service using a Web Setup project.

Deploying a Windows Service

Deploying a Windows service using a Visual Studio .NET Setup project requires performing several tasks, which are described in this section.

Creating a Windows Service

To create a Windows service, use the following procedure:

1. Start Visual Studio .NET and open a new project.
2. Select Visual Basic Projects or Visual C# Projects from the Project Types pane in the New Project dialog box.
3. Select Windows Service from the Templates pane.
4. Type **WindowsServiceExample** in the Name box and click OK. A new .NET solution named WindowsServiceExample is created.
5. Rename Service1.vb or Service1.cs to WindowsServiceExample.vb or WindowsServiceExample.cs. In this Windows service, you insert code that writes a message into a log file every time you start or stop the service.

Visual Basic .NET

```vb
Imports System.ServiceProcess

Public Class WindowsServiceExample
    Inherits System.ServiceProcess.ServiceBase

    Dim fs As New System.IO.FileStream("C:\TestService.log", _
        IO.FileMode.Append)
    Dim myTraceListener As New TextWriterTraceListener(fs)

#Region " Component Designer generated code "

    Public Sub New()
        MyBase.New()
        ' This call is required by the Component Designer.
        InitializeComponent()
        ' Add any initialization after the InitializeComponent() call
    End Sub

    ' UserService overrides dispose to clean up the component list.
    Protected Overloads Overrides Sub Dispose(ByVal disposing As Boolean)
        If disposing Then
            If Not (components Is Nothing) Then
                components.Dispose()
            End If
        End If
        MyBase.Dispose(disposing)
    End Sub
```

(continued)

```vbnet
' The main entry point for the process
<MTAThread()> _
Shared Sub Main()
    Dim ServicesToRun() As System.ServiceProcess.ServiceBase
    ServicesToRun = New System.ServiceProcess.ServiceBase() _
        {New WindowsServiceExample()}
    System.ServiceProcess.ServiceBase.Run(ServicesToRun)
End Sub


' Required by the Component Designer
Private components As System.ComponentModel.IContainer
<System.Diagnostics.DebuggerStepThrough()> Private Sub _
    InitializeComponent()
    Me.ServiceName = "My New VB Service"
End Sub

#End Region

Protected Overrides Sub OnStart(ByVal args() As String)
    ' Add code here to start your service. This method should set
    ' things in motion so your service can do its work.
    myTraceListener.WriteLine("Service Started Successfully.")
    Trace.Listeners.Add(myTraceListener)
    Trace.Flush()
    myTraceListener.Flush()
End Sub

Protected Overrides Sub OnStop()
    myTraceListener.WriteLine("Service Stopped Successfully.")
    Trace.Listeners.Add(myTraceListener)
    Trace.Flush()
    myTraceListener.Flush()
End Sub
End Class
```

Visual C#

```csharp
using System;
using System.Collections;
using System.ComponentModel;
using System.Data;
using System.Diagnostics;
using System.ServiceProcess;
using System.IO;

namespace WindowsServiceExample
{
    public class WindowsServiceExample : System.ServiceProcess.ServiceBase
    {
        System.IO.FileStream fs = new
            System.IO.FileStream("C:\\TestService.log", FileMode.Append);
```

```
TextWriterTraceListener myTraceListener;
/// <summary>
/// Required designer variable.
/// </summary>
private System.ComponentModel.Container components = null;

public WindowsServiceExample()
{
    InitializeComponent();
}

// The main entry point for the process
static void Main()
{
    System.ServiceProcess.ServiceBase[] ServicesToRun;
    ServicesToRun = new System.ServiceProcess.ServiceBase[]
    { new WindowsServiceExample() };
    System.ServiceProcess.ServiceBase.Run(ServicesToRun);
}

/// <summary>
/// Required method for Designer support - do not modify
/// the contents of this method with the code editor.
/// </summary>
private void InitializeComponent()
{
    //
    // WindowsServiceExample
    //
    this.ServiceName = "My New C# Service";
}

/// <summary>
/// Clean up any resources being used.
/// </summary>
protected override void Dispose( bool disposing )
{
    if( disposing )
    {
        if (components != null)
        {
            components.Dispose();
        }
    }
    base.Dispose( disposing );
}

/// <summary>
/// Set things in motion so your service can do its work.
/// </summary>
```

(continued)

```
protected override void OnStart(string[] args)
{
    // TODO: Add code here to start your service.
    myTraceListener = new TextWriterTraceListener(fs);
    myTraceListener.WriteLine("Service Started Successfully.");
    Trace.Listeners.Add(myTraceListener);
    Trace.Flush();
    myTraceListener.Flush();
}

/// <summary>
/// Stop this service.
/// </summary>
protected override void OnStop()
{
    myTraceListener = new TextWriterTraceListener(fs);
    myTraceListener.WriteLine("Service Stopped Successfully.");
    Trace.Listeners.Add(myTraceListener);
    Trace.Flush();
    myTraceListener.Flush();
}
    }
}
```

Once you have added the required functionality, you need to add the service-Installer and serviceProcessInstaller components to your Windows service application by following these steps:

1. Navigate to the Solution Explorer.
2. Double-click WindowsServiceExample.vb or WindowsServiceExample.cs.
3. Right-click in the Design window of the WindowsServiceExample project, and choose Add Installer.
4. Build the WindowsServiceExample project.

Creating a Setup Project

Once you have created the Windows service, you need to add a Setup project to install the service on a target computer. To create a Setup project for WindowsServiceExample, use the following procedure:

1. From the File menu, point to Add Project and click New Project. The Add New Project dialog box appears.
2. In the Add New Project dialog box, select Setup And Deployment Projects from the Project Types pane.
3. In the Templates pane, select Setup Project.

4. In the Name box, type **ServiceSetup** and click OK. After adding the Setup project to the solution, you add WindowsServiceExample.exe to the Setup project. Figure 10.1 displays the file system of the ServiceSetup project.

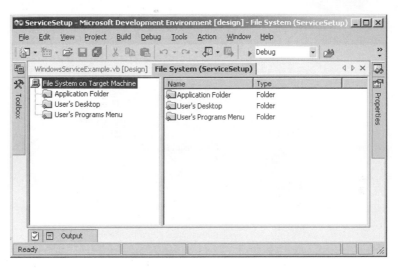

Figure 10.1   The file system of the ServiceSetup project

5. Navigate to the Solution Explorer, right-click the ServiceSetup project, point to Add, and click Project Output. Figure 10.2 shows how to add project output.

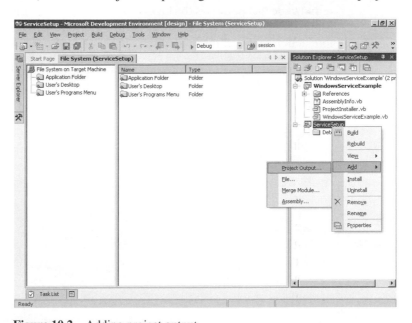

Figure 10.2   Adding project output

6. In the Add Project Output Group dialog box, ensure that WindowsService-
Example is selected in the Project box. From the list, select Primary Output and
click OK. Figure 10.3 shows the Add Project Output Group dialog box.

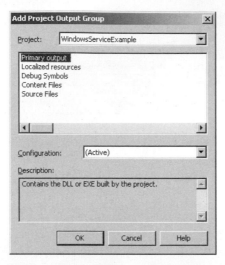

Figure 10.3   The Add Project Output Group dialog box

A project item for the primary output of WindowsServiceExample is added to the
Setup project. You can add a custom action, which is a Windows Installer feature,
to run code that performs the tasks that cannot be performed during the installation.
The code can exist in the form of a .dll, .exe, script, or an assembly. To add a custom action to install the WindowsServiceExample.exe file, follow these steps:

1. Navigate to the Solution Explorer, right-click the ServiceSetup project, point to
View, and click Custom Actions from the shortcut menu. Figure 10.4 shows the
Custom Actions menu item.

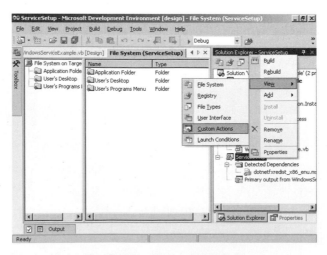

Figure 10.4   The Custom Actions menu item

2. In Custom Actions (ServiceSetup), right-click Custom Actions and click Add Custom Action from the shortcut menu. Figure 10.5 shows how to add a custom action.

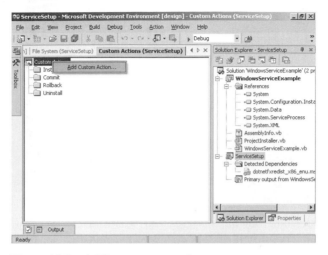

Figure 10.5   Adding a custom action

3. In the Select Item In Project dialog box, double-click Application Folder, select Primary Output From WindowsServiceExample (Active), and click OK. Figure 10.6 shows the Select Item In Project dialog box.

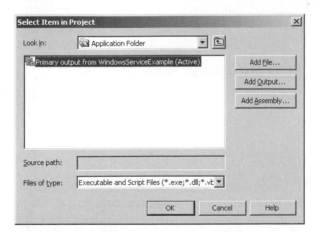

Figure 10.6   The Select Item In Project dialog box

The primary output is added to all four nodes of the custom actions: Install, Commit, Rollback, and Uninstall.

4. To build the Setup project, right-click the ServiceSetup project and click Build. Figure 10.7 shows how to build the ServiceSetup project. When you build the ServiceSetup project, the compiler creates the ServiceSetup.msi file. The figure also shows the primary output for each of the custom actions.

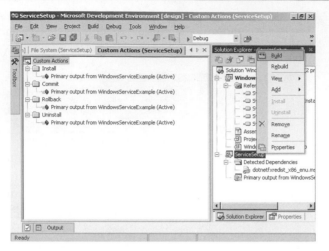

Figure 10.7   Building the ServiceSetup project

After you create the .msi file, you can install the WindowsServiceExample service on any computer.

Important   The applications you create using the .NET Framework require the common language runtime to execute on the target computer. Therefore, if the target machine does not have the .NET Framework, you need to redistribute it along with your application. A redistributable package exists for the .NET Framework and is available with the current version of .NET. The redistributable package for the .NET Framework supports the following platforms:

- Microsoft Windows 98
- Microsoft Windows 98 Second Edition
- Microsoft Windows Millennium Edition (Windows Me)
- Microsoft Windows NT 4.0 (Workstation or Server) with Service Pack 6a
- Microsoft Windows 2000 (Professional, Server, or Advanced Server)
- Microsoft Windows XP (Personal and Professional)
- Microsoft Windows .NET Server 2003

You also need to install the following software required by the .NET Framework on the servers on which you install the redistributable package of the .NET Framework:

- Microsoft Data Access Components (MDAC) 2.6 (MDAC 2.7 is recommended) on the server
- Microsoft Internet Information Services (IIS) on Windows 2000, Windows XP Professional, and Windows .NET Server 2003, for Web-based applications

---

Deploying an XML Web Service

Deploying an XML Web service requires performing several tasks, which are described in this section.

Creating an XML Web Service

To create an XML Web service, use the following procedure:

1. Start Visual Studio .NET and open a new project.
2. Select Visual Basic Projects or Visual C# Projects from the Project Types pane in the New Project dialog box.
3. Select ASP.NET Web Service from the Templates pane.
4. Type **WebServiceExample** in the Name box and click OK. A new .NET solution named WebServiceExample is created. Figure 10.8 displays the New Project dialog box.

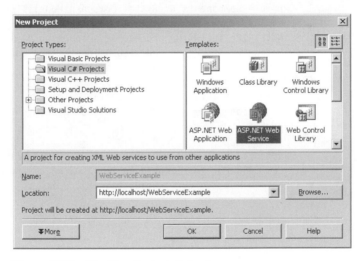

Figure 10.8   The New Project dialog box

5. Rename Service1.asmx.vb or Service1.asmx.cs to WebServiceExample.asmx.vb or WebServiceExample.asmx.cs. In this XML Web service, you add code that writes a message into a log file.

Visual Basic .NET

```
Imports System.Web.Services
Imports System.IO

<WebService(Namespace := "http://tempuri.org/")> _
```

(continued)

```vbnet
Public Class Service1
    Inherits System.Web.Services.WebService
    Dim fs As New System.IO.FileStream("C:\\TestServiceVB.log", _
        FileMode.Append)
    Dim myTraceListener As New TextWriterTraceListener(fs)

#Region " Web Services Designer Generated Code "

    Public Sub New()
        MyBase.New()

        'This call is required by the Web Services Designer.
        InitializeComponent()

    End Sub

    'Required by the Web Services Designer
    Private components As System.ComponentModel.IContainer

    'NOTE: The following procedure is required by the Web Services
    'Designer. It can be modified using the Web Services Designer.
    'Do not modify it using the code editor.
    <System.Diagnostics.DebuggerStepThrough()> _
    Private Sub InitializeComponent()
        components = New System.ComponentModel.Container()
    End Sub

    Protected Overloads Overrides Sub Dispose(ByVal disposing As Boolean)
        'CODEGEN: This procedure is required by the Web Services Designer
        'Do not modify it using the code editor.
        If disposing Then
            If Not (components Is Nothing) Then
                components.Dispose()
            End If
        End If
        MyBase.Dispose(disposing)
    End Sub

#End Region

    <WebMethod()> Public Function WriteTraceListener() As String
        myTraceListener.WriteLine("Trace Written Successfully.")
        Trace.Listeners.Add(myTraceListener)
        Trace.Flush()
        myTraceListener.Flush()
        Return ("Trace Written Successfully.")
    End Function
End Class
```

Visual C#

```csharp
using System;
using System.Collections;
using System.ComponentModel;
using System.Data;
using System.Diagnostics;
using System.Web;
using System.Web.Services;
using System.IO;

namespace WebServiceExample
{
    /// <summary>
    /// Summary description for Service1.
    /// </summary>
    public class Service1 : System.Web.Services.WebService
    {
        System.IO.FileStream fs = new
            System.IO.FileStream("C:\\TestService.log", FileMode.Append);
        TextWriterTraceListener myTraceListener;

        public Service1()
        {
            InitializeComponent();
        }

        #region Component Designer generated code

        //Required by the Web Services Designer
        private IContainer components = null;

        /// <summary>
        /// Required method for Designer support - do not modify
        /// the contents of this method with the code editor.
        /// </summary>
        private void InitializeComponent()
        {
        }

        /// <summary>
        /// Clean up any resources being used.
        /// </summary>
        protected override void Dispose( bool disposing )
        {
            if(disposing && components != null)
            {
                components.Dispose();
```

(continued)

```
        }
        base.Dispose(disposing);
    }

    #endregion

    [WebMethod]
    public string WriteTraceListener()
    {
        myTraceListener = new TextWriterTraceListener(fs);
        myTraceListener.WriteLine("Trace Written Successfully.");
        Trace.Listeners.Add(myTraceListener);
        Trace.Flush();
        myTraceListener.Flush();
        return ("Trace Written Successfully.");
    }
    }
}
```

Once you have added the required functionality, you can build the WebService-Example project.

Creating a Web Setup Project

You deploy the WebServiceExample project by using a Web Setup project. To create a Web Setup project, use the following procedure:

1. From the File menu, point to Add Project, and click New Project. The Add New Project dialog box appears.

2. In the Add New Project dialog box, select Setup And Deployment Projects from the Project Types pane.

3. In the Templates pane, select Web Setup Project.

4. In the Name box, type **WebServiceSetup** and click OK. After adding the Web Setup project to the solution, you add the service WebServiceExample to the Web Setup project. Figure 10.9 displays the file system of the WebService-Setup project.

5. To add WebServiceExample to the Web Setup project, navigate to the Solution Explorer, right-click the WebServiceSetup project, point to Add, and click Project Output, as shown in Figure 10.10.

6. In the Add Project Output Group dialog box, ensure that WebServiceExample is selected in the Project box. From the list, select Primary Output, Debug Symbols, and Content Files, and then click OK. Figure 10.11 shows the Add Project Output Group dialog box.

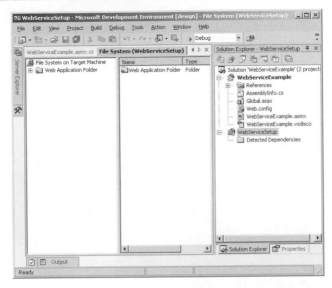

Figure 10.9   The file system of the WebServiceSetup project

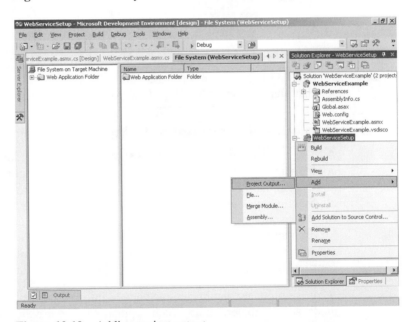

Figure 10.10   Adding project output

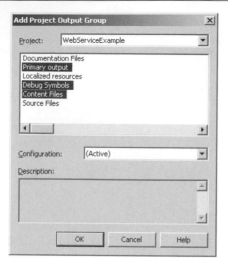

Figure 10.11   The Add Project Output Group dialog box

7. Build the WebServiceSetup project. The WebServiceSetup.msi file is created. To deploy the XML Web service, execute the WebServiceSetup.msi file on the target computer.

Note   Before you execute the WebServiceSetup.msi file, you need to install the .NET Framework on the target computer. You also need to have Windows Installer version 2 and IIS installed on the target computer.

Deploying Components Using a Merge Module Project

A Merge Module project provides a standard method for installing and deploying components. It ensures that the correct version of a component is installed on the target computer. A Merge Module project contains a component such as a DLL along with any dependent files, resources, registry entries, and setup logic. You cannot install merge modules directly. The modules are merged with an .msi file for each application that uses the component. This ensures that the component is installed consistently for all applications, eliminating problems such as version conflicts, missing registry entries, and improperly installed files.

A merge module contains unique version information that the Windows Installer database uses to determine which applications can use the component, preventing the premature removal of a component. Therefore, a new merge module is created for every incremental version of a component. You should not update a merge module after including the module in an installer. The deployment tools in Visual Studio .NET make it easy to create merge modules and include them in installers for your applications.

To deploy a component on a target computer, you first create a component. Next, you add a Merge Module project to the solution, and then merge the merge module file with the Windows Installer file. Deploying components using merge modules requires performing several tasks, which are described in this section.

Creating a Class Library

To create a class library, use the following procedure:

1. Start Visual Studio .NET and open a new project.
2. Select Visual Basic Projects or Visual C# Projects from the Project Types pane in the New Project dialog box.
3. Select Class Library from the Templates pane.
4. Type **ComponentExample** in the Name box and click OK. A new .NET solution named ComponentExample is created.
5. Type the following code in the window.

Visual Basic .NET

```
Imports System
Imports System.Collections
Imports System.ComponentModel
Imports System.Data
Imports System.Diagnostics
Imports System.IO

Public Class Class1
    Sub New()
        Dim fs As New FileStream("C:\\TestComponent.log", _
            FileMode.Append)
        Dim myTraceListener As New TextWriterTraceListener(fs)
        myTraceListener.WriteLine("Trace Written Successfully.")
        Trace.Listeners.Add(myTraceListener)
        Trace.Flush()
        myTraceListener.Flush()
    End Sub
End Class
```

Visual C#

```
using System;
using System.Collections;
using System.ComponentModel;
using System.Data;
using System.Diagnostics;
using System.IO;

namespace ComponentExample
{
    public class Class1
```

(continued)

```
        {
            public Class1()
            {
                System.IO.FileStream fs = new
                    System.IO.FileStream("C:\\Test.log", FileMode.Append);
                TextWriterTraceListener myTraceListener;
                myTraceListener = new TextWriterTraceListener(fs);
                myTraceListener.WriteLine("Trace Written Successfully.");
                Trace.Listeners.Add(myTraceListener);
                Trace.Flush();
                myTraceListener.Flush();
            }
        }
    }
```

6. Build the ComponentExample project.

Creating a Merge Module Project

After building the ComponentExample project, you can then add the Merge Module project. To create a Merge Module project, use the following procedure:

1. Add the Merge Module project from the Add New Project dialog box.
2. In the File System editor pane, select Module Retargetable Folder. From the Action menu, point to Add, and choose Project Output. Figure 10.12 shows how to add project output. The Add Project Output Group dialog box appears.

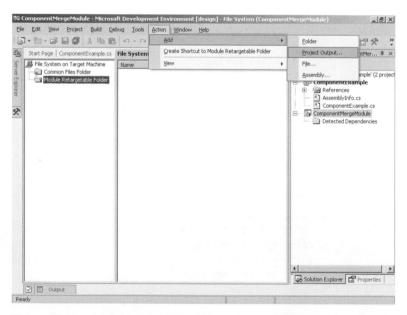

Figure 10.12   Adding project output

3. In the Add Project Output Group dialog box, select Primary Output of the ComponentExample project.

4. Build ComponentMergeModule to create the merge module.

Adding a Merge Module

A merge module cannot be installed directly. You need to add a merge module to the installer of each application that uses the components in the merge module. To add a Setup project that consumes the merge module, you add a Setup project to the solution as described in the "Deploying a Windows Service" section at the beginning of this lesson. Next, you add a merge module to the Setup project. To add a merge module to a Setup project, perform the following steps:

1. From the File menu, point to Add Project, and click New Project.

2. In the Add New Project dialog box, select Setup And Deployment Projects in the Project Types pane, and then choose Setup Project in the Templates pane. In the Name box, type **MergeModuleInstaller**.

3. In the File System editor pane, select Application Folder. From the Action menu, point to Add, and choose Project Output.

4. In the Add Project Output Group dialog box, select the ComponentMergeModule project, and then select Merge Module and click OK.

5. Select the Merge Module in the Solution Explorer. In the Properties window, select the KeyOutput property and expand the node to display the Merge Module Properties node. Expand that node and select the Module Retargetable Folder property.

Note   The properties included in the KeyOutput property are dynamic and do not appear until you build the merge module.

---

6. From the Module Retargetable Folder property click Browse from the drop-down list to display the Select Folder dialog box. Figure 10.13 shows the Browse option in the Module Retargetable Folder property.

7. In the Select Folder dialog box, select Application Folder and click OK.

8. Build MergeModuleInstaller.

9. To install MergeModuleInstaller on your development computer, select the MergeModuleInstaller project in the Solution Explorer. From the Project menu, choose Install, as shown in Figure 10.14.

    This runs the installer and installs MergeModuleInstaller on your development computer. The installer installs the component from the merge module in the application's directory.

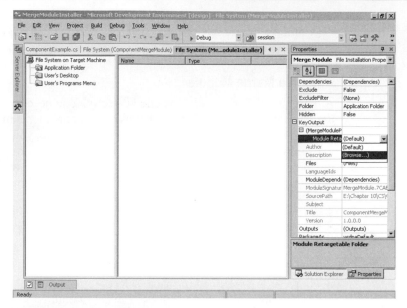

Figure 10.13   The Browse option

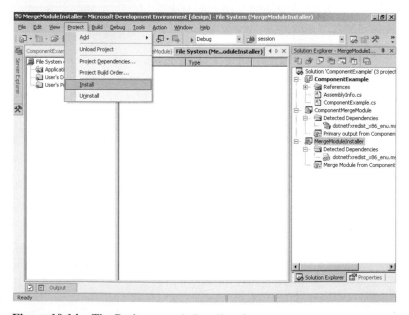

Figure 10.14   The Project menu's Install option

Deploying MergeModuleInstaller

To deploy MergeModuleInstaller on another computer, follow these steps:

1. In Windows Explorer, navigate to the MergeModuleInstaller project, and copy the MergeModuleInstaller.msi file and all other files and subdirectories into a directory on the target computer.

Note   To install MergeModuleInstaller on a computer that is not on a network, copy the files to a portable medium such as a CD-ROM.

---

2. On the target computer, double-click the Setup.exe file to run the installer. This installs the component by using the Merge Module project.

Deploying .NET Components and Applications Using a Cabinet Project

You can create .cab files to package .NET components and applications by using Cabinet projects. You can download these .cab files from a Web server to a Web browser. You can add files and project outputs to a Cabinet project in the Solution Explorer and set properties in the Properties window or the project's properties dialog box. The properties of Cabinet projects allow you to specify a level of compression, implement Authenticode signing, set the display name and version information, and specify the location of dependent files on the Web.

To create a Cabinet project, use the following procedure:

1. Start Visual Studio .NET and open a new project.
2. Select Setup And Deployment Projects from the Project Types pane in the New Project dialog box.
3. Select Cab Project from the Templates pane.
4. Type **CabExample** in the Name box and click OK. A new .NET solution named CabExample is created.
5. Navigate to the Solution Explorer, right-click the CabExample project, point to Add, and choose File from the submenu. Figure 10.15 shows how to add a file to the CabExample project.
6. In the Add Files dialog box, find the file (.dll or .exe) containing your components or application and add it to the project.
7. In the project's properties dialog box, select the Authenticode Signing option, and enter the certificate file, private key file, and timestamp server URL.

Note   Authenticode signing determines whether the outputs of the deployment project will be signed using a certificate file, private key file, or timestamp server.

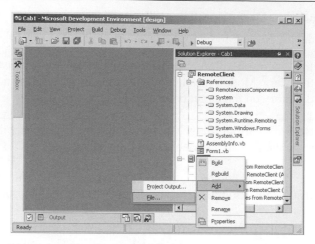

Figure 10.15   Adding a file

8. Choose Build Solution from the Build menu to build the CabExample project.

9. You can save the output of the CAB project on a Web server. Web browsers can download the .cab file from the Web server.

Lesson 3: Registering and Locating Components and Assemblies

The assemblies that you create using the .NET Framework do not require registration. However, to enable COM components to access the functionality that an assembly provides, you need to export the types contained in the assembly to a type library (.tlb file) and register the type library with the Windows registry. In this lesson, you will learn how to export the types contained in an assembly into a type library and register the type library. In addition, you will learn how the .NET Framework locates assemblies when you run an application.

After completing this lesson, you will be able to

- Export .NET components to type libraries
- Register type libraries
- Describe how the .NET Framework locates assemblies

Estimated lesson time: 30 minutes

Registering Components and Assemblies

The .NET Framework does not require you to register components with the Windows registry because the common language runtime uses metadata information contained in an assembly manifest to locate the components and types that an application uses. However, if you want COM components to access managed components, you need to export the managed types to a type library, a .tlb file, and register the type library with the Windows registry. The .NET Framework provides tools that allow you to export the types to a type library and register the type library. These tools include the Type Library Exporter (Tlbexp.exe) and the Assembly Registration Tool (Regasm.exe). The Type Library Exporter creates a type library that describes the types defined by a common language runtime assembly. You use the following command to export the types defined in a common language runtime assembly into a type library:

    tlbexp *assemblyName* [/out:*file*] [/nologo] [/silent] [/verbose]

In the preceding command, *assemblyName* is the assembly for which you want to export the types to a type library. The options that you can use with the tlbexp command are shown in Table 10.1.

Table 10.1   Tlbexp Command Options

Option	Description
/help or /?	Displays the command syntax and options for the tool.
/names:*filename*	Specifies the capitalization that the names in a type library should follow. The *filename* argument is a text file. Each line in the file specifies the capitalization format for one name in the type library.
/nologo	Suppresses the display of the Microsoft startup banner.
/out:*file*	Specifies the name of the type library file to generate. If you omit this option, Tlbexp.exe generates a type library with the same name as the assembly (the actual assembly name, which might not necessarily be the same as the file containing the assembly) and a .tlb extension.
/silent	Suppresses the display of success messages.
/verbose	Specifies verbose mode; displays a list of referenced assemblies for which a type library needs to be generated.

The following command creates a type library named MyLib.tlb from the MyLib.dll assembly.

    tlbexp MyLib.dll

You can also specify the name of the output file that the Tlbexp.exe tool creates, as shown in the following command:

    tlbexp MyLib.dll /out: MyTypeLib.tlb

Note   The .NET Framework provides another tool called Type Library Importer (Tlbimp.exe), which allows you to import types from a type library into a common language runtime assembly. The syntax to import types from a type library is
    tlbimp tlbFile [*options*]
For example, the command
    tlbimp MyTypeLib.tlb /out: MyLib.dll
imports types from MyTypeLib.tlb into the MyLib.dll assembly.

After the types have been exported into a type library, you can use them to create COM components using languages such as Microsoft Visual Basic 6.0. The Tlbexp.exe tool only creates the type library; it does not register the library. You can use the Assembly Registration Tool (Regasm.exe) to create as well as register a type library with COM. The Assembly Registration Tool uses the information provided by the assembly manifest to register the types that a common language runtime assembly contains. The syntax for using the regasm command is

    regasm *assemblyFile* [*options*]

In the preceding command, *assemblyFile* is the assembly to be registered with COM. Table 10.2 shows the options that you can use with the regasm command.

Table 10.2   Regasm Command Options

Option	Description
/tlb [:*typeLibFile*]	Creates a type library from the specified common language runtime by using the definitions of the accessible types defined within the assembly.
/regfile [:*regFile*]	Creates a .reg file for the assembly, which contains the registry entries required to register types. This option does not change the registry. You cannot use this option with the /u or /tlb options.
/unregister or /u	Unregisters the creatable classes that the assemblyFile contains. Omitting this option causes Regasm.exe to register the creatable classes in the assembly.
/codebase	Creates a Codebase entry in the registry. The Codebase entry specifies the file path for an assembly that is not installed in the global assembly cache. The *assemblyFile* argument that you specify with the /codebase option must be a strong-named assembly.
/help or /?	Displays command syntax and options for the tool.
/nologo	Suppresses the display of the Microsoft startup banner.
/silent or /s	Suppresses the display of success messages.
/verbose	Specifies verbose mode; displays a list of any referenced assemblies for which a type library needs to be generated (when specified with the /tlb option).

The following example shows how to register the public classes defined in the MyLib.dll file with COM.

    regasm MyLib.dll

The following command creates a MyTypes.reg file containing registry entries that are required to register the public classes defined in the MyLib.dll file.

    regasm MyLib.dll /regfile: MyTypes.reg

The preceding command does not register types. You can register types by importing registry entries from the MyTypes.reg file using the Registry Editor tool.

The following command registers all public classes contained in MyLib.dll. It also generates and registers the type library, MyTypes.dll, which contains definitions of all the public types defined in MyLib.dll.

    regasm MyLib.dll /tlb: MyTypes.tlb

Locating Assemblies

When deploying your applications on the .NET Framework, you must know how the common language runtime locates and binds assemblies to your application. The common language runtime uses the information contained in an assembly manifest to determine an application's dependency on assemblies. When you start an application, the common language runtime tries to locate and bind the exact version of the assemblies that the application was built with. The common language runtime performs the following tasks, in the order listed, to locate and bind to assemblies:

- Determines the correct assembly version
- Checks for the previously loaded assembly
- Checks the global assembly cache
- Locates the assembly through the codebase setting or probing

Determining the Correct Assembly Version

The common language runtime examines the configurations defined in application configuration, publisher policy, and machine configuration files to determine the correct version of the assembly to locate and bind.

The common language runtime first examines the application configuration file to determine the version of the assembly. The version information in the application configuration file overrides the version information in the calling assembly's manifest.

Next, the common language runtime examines the publisher policy file, if one exists. A *publisher policy file* contains information that directs an assembly reference to the new version of the assembly that contains shared components. After you create a new version of an assembly that contains shared components, you need to install the new version in the global assembly cache. The new version of the assembly should also contain a publisher policy file that directs the callers of the old version of the assembly to the new version of the assembly. The version information contained in the publisher policy file overrides the version information that comes from the application configuration file or the calling assembly's assembly manifest.

Finally, the common language runtime examines the version information in the machine configuration file, which overrides the version information from the publisher policy file as well the version information that comes from the application.

Checking for the Previously Loaded Assembly

After the common language runtime determines the correct version of the assembly being requested, it checks whether or not the assembly is already loaded. If the common language runtime finds that the assembly is loaded, it binds the already loaded assembly for the application.

Checking the Global Assembly Cache

If the common language runtime does not find the requested assembly among the loaded assemblies, it checks the global assembly cache to locate the requested assembly with the correct version. The common language runtime checks the global assembly cache only if the calling assembly requests a strong-named assembly.

Locating Assemblies Through the Codebase Setting or Probing

After the common language runtime determines the correct version of the assembly by using the calling assembly's manifest and configuration files, and checks the global assembly cache (only for strong-named assemblies), it tries to find the requested assembly by using the codebase setting if the codebase element is present in the application configuration file. Upon finding the assembly, the common language runtime binds the assembly. However, if the common language runtime is unable to find the requested assembly in the specified codebase setting, the binding process fails.

If the codebase information is not present in the calling assembly's application configuration file, the common language runtime then tries to locate the requested assembly through probing. When probing, the common language runtime uses the following criteria to locate the assembly:

- **Application base.**   The root location where the application executes.
- **Culture.**   The culture of the assembly being referenced as determined by the culture attribute.
- **Name**   The name of the assembly.
- **Private binpath.**   The list of subdirectories that you can define under the root location. You can specify the binpath by using the application configuration file or by using the AppendPrivatePath property of the application domain in the code.

The common language runtime starts probing in the application's base, which can either be a URL or the application's root directory on a computer. If the referenced assembly is not found in the application base and no culture information is provided, the common language runtime searches the subdirectories, if any, for the assembly name. The directories probed include

- [application base] / [assembly name].dll
- [application base] / [assembly name] / [assembly name].dll

If culture information is specified for the referenced assembly, only the following directories are probed:

- [application base] / [culture] / [assembly name].dll
- [application base] / [culture] / [assembly name] / [assembly name].dll

If you specify the binpath in the application configuration file or by using the AppendPrivatePath property of the application domain in the managed code, the following paths are searched:

- [application base] / [binpath] / [assembly name].dll
- [application base] / [binpath] / [assembly name] / [assembly name].dll

If culture information is also specified, the common language runtime probes the following paths:

- [application base] / [binpath] / [culture] / [assembly name].dll
- [application base] / [binpath] / [culture] / [assembly name] / [assembly name].dll

Lesson 4: Implementing Versioning and Side-by-Side Deployment

In the previous lesson, you learned how to register components and assemblies. You also learned how the .NET Framework locates assemblies. In this lesson, you will learn how to implement versioning in assemblies. You will also learn how to deploy multiple versions of an assembly simultaneously.

After this lesson, you will be able to
- Implement versioning in assemblies
- Deploy assemblies simultaneously

Estimated lesson time: 15 minutes

Implementing Versioning in Assemblies

As mentioned in Lesson 1, the versioning of assemblies is performed at the assembly level. The assembly version and the versions of all dependent assemblies are recorded in the assembly manifest.

You can specify the version for an assembly by updating the AssemblyVersion() attribute in the AssemblyInfo file of an application. The assembly version is a set of four numbers. The format of an assembly version is

<major version>.<minor version>.<build number>.<revision>

You can open the AssemblyInfo file and specify the version number in the preceding format. The following code displays the AssemblyInfo file for an application.

Visual Basic .NET (AssemblyInfo.vb)

```
Imports System.Reflection
Imports System.Runtime.InteropServices

<Assembly: AssemblyTitle("")>
<Assembly: AssemblyDescription("")>
<Assembly: AssemblyCompany("")>
<Assembly: AssemblyProduct("")>
<Assembly: AssemblyCopyright("")>
<Assembly: AssemblyTrademark("")>
<Assembly: CLSCompliant(True)>

' Version information for an assembly consists of the
' following four values:
'    Major Version
```

(continued)

```
'      Minor Version
'      Build Number
'      Revision
'
<Assembly: AssemblyVersion("1.1.1.0")>
```

Visual C# (AssemblyInfo.cs)

```csharp
using System.Reflection;
using System.Runtime.CompilerServices;

[assembly: AssemblyTitle("")]
[assembly: AssemblyDescription("")]
[assembly: AssemblyConfiguration("")]
[assembly: AssemblyCompany("")]
[assembly: AssemblyProduct("")]
[assembly: AssemblyCopyright("")]
[assembly: AssemblyTrademark("")]
[assembly: AssemblyCulture("")]
//
// Version information for an assembly consists of the
// following four values:
//      Major Version
//      Minor Version
//      Build Number
//      Revision
//
[assembly: AssemblyVersion("1.1.1.0")]
```

In addition to specifying the version for an assembly in the AssemblyInfo file, you can include the AssemblyVersion() attribute in the source code of your application. However, to include the AssemblyVersion() attribute in the source code, you need to include the System.Reflection namespace in your project as shown here.

Visual Basic .NET

```vbnet
Imports System.Reflection

<Assembly: AssemblyVersion("1.1.1.0")>
Public Class MyClass
End Class
```

Visual C#

```csharp
using System;
using System.Reflection;

[assembly: AssemblyVersion("1.1.1.0")]
public class MyClass
{
}
```

After you specify the version for an assembly, you can deploy the assembly as a private assembly in the folder that contains executable code for the application. In addition, you can deploy an assembly as a public assembly in the global assembly cache.

Deploying Multiple Versions of an Assembly in the Global Assembly Cache

Assemblies deployed in the global assembly cache are shared assemblies that multiple applications can access. To deploy an assembly as a shared assembly, you sign the assembly using a strong name. You can specify the strong-named key file in the AssemblyKeyFile() attribute. To place an assembly in the global assembly cache, drag the .dll file to the assembly folder within the Windows folder.

At times, you might need to add functionality to existing assemblies. You can add functions to an assembly and compile the assembly using a new version. You can then deploy the new version of the assembly in the global assembly cache. The new version of the assembly can exist along with the previous version of the same assembly in the global assembly cache. Figure 10.16 displays two versions of the same assembly in the global assembly cache.

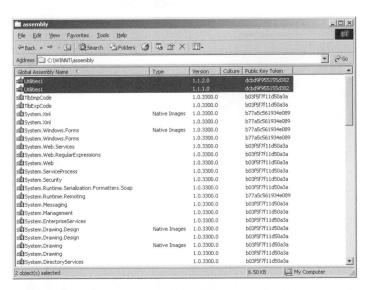

Figure 10.16   The global assembly cache with multiple versions of the same assembly

When you deploy multiple versions of the same assembly, all versions can execute simultaneously. Different versions of the same client can access the respective assembly to which they were bound. This enables you to release newer versions of your application, which users can run along with the previous versions of the application. Figure 10.17 displays different client applications accessing different versions of the same assembly.

Figure 10.17   Client applications accessing different versions of the same assembly on the same machine

After you compile the assembly and deploy it in the global assembly cache, you add a reference of the assembly to the client application by using the Add Reference dialog box. In the Add Reference dialog box, you specify the location of the assembly.

In the following code samples, two assembly versions, 1.1.1.0 and 1.1.2.0, are shown. The 1.1.1.0 version is accessed by version 1.1.1.0 of the client application, and the 1.1.2.0 version is accessed by version 1.1.2.0 of the client application.

Visual Basic .NET

```
Imports System.Reflection
<Assembly: AssemblyVersion("1.1.1.0")>

Public Class Util
    Public Function Util1() As String
        Return ("Hello from Util1 Version 1.1.1.0")
    End Function
End Class
```

Visual C#

```
using System;
using System.Reflection;

[assembly: AssemblyVersion("1.1.1.0")]

namespace Utilities1
{
    public class Util
    {
        public string Util1()
        {
            return("Hello from Util1 Version 1.1.1.0");
        }
    }
}
```

Visual Basic .NET

```
Imports System.Reflection
<Assembly: AssemblyVersion("1.1.2.0")>

Public Class Util
    Public Function Util1() As String
        Return ("Hello from Util1 Version 1.1.2.0")
    End Function
End Class
```

Visual C#

```
using System;
using System.Reflection;

[assembly: AssemblyVersion("1.1.2.0")]

namespace Utilities1
{
    public class Util
    {
        public string Util1()
        {
            return("Hello from Util1 Version 1.1.2.0");
        }
    }
}
```

The assembly manifests for each version of a client application maintain the version details of the assemblies referenced in that version of the client application. Figure 10.18 displays the assembly version entries in the assembly manifests of two versions of the same client application, which use different versions of the same assembly.

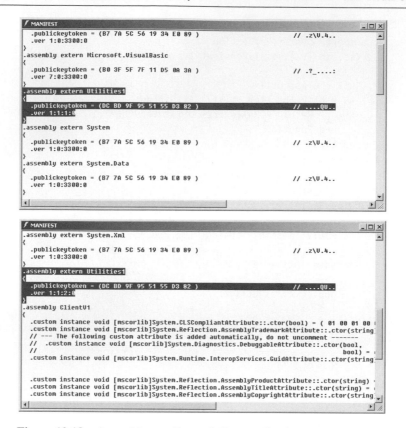

Figure 10.18   Assembly manifests of client application versions 1.1.1.0 and 1.1.2.0, accessing versions 1.1.1.0 and 1.1.2.0 of the Utilities1 assembly

Summary

- The .NET Framework provides various features and tools that you can use to deploy applications. These features and tools enable you to deploy different types of applications to a large number of users. These features include no-impact installation, private components, side-by-side execution, enterprise deployment, controlled code sharing, on-the-fly updates, downloading and caching, and Xcopy deployment.

- Visual Studio .NET consists of four types of project templates that you can use to deploy different types of projects. The four types of deployment projects are Setup, Web Setup, Cab, and Merge Module.

- The .NET Framework does not require you to register components with the Windows registry because the common language runtime uses metadata information contained in an assembly manifest to locate the components and types that an application uses. However, if you want COM components to access managed components, you need to export the managed types to a type library, a .tlb file, and register the type library with the Windows registry.

- Versioning enables you to implement side-by-side deployment.

Lab: Creating Setup Projects

In this lab, you will learn to deploy various projects such as a Windows application, Windows services, and a class library. You will deploy the application that you created in the lab in Chapter 5 using Visual Studio .NET Setup projects. The solutions to the exercises in this lab can be found in the \Solution folder on the Supplemental Course Materials CD-ROM.

Estimated lab time: 30 minutes

Exercise 1: Creating a Setup Project

In this exercise, you will create the Setup project for deploying the entire solution of the lab in Chapter 5. The solution contains four objects:

- RemoteClient, a Windows application
- RemoteAccessComponents, a class library
- RemoteAccessAgent, a Windows service
- BusinessComponent, a class library

To deploy this solution, perform the following steps:

1. Open Visual Studio .NET.
2. From the File menu, open the Open Project dialog box.
3. Navigate to the Solution.sln file in the \Solutions\Ch05\ folder on the CD-ROM.
4. Click Open.
5. Open the Add New Project dialog box. From the Project Types pane, select Setup And Deployment Projects, and then select Setup Project from the Templates pane.
6. Type **Setup** in the Name box and click OK. The Setup project is now added to the solution.
7. To configure the Setup project, navigate to the Solution Explorer. Right-click Setup, point to Add on the shortcut menu, and click Project Output.
8. In the Add Project Output Group dialog box, select BusinessComponents from the Project list, and then select Primary Output. Click OK.
9. Repeat steps 7 and 8 for the other three projects in the solution: RemoteAccess-Agent, RemoteAccessComponents, and RemoteClient. The File System editor after adding the project output of all four projects in the solution is shown next.

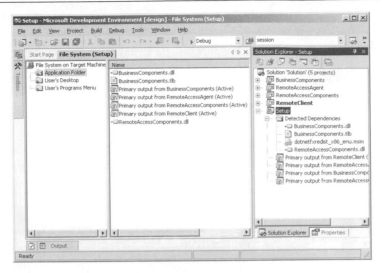

After adding the project output, you need to add a custom action. The custom action is specified for the Windows service component, RemoteAccessAgent. Because you need to install the Windows service after deploying it on the target computer, you need to add the custom action.

10. To add the custom action, navigate to the Solution Explorer, right-click Setup, point to View on the shortcut menu, and click Custom Actions.

11. In the Custom Actions editor, right-click Custom Actions, and click Add Custom Action from the shortcut menu.

12. In the Select Item In Project dialog box, double-click Application Folder, select Primary Output From RemoteAccessAgent (Active), and click OK.

13. In the Custom Actions editor, shown here, you can see that all four actions, Install, Commit, Rollback, and Uninstall, are available for the RemoteAccess-Agent component.

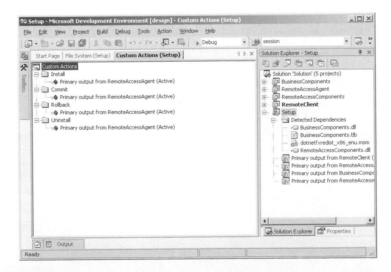

14. Select Build Solution from the Build menu to build the Setup project and the entire solution.

15. Execute the Setup.msi file to deploy the application.

Exercise 2: Deploying a Web Service with a Web Setup Project

In this exercise, you will learn to deploy an XML Web service with a Web Setup project. To deploy an XML Web service, you use the Web Setup Project template available in Visual Studio .NET. To deploy an XML Web service, perform the following steps:

1. Start Visual Studio .NET and open a new project.

2. Select Visual Basic Projects or Visual C# Projects from the Project Types pane in the New Project dialog box.

3. Select ASP.NET Web Service from the Templates pane.

4. Type **WebServiceExample** in the Name box and click OK. A new .NET solution named WebServiceExample is created.

5. Rename Service1.asmx.vb or Service1.asmx.cs to DeployedService.asmx.vb or DeployedService.asmx.cs.

6. To deploy an XML Web service, you need to add a Web Setup project. From the File menu, point to Add Project, and click New Project. The Add New Project dialog box appears.

7. In the Add New Project dialog box, locate the Project Types pane and select Setup And Deployment Projects. In the Templates pane, select Web Setup Project.

8. In the Name box, type **WebServiceSetup** and click OK.

9. To add DeployedService to the Web Setup project, navigate to Solution Explorer, right-click the WebServiceSetup project, point to Add, and click Project Output.

10. In the Add Project Output Group dialog box, ensure that WebServiceSetup is selected in the Project list. From the list, select Primary Output, Debug Symbols, and Content Files, and then click OK.

11. Right-click on the WebServiceSetup project and choose Build from the shortcut menu to build the WebServiceSetup project. The WebServiceSetup.msi file is created. To deploy the XML Web service, execute the WebServiceSetup.msi file on the target computer.

Review

The questions in this section reinforce key information presented in this chapter. If you are unable to answer a question, review the appropriate lesson, and then try answering the question again. Answers to the questions can be found in Appendix A, "Questions and Answers."

1. What are the deployment features of the .NET Framework?

2. What is the format of the assembly version stored in the AssemblyInfo file?

3. Which attribute do you use to specify the version number of an assembly?

4. What are Merge Module projects?

5. What type of Setup project do you create to deploy XML Web services?

6. Which tools does the .NET Framework provide to export types defined in an assembly to a type library?

7. Which tool can you use to register managed types with the Windows registry?

8. What tasks does the common language runtime perform to locate and bind an assembly?

A P P E N D I X   A

Questions and Answers

Chapter 1: Understanding the .NET Framework

Lab: Creating Assemblies and Examining MSIL

Page 41   ▶   **Exercise 2: Using Ildasm to Examine the MSIL Code**

3. Double-click MANIFEST under MyConsoleApp.exe to view the assembly manifest. The assembly manifest for the application created in Visual Basic .NET is shown in the following graphic.

```
.assembly extern mscorlib
{
  .publickeytoken = (B7 7A 5C 56 19 34 E0 89 )
  .ver 1:0:3300:0
}
.assembly extern Microsoft.VisualBasic
{
  .publickeytoken = (B0 3F 5F 7F 11 D5 0A 3A )
  .ver 7:0:3300:0
}
.assembly MyConsoleApp
{
  .hash algorithm 0x00008004
  .ver 1:1:1:33394
}
.module MyConsoleApp.exe
// MVID: {1757E216-194B-427B-A18F-830D426E160E}
.imagebase 0x00400000
.subsystem 0x00000003
.file alignment 512
.corflags 0x00000001
// Image base: 0x03090000
```

What does the assembly manifest contain?

It contains the assembly information such as the version number and hash of the file that make up the assembly. It also contains the name, version, and the public key information of the assemblies, which the application requires at run time. The MyConsoleApp assembly created earlier depends on the mscorlib and Microsoft.VisualBasic assemblies.

The following graphic shows the assembly manifest for the file created in C#.

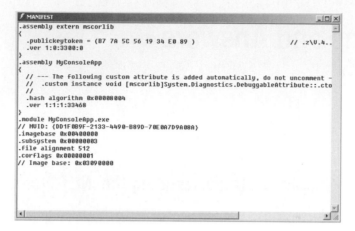

What are the similarities and the differences between the assembly manifests contained within the two assemblies?

The assembly manifests of both assemblies contain the name, version, and public key token information of the assemblies that they depend upon. Both assemblies depend on the mscorlib assembly. However, the assembly created in Visual Basic .NET additionally depends on the Microsoft.VisualBasic assembly.

4. Double-click the Main method in the MSIL window to view the MSIL code. Is it marked as the entry point for the assembly?

Yes.

Page 46

Review Questions

1. What are the development tools and operational systems that .NET provides to build, deploy, and integrate applications?

.NET provides the following development tools and operational systems:

- **Smart Client Software**
- **.NET Server Infrastructure**
- **XML Web Services**
- **Microsoft Visual Studio .NET and the .NET Framework**

2. What are the functions of the components of the common language runtime?

The components of the common language runtime provide the run-time environment and run-time services for .NET applications. These components also load the IL code of a .NET application into the runtime, compile the IL code into native code, execute the code, and enforce security. In addition, these components implement type safety and provide automatic memory management.

3. What are the different types of assemblies?

   The different types of assemblies include

   - **Static and dynamic assemblies**
   - **Private and shared assemblies**
   - **Single-file and multiple-file assemblies**

4. What are the different types of configuration files that the .NET Framework provides?

   Machine configuration file. **This file is located in the %runtime installation path%\Config directory. The machine configuration file contains settings that affect all the applications that run on the machine.**

   Application configuration file. **This file contains the settings required to configure an individual application. ASP.NET configuration files are named Web.config, and application configuration files are named** *App.exe***.config, where** *App.exe* **is the name of the executable.**

   Security configuration file. **The security configuration files contain security permissions for a hierarchy of code groups. The security configuration files define the enterprise-level, machine-level, and user-level security policies. The Enterprisesec.config file defines the security policies for the enterprise. The machine-level Security.config file defines the security policy for the machine, whereas the user-level Security.config file defines the security policy for a user.**

5. What are application domains?

   Application domains are the boundaries within which applications run. A process can contain multiple application domains. Application domains provide an isolated environment to applications that is similar to the isolation provided by processes. An application running inside one application domain cannot directly access the code running inside another application domain. To access the code running in another application domain, an application needs to use a proxy.

Chapter 2: Creating and Managing Windows Services

Page 122

Review Questions

1. What are the states of a service application?

   The states in which a service application can remain are running, paused, stopped, and pending.

2. What are the different types of Windows services?

   Windows services are of two types: Win32OwnProcess and Win32ShareProcess services. Each Win32OwnProcess runs in its own process space, whereas Win32ShareProcess services share a process space with other services.

3. What are the tasks that you perform to create a Windows service?

These tasks are performed when creating a Windows service:

- **Create a blank Windows service by using the Windows Service template for Visual Studio .NET.**
- **Change the default properties of the Windows Service template according to your requirements.**
- **Write code in the service application project to handle various events.**
- **Add installers to your service application.**
- **Install your service application by using the installation tools.**

4. How do you add functionality to a service application?

To add functionality to a service application, you override the OnStart and OnStop methods of the ServiceBase class. You can also override the OnPause, OnContinue, and OnCustomCommand methods of the Service-Base class to increase the functionality of a service application.

5. Write code to specify that a service application create an entry in the file named C:\Temp\ServiceStartStatus.log every time the service application starts.

Visual Basic .NET

```
Protected Overrides Sub OnStart(ByVal args() As String)
    Dim FS As New FileStream("C:\temp\ServiceStartStatus.log", _
        FileMode.Append, FileAccess.Write)
    Dim SR As New StreamWriter(FS)
    SR.WriteLine("Service Started")
    SR.Flush()
End Sub
```

Visual C#

```
protected override void OnStart(string[] args)
{
    FileStream fs = new FileStream(@"C:\temp\ServiceStartStatus.log",
        FileMode.OpenOrCreate, FileAccess.Write);
    StreamWriter SR = new StreamWriter(fs);
    SR.WriteLine("Service Started");
    SR.Flush();
}
```

6. How do you log custom information in the default event logs?

To enable your service application to access the default event logs and write information in them, set the AutoLog property of a service application to False. You then use the WriteEntry method of the EventLog class log to write information in the default event logs.

7. Why do you need to include installers in your service application?

   The installers enable you to install a Windows service and resources, such as custom logs and performance counters, that a service application uses on a computer. The installers automatically install these resources when you install a service application using the Installutil tool.

8. Why do you need to add instances of both the ServiceProcessInstaller and ServiceInstaller classes to install your service application?

   A service application can contain more than one service. The methods of the ServiceProcessInstaller class perform the tasks that are common for all the services within a service application, such as writing entries in the system registry for all the services within the service application. The Service-Installer class performs tasks specific to a service, such as creating an entry for a service in the registry of a computer.

9. How do you specify the security context of a user account within which a service application runs?

   You use the Account property of the ServiceProcessInstaller class to specify the security context for your service application. To specify the security context of a user account, set the Account property to User. You then need to specify the user name and password of a user account when you install the service application.

10. What administrative tasks can you perform on your service using the SCM?

    You can perform the following administrative tasks using the SCM:

    - **Change the state of a service**
    - **Specify how to start a service**
    - **Specify the recovery actions in case of a service failure**
    - **Specify a user account for a service**
    - **View service dependencies**

11. What are the steps to run custom commands on your service application?

    The steps to run custom commands on your service application are

    1. **Create a Windows application that you use to control your service application.**
    2. **Create a method that calls the ServiceController.ExecuteCommand method in the Windows application.**
    3. **Override the OnCustomCommand method in your service application to specify the tasks that you want your service application to perform.**

12. What are the steps to attach a debugger to your service application?

The steps to attach a debugger to your service application are:

1. **Start your service application using the SCM.**

2. **Choose Processes from the Debug menu.**

3. **Select Show System Processes.**

4. **Select the process for your service application and click Attach. The Attach To Process dialog box appears.**

5. **Select Common Language Runtime, click OK to specify a debugger, and close the Attach To Process dialog box.**

Chapter 3: Creating and Consuming Serviced Components

Lab: Creating, Configuring, and Managing Serviced Components

Page 191   ▶   **Exercise 4: Configuring Serviced
Components Using the Component Services Tool**

6. Under the BankAccounts application, expand the Components node, and view the properties for the BankAccount.Account component. Examine properties such as transaction, object pooling, and object construction. What is the default value of the constructor string?

server=localhost; integrated security=sspi; database=Northwind

7. What role is created for the BankAccounts application?

Authorized Users

8. Add users to the Authenticated Users role. These users will have access to the BankAccount.Account component.

9. Run TransactionApp.exe using a user account that is not included in the Authenticated Users role. What error do you receive?

Access is denied.

Page 193   ## Review Questions

1. How is COM+ related to the DNA architecture?

Windows DNA provides the infrastructure and services that enable you to create and deploy applications based on the three-tier architecture. COM+ services, which are an integral part of Windows DNA, include services such as transactions, queued components (QC), security, loosely coupled events, JIT activation, and object pooling.

2. Briefly explain the use of the following COM+ services:

- JIT activation

- Queued components

- Object pooling

Just-in-time activation. The Just-In-Time (JIT) Activation services of COM+ ensure that the client application has references to objects as long as they require them. As a result, the client application does not need to use the valuable memory resources of the server to save the object references.

Queued components. The Queued Component service of COM+ is based on the Microsoft Message Queue Server (MSMQ) model that is a part of Windows 2000 and Windows XP. MSMQ is a middle-tier service that facilitates the asynchronous delivery of messages to named queues. The MSMQ system queues up the method calls and executes them automatically as and when the component is available. You can, therefore, use queued components to execute client methods even after the component is unavailable or offline, ensuring the continuous running of a distributed application.

Object pooling. COM+ provides an automated service for configuring a component so that it can maintain ready-to-use and active object instances in a pool to process client requests. To configure and monitor the pool, you specify characteristics such as the pool size and the creation request time-out values. Next, the COM+ service is responsible for managing the pool and ensuring the activation and reuse of the pool objects according to the configured specifications.

3. What is a serviced component?

    A serviced component is a class that derives from the System.Enterprise-Services.ServicedComponent class, which is the base class for all classes that use COM+ component services. You create and register each service component before it can access the COM+ services.

4. Which class do you need to define when creating serviced components?

    To create a serviced component, you need to define a class that is derived directly from the ServicedComponent base class.

5. How do you assign a name and ID to a COM+ application?

    The application ID serves as an index for all application searches made during the registration process. The application ID is assigned by using the ApplicationID attribute that is derived from the System.EnterpriseServices namespace.

6. What is the importance of the activation type attribute in the registration of a serviced component?

    You use the activation type attribute to specify whether the created serviced component is created in the library of the caller process or in a new process of the server.

7. Which tool is used to add a strong name to an assembly?

    You can use the Strong Name Tool (sn.exe) to create the file containing the public key information.

8. Which procedures can be used to register serviced components?

COM+ services use the following three types of registration for a serviced component:

- **Manual registration**
- **Dynamic registration**
- **Programmatic registration**

9. How do you configure a serviced component for implementation of role-based security at the interface level?

To assign roles to a component, method, or interface, complete the following steps:

1. **In the console tree of the Component Services tool, locate the COM+ application for which the role is defined.**
2. **Expand the tree to view the components, interfaces, or methods of the application, depending on whom you are assigning the role.**
3. **Right-click the item to which you want to assign the role and click Properties.**
4. **In the properties dialog box, click the Security tab.**
5. **In the Roles Explicitly Set For Selected Item(s) list box, select the roles that you want to assign to the item.**
6. **Click OK.**

10. The following is the code for a transaction component. Add the appropriate methods to the Public class to have the component participate in a transaction. In addition, add the appropriate method to continue with the transaction or abort the transaction based on the occurrence of exceptions.

Visual Basic .NET

```
Imports System.EnterpriseServices
Imports System.Reflection

' Providing a name for the COM+ application
<Assembly: ApplicationNameAttribute("MyFirstComPlusExample")>

' Providing a strong-name for the assembly
<Assembly: AssemblyKeyFileAttribute("bin/MyFirstComPlusExample.snk")>

Public Class MyFirstCOMPlusServices
    Inherits ServicedComponent

    Public Sub New()
        MyBase.New()
    End Sub
```

```
      Public Function DoTransaction() As String
          Return "SUCCESSFUL"
      End Function
End Class
```

Visual C#

```csharp
using System.EnterpriseServices;
using System.Reflection;

//Providing a name for the COM+ application
[assembly: ApplicationNameAttribute("MyFirstComPlusExample")]

//Providing a strong-name for the assembly
[assembly: AssemblyKeyFileAttribute("bin/MyFirstComPlusExample.snk")]

public class MyFirstCOMPlusServices :ServicedComponent
{

    public  MyFirstCOMPlusServices()
    {
    }

    public string DoTransaction()
    {
        return "SUCCESSFUL";
    }
}
```

The completed code is shown below. Lines in bold italic type show additions or changes to the original code.

Visual Basic .NET

```vbnet
Imports System.EnterpriseServices
Imports System.Reflection

' Providing a name for the COM+ application
<Assembly: ApplicationNameAttribute("MyFirstComPlusExample")>

' Providing a strong-name for the assembly
<Assembly: AssemblyKeyFileAttribute("bin/MyFirstComPlusExample.snk")>

<TransactionAttribute(TransactionOption.Required)> _
Public Class MyFirstCOMPlusServices
    Inherits ServicedComponent

    Public Sub New()
        MyBase.New()
    End Sub
```

(continued)

```
<AutoComplete()> _
Public Function DoTransaction() As String
    Return "SUCCESSFUL"
End Function
End Class
```

Visual C#

```csharp
using System.EnterpriseServices;
using System.Reflection;

//Providing a name for the COM+ application
[assembly: ApplicationNameAttribute("MyFirstComPlusExample")]

//Providing a strong-name for the assembly
[assembly: AssemblyKeyFileAttribute("bin/MyFirstComPlusExample.snk")]

[TransactionAttribute(TransactionOption.Required)]
public class MyFirstCOMPlusServices :ServicedComponent
{

    public  MyFirstCOMPlusServices()
    {
    }

    [AutoComplete()]
    public string DoTransaction()
    {
        return "SUCCESSFUL";
    }
}
```

11. Write the code for implementing role-based security at the component level. In the code, add a new method to a class called IsSeniorLecturer to check whether the user is a member of the role IsSeniorLecturer.

Visual Basic .NET

```vbnet
Public Function IsSeniorLecturer() As Boolean

    Dim MyObjCallContext As SecurityCallContext = _
        SecurityCallContext.CurrentCall

    IsSeniorLecturer = _
        MyObjCallContext.IsCallerInRole("Senior Lecturer")

End Function
```

Visual C#

```
public bool IsSeniorLecturer()
{

    SecurityCallContext MyObjCallContext=
        SecurityCallContext.CurrentCall;

    return MyObjCallContext.IsCallerInRole("Senior Lecturer");

}
```

Chapter 4: Creating and Consuming .NET Remoting Objects

Page 247

Review Questions

1. What are the requirements to enable communication between objects across remoting boundaries?

   To enable communication between objects across remoting boundaries, you need

   - **A server object that exposes the functionality to callers outside its boundary**
   - **A client that makes calls to the server object**
   - **A transportation mechanism to pass the calls from one end to the other**

2. Describe the two types of remotable objects.

   The two types of remotable objects are

   - *Marshal-by-value objects.* **These objects are copied and passed by value out of the application domain.**
   - *Marshal-by-reference objects.* **The clients that use these objects need a proxy to access the object remotely.**

3. Describe the two types of activation modes of the .NET Remoting system.

   The two types of activation modes in the .NET Remoting system are

   - *Server activation.* **In server activation, objects are created on the server when you call a method in the server class. However, objects are not created when you use the *new* keyword to create an instance of the server class.**
   - *Client activation.* **In client activation, objects are created on the server when you create an instance using the *new* keyword.**

4. How can you renew lifetime leases of objects?

   You can renew the lifetime lease of an object in the following two ways:

   - **A client application calls the ILease.Renew method.**
   - **A sponsor renews the lease.**

5. What are channels?

Channels enable an application that is running in one application domain, process, or computer to send messages to an application running in a different application domain, process, or computer. In addition, channels allow applications to send and receive messages using protocols, such as TCP and HTTP.

6. List the tasks you need to perform to publish a service outside the service domain.

To publish a service outside the service domain, you need to:

   1. Identify the application domain that will host the service.

   2. Identify the activation model: server activation or client activation.

   3. Identify and create a channel and a port.

   4. Identify how the client application obtains the metadata information about the service.

7. Why do you use delegates in your remoting applications?

You use delegates to implement callback functions, event programming, and asynchronous programming in your remoting applications. Events use delegates to enable callback functions to the client in remoting applications. This enables the client and the remote application to function as domain servers. Therefore, you need to design a server/server application instead of designing a client/server application.

8. What steps do you perform to implement asynchronous programming in a remoting application?

The steps to implement asynchronous programming in a remoting application are

   1. Create an instance of an object that can receive a remote call to a method.

   2. Wrap that instance method with an AsyncDelegate method.

   3. Wrap the remote method with another delegate.

   4. Call the BeginInvoke method on the second delegate, passing any arguments, the AsyncDelegate method, and some object to hold the state.

   5. Wait for the server object to call your callback method.

9. What information do you need to provide to the .NET Remoting system to configure remote objects?

You must provide the .NET Remoting system with the following information to configure remote objects:

   ■ **The activation type for the remote object**

   ■ **The channels that the remote object will use to receive messages from clients**

   ■ **The URL of the remote object**

   ■ **The type metadata that describes the type of your remote object**

Chapter 5: Database Programming Using ADO.NET

Page 303

Review Questions

1. What are the components of an ADO.NET data provider?

   The components of an ADO.NET data provider include:

   - **Connection object**
   - **Command object**
   - **DataReader object**
   - **DataAdapter object**

2. What tasks do the data providers enable you to perform?

   The classes of each data provider contain methods that enable you to perform the following tasks:

   - **Create a connection with a database**
   - **Execute a SQL statement or stored procedure on a database**
   - **Read data rows from a database in a forward-only mode**
   - **Transfer data between a database and a DataSet**
   - **Display error messages and warnings that a database returns**
   - **Handle exceptions when a database returns an error or warning**
   - **Execute Transact-SQL statements on a database**

3. What are the options you need to specify when you set the ConnectionString property of a SqlConnection object?

   You need to specify the following options when you set the Connection-String property of the SqlConnection object:

   - **Data Source**
   - **User ID**
   - **Password**
   - **Initial Catalog**

4. Which method of the Command object is best suited for when you are using aggregate functions such as COUNT, MAX, and MIN in a SELECT statement?

   You use the ExecuteScalar method of the Command object when you are using aggregate functions in a SELECT statement because aggregate functions return one value.

5. Which object holds read-only and forward-only data that you retrieve from a data source?

   The DataReader object holds read-only and forward-only data that you retrieve from a data source.

6. How do you create relationships between two tables in a DataSet?

   You use the Add method of the Data Relation object to create a relationship between two tables in a DataSet. The Add method assumes a name for

the relationship being created, and the DataColumn references the columns that you want to define as the parent and child columns in the relationship.

7. What events are exposed by the DataTable object?

The events of the DataTable object are ColumnChanged, ColumnChanging, RowChanged, RowChanging, RowDeleted, and RowDeleting.

Chapter 6: Accessing and Manipulating XML Data

Page 367

Review Questions

1. Which method will you use to load the contents of an XML file into an XmlDocument object?

You need to use the Load method to load the contents of an XML file into an XmlDocument object. Alternatively, you can use the LoadXml method to load the XML data from a string format into the XmlDocument object.

2. Which method will you use to write the contents of the XmlDocument object into an XML file?

You need to use the Save method of the XmlDocument class to write the contents of the XmlDocument object into an XML file.

3. How do you read the contents of an XML document using XmlTextReader?

You need to perform the following tasks to read the contents of an XML document using XmlTextReader:

- **Create an object of the XmlTextReader class.**

- **Call the Read() method on the reader object until all the data is read.**

- **While reading the data from the XML document, check the type of the data being read using the XmlTextReader.NodeType property.**

4. Which class do you use to write data to an XML file?

You use the XmlTextWriter class to write to an XML file. The XmlTextWriter class provides methods such as WriteStartDocument, WriteStartElement, WriteAttributeString, WriteEndElement, and WriteEndAttribute, which you use to write data in a well-formed XML document.

5. How does XPathNavigator read data from an XML document?

The XPathNavigator object reads data from an XML document by using a cursor that enables forward and backward navigation within the nodes. XPathNavigator enables you to randomly access any node in an XML document. However, the XPathNavigator cursor is read-only; therefore, you cannot edit an XML document with XPathNavigator.

6. Which methods of the XPathNavigator class do you use to navigate within the nodes selected from an XML document?

You can use the MoveTo, MoveToNext, MoveToPrevious, MoveToFirst, MoveToFirstChild, MoveToParent, MoveToRoot, and MoveToId methods to navigate within the nodes selected from an XML document.

7. What objects are used to create the structure of an XML document within a schema?

   The simpleType and complexType elements are used to specify the structure of the XML document in the XSD schema file.

8. Which event is raised for validating the semantics of the XML Schema?

   The XmlValidatingReader.ValidationEventHandler event for the Compile method is raised for semantic validation checking of the XML Schema.

9. How can you ensure your XML document is valid?

   You can ensure the validity of XML documents by using the XmlValidatingReader class. The XmlValidatingReader class provides DTD, XDR, and XSD schema validation services. The XmlValidatingReader class takes XmlTextReader as input. XmlValidatingReader applies the property that you specify in XmlTextReader.

10. How can you read fragments of an XML document?

    You can use XmlValidatingReader to read XML fragments. XmlValidatingReader parses a given string as a fragment of XML. This enables you to bypass the root-level rules of an XML document. The value you pass to the XmlNodeType parameter of XmlValidatingReader determines how to parse an XML string.

11. Which method enables you to retrieve the XSD schema for the XML representation of the data stored in the DataSet?

    The GetXmlSchema method enables you to retrieve the XSD schema for the XML representation of the data stored in the DataSet.

12. Which method of the DataSet class enables you to write the contents of a DataSet into an XML file?

    The WriteXml method of the DataSet class enables you to write the contents of a DataSet into an XML file.

Chapter 7: Creating and Consuming XML Web Services

Page 429

Review Questions

1. What is an XML Web service?

   XML Web services are program components that allow you to build scalable, loosely coupled, platform-independent applications. XML Web services enable disparate applications to exchange messages using standard protocols such as HTTP, XML, XSD, SOAP, and Web Services Description Language (WSDL).

2. What are the components of the XML Web service infrastructure?

   The components of the XML Web service infrastructure include XML Web services directories, XML Web services discovery, XML Web services description, and XML Web service wire formats.

3. What are the steps to deploy a Web service?

Follow these steps to deploy a Web service:

1. **Copy the files for your XML Web service application to the Inetpub\Wwwroot folder.**
2. **Open Internet Services Manager from the Administrative Tools folder.**
3. **Expand the Default Web Site node.**
4. **Right-click the Web service folder you copied to the Inetpub\Wwwroot folder to open its properties dialog box.**
5. **Click Create in the properties dialog box to configure the virtual folder as the root of your Web application.**

4. What are the components that are published when you deploy a Web service?

The components that are published when you deploy a Web service are

- **The Web application directory**
- **The <WebService>.asmx file**
- **The <WebService>.disco file**
- **The Web.config file**
- **The \Bin directory**

5. What does the .disco file contain?

A .disco file contains links to other resources that describe your XML Web service and enables clients to discover an XML Web service. The discovery document contains information regarding other XML Web services that reside on the same or a different Web server.

6. What are the steps to configure discovery information for an XML Web service?

To configure discovery information for an XML Web service, perform the following tasks:

1. **Create an XML document and insert the <?xml version="1.0" ?> tag in the first line.**
2. **Add a <discovery> element.**
3. **Add references to service descriptions, XSD schemas, and other discovery documents within the <discovery> element.**
4. **Deploy the discovery document to a Web server.**

7. What tasks do you need to perform to consume a Web service in a client application?

To consume a Web service from a client application, you need to perform the following tasks:

    1. Add a Web reference to the XML Web service in the client application by discovering the XML Web service you want to consume.

    2. Generate a proxy class for the XML Web service.

    3. Create an object of the XML Web service proxy class in the client application.

    4. Access the XML Web service by using the proxy object.

8. Which attribute is used to create a Web method?

In C# you use the [WebMethod] attribute to declare a Web method that exposes the functionality of the XML Web service. In Visual Basic .NET, you use the <WebMethod> attribute to create a Web method.

9. Which file contains configuration information, such as debug mode?

The Web.config file contains configuration information, such as the debug mode and the authentication mode for a Web project. It also includes information about whether to display custom errors for a Web project.

10. Which file allows you to handle application-level events?

The Global.asax file enables you to manage application-level events. This file resides in the root directory of an ASP.NET Web application or ASP.NET Web service. The Global.asax.cs or Global.asax.vb class file is a hidden, dependent file of Global.asax, which contains the code for handling application events such as the Application_OnError event.

Chapter 8: Advanced XML Web Services Programming

Page 487

Review Questions

1. Which property of the WebMethod attribute allows you to maintain the state of objects across sessions in a Web method?

The EnableSession property of the WebMethod attribute allows you to enable session state for a Web method.

2. What steps do you need to perform to enable transactions in a Web method?

To enable transactions in a Web method, you need to perform the following steps:

    1. Add a reference to the System.EnterpriseServices.dll by using the Solution Explorer.

    2. Include the System.EnterpriseServices namespace in the XML Web service project.

    3. Set the TransactionOption property to an appropriate value.

3. When should you use asynchronous programming?

You should use asynchronous programming when your application calls a method on an object that takes significant time to execute and you do not want the program to wait for the method to return.

4. Explain how you implement asynchronous programming using callbacks.

   A client calls the Begin method on the server object and passes a reference to the callback method. When the asynchronous method finishes execution, the server object calls the callback method on the client object. The callback method in turn calls the End method on the server object. The End method returns a value to the client.

5. Which method do you call for the first time when you access an XML Web service or service method with which the SOAP extension is configured to execute?

   You call the GetInitializer method the first time when you access an XML Web service or service method with which the SOAP extension is configured to execute.

6. What are the different properties of the <add> XML element?

   Type, Priority, and Group are the three properties of the <add> XML element. The Type property of the <add> element represents the type of SOAP extension. The Priority property represents the relative priority of the SOAP extension within a group. The Group property represents the group name to which the SOAP extension belongs.

7. Which element in the Web.config file do you use to manage custom error messages?

   You use the <customErrors/> element to manage custom error messages. You can set the <customErrors> mode attribute to On or RemoteOnly to enable custom error messages, and Off to disable the error messages.

8. How can you ensure that only authorized users access your Web service?

   You can use the <authorization> element to specify the users and roles that can access your Web service. This element enables you to implement both positive and negative authorization assertions. You can use this element to allow or deny access to your Web service based on specific users or roles.

Chapter 9: Testing and Debugging XML Web Services

Page 532

Review Questions

1. What are the different approaches to testing?

   There are two different approaches to testing: the waterfall approach and the evolutionary approach.

2. Explain the waterfall approach.

   The waterfall approach is a traditional approach in which each developer in the development team works in phases. These phases cover requirement analysis, design and specifications requirements, coding, final testing, and release.

3. Explain the evolutionary approach.

   In the evolutionary approach, you develop a modular piece or unit of

application, test it, fix it, and then add another small piece that adds functionality. You then test the two units as an integrated component, increasing the complexity as you proceed.

4. How does the Visual Studio .NET debugger work?

When you debug a Visual Studio .NET application, the debugger first maps the native code to MSIL, and then maps the MSIL code to source code by using a PDB file.

5. What are the main windows and dialog boxes that you use to debug a Visual Studio .NET application?

The main windows and dialog boxes that you use to debug a Visual Studio .NET application are the Visual Studio .NET debugger window, Breakpoints window, Watch window, Call Stack window, Locals window, Autos window, and Processes window.

6. What is code instrumentation?

Code instrumentation is a set of tasks that you perform to monitor and analyze information about the performance of your applications. It involves activities such as writing tracing code for the application, collecting trace information, analyzing the trace output, and troubleshooting the problems that occur at run time.

7. How do you implement code instrumentation?

You can implement code instrumentation by using tracing, debugging, performance counters, and event logs.

8. Which tool do you need to use to convert .txt files to .resources files?

If you have text files as resources, then you can use the ResGen.exe tool to convert .txt files to .resources files. The syntax for using the ResGen.exe tool is

ResGen strings.txt myResources.resource

9. Which tool do you need to use to compile the .resources files into satellite assemblies?

Once you have created .resources files, you can compile them into satellite assemblies by using Al.exe, the Assembly Linker (AL) tool. The AL tool creates satellite assemblies from the .resources files that you specify. As you know, satellite assemblies cannot contain any executable code and can contain only resources.

The following command shows you how to use the Al.exe tool to generate a satellite assembly:

al /t:lib /embed:myResource.resources /culture:de /out:MyRes.resources.dll

Chapter 10: Deploying XML Web Services and Windows Services

Page 577

Review Questions

1. What are the deployment features of the .NET Framework?

    The .NET Framework provides the following deployment features:

    - **No-impact applications**
    - **Private components**
    - **Controlled code sharing**
    - **Side-by-side versioning**
    - **Xcopy deployment**
    - **On-the-fly updates**
    - **Integration with Microsoft Windows Installer**
    - **Enterprise deployment**
    - **Downloading and caching**
    - **Partially trusted code**

2. What is the format of the assembly version stored in the AssemblyInfo file?

    The assembly version number is a four-part number. The format of the version number is

    <major version>.<minor version>.<build number>.<revision>

3. Which attribute do you use to specify the version number of an assembly?

    You use the AssemblyVersion() attribute to specify the version of an assembly.

4. What are Merge Module projects?

    Merge Module projects enable you to install and deploy components consistently. Merge Module projects ensure that the correct version of a component is installed on the target computer. A Merge Module project contains a component such as a DLL along with dependent files, resources, registry entries, and setup logic. You cannot install merge modules directly. The modules are merged with an .msi file for each application that uses the component. This ensures that the component is installed consistently for all applications, eliminating problems such as version conflicts, missing registry entries, and improperly installed files. A merge module contains unique version information that the Windows Installer database uses to determine which applications can use the component, preventing the premature removal of a component. Therefore, a new merge module is created for every incremental version of a component. You should not update a merge module after including the module in an

installer. The deployment tools in Visual Studio .NET make it easy to create Merge Modules and include them in installers for your applications.

5. What type of Setup project do you create to deploy XML Web services?

To deploy XML Web services, you create a Web Setup project.

6. Which tools does the .NET Framework provide to export types defined in an assembly to a type library?

The .NET Framework provides the Type Library Exporter (Tlbexp.exe) to export types defined in an assembly to a type library.

7. Which tool can you use to register managed types with the Windows registry?

You can use the Assembly Registration Tool (Regasm.exe) to register managed types with the Windows registry.

8. What tasks does the common language runtime perform to locate and bind an assembly?

The common language runtime performs the following tasks, in the order listed, to locate and bind to assemblies:

- **Determines the correct assembly version**
- **Checks for the previously loaded assembly**
- **Checks the global assembly cache**
- **Locates the assembly through the codebase setting or probing**

A P P E N D I X   B

COM Interoperability

The applications that you develop using the Microsoft .NET Framework might contain managed as well as unmanaged code. Managed code executes inside the common language runtime, and the garbage collection process manages the allocation and deallocation of memory for managed objects. Unmanaged code runs outside the common language runtime and does not benefit from garbage collection. The .NET Framework and Microsoft Visual Studio .NET enable you to create applications that access managed as well as unmanaged objects. The interoperability that the .NET Framework provides between managed and unmanaged code enables .NET components to call methods on COM components and vice versa.

Note   You can enable COM components to access managed components by exporting the types from a .NET assembly to a COM type library. For a detailed discussion on exporting and registering managed components to make them accessible to COM objects, refer to Chapter 10, "Deploying XML Web Services and Windows Services."

Accessing COM Components from Managed Code

COM types are defined in type libraries. Type libraries contain information, such as member names and data types of COM objects, that you need to create an application. However, the structure of type libraries is different from the structure of .NET assemblies. Therefore, you cannot directly use the type definitions from a type library in your .NET application. Before you can use COM types in your applications, you need to import the type information from a COM type library into a .NET assembly. The resulting assembly containing the definitions of COM types is called an *interop assembly*. You can use the types from an interop assembly in your managed code in the same way that you use types from a .NET assembly. The following sections explain how to access a COM object from managed code.

Create a COM Type Library

The following code shows the Microsoft Visual Basic 6.0 code that is compiled to create the Math.dll file.

Visual Basic 6.0

```
Public Function Add(ByVal number1 As Integer, ByVal number2 As Integer) _
    As Integer
    Add = number1 + number2
End Function

Public Function Subtract(ByVal number1 As Integer, ByVal number2 _
    As Integer) As Integer
    Subtract = number1 - number2
End Function

Public Function Multiply(ByVal number1 As Integer, ByVal number2 _
    As Integer) As Integer
    Multiply = number1 * number2
End Function

Public Function Divide(ByVal number1 As Integer, ByVal number2 As _
    Integer) As Integer
    Divide = CInt(number1 / number2)
End Function
```

Create an Interop Assembly from the Type Library

You can create an interop assembly by using either Visual Studio .NET or the Type Library Importer (Tlbimp.exe) tool. To create an interop assembly using Visual Studio .NET, you would do the following:

1. Install the COM DLL and register the type library on your computer. The following command, executed from the command prompt, registers the types in the Math.dll file:

   Regsvr32 Math.dll

2. In the Solution Explorer, right-click References under your project, and choose Add Reference from the shortcut menu to open the Add Reference dialog box.
3. In the Add Reference dialog box, select the COM tab.
4. Select the type library from the list of references, or click Browse to locate the .tlb or .dll file containing the type definitions.
5. Click OK.

Visual Studio .NET creates an interop assembly and adds it to the list of referenced assemblies.

The Type Library Importer (Tlbimp.exe) is a command-line tool that converts the co-classes and interfaces in a COM type library to metadata. You can use this tool to create an interop assembly and a namespace for all the types in a COM type library. The following command creates an interop assembly for the types contained in Math.dll:

    tlbimp Math.dll

The interop assembly created by the preceding command also has the name Math.dll. To create an interop assembly with a different name, such as InteropMath.dll in this example, use the following command:

    tlbimp Math.dll /out:InteropMath.dll

After creating the interop assembly, you need to add a reference to the new assembly in your project. To add a reference to the interop assembly in your project in Visual Studio .NET, perform the following steps:

1. In the Solution Explorer, right-click References under your project, and choose Add Reference from the shortcut menu to open the Add Reference dialog box.
2. From the .NET tab, click Browse, and select the .dll file containing the interop assembly.
3. Click OK.

After adding a reference to the interop assembly in your project, you can use the COM types in your managed code.

Creating COM Objects in Managed Code

After you create the interop assembly InteropMath.dll and add the reference to your project, you can create an instance of the COM type in your managed code as shown in the following code.

Visual Basic .NET

```
' Namespace that contains the types imported from COM type library
Imports InteropMath
Module COMInterop

    Sub Main()
        Dim obj As New Math()
        Console.WriteLine("Sum of 10 and 20 is " & _
            obj.Add(10, 20).ToString)
        Console.WriteLine("Difference between 10 and 20 is " & _
            obj.Subtract(10, 20).ToString)
        Console.WriteLine("Product of 10 and 20 is " & _
            obj.Multiply(10, 20).ToString)
        Console.WriteLine("Result of 20/10 is " & obj.Divide(20, _
            10).ToString)
        Console.Read()
    End Sub

End Module
```

Visual C#

```csharp
// Namespace that contains the types imported from COM type library
using InteropMath;
using System;

class COMInteropDemo
{
    [STAThread]
    static void Main(string[] args)
    {
        Math obj=new Math();
        Console.WriteLine("Sum of 10 and 20 is " + obj.Add(10,
            20).ToString());
        Console.WriteLine("Difference between 10 and 20 is "
            + obj.Subtract(10, 20).ToString());
        Console.WriteLine("Product of 10 and 20 is " + obj.Multiply(10,
            20).ToString());
        Console.WriteLine("Result of 20/10 is " + obj.Divide(20,
            10).ToString());
        Console.Read();
    }
}
```

You can then build your application and run it to view the output of the application. The output of the preceding code appears as shown here.

Glossary

A

ADO.NET Enables datacentric applications to connect to various data sources to retrieve, manipulate, and update data. ADO.NET uses XML to transfer data across applications and data sources.

application activation The application type attribute that specifies whether the serviced component is created in the library of the caller process or in a new process on the server.

application configuration file Contains the settings required to configure an individual application. For Windows applications this file is named App.exe.config, and for ASP.NET applications it is named Web.config.

application domain The boundary within which an application runs. A process can contain multiple application domains. Application domains provide an isolated environment to applications that is similar to the isolation provided by processes. An application running inside one application domain cannot directly access the code running inside another application domain. To access the code running in another application domain, an application needs to use a proxy.

Application event log Contains messages regarding the events that occur in the applications installed on the computer. You can access the Application event log from within the Event Viewer.

application roots Point to the storage location on the managed heap. Each root either refers to an object on the managed heap or is set to null.

assemblies The fundamental units for application development and deployment in the .NET Framework. An assembly contains the types and resources that an application uses.

Assembly Linker (AL) tool or Al.exe Creates an assembly with the manifest in a separate file. You can use the assembly linker to link satellite assemblies to your main assembly.

assembly manifest Contains the assembly metadata. An assembly manifest contains the information about the identity and version of the assembly. It also contains the information required to resolve references to types and resources.

assembly version The version of an assembly enables the runtime to determine the version of the types and the other resources in an assembly. The assembly version is represented as a four-part number, which represents: *<major version>.<minor version>.<build number>.<revision>*. The version of an assembly is stored in the assembly manifest along with other information, such as the assembly name, public key, and identities of other assemblies connected with the application.

automatic memory management The feature that enables you to focus on the solution to the real problem. The process of automatic memory management involves tasks such as allocating memory, releasing memory, and implementing finalizers.

Autos window A window provided by the Visual Studio .NET debugger, DbgClr, to debug a Visual Studio .NET application. You can use the Autos window to view variables in the current and previous statements.

B

Breakpoints window A window provided by the Visual Studio .NET debugger, DbgClr, to debug a Visual Studio .NET application. You can use the Breakpoints window to list all the breakpoints in your Visual Studio .NET application and to display the properties of the breakpoints. You can also use the Breakpoints window to delete and set new breakpoints.

buffer responses Improve the performance of an application by reducing communication between the worker process and the IIS process.

C

cabinet (.cab) files An option for packaging a Visual Studio .NET application that allows you to compress the executable code files, reducing the time it takes to distribute or download the application.

Cab project Enables you to create .cab files to package ActiveX controls. After creating the .cab files, you can download them from a Web server using a Web browser.

Callback function A reference to a method that you pass to another method. When the second method calls the referenced method, it actually calls back the first method.

Call Stack window A window provided by the Visual Studio .NET debugger, DbgClr, to debug a Visual Studio .NET application. You can use the Call Stack window to view the function or procedure calls that are currently on the stack.

Caspol tool or Caspol.exe A tool that allows you to grant and modify permissions to code groups at the user policy, machine policy, and enterprise policy levels.

channel Allows an application running in one application domain, process, or computer to send messages to an application running in a different application domain, process, or computer. The System.Runtime.Remoting.Channels namespace includes the interfaces and classes that you use to work with channels.

channel sink Performs certain functions on a message before forwarding the message to the next channel sink in the chain. The messages carried by channels pass through a chain of channel sinks.

client activation A type of activation mode in the .NET Remoting system in which objects are created on the server when you create an instance using the *new* keyword.

codeBase element A predefined element of the configuration file that determines the location of the assembly.

code instrumentation The task of including code in programs to monitor the performance of .NET applications. You use code instrumentation to display messages or write to event logs in case a failure occurs during the execution of an application at run time.

code manager Calls the entry-point method, which is the Main, WinMain, or DllMain method, after the MSIL code and the metadata are loaded into memory.

COM marshaler Performs marshaling of data when data passes between managed and unmanaged execution environments.

COM+ security A role-based security service that reduces the complexity of administration issues in middle-tier components.

COM+ services Provide a standard set of frequently required services that focus on developing the business components of an application.

Common Language Infrastructure (CLI) Defines the specifications for the infrastructure that the IL code requires for execution.

common language runtime Includes the CLI and provides the execution environment to .NET applications. All .NET language compilers compile the source code into an intermediate code called Microsoft Intermediate Language (MSIL), which the common language runtime loads and executes when you run an application.

Common Type System (CTS) Provides the necessary data types, Value and Object, that you need to develop applications in different languages. All .NET languages share a CTS.

Component Services tool A Microsoft Management Console (MMC) snap-in tool that allows administrators and developers to create, configure, and maintain COM+ applications.

CorDbg tool A command-line–based debugging tool.

D

DataReader class Provides read-only and forward-only access to data from a data source.

DataSet A cache of records that you retrieve from a data source in ADO.NET. A DataSet can contain records from one or more tables and data sources.

DbgClr tool A GUI-based tool and the default debugger for Visual Studio .NET.

debug engine Provided by the common language runtime; enables you to debug an application written in any language supported by the .NET Framework.

debugging Allows you to troubleshoot the programming and logical errors in code. You use debugging tools, such as CorDbg.exe or Dbg-Clr.exe, to debug applications.

Delegate A class that holds a reference to the method that is called when an event is triggered. In other words, delegates call methods, which handle events.

Description attribute Enables you to add a descriptive field describing the assembly, class, interface, and method used in a particular component.

document type definition (DTD) Specifies the content and values in an XML document. XML documents can have either an inline DTD or a reference to an external DTD file.

dynamic assembly Created dynamically at run time when an application requires the types within these assemblies.

E

event Triggered when an action, such as a mouse click, occurs on an interface element in GUI applications.

event log A feature that allows you to log software and hardware events, such as the failure of a service, low-memory conditions, or the pausing of a service. This information can then help you to determine the type and cause of the error.

evolutionary testing Enables you to develop a modular piece or unit of an application, test it, fix it, and then attach another small piece to add functionality. The two units are then tested as an integrated component, increasing in complexity as testing progresses.

exception manager Handles exceptions that arise from managed and unmanaged method calls.

ExecuteNonQuery A method exposed by the ADO.NET Command class that executes an INSERT, UPDATE, or DELETE statement.

ExecuteReader A method exposed by the ADO.NET Command class that executes a SQL statement or a stored procedure against the available data source and returns a DataReader object.

ExecuteScalar A method exposed by the ADO.NET Command class that executes a SQL statement against a specified data source and returns a single value.

F

finalizers Methods that contain the cleanup code that is executed before the object is claimed by the garbage collector. Examples of finalizers are the Dispose and Finalize methods.

G

garbage collector (GC) Performs periodic checks on the managed heap to identify objects that are no longer required by the program and removes them from memory.

generations The division of objects on the managed heap used by the garbage collector. This mechanism allows the garbage collector to perform highly optimized garbage collection. The unreachable objects are placed in generation 0, the reachable objects are placed in generation 1, and the objects that survive the collection process are promoted to higher generations.

global assembly cache tool or Gacutil.exe Allows you to view and manipulate the contents of the global assembly cache. You can install or uninstall a strong-named assembly into the global assembly cache using this tool.

globalization The process of enabling your application to accept, process, and display various types of scripts, data formats, and languages.

I

Ilasm tool or Ilasm.exe A tool that generates PE files from MSIL code. You can run the resulting executable to determine whether the MSIL code performs as expected.

IL to native code compiler The IL to native code compiler contains JIT compilers for different CPU architectures and compiles the IL code into a native instructions set.

Installutil.exe A tool that enables you to install a Windows service application.

J

JIT activation A COM+ service that ensures that the client application can reference objects whenever required.

L

localization The process of separating culture-specific data from an application. The data that is specific to a particular culture is stored separately in assemblies called satellite assemblies and does not become part of the main application.

Locals window A window provided by the Visual Studio .NET debugger, DbgClr, which enables you to debug a Visual Studio .NET application. The Locals window displays variables that are local to the current context.

loosely coupled events (LCE) A COM+ service that enables an application to send notification about the change in its state using events.

M

Machine.config file A file located in the %runtime installation path%\Config directory, which contains the settings that affect all the managed applications running on the machine.

managed code The code that runs within the common language runtime.

managed execution The process by which the runtime loads, executes, and provides automatic memory management.

marshal-by-reference (MBR) objects Remotable objects that extend the System.MarshalByRef-Object class.

marshaling Manages different representations of data across different execution environments by performing the necessary conversions in data formats between managed and unmanaged code.

Merge Module projects Provide a standard method for installing and deploying components. This type of project template ensures that the correct version of a component is installed on the target computer.

metadata Binary information that describes a program. Metadata is stored with the MSIL code of the program in a common language runtime P Efile.

Microsoft Windows Installer packages An option for packaging a Visual Studio .NET application that allows you to create .msi files. You can use the .msi files with Windows Installer 2.0. You can also use another installer to package .msi files.

Mscorcfg.mmc or the .NET Framework configuration tool A tool that enables you to manage and configure assemblies located in the global assembly cache.

MSIL code Intermediate code generated by the compilers of CLS-compliant languages. MSIL code contains a CPU-independent set of instructions, which describes how to load, store, initialize, and call methods on objects.

MSIL disassembler tool or Ildasm.exe A tool that takes a PE file containing the MSIL code as a parameter and creates a text file that contains managed code.

N

namespace Namespaces create logically and functionally related groups of classes and types, making it easier to locate a particular type.

.NET asynchronous programming Enables you to call and execute a method while the program that calls the methods continues to execute. As a result, methods continue to execute without having to wait for the called methods to finish executing, which increases the speed and responsiveness of applications.

.NET data providers Data providers enable an application to connect to a data source, execute commands, and retrieve results.

.NET Framework class library Provides the types that are common to all .NET languages. Programmers can use these types to develop different kinds of applications, such as console applications, Windows and Web Forms, and XML Web services.

.NET Remoting A system that enables communication between different applications regardless of whether they reside on the same computer or on different computers.

.NET server infrastructure Provides a highly secure and scalable platform for deploying .NET applications. The server infrastructure includes Windows 2000 Servers, Windows .NET Servers, and .NET Enterprise Servers.

O

object pooling A COM+ service that provides an automated service for configuring a component so that it can maintain ready-to-use and active object instances in a pool to process client requests.

P

portable executable (PE) file A file that contains MSIL code and metadata and requires the common language runtime to execute.

private assembly Installed in the installation directory of an application and is accessible to that application only.

process The execution boundary within which an application runs.

proxy An object that enables interprocess communication.

Q

queued component service A service of COM+ that is based on the Microsoft Message Queuing (MSMQ) server model. MSMQ is a middle-tier service that enables the asynchronous delivery of messages to named queues.

R

resource file generator or ResGen.exe tool A tool that is used to convert resource files in the form of .txt or .resx files to common language runtime binary .resources files that can be compiled into satellite assemblies.

role-based security An automatic, flexible, and configurable security model provided by COM+ to enforce access control for COM+ applications.

S

Schema Object Model (SOM) Consists of a set of classes that allow you read the schema definition from a file. In addition, you can use the classes in the SOM to create the schema definition files programmatically.

security engine Enforces restrictions on code and controls access to system resources such as the hard disk, network connections, and other system resources.

Security event log Contains messages regarding security changes. You can access the Security event log from within the Event Viewer

server activation A type of activation mode in the .NET Remoting system in which objects are created on the server when you call a method in the server class.

Service Control Manager (SCM) A remote procedure call (RPC) server that manages the Windows service applications and also supports the local or remote management of a service.

serviced components Components in the .NET Framework that can use COM+ services. These components run within the managed execution environment of the .NET Framework and share their context with the COM+ application.

Setup projects A type of project template that you use to deploy different types of projects. Setup projects allow you to create installation files to distribute an application.

shared assembly Shared by multiple applications, has a strong name, and is installed in the global assembly cache.

side-by-side execution Enables you to run multiple versions of the same assembly simultaneously. The common language runtime provides the infrastructure that allows multiple versions of the same assembly to run on the same computer.

SingleCall object A server-activated object that the remoting system creates each time a client method invokes a remote object.

Singleton objects The server-activated objects that can have only one instance regardless of the number of clients. These objects also have a default lifetime.

static assembl y An assembly that is created when you compile a program using a .NET language compiler.

Strong Name Tool or Sn.exe A tool provided by the .NET Framework that allows verification as well as key pair and signature generation.

System event log Contains messages regarding the events that occur on system components such as device drivers. You can access the System event log from within the Event Viewer.

T

test case Includes sample data that is required as input for the application. Test cases consists of sample data and its expected output, which you can then compare against actual results.

test plan A plan that outlines the entire testing process and includes individual test cases.

Tlbexp.exe A tool that generates a type library that describes the public types defined in a common language runtime assembly. Unmanaged applications can then use the generated type library to bind to the .NET type in the assembly.

tracing Enables you to write code in an application that allows you to collect information about code execution at run time. You use tracing information to troubleshoot an application after it is deployed.

transaction Groups a set of tasks into a single execution unit and ensures that all the tasks execute successfully or they all roll back if any of the individual units fail.

Transaction attributes You can control an object's transactional behavior by setting a transaction attribute value on the page, XML Web service method, or class. The attribute value determines the transactional behavior of the instantiated object.

transport channel A combination of technologies in .NET Remoting that perform low-level tasks such as opening a network connection, formatting messages, writing messages into streams, and sending bytes to the receiving application.

type checker Ensures that all objects and values and the references to those objects and values have a valid type. Type checking also ensures that only valid operations are performed on objects or values.

typed DataSet A class that is derived from the DataSet class and has an associated XML Schema.

type-safe code The code that passes the verification process performed during JIT compilation.

U

UDDI Provides a central place to store published information about XML Web services.

unmanaged code The code that runs outside the common language runtime.

untyped DataSet A DataSet that has no XML Schema associated with it.

W

Watch window A window provided by the Visual Studio .NET debugger, DbgClr, to debug a Visual Studio .NET application. You can use the Watch window to evaluate variables and expressions and maintain the results. You can also use the Watch window to edit the value of a variable or a register.

waterfall methodology A traditional approach to testing in which each person works in phases. The phases cover requirement analysis, design and specification requirements, coding, final testing, and release.

Web.config file The configuration file for ASP.NET-hosted applications, including Web services. This configuration file overrides the default configuration settings of your XML Web service.

WebMethod attribute Enables a client application to use standard Internet protocols to access an exposed .NET method.

<WebService>.asmx file A component that is published on the Web when you deploy an XML Web service as the base URL for the clients who access your service.

<WebService>.disco file An optional file published on the Web that describes the discovery mechanism for an XML Web service.

Web Services Description Language (WSDL) Contains information about the capabilities of an XML Web service, its location, and how to interact with it.

Windows Installer 2.0 Allows you to install, repair, or remove the .NET Framework assemblies located in the global assembly cache and in private directories. This is the simplest method for an end user to install a Visual Studio .NET application.

Windows service applications Run as background processes and are created and managed by the operating system to perform such tasks such as managing network connections and monitoring resource access and utilization.

WSDL.exe A tool that enables you to manually generate a proxy class for the XML Web service from the command line.

X

Xcopy deployment You use the Xcopy command to easily copy all the files of a .NET application to a target installation directory. For applications that do not require any further registration of components, the Xcopy command is the simplest way to distribute your .NET applications.

XML Document Object Model (XML DOM) A representation of the XML document in memory. The DOM lets you easily read, write, and manipulate an XML document.

XmlReader class Enables you to access XML data from a stream or XML document. This class provides fast, noncacheable, read-only, and forward-only access to XML data.

XML Schema or the XSD file Contains the rules that are the basis for the structure of XML documents. These rules are also known as grammar.

XML Web services A component that implements program logic and provides functionality for disparate applications. These applications use standard protocols, such as HTTP, XML, and SOAP, to access that functionality. XML Web services use XML-based messaging to send and receive data, enabling heterogeneous applications to interoperate with each other.

XML Web services description Provides information that enables you to know which operations to perform on an XML Web service.

XML Web services discovery A process that clients use to locate the documents that describe an XML Web service using the Web Services Description Language (WSDL).

XML Web service wire formats The open wire formats that enable communication between disparate systems.

XmlWriter class An abstract class that provides a fast, non-cached, forward-only means of generating streams or files containing well-formed XML.

XPath Enables you to access a node or a set of nodes in an XML document. In addition, XPath enables you to create expressions that can manipulate strings, numbers, and Boolean values.

Index